Towards Renewing Church and World

*Revisiting Vatican Council II
through the Eyes of Pope Francis*

Towards Renewing Church and World
Revisiting Vatican Council II through the Eyes of Pope Francis

EDITORS
Francis Gonsalves SJ,
Arjen Tete SJ,
Dinesh Braganza SJ

2020

Towards Renewing Church and World: Revisiting Vatican Council II through the Eyes of Pope Francis – Jointly published by Jnana Deepa (JD), Institute of Philosophy and Theology, Ramwadi, Nagar Road, Pune 411014 and Indian Society for Promoting Christian Knowledge(ISPCK) Post Box 1585, Kashmere Gate, Madarsa Road, Delhi-110006 under JD - ISPCK Theological Publications' Series no. 1.

© Editors, 2020

All rights reserved. No part of this book may be reproduced or transmitted in any form or by any means, electronic, mechanical, photocopying, recording, or by any information storage and retrieval system, without the prior permission in writing from the publisher.

The views expressed in the book are those of the contributors and the publisher takes no responsibility for any of the statements.

Online order: http://ispck.org.in/book.php

Also available on amazon.com

ISBN: 978-93-90569-07-6

Laser typeset by
ISPCK, Post Box 1585, 1654, Madarsa Road, Kashmere Gate, Delhi-110006 • Tel: 23866323
e-mail: ashish@ispck.org.in • ella@ispck.org.in
website: www.ispck.org.in

Contents

Preface ... xi

I

Pope Francis: Keynote and Interpretative Keys

1. What It Costs to Be Pope Francis
   Felix Wilfred ... 3

2. Not a Reformer but a Renewalist:
   Pope Francis Resumes the Conciliar Process
   after a Long Hibernation
   Aloysius Pieris, SJ ... 22

3. Pope Francis and the Reception of VC II in a
   New Global Historical Context
   Massimo Faggioli ... 38

II

Pope Francis' Aggiornamento: Opening Doors to Go Forth

4. The Church Open to The World from Vatican Council II
   to Pope Francis With Special Reference to Asia
   Michael Amaladoss, SJ ... 59

5. Go Forth, Face the World! How Pope Francis
   Embodies Vatican Council II
   Francis Gonsalves, SJ ... 70

6. Pope Francis: A Missionary by His Very Nature
   Recapturing the Missionary Spirit of Vatican Council II
   Anil Thomas, CM ... 93

7. Pope Francis: A Master Communicator
   Renewing Church and World Through Communication
   Joseph Scaria Palakeel, MST ... 109

III

Pope for the People of God: Family, Women, Youth

8. Building Joyful Families
   Walking with Pope Francis through *Amoris Laetitia*
   Deacon Jaime and Ligia da Fonseca ... 131

9. Envisaging an All-Inclusive Vibrant Church with
   Greater Involvement of Women in Decision-Making
   Roles and Sacred Ministries
   Patricia H. Santos, RJM ... 148

10. Mercy and Compassion for an Ailing World:
    Pope Francis' Role in Fostering a Feminist Perspective
    Shalini Mulackal, PBVM ... 162

11. Pope Francis' Vision for a Youthful Church:
    An Ecclesiology for Young Millennials
    Malleswararao Gh. (Jayaraj), SJ ... 178

12. Called to Be Friends of Christ: Pope Francis' Call
    to Youth to Humanize the World
    Thomas Karimundackal, SJ ... 192

IV

Pope Francis' Poor Church for Migrants & Politically Marginalized

13. Can the Church Speak Out? Pope Francis'
    Aggiornamento for Greater Global Involvement
    Joseph Lobo, SJ ... 215

14. The Authentic Option for the Poor:
    A Political Dimension of Pope Francis' Faith
    George A. Sebastin Babu, HGN ... 237

15. Strangers No More: Pope Francis Carries the Torch
    of Vatican Council II
    Mohan Doss, SVD ... 254

16. Being a Poor Church of the Poor and the Periphery:
    The Contribution of Pope Francis
    M. Surekha Lobo, BS ... 279

17. The Political Involvement of the Church
    Nishant A. Irudayadason ... 296

V

Pope Francis' Renewal of Religious Life and Priesthood

18. Pope Francis' Call to Renew Consecrated Life in India:
    By Reviewing Vatican Council II
    Fabian Jose, UMI ... 315

19. Actualization of the Conciliar Spring:
    Pope Francis' Vision of Ministry
    Arjen Tete, SJ ... 341

20. Tracing the Roots of Clericalism
    Jesuraj Rayappan, SVD ... 357

VI

Pope Francis' Dialogue with Religions and Science

21. Pope Francis' Encyclical *Laudato Si'* in Dialogue
    with Asian Religions
    Peter C. Phan ... 377

22. The Documents of VC II: Pope Francis' Springboard
    for Recovering Catholic Foundations for a Profitable
    Dialogue between Science and Catholic Theology and
    Science's Appropriate Place in Seminary Formation
    Richard Benson, CM ... 398

23. Building Bridges between Religions:
    Reading *Nostra Aetate* through the Lens of Pope Francis
    Midhun J. Francis, SJ ... 413

24. The Joys and the Hopes, the Griefs and the Anxieties
    Being in, with and for our Common Home
    Kuruvilla Pandikattu, SJ ... 429

VII

Pope Francis & the Oikos: Ecumenism and Ecology

25. Pope Francis' Enriching of the Ecumenical Movement:
    Moving Ahead after Vatican Council II
    Archbishop Felix Machado ... 453

26. Pope Francis Charts a Different Ecological Way
    Bishop Allwyn D'Silva ... 468

27. Self-Concern versus Concern for Christ:
    Pope Francis' Impetus to the Ecumenical Movement
    Shajan Kuttiyil, OIC ... 484

28. Towards an Environmental Spirituality in the
    Light of *Laudato Si'*
    Isaac Parackal, OIC ... 499

29. From *Cenozoic* Period to *Ecozoic* Era:
    A New Consciousness on Eco-justice
    George Kalapurackal ... 518

Contributors ... 535

Preface

On March 13, 2013, when Argentinian Cardinal Jorge M. Bergoglio chose the name 'Francis'—after the globally acclaimed '*il poverello*' of Assisi—many sensed that he would strive for renewal in the Church plagued with innumerable problems—internal and external. After the euphoria of the papal election and early successes subsided, when Pope Francis began to tackle the tough questions head-on, the backlash he received was backbreaking. Yet, Pope Francis has confidently continued to proclaim the *evangelii gaudium*—the joy of the gospel of Jesus Christ.

While a few have reacted vehemently to the changes being introduced by Pope Francis, a majority of Christians solidly support him, for they know that he 'walks the talk' and seeks to be 'radical', not 'liberal', as his adversaries allege him to be. Being radical entails rereading Jesus' gospel from the perspective of the '*least*' of his sisters and brothers (Mt 25:31ff) whom he loved, lived for, and sacrificed himself in 'the scandal of the cross'. Moreover, being radical also demands going back to the basics of Christian Tradition where, in the power of the Pentecostal Spirit, the apostolic community ensured that "there was not a needy person among them" (Acts 4:34), while "turning the world upside down" (Acts 17:6) with the power of God's word. Today, more than ever before, there's need to delve into Scripture and Tradition anew. It is precisely this that the aggiornamento of Vatican Council II (hereinafter VC II) sought to catalyze so as to keep abreast with a fast-changing world. However, many will agree that we have not gone beyond lip service and cosmetic changes to the radicality that VC II demanded of Christians and Church. There's need for more.

In view of what is happening in the Church, in particular, in order to reflect upon and respond to crucial concerns that affect us all, an international interdisciplinary symposium titled, *'Towards Renewing Church and World Revisiting VC II through the Eyes of Pope Francis'* was held at the aegis of Jnana Deepa (hereinafter abbreviated as JD), Pune, and the Conference of Catholic Bishops of India's (CCBI) Commission for Theology and Doctrine on November 29 and November 30, 2019. The symposium reflected upon this pointed question: How is Pope Francis taking the Church forward in the direction of VC II? Bishops, scholars, lay faithful and social activists from India and abroad presented papers. Some of the JD postgrad students, too, contributed their mite to revisit the pronouncements of VC II and looked at the Church and the world through the eyes and pen of Pope Francis.

This volume that retains the title of the Symposium and collects the papers presented under seven parts, as follows: (I) Pope Francis: Keynote and Interpretative Keys [articles of Felix Wilfred, Aloysius Pieris and Massimo Faggioli]; (II) Pope Francis' Aggiornamento: Opening Doors to Go Forth [articles of Michael Amaladoss, Francis Gonsalves, Anil Thomas and Joseph Palakeel]; (III) Pope for the People of God: Family, Women, Youth [articles of Deacon Jaime & Ligia da Fonseca, Patricia Santos, Shalini Mulackal, Malleswararao Gh. and Thomas Karimundackal]; (IV) Pope Francis' Poor Church for Migrants & Politically Marginalized [articles of Joseph Lobo, G. S. Babu, Mohan Doss, Surekha Lobo and Nishant I.]; (V) Pope Francis' Renewal of Religious Life and Priesthood [articles of Fabian Jose, Arjen Tete and Jesuraj Rayappan]; (VI) Pope Francis' Dialogue with Religions and Science [articles of Peter C Phan, Richard Benson, Midhun Francis and Kuruvilla Pandikattu]; (VII) Pope Francis & the *Oikos*: Ecumenism and Ecology [articles of Felix Machado, Allwyn D'Silva, Shajan Kuttiyil, Isaac Parackal, George Kalapurackal]. Here's a brief summary of all the articles.

In *'What it Costs to be Pope Francis,'* keynote speaker Felix Wilfred shows why Pope Francis is one of the most hated persons in the Church. Reflecting on the influences—both inside and outside church circles—

that seem to have led to this situation, he argues that Pope Francis is paying the price for daring to be different. He demonstrates how by not travelling the 'highway of theological debates' but by entering 'the byways and lanes of life,' relocating the poor at the centre, denouncing 'unbridled capitalism' and challenging the right-wing populists, Pope Francis has unsettled those rooted in orthodoxy, tradition, and power. Subsequently, he highlights Pope Francis' contextual vision of faith and theology, his understanding of the Church and its ministry, his advocacy for synodality and collegiality that takes immense risks with deep faith.

Aloysius Pieris' paper, *Not a Reformer but a Renewalist: Pope Francis Renews the Conciliar Process after 35 Years of Hibernation,'* argues that, after the Council of Jerusalem (Acts, chapter 15), VC II was the second council of 'renewal,' not just 'reform' since change was sought from the periphery to the centre, and from down to up—not the other way around. Pieris argues that by adopting a synodal mode of governance and by tending to the peripheries, Pope Francis is daringly leading the Church in ways amenable to Asian churches, thereby resuscitating the VC II spirit that had all but died down under the governance of two of his papal predecessors.

In his paper, *'Pope Francis and the Reception of VC II in a New Global Historical Context,'* Massimo Faggioli shows that from the beginning of Francis' pontificate (unlike that of his predecessor), the presence of VC II has been more mediated and non-textual rather than explicit in programmatic texts; more a matter of implementation than of interpretation of the Council. Affirming that Francis quotes VC II rarely and surely not more often than his predecessors, Faggioli argues that his modality of reception of VC II is a complex mix of both the *reception of the documents* of the council and *of the act* of the council.

In *'The Church Open to the World: From Vatican II to Pope Francis with Reference to Asia,'* Michael Amaladoss reflects upon a twofold opening of the Church to the World, namely, the Roman Church, though still centered in Rome, opening out to be a World Church and the Church opening out to the world. Amaladoss notes that already in

1974, the Federation of Asian Bishops' Conferences (FABC) had spoken about the 3-fold dialogue of the Gospel with Asia's poor, rich cultures, and living religions. Hence, lauding Pope Francis' call to go forth to the world's peripheries and citing his bold pastoral and consultative approach from below, he concludes that Pope Francis may be launching a new kind of Church in which the Asian Churches will feel at home and more empowered in their mission towards God's Kingdom.

In his paper *'Go Forth, Face the World! How Pope Francis Embodies Vatican Council II'* Francis Gonsalves first builds a 'body-framework', so to say, stressing the importance of the body in Christianity and then specifically looks at VC II documents—especially VC II's 'Pastoral Constitution on the Church in the Modern World' *Gaudium et Spes*—to see what was dreamt of therein. He then argues that Pope Francis not only effectively uses words like face, heart, body and flesh in his words and works, but also enfleshes them in his theology, pastoral praxis and lifestyle. By so doing, the pope gives both, church and world, Christians and believers in other religions—especially in Asia and India—a *darshan* of who God is, and who we are called to '*be*' and '*do*' as individual Christians and as Church, at large.

Anil Thomas presents Pope Francis as a missionary by his very nature. Highlighting the missionary spirit of the VC II documents, he argues that the missionary concern of Pope Francis for the Church springs straight from the teachings of VC II. Elaborating Pope Francis' words that all Christians are always and everywhere "missionary disciples" of Jesus (EG 120), Anil demonstrates how through his life and works Pope Francis is recapturing the missionary spirit of VC II.

In his paper, *'Pope Francis: A Master Communicator,'* Joseph Scaria Palakeel portrays the Pope as someone who has joyfully welcomed the Good News of salvation and is capable of communicating it to the whole of humankind effectively. Exploring the Francis-effect from communication theology perspective, particularly his distinctive communication strategies and skills in his effort to renew the Church and the world, Palakeel argues that Pope Francis is, undoubtedly, the most influential world leader today.

Deacon Jaime and Ligia da Fonseca—a Catholic couple, married for forty years—reflect upon Pope Francis' 2016 Apostolic Exhortation *Amoris Laetitia*. Giving an overview of the teachings of the two predecessors of Pope Francis on family life and Francis' *Amoris Laetitia* as the joy of love and the vocation of the family as proclamation of the gospel of love, Jaime and Ligia share their experiential insights in accompanying families, forming youth and young adults, strengthening married couples, creating a culture of life for children, and accompanying newlyweds and couples in irregular situations in order to build joyful families.

Patricia Santos envisages actualization of an all-inclusive vibrant Church, but only possible with greater involvement of women in decision-making roles and sacred ministries. Despite acknowledging the changing role of women in the Church and world, the ecclesiastical hierarchs obstruct their visibility and voice in church. By contrast, while slow and cautious to tackle the issues of women's participation in the Church, Pope Francis is appointing some women in ecclesial offices and is ensuring that all forms of abuse and discrimination against women is stopped. Notably, even though women continue to be sidelined and subordinated in the Church, they persevere in strongly resisting, actively participating and making their voices heard in the hope of envisioning and enforcing a renewed humanity and a flourishing creation.

In her paper, '*Mercy and Compassion for an Ailing World: Pope Francis' Role in Fostering a Feminist Perspective*,' Shalini Mulackal analyses the various ills afflicting humanity and the world today and prescribes the medicine of mercy and compassion as a remedy for the ailing world as proposed by Pope Francis in *Misericordiae Vultus*. She underscores Pope Francis' constant invitation to us to develop the feminine aspect of our psyche so that we may look at the ailing world with a maternal heart.

In his paper, '*Pope Francis' Vision for a Youthful Church: An Ecclesiology for Young Millennials*,' Malleswararao Gh. analyzes how the Church encounters youth in the postmodern world and how Catholic young people envision a new Church that listens to their voices. Having analyzed the dreams of the young Catholics as implanted in Pope Francis' summons for the Synod of Bishops on young people October 2018, preparatory documents, apostolic exhortations, like *Evangelii Gaudium* and *Christus Vivit*, he lauds the pope's vision for a dynamic Church of young millennials.

Thomas Karimundackal studies *Christus Vivit* and highlights Pope Francis' invitation to the youth to be alive in and with Christ for the service of the humanization of the world. Stressing the importance of having a correct relationship with God and humanity, he amplifies Pope Francis' call to be open to the Spirit so that young people may recognize their personal vocation and mission.

Joseph Lobo, in '*Can the Church Speak Out? Pope Francis' Aggiornamento for Greater Global Involvement*', explores the current specificities of a strong and a well interwoven wave of political populism, dictatorship of the market economy and the religio-cultural 'fascism' in significant parts of the globe. Taking cue from the celebrated book of Gayatri Spivak – *Can the Subaltern Speak*? Lobo asks: *Can the Church speak out* in a context that is explicated above? Underscoring the political, economic, and pastoral stances and personal charisma of Pope Francis as authentic expressions of today's subalterns' identity and interests, he supports the pope's positions and deplores concerted efforts from certain groups of people to ignore, ridicule, rebut and even attack them.

In '*The Authentic Option for the Poor: A Political Dimension of Pope Francis' Faith*,' G. Arokia Sebastin Babu presents Pope Francis as a politically-informed leader and a radical theologian who raises a political voice against the systemic oppression of the politics by way of his authentic writing, teaching and preaching. Surveying his encyclicals, apostolic exhortations, and messages, Babu affirms that the political dimensions of a Christian faith demand an 'authentic option for the poor'.

In '*Strangers No More: Pope Francis Carries the Torch of VC II*,' Mohan Doss illustrates how Pope Francis has carried the flame of VC II and his predecessors' concern for the welfare of migrants and refugees through his passionate teachings and powerful symbolic actions. Reviewing the magisterial teaching till the years of Pope Benedict XVI, he highlights Pope Francis' prophetic role in awakening the conscience of the world to accept migrants as brothers and sisters and embrace them as gifts to be nourished for the enrichment of the human community.

M. Surekha Lobo explores how Pope Francis is taking forward the agenda of VC II and its vision of Church and human family more concretely and radically in the footsteps of Jesus. Highlighting God's fundamental option towards human beings in the Exodus experience, concentrating on Jesus' walk with the poor, and examining the development of the idea of 'Church of the poor' as envisioned by Pope Francis, she argues that it is possible and necessary to embark upon building a poor Church for the poor.

Nishant A. Irudayadason discusses the prominent theological views of the twentieth century that have laid emphases on responsibility of faith in the political domain without nourishing the dream of a return to the old theocratic regime. Discussing briefly the theological standpoints of contemporary theologians like Erik Peterson, Carl Schmidt, Johann Baptist Metz and Jacques Maritain, he explores how the mission of the Church goes beyond the exercise of "critical resistance" and opens up a broader perspective of contributing to the "invention" of the society, a task that can be said to be "political" in a broader sense.

In her paper, '*Pope Francis' Call to Renew Consecrated Life in India: By Reviewing VC II*,' Fabian Jose explores the beauty, challenges, and relevance of consecrated life by reviewing VC II through the eyes of Pope Francis. Listing the challenges to consecrated life in India, she emphasizes its relevance by drawing strength and spirit from *Perfectae Caritatis, Evangelii Gaudium, Gaudete Et Exultate*, etc., so as to inspire consecrated people to creatively contribute towards building a new Church in India.

In '*Actualization of the Conciliar Spring: Pope Francis' Vision of Ministry*,' Arjen Tete studies the document that addresses priesthood—*Presbyterorum Ordinis*—through the lens of the primary doctrinal document of VC II, *Lumen Gentium* and Pope Francis' *Evangelii Gaudium*. Mapping out the major focal points of VC II and correlating them with pivotal points of Francis' "priestly thoughts," Tete argues that there is a definitive movement from cultic and sacerdotal dimension of priesthood to a broader vision of priestly ministry of preaching and pastoral activities so necessary for the full blooming of the Church.

Looking at the contemporary clerical lifestyle of priests who see themselves as part of a separate class and often tend to resist collaborative and pluralistic approaches of reforms introduced at VC II, Jesuraj Rayappan analyzes critically some of the historical data to understand clericalism and its impact on the Church, at large.

In '*Pope Francis' Encyclical Laudato Si' in Dialogue with Asian Religions*,' Peter C. Phan reads *Laudato Si'* with Asian eyes, from the Asian perspective, in dialogue with Asian religions. Acknowledging and appreciating the way Asians and Asian Catholics take initiatives to save their continent from ecological destruction, he argues that *Laudato Si'* could be further enriched by adding perspectives from the Asian religions, especially Buddhism and Daoism.

Richard Benson demonstrates the relationship between science and theology, and specifically Catholic theology. Highlighting the progress in dialogue between science and theology, challenges posed by some scientific developments, and the aggiornamento of the documents of VC II, Benson argues that science ought to be given an appropriate place in priestly formation.

To champion Pope Francis' cause of '*Building Bridges between Religions*,' Midhun J. Francis reads *Nostra Aetate* in the context of today's evangelization. He elaborates Pope Francis' attempt to implement this document in his encyclicals like *Evangelii Gaudium* and the document on '*Human Fraternity for World Peace and Living Together*'.

In his paper, Kuruvilla Pandikattu borrows some insights of *Gaudium et Spes*, no. 1, to demonstrate how Pope Francis has been able to feel this joy and grief intensely and intimately with hope and love. Discussing the reality of the Fourth Industrial Revolution and the fear of the possible Sixth Mass Extinction, Pandikattu seeks moral and spiritual resources in the prophetic, hopeful and joyful message of Christianity, VC II and the words and actions of Pope Francis. These, he argues, can enable us human beings to survive collectively as a species.

In '*Pope Francis' Enriching of the Ecumenical Movement Moving Ahead after Vatican Council II*,' Archbishop Felix Machado presents Pope Francis' contribution to the deepening and enriching of the ecumenical movement. Citing extensively from the addresses of St John XXIII and the homilies of Pope Francis, Archbishop Machado emphasizes the importance of building bridges between the Catholic Church and other Churches. He also provides many 'practical ways' of fostering ecumenism.

In his paper '*Pope Francis Charts a Different Ecological Way*,' CCBI's chairperson for Commission of Ecology Bishop Allwyn D'Silva highlights the ecological problems that we are facing worldwide. Showing how Pope Francis' eco-theology—especially as seen in *Laudato Si'*—provides us with insight to respond to these crises, he charts roadmaps for those in priestly formation, encouraging simplicity of life, contemplation of God, concern for the poor, and protection of the environment. Describing 'Green Initiatives' that the Archdiocese of Mumbai has started to effectively combat this crisis, he offers a few practical suggestions for an eco-friendly lifestyle.

In his paper, '*Self-Concern versus Concern for Christ: Pope Francis' Impetus to the Ecumenical Movement*,' Shajan Kuttiyil offers a bird's eye view of Pope Francis' stance on ecumenism, particularly focusing on his pastoral approach, which is Christocentric and deeply rooted in the teachings of VC II. Affirming love and friendship as basics of ecumenism, Shajan underscores Pope Francis' approach and his way of communicating with other churches is one of a heart speaking to the heart which avoids sentimentalism and emotional ploys.

Isaac Parackal analyses Pope Francis' eco vision as depicted in his 2015 encyclical letter *Laudato Si'* and augments his challenge to think in terms of an environmental spirituality that integrates all beings in the thread of harmony and love. Giving a brief overview of the ecological legacy of Christianity, ecological crisis, human responsibility of caring for creation, Parackal amplifies Pope Francis' call for a spirituality of radical conversion (*metanoia*).

In his paper, '*From Cenozoic Period to Ecozoic Era: A New Consciousness on Eco-justice*,' George Kalapurackal unravels the sacred and sacramental dimension of the creation. Examining VC II's *Dignitatis Humanae* and Pope Francis' *Laudato Si'*, he advocates for a change in the consciousness; a transition from *Cenozoic* period to *Ecozoic* era (a call for *metanoia*).

Apart from the papers appearing in this volume, there were other shorter presentations by panelists and grassroot activists who provided invaluable insights into the life, praxis and projects of Pope Francis. We are especially grateful to Rt Rev. Dr Thomas Dabre, Bishop of the Poona Diocese; Prof. Dr Brinelle D'Souza from TISS, Mumbai; Ms. Grace David from the Archdiocese of Delhi; Fr Cedric Prakash from Ahmedabad; and JD professors: Dr V M Jose, Dr Konrad Noronha, Dr Sebastian Vazhapilly, Dr Henry D'Almeida and Dr Shiju Joseph whose viewpoints contributed immensely to the discussions.

A million thanks also to the JD management—especially Prof. Dr Selva Rathinam and Prof. Dr Jose Thayil—and to the Chairman and members of the CCBI Commission for Theology and Doctrine: His Grace Archbishop Felix Toppo of Ranchi, His Grace Albert D'Souza of Agra and Rt Rev Lawrence Pius, Bishop of Dharmapuri. Thanks also to the many archbishops and bishops who contributed to the success of the symposium in many ways. Besides those who presented papers, we are grateful to His Grace Anil J.T. Couto of Delhi; His Grace Filipe

Neri Ferrão of Goa and Daman; His Grace Raphy Manjaly, Archbishop of Agra; Rt Rev. Eugene Joseph, Bishop of Varanasi and Rt Rev. Gerard Mathias, Bishop of Lucknow.

Summarizing the Symposium in six points the 'observer' Dr Shiju Joseph said: (i) Pope Francis is unafraid of saying what must be said—whether to world leaders or to his own clerical brethren; (ii) Pope Francis is Christocentric; for him, Christ is a flesh-and-blood person, not an abstract divinity; (iii) He is keenly aware of happenings in different parts of the world today, and taps local wisdom to address them; (iv) He does not come across as a know-it-all leader but is open to learn from others through synodality; (v) Pope Francis' capacity to dialogue—with women, prisoners, refugees, migrants, youth, families, world leaders, believers of other churches and other religions—is immense and incredible; and, (vi) He is deeply concerned about our 'Common Home', mother earth. Endorsing these points wholeheartedly, we can only exclaim: *Viva il papa!* Long live Pope Francis! May we assist him in renewing church and world way beyond what VC II dreamt of, and may God's Spirit be our driving force.

Prof. Dr Francis Gonsalves, SJ **Dr Arjen Tete, SJ** **Dr Dinesh Braganza, SJ**
francis.gonsalves@jdv.edu.in *arjen.tete@jdv.edu.in* *dinesh.braganza@jdv.edu.in*

Jnana Deepa, Pune
Birthday of Pope Francis
December 17, 2020

I

Pope Francis: Keynote and Interpretative Keys

"The world tells us to seek success, power and money;
God tells us to seek humility, service and love"

(Pope Francis)

1.
What It Costs to Be Pope Francis
Felix Wilfred

Introduction: A Besieged Pope

Arguably, Pope Francis is one of the most hated persons in the Church today. He also seems to be one of the most detested and despised leaders in the world, at large. There is a war against Pope Francis, which he calmly seems to withstand. In this keynote presentation, I shall strive to show why this is so by reflecting on the factors and influences—both inside and outside church circles—that seem to have led to this situation.

1.   Surveying the Siege Within

The hostility against Pope Francis begins with his own closest collaborators. You may remember that in 2016 four cardinals—Joachim Meisner, Walter Brandmüller, Carlo Caffara, and Raymond Burke—raised critical questions regarding the pope's stand on family and morality expressed in *Amoris Laetitia*. Pope Francis was accused of heresy; thus, these cardinals sought to offer so-called 'filial correction' to an errant pope through their infamous letter of '*dubia*' (literally, 'doubts'). Others go to the extent of unearthing irregularities in the conclave and questioning the validity of his papal election. A former papal nuncio to the United States, Archbishop Carlo Maria Viganò, openly asks Francis to resign. He is joined by other prelates of no less influence and weight. There are many foul and vitriolic accusations hurled against Francis. For his deriders, his words and acts are not in keeping with the orthodox tradition of the Church. His teachings are found to be "ambiguous", "modernist" and "syncretistic". He has, according to his detractors, disrupted the tradition of the Church and its teaching. One of the vicious narratives—a small but potent minority of Church leaders and Catholic fundamentalists are trying to weave—is that his pontificate is heading for a schism in the Church.

Viganò's Cassandric language characterising the pontificate of Francis seems to present an impending apocalyptic doom. This is what he says,

> Now the Church is lifeless, covered by metastasis, devastated. The people of God grope, illiterate and robbed of their faith, in the darkness of chaos and division. In recent decades, the enemies of God have progressively burned two thousand years of tradition. With unprecedented acceleration,thanks to the subversive goal of this pontificate supported by the powerful Jesuit Apparatus, a deadly *coup de grace* is being prepared against the Church.

For his denigrators in the Church, Pope Francis woefully lacks deep theological knowledge and scholarly background. They contrast his teachings with that of Pope John Paul II in whom they find the embodiment of Catholic orthodoxy. Those who are beholden by Pope Benedict XVI, like the club of his disciples (*Schülerkreis*), think that he is a theological giant whereas Pope Francis is theologically a dwarf, a light-weight pussycat. For many such people, the theology of Francis is ephemeral and superficial. There is a legion of Catholic fundamentalists belonging to tribal and militant Catholicism who find the best only in the past and are wary of the surprises of God every new moment. They find the thoughts and ways of Francis abominable and abhorring. They even dare to warn the pope and hope for a natural biological solution: his death.

2. Reasons Behind this Siege from Within

A question certainly rises in all our minds: Why this aggressive posture, and passionate and full-blooded opposition to Francis in the Church?

There is a need to dig deeper. I attempt to propose a few points for our studied consideration.

I think we may not be able to gauge the epochal significance of this papacy if we relate Francis to the teachings of Vatican Council II (hereinafter VC II) alone. Under the past two pontificates—of John Paul II and Benedict XVI—theological debates abounded on the reception and hermeneutics of VC II: whether VC II is to be interpreted in continuation with the Councils of Trent and Vatican Council I, or whether it represents a caesura, a break with this tradition. This was the pivotal point at the Extraordinary Synod of 1985.

There was a heated discussion on whether the Universal Church comes first or the Local Church. Western theological titans like Joseph Ratzinger and Walter Kasper clashed on these points. The Congregation for the Doctrine of the Faith (CDF) drew up a document in which it affirmed the *chronological* and *ontological* priority of the Universal Church. Theologians are racking their brains as to what all that means. Further, people from Asia, Africa and Latin America were warned that their project of inculturation should not be at the risk of losing the Greco-Roman heritage which, they were told, is an integral part of the Christian kerygma itself. Asian theologians and others from the Global South were flabbergasted.

Francis does not entertain any jugglery of theological concepts to awe his audience. He does not want to drive through the highway of theological debates about VC II in which case the opposition to him may not have been as fierce as we are witnessing. His would have been simply an inflexion within a basic theological model of VC II. One could debate with Francis on the significance of VC II with the hope that he would be speaking a conventional idiom and language, and any differences on the matter could be sorted out. But the problem with Francis is that he treads the rough ground of everyday life and enters into the byways and lanes of life. He relates the core of the Gospel to down-to-earth realities of life. This is not something new to him. This was what he was doing as a shepherd in Buenos Aires; in short, he interprets VC II from the margins, from life at the periphery.

Pope Francis draws on his personal experiences. All this is unpalatable. He views his mission not only to put into practice the teachings of VC II. These teachings are now cramped by hermeneutical debates and minutiae. He also wants to come to terms with something that did not emerge forcefully enough in VC II, the poor, who make up the very heart of the Gospel. The Good News to the poor to whom Jesus promised the Kingdom of God, is Pope Francis' central agenda. He is not simply trying to do reforms and renewal but is attempting, against many odds, a paradigm shift in the life and engagement of the Church. The radical consequences of this commitment to the poor unsettle the establishment, both in the Church and in the present world-order. It challenges clericalism and careerism, the evils of which he never ceases to decry and castigate. No wonder, he has become too unsavoury to the acolytes of a constricted tribal Catholicism ruled by an elitist clergy. This seems to explain the high voltage of censure and resistance from within.

I must add that what is at stake is not orthodoxy and tradition. In reality, it is the call of Francis for *greater accountability and transparency* (including financial transactions) in the Church and in its leadership, beginning with the Roman Curia. This causes heartburns and stirs up fierce resistance. But there is an effort to camouflage these deeper roots as a matter of doctrine and of orthodoxy, thereby trying to strike Francis with this weapon in the hope that it will garner support in their battle against him.

3. Capitalism and Capitalists Up in Arms

Francis is hated because of his stinging criticism of laissez-faire capitalism and the global market. What he says and does is so challenging that capitalists and market-ideologues and practitioners feel unnerved. Pope Francis takes Wall Street head on. He does not mince words in chastising an impersonal and deterministic economy bereft of humanising purposes.

In this economy, values vanish into thin air. His call for equality and justice, and denunciation of structures of injustice has infuriated the elites, the corporates and the capitalist lobby. In his Apostolic Exhortation, *Evangelii Gaudium* (hereinafter *EG*), Francis calls the market economy "a murderous system which kills people." It is capitalism that has caused increasing inequality in the world and the impoverishment of developing countries. For him, unbridled capitalism and greedy accumulation of money and wealth are "dung of the devil". No wonder that he has gained many enemies in the capitalist world. Notorious among these are many North American conservative Catholics, and even some ecclesiastics. Steve Bannon, former adviser to Trump at the White House, is the leader who galvanises the anti-Francis crusade. For him Pope Francis is bad for business. He supports populist politicians masquerading to defend the so-called 'Christian West' against migrants, and instigates xenophobia.

While Francis was flying to Maputo, Mozambique, a journalist told him, "Holy Father, the Americans hate you." His reply was, "I am honoured that the Americans attack me." It meant that he was speaking some uncomfortable truths to the capitalist system and its driving force of the market. The argument of his capitalist critics rests on shaky grounds: First, the pope lacks knowledge of economics; so, he should not venture into a realm which he is not familiar with. Second, he is a person of religion, and he should confine himself to his turf—the religious realm—and not meddle with issues of the economy that are not within his area of competence. We need to investigate deeper into the anti-Francis mood of capitalists. By the way, the arguments against the pope speaking about ecology—in *Laudato Si'*—are the same.

American capitalists see in this Jesuit Pope Francis the heritage and the legacy of the six Jesuits murdered at the Central American University (UCA) in El Salvador on the night between November 15–16, 1989. Fr Ignacio Ellacuría and his five companions of UCA in San Salvador were dragged out from their rooms in the middle of the night and brutally shot dead, along with the woman who cooked for the community and her daughter. Some years later, I visited San Salvador on the invitation of my long-time theologian-friend, Jon Sobrino, who was part of that community but escaped death, because he was away on that night. Sobrino showed me around. I was deeply moved when I saw the blood-stained clothes of these martyrs.

During the civil war, Ellacuría and his companions became the powerful voice of the powerless, the poor, the kidnapped, and the murdered. They were against exploitative capitalism and ruthless imperialism; they were against the terror unleashed by the armed forces against the poor. Ellacuría was the chief advisor to Archbishop (now Saint) Oscar Romero. The inspiration to stand up for justice, for the poor, led to the massacre of these exemplary Christian witnesses by the army personnel trained in the USA with the blessings of the USA administration. Ellacuría, the rector of UCA, and his companions were branded as 'communists' and as the inspiration behind the guerillas. In the minds of the imperialists, Pope Francis standing up for the poor and the marginalised evokes the image of the martyrs of El Salvador and their fearless resistance. Francis is the scapegoat upon whom is heaped the long-harboured resentment of North American capitalism, imperialism and militarism. They see in Pope Francis the revival of the old enemy of liberation in Latin America.

Some prominent members of the American Catholic episcopacy too seem to be soft-pedalling on capitalism and playing second fiddle. As more than one American bishop stated, the critique of the pope does not apply to American capitalism which is 'soft-capitalism'!

4. Right-Wing Populists: New Defenders of Christianity

Pope Francis is hated by right-wing populists and nationalists in Europe and elsewhere. Reason? He speaks out on the plight of the immigrants and refugees, and appeals for a welcome policy towards them. In one of his speeches, the pope said how he is concerned about "the reemergence, somewhat throughout the world, of aggressive tendencies toward foreigners, migrants, as well as that growing nationalism that disregards the common good." He is opposed by right-wing political outfits like the Northern League party in Italy headed by Matteo Salvini, till September 2019 deputy prime minister and home minister of Italy. Salvini, a divorcee, is never known as a practising Catholic, but holds a rosary in his hands at public appearances on TV; holds a crucifix while addressing press-conferences; and invokes the Virgin of Immaculate Conception for his political victory. He is someone staunchly opposed to Pope Francis and his policies in the Church and in the world. Unfortunately, populists like Matteo Salvini are supported by people in the Church who oppose Pope Francis.

The recent victory of the far-right in the parliamentary elections of the European Union has further strengthened the increasing opposition to Francis. These right-wing politicians seem to enjoy the blessings and ecclesiastical patronage of some prelates since these politicians are viewed by them (prelates) as defenders of Western Christianity against the invasion of Islamic migrants. Such an ecclesiastical sponsorship projects these populist politicians in a favourable light among the conservative Catholics voters.

5.   **Papacy with a Contextual Vision of Faith and Theology**
Papacy, like all other ministries in the Church, is in service of faith. The vision of faith inspires Pope Francis and leads him to adopt a different approach of the Church to the world. The new relationship he envisages also marks his theological orientation.

Faith is a way of seeing. Like the external eyes, faith is an inner eye or the third eye. It lets us see the reality in a different light. It is like the enlightenment of Siddhartha under the peepal tree. That experience made him the enlightened one: the Buddha. Without going into details, let me simply refer here to the allegory of the cave in Plato's *Republic*, which is also a story of enlightenment. No wonder, that the early Church called the sacrament of faith, baptism, as *photismos*, meaning, illumination or enlightenment. Well-known are the transformation of Paul on the way to Damascus and the conversion of St Augustine. If we hold all these in mind, we will understand what faith means as a new way of seeing. Everything looks different. Communicating this enlightenment is true evangelisation.

This is very different from the understanding of faith as a set of propositions to believe in, to be preserved and transmitted. St Thomas Aquinas rightly reminds us "*Actus credentis non terminatur ad enuntiabile sed ad rem*" (the act of faith does not end in propositions but in reality). When we conceive faith in terms of statements to be believed in, we will end up in such a curious situation as the one that caused an infelicitous schism in the Church. I am referring here to the theological dispute '*filioque*' which split Eastern Christianity from the West. The dispute was whether the Spirit proceeds from the Father alone, or from the Father and the Son. Consequence? A divided Christendom. To be credible any belief needs to have reference to our life and the life and salvation of the world. The connection between doctrinal tenets and what they imply for the wellbeing of humanity and nature should become more evident today in order to be credible.

This tells us about the importance of context in the exercise of faith and in doing theology. Undoubtedly, Karl Rahner was an outstanding theologian. I am proud that he was my teacher too. His explanations of the meaning of articles of faith by applying the transcendental method were very profound and refreshing. And yet his theology had no reference to contexts like World War II or to crimes against humanity such as the holocaust or genocide in which six million Jews were systematically and in a planned way eliminated.

For Pope Francis, faith and theology are dynamic and contextual. They need to be lived and practised with reference to our experiences today, with reference to our struggles, hopes and aspirations. Faith and theology are responses to God's continuous speaking. By his deep engagement with all that touches the people, especially the poor at the margins, the vision of Pope Francis' faith and theology acquire great vitality and dynamism.

6. Francis' Understanding of the Church and Its Ministry

The traditional image of the Church could be likened to a fortress: unassailable and unchanging. I am reminded about the episcopal motto of Cardinal Ottaviani who played the leader of traditional Catholicism at VC II. It read: "*Semper Idem*" (ever the same!). Compare the fortress image with that of Pope Francis: Church as a field hospital—attending to urgent needs of people in critical situations.

When I hear accusations that Pope Francis does not follow the traditional teaching, I am reminded of the words of the great Cardinal Augustine Bea who made an immense contribution at VC II. When he presented some of his views at the Council, he was opposed saying that what he was saying was not traditional teaching. Cardinal Bea answered, "well, *this is not traditional teaching, but life today is not traditional!*". The expectation from the pope is that he keeps to tradition in his teachings. But what these Catholic fundamentalists do not understand is the fact that in the history of the teachings of the Church, continuity has not always been the norm. There have also been instances of a breakthrough in tradition and traditional teaching. It is illuminating to see, for example, how the Church—from the negation of religious freedom which was included as one of the errors in the Syllabus of Errors of Pope Pius IX—came to uphold and defend religious freedom as it happened with *Dignitatis Humanae* in VC II. Some of the things Pope Francis says and does fall in this tradition of breakthrough, and may not be fitted into the tradition of continuity. The breakthrough is painful for many, but like the birth-pangs, it brings new life to the Church, society and the world. The breakthrough moments have been most significant in the growth of the Church and its mission. With Francis, we are experiencing such a breakthrough in the history of the Church.

7. A Pope who Dares to be Different

I am not comparing popes. Surely, each one is different. They come from different contexts and varied worlds of experience. These inevitably affect their way of thinking, their vision of the Church, their relationship to the world and society.

Pope John Paul II took up his papal ministry as someone who had experienced first-hand the world of communism, atheism and the tensions of the cold war. He lived in a country of an oppressive totalitarian state with allegiance to Marxist ideology. No wonder, he tended to see the rest of the world in danger of communism and exposed to Marxist atheism. He interpreted that communism and Marxism were insidiously at work in Latin America, while people were, in fact, struggling against dictatorships, oppression, kidnappings, tortures and killings.

Pope Benedict XVI experienced painfully the revolution of 1968, the student protests of the time, and the sexual revolution of the 1960s. He witnessed in his own native country Germany and all over Europe, the decline of traditional Catholic Christianity with a mass exodus of people from the Church. He interpreted such developments as resulting from secularism and relativism, and as signs of the absence of God. Hence it was important for him to restore the traditional faith and Catholicism in their pristine glory. This was evident already when he was Prefect of the Congregation of the Doctrine of the Faith (CDF), preceding his papal ministry. Before the conclave, he could warn the cardinals about the danger the "dictatorship of relativism" poses to the Church. All these experiences and thoughts influenced his decisions and policies as the pope.

One of the leading psychologists of the twentieth century, Abraham Maslow (1966), made a very telling statement which, I think, has considerable hermeneutical implications. He said, "*A man with a hammer can see only nails everywhere*". Orthodoxy has been the primary agenda of the CDF. It has been known in history for denouncing and ostracising any shade of doctrinal deflection or woolly expression. This curial institution gave the impression of a tomb where the doctrines of the Church were embalmed and preserved.

Things seem to have quite perceptibly changed with the advent of Pope Francis who accords primacy to orthopraxis, namely, following the path of the Gospel and putting it into practice. Fortunately, the overblown importance the CDF enjoyed has abated by now, and it is being downsized to its right proportions. This will materialise further, hopefully, when Pope Francis brings to fruition the much-awaited reform of the Roman Curia.

Pope Francis is someone with both his feet on the ground; he is not lost in the Platonic world of ideas. This does not mean that he has no vision. He is a pope of true Gospel-vision. With this vision, we hope the pope will introduce much-desired reform in the communication with the local Churches and respond to their exigencies and experiences. The curia is a service apparatus, and this should become evident in its attitude and the way it deals with the local Churches and the bishops leading them.

We can only pity the papal nuncios who are shunted from one country to the other without being able to strike root anywhere. Many of them, despite their best intentions, are not adept in assessing the situation of the local churches—often due to their lack of knowledge about and familiarity with the culture, social structure, language, life-situation and history of the local people—and yet expected to play a crucial role in matters of such gravity as the selection of bishops for the local Churches. Pope Francis has started to bring more and more pastorally seasoned bishops from the local Churches for leadership roles at Vatican curial offices. That helps avoid careerism in the Roman Curia. But then he is bearing the brunt of all these moves.

On the one hand, the Roman Curia often projects its identity in the image of an institution meant for the self-preservation of the Church; and, on the other hand, Francis' engagement for the reform of the Roman Curia, stems from his vision of the Gospel, from the dream of a purified and transformed Church. We could read between the lines his reformist agenda when he says in his very first Apostolic Exhortation, *Evangelii Gaudium*:

> I dream of a 'missionary option', that is a missionary impulse capable of transforming everything, so that the Church's customs, ways of doing things,

times and schedules, language and structures can be suitably channeled for the evangelization of today's world rather than for her self-preservation (*EG* 27).

8. Shouldering a Burdensome Legacy

What has happened in the Church for the past forty years, before Francis appeared on the scene, constitutes a problematic and complicated legacy. Many collaborators Francis has inherited in the Curia, and many bishops appointed all over the world during the last few decades, unfortunately, do not chime with the spirit of Francis. They were trained and brought up in a different legacy. In the immediate post-VC II period, the criterion for the choice of bishops was whether the candidate was open to dialogue, had the aptitude to put into practice the teachings of VC II, and had the skills to guide the local Church in the spirit of collaboration and co-responsibility. In the last few decades, the criteria, instead, seems to have dramatically shifted to loyalty—whether someone adheres to doctrinal tradition and orthodoxy. People were appointed whose orthodoxy was tested, on the basis, for example, of their views on reproductive and sexual morality, their stance vis-à-vis liberation theology, communism, relativism, and their stance on communion for the re-married divorcees, and so on.

Another most disturbing legacy Francis inherited is the clerical sexual abuse which continues to vex the Church and drain a lot of its energy and resources. I think, we need to also ask whether the traditional theology of Holy Orders has not also been responsible for the present quagmire in which the Church finds itself with the issue of clerical sexual abuse. I mean the theology of *ex opere operato*. This theology, as is well-known, originated in the polemics against Donatism. It was a completely different context. Transported lock, stock and barrel to our times, without discernment of changing times, this theology gave the impression that the sacramental seal trumps the failings and misdeeds of a cleric, even when these go manifestly against human dignity and rights as is the case with clerical sexual abuse. Further, in medieval Canon Law, there was a provision called *privilegium clericale*. It was the exemption of the clergy from the temporal justice of the state. Civil courts were to have no jurisdiction over the clergy even in criminal cases, and they could not be punished by civil courts. Their misdeeds could only be tackled in ecclesiastical courts. This legal tradition created a mindset of protecting the clerics at all costs. Its effects spilt over in the case of today's issues of clerical sexual abuse.

We could identify a general template at work in handling this issue. Instead of taking to task the perpetrator of sexual abuse, the clerics were shunted from one place to the other in a bid to protect them. All these shoddy dealings were shrouded in secrecy with no room for transparency. This is due to the fact that many ecclesiastics think that sexual abuse is a sin to confess in secret and to repent from and to be forgiven, and not a matter of public crime to be prosecuted. Sexual abuse is a serious matter of human dignity and involves a violation of basic human rights. To claim that the Church is a different society with the implicit understanding that its clerics are not subjected to civil jurisdiction when they violate human rights is something totally unacceptable. But this seems to have been the ideology behind the cover-ups of most cases of clerical sexual abuse.

Francis stepped into his pontificate burdened with the enormous weight of clerical sexual abuse on his back. The media was digging out embarrassing materials and publicising outrageous cases from different parts of the world, and even from unsuspected quarters in the Church. It was a moral pandemic which Francis inherited and had to face a world that was becoming ever more stridently critical of how clerical sexual abuses were handled under his predecessors. Pope Francis realized the gravity of the matter. But he is not someone who thinks problems could be solved through magisterial statements and declarations. In trying to respond to the crisis, he took into confidence the entire Church and the world-episcopate. In February 2019, he convened a four-day extraordinary consultative meeting with the presidents of bishop's conferences as how to go about with the issue of clerical sexual abuse which was eroding the Church and its credibility. It was the most open step to address an issue which has been devastating for the Church.

Francis continues to bear the brunt of the inherited policy-failures in this matter.

9. Facing Risks and Addressing Ambiguities

We have too many 'goody-goody' Church-leaders who act in a 'touch-me-not' fashion. If these prelates make any mistake, instead of honestly owning it up, they pretend that they are unblemished and perfect, and pass on the blame to someone else. I am reminded of an old saying. *"senatus non errat, et si errat, non corrigit ne videatur errasse"* (The senate does not err, and if it errs it does not correct, so that it is not seen to have erred!). It is the fear of making mistakes and ignorance that prevent many Church-leaders from taking bold decisions. It requires a lot of courage to own one's mistakes. Indeed, it takes a lot of courage to speak the truth. Here Pope Francis has set a model for Church-leaders to take risks, as he famously said, "I prefer a Church which is bruised, hurting and dirty because it has been out on the streets, rather than a Church which is unhealthy from being confined and from clinging to its own security" (*EG* 49). It is this open and courageous vision of the Church that leads Francis to take risks and to face puzzling and ambiguous situations. Let me illustrate this with some instances.

On September 21, 2018, Pope Francis signed a historic agreement with the Chinese state. Ever since the Chinese Communist Party (CCP) came to power, the relationship with the Vatican has undergone severe tensions and strains, causing an unfortunate split in the Chinese Church between the so-called underground Church and the open Church. Pope Francis faced a dilemma. If you give in to the Chinese government, then the freedom of the Church and its mission will be seriously hampered. On the other hand, if you refuse any negotiation with the CCP, then the split in the Chinese Church will continue and cause a lot of confusion among the faithful. It is a highly risky situation. There was opposition. Cardinal Joseph Zen, emeritus bishop of Hong Kong, felt that a deal with the CCP would be "to send the flocks into the mouth of wolves". He even named it a betrayal—a betrayal of the loyal Chinese underground Church.

Pope Francis could have postponed a decision on the matter, saying, that it was not yet the opportune moment to take one. This is what most administrators do in the Church: postpone, instead of engaging with difficult problems. As it is said, for the coward, the opportune moment never comes! The pope is aware of the importance of the present moment to arrive at a decision; which he took indeed amid contestations. There is a risk. In hindsight of history, the agreement with China could be the most outstanding achievement of Pope Francis' papacy, but could also turn out to be the most monumental blunder. The pope was aware of the risks and yet took a clear decision.

On January 4, 2019, Pope Francis goes to Dubai and meets with the Great Imam at Al Azhar with whom he makes a joint historic declaration of peace and religious harmony. The meeting was historic, so too the content of the joint statement. This statement acknowledges the plurality of religions as willed by God: a revolutionary statement! Henceforth Christian relationship to other religions takes on a new dimension and calls for a different approach. Let me quote from this statement:

> Freedom is a right of every person; each individual enjoys the freedom of belief, thought, expression and action. The pluralism and the diversity of religions, colour, sex, race and language are willed by God in His wisdom, through which He created human beings. This divine wisdom is the source from which the right to freedom of belief and the freedom to be different derives. Therefore, the fact that people are forced to adhere to a certain religion or culture must be rejected as too the imposition of a cultural way of life that others do not accept.
>
> Far-reaching are the consequences of this common declaration for the theology of religions. Here is a landmark in the Christian theology of religions. If the religions are willed by God like race, gender difference, the colour of the skin, and so on, then we need to take them very seriously and work with them (religions) for the salvation of the world.

The significance of this meeting with the Imam of Al-Azhar and the signing of the declaration stands out in bold relief against the background of the controversial lecture of Benedict XVI in Regensburg on September, 12, 2006, which allegedly stated that Christianity is rational. In contrast, Islam is not (quoting the last Christian Byzantine Emperor Manuel II).

In Muslim perception, the claims made in this lecture were an insult to Islam. Coming indeed from none other than the head of the Roman Catholic Church, the claims added to the gravity of the issue. It caused a huge commotion and street protests in many Islamic countries. A Pakistan-based Islamic body issued a fatwa against the pope. Thanks to quick diplomatic moves of the Vatican, the situation was diffused, and the Church was saved from further embarrassment. In any genuine dialogue, it is not only a matter of what I am saying is right or not. It is important how what I am saying is perceived by my dialogue partner. I think the recent visit of Pope Francis to Al Azhar and the common declaration with the Imam there has contributed to healing the wounds of the past and has helped to win back the trust of our Islamic brothers and sisters.

Pope Francis does not gloss over difficult issues but takes the bull by its horns. One clear example is the issue of homosexuality which is not simply a moral issue but a humanistic issue. That there are people who have innate homosexual tendencies similar to heterosexuality is something no one can ignore. Simply by this fact of possessing the tendency and inclination, homosexuals automatically do not become sinners. In this case, the Pope showed that everything need not be subjected to moral judgement. We leave certain things to God to judge. Hence his reply to the journalist as he was travelling back from Brazil after his first visit abroad as pope "If a person is gay and seeks God and has goodwill, who am I to judge?" It implied that homosexuals should not be marginalised but accepted and integrated into society.

Besides the issue of homosexuality, he has confronted boldly the long-standing pastoral issues connected with family. He convoked two synods on this issue. One of the most disputed questions at these two synods was about giving communion to the divorcees who are remarried. It was an extremely sensitive issue with opinions very divided. When he drew up his post-synodal exhortation, he did not avoid this thorn in the flesh. He faced it and made his view known with solid arguments. A footnote in *Amoris Laetitia* (footnote 351 no. 305) where the pope expresses the possibility of communion to the divorcees and remarried due to mitigating situations. His argument is in the spirit of the Gospel. Quoting *Evangelii Gaudium* the pope says, "The Eucharist, although it is the fullness of sacramental life, is not a prize for the perfect, but a powerful medicine and nourishment for the weak" (*EG* 47). Indeed, the Eucharist is not only for the healthy and the holy, but has also therapeutic or curing effect. All hell broke loose from this footnote! Pope Francis was accused of turning against the orthodoxy of the Catholic faith and tradition. His understanding of faith is much broader and deeper; and he stands his ground.

Let me cite one more instance which speaks volumes about the boldness of Pope Francis to act amid uncertainties and ambiguities. I am referring here to the convocation of the Synod of Amazonia (October 6–27, 2019). Such a regional synod itself was a bold innovation. The pope created an environment of freedom of thought and expression and gave the synodal reflections and proposals considerable attention and thought. For example, he let such recommendations be made as the ordination of married men, the ministry of women. But the synod was marred by a controversy around the wooden statue of a lady (*Pachamamma*) presented to the pope. The two-foot-high figurine became the focus of ire and wanton vandalism. For those who presented it, the statue in question had multivalent meaning—mother earth, Virgin Mary, fertility and life in Amazonia—whereas it was a provocation for those who saw just one thing in the statue: an idol!

If we analyse deep, we will note that there was a resistance to this synod by the Euro-centric Catholicism which believes the legacy of Plato and Aristotle are an integral part of the Christian kerygma. This Catholicism and *ancien régime* Christianity look with cynicism at efforts like that of indigenous peoples of Amazonia who live and understand faith according to their ethos and genius. The resistance, fear and anger of Euro-centric Catholicism has discredited the synod and trivialized the initiative of Pope Francis. Through this synod, Pope Francis allowed the face of another way of being Christian and Catholic be manifested at the heart of Rome. It proved to be a provocation for Euro-centric Christianity who consider their culture, languages, Churches, etc., as unchangeable criterion for judging all other forms of Christianity.

Conclusion: Pope Francis Leading a Listening, Poor Church

The Church is a tent; it moves with the people. It shifts. This is not a weakness. Faith in God turns the Church into a pilgrim, a Church always on the way. Hence there is no room for any sense of triumph as if one has reached the final goal. True to the pilgrim nature of the Church, we have a universal pastor in the Church who does not use his formal authority to impose. Here is a pope who listens – listens to the local Churches and to Bishops' Conferences worldwide. Pope Francis listens to the voices of the indigenous peoples (Synod of Amazonia), voices of the victims of clerical sexual abuse, voices of prisoners, of the physically challenged, the voices of peoples of other faiths, the voices of refugees and migrants. The result is a different papacy. It is not a papacy of ermine cape, silk and fine red shoes, a life of aloofness in the cultural ambience of nobility, but a life lived in elegant simplicity residing in the community of Santa Marta, settling his own hotel bills, buying his spectacles in an optical shop, and carrying his own bag on travel, like most people.

Pope Francis is at the same time battling to carry forward the spirit of VC II and its legacy with a new focus on the poor and the marginalised. The major stumbling block he encounters on this journey is the stiff resistance to change among a powerful segment within the Church. There is a fixated mindset among Church-leaders and Church-institutions. Any radical reform takes place when there comes into being a new mindset: *novus habitus mentis*. To inculcate the flexibility of mind and openness to change, Francis refers to the words of Cardinal John Henry Newman, whom he recently canonised. "Here on earth to live is to change, and to change often is to become more perfect". Francis' efforts at decentralisation and synodal governance in the Church provoke a reaction. This difficulty he encounters both in the Roman Curia and in the leadership of local Churches, infected with feudal trappings and medieval mindset.

From what I have said, it should be clear now, to be Pope Francis is not a bed of roses, but of thorns. It is a terrible experience of even isolation and loneliness. Marco Politi, a biographer of Pope Francis, has titled his work *"Francis's Loneliness. A Prophetic Pope. A Church in Stormy Seas"*. In his own house, in his own Curia, Pope Francis is misunderstood and sidelined. Pope Francis needs the support of all of us. We support him in that we follow his vision of faith, his path of the Gospel and his image of the Church and his continuing engagement with society and the world, at large.

The Pope is working on the Reform of the Roman Curia. When I was president of the International Theological Journal *Concilium*, we prepared a special issue on 'Reform of the Roman Curia' (*Concilium* 2013/5) to support the pope in his initiative of reform. We released the volume in Rome. Copies in Italian and Spanish were handed over to the Pope. Later we came to the conclusion, that to carry out the renewal of the Church, the existing Code of Canon Law is inadequate. Hence, we brought out an issue on 'Revision of Canon Law' (*Concilium* 2016/5). The idea proposed was to reshape Canon Law in such a way that it supports the initiatives of the pope for renewing the Church.

I think that the voice of Asia, Africa, Latin America and Oceania is not loud enough. It is time that the voices from the global South resound. We need to tell Euro-centric Christianity and Catholic fundamentalists that we stand by the vision and praxis of Pope Francis because we see the splendour and joy of the Gospel reflected in his words and actions. What Francis says and does vibrates with our own experiences in this part of the world. Yes, he is, indeed, a pope from "the end of the earth".

2.

Not a Reformer but a Renewalist

Pope Francis Resumes the Conciliar Process after a Long Hibernation

Aloysius Pieris, SJ

0. Renewal: Fruit of Responding to a Crisigenic Option Originating in the Periphery

When one thinks of Francis coming from the periphery and creating a storm in the institutional centre of the Church and getting blamed for dividing the faithful into two camps, one recalls a somewhat similar event from the Book of Acts, chapter 15. When Paul and Barnabas brought from the periphery (Antioch) to the centre (Jerusalem) the news of their bold decision to exempt non-Jewish neophytes from undergoing circumcision—a gender and race based rite of initiation—the assembly listened to Peter the Leader of the Church, who spoke in support of the new praxis, appealing to his own experience of seeing the Spirit descending on gentiles. His intervention created an atmosphere of openness that allowed the voice of the periphery (of Paul and Barnabas) to be heard at the centre "in silence" (Acts 15:1-12) i.e., with rapt attention.

The immediate aftermath of this 'Conciliar' deliberation was a widespread disarray among the rest of the Christians, polarizing them between Judaizers and the universalists. It was the gradual resolution of this 'post-conciliar' crisis that brought about the desired renewal in the nascent Church. Note also that during this critical period, it was Paul who helped Peter not to waver in his decision (Gal 2:11-14). Consequently, the Church was prevented from being a mere sect within Judaism and became what Christ had willed it to be: a universal sacrament of salvation—to borrow a happy phrase from Vatican Council II (hereinafter VC II).

This then is the prototype of church renewal: a crisigenic decision precipitated by the demands made in the periphery and the resultant crisis resolved in the subsequent era thanks to the exercise of the dialectical leadership played by Peter and Paul. This observation is essential to appreciate the renewalist project of Pope Francis, who has begun to re-live in his person and office the original charisma of papacy: a dual charisma couched in the ancient traditional understanding of the Bishop of Rome as "Vicar of Peter in the See of Peter and Paul."[1]

While 'reform' is a smooth flow of changes from the top to the base or from the centre to the periphery, leaving the institution structurally untouched, *'renewal'* is a centrifugal movement storming from the periphery as well as a base-to-top eruption of a transformative force that ends up in an attitudinal as well as a structural revolution in the ecclesial institution itself—not before resolving the initial crisis created by those who reject the proposed 'newness' as a violation of orthodoxy,[2] a delicate process in which Peter needs the cooperation of Paul.

The so-called Council of Jerusalem, where this process is first witnessed, is probably the one and only renewalist 'council' recorded in pre-VC II history. It was John XXIII who convoked the second Renovational Council, which judiciously accommodated within its teaching the insights derived from neo-praxes prevalent in the margins!

It too created a pan-ecclesial crisis as was to be expected both during and after its four sessions. Paul VI did a balancing act by making some compromises in order to bring VC II to a relatively successful finale.

But under the two successive papacies, which lasted thirty-five years, the Vatican Curia regrettably reversed the Conciliar process so that the chance of resolving the post-Conciliar crisis, which the renewalist movement from the periphery had created, was averted and consequently the intended renewal was aborted. What happened in the universal Church during this thirty-five-year period has been aptly summed up in the Editorial of a Catholic Journal:

> A lack of leadership was also baked into the character of bishops appointed during the 35-year span of the papacies of John Paul II and Benedict XVI. It became clear shortly after John Paul was elected in 1978, as the Congregation for the Doctrine of the Faith under him hauled in a string of distinguished theologians for disciplining and silencing, that his preferred candidates for the episcopacy would be submissive, devoid of questions or the slightest challenge to [curial] authority. Decades of appointments of men who generally conformed to those preferences and resisted anything that could be construed as dissent resulted in a conference acquiescent to Rome's [= the Vatican's] every wish.[3]

Hence we deem it providential that Francis, a genuine product of VC II, has rekindled the fire of renewal from the embers, allowing the aborted post-Conciliar crisis a fresh chance to take its own course through a 'synodal' procedure, i.e., bringing the centre face-to-face with the periphery and deftly employing the soft glove of Peter covering the iron hand of Paul. Rome has now become sensitive to the issues in the periphery as never before; for this Pope firmly believes that renewal originates in the periphery. Francis himself hails from the periphery; he exhorts the Church's ministers and the religious to go to the periphery; all his visits outside the Vatican, barring the one to the USA have been to the peripheries;[4] and most of his new cardinals represent the periphery. Therefore, he is in every sense a Renewalist Pope with a strong Pauline charisma energizing his Petrine leadership and ensuring that the periphery is vibrantly present in the centre.

(I)

Amazon Synod: Periphery Calling for a Crisigenic Decision from the Centre

Synodality, which was the mode in which VC II was launched and conducted,[5] became in the mind of Paul VI, the way to continue the Conciliar renewal in the post-conciliar years. In other words, VC II was conceived as the 'last Council' and a 'lasting Council'! Periodic Synodal consultation of the royal, prophetic and priestly people, who are the Church, accompanied by collegial deliberation among the bishops leading eventually to papal approval and promulgation seemed to be the most effective method of ensuring an incessant renewal that would dispense with the need of convoking another Council.

But no Synod, not even under Paul VI, followed this procedure to the letter; all of them were of a mere consultative nature. Hence it is the Amazon Synod, preceded by the one on Marriage and Family, that responded to the spirit of VC II and triggered off the process of *ecclesia semper renovanda*. In fact Archbishop Robert McElroy of San Diego, USA, who gratefully recalls his participation in this Synod, makes this confession: "My suggestion would be to embrace the type of synodal pathway that the church in the Amazon has been undergoing —one filled with deep and broad consultation, the willingness to accept arduous choices, the search for renewal and reform at every level, and unswerving faith in the constancy of God's presence in the community".[6] The American theologian, Massimo Faggioli, seems to recommend synodality not only for church-renewal but also for rescuing democracy from its present crisis [in the secular sector] since violation of justice is the first casualty of this crisis.[7]

The effectiveness of the synodal process rests in the art of engaging the peripheries. If, for instance, an element of renewal recognized as important in the peripheries had failed to enter the deliberations of the Council gathered at the centre, a subsequent Synod would have to take it up and continue the Conciliar renewal. In fact, the Amazon Synod has taken up a series of renewal that the bishops and theologians of VC II had overlooked. Let me illustrate this observation:

Though VC II was a response to several decades of agitation on the part of Catholic renewalists for a return to the Sources of Revelation (*reditus ad fontes*)—echoing the Reformed Churches' 'Back to the Bible' movement of the previous century but incorporating Tradition with the written Word—VC II did not formally take up for deliberation the biblical narrative on creation and the new creation. The Pastoral Constitution *Gaudium et Spes*—initially known as 'Church in the Modern World'—dealt with the Church in the contemporary social context, but the observation point was the '*modern*' secularized part of the globe rather than the so-called '*developing*' world—where, the ancient tradition of sacralizing nature rather than vandalizing it is still maintained to some extent. The Council Fathers' standpoint had affected their viewpoint. For, what one sees is determined by where one stands! Hence the Christian obligation towards creation (or nature or the universe as a whole) was not adequately and directly addressed by the participants of VC II and consequently the eco-spirituality still surviving in South America, Africa and Asia hardly entered the teaching of VC II.

It is the South American Francis, the first pope from the periphery, who filled the vacuum left by VC II, first by issuing the classic exhortation *Laudato Si'* and then by summoning the Amazon Synod, courageously braving waves of fiercely orchestrated protests from a few wealthy and fanatical critics living in the desacralized part of the globe—those who most need to hear the Good News about the sacredness of God's Creation.

The reason for this dissension today is not difficult to see. 'Secularism'—not in the sense of *secularity* but in the sense or 'anti-religious this-worldliness'—seems to have settled down for good in the West and also in the Westernized Christian enclaves elsewhere ever since both the Reformers and counter-Reformers 'cleansed' the Church of what they thought were the last vestiges of 'superstition' or 'nature worship' —a prejudice that many opponents of the Amazon Synod are parroting ad nauseam. By contrast, we in the Southern Hemisphere still experience a sacred this-worldliness, that is to say, a "this worldly religiousness" or, to use my own neologism, a *'cosmic religiosity'*.[8]

The complaint that Western missionaries had imported their secularism into the Asia-Pacific churches, suppressing the eco-religiosity of the indigenous masses as 'paganism', has been reiterated by our Asian Bishops, who went even further by advocating the promotion and preservation of that Asian legacy.[9] It is quite intriguing, therefore, to notice that a few eco-sensitive theologians in the West have come to recognize their regrettable oversight and have been striving hard to restore the lost heritage under the name of "Creation Theology".[10]

The Amazon, too, is a periphery that maintains this eco-spirituality in the midst of a losing battle against the onslaught of Mammon worshipers of the Secular West and their local (South American) accomplices. Once more we hear from ecclesiastics of the affluent and desacralized sector of the globe—e.g., Cardinals Brandmüeller, Mueller, Burke, etc.—that the Synod on Amazon is fostering superstition, pantheism and paganism. Hence it is all the more significant that thanks to this Synod the humanly induced fate of the infrahuman universe —felt deeply in the periphery but affecting the entire globe— had been boldly taken up at the Centre with evangelical daring (*parrhesia*), which is characteristic of this papacy. For this Pope reads God's Word in the Scriptures (i.e., in the History of Israel and of its neighbours) and, in its light, he also listens to the "increasingly desperate cries of the earth and the poor".[11] Earth and the poor! The Pope's critics cannot recognize this voice of the desecrated creation and dehumanized masses because these men—they are mostly men—have ceased to hear that same word in the Scriptures for the following reason:

According to an anti-biblical perception of creation prevalent in the West—here I am echoing the recurrent complaint hurled by the renowned British Biblical Scholar N.T. Wright against his own colleagues in the West[12]— namely, that this is destined to be destroyed for good by God at the end of time so that all the good 'souls' would go to 'heaven' which is a non-material or ethereally spiritual abode somewhere *outside* this creation. The logical consequence of subscribing to this false eschatology borrowed from Greek philosophers like Plato and Plutarch is to believe that since God is alleged to destroy this universe forever at the end of time, we might as well exploit it to the maximum for human use! This is a kind of anti-scriptural 'theology' that militates against *Laudato Si'* as well as the Amazon Synod, and obviously against the 'renewalist mission' of the Pope who spearheads both these initiatives.

The British theologian, Bishop N. T. Wright goes further (*ibid.*) in maintaining that the Book of Genesis presents the created universe as 'heaven and earth', a technical term that conveys the idea that creation was intended to be the abode of God (heaven) as well as of humans (earth), thus insinuating that the universe was conceived and created by God as a sacred place of worship. In any shrine dedicated to a god, the builder of that shrine installs a man-made image of that god for worship. But in this sacred temple of creation God Herself has placed Her own authentic *icon* to be revered, namely, *hā ādām*, the human person who is both male and female. Creation therefore is a sacred temple for rendering 'worship' ('*ăbôdah*) to God as well as rendering 'service' ('*ăbôdah*) to humanity.[13] Hence the human being who reflects God's own image is immediately entrusted with the mission of sharing God's sovereignty over infrahuman beings, namely, bearing the *human responsibility* for caring for the rest of creation (Gen 1:26-28).

The human rights theory derived from the traditional scholastic understanding of justice, valid and essential in itself, has been wrongly invoked by many theologians to suggest human ownership rather than humanity's stewardship over nature. This had led to fierce protests on the part of the Animal Rights' Lobby against Christian theologians.[14] This eco-hostile theory is based on a misinterpretation of Gen 1:26-28 cited above, namely, that human dignity, which we humans possess thanks to the Creator's image we bear, consists of human *rights*—a Scripturally unwarranted assumption, indeed! For this very Scriptural text as well as its context explicitly mentions the *responsibility that God shares with humans over all creation;* for immediately after creating humanity (*hā* ādām who is both male and female) according to the divine image and likeness, the Creator invites humanity to 'rule over', i.e., *take charge of the infrahuman world*, thus conferring upon the human species a *co-responsibility* with God for the entire universe! This is confirmed in the code of holiness enjoined in the Leviticus chapter 25 requiring that the Sabbath and the Jubilee laws concerning periodic rest be applied, not exclusively to the humans but to animals and fields as well. The rights theory, in other words, has to be subsumed under the theology of responsibility.[15]

The responsibility or the obligation of humans to conserve creation is based equally on another biblical teaching, namely, that there is *no experience of salvation above or apart from this very universe.* Thus, the Jews never spoke of another non-material existence or another spiritual realm as imagined by Greek thinkers, but of 'the age to come' ('*ôlām habā*), in contrast with 'the present age ('ôlām *hazeh*); not another world as such but a new age to this very world. This same creation together with its human stewards will re-appear in a radically renewed form, which is already anticipated in the bodily Risen Jesus who is the *New Creation,* which is to say, the *New Temple* in which the Divine and the Human coexist anew.

The Western theologies that Bishop Wright has rightly criticized for having abandoned this biblical vision of creation, prevent their advocates from comprehending the eco-theology of Francis which resonates with the content of Revelation. We hope firmly that the virulent protests heard from the vocal minority of Northern 'theologians', whose scholasticism prevents them from going back to the Sources of Revelation (as recommended in VC II), will subside (as all post-renewal crises must) thanks to the sense of *hope* with which Francis handles dissent —a theme I take up in Part III.

(II)

Migratory Rights:
Humanity's *Universal* Stewardship Over the Earth

The present Pontiff's strong stand on the care of the Earth as our common home is equally visible in his clear stance on the *rights* of migrants, or more poignantly, on the *responsibility* of rich countries to accommodate the 'dregs of society' emigrating from the nations which they had economically colonized. This papal plea is a gesture of obedience to the Word of God in the Holy Scriptures discerned in the context of today's Mammon worshippers manufacturing destitute masses by usurping and exploiting their natural resources.

The central take-off point in the Hebrew Scriptures is the Exodus, the story of poor hungry children of Jacob migrating to a rich country in the West (Egypt) in search of economic aid and becoming that rich Western nation's political slaves. YHWH, consistent with Her own nature, took the side of the enslaved migrants as their deliverer through the ministry of his chosen servant Moses—a humble person suffering from a poor self-image owing to an unsettling childhood-experience but transformed by God's grace into a giant of a leader, who dared to challenge the exploiter for a showdown. It is such leadership that people within and beyond ecclesiastical boundaries expect today in the face of the Pharaohs who enslave nations by misappropriating and misusing their natural resources. Francis has once more accepted this leadership role with evangelical daring (*parrhesia*).

Note that *powerful* colonizers are driven by *greed* to encroach into lands on which nature has poured out its blessings, whereas *powerless* migrants are driven by dire *need* for survival when entering a country that has become prosperous at their own nation's expense, only to end up becoming an object of that country's contemptuous discrimination. An example is the climatic disaster in the coffee plantations in Guatemala, reported to be entirely created by the so-called 'developed North' and resulting in an exodus of migrants into the land of the exploiters—the exploiters who had already threatened 'zero-tolerance' on their victims.[16]

In this case, the leaders of the colonizer nation which claims a Christian affiliation have conveniently forgotten that they too had migrated into that country and are obliged by God, as were the migratory children of Jacob, to welcome and accommodate alien migrants into the land that God has given them (Ex 22:21 [23:9], Lev 19:10 [23:22]; Deut 10:18-19; 24:17 [17:19]; 1 Chron 29:15; Jer 7:6; 22:3). It is providential, therefore, that there is a prophetic voice crying out in the wilderness, boldly taking to task the powerful nations that own and abuse the rich inheritance of poor nations and reject these displaced citizens' plea for accommodation. It is the obligation of all Christians in the South —for the Church is no more vibrant in the North—to join him in this noble but risky mission, with full awareness that the impending cosmic disaster has already begun in the South too.

The aforementioned papal protest is founded on the Creator's intention that the humans are stewards and not owners of creation. Christ's response to the question about paying taxes to Caesar (Mt 27:17; Mk 12:14; Lk 20:22) cannot be understood except against this biblical backdrop. Only the coin which bears 'Caesar's image' and his pompous inscription—*Tiberius son of divine Augustus*—belongs to Caesar who created it; whereas humans who bear "God's image" and are tattooed from eternity as sons and daughters of the one and true God who created them, belong to their Creator, not to Caesar. The human rulers are not God and therefore they own neither the humans nor their land.

It was, therefore, with tongue in cheek that the evangelist mentions Jesus tossing a coin to the treasury (of the Temple?),[17] a coin that is cynically alluded to be something a fish had swallowed, obviously from the dirt dumped in or around the Sea of Galilee— dirty money which Peter and Paul would call filthy lucre (1 Pet 5:2; 1 Tim 3:8; Tit 1:7, 11). The backdrop of these sayings and doings of Jesus is that the entire creation is meant to be a sacred space for God and humans to encounter each other rather than to be owned, valued and used by Mammon worshippers as a commercial good that amasses wealth in the hands of the few and creates landless migrants.

Thus, the countries that make filthy lucre by manufacturing and selling weapons of mass destruction—weapons that desecrate the Cosmic Temple and decimate its inhabitants— are the very nations that feign to be mediators of international peace in and between poorer countries. Any wonder that they are irritated by Pope Francis' bluntness that exposes their hypocrisy? What the American novelist, E.L. Doctorow had observed about his own country might soon be true of Asian countries that have joined the nuclear power race:

> We have had the bomb on our minds since 1945. It was first our *weaponry*, then our *diplomacy* and now it's our *economy*. How can we suppose that something so monstrously powerful would not, after years, compose our identity? [italics added] [18]

Already Pope John XXIII, who questioned the ethical validity of 'the just war theory', especially in this nuclear age,[19] knocked sense into Kennedy and Kruschev during the Cuban missiles crisis by appealing to their responsibility for the preservation of both humanity and creation. Francis has resumed this legacy with such evangelical passion as to seem annoyingly 'belligerent' in the eyes of powerful *warmongers*; but the weapon he wields in this 'warfare' against principalities and powers of this world is his dogged reiteration of the saving truth that hurts before it liberates.[20]

(III)

Pregnant Mother: A Symbol of Hope —
Eco-Feminism or Gyne-ecology

The Jewish world which Jesus and Christianity were born into was deeply affected by the cultural impact of Alexander's thoroughgoing colonialism that lasted three centuries. We have already noted in Part I the negative effect of Greek eschatology which created in the Church a theological stream that abandoned the biblical teaching on the salvific destiny of the whole of creation and advocated a utopia supposedly uncontaminated by this material universe. Now there is also another danger, aligned to that same source: a pessimism orchestrated in the

Greek dramatic tradition which invariably depicted life on earth as a *tragedy—a* serious threat indeed to the sense of *hope* that must invariably accompany one's *faith* in Christ since both these 'theological virtues' are derivatives of God's unfailing *love.*

'Hope' was another theme that characterized VC II as well as the Pope who convoked it. 'Prophets of doom' was how Pope John XXIII alluded to Christians who lacked this specifically Christian virtue and suffered from a negativity about the Church and Creation. John Paul I's brief pontificate of 33 days was an epitome of two things that go together: hope and humour. Francis has resumed this as the leitmotif of his kerygma. "Never to lose *hope* in the promises of Jesus" and to maintain a "sense of *humour*" were the fruit of the Lenten retreat that Francis had made with the members of the curia at the end of his first year in office.[21] In the homily he preached to the earthquake victims in Camerino, his mouth spoke out of his heart, with an appeal to exercise *hope* in the midst of tragedy trusting in the assurance of assistance from the Holy Spirit, the Comforter.[22] To the question raised by the Jesuits in Ireland after he was treacherously subjected to a public humiliation engineered by Viganò, 'the accuser', Francis said he was in deep consolation! His trust in the God of justice was so great that he had an unshakeable hope that he would be vindicated in God's good time; and his hope bore fruit.[23] In his recent exhortation to the Jesuits—commemorating and celebrating GC 32 decree 4—he was even more emphatic: "Share your hope wherever you are, encourage, console, comfort and invigorate. Open up the future, raise possibilities, generate alternatives, help to think and act differently"[24]

Some Roman citizens —baptized but not catechized— could not perceive the *message of hope* that a *pregnant mother* offers to any sensitive and cultured human person. The covert 'paganism' of these 'Christians' who vandalized the indigenous people's sacred icon by dumping it into the River Tiber reveals their failure to see a God-given sign of *Hope* in an 'expectant mother'. For, hope is not the wishful thinking of someone who had taken a lottery ticket but is the firm assurance of having already received what is desired; for a pregnant woman possesses within her that which she is 'expecting' to see in the near future!

Have the post-Christian nations forgotten that the fulfilment of the millennial *hope* in the arrival of the long awaited Messiah-Saviour is recounted in the Holy Writ within the personal histories of two pregnant mothers (Lk 1:1-80) and that the final birth pangs of the New Creation is also symbolized by the figure of an expectant mother (Rev 12:1-6)? Hence in *Laudato Si'* and the Amazon Synod, the Pope sends this message to his critics: "Return to the Christian sources and listen to the periphery." They are two conditions that foster the *hope* of ushering in a renewed church and a renewed creation.

The term 'ecofeminism' and Mary Daly's clever pun 'gyne-ecology', which I have cited in the subtitle above, are two neologisms coined by women who had perceived themselves and nature as co-victims of androcracy. The Chipko movement in India has been cited as one of many powerful examples of women defending nature against the combined forces of androcracy and technocracy. Notwithstanding such radical movements, Asia too is in danger of falling prey to this dual enemy—a peril about which I had offered an exhaustive analysis plus a warning followed by a tentative solution way back in 2005 at the Tenth International Congress of Marist Brothers, addressing them as Catholic Educationists.[25] Since then this crisis has trebled. Hence, I believe that the Amazon Synod sends a timely message to the Asian Churches as well.

It is therefore not surprising that the prospect of women strengthening the faith of Christians and maintaining our earthly home as a sanctuary for God-Human encounter, has come up in the Amazon Synod in the form of two suggestions:

(a) women as sensitive *leaders* in the Amazon mission and

(b) women as life-long *spouses* of "ordained community leaders".

Here again Francis is listening to the Spirit both in the Scriptures and in God's People in the periphery and is still in the process of discerning how and when that twofold request of the Amazon Church is to be complied with. For the New Testament testifies to the existence of female leaders such as Phoebe a minister in the church of Cenchreae (Rom 16:1); Junia, an Apostle (Rom 16:7),[26] —"apostle" in the sense of 'missionaries' such as were Paul and Barnabas; the lady mentioned in 2 Jn 1:1 and receiving instructions (2 Jn 1:10) that usually describe duties of Church leaders in Acts, 20:17, 28-31; teachers such as Priscilla who with her husband Aquila established and maintained a household church (1 Cor 16:19) and was knowledgeable enough to instruct the future evangelizer Apollo in Ephesus (Acts 18:24-26).

As for the second suggestion, the same New Testament mentions that the community leaders (presbyters and bishops) were chosen by the People of God from among exemplary married men—an ecclesiastical tradition that lasted more than a millennium in the Roman Communion until celibacy was officially introduced to presbyters and bishops in the 12th century. Once again, the Francis-bashers reveal their culpable ignorance of both Scriptures and Tradition, each of which accords with each of the two requests made by the Amazon Churches.

Hence our hope and our plea—which is also that of the Pope— is that even the dissenters listen to the delegates from the periphery "in silence" in the way the earliest Christians in Jerusalem did in listening to Paul and Barnabas from Antioch (Acts 15:12), given the fact that this openness came about after Peter, the leader of Apostles, had authoritatively explained the providential nature of their message to the rest of the Church (Acts 15:6-11). Peter has done it again; it is now for the rest of the Church to listen "in silence" to the apostles hailing from the periphery.

Endnotes

[1] J.M.R. Tillard, *The Bishop of Rome*, SPCK, London, 1983, 93-101.

[2] Cf. "Vatican II, A Crisigenic Council with an Unwritten Agenda "being Chapter III of my book *Give Vatican II a Chance: Yes to Incessant Renewal, No to Reform of the Reforms*, Kelaniya 2010, 69-94; (reprint, Bangalore 2012), 63-86.

[3] "Money Shapes the US Catholic Narrative", Editorial, *National Catholic Reporter*, October 25, 2019. [the parenthesis is added by me].

[4] The visit to WCC headquarters in Switzerland was also an unprecedented papal act of solidarity shown towards churches regarded as 'outside' the Roman Communion and unecumenically alleged to be peripheral to the Catholic Church.

[5] This Council and its sessions were preceded and accompanied by a search for the mind of God's People through the circulation of questionnaires etc.

[6] *National Catholic Reporter*, November 11, 2019.

[7] *La Croix Internationale*, November 13, 2019.

[8] I invented this word way back in the 1970s to differentiate it not only from *metacosmic religiosity* (by which I refer to religions that posit a transcendent horizon as the source and summit of salvation), but also from secularism of Western provenance. Cf. *An Asian Theology of Liberation*, Orbis Books, Maryknoll, NY,1988, 71-73 and *passim; The Genesis of an Asian Theology of Liberation*, Kelaniya Sri Lanka 2013, chapter 14. I have already expressed my gratitude to Jacques Dupuis, SJ and M. Zago, OMI who, in preparing the first draft of John Paul II's *Redemptoris Missio*, introduced these terms 'cosmic' and 'metacosmic' into this pontifical document so that now it is part of the Magisterium's vocabulary!

[9] See FABC papers, n.81, Hong Kong, 25.

[10] This is briefly discussed in my article "Towards a Theology of Religious Pluralism: Fidelity and Fairness in Inter-Faith Fellowship," in Jose Maria Vigil (ed.), *Towards a Planetary Theology along the Many Paths of God*, Dunamis Publishers, Montreal, 2010, 124-127.

[11] These are the very words that Francis used when appealing to the Chief Executives of Companies such as BP, Exxon, Mobil, Shell, Total, Chevron, Black and Hermes. See *The Tablet* 20/10/2019, 5.

[12] In his numerous talks easily accessible in the internet by googling "N.T. Wright".

[13] I have discussed this Hebrew term within the purview of Ignatian spirituality in *A Gist of Jesuitness: A Thesis and a Hypothesis*, Tulana Centre, Kelaniya, Sri Lanka, 2015, 5-10.

[14] See the controversy that resulted from advocating this traditional Catholic theory in *Civilta Cattolica*, 1999/I, 319-331, 532-543; 1999/II, 477-481.

[15] As I have argued in my trilogy on Human Rights [soon to be re-printed as one volume], the rights belong to the realm of the Law, which (according to Paul) exposes sin (and thus prevent violations of justice) whereas responsibility is a derivative of

love which alone saves sinners. For a jejune summary of this view, see my "Justice and Faith: Clearing a Cloud of Confusion", *Social Justice*, CSR, Colombo, June-July (vol 39, n.194), 8-9.

[16] *National Catholic Reporter*, October 18-31, 2019, 1 and 8.

[17] Probably a shekel as part of the Temple Tax according to some exegetes; see, e.g., D.A.C.R.T France, J.A, MG.J. Wenham (consulting editors), *New Bible Commentary*, 21st century edition, reprint, Hyderabad, 2015, 927.

[18] Zia Mian, "Lingering Shadows" [Letter from America], *Economic and Political Weekly*, May 28-June 4, 2005, 2219.

[19] *Pacem in terris*, nn. 111ff.

[20] https://www.armscontrol.org/act/.../pope-calls-nuclear-weapons-ban; https://www.japantimes.co.jp/.../hopes-high-pope-francis-will-send-message- bombed-cities-support-nuclear-weapons-ban-treaty; https://www.vaticannews.va/.../holy-see-united-nations-auza-prohibition- nuclear-weapons.html ...... etc.

[21] C. Wooden, *Catholic News Service*, March 14, 2014.

[22] *Vatican Media*, 16 June 2019.

[23] See A. Pieris, *Helping Francis Renew the Church*, Kelaniya, Sri Lanka, 2019, 15-16.

[24] Pope Francis' Audience with Jesuit Social Justice and Ecology Secretariat, *Vatican News*, November 7, 2019.

[25] "Religion, Nature and Violence: The Restoration of an Eco-Spirituality in Asia", being Part III of my article, "Asian Reality and the Christian Option: A Plea for a Paradigm Shift in Christian Education in Asia," *Dialogue NS*, vols. 32/33 (2005/06), 158-196. For Part III, refer to 180-196.

[26] The masculine form 'Junias' is never found in contemporary literature and is therefore a later interpolation inserted by an androcrat! Junia was therefore a woman, probably the wife of Andronicus.

3.

Pope Francis and the Reception of VC II in a New Global Historical Context

Massimo Faggioli

Introduction:[1]

The conclave of March 2013 took place in a very particular period in the history of the reception of the Second Vatican Council (hereinafter VC II): after a pontificate, Benedict XVI's, whose overarching message was clearly about the intention to revisit VC II and its reception and application in the life of the Church. In this sense, the election of the successor of Benedict XVI was not just the election of the new bishop of Rome, but it was also framed in the context of the debate on VC II—a debate in which Benedict XVI had played a very visible role, because the debate had been prompted by him at the beginning of his pontificate with the famous speech to the Roman Curia on the 'two hermeneutics' of December 22, 2005.[1]

The pontificate of Benedict XVI represented the culmination of a trend inaugurated before his election. Already toward the end of the

---

[*] This article develops a chapter from Massimo Faggioli, *The Liminal Papacy of Pope Francis. Moving Toward Global Catholicity* (Maryknoll New York: Orbis Books, 2020).

pontificate of John Paul II, that is, in the early 2000s, one could see signs of a 'policy review' of the Roman Curia about the interpretation and reception of VC II—the most consequential being the instructions of the Congregation for Divine Worship *Liturgiam Authenticam* of March 28, 2001 (that inspired and caused a new trend in the translation of liturgical texts, whose fruits are very well known in the English-speaking world) and *Redemptionis Sacramentum*, of April 23, 2004, about liturgical abuses.[2] This trend became even stronger with the election of Benedict XVI. From 2005 onward, Benedict XIV's interpretation of VC II was summarized by commentators on the one side as a polarity between 'continuity and reform' and between 'discontinuity and rupture' on the other. This simplistic caricature of the hermeneutical complexity of VC II penetrated and shaped the language of the discourse of the Catholic Church on VC II, especially at the level of theological studies and seminaries, but also in the theological orientation of bishops and cardinals.

This is a key element for understanding how Francis' theology interacted with the theological culture identified with the papacy in 2013, and it helps to explain the reception of Francis in the global Church today. Pope Francis inaugurated a new phase in the reception of VC II, partly due to the disappearance of traditionalist issues from his agenda, which affected his handling of liturgical and other matters.[3] The pontificates of the popes elected since 1939 have all been defined (in different measures) by the historical-theological debate in relation to the council—from Pius XII's decision not to reconvene Vatican I in 1948–1949 to John Paul II, the last pope who had been a member and a key figure of VC II and, at the same time, a stabilizer of the council in the post-VC II period, to Benedict XVI, one of the most influential theologians at VC II.[4] Pope Francis, ordained priest in 1969, does not belong in this line of popes involved in VC II for biographical reasons. But there is also the specific heritage of the Catholic Church in Latin America and the legacy of VC II for Latin American Catholicism throughout these last fifty years. Clearly, the Argentinian Jesuit Bergoglio perceives VC II as a matter that should not be reinterpreted or restricted, but implemented and expanded.[5]

There was also something very visible from the very beginning of his pontificate. In the words addressed to the people in Saint Peter's Square after the election, on the evening of March 13, 2013, Francis presented himself as the "bishop of Rome": the binomial "bishop and people," crucial to Francis' ecclesiology, signified from the beginning an emphasis on the ecclesiology of the local Church and on the diocese of Rome as a local Church.

Francis' quotations of VC II have been rarer than in his predecessors, but have always been carefully chosen to mark particularly important moments during the pontificate. Remarkably, the first quotation of VC II during his pontificate was one week after his election, March 20, 2013—during a meeting with the fraternal delegates from other churches and religions, Francis mentioned for the first time VC II and in particular the declaration *Nostra Aetate* (October 28, 1965) on non-Christian religions.

From the beginning of Francis' pontificate, the presence of VC II has been more mediated and non-textual than explicit in programmatic texts; more a matter of implementation than of interpretation of the council. This is why it is impossible to assess Francis' relationship with VC II simply from the textual references to the council in the texts of his teaching. As a matter of fact, Francis quotes VC II rarely and surely not more often than his predecessors. His modality of reception of VC II is a complex mix of both the *reception of the documents* of the council and *of the act* of the council.

1. A Spiritual-Theological and Ecclesiological Reception of VC II

The two ecclesiological constitutions, *Lumen Gentium* and *Gaudium et Spes*, are the most important textual references to VC II in Pope Francis' teaching: it can be said that Francis' reception of VC II is ecclesiological in the sense of a missionary reform of the Church. There is also an ecclesiological intention in the selections of the sources in Francis' teachings: in the 217 endnotes of *Evangelii Gaudium* there are only seven quotations from documents issued by the Roman Curia (four from the *Compendium of the Social Doctrine of the Church* by the Pontifical Council for Justice and Peace; three from the Congregation for the Doctrine of the Faith, all from the instruction *Libertatis Nuntio* about theology of liberation, 1984), fifteen quotations from VC II, and twenty-three from documents of national or continental bishops' conferences. But Francis' response is, above all, a spiritual-theological reception of VC II and of its ecclesiology.[6] We can see that from his reception of *Lumen Gentium*.

1.1. Lumen Gentium: Papal Teaching and the Church

The conciliar constitution on the Church, *Lumen Gentium* (November 21, 1964; hereinafter, *LG*), plays a special role in the relationship between Francis and VC II. Pope Francis' apostolic exhortation *Evangelii Gaudium* (hereinafter, *EG*), which is akin to a programmatic document for his pontificate, quotes the documents of VC II twenty times, and the most-quoted is the constitution on the Church, *LG*.

Paragraph 12 of *LG* is particularly significant for Francis. In *Evangelii Gaudium*, it is clearly his intent to rephrase the infallibility of the magisterium as based on the infallibility of the people of God:

> In all the baptized, from first to last, the sanctifying power of the Spirit is at work, impelling us to evangelization. The people of God is holy thanks to this anointing, which makes it infallible *in credendo*. This means that it does not err in faith, even though it may not find words to explain that faith (*EG* 119).

This passage about the *sensus fidei* is even more remarkable because this is the only passage of the exhortation that talks about infallibility, and it does that in terms of infallibility *in credendo* of the people of God. Francis' choice is clear in favor of an ecclesiology of the people as missionary people that is more accentuated in *EG* than in VC II itself (*LG* 17 and *Ad Gentes* 5–6, hereinafter *AG*). This is also an ecclesiology that has in mind a practical restructuring of ordained ministry in the Church, beginning with the bishops:

He [the bishop] will sometimes go *before his people*, pointing the way and keeping their hope vibrant. At other times, he will simply be *in their midst* with his unassuming and merciful presence. At yet other times, he will have to *walk after them*, helping those who lag behind and—above all—allowing the flock to strike out on new paths" (*EG* 31).

The local level is emphasized not only here in the relations between the bishop and the people, but also in the way *EG* operates theologically. The sources of the exhortation—much more abundantly than in previous papal teachings, now coming from documents approved by national and continental bishops' conferences—presupposes a *communio ecclesiae* (the communion of the local Churches with Rome) not absorbing totally the *communio ecclesiarum* (the communion of the local Churches between themselves).[7]

The connection between reform ecclesiology and local ecclesiology leads in *EG* to a paragraph on the reform of the Petrine ministry, which Pope Francis connects to the "conversion of the papacy." Francis admits that little progress has been made since VC II and since John Paul II's encyclical on ecumenism *Ut Unum Sint* (1995): "Pope John Paul II asked for help in finding "a way of exercising the primacy which, while in no way renouncing what is essential to its mission, is nonetheless open to a new situation" [quot. of John Paul II, encyclical *Ut Unum Sint* 1995, par. 95]. We have made little progress in this regard. The papacy and the central structures of the universal Church also need to hear the call to pastoral conversion". (*EG* 32)

Evangelii Gaudium is not the only major teaching of Francis that draws from VC II. The encyclical *Laudato si'* does not quote *Lumen Gentium* but contains indirectly a reception of the ecumenical ecclesiology of VC II, expressed also in *LG*, with its inter-Christian appeal and sources.

It is in the post-synodal exhortation *Amoris Laetitia* (March 19, 2016; hereinafter *AL*) that Francis makes progress regarding the reception of the ecclesiology of *Lumen Gentium*. From the very beginning of the exhortation, Francis reframes the relationship between the papacy and the teaching of the Church:

> I would make it clear that not all discussions of doctrinal, moral or pastoral issues need to be settled by interventions of the magisterium. Unity of teaching and practice is certainly necessary in the Church, but this does not preclude various ways of interpreting some aspects of that teaching or drawing certain consequences from it (*AL* 3).

This is by far the most important ecclesiological development in a papal document issued after the very eventful, two-year and two-session Bishops' Synod (2014 and 2015) on family and marriage.

1.2. Gaudium et Spes: Recontextualization of the Catholic Church

The reception of *GS* in Francis' pontificate presents a remarkable reversal of fortune for the last document of VC II, the pastoral constitution, from the pontificate of Benedict XVI, who quoted *Gaudium et Spes*, but often in a critical way.[8] Francis' theological thrust is about the recovery of a Catholic universality that is free from Latin universalism and not about a cultural resistance against modernity and post-modernity.

The legacy of *Gaudium et Spes* is evident in paragraphs 222 and 233, where we have a condensed summary of the worldview of VC II in four axioms: "Time is greater than space"; "unity prevails over conflict"; "realities are more important than ideas"; and "the whole is greater than the part."[9] Francis writes, "Giving priority to time means being concerned about initiating processes rather than possessing spaces" (*EG* 223)—a reception of the new awareness expressed by VC II about historicity. Then in *EG* 233: "Realities are greater than ideas. This principle has to do with incarnation of the word and its being put into practice"—this is closest to the core of *Gaudium et Spes*'s existential-ontological thesis: also in the realm of concrete spiritual decisions, the particular and individual element cannot, despite the real validity of general principles, be simply-drawn general principles. "Time is greater than space" embodies the shift from a purely metaphysical approach to God's revelation to a more tangible "history of salvation." "Realities are more important than ideas" embodies the shift from the deductive to the inductive method.

Francis' pontificate deals with this shift most specifically in his remarkable description of the Church as a polyhedron:

> Here our model is not the sphere, which is no greater than its parts, where every point is equidistant from the centre, and there are no differences between them. Instead, it is the polyhedron, which reflects the convergence of all its parts, each of which preserves its distinctiveness. Pastoral and political activity alike seek to gather in this polyhedron the best of each. There is a place for the poor and their culture, their aspirations and their potential. Even people who can be considered dubious on account of their errors have something to offer which must not be overlooked. It is the convergence of peoples who, within the universal order, maintain their own individuality; it is the sum total of persons within a society which pursues the common good, which truly has a place for everyone (*EG* 236).

The universality Francis has in mind means a big-tent Church open to the world and against the temptations of creating a smaller, purer Church made of smaller communities—with some remarkable consequences for the link, often made by papal magisterium in the post-VC II period, between the council and the flourishing of post-conciliar lay Catholic movements.[10] But what is especially typical of Francis' reception of VC II is not only this anti-elitism, but also the retrieval of the almost forgotten emphasis on the poor and the "preferential option for the poor" that finds its source in VC II (*LG* 8, *GS* 1, *AG* 3).

The conciliar ecclesiology of the relationship between the Church and the world, rooted in *GS*, is received in *EG* 114: "Jesus did not tell the apostles to form an exclusive and elite group." Also, the discussion in *EG* 115 about Christian faith and plurality of cultures demonstrates a full and unembarrassed reception of the pastoral constitution of VC II by Francis.[11]

The encyclical *Laudato si'* draws from *GS*, although, typical of Francis, its text is not overloaded with conciliar quotations, which are mostly mediated through the use of post-conciliar teaching—especially that of Paul VI and the national and continental bishops' conferences.[12] It is remarkable that all quotations from VC II in *LS* are from *GS*.

Of all the major documents issued by Francis, *GS* plays the most prominent role in the exhortation *Amoris Laetitia*. In *AL*, Francis quotes *Evangelii Gaudium* (10 times), the constitution *Gaudium et Spes* of VC II (19 times), and John Paul II's exhortation *Familiaris Consortio* of 1981 (26 times). As in his previous documents, in *AL*, Francis cites often from documents of national bishops' conferences (Spain, Korea, Argentina, Mexico, Colombia, Chile, Australia, CELAM, Italy, and Kenya) and, in this particular case, very often from the catechesis of John Paul II. But *GS* plays a pivotal role for the exhortation, as it did during the entire synodal process of the Bishops' Synod of October 2014 and October 2015. *AL* draws from *GS* for the paragraphs of the pastoral constitution on family and marriage,[13] but also from *GS* 22 on "Christ the new Adam" (cf. *AL* 77–78), *GS* 16 on conscience, and *GS* 17 on freedom and human dignity.

1.3. *Sacrosanctum Concilium: Liturgy and Ecclesiology*

The reception of the liturgical constitution of VC II presents a particular aspect of Francis' overall reception of the council: on the one hand, the liturgical issue in the Catholic Church had been one of the most affected by the pontificate of Francis' predecessor;[14] on the other hand, regarding the liturgical issue, Francis' pontificate has been marked by a reception of the teaching of VC II that does not reduce the council to a corpus of texts and at the same time is faithful to its trajectories—in this case, to the path toward liturgical reform introduced by VC II. This is one way to read the notable absence of quotations of *SC* in *EG*—a document which contains a long section on the homily.

However, Francis' attention to the liturgical issue and its connections to the ecclesiology of VC II are evident in *EG*. As Francis notes, liturgy is evangelizing and not part of a power struggle in the Church, or a way to express an exclusive ecclesiology, or to use the gospel to ignore the deep solidarity between the Church and the world:

> This insidious worldliness is evident in a number of attitudes which appear opposed, yet all have the same pretence of 'taking over the space of the Church.' In some people we see an ostentatious preoccupation for the liturgy, for doctrine and for the Church's prestige, but without any concern that the Gospel have a real impact on God's faithful people and the concrete needs of the present time. In this way, the life of the Church turns into a museum piece or something which is the property of a select few (*EG* 95).

In *Laudato Si'*, Francis expresses (quoting John Paul II's exhortation *Ecclesia de Eucharestia*, 2003) the link between liturgy and a new Church-world relationship, speaking of creation and the Eucharist "as an act of cosmic love" (*LS* 236). Also in *Amoris Laetitia*, quoting again from the teaching of John Paul II, Francis emphasizes an understanding of the liturgy that connects human love and divine love, thus extending the definition of "liturgical" beyond the boundaries of the liturgical rites of the Church: "The procreative meaning of sexuality, the language of the body, and the signs of love shown throughout married life, all become an 'uninterrupted continuity of liturgical language' and 'conjugal life becomes in a certain sense liturgical'" (*AL* 215). This has been a constant impulse coming from Francis: the visible statements about the liturgical reform of VC II—in the direction of a rejection of the plans for a "reform of the liturgical reform" of VC II—are substantiated by a much larger body of theology of the liturgy in his pontificate.[15]

1.4. *Dei Verbum: Exegetes, Theologians, and the Church as a People*

Among all the major documents of VC II that need to be examined to understand Francis' reception of the council, the dogmatic constitution on revelation offers a particular comparison with his predecessor, Benedict XVI, for whom *Dei Verbum* (hereinafter, *DV*) was probably the keystone of the conciliar teaching.[16]

Francis' theological profile is not that of a biblical scholar. But certainly his preaching is in line with the conciliar re-centering on the gospel of Jesus Christ as the "generative grammar" of Catholic theology and magisterium.[17] This passage from *DV*: "Through this revelation, therefore, the invisible God (see Col 1:15, 1 Tim 1:17) out of the abundance of His love speaks to men [and women] as friends"

(2) represents Francis' new incarnation of the papacy as a way to be the Church not based on the gospel or about the gospel, but the Church *of* the gospel. In the famous passages of *EG* 222 and 233—"time is greater than space" and "realities are greater than ideas"—there is an indirect but unquestionable reception of the theological insight of *DV* 8 about the relationship between human experience and God's revelation.[18]

2. A Generative Reception

The marker of Pope Francis' reception of VC II is not a textual one, but a "generative reception" of the council. In his pontificate, the legacy of the council lives not through quotations from the final documents, but in a reception of various conciliar sources and in various ways.

2.1. The Key Role of John XXIII's '*Gaudet Mater Ecclesia*'

The first way that Pope Francis demonstrates his generative reception of the council is through the use of the texts of VC II that do not belong to the formal corpus of the final documents of the council. The most important example of this is found in paragraph 41 of *Evangelii Gaudium*, where he discusses the relationship between the deposit of faith and ways to express it. Here, Pope Francis quotes from John XXIII's opening speech of the council delivered on October 11, 1962, *Gaudet Mater Ecclesia*—a key (and not at all obvious) source from the history of VC II from a hermeneutical point of view:[19] "At the same time, today's vast and rapid cultural changes demand that we constantly seek ways of expressing unchanging truths in a language which brings out their abiding newness. 'The deposit of the faith is one thing...the way it is expressed is another' [*Gaudet Mater Ecclesia*]. There are times when the faithful, in listening to completely orthodox language, take away something alien to the authentic Gospel of Jesus Christ, because that language is alien to their own way of speaking to and understanding one another. With the holy intent of communicating the truth about God and humanity, we sometimes give them a false god or a human ideal which is not really Christian. In this way, we hold fast to a formulation while failing to convey its substance. This is the greatest danger. Let us never forget that 'the expression of truth can take different forms. The renewal of these forms of expression becomes necessary for the sake of transmitting to the people of today the Gospel message in its unchanging meaning.'" [John Paul II, encyclical *Ut Unum Sint* (1995) par. 19].

The other most important quotation of *Gaudet Mater Ecclesia*, however, is in *EG* 84 about the challenges to evangelization and the lack of hope that is typical of our times:

> The joy of the Gospel is such that it cannot be taken away from us by anyone or anything (cf. *Jn* 16:22). The evils of our world—and those of the Church—must not be excuses for diminishing our commitment and our fervor. Let us look upon them as challenges which can help us to grow. With the eyes of faith, we can see the light which the Holy Spirit always radiates in the midst of darkness, never forgetting that 'where sin increased, grace has abounded all the more' (*Rom* 5:20). Our faith is challenged to discern how wine can come from water and how wheat can grow in the midst of weeds. Fifty years after the Second Vatican Council, we are distressed by the troubles of our age and far from naïve optimism; yet the fact that we are more realistic must not mean that we are any less trusting in the Spirit or less generous. In this sense, we can once again listen to the words of Blessed John XXIII on the memorable day of 11 October 1962: "At times we have to listen, much to our regret, to the voices of people who, though burning with zeal, lack a sense of discretion and measure. In this modern age they can see nothing but prevarication and ruin.... We feel that we must disagree with those prophets of doom who are always forecasting disaster, as though the end of the world were at hand. In our times, divine Providence is leading us to a new order of human relations which, by human effort and even beyond all expectations, are directed to the fulfillment of God's superior and inscrutable designs, in which everything, even human setbacks, leads to the greater good of the Church.

In this section of *Evangelii Gaudium*, with the quotations from *Gaudet Mater Ecclesia*, Pope Francis is re-enacting Pope John XXIII's reorientation of the Church's message, thus showing many parallels between the Church at the end of Pius XII's pontificate and at the beginning of his own.[20] Like John XXIII, the election of Francis happened in difficult times for the Church not only because of the external circumstances, but also because of the unstated but clear sense of exhaustion of a given theological-cultural paradigm, and the need to reframe and rephrase the message of the Church in a new paradigm. It is no surprise, then, that the resistance and fear of change met by John XXIII at the time of the council is similar to the reception of Pope Francis in some quarters of the Catholic Church today.

The bull of indiction of the extraordinary jubilee of mercy *Misericordiae Vultus* (April 11, 2015) quotes once again from John XXIII's opening speech of VC II, *Gaudet Mater Ecclesia*:

> I have chosen the date of 8 December because of its rich meaning in the recent history of the Church. In fact, I will open the Holy Door on the fiftieth anniversary of the closing of the Second Vatican Ecumenical Council. The Church feels a great need to keep this event alive. With the Council, the Church entered a new phase of her history. The Council Fathers strongly perceived, as a true breath of the Holy Spirit, a need to talk about God to men and women of their time in a more accessible way. The walls which for too long had made the Church a kind of fortress were torn down and the time had come to proclaim the Gospel in a new way. It was a new phase of the same evangelization that had existed from the beginning. It was a fresh undertaking for all Christians to bear witness to their faith with greater enthusiasm and conviction. The Church sensed a responsibility to be a living sign of the Father's love in the world. We recall the poignant words of Saint John XXIII when, opening the Council, he indicated the path to follow: 'Now the Bride of Christ wishes to use the medicine of mercy rather than taking up arms of severity.... The Catholic Church, as she holds high the torch of Catholic truth at this Ecumenical Council, wants to show herself a loving mother to all; patient, kind, moved by compassion and goodness toward her separated children'.[21]

And since *EG*, Francis has continued to stress the parallels between John XXIII and himself.[22]

2.2. A Reception in Acts and Gestures

The second way that Francis demonstrates his generative reception of VC II is his interpretation of the council *as an act* and not simply as a corpus of final documents—as a reception in acts and gestures. Francis' pontificate is part of the new papacy shaped by VC II together with the new global media culture, globalization of religion, and the comeback of religion in international affairs. In this sense, Francis' pontificate is not phenomenically different from the "magisterium of gestures" of his predecessors, at least since John XXIII. But there are gestures that speak specifically to Francis' global reception of the message of VC II:

- His visit to the island of Lampedusa in the Mediterranean Sea on July 8, 2013, to commemorate thousands of migrants who had died crossing the sea, as a sign of a Church attentive to the signs of our times;

- The decision to open the Extraordinary Jubilee of Mercy on November 29, 2015, in Bangui, in the Central African Republic, as a sign of a Church decentralizing from Rome;

- The visit to migrants and refugees detained on the Greek Island of Lesbos on April 16, 2016, as a sign of the ecumenical engagement of the churches on the humanitarian crisis of our time;

- The washing of the feet of a young Muslim woman prisoner beginning in March 2013. Francis' reception of VC II as an act is key to understanding his pontificate as rejection of a neo-exclusivist Catholic ecclesiology.[23]

Gaudium et Spes plays a special role in the textual as well as the non-textual, performative reception of VC II in Francis' pontificate, beginning with the trip to the island of Lampedusa in July 2013. But the textual reception of *Gaudium et Spes* constitutes an important part of his teaching for the effort of *re-contextualization* of the Church against the current *de-contextualization* (ideologization and virtualization of the faith experience), and also in terms of re-contextualization of the Church's teaching in its own tradition: different moments and different voices. In this respect, the use of VC II documents in *AL* cannot be examined without a careful look at the complex relations between different sources: the systematic recourse to Jesus' preaching of the gospel; the tradition of the Church, especially the papal teaching of the twentieth century; and the post-VC II teaching of the bishops' conferences.

Francis' non-textual reception of VC II was not found just in personal gestures, but also in institutional acts. In Francis' pontificate, the most interesting reception of VC II as an act has surely been the synodal process of 2014 and 2015 leading to the exhortation *Amoris Laetitia*. It is telling of Francis' reception of VC II that *AL* relies heavily and creatively on the two 2014 and 2015 Synod final reports: Francis chose which texts of the final reports he wanted to quote, and he clearly takes risks vis-à-vis his opposition, making clear his mind and his ecclesiology. Francis quotes from the three paragraphs of the final 2015 report that received the highest number of negative votes.[24] They are significantly used for *AL*'s section on the pastoral accompaniment of difficult situations. But all this is in the context of a reception of the synodal process that follows the intention of VC II for the Bishops' Synod as a body representing effectively the Church through the episcopate.

2.3. Ecumenism and the New Signs of Our Times

The third demonstration of Francis' "generative reception" of the council is his understanding of the message of VC II *according to the new signs of our times*. This is evident in the example of the "ecumenism of blood," which Francis talked about from the beginning of his pontificate. There is an ecumenical landscape that has changed tragically as a consequence of the wars that target religious minorities—Christians included—in Africa, the Middle East, and Asia. What Francis called the "ecumenism of blood" is certainly part of his ecumenical outlook, as he said many times and especially in his December 2013 interview with Italian journalist Andrea Tornielli: "For me, ecumenism is a priority. Today, there's the ecumenism of blood. In some countries they kill Christians because they wear a cross or have a Bible, and before killing them they don't ask if they're Anglicans, Lutherans, Catholic or Orthodox. The blood is mixed. For those who kill, we're Christians.... That's the ecumenism of blood. It exists today too, all you have to do is read the papers."[25] But it is also evident in Francis' reception of the theological message of VC II on ecumenism and religious freedom, with the conciliar intuition of the need for a deeper look at the signs of our times, in an inter-textual reception of the council.

This has made of Francis a global spokesperson for the defense of the religious freedom of persecuted minorities, such as the *Rohingya* Muslims in Myanmar,[26] and also a general spokesperson for a Catholic Church that is not concerned about its particular position in the world, but about being able to advocate for causes that concern the human person today.

Conclusion

Scholars of VC II saw in the election of Jorge Mario Bergoglio–Francis to the papacy something that eluded those who had dismissed the council as an anomaly in the way Catholicism works. Words, symbols, and acts of the 2013 conclave and of the beginning of Francis' pontificate were clearly an echo of the 1958 conclave and of the beginning of John XXIII's pontificate.[27]

There is something especially relevant in this moment of reception of VC II at sixty years, that is, a fundamental shift in the status of the council as a point of reference for Catholic theologians and Church leaders. There is no question that all the successors of John XXIII were "VC II popes" (Paul VI brought the council to a conclusion; John Paul I and John Paul II were council fathers; and Benedict XVI was one of the most important theological *periti* at the council). But the election of Francis on March 13, 2013, has indubitably changed the landscape of the Church and especially of the debate on VC II. The fact that Jorge Mario Bergoglio–Francis is a VC II Catholic—and, in a sense, the first post-VC II pope—has changed the nature of the debate on the council.

What is typical of Francis is the idea that the interpretation of VC II as an exercise of textual exegesis made in a historical vacuum is not only a reduction of its meaning, it is also the subtlest form of rejection of the council. The same form of rejection can be seen in those attempts to interpret Francis' papacy outside of the history of the hermeneutics of VC II as an act and not just as a series of documents.

Endnotes

[1] Benedict XVI's speech made indirect but unmistakable references to Giuseppe Alberigo, ed., *Storia del Concilio Vaticano II*, 5 vols. (Bologna: Il Mulino; Leuven: Peeters, 1995-2001), published in English as *History of VC II*, ed. Joseph Komonchak (Maryknoll, NY: Orbis Books, 1995-2006) and Peter Hünermann and Bernd Jochen Hilberath, eds., *Herders theologischer Kommentar zum Zweiten Vatikanischen Konzil*, 5 vols., (Freiburg i.B.: Herder, 2004-2005).

[2] About this see Massimo Faggioli, "The Liturgical Reform from 1963 until Today... and Beyond," *Toronto Journal of Theology*, 32(2) 2016: 201-217.

[3] See for example Francis' speech to Italian liturgists gathered for the 68th National Liturgical Week, August 24, 2017, on the irreversibility and ongoing process of the liturgical reform of VC II: http://w2.vatican.va/content/francesco/en/speeches/2017/august/documents/papa-francesco_20170824_settimana-liturgica-nazionale.html. About this see also Cesare Giraudo, SJ, "La riforma liturgica a 50 anni dal Vaticano II. 'Parlare di "riforma della riforma" è un errore'," *La Civiltà Cattolica*, 2016 IV (3995, December 10, 2016): 432-45.

[4] See Enrico Galavotti, "Il Concilio di papa Francesco," in *Il Conclave e papa Francesco. Il primo anno di pontificato*, ed. Alberto Melloni (Rome: Istituto della Enciclopedia Italiana, 2014), 35-69; Id. "Jorge Mario Bergoglio e il concilio Vaticano II: fonte e metodo", *Rivista di Teologia dell'Evangelizzazione*, XXII (2018) 43: 61-88.

[5] About this, see Massimo Faggioli, *Pope Francis: Tradition in Transition* (New York: Paulist, 2015).

[6] For the distinction between *kerygmatic*, *theological*, and *spiritual* reception of a council, see Alois Grillmeier, "The Reception of Chalcedon in the Roman Catholic Church," *Ecumenical Review* 22 (1970): 383-411.

[7] This is one of the "building sites" left unfinished by VC II: see Hervé Legrand, "Communio ecclesiae, communio ecclesiarum, collegium episcoporum", in *La riforma e le riforme nella chiesa*, eds. Antonio Spadaro and Carlos Maria Galli (Brescia: Queriniana, 2016), 159-188.

[8] About Joseph Ratzinger's very critical approach to *Gaudium et Spes* see his introduction, in the series of his complete works, to the first of the two volumes dedicated to VC II: "Vorwort", in *Zur Lehre des Zweiten Vatikanischen Konzils. Formulierung—Vermittlung—Deutung* (series Joseph Ratzinger Gesammelte Schriften, Band 7/1) (Freiburg i.B.: Herder, 2012), 5-9, esp. 6-7. See Carlos Schickendantz, "¿Una transformación metodológica inadvertida? La novedad introducida por *Gaudium et Spes* en los escritos de Joseph Ratzinger," *Teología y Vida* 57, no. 1 (2016): 9-37.

[9] See Drew Christiansen, SJ, "The Church Encounters the World." *America* (January 6-13, 2014), 20-21.

[10] For more on Francis and the new Catholic movements, see Massimo Faggioli, *The Rising Laity: Ecclesial Movements since VC II* (Mahwah, NJ: Paulist Press, 2016), 131-153.

[11] It is not an accident that in the footnote to *GS* 36 there is an indirect reference to the case of Galileo Galilei when the text talks about the compatibility between faith and science. The reference in the footnote of *GS* is to the book by Pio Paschini, *Vita e opere di Galileo Galilei*, 2 vols. (Pontificia Accademia delle Scienze, Città del Vaticano 1964). About this see Alberto Melloni, "Galileo al Vaticano II. Storia d'una citazione e della sua ombra," *Cristianesimo nella Storia*, XXXI/1 (2010): 131–164.

[12] Like, for example, the quotation from Paul VI's encyclical *Populorum Progressio* (1967) in *LS* 127.

[13] *GS* 48–50 in *AL* 80, 125, 126, 134, 142, 154, 166, 172, 178, 222, 298, and 315.

[14] See Faggioli, "The Liturgical Reform from 1963 until Today...and Beyond."

[15] Pope Francis, *Address to the participants of the 68th National Liturgical Week in Italy*, August 24, 2017: "There is still work to be done in this direction, in particular by rediscovering the reasons for the decisions taken with regard to the liturgical reform, by overcoming unfounded and superficial readings, a partial reception, and practices that disfigure it. It is not a matter of rethinking the reform by reviewing the choices in its regard, but of knowing better the underlying reasons, through historical documentation, as well as of internalizing its inspirational principles and of observing the discipline that governs it. After this magisterium, after this long journey, we can affirm with certainty and with magisterial authority that the liturgical reform is irreversible": http://w2.vatican.va/content/francesco/it/speeches/2017/august/documents/papa-francesco_20170824_settimana-liturgica-nazionale.html. See also the Holy See Press Office communiqué on July 11, 2016, which disavowed the statement by cardinal Robert Sarah (Prefect of the Congregation for the Divine Worship) and the agenda of the "reform of the liturgical reform" (an expression that the Holy See statement says "may at times give rise to error"), which the cardinal recommended to the clergy in a public lecture in London a few days before: http://press.vatican.va/content/salastampa/it/bollettino/pubblico/2016/07/11/0515/01177.html#en.

[16] See the still reliable and very fascinating commentary to *Dei Verbum* by Joseph Ratzinger, in *Commentary on the Documents of VC II*, volume III, trans. and ed. Herbert Vorgrimler, (New York: Herder & Herder, 1968).

[17] About the "generative grammar" of VC II, see Christoph Theobald, *La réception du concile VC II. Vol. I. Accéder à la source* (Paris: Cerf, 2009), 894–900.

[18] About this see Severino Dianich, *Magistero in movimento. Il caso papa Francesco* (Bologna: EDB, 2016), 63–64.

[19] See Giuseppe Alberigo, "Criteri ermeneutici per una storia del Vaticano II," in Giuseppe Alberigo, *Transizione epocale: Studi sul Concilio Vaticano II* (Bologna: Il Mulino, 2009), 29–45. About Francis and John XXIII's *Gaudet Mater Ecclesia*, see Ormond Rush, *The Vision of VC II. Its Fundamental Principles* (Collegeville MN: Liturgical Press, 2019), 531-545.

[20] About the impact of John XXIII's *Gaudet Mater Ecclesia* on VC II, see John W. O'Malley, *What Happened at VC II* (Cambridge MA: Belknap Press of Harvard University Press, 2008), 93-96; Andrea Riccardi, "The Tumultuous Opening Days

of the Council," in *History of VC II*, dir. Giuseppe Alberigo, English ed. Joseph A. Komonchak, vol. 2 (Maryknoll, NY: Orbis Books, 1997), 14–19.

[21] Pope Francis, *Misericordiae Vultus* (April 11, 2015), par. 4, http://w2.vatican.va/content/francesco/en/apost_letters/documents/papa-francesco_bolla_20150411_misericordiae-vultus.html.

[22] It is interesting to see that VC II is very present in the final document of the Aparecida conference of 2007, but in that document (largely the fruit of Bergoglio's crucial role at that conference of CELAM) John XXIII is not mentioned. Bergoglio's closeness to Roncalli seemed to have been activated, if not caused, by the conclave of 2013. Francis quotes John XXIII's theological testament and last encyclical, *Pacem in terris* (April 11, 1963), in the beginning of the encyclical "On Our Common Home," in *LS* 3.

[23] About this see Gerard Mannion, *Ecclesiology and Postmodernity: Questions for the Church in Our Time* (Collegeville, MN: Liturgical Press, 2007).

[24] N. 84 (72 no votes), n. 85 (80 no votes), and n. 86 (64 no votes).

[25] See Pope Francis' interview with Andrea Tornielli of the Italian newspaper *La Stampa*, December 14, 2013 http://www.lastampa.it/2013/12/15/esteri/vatican-insider/it/mai-avere-paura-della-tenerezza-1vmuRIcbjQlD5BzTsnVuvK/pagina.html.

[26] See Pope Francis, "Angelus" prayer of Sunday, August 27, 2017.

[27] About this, see Massimo Faggioli, *A Council for the Global Church: Receiving VC II in History* (Minneapolis, MN: Fortress Press, 2015), esp. 329-335.

II

Pope Francis' Aggiornamento: Opening Doors to Go Forth

"Mission is part of the 'grammar' of faith, something essential for those who listen to the voice of the Spirit who whispers 'Come' and 'Go forth'. Those who follow Christ cannot fail to be missionaries, for they know that Jesus walks with them, speaks to them, breathes with them."

(Pope Francis)

4.

The Church Open to The World from Vatican Council II to Pope Francis

With Special Reference to Asia

Michael Amaladoss, SJ

Introduction: The Second Vatican Council's Dual Opening

Pope John XXIII was said to have opened the windows of the Church to the World—a true aggiornamento—by convoking the Second Vatican Council (hereinafter VC II). Pope Paul VI finished the process, though he was more careful. Now, with Pope Francis we have a new start in a different manner. VC II can be said to have opened the Church to the World in two ways. First, before the Council the Church was primarily a Roman Church. During the Council, it becomes aware of itself as a universal Church which is a communion of local Churches, spread across the world, though still centred in Rome. Second, was the opening of the Church to the World as distinct from or even opposed, sometimes, to the Church. I shall reflect upon this twofold opening one after the other.

1. The Roman Church Opening Out to be a World Church

The very first document on the Liturgy opened the door to inculturation and pluralism. For example, the Council declares in no. 4 of the document: The "Holy Mother Church holds all lawfully recognized rites to be of equal right and dignity." An expert present at the Council told us students that the word 'recognized' was used in the place of 'existing' found in the first draft to indicate that the Church was open to the emergence of new rites like the Indian, Chinese, African, etc. That this has not happened is, of course, a problem.

The document on Liturgy set as the goal of liturgical reform 'the full, conscious and active participation' by the people (14).[1] It was recognized that 'the liturgy is made up of unchangeable elements divinely instituted, and of elements subject to change.' These latter ought to be changed (21). While refusing to impose a rigid uniformity (37), it makes provision for 'legitimate variations and adaptations to different groups, regions and peoples, especially in mission countries' (38). 'In some places and circumstances, however, a more radical adaptation of the liturgy is needed' and this is entrusted to the competent territorial ecclesiastical authority (40), which are the bishops' conferences, legitimately established (22). What we see here is the recognition of a diversity of situations, needs and agents. The Church discovers itself as a communion of local Churches. However, it is a pity that the openness to inculturation manifested in the first fifteen years or so after VC II did not last. Now the local Churches are reduced to branches of the universal Church. All they can do is to translate literally the Latin liturgical texts produced by Rome. What keeps the diversity alive, however, is the popular religiosity that we find, especially in pilgrim centres and during festivals.

The *Decree on the Pastoral Office of Bishops in the Church* makes provision for the formation and functioning of episcopal conferences

---

[1] The numbers throughout the article refer to the Documents of Vatican Council II mentioned in the text.

(36-38). These are usually organized nation-wise. Many episcopal conferences also come together on a regional basis. There are for example the *FABC* in Asia, *SECAM* in Africa and *CELAM* in Latin America and similar units elsewhere. These help coordination, common reflection and mutual help. Such organisations help us to see the universal Church as a communion of local Churches. The *Federation of Asian Bishops' Conferences* (FABC), for example, has been active through its various offices reflecting on its mission in Asia and animating it with documents and meetings.

St Paul VI launched the Synod of Bishops at the universal level, but as a consultative body. These synods have been organised regularly to reflect over the situation and mission of the Church. But unfortunately, after the first few meetings, they have been controlled, not to say manipulated, by the central offices in the Vatican. The first one or two synods published their own statements. Later they have been submitting their papers to the Pope who writes a document later on his own authority. The synods have thus lost their autonomy. Pope Francis, however, has restored it. These synods, even in an imperfect way, manifest the global unity in pluralism of the Church and have provided a platform to evoke pastoral problems that concern the universal mission of the Church.

These are some of the ways in which the Church is becoming aware of itself as a world body and is coordinating its mission at that level. The appropriate structures exist. But their functioning can certainly be improved. It is in this context that the Amazonian synod and its demand for an Amazonian rite offer some hope, as they revive the original inspiration of VC II.

2. The Church Opening Out to the World

Now let us explore how the Church is opening itself to the world to which it is on mission to proclaim and witness to the Gospel. VC II was the first to focus on the world outside the Church. Of course, there have been social encyclicals for more than a hundred years starting with *Rerum Novarum* of Pope Leo XIII in 1891. Likewise, Pope Pius XII was known to address many different groups with special reference to moral and religious issues. But VC II really widened church horizons to look at the world beyond doctrinal and pastoral issues.

The document on *Religious Freedom* affirmed and defended the freedom of conscience to practice any religion of one's choice. Its recognition of the freedom of conscience was significant. The decree on *Other Religions* opened the way to interreligious dialogue. Christians were encouraged "to acknowledge, preserve and encourage the spiritual and moral truths found among non-Christians, also their social life and culture". The reference to 'social life and culture' underlines the fact that interreligious dialogue need not focus only on religious issues.

The decree on *Ecumenism* recognized that all who are baptized are incorporated into Christ and are our brothers, though separated. They have precious gifts like "the written Word of God, the life of grace, faith, hope and charity, with the other interior gifts of the Holy Spirit." Though the document implies that they have to come back to our Church, it also indicates the need to work together in the social field: "Since cooperation in social matters is so widespread today, all men [sic] without exception are called to work together; with much greater reason is this true of all who believe in God, but most of all, it is especially true of all Christians, since they bear the seal of Christ's name" (12). The document on *Mission* gave priority to God's universal mission, sending the Son and the Spirit. We are called to dialogue with God in mission. The focus, however, remains witnessing to and proclaiming the Gospel in view of spreading the Church.

The document on the *Church in the Modern World* is the finest example of the Church opening out to serve the world, at large. It shows great openness from its very first paragraphs: "The joy and the hope, the grief and anguish of the men [sic] of our time, especially of those who are poor or afflicted in any way, are the joy and hope, the grief and anguish of the followers of Christ as well. Nothing that is genuinely human fails to find an echo in their hearts" (1). It addresses all the people in the world and wishes to enter into dialogue with them (2-3). "The sacred Synod, in proclaiming the noble destiny of man [*sic*] and affirming an element of the divine in him, offers to cooperate unreservedly with mankind in fostering a sense of brotherhood to correspond to this destiny of theirs" (3).

The document recognises the changes and the tensions at the personal, economic and socio-cultural levels. It notes "a growing conviction of mankind's ability and duty to strengthen its mastery over nature and of the need to establish a political, social, and economic order at the service of man [*sic*] to assert and develop the dignity proper to individuals and to societies" (9). It affirms again the dignity of moral conscience and explores the problem of atheism, the challenge to build community, respecting persons as well as the common good and the rightful autonomy of earthly affairs. It insists that "by its nature and mission the Church is universal in that it is not committed to any one culture or to any political, economic or social system." Besides, "whatever truth, goodness, and justice is to be found in past or present human institutions is held in high esteem by the Council" (42). It goes on to affirm how much it has learnt from the world—an admission that is very much relevant to our theme.

Just as it is in the world's interest to acknowledge the Church as a social reality and a driving force in history, so too the Church is not unaware how much it has profited from the history and development of humankind. It profits from the experience of past ages, from the progress of the sciences, and from the riches hidden in various cultures, through which greater light is thrown on the nature of man and new avenues to truth are opened up (44). It is honest enough to admit that "the Church itself also recognizes that it has benefited and is still benefiting from the opposition of its enemies and persecutors." (44)

In this first section of the document, after pointing out how Christians are conformed to the image of the Son of God through the Holy Spirit, it goes on to open up this 'privilege' to everyone in the following words:

> All this holds true not for Christians only but also for all men [sic] of good will in whose hearts grace is active invisibly. For since Christ died for all, and since all men are in fact called to one and the same destiny, which is divine, we must hold that the Holy Spirit offers to all the possibility of being made partners, in a way known to God in the paschal mystery. (22)

In the second part of the document, the Council addresses some more urgent problems. These are: the dignity of marriage and the family, the proper development of culture, economic and social life, the political community and fostering of peace and establishment of a community of nations. Finally, the conclusion opens up the document to all peoples. This is extremely significant.

> Drawn from the treasures of the teaching of the Church, the proposals of this Council are intended for all people, whether they believe in God or whether they do not explicitly acknowledge him; they are intended to help them to a keener awareness of their own destiny, to make the world to conform better to the surpassing dignity of humankind, to strive for a more deeply rooted sense of universal brotherhood, and to meet the pressing appeal of our times with a generous and common effort of love (91).

3. Turning to Asia: Dialogue of the Gospel with the Poor, the Cultures and Religions

Let me now turn my attention to Asia. Almost ten years after the Council, in its first general assembly in 1974, the *FABC* described the mission of the Church in Asia as an ongoing dialogue of the Gospel with its many poor, the rich cultures and the living religions. The focus of this triple dialogue has evolved with time. If I can take the dialogue of the Gospel with culture as an example, in an earlier period, we were talking more about inculturation. The discussion was about how we can develop an Indian liturgy, an Indian theology, etc. Now the focus is not so much on inculturation, but on, what can be called, transculturation: that is, how can the Gospel prophetically transform culture.

The Indian vision of society and way of life, for example, is still very much characterised by the caste system. Though Christianity—and also the Indian Constitution—speaks about the equality of all people, the Indian social system is still hierarchical. Besides the four major caste groups, we have the outcastes, who call themselves the Dalits, literally, people who are ground down or crushed. Though the government has many affirmative action programmes for them and they are slowly coming up in terms of education and job opportunities, they are still not recognised as equals. This is true not only among the Hindus, but also among Muslims, Christians and those of other religious groups. Religious vision is not able to overcome social divisions. In the Eucharist we may break bread together, made easy because we are not actually sharing bread, but it is given to us by the priest or minister. But we may not occupy the same area even within the Church, especially in the villages. The women too are oppressed. Every day the papers carry the news of girl children being violated and even killed. The dowry system is still operative. Women are mostly at the service of men and children. Their identity and dignity are not respected. Divorces are becoming common. Then there is the impact of globalisation and the mass, and also the social, media. As a matter of fact, we do not talk much about how culture impacts or suffers from such situations. Finally, there is the growing process of secularisation in which religious approaches may even be rejected.

The Christian community has a lot of educational institutions. How much are they sensitive to the contemporary developments in science and technology and the impact they have on life? While faith is no longer disturbed by new discoveries in science, new developments in areas like bio-technology challenge the ways we respect and promote life in its wholeness and resist all sorts of manipulation. The proper use and protection of the earth is becoming an urgent responsibility for our own life and the wellbeing of future generations. The stability of families seems to be under threat, affecting particularly women and children. Contraception used to be a big issue a few decades ago. Now, no one seems to talk about it. Being a minority community, any critical approach of Christians to political issues seems non-existent unless their own interests are affected. Nonetheless, promoting peace and harmony in the world remains a prophetic task of the Church. What we are experiencing now is an artificial and tense calm imposed by armed might.

In the Christian community, helping the poor has always been a tradition. Often this was done by and through the clergy and the religious. These often run educational, medical and social service institutions. The poor were at the receiving end. But the situation has changed today. The poor are migrating to the cities for jobs and their situation is worse, living in the slums. Though the Indian economy is growing, it is the rich who are growing and prospering with it, while the poor are becoming poorer. However, the poor are no longer resigned to the situation. They get organised and agitate. Today we have many liberation movements and theologies across Asia: Minjung theology in Korea, the theology of Struggle in the Philippines, Dalit theology in India and Tribal theologies under various names elsewhere. The poor are no longer simply at the receiving end; they have started to protest and to demand. What is special in Asia is that these struggles and theologies are today multi-religious or, at least, multi-ideological, where there are non-believers involved.

Immediately after VC II, while interreligious dialogue was still promoted, it was related to proclamation. One started to dialogue with the other believers with the hope that, once Christianity is understood and respected, we can move towards proclamation and possible conversion. I have heard this motivation from some of the early ashramites. Today we have a growing positive view of other religions. We believe that salvation may also be facilitated through other religions. St. John Paul II declared in his encyclical *The Mission of the Redeemer* very clearly that the Spirit of God is present and active in other religions. His invitation in October 1986 to the leaders of all religions to come together to Assisi to pray for world peace had a global impact. When Benedict XVI repeated the invitation 25 years later, the focus was not on prayer but on a commitment to promote world peace and development. While there were some regrets that the religions were not recognised in relation to their spiritual orientation, we had to recognise that religious groups have started to come together to collaborate in the promotion of peace and justice in the world. In this process they may also have to relate to and work with non-religious groups. So, the scope of dialogue has widened. At the same time, with the growing realisation that all religions can facilitate salvific divine-human encounter, the goal of dialogue is no longer the Church, but the Kingdom of God. Asian bishops began saying that all the religions are co-pilgrims towards the Kingdom. Such a collaborative approach, however, has to contend with religious fundamentalism and communalism that are divisive and sometimes violent. All these developments show how the Church has been opening up to the world in new ways and in new directions.

Pope Francis: Call to Go Forth to the World's Peripheries

The Church is once again being opened to the world by Pope Francis. He is challenging the Eurocentric character of the Church and empowering the peripheries. He is encouraging, not a scholarly approach to problems from above, but a pastoral and consultative approach from below. In preparing the Synods, for instance, he has been insisting on consulting the people at the preparatory phase. The Amazon synod was prepared, not by the experts in the Vatican, but by a series of consultations in the region and the preparatory document was written by the people involved in the consultations.

A good example of how Pope Francis' pastoral-theological approach works is the question of the possible ordination to the priesthood of married people. He did not ask theological experts to explore the problem and offer possible solutions. They would have focused on the importance and meaning of celibacy for the priests. He rather focuses on the scattered communities in the Amazon and their need for the Eucharist. A request for ordaining married deacons emerges from below and gains approval. We saw above how the inculturation of the liturgy was blocked from above about 10-15 years after VC II. Now a request for a new Rite for the Amazon has emerged from below and again has gained approval. It opens the space for Africans and Asians to make similar requests; the Amazonian Rite becoming a precedent. It is the periphery that is challenging and changing the centre and opening it to the world. Earlier, in the Synod on the Family focusing on the divorced-remarried persons, after affirming that the priests are supposed to form the consciences of the people and make them free and not to replace them, a small footnote enables the people to participate in the Eucharist guided by their conscience. Pope Francis is not laying down general and universal rules of behaviour.

Pope Francis is also opening up the Synod process. The control from above is disappearing. The Synods now vote on and publish their conclusions, as they did at the beginning. There are now more representatives of the People of God at the Synod, though they still do not have the power of vote, making it slowly a Synod of the Church and not of the Bishops only. The Amazon Synod has opened a pastoral approach to problems encouraging an Amazonian Rite and the possibility of ordaining married men to meet a pastoral need. By quietly allowing a Synod of the Church in Germany where the Bishops and an organization of the People of God are preparing it jointly and are equal participants with the power of vote, Pope Francis may be launching a new kind of Church where the People of God are equal participants. I think that the Asian churches will feel at home in it and more empowered in their mission towards the Kingdom!

Pope Francis is visiting the local Churches at the periphery. He has not visited any of the big Christian countries. He follows the same policy in visiting Muslim countries. As a matter of fact, he has shown special interest in reaching out to the Muslims. His joint publication of a document on interreligious dialogue with the President of the Islamic University Al Azhar in Egypt is also noteworthy. It has been condemned as heretical by some groups in the Church. He has had joint meetings with Jewish and Muslim leaders, even praying with them. He is focusing on smaller meetings than on big events that attract media attention. He has also planned joint activities with the head of the Anglican Church. He is reaching out to the Orthodox Churches. He seems less interested in expert commissions for study, which go nowhere; rather, he prefers small significant actions on the field at the grassroot level. All these gestures, not only indicate a new openness, but a new way of opening out to the world, as well as to other Churches and religions.

5.

Go Forth, Face the World!

How Pope Francis Embodies Vatican Council II

Francis Gonsalves, SJ

Introduction: The Challenge to Make Words Flesh

"The Word became flesh and lived among us" (Jn 1:14) is a core Christian belief. "Being a Christian is not the result of an ethical choice or a lofty idea, but the encounter with an event, a *person*, which gives life a new horizon and a decisive direction."[1] These words of emeritus Pope Benedict XVI find person-centered, fleshy, bodily expression not only in Pope Francis' words,[2] but also in his work and the witness of his life. This symposium juxtaposes two spaces: church and world; and three faces, namely, of Pope John XXIII and Pope Paul VI who conceived and carried to completion Vatican Council II (hereinafter VC II), respectively, and Pope Francis who, I shall try to show, is deftly demonstrating what these documents demand in deeds, not merely in words.

This paper is divided into three parts. In the first part, I shall build a body-framework, so to say, establishing the significance of 'face' and 'body' in Christianity. In the second, I will examine VC II's 'Pastoral Constitution on the Church in the Modern World' *Gaudium et Spes* (hereinafter GS), examining how the two 'spaces'—church and world—could more effectively interact. Finally, in the third part, I will turn the spotlight on Pope Francis, arguing that in his use of words like face, heart, body and flesh, and in his incarnating these in his theology and pastoral praxis, he gives both, church and world, a glimpse or a *darshan* of who God is, and who you and I are called to '*be*' and '*do*' as individual Christians and as Church, at large. My reflections will be made in the light of the Asian/Indian context.

1. The Body, Nobodies and Some Bodies in Christianity

Christianity is a body-creed that values the human body and other bodies, too.[3] In incarnating Godself as Jesus of Nazareth, God was reiterating the beauty and blessedness of the human body. Indeed, Genesis tells us that we are all created in the "image and likeness of God" (Gen 1:26-27). Moreover, in the gospels we see God's face and body in Jesus who makes unprecedented claims like: "Whoever has seen me has seen the Father" (Jn 14:9) and "The Father and I are one" (Jn 10:30), which were validated with his resurrection from the dead.

Bodies link all human beings, worldwide. Moreover, our flesh makes everyone *feel* heat, cold, pain, old age and suffering in much the same way as everyone else, though the way we *think* about these realities differ. Christianity differs from other world religions and philosophies in that it is not a creed of words as much as it is a creed of the body,[4] wherein the flesh becomes an instrument of salvation, so to say.[5] The conceptions of God, salvation and human person in the Judeo-Christian tradition are strikingly different from the once-influential dualistic Greek philosophical tradition that privileged spirit over matter, the immutable over the changing, eternal over the spatiotemporal. In Greek imagination, the highest reality was impersonal, universal nature such as Plato's world of the forms, with the divine conceived as unbegotten, immutable, ineffable, impassible and utterly transcendental. By contrast, Yahweh was revealed as *Deus in nobis*—active in history, walking and talking with people, inspiring them to be holy and whole.

Corresponding to the divergences in the Greek and Jewish conceptions of divinity, there were also differences in the way the human person and one's body were perceived. Since the Biblical worldview was holistic with no distinction between matter and the substance out of which matter was made, Judaism used but one word, *basar*, to speak of the body in contrast to the Greek tradition that used two words, i.e., *soma* and *sarx*, to distinguish body from flesh,[6] with contempt for the body, which by its very materiality was enmeshed in the world of becoming and change. Conversely, in the Hebrew worldview, the human person was a somatic unity, an integral living being that related to the world. Wo/man '*is*' body: s/he does not merely '*have*' body by which s/he lives, loves and interacts with others and the world.

While everybody '*is*' somebody, there is also the 'nobody' or 'nonperson' who the Oxford Dictionary describes as "a person regarded as nonexistent or unimportant, or as having no rights; an ignored or forgotten person."[7] The biblical *anawim*—widows, orphans, aliens—can be considered archetype of these people who, being spouseless, parentless and friendless, experience a 'lack' in their lives. As a people, the Israelites would confess: "A wandering Aramean was my ancestor; he went down into Egypt and lived there as an alien, few in number …." (Deut 26:5), while Jesus would refer to the poor and needy as "the *least* of my sisters and brothers" (Mt 25:40). Today's 'nobodies' are those bearing backbreaking burdens: the sick, lepers, refugees, bonded labourers, abused women and children, those discriminated against like the LGBTQI and so on. In the Indian context, there are millions of these nobodies, nonpersons or broken bodies whose faces never appear on TV screens and who struggle at Indian peripheries. Finally, as a corporate term, we can think of other bodies: familial, ecclesial, societal, local, national, global and cosmic.

Every 'body' has a 'face', which makes one see and be seen, hear and be heard, smell, taste and be touched. 'Every face tells a story, it never tells a lie,' is the title of a popular English song. Besides its visual and carnal aspects, 'face' is a rich biblical symbol with many meanings, as follows:[8]

[a] Face stands for the 'self'. To honour one's face is to honour the person (Lev 19:32). When the king asks: "Why is your face sad?" it means, "Why are you sad?" (Neh 2:2). With childlike simplicity when Moses desires to hide himself, he covers his face (Ex 3:6) and Moses' radiant face indicates that he has seen God (Ex 34:29). [b] Face reveals nature and character. Luke describes the face of Christianity's first martyr, Stephen, as the "face of an angel" (Acts 6:15) and the face of Jesus at the Transfiguration "shone like the sun" (Mt 17:2) indicating his divine nature. [c] Face indicates presence. To "see the face" simply means to be in front of, before or in the presence of (Gen 32:20; Acts 20:25); and, the psalmist "seeks the face of God" ever yearning to experience divine presence and power. [d] Face stands for light and blessing. "O God, let thy face shine upon us that we may be saved (Ps 80:19) and "May the Lord make his face to shine upon you" (Num 6:25). [e] Face reveals emotions: "No longer shall Jacob be ashamed, no longer shall his face grow pale" (Isa 29:22) and "a glad heart makes a cheerful countenance" (Prov 15:13). Ezekiel reproaches those who because of their abominations have their faces covered with horror and shame (7:18).

Having stressed the importance of body, bodies, nobodies and face, let us now see how the Body of Christ, the Church, sought to respond to what was happening in the 1960s in another body: the world, at large.

2. The Body of Christ, Church, Eager to Love and Serve the World at VC II

Two faces always appear side-by-side when reminiscing about VC II: of Popes John XXIII and Paul VI. Inaugurating VC II on October 11, 1962, with his *'Gaudet Mater Ecclesia'*, Pope John XXIII expressed his desire that it be: "not a discussion of one article or another of the fundamental doctrine of the Church...... but teaching of a predominantly *pastoral* nature."[9] Two years later in December 1964, his successor Pope Paul VI visited Mumbai for the 38th International Eucharistic Congress. Addressing a meeting with representatives of other churches and religions, he said:

> This visit to India is the fulfilment of a long, cherished desire. Yours is a land of ancient culture, the cradle of great religions, the home of a nation that has sought God with a relentless desire, in deep meditation and silence, and in hymns of fervent prayer. Rarely has this longing for God been expressed with words so full of the spirit of Advent as in the words written in your sacred books many centuries before Christ: "From the unreal lead me to the real; from darkness lead me to light; from death lead me to immortality". This is a prayer which belongs also to our time. Today more than ever it should rise from every human heart.[10]

This first ever visit by a pope to India and his quoting of Hindu scriptures indicated a resolve of the Church's highest authority to break away from an exclusivist Eurocentric enclave to build bridges across cultures, religions and viewpoints. Moreover, since, "on the one hand the massive presence of diverse religious traditions and ideologies and, on the other, its widespread poverty and political oppression"[11] characterize India, VC II was expected mainly to: (a) provide a roadmap to dialogue with other religions and (b) respond to poverty. Among other contributions, five of the following points appear to me as pathbreaking and inspirational for Asia/India in GS:

2.1. GS methodology as secular-dialogic

Unlike most other documents that saw the Church as active subject and the world as an object to act upon and influence, GS's premise was 'secular-dialogic' — secular, because for the first time the Church saw the world as a proper theological locus; and, dialogic since it sought to operate in the interstices between the modern world and Christian Tradition rather than simply apply the latter as a measure of the former.[12] For instance, the text of GS 3 reads: "[T]his council can provide no more eloquent proof of its solidarity with, as well as its respect and love for, the entire human family with which it is bound up, than by engaging with it in *dialogue* about these various problems." Similarly, GS 21 stresses: "The Church sincerely professes that all men [*sic*], believers and unbelievers alike, ought to work for the rightful betterment of this world in which all alike live; such an ideal cannot be realized, however, apart from sincere and prudent *dialogue*. This idea of openness to ecumenical and interfaith dialogue is reiterated in GS 92.

2.2. GS condemns excessive wealth and opts for the poor, like Jesus

GS 31 reads: "[H]uman freedom is often crippled by extreme destitution just as it can wither when in an ivory-tower isolation brought on by overindulgence in the good things of life." Moreover, the Church made a definite option for the poor, with the opening line of GS 1 stating: "The joys and the hopes, the griefs and the anxieties of the men [*sic*] of this age, *especially those who are poor or in any way afflicted*, these are the joys and hopes, the griefs and anxieties of the followers of Christ." Likewise, GS 72 reads: "Thus their [Christians'] whole life, both individual and social, will be permeated with the spirit of the beatitudes, notably with *a spirit of poverty*." Indeed, the reason for desiring to have a church "for the poor" was Jesus, God's poor Son. Thus, GS 88 reads:

> Christians should cooperate willingly and wholeheartedly in establishing an international order that includes a genuine respect for all freedoms and amicable brotherhood between all. This is all the more pressing since the *greater part of the world is still suffering from so much poverty that it is as if Christ Himself were crying out in these poor to beg the charity of the disciples. The spirit of poverty* and charity are the glory and witness of the Church of Christ.

2.3. Servant-model church envisioned

GS proposed a 'servant model' for ecclesial identity and mission.[13] The text of GS 3 reads: "[T]he Church seeks but a solitary goal: to carry forward the work of Christ under the lead of the befriending Spirit. And Christ entered this world to give witness to the truth, to rescue and not to sit in judgment, *to serve and not to be served*." Echoing similar sentiments, GS 89 reads: "[T]he Church must be clearly present in the midst of the community of nations both through her official channels and through the full and sincere collaboration of all Christians—a collaboration motivated solely by the desire to be *of service* to all." Identifying itself strikingly as a 'servant-church' was unique in those times.

2.4. From church as teacher to a listening church open to learn

Fourth, rather than merely be a teacher who has everything to teach and nothing to learn, the GS church aspired also to be a 'learner', listening, and seeking help from others. GS 44 states:

> She [the Church] gratefully understands that in her community life no less than in her individual sons [*sic*], she receives a variety of helps from men [*sic*] of every rank and condition, for whoever promotes the human community at the family level, culturally, in its economic, social and political dimensions, both nationally and internationally, such a one, according to God's design, is contributing greatly to the Church as well …

The Church also began to appreciate the contributions of the sciences, arts and other disciplines. GS 36 and GS 59 accorded "legitimate autonomy" to culture in its myriad manifestations; while GS 62 stated: "Theologians are invited to seek continually for more suitable ways of communicating doctrine … In pastoral care, appropriate use must be made not only of theological principles, but also of *the findings of the secular sciences, especially of psychology and sociology.*"

2.5. Dialogue and Collaboration as the GS key to universal solidarity

Fifth, rather than 'go up' in ivory-tower isolation, the Church sought to 'go forth' for co-planning and cooperation,[14] co-working or '*co-laboring*' with all peoples of goodwill. GS 89 says: "[T]he Church must be clearly present in the midst of the community of nations both through her official channels and through the full and sincere collaboration of all Christians: collaboration motivated solely by the desire to be of service to all." Furthermore, GS 90 promotes 'joint efforts':

> An outstanding form of international activity on the part of Christians is found in *the joint efforts* which, both as individuals and in groups, they contribute to institutes *already established* or to be established for the encouragement of

cooperation among nations. ... For today both effective action and *the need for dialogue demand joint projects*. Moreover, such associations contribute much to the development of a universal outlook—something certainly appropriate for Catholics. They also help to form an awareness of genuine universal solidarity and responsibility.

In sum, GS expanded the horizons of the 'fullness of life' that Jesus came to bring so as to be an agent of salvation not only for baptized Christians, but for all men and women who (explicitly or implicitly) live the paschal mystery (life-death-resurrection) of Our Lord Jesus. This is strikingly stressed in GS 22, which explains salvation mediated by Jesus Christ as follows:

> All this holds true not only for Christians, but for all men [sic] of good will in whose hearts grace works in an unseen way. For, since Christ died for all men [sic], and since the ultimate vocation of man [sic] is in fact one, and divine, we ought to believe that the Holy Spirit in a manner known only to God offers to every man [sic] the possibility of being associated with this paschal mystery.

In the light of the aforementioned revolutionary shifts that GS proposed, one can say that there were some efforts made in India to translate words into works.[15] A clear change was certainly noticed in the liturgical and sacramental life of the Indian Church.[16] But, after the initial euphoria of the 1960's and 1970s subsided, from the 1980s onwards, the Church in India seems to be groping around for an identity, struggling to dialogue and collaborate with others, and is busy with ministries that often hardly benefit Christ's least brethren. In this context, Pope Francis' words and life are inspirational, especially for Asia/India.

3. Pope Francis' Words and Works Calling for Flesh-and-Blood Discipleship

Indians are tired of Christian preachers who sermonize about liberation, salvation, church-planting, harvest of souls, etc. They want to see, hear and encounter flesh-and-blood Christians who are free from attachments: merciful, compassionate, ready to love and even die so that others might live, fully. For most Indians, Jesus is the finest *prem-avatar*: icon of divine love made visible. Similarly, Pope Francis seems to be Christ's most admired and appreciated avatar for millions, worldwide. Let us see how he enfleshes the ideals mentioned in the previous section.

3.1. Pope Francis' secular-dialogic mindset and modus operandi

One of the most difficult theological issues to resolve is that of the centrality of Christ for salvation, the role of the Church and the mission of Christians vis-à-vis the immense majority of people worldwide who neither know Christ nor are Christians. This is particularly true of India with a miniscule 2.35% Christian population in a majoritarian Hindu country where Hindutva or militant religious nationalism is gaining ground. Put bluntly: Is the gospel relevant to everyone?

Pope Francis writes in EG 113, "The salvation which God has wrought, and the Church joyfully proclaims, is for *everyone*. God has found a way to unite himself to every human being in every age." Here in footnote 82 he quotes GS 22, which provides a key to unlock doors leading to ecclesial extroversion and engaging with others in society. The way that God has found to unite Godself with all of humanity is to make Word flesh and dwell in our midst. Thus, the pope says:

> Everything that the Church has to offer must become *incarnate* in a distinctive way in each part of the world, so that the Bride of Christ can take on *a variety of faces* that better manifest the inexhaustible riches of God's grace. Preaching must become *incarnate*, spirituality must become *incarnate*, ecclesial structures must become *incarnate*.[17]

Pope Francis repeatedly rejects all forms of dualism and what he terms 'neo-Gnosticism'—whether in matters of faith,[18] or belief,[19] or as hindrance to holiness, where he condemns neo-Gnostics, for: "They think of the intellect as separate from the flesh, and thus become incapable of touching Christ's suffering flesh in others…. In the end, by disembodying the mystery, they prefer a God without Christ, a Christ without the Church, a Church without her people."[20] The danger to be avoided, then, is to avoid all dualisms and dichotomy, and instead adopt an *advaitic*, nondual approach to all reality which can facilitate dialogue. Dialogue then becomes the means by which we discern and decide on how to build a better world for all people, especially the poor.

3.2. Pope Francis' dream of a poor church, for the poor, revealing the face of Christ

Before drawing up any church agenda on paper, Pope Francis draws the face of Christ for all peoples to see. Upon election as pope, he assumed the name 'Francis' after *il poverello* from Assisi: poor, peacemaker, church-builder and dialoguer. Like his patron, he transports us to the periphery, the crib of God's child at Bethlehem: "to 'feel' and 'touch' the poverty that God's Son took upon himself in the Incarnation."[21] Moreover, he writes, "Jesus Christ is the face of the Father's mercy ... By his words, his actions, and his entire person, Jesus of Nazareth reveals the mercy of God". These were the opening words of his *Misericordiae Vultus*—meaning, 'The Face of Mercy'[22]—heralding the great 'Jubilee of Mercy'. In the same document, calling Mary the 'Mother of Mercy', he added: "No one has penetrated the profound mystery of the incarnation like Mary. Her entire life was patterned after the presence of mercy made flesh."[23]

Pope Francis preaches in no unclear terms that the Church should 'be' a poor church and a 'church *for* the poor' because "God's heart has a special place for the poor", so much so that God himself "became poor" (2 Cor 8:9).[24] Notably, while GS condemned excessive wealth, made an option '*for*' the poor and even exhorted Christians to imbibe a spirit of the beatitudes, Pope Francis goes a step further in EG 198, saying, "I want a Church which *is* poor and for the poor. They have much to teach us. Not only do they share in the *sensus fidei*, but in their difficulties they know the suffering Christ. We need to let ourselves be evangelized by them."

Besides *being* poor himself, Pope Francis' being '*for*' the poor is seen in his option to unfailingly embrace the poor or direct society's attention to heed their woes.[25] Therefore, whether it be him hugging the sore-covered Vincio Riva suffering from neurofibromatosis,[26] or his Mass at Lampedusa in July 2013, to comfort the families of victim-refugees who drowned off the Sicilian coast when he preached about the 'globalization of indifference',[27] or his critique of efforts to build a wall along the USA-Mexican border and his donation of 500,000 US dollars to alleviate refugee woes,[28] Francis always acts '*for*' the poor and stands alongside them, in solidarity with them.

In terms of initiating programmes, Pope Francis has instituted the 'World Day for the Poor' to be commemorated on the 33rd Sunday of the Liturgical Year; and, every year, he publishes a Document on the 'World Day of Migrants and Refugees' on the last Sunday of September bringing world attention to this huge problem, urging people to: *welcome, protect, promote* and *integrate*[29] refugees and migrants into their own societies and countries. In one of these messages he writes:

> In each of these people, forced to flee to safety, Jesus is present as he was at the time of Herod. In the faces of the hungry, the thirsty, the naked, the sick, strangers and prisoners, we are called to see the face of Christ who pleads with us to help (cf. Mt 25:31-46). If we can recognise him in those faces, we will be the ones to thank him for having been able to meet, love and serve him in them.[30]

3.3. Pope Francis as the servant who wants Church to be a servant, mother and revolutionary

From the beginning of his papacy, Pope Francis showed the world what the title '*servus servorum dei*' really demands in a striking prophetic symbolic action of washing the feet, not of priests—as is traditionally done at the Roman Basilicas on Maundy Thursday—but of prisoners, men and women alike, irrespective of their religion. He said in his homily, "Washing feet means 'I am at your service ...' Help one another. This is what Jesus teaches us. This is what I do. And I do it with my heart. I do this with my heart because it is my duty, as a priest and bishop I must be at your service."[31] Reportedly, "Francis, who suffers from sciatica, which causes back pain, needed help from his aides to stand up and kneel down before each prisoner." Though "in the past, conservative Catholics criticised the pope for washing the feet of women and Muslim inmates,"[32] this bodily symbolism has had a huge impact on people of other religions.

Pope Francis sees the beatitudes and Jesus' teachings on the Last Judgment as the criteria by which one can measure the authenticity of one's discipleship. He said:

> Every disciple's point of reference should be what Jesus preached in those two columns of Christianity: the Beatitudes and the 'protocol' by which we will be judged, namely that indicated by Matthew in chapter 25. This is the 'framework' of 'evangelical service'. ... If a disciple does not walk in order to serve, his walking is of no use. If his life is not in service, his life is of no use, as a Christian .... There are those who say: "I'm a Christian, I'm at peace, I confess, I go to Mass, I follow the Commandments". But where is the service to others? Where is the service to Jesus in the sick, in the imprisoned, in the hungry, in the naked"? And this is precisely what "Jesus told us we must do because he is there".[33]

The idea of love and service also emerges through Pope Francis' vision of the Church as "a true mother who gives us life in Christ and, in the communion of the Holy Spirit, brings us into a common life with our brothers and sisters ...She is a mother who has at heart the good of her children."[34] Pope Francis says: "The Church is Mother and talks to the people as a mother talks to her child, with that confidence that the child already knows that everything is being taught for its good, because the child knows that it is loved."[35] This requires face-to-face encounters:

> The Gospel tells us constantly to run the risk of a face-to-face encounter with others, with their physical presence which challenges us, with their pain and their pleas, with their joy which infects us in our close and continuous interaction. True faith in the incarnate Son of God is inseparable from self-giving, from membership in the community, from service, from reconciliation with others. The Son of God, by becoming flesh, summoned us to the *revolution of tenderness*.[36]

This term 'revolution of tender love' has captivated me and inspired me to dwell at greater length on this idea elsewhere,[37] which can only be introduced in brief as follows.

In a TED talk entitled: "Why the only future worth building includes everyone," Pope Francis expressed his dream for each and every human being—not only Christians—to be committed to a 'revolution of tenderness'.[38] He said, first, that each one of us must be personally convinced about the need for caring, sharing and serving. Second, after '*I*' am convinced of and converted to this cause, I can strive to inspire '*You*'. Third, when many '*Yous*' are transformed, we can construct a common '*We*' and '*Us*'. Finally, this will snowball into a revolution of tenderness and love engulfing peoples, nations and the whole world. He explained that the revolution of tenderness begins in the terrains of the human heart and travels through one's eyes, ears, hands and feet, enabling one to see and hear the other, so as to specially respond to the cries of the poorest of poor, including the cries of our poor, poisoned mother earth who cries out for our care.

3.4. Collegiality and synodality for listening, learning and conversion

While GS and VC II, in general, wanted the Church to be aware of its mission to make Christ come alive anew and be of service to the world, at large, especially the poor, it was difficult to change the mindsets and mission priorities of the ecclesial hierarchy and the clergy. While John XXIII and Paul VI sought to open doors, build bridges and renew the Church radically, it was felt by some that the papacy of John Paul II and Benedict XVI "comprised a three-and-a-half-decade attempt to rein in the impulses of the Second Vatican Council.... Both popes spent an inordinate amount of time and energy going after those who raised inconvenient questions or explored areas of theology that didn't fit their prescriptions of church."[39] Sadly, not much was done to address real church-and-world issues. However, Pope Francis changed things.

A month after his election to the papacy, by appointing nine cardinals from diverse continents and cultures as his advisors, Pope Francis was transferring power and spreading the decision-making processes over a larger area. Besides this collegiality, building upon Pope Paul VI's synodal principles in *Apostolica Sollicitudo*,[40] he widened the circles of synodality with greater outreach to families and youth, worldwide, so as to listen to God's Spirit. He writes:

> A synodal Church is a Church which *listens*, which realizes that *listening* 'is more than simply hearing'. It is a mutual *listening* in which everyone has something to learn. The faithful people, the college of bishops, the Bishop of Rome: all *listening* to each other, and all *listening* to the Holy Spirit, the 'Spirit of truth' (Jn 14:17), in order to know what he 'says to the Churches' (Rev 2:7).[41]

Pope Francis explains that synodality is built on a: '*Quod omnes tangit ab omnibus tractari debet*' principle – 'What touches all should be considered and approved by all'. He affirms that: "It is precisely this path of *synodality* which God expects of the Church of the third millennium. What the Lord is asking of us is already in some sense present in the very word 'synod'. Journeying together—laity, pastors, the Bishop of Rome." He also says: "This (synod) is an easy concept to put into words, but not so easy to put into practice."[42]

Inspired by Pope Francis' insistence on initiating participatory processes in the Church, the 'Congregation for the Doctrine of the Faith' (CDF) published a document entitled: '*Synodality in the Life and Mission of the Church*' in March 2018.[43] It states that: "Although synodality is not explicitly found as a term or as a concept in the teaching of Vatican II, it is fair to say that synodality is at the heart of the work of renewal the Council was encouraging."[44] The synodal process was set in motion in the Synods of the Family (2015) and Youth (2018). The Final Document of the latter synod specifically described a "church that listens,"[45] saying: "Listening is an encounter in freedom ... Listening transforms the hearts of those who do it, especially when it takes place with an inner disposition of harmony and docility to the Spirit. .... The Church, by her listening, enters into the movement of God who, in his Son, draws near to every human being."

Synodality is also stressed in the Final Document of the Synod of Bishops' Special Assembly for the Pan-Amazonian Region issued on October 26, 2019.[46] Chapter 1 is entitled 'From Listening to *Conversion*' and chapter 5 describes 'New Paths of Synodal *Conversion*' with the opening line: "To walk together the Church requires a synodal *conversion"*.⁴⁷ Pope Francis never tires of exhorting Christians to conversion, first, of one's mind and heart, which will lead to change in missionary outreach. He seeks conversion himself, confessing: "Since I am called to put into practice what I ask of others, I too must think about a conversion of the papacy."⁴⁸ He has chosen 'synodality' as the theme for the next synod in 2022.⁴⁹ Much is expected from it.

3.5. *Dialogue and collaboration for all bodies to work jointly for our common home*

Along with synodality, Pope Francis fosters ecumenical and interreligious dialogue and collaboration in a significant way, with the 'common good' as the starting point. In EG 217-237, he first draws up principles for ensuring peace and the common good, and then in EG 238 he points out "three areas of dialogue": (a) dialogue with states, (b) dialogue with society—including dialogue with cultures and the sciences, and (c) dialogue with other believers who are not part of the Catholic Church. Pope Francis' idea of dialogue is not arm-chair conversations among ideologues; for, one of the principles he lays down is: "realities are more important than ideas."⁵⁰

By way of methodology, in the document that Pope Francis publishes, he moves in ever-widening concentric circles beginning with revealing Christ's face anew for Christians, and then proceeds to invite other churches and religions to tap the treasures of their own scriptures and traditions, which widely differ; yet, the concerns of hunger, poverty, violence, fundamentalism, abuse of the weak and ravaging of mother earth are everywhere the same. These evils are felt especially by the poor, in their bodies—the substratum that we all share. In humility and honesty, in EG 241, he writes: "In her dialogue with the State and with society, the Church does not have solutions for every particular issue. Together with the various sectors of society, she supports those programmes which best respond to the dignity of each person and the common good."

Pope Francis wields immense influence on the world stage as seen in the reception he received at the UN and the USA, and even in a predominantly Buddhist country like Sri Lanka and a Muslim-dominated UAE with the signing of the historic 'Document on Human Fraternity for World Peace' with the Grand Imam of Al-Azhar, Ahmad Al-Tayyeb at Abu Dhabi on February 4, 2019.[51] Both his predecessors had created controversies with their simplistic views on these two religions—John Paul in 1995,[52] and Benedict XVI in 2006.[53] In speaking about ecumenical dialogue Francis writes: "We must never forget that we are pilgrims journeying alongside one another. This means that we must have sincere trust in our fellow pilgrims, putting aside all suspicion or mistrust, and turn our gaze to what we are all seeking: the radiant peace of God's face."[54] Once again God's face is what motivates and energizes ecumenical actions.

In the countries he visits, Francis draws attention to our shared humanity, insisting on dialogue, always pointing out to people, faces, bodies, hands and hearts. To Asian bishops he said:

> Dialogue demands of us a truly contemplative spirit of openness and receptivity to the other. I cannot engage in dialogue if I am closed to others. Openness? Even more: acceptance! Come to my house, enter my heart. My heart welcomes you. It wants to hear you. This capacity for empathy enables a true human dialogue in which words, ideas and questions arise from an experience of fraternity and shared humanity.[55]

He exhorted his fellow bishops in the USA, as follows:

> The path ahead, then, is dialogue among yourselves, dialogue in your presbyterates, dialogue with lay persons, dialogue with families, dialogue with society. I cannot ever tire of encouraging you to dialogue fearlessly.... Do not be afraid to set out on that "exodus" which is necessary for all authentic dialogue. ... Harsh and divisive language does not befit the tongue of a pastor, it has no place in his heart; although it may momentarily seem to win the day, only the enduring allure of goodness and love remains truly convincing.[56]

In dialogue, Pope Francis is deeply aware that, without genuine inculturation, the face and gospel of Christ will never bring joy to the world's peoples.[57] Thus, describing Church as: "a people of *many faces*," he writes, "the People of God is *incarnate* in the peoples of the earth" and speaks of "legitimate autonomy" of culture quoting GS's views on culture.[58] In the Final Document of the Amazon Synod, he refers to GS thrice: [a] "Pastoral action is based on a spirituality founded on listening to the word of God and the cry of his people .... We recognize that the Church which hears the voice of the Spirit in the cry of the Amazon can take to heart the joys and the hopes, the griefs and the anxieties of everyone, but especially of the poorest (cf. *GS* 1), who are God's beloved sons and daughters."[59] [b] With regard to "inculturated theology" he says: "The evangelization of the Church is not a process of destruction, but of consolidation and strengthening of these values; a contribution to the growth of the 'seeds of the Word'" (*DP* 401, cf. *GS* 57) present in various cultures."[60] and, [c] "Although mission in the world is the task of every baptized person, the Second Vatican Council emphasized the mission of the laity: 'the expectation of a new earth must not weaken but rather stimulate our concern for cultivating this one' (*GS* 39). It is urgent for the Church in the Amazon to promote and confer ministries for men and women in an equitable manner."[61] The thrust for synodality will hopefully allow for more participation of the laity.

It is clear then, that Pope Francis drives VC II agenda forward not only by advocating dialogue at every level—with states, with the sciences,[62] with art and poetry,[63] with cultures, with diverse peoples, with sociopolitical contexts and many religions—but also understands the complexities involved in each of these realms. Thus, all the "professional theologians [who] seem to think Pope Francis is barely literate in theology.... are very much mistaken ... It is important to note that Francis believes theology can only be done in a real, flesh-and-blood context. It can never be exercised as a mere idea or ideal."[64]

Conclusion: You and I '*are*' Mission Bearing Good News in Our Bodies
Having argued that Pope Francis strives to enflesh or incarnate much of what VC II documents have to say, we must note that he places mission not merely at the level of functionality, i.e., mere '*doing*' but situates mission in the realm of ontology: '*being*'. He writes: [65]

> My mission of being in the heart of the people is not just a part of my life or a badge I can take off; it is not an 'extra' or just another moment in life. Instead, it is something I cannot uproot from my being without destroying my very self. *I am a mission* on this earth; that is the reason why I am here in this world.

By asserting that: "I *am* a mission on this earth," Francis seems to say that mission inheres in our genes; it's our self-defining DNA. In other words, every "missionary disciple"[66] has a face and a body to go forth and mirror the face of Christ. Indeed, his theology circularly proceeds from Christology to Ecclesiology to Missiology, and then back to Christology, for that is the way that one will recognize oneself and help Christ to redeem the world. He says: "How many have forgotten and urgently need to see the face of the Lord in order to find themselves again!" and adds, "Here then, is the secret of life, that which brings us out of anonymity: to fix our gaze on Jesus' face and become familiar with Him."[67] Prayer is an indispensable part of theology.

Pope Francis is a 'dreamer' in the best sense of the term, dreaming social, cultural, ecological and ecclesial dreams for the churches at the periphery, one of which is: The Beloved Amazon.[68] He dreams "of Christian communities capable of generous commitment, *incarnate* in the Amazon region, and giving the Church *new faces* with Amazonian features;"[69] and in his ecclesial dream, he calls the Church "to journey alongside the people of the Amazon region …. to develop a Church with an Amazonian *face*."[70] How about substituting 'Amazon' with 'India'? Before leaving for India as a missionary, Jesuit St Francis Xavier once dreamt that he was carrying an Indian on his shoulders. Though Pope Francis has expressed his desire to visit India, given the present political scenario, his dream may never be realized. Nonetheless, he has provided us, Asians and Indians, with inspiration to do flesh-and-blood contextual theology and to reveal the Indian face of Christ to all Indians and to global citizens, too.

"We need to initiate processes and not just occupy spaces,"[71] is a sentence that Pope Francis repeats.[72] Presenting Christ's youthful face to the youth he began '*Christus Vivit*', his apostolic exhortation, proclaiming: "Christ is alive! ... and he wants you to be alive!"[73] He concluded his exhortation saying: "Keep running, attracted by the face of Christ, whom we love so much, ... and acknowledge in the flesh of our suffering brothers and sisters. May the Holy Spirit urge you on as you run this race."[74] We, in India, whisper, "Amen!"

Endnotes

[1] See his Encyclical Letter: *Deus Caritas Est* n.1, of December 25, 2005; italics added.

[2] This is reiterated by Pope Francis in his 2013 Apostolic Exhortation: *Evangelii Gaudium*, n.7, hereinafter EG.

[3] I have developed this point in depth in my book *Body Broken for Body Building: Christic Living in a Broken, Global Village*, Bandra, Mumbai, St Pauls, 2013.

[4] Angela Burr, *I Am Not My Body: A Study of the International Hare Krishna Sect*, Delhi, Vikas Publishing House, 1984, has a contrary view of a Hindu *panth* that (p.9): "throws into relief and sheds light on an important new social variable that is developing in western society, namely, the 'body' and bodily symbolism."

[5] Cipriano Vagaggini, *The Flesh: Instrument of Salvation. A Theology of the Human Body*, New York, Society of St. Paul, 1969, develops a 'theology of the body' in the light of it being basic to salvation. See also Jose Kuttianimattathil, 'Towards a Theology of the Body - I and II', *Vidyajyoti Journal of Theology* 65/1,2 (January & February 2001): 27-39, 98-104, for insights on this theme.

[6] For details, see Gregory Arby, 'Body as Locus of Divine Revelation of Love: Exploring Communion through the Theology of the Body', *The Living Word* 114/4 (July-August 2008): 304-323.

[7] See https://www.lexico.com/en/definition/nonperson.

[8] See Leland Ryken, James C. Wilhoit, and Tremper Longman III, eds., *Dictionary of Biblical Imagery*, Illinois and Leicester, InterVarsity Press, 1998, 259-261, s.v. 'Face, Facial Expressions'.

[9] https://jakomonchak.files.wordpress.com/2012/10/john-xxiii-opening-speech.pdf, for the text, n.15.

[10] See Jacques Dupuis, ed., *The Christian Faith in the Doctrinal Documents of the Catholic Church*, 6th ed., New York, Alba House, 1995, n.1031, 399. This hymn is from the *Brihadaranyaka Upanisad* 1,3,28, of Hinduism.

[11] See "Statement of the Sixth Bishops' Institute for Interreligious Affairs [BIRA] on the Theology of Dialogue," in *For All the Peoples of Asia: Federation of Asian Bishops' Conferences Documents from 1970 to 1991*, ed. G. B. Rosales & C. G. Arevalo, New York, Orbis Books and Quezon City, Claretian Publications, 1992, 3030.

[12] I take 'dialogic' to mean a conversation or dialogue to explore the meaning of something. Dialogic communication would therefore mean sharing between two parties, both of them contributing to the emergence of truth.

¹³ See Avery Dulles, *Models of the Church*, New York & London, Doubleday, 1987, 89-102, for details of this model.

¹⁴ GS seeks co-operation at various levels: (a) to spread Life-giving family values [GS, 52]; (b) to guarantee the fundamental rights of all people [GS, 73]; (c) to ensure peace and prosperity for all it also seeks to cooperate with the political state. See GS, 76: "The Church and the political community in their own fields are autonomous and independent from each other. Yet both, under different titles, are devoted to the personal and social vocation of the same men [*sic*]. The more that both foster sounder cooperation between themselves with due consideration for the circumstances of time and place, the more effective will their service be exercised for the good of all."

¹⁵ As outcome of VC II, the Catholic Bishops Conference of India (CBCI) instituted the 'National Biblical, Catechetical and Liturgical Centre' (NBCLC) in Bangalore in 1967, in order to: "promote and co-ordinate the renewal of Christian life in the Church according to the principles outlined by Vatican II."

¹⁶ Some of the significant contributions in the line of liturgy are mentioned by Peter C. Phan, "Reception of Vatican II in Asia: Historical and Theological Analysis," in *Exploring the Treasures of Vatican II*, Quezon City, Claretian Publications and Jesuit Communications, 2011, 164-168.

¹⁷ See n. 6 of *Querida Amazonia*, his 2020 Post Synodal Apostolic Exhortation; italics added. Hereinafter QA.

¹⁸ See his first encyclical letter in 2013 *Lumen Fidei*, n.47, wherein quoting Irenaeus he writes: "[T]here is but one faith, for it is grounded in the concrete event of the incarnation and can never transcend the flesh and history of Christ, inasmuch as God willed to reveal himself fully in that flesh."

¹⁹ In EG 233, he writes: "Not to put the word into practice, not to make it reality, is to build on sand, to remain in the realm of pure ideas and to end up in a lifeless and unfruitful self-centredness and Gnosticism." See also EG 94.

²⁰ See his 2018 apostolic exhortation *Gaudete et Exsultate* on the 'Call to Holiness in Today's World,' n.37. This will hereinafter be abbreviated as GE. See also see GE 35-46, where he explains this neo-heresy in detail.

²¹ See his 2019 Apostolic Letter *Admirabile Signum* on the Meaning and Importance of the Nativity Scene, n.3.

²² This 'Papal Bull of Induction' helps us to reflect upon what 'mercy' actually means in theory and entails in praxis. This document will hereinafter be abbreviated as MV.

²³ MV 24.

²⁴ See his 2013 Apostolic Exhortation, *Evangelii Gaudium: The Joy of the Gospel*, nn.197-201, for details of the need for the ecclesial option for the poor and the rationale behind it.

²⁵ See Clemens Sedmak, *A Church of the Poor: Pope Francis and the Transformation of Orthodoxy*, Maryknoll, New York, Orbis Books, 2016, for an analysis of what being a poor church will entail for the local and global church.

[26] Sedmak, *A Church of the Poor: Pope Francis and the Transformation of Orthodoxy*, p.vii.

[27] See https://www.vaticannews.va/en/pope/news/2018-07/pope-francis-mass-lampedusa-5-anniversary.html for details; accessed on May 22, 2019.

[28] See https://edition.cnn.com/2019/04/27/politics/pope-francis-migrants-aid/index.html accessed on May 22, 2019.

[29] These four words were focused upon in his message for World Day for Refugees and Migrants, 2019. See https://www.vaticannews.va/en/pope/news/2019-05/pope-francis-message-world-day-migrants-refugees-full-text.html

[30] From his message on the 106th World Day of Migrants and Refugees, September 27, 2020.... Accessible at: http://www.vatican.va/content/francesco/en/messages/migration/documents/papa-francesco_20200513_world-migrants-day-2020.html

[31] Homily on March 28, 2013; accessible at: https://saltandlighttv.org/blogfeed/getpost.php?id=46470

[32] https://www.aljazeera.com/news/2019/4/18/pope-tells-prisoners-at-foot-washing-rite-shun-inmate-hierarchy.

[33] See https://insidethevatican.com/popeswords/morningmass/missionaries-of-the-good-news-a-disciple-who-doesnt-serve-others-is-not-a-christian/

[34] See Pope Francis, *The Church of Mercy: A Vision for the Church*, Chicago, Illinois, Loyola Press, 2014, for a compilation of essays, speeches, and homilies on church.

[35] In a homily of January 19, 2005; reproduced in *Pope Francis in His Own Words*, ed. J. S. Collazo & L. Rogak, London, William Collins, 2013, 35.

[36] EG 88.

[37] See my *Saint Romero and Pope Francis: Revolutionaries of Tender Love*, Mumbai, Pauline Publications, 2019.

[38] See website: https://www.google.com/search?q=TED%20talk%20%2B%20pope%20Francis&ie=utf-8&oe=utf-8&aq=t&rls=org.mozilla:en-US:official&client=firefox-a&channel=np&source=hp; accessed on July 31, 2018.

[39] See Editorial of National Catholic Reporter "Francis' election full of symbols, signs of new era," March 23, 2013. Accessible at https://www.ncronline.org/news/vatican/editorial-francis-election-full-symbols-signs-new-era. This point is argued even more forcefully by Sri Lankan theologian Aloysius Pieris in the article in this volume, as well as in his e-book entitled: *Background Information Necessary for Helping Francis Renew the Church*, Kelaniya, Sri Lanka, Tulana Jubilee Publications, 2019.

[40] Text available on the internet at http://w2.vatican.va/content/paul-vi/en/motu_proprio/documents/hf_p-vi_motu-proprio_19650915_apostolica-sollicitudo.html. The focus is on starting the 'Synod of Bishops'.

[41] See the Address of Pope Francis at the ceremony commemorating the 50th Anniversary of the Institution of the Synod of Bishops at the Vatican on October 17, 2015. Text available on the internet; italics added.

⁴² Ibid.

⁴³ See http://www.vatican.va/roman_curia/congregations/cfaith/cti_documents/rc_cti_20180302_sinodalita_en.html

⁴⁴ See CDF's document: *Synodality in the Life and Mission of the Church*, March 2018, n.6.

⁴⁵ See Final Document of the Synod of Bishops on Young People, Faith and Vocational Discernment (2018); text available at: http://www.synod.va/content/synod2018/en/fede-discernimento-vocazione/final-document-of-the-synod-of-bishops-on-young-people—faith-an.html

⁴⁶ Text available at: http://www.vatican.va/roman_curia/synod/documents/rc_synod_doc_20191026_sinodo-amazzonia_en.html

⁴⁷ See Final Document of the Synod of Bishops' Special Assembly for the Pan-Amazonian Region issued on October 26, 2019, n.86.

⁴⁸ See EG 32.

⁴⁹ See https://cruxnow.com/vatican/2020/03/pope-chooses-synodality-as-theme-for-2022-synod/ for details.

⁵⁰ See EG 231, which goes on to say: "There exists a constant tension between ideas and realities. Realities simply are, whereas ideas are worked out. ... realities are greater than ideas. This calls for rejecting the various means of masking reality: angelic forms of purity, dictatorships of relativism, empty rhetoric, objectives more ideal than real, brands of ahistorical fundamentalism, ethical systems bereft of kindness, intellectual discourse bereft of wisdom

⁵¹ Text available at: http://www.vatican.va/content/francesco/en/travels/2019/outside/documents/papa-francesco_20190204_documento-fratellanza-umana.html

⁵² See report by John-Thor Dahlburg, "Pope's Remarks on Buddhism May Mar His Sri Lanka Visit," in the Los Angeles Times, online, Jan 13, 1995; accessible: https://www.latimes.com/archives/la-xpm-1995-01-13-mn-19567-story.html

⁵³ See report by Ian Fisher, "Muslims Condemn Pope's Remarks on Islam" in The New York Times, online, Sept. 15, 2006; accessible at: https://www.nytimes.com/2006/09/15/world/europe/15papal.html

⁵⁴ See EG 244.

⁵⁵ See his Address to the Bishops of Asia assembled at the Shrine of Haemi, South Korea on

August 17, 2014; accessible at: http://www.vatican.va/content/francesco/en/speeches/2014/august/documents/papa-francesco_20140817_corea-vescovi-asia.html

⁵⁶ See Address at the Meeting with the Bishops of the United States of America, Cathedral of Saint Matthew, Washington, D.C., Wednesday, September 23, 2015.

⁵⁷ In QA n. 66 on "inculturation" in footnote n.84, Pope Francis quotes GS 44 with regard to Inculturation so that it "is possible to create in every country the

possibility of expressing the message of Christ in suitable terms and to foster vital contact and exchange between the Church and different cultures".

[58] See EG 115, wherein in footnote n.85 he refers to GS of VC II where the "autonomy" that cultures must enjoy is upheld. This ensures that the Church does not impose a uniform culture on all believers, worldwide. He refers to this once again in *Laudato Si'* 80, referring to GS 36 in footnote n.50.

[59] See Final Document of the Synod of Bishops' Special Assembly for the Pan-Amazonian Region, n.38.

[60] See Final Document of the Synod of Bishops' Special Assembly for the Pan-Amazonian Region, n.54.

[61] See Final Document of the Synod of Bishops' Special Assembly for the Pan-Amazonian Region, n.95.

[62] See EG 132, 133, 182, 242, 243; also, LS 62, 63, 102, 107, 110, 131, 132, etc.

[63] This is clearly seen in QA wherein the pope quotes 16 writers and poets of South American origin or adoption.

[64] Robert Mickens, "The Radical Theological Vision of Pope Francis," in *La Croix International* online, July 5, 2019.

[65] See EG 273. Italics added.

[66] We are all "missionary disciples" according to Pope Francis. See EG 24, 40, 50, 119-121 and 173.

[67] https://licatholic.org/pope-francis-tells-the-secret-of-life-fix-your-gaze-on-jesus/ from a homily of August 17, 2019.

[68] See QA 5-80.

[69] QA 7.

[70] QA 61.

[71] EG 223.

[72] Insisting on change and conversion, he repeated this to the Roman Curia on December 21, 2019, when he received the cardinals and superiors at the Vatican Apostolic Palace for the presentation of Christmas wishes.

[73] See his 2019 Apostolic Exhortation to Youth, *Christus Vivit*, n.1.

[74] *Christus Vivit* 299.

6.

Pope Francis: A Missionary by His Very Nature

Recapturing the Missionary Spirit of Vatican Council II

Anil Thomas, CM

Introduction

On December 8, 1965, the Second Vatican Council (hereinafter VC II) came to an end. This marked the beginning of a new process of debate concerning the interpretation and implementation of the final texts of the Council. Consequently, there emerged a multitude of different interpretations and commentaries by theologians, bishops, priests, seminarians, religious men and women and lay people who were trying to comprehend the Council documents. This gave rise to many controversies and damaged even the smooth reception of the Council documents. The post-conciliar debates over the letter and the spirit of VC II, between the hermeneutic of continuity and discontinuity, liberal and conservative views and tradition and modernity and so on are still going on. Popes Paul VI, John Paul II and Benedict XVI were council fathers and made tremendous contribution in the correct interpretation and implementation of the documents. The contribution of Pope Francis is the latest in this list.

Archbishop Jorge Mario Bergoglio was always known for his simplicity and great missionary zeal. Right from the beginning of his pontificate Pope Francis has exhibited his desire to lead the Church after the example of Jesus Christ the evangelizer (missionary) par excellence. The missionary concern of Pope Francis for the Church springs straight from the teachings of VC II whose Decree on the Church's Missionary Activity *Ad Gentes Divinitus* states, "The Church on earth is by its very nature missionary since, according to the plan of the Father, it has its origin in the mission of the Son and the Holy Spirit."[1] Giving his own explanation of this statement, in his apostolic exhortation *Evangelii Gaudium* Pope Francis stated that all Christians are always and everywhere "missionary disciples" of Jesus. The paper tries to unpack this concept and demonstrate how through his life and works Pope Francis is recapturing the missionary spirit of VC II.

1. The Missionary Purpose of Vatican Council II

At the outset it is important to realize and comprehend the real purpose of VC II. The original purpose of the Council can be grasped from the life and works of Pope John XXIII who convoked it, from the Bull convoking the Council, from his opening address, from his writings during the Council and above all from the documents of the Council. On January 25, 1959, Pope John XXIII expressed his decision to convoke VC II for the universal Church as a necessary response to the then situation of the modern world.

1.1. Life and Experience of Pope John XXIII

John XXIII was a man of great pastoral experience. As a young priest Pope John was called to military service as a sergeant medic in 1915. One year later he became a military chaplain serving military hospitals during the First World War when Christians were killing Christians in the name of different nation states.[2] He also lived through the experiences of the Russian Revolution when classes were killing other classes in the name of social justice. He had witnessed the horrible crimes of the Nazi experiments of extermination of races and the other bitter consequences of the Second World War. He had personally intervened to ease the conflict and tension between Soviet Union and United States during the Cuban Missile Crisis and successfully contributed to save the world from the verge of a nuclear war. In short, he had seen and lived through different forms of conflicts and dangers of the modern humanity.

From the beginning of his pontificate one important concern of Pope John XXIII was how the Church could carry out her mission in the modern world. He demonstrated in his own words and actions the compassion of Christ and the Church for the modern world. As a genuine pastor he desired that VC II would be a pastoral one and different from the past councils of the Church that used more legalistic and juridical approaches. He wanted VC II to follow the example of Christ to make the Church more effective in evangelizing the modern world. This conviction emerged mostly from his experiences as a pastor for a long time.

Pope John realized that the world was at war with itself and was on the verge of self-destruction. So he was concerned with peace and unity of the contemporary world. It was out of this conviction that he wrote his famous encyclical *Pacem in Terris*. He recognized that someone should take up this challenge of directing and guiding the ways of the modern world at war with itself and teach nations and individuals that we are one human family. As the supreme pastor of the Church of Christ he thought that this was the duty of the universal Church. Therefore, we can say, in convoking the Council, Pope John XXIII was primarily looking at a divided world.

1.2. *Humanae Salutis*

Pope John XXIII officially convoked VC II through the Bull *Humanae Salutis* in which he laid down the reasons for convoking it. First, he stated that the Church was witnessing a crisis within society (humanity) that was at the threshold of a new age; then he enumerated some significant reasons for this crisis.³ Having analyzed the modern world and its characteristics, Pope John turned his attention to the Church's duty and role in the present situation and observed that "immensely serious and broad tasks await the Church..."⁴ He went on to substantiate, "It is a question in fact of bringing the perennial life-giving energies of the Gospel to the modern world, a world that boasts of its technical and scientific conquests but also bears the effects of a temporal order that some have wanted to reorganize by excluding God."⁵ The Holy Father reiterated that the modern world was characterized by great material progress but without a corresponding progress in the moral and spiritual sphere. The disturbing fact he pointed out was that there was a growing tendency in society to seek only the earthly pleasures that technological progress could bring. Making his own the recommendation of Jesus that we must learn to discern "the signs of the times" Pope John XXIII reminded the Church of her duty and responsibility in the modern world.

In the section, *the Present Vitality of the Church*, Pope John XXIII makes it clear that the Church has never remained a lifeless spectator in the face of such events. The Church is ever ready to carry out her mission in the new circumstances and situations created by the contemporary world. It is worth observing that Pope John does not say anywhere in *Humanae Salutis* that in order to carry out her mission in the modern world the Church needs to undergo modernization. On the contrary he declares, "Thus if the world seems to have changed profoundly, the Christian community has also in great part been transformed and renewed: that is, it has been strengthened in its social unity, reinvigorated intellectually, interiorly purified. It is ready for any trial."⁶

In the light of the above two realities, "a world which displays a serious state of spiritual poverty and the Church of Christ, still so vibrant with vitality," Pope John XXIII stated that the primary purpose of the Council was pastoral and missionary. He wrote that the Council was called "to give the Church the possibility to contribute more effectively to the solution of the problems of the modern age."⁷ Therefore, it must be emphatically stated that VC II was not called in order to modernize the Church. Of course, some modernization of the Church did indeed happen. However that was not the primary purpose of the Council. VC II was not called so as to enable to Church to catch up with a fast progressing modern world. The world can never set the agenda for the renewal of the Church.

1.3. *Gaudet Mater Ecclesiae*

The famous opening speech of Pope John XXIII at the solemn inauguration of VC II known as *Gaudet Mater Ecclesia* (Mother Church Rejoices), sets the tone of the Council. The pastoral and missionary intent of the Council becomes much clearer in *Gaudet Mater Ecclesia*. The Holy Father reiterates his outright criticism of the one-sided progress of the modern world and his conviction of the significance of the Church's mission in modern world in this critical juncture. He states that the main objective of the Council is that the "sacred deposit of Christian doctrine be guarded and taught in an increasingly effective way."[8] It is the responsibility of the Church to assist modern men and women to attain heavenly goods. The Church following the command of her founder has this fundamental duty and responsibility to teach the contemporary world to "seek first the Kingdom of God and its righteousness."[9] It is essential that the Church's teaching must reach different fields of human activity. In order to achieve this, it is necessary that the Church never turn her eyes from the sacred heritage of truth which she has received and at the same time "she must look at the present times which have introduced new conditions and new forms of life, and have opened new avenues for the Catholic apostolate."[10]

The Church takes note of the fact that modern man and woman is gradually turning away from God and therefore she reminds them to turn their eyes to God who is the source of all wisdom and beauty, "lest those to whom it was said "Subdue the earth and dominate it" (Gen 1:28), ever forget that most serious command: "The Lord your God you shall worship, and him alone you shall serve" (Mt 4:10; Lk 4:8)."[11] Pope John observes that on the basis of these concerns it is clear what is expected of the Council. "The main task of this Council is not the discussion of this or that theme of the fundamental doctrine of the Church, repeating diffusely the teaching of ancient and modern Fathers and theologians, which is very well known to you and with that you are so familiar with."[12] In order to have only such discussions there would have been no need to call an Ecumenical Council. "What instead is necessary today is that the whole of Christian doctrine, with no part of it lost, be received in our times by all with a new fervour, in serenity and peace...One thing is the substance of the old doctrine of the *depositum fidei* and another the way to formulate its expression; and of this we must take great account..."[13] It becomes clear, therefore, that the primary concern of the Council is one of properly exposing and effectively communicating the perennial and life-giving message of the Gospel to the modern men [sic] and women and to the contemporary society.

In this inaugural address Pope John XXIII boldly stated the way the Council and so the Church should deal with the modern world and its errors. "The Church has always opposed these errors. Frequently she condemned them with the greatest severity. In our time, however, the Bride of Christ prefers to use the medicine of mercy rather than severity."[14] The Church has a message for the modern world. She does not promise an earthly happiness. She has to offer humanity the divine grace and elevate them to the dignity of the children of God. In and through the Council the Church "wishes to show herself to be the most loving mother of all, kind, patient, and moved by mercy and goodness towards her separated children."[15] From Pope John XXIII's opening speech it becomes crystal clear that to him the primary reason for convoking VC II was "modernity" and a concern to effectively evangelize this modern world. Pope John XXIII was right in his desire for a renewal and revision of the relation between the Church and the modern world.

1.4. Lumen Gentium

The missionary intent of VC II becomes clear in different documents of the Council. *Lumen Gentium*—the Dogmatic Constitution on the Church—begins by emphatically stating this missionary purpose of the Council: "Christ is the light of humanity; and it is, accordingly, the heartfelt desire of this sacred Council, ... by proclaiming his Gospel to every creature (cf. Mk. 16:15), it may bring to all men [sic] that light of Christ which shines out visibly from the Church."[16] The aim of the Council is to bring the light of Christ to the whole world.

Lumen Gentium has defined the Church in many ways; stating that "the Church, in Christ, is in the nature of a sacrament — a sign and instrument, that is, of communion with God and unity among all men [sic]..."[17] This definition of Church exposed by the Council unfortunately did not attract the attention it deserved from the theologians. The Church got more preoccupied with matter concerning *ad intra* and almost neglected the *ad extra* aspect of this missionary commitment to which the Council wanted to direct the Church. However, from the point of view of mission and mission theology, this understanding of Church as the sacrament, sign and instrument of communion with God and unity among human beings is of enormous significance.

The Church is sent forth to bring human beings to God (communion with God) and to bring human beings to one another. Indeed this is her identity, her mission and the primary purpose of her existence. A Christian's deepest identity emerges from this fundamental definition of the Church set forth in *Lumen Gentium*. In the same way the entire second chapter of *Lumen Gentium* dealing with the Church as the People of God manifests the Council's understanding of the Church's missionary nature and her evangelical commitment to the entire human race.

1.5. Ad Gentes

In *Ad Gentes*, its famous decree on the 'Church's Missionary Activity', VC II categorically states, "The Church on earth is by its very nature missionary since, according to the plan of the Father, it has its origin in the mission of the Son and the Holy Spirit according to the will of the Father."[18] This indeed was substantially a radical statement in the sense that it greatly influenced the way the post-conciliar Church understood and explained what it means to be a member of the Church and more specifically what it means to be a missionary. Mission is a participation in the life of the Trinity and this participation begins in and through one's baptism. Thus, the Church, which VC II defined as the "People of God" (LG 9-17), is missionary by its very nature.

In *Ad Gentes*, the Church teaches that the Church's mission (and her missionary nature) is rooted in the mission of God. Mission springs from the very nature of God who is love. The Church and her mission spring from the "fountain-like love" of God the Father. This teaching of *Ad Gentes* has two essential implications from the perspective of practical evangelization. First, all the disciples of Christ are called to be missionaries by participating in the very life of God in and through baptism. Second, this divine mission (divine life) entrusted to the Church in general and to every Christian in particular reaches out to all, especially those who are poor or in need. "The Church, sent by Christ to reveal and communicate the love of God to all men [*sic*] and all peoples, is aware that for her a tremendous missionary work still remains to be done."[19]

Like our God we are also meant to reach out to others without measuring our love and without expecting anything in return. Jesus asks: "If you love only those who love you, what reward will you have? Even the tax collectors do the same. If you greet only your brothers, what is unusual about that? Even the pagans do the same. So be perfect just as your heavenly Father is perfect" (Mt 5:46-48). Thus, having the divine life in us, we are meant to love God and others in a radical way. This is an important implication of the conciliar teaching that we are missionaries by our very nature. *Ad Gentes* goes on to state that if the Church has to be effective in carrying out the mission entrusted to her by Christ the Lord, "then the Church, urged on by the Spirit of Christ, must walk the road Christ himself walked, a way of poverty and obedience, of service and self-sacrifice even to death, a death from which he emerged victorious by his resurrection."[20]

1.6. *Gaudium et Spes*

Gaudium et Spes, VC II's famous 'Pastoral Constitution on the Church in the Modern World' substantiates and reiterates the Church's missionary nature and her missionary commitment to the entire world. In this document it becomes evident that the Church is not for herself but for others. She reaches out to one and all in her resolve to remain faithful to the missionary character. Thus, in the very opening sentence *Gaudium et Spes* declares: "The joy and hope, the grief and anguish of the men [*sic*] of our time, especially of those who are poor or afflicted in any way, are the joy and hope, the grief and anguish of the followers of Christ as well. Nothing that is genuinely human fails to find an echo in their hearts."[21]

The Church is depicted as a community of disciples of Christ moving forward to the kingdom of the Father and bears a "message of salvation intended for all men" [*sic*] because of which "Christians cherish a feeling of deep solidarity with the human race."[22] Having deeply studied the mystery of the Church the Council is interested not only in the sons and daughters of the Church but the whole of humanity as well.[23] Today the human race is troubled and perplexed due to various reasons. With solidarity and respectful affection for the whole humanity, the Church desires to enter into dialogue with them. She "offers to cooperate unreservedly with mankind in fostering a sense of brotherhood to correspond to this destiny of theirs."[24]

After VC II all the four Popes have deliberately carried forward this conciliar emphasis on the missionary nature of the People of God and the Church's missionary commitment and approach to humanity as a whole.

2. Pope Francis Recapturing the Missionary Spirit of VC II

A deeper analysis of the life and works of Cardinal Jorge Mario Bergoglio, Archbishop of Buenos Aires, Argentina, shows that he was a person really influenced by the teachings of VC II even though he had not taken part in the proceedings of the Council. He had succeeded to a great extent in implementing the teachings of the Council in his archdiocese as well as in his personal life. Therefore, it is not surprising that when he was elected Pope on March 13, 2013, he began another phase of that implementation.

2.1. Evangelii Gaudium

On November 24, 2013, Pope Francis issued his first Apostolic Exhortation *Evangelii Gaudium* (EG), a document that in line with the teachings of VC II—especially that of *Ad Gentes and Lumen Gentium*—proposes a program of evangelization of the contemporary world and reform of the Church. It has reminded the whole Church of the great missionary commitment and responsibility. In the very opening paragraph of the document Pope Francis says, "In this Exhortation I wish to encourage the Christian faithful to embark upon a new chapter of evangelization marked by this joy, while pointing out new paths for the Church's journey in years to come."[25] In EG 27 the Holy Father speaks of choosing a missionary option in everything that we do as disciples of Jesus Christ. "I dream of a missionary option, that is a missionary impulse capable of transforming everything, so that the Church's customs, ways of doing things, times and schedules, language and structures can be suitably channeled for the evangelization of today's world rather than for her self-preservation."[26]

Reiterating the views of Pope John Paul II, Pope Francis said, "there must be no lessening of the impetus to preach the Gospel to those who are far from Christ, because this is the first task of the Church... missionary outreach is paradigmatic for all the Church's activity."[27] He has repeatedly demonstrated what it means to be a missionary by nature. "In all the baptized, from first to last, the sanctifying power of the Spirit is at work, impelling us to evangelization."[28] In his opinion, all Christians are missionary disciples of Jesus and therefore, the Church is the community of the missionary disciples of Christ. "In virtue of their baptism, all the members of the People of God have become missionary disciples (cf. Mt 28: 19). All the baptized, whatever their position in the Church or their level of instruction in the faith, are agents of evangelization, and it would be insufficient to envisage a plan of evangelization to be carried out by professionals while the rest of the faithful would simply be passive recipients. The new evangelization calls for personal involvement on the part of each of the baptized. Every Christian is challenged, here and now, to be actively engaged in evangelization."[29] From the magisterium of Pope Francis it becomes all the more clear that it is baptism that really makes us missionaries.

To be a Christian is to be missionary and to be a missionary means to be caught up in the very life of God, the Trinity. In the sacred scripture we encounter God as one who invites us to share his life and glory and reaches out to everyone especially the "poor" with his saving presence and unconditional love (Lk 4:18-19). This missionary outreach is "paradigmatic for all the Church's activity."[30]

His advice to the theologians is worth observing. "I call on theologians to carry out this service as part of the Church's saving mission. In doing so, however, they must always remember that the Church and theology exists to evangelize, and not to be content with a desk-bound theology."[31] The entire Church is permanently on a state of mission. Pope Francis exhorts all the baptized not to lose the missionary enthusiasm entrusted to us in our baptism: "Let us not allow ourselves to be robbed of missionary enthusiasm."[32]

In *Evangelii Gaudium* Pope Francis succeeds in presenting the broadest possible understanding, after *Ad Gentes*, of the Church's mission and her missionary nature. Pope Paul VI, Pope John Paul II and Pope Benedict XVI explained this conciliar concept of mission in different ways and tried to implement it. However, it seems to me that the definition and explanation of Pope Francis stand closer to the *Ad Gentes*' concept of mission. He gives a new expression to capture the entire meaning of mission presented in VC II. The new expression includes all the aspects of the one, complex mission of the Church.

2.2. Year of Mercy

Pope Francis can be easily described as the 'Pope of Mercy'. Emphasizing God's mercy is a repeated theme in his teachings and writings. He considers it so important that he announced an 'Extraordinary Jubilee Year of Mercy' from December 8, 2015 to November 20, 2016. In *Misericordiae Vultus*, the Bull of Indiction of this Extraordinary Jubilee of Mercy, Pope Francis reminded the Church that in Jesus Christ God's mercy has become living and visible. Therefore, we constantly need to contemplate the mystery of mercy. He stated that the Jubilee Year of Mercy is directly related to the Church's mission and to VC II: "At times we are called to gaze even more attentively on mercy so that we may become a more effective sign of the Father's action in our lives. For this reason I have proclaimed an Extraordinary Jubilee of Mercy as a special time for the Church, a time when the witness of believers might grow stronger and more effective."[33]

The missionary purpose of VC II and its relation to the year of mercy is powerfully demonstrated in *Misericordiae Vultus* 4, the text of which runs as follows:

> I have chosen the date of December 8 because of its rich meaning in the recent history of the Church. In fact, I will open the Holy Door on the fiftieth anniversary of the closing of the Second Vatican Ecumenical Council. The Church feels a great need to keep this even alive. With the Council the Church entered a new phase of her history. The Council Fathers strongly perceived, as a true breath of the Holy Spirit, a need to talk about God to men and women of their time in a more accessible way. The walls which for too long had made the Church a kind of fortress were torn down and the time had come to proclaim the Gospel in a new way. It was a new phase of the same evangelization that had existed from the beginning. It was a fresh undertaking for all Christians to bear witness to their faith with greater enthusiasm and conviction. The Church sensed a responsibility to be a living sign of the Father's love in the world.

From the above citation it becomes evident that to Pope Francis the Extraordinary Jubilee Year of Mercy is directly related to VC II and its missionary nature and purpose. Further, in *Misericordiae Vultus* Pope Francis makes explicit reference to two pivotal ideas that Pope John

XXIII presented before the Council Fathers in his famous opening address *Gaudet Mater Ecclesia*. "We recall the poignant words of Saint John XXIII when, opening the Council, he indicated the path to follow: Now the Bride of Christ wishes to use the medicine of mercy rather than taking up arms of severity.... The Catholic Church, as she holds high the torch of Catholic truth at this Ecumenical Council, wants to show herself a loving mother to all; patient, kind, moved by compassion and goodness towards her separated children."[34] Referring to Pope Paul VI's closing address at VC II, Pope Francis observes that charity had been the main religious feature of the Council.

Pope Francis has emphasized the significance of reaching out to everyone especially those on the margins of the society. Mercy, in the Christian theological understanding, has a direct relation to sin. When and where sin becomes a serious issue mercy becomes relevant and necessary. God is merciful to the sinner. St. John teaches us that God is love (1 Jn. 4:7-8). When God turns to the sinner what appears is mercy. In other words, mercy appears when love meets the sinner. So it is important not to misunderstand Pope Francis's emphasis on God's mercy. He never intends to say that sin does not matter because God is merciful. Mercy and sin are two sides of the same coin. The call to use the medicine of mercy to heal the sickness of the world was the invitation of Pope John XXIII and the proposal of VC II.

2.3. Baptized and Sent

In order to celebrate the hundredth anniversary of the promulgation of the Apostolic Letter *Maximum Illud*, Pope Francis called for an 'Extraordinary Missionary Month' that was celebrated in October 2019, with the aim of fostering and reviving the Church's missionary awareness and commitment. In his message for the World Mission Day 2019 titled: 'Baptized and Sent: The Church of Christ on Mission in the World', Pope Francis once again spoke about the importance of renewing the Church's missionary commitment.[35] He envisions a Church that goes out with a renewed missionary commitment. The Church is sent by Christ to reveal and to communicate the love of God to all human beings. He invites us to have a sense of duty towards the mission.

Pope Francis said that the 'Extraordinary Missionary Month' was an invitation "to rediscover the missionary dimension of our faith in Jesus Christ, a faith graciously bestowed on us in baptism."[36] In baptism we are born to new life and are invited to share this new life of love with those around us. Pope Francis understands this to be the proper meaning of mission. "This missionary mandate touches us personally: I am a mission, always; you are a mission, always; every baptized man and woman is a mission."[37] The Church of Christ is on a mission in the world. "Each of us is a mission to the world, for each of us is the fruit of God's love."[38] The missionary mandate of Christ touches all Christians personally. "Our mission, then, is rooted in the Fatherhood of God and the motherhood of the Church. The mandate given by the Risen Jesus at Easter is inherent in Baptism: as the Father has sent me, so I send you...This mission is part of our identity as Christians."[39] In this way Pope Francis further develops and explains the concept of mission and missionary nature of the Church presented in *Ad Gentes* and *Lumen Gentium*.

Conclusion: We are all Called to be Missionary Disciples

Being a missionary disciple is of paramount importance as far as Pope Francis is concerned. All the baptized are disciples of Christ sent out into the world to preach the good news. So evangelical proclamation is the central preoccupation of the Church; therefore, all other elements and aspects in the life of the Church should come after this essential and central reality. Proclaiming the good news that the Son of God died for our sins and rose from the dead is to be communicated to everyone. This was the fundamental driving force of the Church from the very beginning, for the apostles and the early Church. In the course of time this was somewhat sidelined. Going back to the scripture and fathers of the Church, VC II recaptured it and asked us to put into practice. Pope Francis appropriated this teaching of the Council and began courageously implementing it. He reminds us that we are sent out precisely for this proclamation. Therefore, we must feel like St Paul: "Woe to me if I do not proclaim the gospel!" (1 Cor 9:16).

Today with Pope Francis the Church is not radically different from what it was in the time of Pope Benedict XVI or Pope John Paul II or Pope Paul VI. Of course the positive approach of Pope Francis is much more appealing to everyone. His lifestyle and language attract the attention of the whole world. Thus, no one should think that Pope Francis represents some major revolution in the Church's self-understanding. His is an attempt to adopt the simple and humble lifestyle and spirit of Jesus and the Gospel.

Greatly influenced by the recommendations of *Gaudium et Spes* and *Ad Gentes,* Pope Francis invites us to see the world through the eyes of the poor. He wants a Church for the poor, a Church that goes forth to all, but first of all to the poor and a Church where the poor can feel at home. VC II was a pastoral Council. Pope Francis is becoming an embodiment of this new pastoral concept of leading the Church and evangelizing the modern world. This is how he carries forward the vision of reform and evangelization proposed by VC II.

Endnotes

[1] The Second Vatican Council's Decree on the Church's Missionary Activity *Ad Gentes Divinitus* (AG), n.2.

[2] https://w2.vatican.va/content/john-xxiii/en/biography/documents/hf_j-xxiii_bio_20190722_biografia.html (accessed November 19, 2019).

[3] Pope John XXIII, Apostolic Constitution *Humanae Salutis* (HS), December 25, 1961, n.3.

[4] HS n.3.

[5] HS n.3.

[6] HS n.5.

[7] HS n.6.

[8] Pope John XXIII, Opening Speech to the Council *Gaudet Mater Ecclesia* (GME), October 11, 1962, n.11.

[9] GME n.11. Mt 6:33.

[10] GME n.12.

[11] GME n.13.
[12] GME n.15.
[13] GME n.15.
[14] GME n.16.
[15] GME n.17.
[16] Vatican Council II, Dogmatic Constitution on the Church, *Lumen Gentium* (LG), n.1.
[17] LG n.1.
[18] AG n.2.
[19] AG n.10.
[20] AG n.5.
[21] Vatican Council II, Pastoral Constitution on the Church in the Modern World *Gaudium et Spes* (GS), n.1.
[22] GS n.1.
[23] GS n.2.
[24] GS n.3.
[25] Pope Francis, Apostolic Exhortation *Evangelii Gaudium* (EG), n. 1.
[26] EG n.27.
[27] EG n.15.
[28] EG n.119.
[29] EG n.120.
[30] EG no. 15.
[31] EG no. 133.
[32] EG no. 80.
[33] Pope Francis, Bull of Indiction of the Extraordinary Jubilee of Mercy, *Misericordiae Vultus* (MV) no. 3.
[34] MV no. 4; GME Nos.16-17.
[35] Pope Francis, *Baptized and Sent: The Church of Christ on Mission in the World. Message for the World Mission Day 2019* (Mumbai: Better Yourself Books, 2019).
[36] Ibid.
[37] Ibid.
[38] Ibid.
[39] Ibid.

7.

Pope Francis: A Master Communicator

Renewing Church and World Through Communication

Joseph Scaria Palakeel, MST

Introduction: Pope Francis and Church Reform through the Media

Half a century ago, *Gaudium et Spes* (hereinafter GS) outlined the vision of a Church that makes her own "the joys and the hopes, the griefs and the anxieties of the men (*sic*) of this age" and today we have a Pope who communicates the 'Joy of the Gospel', *Evangelii Gaudium* (hereinafter EG) to the entire humanity. Through his symbolic actions and simple language, Pope Francis communicates joy and hope to everyone and infuses new energy and enthusiasm in the Church and the world. From his first appearance at the papal window in 2013, the communication genius of Pope Francis has aroused much interest and debate in both religious and secular circles. His distinctive communication strategies and skills, coupled with his deep devotion to the Gospel, has helped him become the most influential world leader today. *Time Magazine* chose him as the person of the year 2013 and several prestigious journals adorned their cover pages with his images. By designating Pope Francis as the world's greatest leader in 2014, *Fortune Magazine* wrote, "Francis has electrified the church and attracted legions of non-Catholic admirers by energetically setting a new direction."[1]

Pope Francis is not only a public media icon, but also a powerful reformer of the Church in and for our times. He makes productive and transformative use of communication, along with his theological vision, to renew and reorient the Church. By taking the Church back to the Gospel and leading her 'out' to the peripheries of the world through his own emblematic style, Pope Francis calls our attention to the 'discontinuities' introduced by Vatican Council II (hereinafter VC II) for reforming the Church. In this paper, I will briefly examine the distinctive personal and papal (official) communication by Pope Francis from a communication theology perspective and demonstrate how his communication style unveils his vision of the Church and how his theological vision is enfleshed in his communication.

Pope Francis is an accomplished communicator, who wants to usher in a missionary-synodal Church with bottom-up and participatory communication, and thereby, implement the reform-renewal program of VC II. He accomplishes it through visual-spatial-tactile rhetoric coupled with simple words and metaphorical speech, a style unusual to papal communication, as we know it. All his administrative reforms in the Curia follow closely from his vision of a synodal Church. In a unique and original manner, Pope Francis is renewing and reforming the Church through his communication style and strategy.

1. Pope Francis: A Master Communicator for the New World

Pope Francis—the first Pope of the social media era—is rightly described as the Pope from the new world and 'Pope for the new world.'[2] His first appearance on the papal balcony went viral, announcing the *new avatar* of Pope, an icon of hope and an archetypal model for emulation by church leaders. Many of his actions in the very first year of his papacy became events discussed around the world through the photos and videos watched worldwide over million times. With his many gestures of affection towards the poor and the marginalized, as well as his papal communication choices, Pope Francis has endeared himself to the whole world: Catholics, Christians and people of other faiths. No other pope in history has attracted so much media attention and exercised such global influence like Pope Francis. Even after the initial euphoria, Pope Francis continues to fascinate everyone with his visual rhetoric, simple language and profound insights.

1.1. A Pope for the Social Media Age

Pope Francis communicates well in the digital media culture of our times. *Time Magazine* chose him as the person of the year 2013, complimenting his public relations and communication skills: "he understands public opinion, connects easily with all people, speaks from heart in simple language and is at home with technology."[3] His public relation skills and gestures, with an unambiguous tone of openness and transparency, have served to improve the public perception of the Catholic Church especially at a time when the image of church was low due to scandals that plagued the church in recent times.

Pope Francis is one of the most followed and influential leaders in social media like Twitter and Instagram. The Pope's Instagram account *@Franciscus* reaches 5.6 million people and he has 47 million Twitter followers *@Pontifex* – including 17.9 million in English and 16.8 million in Spanish. Pope Francis uses the potential of digital technology to the best to send out simplified yet grand and beautiful messages that would potentially reach everyone. The pope's everyday "pills of wisdom" and "capsules of love" are inspiring to even to believers of other religions and non-believers alike.[4] Francis' spontaneity, good humor, simplicity and generosity convey authenticity in terms of digital media.

Pope Francis' reorganization of the Vatican Communication Offices and his World Communications Day Messages bear testimony to his clear understanding of the communication tools, technologies as well as the communication issues of the digital culture. Through these messages, he addresses the dilemmas in social media culture, especially fake news, connection without presence, and contact without encounter. Above all, the most outstanding trait of Pope Francis' communication is his visual rhetoric, which is ever relevant in the audiovisual age.

1.2. The New Papal Rhetoric for the Audiovisual Age

Pope Francis has "revolutionized the world by communicating with his words, transparency, good mood, closeness and symbolic acts. Furthermore, not only his words, but also his gestures and acts convey a message."[5] In a recent book entitled *The Rhetoric of Pope Francis*, Christopher Oldenburg[6] characterizes Pope Francis as a "well-trained rhetor" (p. 34), a "rhetorically intelligent designer" (p.15) and a "skillful practitioner of rhetoric" (xxxii and epilogue), with a great gift for gesture. He believes that the genius of Pope Francis is best explained in terms of his symbolic-iconic gestures, which he calls "pope tropes" (p.xx). The visual communication of Pope Francis, coupled with his simple and vivid imageries in speech, serves as a kind of "catholic language" not only to 1.2 billion Catholics who speak thousands of different languages but also for the global audience [cf. pp.4-5]

Oldenburg demonstrates further that, Pope Francis is fully aware of the rhetorical power and didactic role of images to attract and convince people [p.4] and he utilizes "deliberate dramatization of visual argument" (p.xx) to articulate his vision of the Church. "Photographs for Pope Francis are visual sermons that aim to reach the heart through the eyes; they are the stained-glass church windows of our time." (p.5). Noting that Francis rhetoric has a transformative capacity for papal and pastoral conversion (p.xviii), Oldenburg portrays Pope as a "living icon of mercy" and describes papal rhetoric as "sacramental semiotics of mercy" to make God's grace visible in the world through material signs of space, physical artifacts and non-verbal communication. (p.34) We may look at a few instances to show how Pope Francis employs a visual argument to impart his vision.

1.2.1. First Appearance Signals a New Vision of Papacy

Pope Francis communicated a new style of papacy and a new vision of the Church by his first appearance at the Papal window in a simple white robe without traditional papal paraphernalia and with a personal greeting and humble request for prayer. He transformed "the ritualized modernist spectacle" of presenting papacy as a medieval, hierarchical and political machination of power and opulence for reinforcing complete authoritative power of papacy to a visual argument in sign and symbols to refocus image of supreme jurisdiction granted by Code of Canon Law 331 to one of shepherd.[7] Similarly, the first Jesuit Pope choosing the name 'Francis'[8] aroused much curiosity and speculation as to the course the new pope would take. Pope Francis' subsequent actions like his choice of residence in Martha's guesthouse instead of the papal palace, his visit to the hotel desk to pay his bills, his travel choices as well as his conduct during papal audiences and visits clearly signal a radical shift in the hierarchical status from 'top' to 'down' and from 'center' to 'periphery'. All these sent out a message to the whole world about the forthcoming "demonarchising, demythologizing, and decentralizing" papacy.[9] Two instances are analyzed here to substantiate what we have been saying.

1.2.2. Hierarchical Transference through Spatial Communication

Pope Francis chose to wash the feet of the inmates in *Casal de Marmo* prison during his first paschal season as Pope. More than a ritualistic reenactment of the last supper, it was a deliberate dramatization of the occasion to point toward a new orientation for the Church and Church leaders. First, Pope's foot-washing ceremony served as a visual spatial demonstration of conversion to servanthood of 'his holiness' and a reenactment of Christ's kenosis beyond church. Second, it served as symbolic enactment of his address to the priests during Chrism Mass on Holy Thursday of 2013 on the "need to 'go out' in order to experience the power and redemptive efficacy of anointing" towards the periphery (from Vatican City to a prison) and towards marginalized people (criminals, people of other faiths, including women). Third, this act served as a new theological interpretation of the "kenotic ecclesiology" that Church should empty herself in service to the world.[10]

By his gesture of moving that first Maundy Thursday ceremony in 2013 from the sacred space of the Church and territory of Vatican to the profane space of a prison, and selecting sinners (prisoners) in place of the just (churchgoers and practitioners of faith), he visually enacted his idea of Church that goes out in search of the lost sheep. Bringing forgiveness and mercy to prison through a ritual ablution, Pope Francis was cleansing the 'sinners' as well as the papacy.[11] These interpretations are further validated through his many travels 'outside' – visiting earthquake sites, slums, homes, Roman parishes, hearing confessions and so on.

1.2.3. Proclaiming Mercy through Proxemics and Tactile Communication

Pope Francis' embrace of Vinicio Riva, a severely disfigured Italian man suffering from neurofibromatosis, during his first weekly audience in St Peter's square was another visual proclamation of mercy. The pope was here using spatial-tactile communication to show his affection and heart for people in the peripheries of pain. Proximity and intimate touch create new emotional connection and closeness for one who enacts it and in all who see it in photographs or video. Pope Francis' compassionate closeness violated the papal contact codes of Public or VVIP distance. However, through this gesture, Pope inverts the idea of "inclusive inner circle, a space traditionally reserved for normative, powerful and privileged." Mercy makes us "pass from exclusion to full inclusion, from estrangement to embrace" (p.54). Likewise, it symbolizes 'going out to the peripheries to administer comforting touch to the suffering and alienated people.

In his address on the First World Day of the Poor Pope Francis said, "if we truly encounter Christ, we have to touch his body in the suffering bodies of the poor". Sharing the joys and hope (GS 1) of the poor and the marginalized, the pope is becoming a living icon of the

Church he heads and shows that he is a missionary par excellence. He is also giving out a teaching in action to "embrace more intentionally the peripheries," going beyond charity and social service (p.54). He was preaching with action and not words in complete fidelity to the Franciscan vision to preach without words.

1.3. Simplicity of Language vs High Theology

Consistent with his symbolic actions—iconic and sometimes ironic—Pope Francis' language is simple and full of popular expressions. In his spoken as well as written communication, he deliberately avoids Church cliché language as well as conceptual theological terminology and construction of arguments. In the Preface to the book *The Vocabulary of Pope Francis*,[12] Cardinal Pietro Parolin, Vatican Secretary of State, writes the following about Pope's new style of communication: "For many Catholics the Pope's communication style is a complete novelty, because they were used to a way of teaching in the Church which usually involved a difficult, sophisticated language and often complicated concepts."[13] "In his speech," the Cardinal added, "there is 'the ability to communicate high content', 'making use of a vocabulary and of images that draw their strength from their closeness to daily life' and thus putting the reader or listener, whoever they may be, on the same level and not at a distance."[14] Pope Francis speaks a language that contemporary people understand and can resonate with, yet making his point in clear catholic doctrine.[15]

Pope Francis is adept in the multimedia and multisensory communication using images, sounds and story, which is characteristic of the digital media culture of today. In *Christus Vivit* 211, he speaks of "ways of incarnating the kerygma in the language of today's youth": "we need to use above all the language of closeness, the language of generous, relational and existential love that touches the heart, impacts life, and awakens hope and desires." His speeches in a familiar conversational, direct, and dialogical style, full of examples from everyday life, evoke the teaching style of Jesus. He speaks in simple and straightforward style using picturesque and imaginative language. Metaphorical thinking and speaking is his forte. His usages like "shepherds who smell like the sheep", "church which is bruised, hurting and dirty", "the memory of God ... is not a 'hard disk' that 'saves' and 'archives' all our data" rather one that "finds joy in 'deleting' from us every trace of evil" (CV 115) resonate powerfully with people and invite them to transformation.

Pope Francis puts profound theological instincts directly from gospel into simple language understandable to all. He sees the Gospel not as a monolithic body of doctrine to be "communicated by fixed formulations... or by words which express an absolutely invariable content" (EG 129, 40) but through inculturated preaching, an incarnated gospel. He speaks from heart and uses the imagery of the heart often (EG 2, 5, 178, 183, 283) and his theology is a "cordial theology in an etymological sense. The recurring theme in his writings is joy, proposing it as the affective infectious response to Good News of God's love. The rationale of his using simple language is clearly laid out in *Evangelii Gaudium* 35: "Pastoral ministry in a missionary style is not obsessed with the disjointed transmission of a multitude of doctrines to be insistently imposed. When we adopt a pastoral goal and a missionary style which would actually reach everyone without exception or exclusion, the message has to concentrate on the essentials, on what is most beautiful, most grand, most appealing and at the same time most necessary. The message is simplified, while losing none of its depth and truth, and thus becomes all the more forceful and convincing" (EG 35). Francis's only true strategy of communication is confident and serene adherence to the Gospel.

1.4. The Francis-Effect: Communication and Image of the Church

The overall impact of the actions and teachings of Pope Francis is depicted as the 'Francis Effect', drawing on from the 2014 documentary[16] on Pope Francis with the same title. The iconic images of Pope and touching stories of his compassion circulated widely by *L'Osservatore Romano* as well as in various print and social media have played major role in creating the so called 'Francis effect'. These narratives visually reinforced his message of the spirit of poverty, humility, and openness of the Church as a whole. While he is highly praised for his communication strategies, he is also criticized often enough for his communication style, along with or apart from his theological standpoints. We could say that the controversies about Pope Francis are mostly due to a lack of sympathetic perception of his communication choices and styles. So also, his widespread appeal to the larger world community—including, believers, non-believers, and people of all walks—is attributable to his communication power, along with his novel vision of the Church.

The 'Francis-effect' is primarily a communication phenomenon, which initiated major theological shifts. Pope Francis' personal and papal communication style and strategy reveal a radically new vision of the Church and its communication. His communication style flows from his ecclesiology and, for all good reasons, his ecclesiology itself is shaped by his personal communication styles and preferences. In other words, the actions and images of Pope Francis are not just a manifestation of papal humility but are also indicative of his ecclesiological shift from a hierarchical to a communion model of church, inspired by the ecclesiology of VC II.

2. Communication Style of Pope Francis and his Vision of the Church: Dialogical, Participatory, Synodal Church with Bottom-up Communication

The apostolic Church was a communicating community of believers. Church acquired a hierarchical structure from the imperial times and the 'perfect society' tag was attributed from the medieval period. These and other elements climaxed in the 'infallibility' doctrine, which gave birth to a traditional, dogmatic, conservative and immutable Church in the twentieth century. VC II spelled out a communion ecclesiology by declaring the Church as "people of God" (*Lumen Gentium* and *Gaudium et Spes*), but no radical change took place until Pope Francis who signaled clear movement downward and outward through his incessant teaching and examples. His communication strategy, along with the predominant social media culture, has initiated a transformation of the hierarchical church into a synodal church, dissolving centuries of hierarchical stability and settling. His call for synodality is a revolution from hierarchical and one-way or 'top-down' to 'bottom-up' communication with lateral and multi-nodal interchange — a mode of communication practiced in the synods.

In his book, *Models of the Church*, a ground breaking survey on ecclesiology, Avery Dulles speaks of an intrinsic mutual connection between the model of the Church (ecclesiology) and church communication style.[17] Following this lead we can say that the administrative and communication style of the Church flows closely from the vision of the Church (ecclesiology). In a hierarchical church, with a monolithic and monologic structure, communication is always institutional and top-down, demanding obedience and submission, whereas in a servant and herald models of church, participatory and dialogical processes mark the internal organization and communication, while the outward communication is simple, attractive, open and transparent. Pope Francis envisions a synodal church, which could be reckoned as a new model which is an amalgamation of the communion, herald and servant models of Church.

2.1. Synodal Church: A Communication Perspective

From the beginning of his ministry as Bishop of Rome, Pope Francis has consistently outlined and pursued a synodal vision of the Church[18] in place of the Rome-centred hierarchical church and has "sought to enhance the Synod, which is one of the most precious legacies of the Second Vatican Council."[19] He firmly believes that "The world in which we live, and which we are called to love and serve, even with its contradictions, demands that the Church strengthen cooperation in all areas of her mission. It is precisely this path of *synodality* which God expects of the Church of the third millennium."[20] In an interview marking the beginning of the fifth year of the pontificate of Pope Francis, Cardinal Wuerl said: "Now comes Pope Francis who's saying, why don't we pick up where we left off: collegiality, synodality? The synodality that Paul VI initiated has flowered under Francis."[21]

In an interview to Belgian Catholic Newspaper *Tertio* in December 2016, Pope Francis stated: "... either there is a pyramidal Church, in which what Peter says is done, or there is a synodal Church, in which Peter is Peter but he accompanies the Church, he lets her grow, he listens to her, he learns from this reality and goes about harmonizing it... It is unity in diversity. This is synodality."[22] He values "*Synodality*, as a constitutive element of the Church," which derives from the nature of Church as a communion rooted in the Trinitarian mystery and effects greater effective communion among men. Synodality is the best form of the exercise of collegiality which includes a process of community discernment or common listening to the Spirit in a dynamic of consensus seeking for fulfilling the mission of the Church. It is in this context that we have to understand the reforms by Pope Francis such as church that is poor and for the poor, disposal of the baroque trappings in liturgical celebrations, and the "revision of the institutional aspects of the church."[23] By constituting a Council of Cardinal Advisers from throughout the world to assist him and making greater use of church synods Pope Francis is moving the church away from legalism, triumphalism, and clericalism.

2.2. Synodality Calls for a Listening Church[24]

A synodal Church is a Church which listens, which realizes that listening "is more than simply hearing" (EG 171). It is a Church that "listens to God, so that with him we may hear the cry of his people; to listen to his people until we are in harmony with the will to which God calls us."[25] It consists of mutual listening in which everyone has something to learn. The faithful people, the college of bishops, the Bishop of Rome; all listening to each other, and all listening to the Holy Spirit, the "Spirit of truth" (Jn 14:17), in order to know what he "says to the Churches" (Rev 2:7)."[26] A Church that listens is a Church in dialogue, a missionary Church, a welcoming Church, a participatory Church, a creative Church, a harmonious Church, an inculturated Church, a Church engaged with the poorest that fights against injustices.[27]

All the synods of Pope Francis are examples of synodality. We saw the synodal process in action in the Synod on Family, Synod on Youth and the Amazonian Synod. Pope Francis reminded the members of the Synod on the Family that the church is called to be "a listening church…in which everyone has something to learn." The pope says, "Such was the conviction underlying my desire that the people of God should be consulted in the preparation of the two phases of the Synod on the family …. how could we speak about the family without engaging families themselves, listening to their joys and their hopes, their sorrows and their anguish?"[28] In this synod, departing from previous customs, Francis facilitated what he describes as the "Synod process," a two-year long effort that involved two assemblies of bishops and several efforts to solicit the input of lay people."[29] "Because each person said what he thought, without fear of feeling judged. And everyone had the attitude of listening, without condemning. And then we discussed, like brothers, in the groups. But it is one thing to debate like brothers and another to condemn *a priori*. There was great freedom of expression. And this is beautiful!"[30] In both content and style, "*Amoris Laetitia*" embodies synodal vision of a dialogical church. In the Amazon Synod too, there was a clear shift from "the method of "seeing, judging and acting" towards "listening, understanding and accompanying."

Pope Francis' inductive approach includes also listening to collective wisdom of humanity as is evident from the many sources that he draws upon, departing from traditional papal teaching which generally only referenced the Bible, magisterial documents and the teachings of saints. Having conducted a survey of the dozens of additional sources in the 391 footnotes to the text of *Amoris Laetitia,* Kevin Ahern points out that "engaging the experiences and wisdom of sources beyond the traditional reference points of Scripture, Popes and saints, Francis models in *Amoris Laetitia* the type of listening and discerning church."[31] *Laudato Si'* and *Amoris Laetitia* make strategic references to statements from Bishops' Conferences in Spain, Korea, Argentina, Mexico, Columbia,

Chile, Australia, Italy and Kenya and includes references of Catholic and non-Christian, protestant and even secular writers and film makers.

2.3. Synodality as Encounter and Journeying Together

Synodality, for Francis, is not just a form of Church government but also a way of being Church. Harping on the literal meaning of the word 'synod', Pope calls synodal process as meeting and "journeying together"[32] with men and women, sharing the travails of history (EG 186ff). Synodality is a communication style that invites to encounter and communion. By incarnation, God privileges encounter (EG 91) and our encounter with Jesus affects and orders all our encounters. Encounter is a key theme of his pontificate: face-to-face; person-to-person relation. For Pope Francis, theology is transformative encounter with Jesus in the gospels and not a set of ideas, texts and theories. He himself relates to people, talk from heart. He criticizes unrelational, individualized, post-modern context (EG 67) and calls for "a 'mystique' of living together, of mingling and encounter, of embracing and supporting each other" (EG 87). Synodal journeying together begins with dioceses, provinces, regions and national conferences and involves finally the universal church as well as the whole of humanity.

2.4. Synodality as Missionary Transformation

The synodal church that Pope Francis envisages is part of missionary transformation of the church. From the beginning of his pontificate, he has urged the church to reach out to the people, especially those at the peripheries. For this he has insisted on moving the church from maintenance mode to "an evangelizing discipleship". The Final Document of the Synod of Bishops on Young People (2018) describes it as a "missionary synodality": "It is in relationships – with Christ, with others, in the community – that faith is handed on. For the sake of mission, too, the Church is called to adopt a relational manner that places emphasis on listening, welcoming, dialogue and common discernment in a process that transforms the lives of those taking part."[33] Cardinal Wuerl puts it succinctly. "The voice of the faith, the voice of the Gospel, isn't going to be announced today to crowds of people waiting to hear. Nor is it going to be announced through the structures of culture, society – all the routine elements that used be part of the Christian culture. It's going to be heard because believers are walking with others and saying, 'You know I think there's a better way; I have a different take on this than you do.'"[34] The proclamation and transmission of faith require a synodal Church, because missionary transformation happens through communication leading to encounter and communion and a mission in dialogue is better practiced in a participatory and co-responsible Church.

2.5. Synodality as a Communication Style

Synodal church is a communication strategy for the meaningful proclamation of the Gospel to invite people to encounter Jesus and enter into communion. The traditional hierarchical and top-down communication style of the Church does not match the cultural conditions of today. Synodality, for Pope Francis, implies a new communication style, which is bottom-up, dialogic and participatory. Through his teachings and personal communication style, he advocates a Church that communicates the joy of the Gospel to the whole world by listening, dialoguing and accompaniment, rather than by one-way proclamation.

Pope Francis' communication style and ecclesial reforms clearly mark an attempt to respond positively to the "new age of human history" (GS 54) with profoundly changed circumstances of life determined by the communication revolution: "new ways of communicating" leading to a "total communication environment" and a "new culture" determined by "new technology", new language", "new psychology" (AN 2).[35] Where Pope Benedict saw relativism, Pope Francis is asking "how is the dynamism and expansion of a new culture to be fostered without losing a living fidelity to the heritage of tradition" (GS 56) and seeking to "present to our contemporaries the doctrine of the Church concerning God, man and the world, in a manner more adapted to them so that they may receive it more willingly" (GS 62). Pope Francis has the broader aspirations of humankind in mind and does not hesitate to declare to the world that Church shares in "the joys and the hopes, the grieves and the anxieties of the men of this age" (GS 1) as "nothing genuinely human fails to raise an echo in their hearts" (GS 2). He is attentive to the signs of the time and engages the world in conversation on ecology, migration, global poverty and injustice, proper governance through his communication.

Conclusion

Pope Francis is renewing the Church with his strategic communication by words, gestures and actions which are full of symbolism and significance. Pope Francis is less formal, quite humble and very approachable as a religious leader who uses powerful tools like identification, inclusion and transparency to reach his audience. His oral communication in simple, direct and inclusive speech goes directly to the heart of people. His written communication, shorn of dogmatic clichés, is readable and understandable to everyone. He is a gifted communicator who brings about change with visual and verbal rhetoric suitable for the audiovisual age of communication. He is able to communicate his convictions in simple and direct language full of anecdotes and experiences from everyday life to which people can easily connect. He is less doctrinal and more open to new ideas. He spreads joy and instills hope through his personality, words and deeds. He is renewing the Church and the world through his intentional communication style and pertinent message. He is a master in religious, personal and strategic communication.

Pope Francis appears deeply committed to take forward the reform and renewal project of VC II especially in the fields of Church administration and Church communication. Pope Francis' vision of a missionary disciple Church, always going out to the peripheries of life, is directly in continuity with the larger ecclesiological vision of VC II. A missionary church will be concerned more with the communication of the Good News rather than on administration and maintenance of a perfect society. His vision of a synodal church and his communication preferences have much in common. He wants to replace the hierarchical church that communicates top-down and centre to periphery synodal church which values sharing, dialogue, participation and communion. Thus, his communication style flows from his ecclesiology and, for all good reasons, his ecclesiology itself is qualified by his personal communication styles and preferences.

Above all, Pope Francis is an accomplished religious communicator, who points beyond himself to the Gospel, so that "the knowledge of God is better manifested and the preaching of the Gospel becomes clearer to human intelligence and shows itself to be relevant to man's (*sic*) actual conditions of life" (GS 62).

Endnotes

[1] *Fortune Magazine* March, 2014, https://fortune.com/2014/03/20/worlds-50-greatest-leaders/ , (accessed January 21, 2020).

[2] Front-page headlines of several publications carried a similar title. For Example, *Time*, March 25, 2013; *The Times*, UK; Michel Cool, *Francis. A new World Pope*, Eerdmans, 2013.

[3] www.poy.time.com, Dec. 23, 2013, (accessed January 21, 2020).

[4] "How does Pope Francis Communicate?", https://clarionherald.org/2018/06/13/how-does-pope-francis-communicate/ ; (retrieved on Nov 22, 2019). One response read: "Can you please stop making me fall more in love with you every day." A Muslim said: "I think you are perfect, Mr. Pope." A non-believer wrote: "This is so inspiring … omg … even though I am an atheist." (Reportedly said by Natasa Govekar, Director of the theological-pastoral department of the Vatican's Secretariat for Communication, to nearly 300 Catholic journalists June 12, 2018, at the Catholic Media Conference in Green Bay).

[5] María Esteve and Paola Gómez, "Pope Francis: master of strategic communication", https://ideasen.llorenteycuenca.com/wp-content/uploads/sites/6/2015/05/150519_DI_article_pope_francisco_ENG.pdf (2015). (consulted on Jan 21, 2020).

[6] Christopher J. Oldenburg, *The Rhetoric of Pope Francis: Critical Mercy and Conversion for the Twenty-First Century*, 2018. This study provides an extensive rhetorical analysis of Pope Francis's visual, spatial, tactile, written, and oral discourse. Each chapter identifies several of Francis' dominant rhetorical strategies and shows how they articulate Francis' vision for the Church. In this book Oldenburg explores Francis' "reinstatement of mercy as the central religious and rhetorical force for conversion" through "a close, in-depth rhetorical criticism" of his interviews, public addresses, speeches, exhortations, encyclicals, to photographs (cf. xviii). The author identifies four dominant conversion therapies, which he calls "pope tropes" – each

of which "operates as a central rhetorical strategy" corresponding to the 4 sites of conversion mentioned, viz., papal, pastoral, political, spatial (xx).

[7] Cf. Oldenburg, *The Rhetoric of Pope Francis*, 3.

[8] His deliberate choice of the name Francis' too served as an explicit indication of his preference for the poor and a poor church as well as his desire to go back to the purity of the Gospel. His later teachings about the church *of* the poor and *for* the poor and his ecological deliberations in *Laudato Si* have proved the point beyond doubt. There is so much in a name, especially when it is a papal name, chosen by deliberate decision.

[9] Christopher Oldenburg, *The Rhetoric of Pope Francis*, 3-4. Oldenburg argues that 'Francis is hyperaware of the rhetorical power of iconography and visual rhetoric.' Pope Francis uses images as a significant medium for reforming the church to match its original simplicity and missionary fervor. [4; Cf. 3-32]

[10] Donald McKinnon's theory of "Kenotic Ecclesiology" as quoted in Oldenburg, *The Rhetoric of Pope Francis*, 42-43; note 42.

[11] Christopher Oldenburg, *The Rhetoric of Pope Francis*, 37-40.

[12] Antonio Carriero (ed.), *Il vocbolario di papa Francesco*, Elledici, Roma, 2016. In this book, 50 journalists have written on 50 words that apply to Pope Francis.

[13] "Communicating in the style of Pope Francis", Salesian Information Agency, April 2016, https://www.infoans.org/en/sections/editorial/item/772-communicating-in-the-style-of-pope-francis, (accessed January 21, 2020).

[14] "Communicating in the style of Pope Francis".

[15] Here we must mention that some of his liberal views and casual comments have aroused criticism and caused damage of sorts to church teachings. He is also accused of populism in moral issues like homosexuality. However, these are sensitive issues and previous popes have shied away from addressing them creatively and with necessary sensitivity.

[16] The usage became popular with the 2014 documentary *The Francis Effect*, a visual chronicle to narrate the pontificate of Pope Francis. A Yale University program on Climate Change Communication is also entitled: *The Francis Effect. How Pope Francis changed the Conversation about Global Warming*. https://environment.yale.edu/climate-communication-OFF/files/The_Francis_Effect.pdf, (accessed January 21, 2020). Another documentary *A Man of his Word* (2018) also uses visual narrative to highlight the global impact of Pope Francis.

[17] Avery Dulles, *Models of the Church*. Image/Doubleday, 1987.

[18] "Address of his Holiness Pope Francis at the ceremony commemorating the 50th anniversary of the institution of the synod of bishops", Paul VI Audience Hall, Saturday, 17 October 2015. Cf. http://www.vatican.va/content/francesco/en/speeches/2015/october/documents/papa-francesco_20151017_50-anniversario-sinodo.html. (accessed January 21, 2020)

¹⁹ Cf. Pope Francis, *Letter to the General Secretary of the Synod of Bishops, Cardinal Lorenzo Baldisseri, on the elevation of the Undersecretary, Mgr Fabio Fabene. to the episcopal dignity*, 1 April 2014. (accessed January 21, 2020).

²⁰ "Address of his Holiness Pope Francis".

²¹ Gerard O'Connell, "Cardinal Wuerl: Pope Francis has reconnected the church with Vatican II", (interview given to the America Magazine on the beginning of the fifth year of the pontificate of Pope Francis in 2017). Cf. https://www.americamagazine.org/faith/2017/03/06/cardinal-wuerl-pope-francis-has-reconnected-church-vatican-ii, (accessed January 21, 2020). In the words of Cardinal Wuerl, "his [Pope Francis'] great contribution to date has been, the reconnecting of the church with the energy of the Second Vatican Council".

²² Interview the Holy Father granted to the Belgian Catholic weekly publication *Tertio*, on the conclusion of the Extraordinary Jubilee of Mercy. See also Massimo Faggioli, "Pope Francis struggle to bring forth a synodal Church", *La Croix International*, published Nov. 5, 2018, https://international.la-croix.com/news/pope-francis-struggle-to-bring-forth-a-synodal-church/8784#. http://press.vatican.va/content/salastampa/en/bollettino/pubblico/2016/12/07/161207a.html (accessed January 21, 2020).

²³ Massimo Faggioli, *Pope Francis: Tradition in Transition* (Translation ed.), Paulist Press, 2015, 32-33.

²⁴ Frances Plude, "A Listening Church: Communication and Collegiality in the Age of Pope Francis", *America Magazine*, April 4-11, 2016, (accessed January 21, 2020)

²⁵ Francis, Address at the Prayer Vigil for the Synod on the Family, 4 October 2014. (accessed January 21, 2020)

²⁶ Cf. "Address of His Holiness Pope Francis".

²⁷ http://www.sinodoamazonico.va/content/sinodoamazonico/en/news/the-upcoming-pan-amazon-synod—a—synod-of-urgency—and—the.html, (accessed January 21, 2020).

²⁸ Cf. *Gaudium et Spes* 1, as referred to in "Address of His Holiness Pope Francis".

²⁹Pope Francis, *Amoris Laetitia*, nos 2,4,7. See also Kevin Ahern "Amoris Laetitia' embodies the pope's vision of a listening church". *America Magazine*, April 08, 2016. Cf. https://www.americamagazine.org/issue/listening-pope, (accessed January 21, 2020).

³⁰ Massimo Faggioli, "Pope Francis' struggle to bring forth a synodal Church", *La Croix International*, published Nov. 5, 2018, (accessed January 21, 2020).

³¹ Kevin Ahern "Amoris Laetitia' embodies the Pope's vision of a listening church".

³² The Synod of Bishops is the point of convergence of this listening process conducted at every level of the Church's life from laity, pastors, bishops and finally bishop of Rome. Pope invokes "the supernatural sense of the faith (*sensus fidei*) of the whole people of God" to support synodality. "The *sensus fidei* prevents a rigid separation between an *Ecclesia docens* and an *Ecclesia discens*". Interprets *cum Petro*

(the bond of episcopal communion), and *sub Petro* (hierarchical connection) not as a limitation of freedom, but a guarantee of unity.

³³ Final Document of the Synod of Bishops on Young People, *Faith and Vocational Discernment*. 119-127, here 121-122. http://www.synod.va/content/synod2018/en/fede-discernimento-vocazione/final-document-of-the-synod-of-bishops-on-young-people—faith-an.pdf, (accessed January 21, 2020).

³⁴ https://www.americamagazine.org/faith/2017/03/06/cardinal-wuerl-pope-francis-has-reconnected-church-vatican-ii. This resonate with *Evangelii Nuntiandi* 41 which said: "Modern man listens more willingly to witnesses than to teachers, and if he does listen to teachers, it is because they are witnesses."

³⁵ Pontifical Council for Social Communications, Pastoral Instruction *Aetatis Novae* (1992).

III

Pope for the People of God: Family, Women, Youth

"To be saints is not a privilege for a few, but a vocation for everyone"

(Pope Francis)

8.
Building Joyful Families
Walking with Pope Francis through *Amoris Laetitia*

Deacon Jaime and Ligia da Fonseca

Introduction

We reflect upon Pope Francis' 2016 Apostolic Exhortation *Amoris Laetitia*—hereinafter, *AL*—as a Catholic couple married for forty years. Of these years, we have been members of an ecclesial movement 'Couples for Christ' for twenty-eight years, besides being actively involved in the Family Apostolate in the Archdiocese of Bombay and outside since the year 2000. Our late Holy Father, St John Paul II made the family a focal point of his teachings throughout his pontificate. Being married in 1980, we consider ourselves to be a couple of the John Paul II generation. In the course of our married life and ministry, we discovered his marvellous teachings on the 'Theology of the Body' and we decided to pass on these teachings to married couples, young adults as well as teenagers, whenever we conducted programmes for such groups.

JP II stated very pointedly that "civilisation depends upon the family". One of the most interesting quotations in *Familiaris Consortio* is one in which the Pope gives a puzzling exhortation: "Family, become what you are!"[1] How can something become what it already is? We believe that what the Holy Father is saying is, first of all, the grace of the sacrament is present, and secondly, the grace of the Magisterium's teaching on sacramental marriage is there; but both are lying dormant and unused. Sadly, often our failure as a Church to communicate these truths is directly linked to the widespread failure of families and helps explain their inability to "become what they are".

Like his predecessor, Pope Benedict XVI continued to emphasise the central role of the family in his special addresses, during his apostolic trip to Brazil, and particularly during his historic trip to Valencia. In 2009, we were appointed by Pope Benedict XVI as Members of the 'Pontifical Council for the Family' in Rome for a period of five years. We felt blessed to have a personal encounter with him in Rome on December 1, 2011. In one of his homilies, he extolled the family as an icon of the most Holy Trinity. He said:[2]

> God has chosen to reveal himself by being born into a human family. And the human family thus became an icon of God! God is the Trinity, He is a communion of love; so is the family despite all the differences that exist between the Mystery of God and His human creatures, an expression that reflects the unfathomable Mystery of God as Love . . . The human family, in a certain sense, is an icon of the Trinity because of its interpersonal love and the fruitfulness of this love.

Echoing and elaborating the viewpoints of his two predecessors, Pope Francis often emphasised the vital role of the family in his Wednesday audiences and his major addresses, which culminated with convoking a special Synod for the Family in Rome in 2015.[3] In making his first pastoral visit to the United States for the World Meeting of Families in 2015, he urged "all married couples, therefore, priests and parish communities, as well as movements and associations to let themselves be led by the Word of God, on which rests the foundation of the holy edifice of the family, the domestic Church and the family of God (cf. *Lumen Gentium*, nn. 6 and 11."[4] Indeed, the key to the Church's teaching on marriage and the family and its role in society lies in the family's identity as a Church in miniature: a domestic Church. This ancient title—*Ecclesia domestica*—was highlighted again in the teaching of Vatican Council II (hereinafter VC II), particularly in *Lumen Gentium*, n.11 and *Gaudium et Spes*, n.48. It also occupies a key position in the 'Catechism of the Catholic Church Part II, nn. 1655-1658. All other discussions—including the role of the family as the foundation of society—stem from this key and fundamental theological concept.

1. An Overview of *Amoris Laetitia*: The Joy of Love

At the very beginning of *AL*, the Pope Francis outlines his intended audience. In a break with traditional openings he states that this Apostolic Exhortation—in addition to being addressed to bishops, priests and deacons, consecrated persons and all the lay faithful—is also addressed to 'Christian Married Couples'. Having read the document and seen how simply and accessibly Pope Francis writes, we think that he really desires to speak directly to those of us who are married.

So, what is Pope Francis trying to say to us as married people? Firstly, he says something that is, we feel, really important. He talks about how often in the Church, marriage is mis-represented. It is presented in such an idealised way that it cannot draw people to want the Sacrament, but rather it seems to be excessively burdensome. We are particularly struck by his statement that the church should be presenting marriage "more as a dynamic path to personal development and fulfilment than as a lifelong burden."[5]

Pope Francis writes that "there is no need to lay upon two limited persons the tremendous burden of having to reproduce perfectly the union existing between Christ and his Church, for marriage as a sign entails a dynamic process... one which advances gradually with the progressive integration of the gifts of God." [6] He adds: "After the love that unites us to God, conjugal love is the 'greatest form of friendship'. It is a union possessing all the traits of a good friendship: concern for the good of the other, reciprocity, intimacy, warmth, stability and the resemblance born of a shared life."[7]

This, it seems to us, is a profoundly hope-filled expression of what the sacrament should be. As we reflect on our own marriage, we are aware that it has been a place in which we have grown and developed. The astonishing gift of motherhood and fatherhood, for which no reading or courses or conversations adequately prepared us, is something that we have pondered and grappled with, both interiorly and in deep conversations in daily life. This strange gift of parenthood has seen change with both of us. Likewise, for us, marriage has been a place of maturing, of growing in inner freedom.

The whole dynamic of aging, of establishing a home, of becoming the generation who are the primary bread-winners, of watching our parents age, and realising the shortness of life have all happened for us within the marital relationship. All through our married life we have been realising that all of this growth and healing is possible only when we, as spouses, are living from a mutual understanding that we are fragile people, with our own wounds and vulnerabilities. It is not possible if we are tied to idealised images of marriage as promulgated by the church or popular culture.

In the chapter entitled 'Love in Marriage' Pope Francis uses St Paul's great hymn to love as a starting point for a series of profound meditations on the nature of love as we married couples are called to live it out. In many ways there is nothing startlingly new in what he writes; it flows out of the stream of Christian ideas about marriage that we have heard over the whole of our life. Yet, at the same time, to read this chapter is to be drawn back again into considering the real nature of the vocational call to marriage. Just as Paul's hymn to love is itself, whenever we read it, a challenge to rethink the nature of how we live and love in the world, so do Pope Francis' insightful and stirring words pose a challenge to us to rethink how we are living and loving.

Another deeply counter cultural message is that of lifelong fidelity and linked with it the demands of compassion and forgiveness. Writing of a love that believes all things, hopes all things and bears all things, Pope Francis asks us to step beyond the narrow margins of a kind of ledger book approach to marriage into one of great generosity and hope. He explores the importance of trust in marriage.

- Writing that it is trust that "enables a relationship to be free.... Love trusts, it sets free, it does not try to control, possess and dominate everything."[8]

- Love that hopes all things, is a love that tries to see the other as God sees them. In marriage "this realization helps us, amid the aggravations of this present life to see the person from a supernatural perspective."[9]

- Love that bears all things is a love "that never gives up."[10] It is an "endurance of the spirit", a "certain dogged heroism" that resists negativity, and is committed to goodness.

These three fundamental attitudes are, it seems to us, completely at odds with the messages about love and sex that we most often hear. Those messages are rooted in our temporal experience, and are often about earning or maintaining trust, or love. Pope Francis reminds us that love and trust, if they are of God, are ultimately gratuitous. They are freely given and rooted in the wellspring of love that is God's own self.

In general, this document is profoundly rich. To be fruitful, this needs to be a document that engages with our lives. To do this we, as the married faithful, must be vulnerable and open to allowing Pope Francis to speak to us in the concrete circumstances of our own lives. Then, with the Church, we too can hope that our marriages may grow into the fullness promised by the sacrament of a "free and mutual self-giving, experienced in tenderness and action, and permeating our entire lives."[11]

1. The Vocation of the Family: Proclaiming a Gospel of Love

Of the vocation of families, Pope Francis writes: "In and among families, the Gospel message should always resound; the core of that message, the kerygma [proclaiming about salvation through Jesus Christ; proclaiming His Life, Death and Resurrection through words and actions], is what . . . we must hear again and again in different ways, and which we must always announce in one form or another."[12] This calls for faith in the Lord's presence "dwelling in real and concrete families, with all their daily troubles and struggles, joys and hopes."[13] The Eucharist being the sacrament of the new covenant, should strengthen the covenant of conjugal love.[14] "Our loved ones merit our complete attention."[15] The love of the family circle is meant to expand further, "by going forth and spreading life by caring for others and seeking their happiness." Thus, "the family lives its spirituality precisely by being one and the same time a domestic church and a vital cell for transforming the world."[16]

Undoubtedly, therefore, the family is the place where the life of faith is first nurtured in young people, because "it is the place where one learns to love"[17] and to accept being loved. Both of these experiences are foundational preconditions if children are to be evangelized. That is why, as Katie Warner has remarked, "the home is truly the epicentre of the New Evangelization."[18] There is a whole body of social science evidence showing that when parents evangelise their children, they are successful at far higher rates than anyone else involved in the evangelisation of young people.[19]

For its part, the parish, by means of fostering contact among families, as well as providing adult catechesis aimed at parents, helps them carry out their duty of educating their children.[20] The parish ought to be at the service of the parents, setting up programmes which favour the evangelisation of children, a commitment which should go well beyond preparing them for the Sacraments of Initiation. Besides serving as a centre for catechesis and sacramental preparation, the parish is also the community where young people participate in the liturgy and join with their peers in charitable work, social activities and missionary outreach.

The nine chapters of *AL* are truly a very rich resource and content for family catechesis. One can find a wide variety of topics that can be used for reflection at various moments of family catechesis. The chapters provide numerous topics such as theology of family, special family situations, roles of couples, family faith, education of children, family spirituality, etc. In fact, the 'General Directory of Catechesis' emphasises the irreplaceable character of family catechesis.[21] It is the catechesis that accompanies, precedes and enriches all other forms of catechesis.[22] Couples and parents should be properly appreciated as active agents in catechesis. Family catechesis is of great assistance as an effective method in training young parents to be aware of their mission as the evangelisers of their own family.[23]

Family catechesis is a 'ministry of accompaniment'. This is the crux of the approach towards family today. An open, warm, merciful, and accompanying Church. The ministry of accompaniment is very dear to Pope Francis. One can notice this ministry mentioned right from his first document *Lumen Fidei* (in 2013) to *Amoris Laetitia*. He points out many ways we could accompany the family today. Some of them are: preparing families for first communion, confirmation, blessing families, pastoral visits to families, etc.[24] In this regard, we also need to accompany young couples during the first years of their married life.[25]

3. Insights into Accompanying Families

Pope Francis tells us: "Learning to love someone does not happen automatically, nor can it be taught in a workshop just prior to the celebration of marriage. For every couple, marriage preparation begins at birth.[26] Those best prepared for marriage are probably those who learned what Christian marriage is from their own parents, who chose each other unconditionally and daily renew this decision."[27] The family is where children grasp the meaning of love, which is the foundation of marriage. Thus, marriage preparation begins right from the time of childhood. Since love can never be 'taught' but only 'caught', it is very important to evaluate what is the general atmosphere in our homes. Marriage counsellors and psychologists agree that the general atmosphere in the family of origin of each spouse will play a significant role in the lives of the newly married couples for better or for worse.

While 'Remote Marriage Preparation' is ultimately the responsibility of the family, they cannot do it by themselves. In this regard, the local parish should offer great assistance and support to families. The main contribution to the pastoral care of families is offered by the parish, which is the *family of families*, where small communities, ecclesial movements and associations live in harmony.[28]

Pope Francis often talks about 'missionary families'. Missionary families are people who have maturity and stability and who feel called to serve other families so they can experience the joy of love. "With the help of missionary families, the couple's own families and a variety of pastoral resources, ways should also be found to offer a remote preparation that, by example and good advice, can help their love to grow and mature. Discussion groups and optional talks on a variety of topics of genuine interest to young people can also prove helpful."[29]

The Pope also laments the fact that sex education is an important area that is often neglected. He recommends that sex needs to be taught in the broader framework of an education for love and mutual lifelong self-giving in marriage. "Sex education should provide information while keeping in mind that children and young people have not yet attained full maturity. The information has to come at a proper time and in a way suited to their age."[30] Young people should not be deceived into confusing two levels of reality: "sexual attraction creates, for the moment, the illusion of union, yet, without love, this 'union' leaves strangers as far apart as they were before."[31]

We must think about the following: Who looks after the 'sex education' of children in our parish? What resources are available in our parish or diocese? How can we use these resources to impart these teachings in our parish? For a parish to actually be a 'family of families' calls for concrete actions of hospitality and generosity.[32] Some points to keep in mind as plans are developed:

1. We can no longer assume that people know their faith. Many pastors are finding it more and more difficult finding qualified volunteers who know and live their faith.

2. At every level, we must develop creative and new ways to engage those listening. Our message must be solid, compelling and consistent. If it is not, people become confused and walk away.

3. We must provide tools to evangelize. To use a term commonly used in the corporate world: 'You must have the tools to do the job'.

In the light of civil courts attempting to redefine marriage, this is not only just a nice thing to do; rather, it is something we *have to do*. Rebuilding a culture of marriage has to be a top priority for our future generations to understand the Gospel and to find true happiness that can only come from Christ.

4. The Need to Form Youth and Young Adults

Renewed catechesis of young people and others preparing for Christian marriage is absolutely necessary in order that the sacrament may be celebrated and lived with the right moral and spiritual dispositions. The religious formation of young people should be integrated, at the right moment and in accordance with the various concrete requirements, with a preparation for life as a couple.[33] Therefore, it is up to parents, the extended family, godparents, adult mentors and educators to monitor this exposure, and to ensure children's imaginations are fortified and fed with wholesome food, with material that protects their innocence, gives them an appetite for the adventure of Christian living, and evokes a vocations approach to life ... But it is even more vital to teach children how to pray, and to give children role models, adult examples for them to witness and aspire toward.[34]

Most recent studies that measure how young people understand the importance of marriage indicate that our millennials have let go of the ideal of traditional or natural marriage. So, the question does arise:

Does our parish provide programmes and effective catechesis that help youth and young adults to discuss, understand and defend the unique meaning of marriage in the face of contemporary challenges?

Another aspect a parish should evaluate is how welcoming it is when the couple approaches the Church for marriage. Hospitality to our young adults is important. Since couples are marrying later in life, many may not have been actively involved in a parish and may be apprehensive about how they will be received. To be welcoming we need to affirm them on their decision to marry in the Church, assure them that we are excited about their decision and that we are willing to work with them.

Couples today are looking for a meaningful and honest exposition on how the Church views marriage. They may not always agree with everything we value as Christians, but they are interested in knowing why we believe what we do. Do we, as a parish community, provide trained mentor couples that walk with them through the process, offer our prayers for their discernment, and provide assistance with preparing a wedding liturgy? Involving the broader parish community in the marriage preparation process can serve the couple well, not only through the discernment process of engagement, but well into the first years of marriage.

5. Creating a Culture of Life for Children

Today in our parishes, we have families of many shapes and sizes. Some families will be inside the framework of a sacramental marriage, some will not. Some will have the learned ability to uphold the teachings of the Church on marriage between one man and one woman, some may not. Some will struggle with time, finances, lack of desire or resources to make their home a domestic church. In view of all this, the parish church has a definite role in assisting parents in fostering the spiritual formation of children.

At one of his general audiences Pope Francis spoke on the education of children:[35]

> I hope that the Lord will give Christian families the faith and freedom and the courage necessary for their mission. If family education rediscovers the pride of its leadership, many things will change for the better, for hesitant parents and disappointed children. It is time that fathers and mothers return from their exile – because they have exiled themselves from the education of their children – and reassume fully their educational role. We hope that the Lord will give parents this grace: not to exile themselves from the education of their children. And only love, tenderness and patience can do this.

If we do not provide constructive tools for parents to be the primary educators they are called to be, and if we do not challenge parents to accept and take up that role, then we will continue to lose our children to the secular humanistic world they are offered at every turn, every day.

6. Strengthening the Married and Accompanying Newly Weds

When couples coming in for marriage preparation classes are asked: How many of you expect that you are marrying for five years and will then divorce? None! They all come with the desire of their hearts wanting a fulfilling, lifelong, happy marriage. If couples going into marriage do sincerely desire this lifelong happy marriage, why then do so many of them fail? In the tough task of ensuring that marriages succeed and bear fruit, how can the church assist couples throughout their lifecycle? Indeed, the first few years of marriage can be the most difficult; and so, their accompaniment is most crucial. Do we, as a parish, consider married couples to be finished products or do we nurture them throughout the lifecycle?

Mature couples can play an important role in accompanying couples in the early years of marriage. The initial years of marriage are a vital and sensitive period during which couples become more aware of the challenges and meaning of married life... "In this regard, experienced couples have an important role to play. The parish is a place where such experienced couples can help younger couples, with the eventual cooperation of associations, ecclesial movements and new communities."[36]

'Ten Tips for Couples from *AL*' worth remembering: (1) Appreciate the other. (2) Learn from the other. (3) Speak with kindness. (4) Learn to dialogue. (5) Empathise with the other. (6) True love is more than just a feeling. (7) The three magic words: please, thanks, sorry are important. (8) Grow in love. (9) An authentic sexuality helps. (10) Believe in the promise of the future.

7. Accompanying Couples in Irregular Situations

Pastoral caring analyses how a parish provides to couples and families in times of difficulty and loss. When a parish is a 'family of families', it makes it a place where people in crisis can go for assistance or referral. Individuals or couples may come to the parish at times of sudden crisis, for example, the loss of a job, miscarriage, financial loss, or death of a loved one. Some may come after short- or long-term trials, such as, infertility, marital conflict, addictions or behaviours (alcohol, drugs, gambling or pornography). Of course, this is not an exhaustive list, but a sampling of possible reasons couples or families find themselves in crises. To meet the needs of those trusting in the Church's wisdom and guidance, pastoral caring requires training and resources for clergy, pastoral staff and mentor couples. For pastors and deacons, it would include intervention skills to help struggling marriages.

This pastoral plan should be part of the way the parish reaches out, urging couples in crisis to turn to the Lord Jesus for help. Parishes must also encourage them to make use of the many resources, including programmes and ministries offered by the Church, that can help to save marriages, even those in serious difficulty. In *AL*, Pope Francis recommends that while dealing with those in 'irregular situations' we can solve their problems using the following four-point criteria: (1) Welcome wounded families. (2) Accompany them. (3) Discern each case and integrate it. (4) Help to make it whole again.

7.1. Welcoming wounded families: Welcoming firstly means not having an attitude of condemnation towards anyone. There are many things that are objectively wrong or even sinful and we cannot encourage such practices. But that does not mean we cannot be merciful towards such people, especially those who still have good will and do not flaunt their irregular situation as model behaviour. Pope Francis writes: "No one can be condemned for ever, because that is not the logic of the Gospel! Here I am not speaking only of the divorced and remarried, but of everyone, in whatever situation they find themselves."[37] He also stresses: "We would like before all else to reaffirm that every person, regardless of sexual orientation, ought to be respected in his or her dignity and treated with consideration, while 'every sign of unjust discrimination' is to be carefully avoided, particularly any form of aggression and violence. Such families should be given respectful pastoral guidance, so that those who manifest a homosexual orientation can receive the assistance they need to understand and fully carry out God's will in their lives."[38]

7.2. Accompanying: means engaging with such persons with an open heart and welcoming arms. It means listening non-judgmentally to their situation without any form of prejudice, understanding the concrete reality of their situation without rushing to give advice. It does not mean blindly accepting all that they are doing, especially if it is objectively wrong, but it also does not mean condemning the persons either.

7.3. Discerning: each case means accepting that every person's situation and reasons for 'why' they do 'what' they are doing are different. Here we can find opportunities to gently guide them towards how they can be fully integrated into the faith, if that is what they wish for. This sometimes can take months or even years; and hence patience is a necessary virtue. Perhaps the person cannot receive Holy Communion but we can invite them to attend Mass and other prayer meetings.

7.4. Helping to make things whole again: is the ultimate goal of all of our efforts. We must strive to help such families to achieve what is best for them and to create an atmosphere where they can thrive physically, emotionally and spiritually. Moreover, should all our efforts seem to be in vain, we must still continue to always be welcoming and kind to everyone.

We must ask ourselves: As a parish, do we provide support for persons going through the initial trauma of separation and divorce? For those who have remarried outside the Church after a divorce, an outreach to those couples is possible. The Vatican document 'On the Pastoral Care of Divorced and Remarried Persons' says, "Pastors are called to provide care in a discreet manner . . ." (no. 2)

The emotional upheaval suffered by children of separated couples who suddenly find themselves with a single parent or in a 'new' family poses a challenge for bishops, pastors, catechists, teachers, and all who are responsible for the young . . . It is not a question of replacing their parents but collaborating with them.[39]

With the heart of a merciful pastor, Pope Francis asks: "Do we feel the weight of the mountain that crushes the soul of a child, in families in which the members treat each other badly and harm each other, to the point of breaking the bonds of conjugal trust? . . . When adults lose their head . . . when the father and mother harm each other, the soul of the child suffers greatly, feeling a sense of desperation. And they are wounds that leave a lifelong mark."[40]

8. Worship, Sacraments and Prayer: Sustenance for the Domestic Church

To be a 'family of families' every parish needs its families to be regularly participating in the source and summit of our faith, the Eucharist. The Eucharist is the prime sacrament where the family finds its support and meaning so that it can build itself into a domestic church. As parish communities, it is also our duty to bring our intentions to our adoration chapels, asking for God's grace and mercy to rebuild a culture of marriage and family. It is only on our knees before the Blessed Sacrament, asking for forgiveness, that we can hope to turn the tide to make marriage relevant again.

Conclusion: Striving to Grow into the Image and Likeness of the Trinity

St John Paul II wrote, "Willed by God in the very act of creation, marriage and the family are interiorly ordained to fulfilment in Christ and have need of His graces in order to be healed from the wounds of sin and restored to their 'beginning', that is, to full understanding and the full realization of God's plan."[41] He also held that, "It is therefore indispensable and urgent that every person of good will should endeavour to save and foster the values and requirements of the family . . . Yes indeed, the families of today must be called back to their original position. They must follow Christ."[42]

Pope Benedict XVI wrote: "The New Evangelization is inseparable from the Christian Family."[43] Finally, Pope Francis reminds us that: "All of us are called to keep striving towards something greater than ourselves and our families, and every family must feel this constant impulse. Let us make this journey as families, let us keep walking together. What we have been promised is greater than we can imagine. May we never lose heart because of our limitations, or ever stop seeking that fullness of love and communion which God holds out before us."[44]

May we enter with joy into that Divine Dance, that we are invited into by the Most Holy Trinity, whose icon our human family (with all its imperfections) is called to be! May the Holy Family of Nazareth bless our families!

Endnotes

[1] See Pope St John Paul II, *Familiaris Consortio,* November 1981. Full text accessible at: http://www.vatican.va/content/john-paul-ii/en/apost_exhortations/documents/hf_jp-ii_exh_19811122_familiaris-consortio.html.

[2] Pope Benedict XVI, Angelus, on the Feast of the Holy Family, December 27, 2009. Full text accessible at: http://www.vatican.va/content/benedict-xvi/en/angelus/2009/documents/hf_ben-xvi_ang_20091227.html.

[3] We felt blessed to have a private audience with His Holiness, Pope Francis, in Rome in October 2013.

[4] From the Letter of Pope Francis for the 8th World Meeting of Families in Philadelphia from September 22 to 27, 2015. Full text accessible at: http://www.vatican.va/content/francesco/en/letters/2014/documents/papa-francesco_20141210_lettera-incontro-mondiale-famiglie.html.

[5] *AL* 37.

[6] *AL* 121.

[7] *AL* 123.

[8] *AL* 115.

[9] *AL* 117.

[10] *AL* 118.

[11] *Gaudium et Spes*, 49.

[12] *AL* 58.

[13] *AL* 315.

[14] *AL* 318-319.

[15] *AL* 323.

[16] *AL* 324.

[17] Pope Francis, Address to the Plenary Assembly of the Pontifical Council for the Family, October 25, 2013.

[18] Katie Warner, *Head and Heart: A Guide to Becoming Strong Spiritual Leaders for Your Family*, Ohio, Emmaus Road Publishing, 2015, 68.

[19] Cf. "Dad Matters! . . . The Spiritual Influence of Fathers": https://formingfaith-wordpress.com!20-15/06/1-8/dad-matters-the-spiritual-influence-of-fathers!

[20] Cf. Congregation for the Clergy, *General Directory for Catechesis (GDC)*, 1997, n.227.

[21] The document says, "Nothing replaces family catechesis". *GDC*, n.178.

[22] *GDC*, n.226.

[23] *AL* 287.

[24] *AL* 230.

[25] *AL* 217-222.

[26] *AL* 208.

[27] *AL* 208.

[28] *AL* 202.

[29] *AL* 208.

[30] *AL* 281.

[31] *AL* 208.

[32] *Love is Our Mission: The Family Fully Alive A Preparatory Catechesis for the World Meeting of Families*, Philadelphia, 2014, n.88.

³³ Pope John Paul II, *Familiaris Consortio*, n.66.

³⁴ *Love is Our Mission*, n.83.

³⁵ Pope Francis, General Audience Address on May 20, 2015. Full text accessible at: https://www.cfcthai.net/catholic-teachings/pope-francis-on-the-education-of-children.

³⁶ *AL* 223.

³⁷ *AL* 297.

³⁸ *AL* 250.

³⁹ *Love is Our Mission*, n.87.

⁴⁰ Pope Francis, General Audience address on Wednesday, June 24, 2015. See Vatican Information Service (VIS) at: http://visnews-en.blogspot.com/2015_06_24_archive.html.

⁴¹ Pope John Paul II, *Familiaris Consortio*, 3.

⁴² Pope John Paul II, *Familiaris Consortio*, 86.

⁴³ Pope Benedict XVI, Address to the Plenary Assembly of the Pontifical Council for the Family, *L'Osservatore Romano*, December 2, 2011.

⁴⁴ *AL* 325.

9.
Envisaging an All-Inclusive Vibrant Church with Greater Involvement of Women in Decision-Making Roles and Sacred Ministries

Patricia H. Santos, RJM

Introduction

[T]he hour is coming, in fact has come, when the vocation of woman is being achieved in its fullness, the hour in which woman acquires in the world an influence, an effect and a power never hitherto achieved.[1]

These were the words of Pope Paul VI to women in his closing address at the Second Vatican Council (hereinafter VC II), acknowledging their contribution and recognizing the great potential they had to be leaders and evangelizers in the Church. He entrusted to women the task of taking "the spirit of this council into institutions, schools, homes and daily life" and to "save the peace of the world." It was Paul VI who had earlier extended the invitation to a few significant women to participate in the third session of the Council, thanks to the intervention of Cardinal Leo Jozef Suenens of Belgium towards the end of the second session of VC II. When discussing the People of God, Suenens realized that more than half the Church was not represented at the Council. Paul VI's closing words to women were not totally novel. They were already expressed by John XIII in his 1963 encyclical, *Pacem in Terris*:

> Women are gaining an increasing awareness of their natural dignity. Far from being content with a purely passive role or allowing themselves to be regarded as a kind of instrument, they are demanding, both in domestic and in public life, the rights and duties which belong to them as human persons.[2]

John XXIII and Paul VI were both aware of the impact of feminism and especially the theological awakening among Catholic women who had begun to study theology. A number of religious and lay women were getting their master's and doctoral degrees in Sacred Theology from St Mary's College in Indiana, the first Graduate School of Sacred Theology for women established by Holy Cross Sister Mary Madeleva Wolff in 1943.[3] This was followed by the opening of Regina Mundi Institute in Rome in 1954 to offer theological education for European and other women.[4] Hence, it would have been only fitting to invite theologically trained women to VC II since some men from among the laity were invited as auditors. Even after women were brought in for the third session, Gerard Mannion (1970–2019), a renowned Irish theologian and ethicist, notes the varied perspectives offered in retelling the stories of VC II from appreciation and admiration to some thinking that the presence of women at the Council "was both 'too little and too late' and by and large a monumental exercise in tokenism."[5] Nonetheless, the very presence of women at the Council was an eye-opener and challenge to a patriarchal androcentric church.

1. Women's Presence at the Second Vatican Council

The women invitees to VC II were educated influential leaders and appeared to be well prepared to undertake any role. Patricia Madigan, a Dominican Sister and executive director of the Dominican Centre for interfaith ministry, education and research in Melbourne, records that the women who attended the Council "were well read and had travelled widely, more widely than many bishops."[6] Of the twenty-four Catholic women who participated in the last two sessions of the Council eight of the ten religious women were major superiors of their Congregations, and the remaining fourteen were women leaders of national and international organizations from among the laity.[7] Despite this, one could witness the men and women receiving differential treatment. There were separate coffee bars – 'Bar-None' only for the women and 'Bar-Jonah' for the men where the male auditors could freely mix with the Bishops while the women were prevented from doing so.[8] However, they did not actually manage to segregate the men and women as they mingled with each other in the bars. In fact, some of these mixed sentiments of the women who attended the Council are recorded by Carmel McEnroy, a religious Sister of Mercy and distinguished professor of theology, in her 1996 work entitled *Guests in their Own House: Women of Vatican II*.[9]

Although the women invitees were initially given minimal roles to play as auditors, they exercised different functions in and around the Council halls and some of the women even contributed to the discussions in the commissions formulating some of the VC II documents: mainly, the Pastoral Constitution on the Church in the Modern World (*Gaudium et Spes*) and the Decree on the Apostolate of the Laity (*Apostolicam Actuositatem*).[10] Prominent among the religious women who formed part of these commissions was an American Loretto religious, Mary Luke Tobin (1908–2006) who was the President of the Conference of Major Superiors at that time and Rosemary Goldie, a woman from Australia who was eloquent and daring. Besides being part of the drafting commissions, the women at the Council interacted with some of the bishops and journalists outside the Council and even offered hospitality through "open houses for the bishops and seminarians."[11] They also met regularly among themselves to read and comment on the draft documents. They were thus a valuable resource to the bishops in giving comments on texts that dealt with the laity and religious.

Owing to the presence of women at the council, there was some effort to acknowledge the discrimination against women and include a few prescriptions to their favour in the documents. In practice though, not much has changed with respect to their roles in the Church. During the Council discussions in October 1964 on the role of women in the world, Madigan notes that there were significant interventions made on the position and place of women in the Church and in society by Gerard Coderre, a Canadian Bishop and Bishop Augustinus Frotz from Germany:[12]

> Bishop Coderre.... emphasized that men should not only give women their proper place in the world but recognize that they are necessary for the completion of the divine plan for human perfection, for the perfection of the family and of society in general. Bishop Frotz said that the Church has not yet become aware of the worldwide implications of the changed position of women in modern society. Women should be accepted as the Church's grown-up daughters, not just children. In the liturgy, they should be addressed directly as 'sisters' and not just submerged in the term 'brothers'.[13]

The plea for inclusive language had already come strongly then from the mouth of a German Bishop. The strongest remarks in favour of women were made by Archbishop Paul Hallinan of Atlanta who confessed that "the Church has been slow to offer women, in the selection of their vocations, any choice but that of mother or nun" and so "we must not continue to perpetuate the secondary place accorded to women in the Church of the 20th century."[14] We can thus observe that even though women came to the Council halfway through the sessions, their presence was noted and it bore a considerable impact in changing the tone of the discussions and even some of the documents.

Role of Women in the Church after VC II

To mark the fiftieth anniversary of VC II, a number of academic events were organized to measure its impact on the Church, Catholic life and theology. Jessica Coblentz, Assistant Professor of Religious Studies at St Mary's College Notre Dame, points out that on November 6 and 7, 2015, theologians, church historians, ministers, and others met at Loyola University Chicago to reflect on "the role of women in Catholicism fifty years after the Council."[15] Some of the questions discussed include:

> What has and has not changed for women in the Church since the Second Vatican Council? What positions do women have and what roles do they play in the Church today? What is the future for women in the Church? What should be the agenda of engagement for the next half century?[16]

It was noted that VC II had affected the everyday experiences of women in diverse ways. On the brighter side there were increased opportunities for women to study theology, contribute to theological discussions and participate in liturgical functions as Eucharistic ministers and lectors. Women religious institutions also renewed their way of life after the Council. However, not much has changed with regard to women's roles in the Church and they still experience challenges in the varied ministries they participate in. They continue to be kept out of decision-making bodies and sacred ministries.

Reflecting on the significant role played by women in the commissions that drafted some of the texts of the documents, Mannion sees their contribution as a clear "exercising of magisterium."[17] He explains the term magisterium as signifying "a function, an act" or "the art of teaching-with-authority…. the multiple aspects and wondrous gifts of the Christian faith" which cannot be restricted only to men.[18] While women are not yet part of the official teaching Magisterium, they do have a significant role to play in the magisterium both as part of the *sensus fidelium* and as theologians and learned women, discerning, interpreting and explaining the faith right from the beginning.[19] The experiences and writings of women have shaped and impacted the Church and theology. Anne Patrick (1941–2016), an American theologian and religious Sister of the Holy Names, affirms that "women's participation in theological education and research has increased dramatically since the Council."[20] Even though women are forbidden from certain sacramental functions they continue to "serve in many pastoral, educational, and administrative capacities today."[21] Feminist theologies have emerged and feminist movements have sprung up across continents.

In India, the Gender Policy came into effect in 2010 because of the committed and consistent efforts of some Indian women theologians who actively resisted the rigid, hierarchical and unjust structures in the Church that favoured mostly men. Although the policy was well-formulated and approved by the bishops, it has not been implemented in most of the dioceses and there is even resistance from some of the clergy and members of the church hierarchy. In 2014, *Streevani* undertook a scientific study on the impact of the Gender Policy of the Catholic Church. They distributed a self-administered questionnaire to parish council members in 95 dioceses across the country. Through this they attempted to establish whether the parish council members were familiar with the Policy, and to gather their perceptions and opinions about the Policy and about gender and justice related issues in general. Of the one thousand respondents who participated in this study, only a small percentage of people, the majority of whom were religious, were familiar with the document. *Streevani*, along with some of the Diocesan Women's Commissions, is persistent in following the Policy through. There is urgent need for the Policy to be widely promoted and practised, creating forums and mechanisms for women's voices to be heard, their concerns to be addressed, and respectful relationships to be fostered. This will serve to bring about a renewed way of being Church, one that is open, inclusive and at the service of the world and all people.

Mary McClintock Fulkerson, professor of theology at Duke University, thinks that even if women are able to influence the Church through their presence and active participation, "there appears to be a deeply embedded structural hierarchy, where males have dominant power and refuse to authorize full access to ministry to the female gender," thereby upholding and valorising maleness for certain employments and ministries.[22] Women's destiny in the Church is still to a great extent determined by their bodies. Jamie Manson, columnist and books editor of the National Catholic Reporter (NCR), USA, notes that Pope Francis too seems to be reinforcing a certain biological determinism in the church with his "nuptial symbolism" and other comments that appear to "reinforce women's fixed place in the church."[23] All the same there is an openness and positive direction in which Francis' pontificate is moving forward in favour of women even if it is slow and gradual.

Role of Women in the Church through the Lens of Pope Francis

With the papacy of Pope Francis one can notice promising initiatives as well as disconcerting perceptions towards women in the Church. Francis is surely ensuring better representation of women in the Vatican offices as well as in other ecclesial bodies and is also promoting the empowerment of women in the Church. He asserts the need of giving women important positions and opportunities in the Church and getting them involved in the public sphere, encouraging them to take more pastoral responsibilities and engage in theological reflection.[24] He appointed seven women to the Vatican Congregation for Religious (officially known as the Congregation for Institutes of Consecrated Life and Societies of Apostolic Life – CICLSAL), which oversees religious orders and sets policies for religious men, women and consecrated members of the laity.[25] This is a noteworthy move since this congregation earlier comprised of only cardinals, bishops and heads of religious men's orders. He made significant appointments in 2014 by approving Sr Mary Melone as the first woman rector of the Franciscan *Pontifical University Antonianum* in Rome and assigning five women to the Vatican's International Theological Commission.[26] He has also included a thirty-seven member Women's Consultation Group to the all-male Pontifical Council for Culture which reflects on diverse global issues.[27] Francis has been continuously advocating for equal wages for men and women.[28]

In April 2015, he met with a delegation of US religious women and brought the long fraught process of the CDF doctrinal investigation to a sudden closure acknowledging the great work and witness of the American women religious congregations.[29] In 2016, he raised the liturgical commemoration of Mary Magdalene to a feast bringing it on par with the feasts of the apostles and affirming her as 'apostle to the apostles' in the preface of the Eucharist on her feast day.[30] In the same year he appointed a Commission to study the possibility of permanent deacons for women and included six women of its twelve members to explore the historical development of the diaconate ministry of women, though this is not something totally new as there were women deacons in the early Church.

With the way things were moving in the pontificate of Pope Francis, Catholic religious women had high hopes and expectations of greater involvement in decision-making and leadership roles, but they soon realized that this was not a significant issue in Francis' agenda. While involving women in some of the ecclesial offices of the Vatican, Francis is cautious and hesitant to tackle the issues of women's full participation in the Church. This is affirmed by Astrid Lobo Gajiwala, an Indian feminist theologian, who observes that Francis either avoids or is vague about women's participation in decision-making in the Church. While she is positive about Francis' sensitivity and denouncement of "women's subordination both in the Church and in the world" she has mixed reactions to his comments and strategies.[31] She is of the opinion that on one hand he advises women to refrain from roles of servitude and advocates their promotion in the public sphere, and on the other, he limits women's role in the Church "to their involvement in pastoral responsibilities, in the accompaniment of persons, families and groups."[32]

It appears that Pope Francis' understanding of women's role in the church is ambiguous and constantly changing. He demonstrates greater clarity with regard to the poor, migrants, refugees and other displaced categories. However, with regard to women Francis often reverts back to exalting the feminine genius of women and reinforcing the theology of complementarity emphasized by Pope John Paul II.[33] For instance, in his address to men and women religious in Rome in 2015, he distinguished between functionality by which women can head certain *dicasteries* and the feminine genius which is about rediscovering the essential role of women in the Church.[34] Francis understands the feminine genius of women and especially consecrated women in terms of maternity, fidelity, concrete love, smiles and tenderness which he relates to Mother Mary and Mother Church. What about the strength, courage and daring of Mary of Nazareth as reflected in the accounts of the evangelists?

Speaking with members of the International Union Superiors General (UISG) in 2016, Francis acknowledged that women are rarely given decision-making roles in the Church. When the women superior generals asked for greater share in decision-making roles in the Church and to separate leadership and preaching from priesthood, they were made aware of the complementarity of the sexes and their differing functions in the Church.[35] Anne Patrick finds that many of Pope Francis' statements about women reiterate Pope John Paul's "'essentialist' understanding of human nature, which sees women as complementary to men in a way that effectively limits women's contributions."[36] Francis also spoke of two dangers that must be avoided: feminism and clericalism. He sees feminism as a temptation and evil that would "reduce a woman's importance" and clericalism as the "clerical spirit" with which a priest solely runs a parish or diocese without implementing 'synodality'.[37] It is interesting to observe the way feminism and clericalism are both seen as dangers since in reality feminists in no way seek to reduce importance to women and actually strive to do away with all forms of clericalism.

Nevertheless, with Pope Francis it is possible for women and all people to work together towards creating an inclusive interdependent Church community to promote the flourishing of all persons and protect the earth since he is open to listen and discern according to the signs of the time. Francis has underscored interdependence and the interrelatedness of life in his encyclical *Laudato Si*, wherein he sees true love as respecting every aspect of reality, since everything is related and connected in and for universal communion.[38] This can provide a way forward for women to push for greater reform and participation.

The Way Forward: Women's Vision and Expectations of Greater Involvement in Decision Making Roles and Sacred Ministries
More than 50 years after VC II acknowledged the changing role of women in the world, their vocation and rightful place in the Church has not yet seen the light of day. When women have assumed significant roles in society as CEO's, senators, governors, politicians, university presidents and so on, why is there reluctance to give women greater

voice, visibility and vital functions in the Church? Women hope for a renewed discipleship of equals where the Church reconsiders and recognises women's roles as prophets, preachers and leaders to ensure relational representation and participatory processes of decision making at every level. Lobo Gajiwala believes that although women appreciate Pope Francis's personal stance in favour of them, they are not totally satisfied. According to Gajiwala:

> They want structured mechanisms that will function in a consistent manner to hold negligent bishops accountable, processes of redress that will be transparent, and most important, a demonstrated, timely and uncompromising concern for the safety of minors and vulnerable adults that supersedes administrative priorities.... What Pope Francis urgently needs to do is sit with women at the table and let them set the agenda. Women will then expose him to the foundational principles of feminism, gender sensitivity and gender mainstreaming. They will let him know why talk of a 'feminine genius' frustrates and limits them, and why a "theology of women" perplexes them. They will share how "complementarity of the sexes" is like an insurmountable wall for them. They will ask for an ecclesiology that includes women so that the Church can truly be a People of God and explore with him avenues for women's leadership in the Church.[39]

I agree with Lobo Gajiwala that much needs to be accomplished with regard to respecting the dignity of women, recognising their contribution in the Church and in society, offering them equal opportunities, promoting the use of inclusive language, and increasing their participation in advisory and decision-making bodies, in liturgical and other sacred ministries. Restoring the dignity and worth of women requires recognising and respecting their bodies, allowing women to take decisions concerning their bodies and re-establishing the wholeness of the human body in relation to sexuality and spirituality. Not much attention has been paid to the working and laboured bodies of women subjected to the *violence of un-rest*.

The Church has a responsibility to see that "every type of discrimination, whether social or cultural, whether based on sex, race, colour, social condition, language or religion, is to be overcome and eradicated."[40] The Church needs to create structures and mechanisms whereby all women can live a more dignified life. While the dignity of the human person has been a major concern in the Church documents,[41] upholding the rights and dignity of women has been explicitly mentioned in a number of documents and letters. Yet, a wide gap exists between well-formulated principles and policies and their actualization in praxis. While engaging in policy reform and advocacy to promote the flourishing of all persons is imperative, the Church needs to find ways in which women's voices are heard, their rights are acknowledged, and they are allowed to share social, cultural and religious spaces with dignity, equality and freedom. There is an urgent need for more dialogue, discussions, collaboration and networking to promote the common good of all. Catholic women across the globe are joining with like-minded people of all faiths to exercise agency in strongly resisting, actively participating and speaking out boldly against any kind of discrimination against women and other marginalised persons. They see the need of a greater feminist consciousness and collaborative action to engender a renewed humanity and flourishing creation.

At the recent National Consultation organized by *Streevani* and Ishvani Kendra from October 4–6, 2019, ninety-five consecrated women gathered to reflect on the theme "Women in the Church: Reading the 'Signs of the Time.'" Some of the key reflections and resolutions revolved around restoring equality and building solidarities across gender, class, caste, religion and other divides. There was a felt need to challenge and counter clericalism, patriarchy, gender stereotypes, binaries and all forms of oppression and discrimination in the Church and society so that authentic partnerships may be established for a revitalised mission in the Church. As we 'dream the impossible dream'[42] to create a just and equitable world order, let us unite in our endeavours, sharing roles and responsibilities to 'right the unrightable wrongs' and to walk humbly and courageously with God and each other, within and across all borders.

Endnotes

[1] Vatican Speeches, "Address of Pope Paul VI to Women: Closing of the Second Vatican Ecumenical Council," Libreria Editrice Vaticana, 1965, http://www.vatican.va/

content/paul-vi/en/speeches/1965/documents/hf_p-vi_spe_19651208_epilogo-concilio-donne.html.Closing address (accessed November 20, 2019).

[2] John XXIII, *Encyclical, Pacem in Terris: On Establishing Universal Peace in Truth, Justice, Charity, and Liberty* (Vatican, Rome: Libreria Editrice Vaticana, 1963), no. 41.

[3] Cf. Helen R. Graham, "Vatican II and Women," *Landas: Journal of Loyola School of Theology* 26, no. 1 (2012): 86.

[4] Cf. ibid.

[5] Gerard Mannion, "Women and the Art of Magisterium: Reflections on Vatican II and the Postconciliar Church," in *Catholicism Opening to the World and Other Confessions: Vatican II and Its Impact*, ed. Vladimir Latinovic, Gerard Mannion, and Jason Welle (London: Palgrave MacMillan, 2018), 121-122.

[6] Patricia Madigan, "Women during and after Vatican II," in *Catholicism Opening to the World and Other Confessions: Vatican II and Its Impact*, ibid., 82.

[7] Cf. ibid. Helen Graham records 23 women at the Council instead of 24. Cf. Graham, "Vatican II and Women," 81.

[8] Madigan, "Women during and after Vatican II," 81.

[9] See Jessica Coblentz, "Women in American Catholic Theology Fifty Years after Vatican II: Introduction," *Journal of Feminist Studies in Religion* 33, no. 1 (2017): 87.

[10] Cf. Mannion, "Women and the Art of Magisterium," 127; See also Graham, "Vatican II and Women."

[11] Madigan, "Women during and after Vatican II," 83, 84.

[12] Cf. ibid., 84.

[13] Ibid.

[14] Placid Jordan, "U.S. Prelate Asks Women Be Given Roles in the Mass," *The Voice (Archdiocese of Miami, Florida)* 7, no. 31 (1965): 4. Quoted in Madigan, "Women during and after Vatican II," 86.

[15] Coblentz, "Women in American Catholic Theology Fifty Years after Vatican II: Introduction," 87.

[16] Ibid., 88.

[17] Mannion, "Women and the Art of Magisterium," 129.

[18] Ibid., 130, 132.

[19] Cf. ibid., 135.

[20] Anne E. Patrick, "Tensions Over 'Feminism,' US Women Religious and the Contested Reception of Vatican II," in *Catholicism Opening to the World and Other Confessions: Vatican II and Its Impact*, 113.

²¹ Ibid., 118.

²² Mary McClintock Fulkerson, "Opening to the World: A Reformed Feminist Posture of Openness," in *Catholicism Opening to the World and Other Confessions: Vatican II and Its Impact*, ibid., 103, 104.

²³ Jamie Manson, "It's Time to Be Honest about Pope Francis and Women," *National Catholic Reporter*, May 19, 2016, https://www.ncronline.org/blogs/grace-margins/its-time-be-honest-about-pope-francis-and-women.

²⁴ Cf. Astrid Lobo Gajiwala, "Women," in *A Pope Francis Lexicon*, ed. Joshua J McElwee and Cindy Wooden (Collegeville, MN: Liturgical Press, 2018), 191.

²⁵ Cf. Thomas Reese, "Pope Francis Gets It Right on Curia Reform and Women," *National Catholic Reporter*, July 18, 2019, https://www.ncronline.org/news/opinion/signs-times/pope-francis-gets-it-right-curia-reform-and-women; See also Lobo Gajiwala, "Women."

²⁶ Cf. Lobo Gajiwala, "Women," 193.

²⁷ Cf. ibid.

²⁸ Cf. Madigan, "Women during and after Vatican II," 91.

²⁹ Cf. Mannion, "Women and the Art of Magisterium," 140.

³⁰ Cf. ibid., 136.

³¹ Lobo Gajiwala, "Women," 190.

³² Ibid., 191.

³³ Cf. Patrick, "Tensions over 'Feminism'"; See also Mannion, "Women and the Art of Magisterium," 140.

³⁴ Cf. Vatican Speeches, "Address of His Holiness Pope Francis to Consecrated Men and Women of the Diocese of Rome," Libreria Editrice Vaticana, 2015, http://www.vatican.va/content/francesco/en/speeches/2015/may/documents/papa-francesco_20150516_religiosi-roma.html; See also Catholic World News, "Pope Francis: 'Feminine Genius,' Not 'Functionalism,' Key to Women's Role in Church," 2015, https://www.catholicculture.org/news/headlines/index.cfm?storyid=24949 (accessed September 30, 2019).

³⁵ Cf. Vatican Speeches, "Address of His Holiness Pope Francis to the International Union of Superiors General (UISG)," Libreria Editrice Vaticana, 2016, https://w2.vatican.va/content/francesco/en/speeches/2016/may/documents/papa-francesco_20160512_uisg.html (accessed September 30, 2019).

³⁶ Patrick, "Tensions over 'Feminism,'" 111.

³⁷ Vatican Speeches, "Address of His Holiness Pope Francis to the International Union of Superiors General (UISG)."

38 Francis, *Encyclical Letter, Laudato Si': On Care for Our Common Home* (Rome: Libreria Editrice Vaticana, 2015), nos. 76, 92.

39 Astrid Lobo Gajiwala, "Are the Women in the Church Really Happy with Pope Francis?," *JIVAN: News and Views of Jesuits in India* (2018): 3,5.

40 Paul VI, "Gaudium et Spes: Pastoral Constitution on the Church in the Modern World," in *Vatican II: The Essential Texts*, ed. Norman Tanner (New York: Image Books, 2012), 189–298.

41 Cf. ibid., 12–19; Cf. John XXIII, *Pacem in Terris*, 6–11.

42 'The impossible dream' is the theme song of the 1965 musical 'Man of La Mancha' based on Miguel Cervantes's novel character Don Quixote. The words 'to right the unrightable wrong' also appear in the song.

10.

Mercy and Compassion for an Ailing World

Pope Francis' Role in Fostering a Feminist Perspective

Shalini Mulackal, PBVM

Introduction: Pope Francis' Response of Mercy to a Broken World

God created our beautiful world and entrusted human beings to take care of it. The beauty of snow-capped mountains and oceans, forests and hills, rivers and lakes, sunrise and sunset, trees and plants, flowers and fruits, animals and fish, birds and insects, is breath-taking. However, not only have we, human beings, failed to nurture and take care of our earth over the centuries, but we have been ruthlessly looting and plundering our common home. We have polluted our rivers, seas, soil and the air. As a result, our world is broken and sick today. Pope Francis vividly describes this situation in the first chapter of his social encyclical *Laudato Si* titled: 'What is happening to our common home?'

Innumerable ills plague planet earth and all its inhabitants. Day by day plant and animal species are getting extinct. Overuse of natural resources has resulted in global warming and climate change, nay, climate emergency! We are witnessing droughts, floods, hurricanes, storms, earthquakes, forest fires, etc., in many parts of the world causing untold misery for a large number of people. Though the world is growing and developing, the benefits of growth are not distributed evenly and justly. As a result, a majority of people worldwide lack sufficient food and water and do not even have clean air to breathe.

The maternal heart of God bleeds looking at the world and its manifold miseries caused by human beings and the sinful structures they have created. Like the Father in the parable of the Lost Son (Lk 15:11-32), God waits with a heart full of mercy and compassion for the return of God's children to wholeness and wellbeing. In this context of an ailing humanity and a broken world, this paper makes a modest attempt to understand the deeper significance of the Biblical terms 'mercy and compassion' with particular reference to Pope Francis' *Misericordiae Vultus*, the Bull of Indiction during the Jubilee year of Mercy. This paper also hopes to look at the broken world and the response it evokes from a feminist lens. There is no doubt that in his teaching and writing Pope Francis uses a feminist perspective in addressing the present-day problems that adversely affect humanity and planet earth, our common home.

The first part of the paper will critically analyse the various ills afflicting humanity and the world today. The second part of the paper will focus on mercy and compassion as a remedy for the ailing world as proposed by Pope Francis in *Misericordiae Vultus*.

1. An Ailing, Bleeding World

A quick glance at what is happening in our country, India, will surely give us an idea of what is happening in the world at large. Farmers in India are in distress for a very long time. Many thousands have ended their lives already. Our Government is least bothered to alleviate their suffering but, on the contrary, is making efforts to get rid of them and hand over the agricultural sector to the monopoly of corporate companies and industrialists for agro-business.

Our economy is going from bad to worse. Unemployment is all time high both in urban and rural areas. The price of essential commodities is rising and ordinary people are getting desperate. There is an unholy alliance between the ruling political party and a handful of business corporates. Laws and policies of the government are made in such a way that both the ruling party and the corporate benefit from each other. The law that makes buying of electoral bonds is a case in point. Anyone can donate to any political party anonymously. There is no transparency in this deal.[1]

We are witnessing an increase in violence in the form of mob lynching, communal riots, road rage, etc. Violence against women too is on the increase. Women and girls are victims of rape, murder, molestation, sex harassment, domestic violence, honour killing, trafficking, sex slavery, etc. The situation of Dalits and Adivasis is pathetic. They are victims of various exploitations. Dalits are systematically excluded from entering the mainstream of society. Any attempt to claim their rights as citizens of this country are ruthlessly suppressed. In the name of development, Adivasis are displaced from their land and are seldom given alternate land as compensation.

The minorities in the country feel insecure and are targeted due to the Hindutva ideology of the present government. The penetration of this ideology into various democratic institutions of the country gives very little hope for India to remain and function as a democratic nation for long.[2]

The people of Kashmir are literally imprisoned for the past number of months in their own homes with their fundamental rights ruthlessly suppressed in the name of law and order. The enmity between India and Pakistan is kept alive and a lot of money is spent in the name of national security. We are accustomed to read every other day newspaper reports such as:

> Pakistan army on Saturday violated ceasefire by resorting to unprovoked firing and shelling on forward posts and villages along the Line of Control (LOC),

in Jammu and Kashmir's Rajouri district. Pakistan initiated the unprovoked ceasefire violation by firing small arms and shelling with mortars at about 11.30 am, prompting befitting retaliation by Indian Army.[3]

It is not an exaggeration to say that the world we live in today has institutionalized violence in every possible way. The arms and ammunition industry thrives on violence and war. Some thrive on the production and sale of sophisticated weaponry. They take pride when a latest missile can wipe out in seconds an entire community: children, women, men with flora and fauna.[4] Sadly, millions of people across the globe are under the grip of war and violence. For instance, countries like Syria, Iraq and several other countries in West Asia have witnessed the cruel reality of war causing untold suffering for years together. The number of refugees and asylum seekers have increased manifold due to these wars. One cannot easily forget the picture of the body of a little boy washed ashore as they were fleeing their war-torn country. The Israeli occupation of Palestine and the resulting conflicts have taken many lives and it continues to this day.

In several parts of Africa, civil wars have claimed thousands of lives. The oil-rich Libya remains fractured after descending into chaos in 2011, when an international military coalition helped rebels overthrow long time autocrat Muammar Gaddafi. Rival armed groups have been fighting there for control of the city Tripoli since April. In September 2019, the US military said it carried out several airstrikes against the Islamic State group in Libya, killing 40 militants.[5]

2. Factors Causing the Malady

The present situation of the world is caused by various factors such as unjust distribution of wealth, exploitation of labour, lack of political will to work for the wellbeing of people, discrimination of people based on caste, race, gender, class, region, religion, etc. The unbridled growth and development have made it possible for the so-called developed nations to enjoy a high standard of living. To maintain such high standards of living, over-exploitation of natural resources becomes a must leading to deforestation, global warming, climate change, extinction of plant and animal species and increase in pollution. The neo-liberal, capitalistic patriarchal ideology sustains these unjust socio-economic and political structures. In this worldview one's happiness is measured by having more, having the latest gadget and accumulating wealth by all means. Profit becomes the only reason for one's economic activities. Things are produced to make profit rather than to serve human needs. Therefore, needs are created so that the producers can make maximum profit.

The capitalistic patriarchal worldview reinforces a consumerist culture, which results in cut-throat competition. In this worldview people are seen as functional, relationship is always hierarchical and money is seen as absolute. Nature is seen as something to be manipulated and exploited by humans without any limits. It suppresses not only women but also the feminine qualities of love, tenderness, compassion and projects God as a patriarch who is all knowing, judging and controlling.

As science and technology make more and more progress, the age-old values cherished by human beings are fast disappearing. Religion has almost lost its grip on human conscience since most organized religions have lost their prophetic edges and their leaders have become corrupt. In most economically developed nations, religion plays very little role in public life. It is relegated to one's private sphere. With the eclipse of religion from the public life, human greed seems to have taken the upper hand. Gradually individualism, materialism, consumerism, etc., replaced community feeling, solidarity, simplicity, care for others and care for the earth. Human greed and selfishness have led the world to its present situation of brokenness, darkness and agony.

3. Theological Reflection

The above discussion makes it clear that our world stands in need of liberation. It does not need a judging and condemning God, but rather a motherly God who looks at her children with tender love and mercy irrespective of their physical, mental, psychological conditions or moral uprightness. Jesus came to such a world of brokenness as Emmanuel "God-with-us" (Mt 1:23) incarnating God's love, compassion and mercy for our world (Jn 3:16). He proclaimed the Reign of God and inaugurated it in his person, words and deeds. Through his deeds he demonstrated how compassionate and merciful is our father-mother God in heaven. Jesus prepared a group of disciples to carry forward his mission of spreading the reign of God to the ends of the earth (Mt 28:18-20). The Church as the body of Christ is commissioned to continue Jesus' compassionate ministry in the world.

Despite Jesus' clear mandate to his disciples to work towards building a loving, caring and compassionate world, there have been ups and downs in the history of the Church. Vatican Council II (hereinafter VC II) has been a landmark for the Church in its self-understanding and mission. It brought a fresh lease of life to a Church that had lost its way. This was clearly expressed by the words of Saint John XXIII at the opening of VC II: "Now the Bride of Christ wishes to use the medicine of mercy rather than taking up arms of severity..."[6] To mark the fiftieth anniversary of the closing of VC II, Pope Francis announced the extraordinary Jubilee Year[7] and called the entire Church to reflect and respond to the present day needs of the world by promulgating *Misericordiae Vultus*—Latin, for The Face of Mercy—the Bull of Indiction of the Extraordinary Jubilee of Mercy.

'Mercy' is a keynote of the pastoral, theological, and ecclesial approach of Pope Francis, who declared 2016 to be the Jubilee Year of Mercy. Announcing the Jubilee in *Misericordiae Vultus*, he called mercy 'a wellspring of joy, serenity, and peace' (n.2), identified mercy as qualities of God and Christ, called mercy 'the very foundation of the Church's life,' and summoned the whole Church 'to bear the weaknesses and struggles of our brothers and sisters' in mercy. Mercy is 'the force that reawakens us to new life and instils in us the courage to look to the future with hope' (n.10).[8]

The theme of mercy and compassion runs through the various documents of VC II and is not confined to any particular document. It was a watershed experience of mercy. For instance, in *Gaudium et Spes*, the Council affirms how the joys, hopes, agonies and aspirations especially of the poor and the afflicted, are the joys, hopes, grief and anxieties of the Church (GS 1). In *Ad Gentes*, we get the most significant insight that God is "the fountain of love" (AG 2). In fact, every document of VC II resonates this understanding of God as loving-kindness. In contrast to the earlier understanding of revelation as God communicating certain truths that humans are to believe, the Constitution of Divine Revelation, *Dei Verbum*, describes revelation as divine self-manifestation through deeds and words (DV 2) beginning with creation (n.3).

Further, the Constitution on the Church, *Lumen Gentium*, presents the Church as a sacrament of the intimate union with God and of the unity of all humankind (LG 1), emphasising its call to service as the initial step of the reign of mercy (LG 5). Liturgy is no more just the observance of laws, but enabling the participation of all "knowingly, actively and fruitfully" (SC 11). The conciliar statement on mission, "Missionary activity is nothing else and nothing less than a manifestation or epiphany of God's will (the reign of mercy) and the fulfilment of that will in the world and in world history" (AG 9).[9]

Misericordiae Vultus of Pope Francis reminds the Church once again that its mission is to be the Face of Mercy in our broken world. It would be in order at this juncture to have a deeper look at mercy and compassion.

3.1. *Mercy and Compassion in Judaism and Christianity*

The word 'mercy' occurs approximately 150 times in the Bible, while 'compassion' appears around 50 times.[10] Moreover, the description of God as: "merciful and gracious, slow to anger and abounding in steadfast love and faithfulness" also appears about a dozen times in the Bible.[11] This description seems to summarize God's mercy. The Hebrew word *hesed* is often translated as 'mercy' but it is also translated as 'loving-kindness' and 'goodness.' The Greek *splagchnizomai* which literally means 'to be moved in one's bowels or intestines' is characteristic of

Jesus, who either provides for the poor or forgives sinners. Mercy and compassion therefore are seen more as heart-felt or gut level emotions.

The Hebrew word for 'mercy,' i.e., *rahamim*, is etymologically related to the word *rehem*, meaning, 'womb.' In Hebrew religious consciousness, the meaning of mercy is rooted in and clarified by the root *rehem*-womb. Many Bible commentaries and dictionaries translate the word *rahamim* as compassion, mercy, affection and love; the word comes from the same root as the noun *rehem*, translated as uterus, mother's womb, maternal covering of life, entrails.[12] Thus, a whole range of merciful affectivity associated with *rahamim* is, as it were, rightly associated with what might be called 'womb-like' love.[13] Reflecting upon mercy as a form of 'womb-like love' can give us deeper insights into the nature of mercy; for, in biblical imagery, the womb is not merely a bodily organ or a receptacle for reproduction but evokes myriad meanings: symbolic, metaphorical, analogical and transcendental.[14]

It is important to notice that *rahamim* is closely related with *rehem*, which gives rise to the verb 'to show mercy' and the adjective 'merciful.' According to Phyllis Trible, 'In its singular form *rehem* means 'breast' or 'womb.' In the plural, *rahamim*, it opens out into abstractions such as compassion, mercy and love. As a result, our metaphor is located in the semantic movement that goes from a physical organ of a female body to a psychic state.[15] Further, "the psychic state, this compassionate concern, can be displayed both by men and by women."[16]

Nonetheless, if we want to refer to being merciful like God, the paradigmatic metaphor is the love a woman feels for her son or daughter of her entrails, as indicated in passages: 'I shall show him my maternal compassion' (Jer 31:20); 'Can a woman forget her nursing-child, or show no compassion for the child of her womb? Even these may forget, yet I will not forget you' (Isa 49:15). The symbol to which both these texts refer, *rehem*, God's uterus, God's maternal womb; although because it is part of a woman's body, it already has a series of stereotypes. Nonetheless the term refers to this area of the body that has the possibility of creating life and protecting its full development. There can be no doubt that this experience brings with it an intimate, deep-rooted, loving feeling of full connection and involvement of two bodies that are completely interconnected, since this new being is the extension of the woman herself.[17]

Indeed, at a most primordial level, God is the sole author of life whose Womb, figuratively speaking, brought forth the world. Then, womb is the place of the origin of life which God can "open"[18] or "close"[19] or reach, so as to delicately "knit together" forms of life (Ps 139:13). The womb is also a place of sacrificial love oriented towards nurturing the weak and vulnerable and a place of relationship where human life is sown through spousal love that will eventually flower in loving God (vertical) and all of creation (horizontal). Finally, the womb is a place of welcome, which militates against the 'culture of death' that Christianity strongly opposes.[20]

Mercy in the Second Testament goes with a cluster of words: love, compassion, pity, forgiveness and justice. Some of these words are: *eleos* (mercy, pity), *splaggnizomai* (having compassion), *dikaiosynē* (righteousness), *charis* (grace), *pistis* (faithful/ness) and *agapē* (love). All these terms speak about the essential property or character of God in relation to sinful, helpless human beings without exception (Rom 3:23). The comprehensive end result of God's mercy is *sōtēria* (salvation) and *eirēnē* (peace, wholeness/shalom) given by God unconditionally as a free gift in Christ.[21]

Mercy comes out clearly in the story when Jesus tells the cured demoniac who wants to follow him: "Go to your house and your people and tell them what the Lord has done for you and how he has shown mercy to you" (Mk 5:19). Pope Francis sees in the parable of the prodigal son (Lk 15:11-32) 'the core of our gospel and faith.'[22] Divine mercy as the new covenant has consequences for all humans. Baptized in Christ into Trinity, and constituted God's children thereby, Christians share substantially in God's life. They are cut into the new covenant in Jesus' humanity as members of his body (1 Cor 12) or branches of his vine

(Jn 15:1-17). They are endowed with the grace and vocation to be a Eucharistic people, people who having received mercy are themselves merciful in memory of Jesus. Being merciful is therefore not an option, or a gift offering or homage done to God. In them and through them Jesus, God's mercy to humanity, remains alive and active in every age.[23]

3.2. Mercy and Compassion in other Faith Traditions

Mercy and compassion are terms rich in meaning in faith traditions other than Christianity, too, as we see below.

3.2.1. The Qur'an

Mercy is one of the most important features of the image of God in the Qur'an. There are over 300 references to mercy, mostly to the mercy of God. In these passages God is called time and again 'the Merciful' (*arraḥmān*) or described as 'compassionate' (*rahim*), or the noun (*rahma*).[24] The Qur'an mentions three main forms of God's mercy, bestowed or at least intended for all human beings: The mercy with which God has constructed the whole creation for the good of human beings and with which he also continues unfailingly to provide them with the necessities of life; the mercy of divine 'guidance' (*hudā*) through revelations that he constantly sent human beings through the course of history through prophets to bring them back from polytheistic aberrations and moral decline to the right path.[25]

In the Qur'anic concept of divine mercy, particular importance is attached to the forgiveness of sins. From the Qur'an and *Hadiths* of the Prophet it is clear that dealing with others compassionately is indispensable for salvation. This enjoins on the believer four tasks: first, to live in gratitude for Allah's mercy, second, to ask for more of Allah's mercy, third, to beg forgiveness for one's forgetfulness and cruelty and fourth, to live intensely in mutual compassion.[26]

3.2.2. The Indic Religions

The Indic religions which originated in India are Hinduism, Buddhism, Jainism, and Sikhism. These religions preach that compassion must flow from the basic premise of reciprocity, that is, the realization that as much as one wants to avoid pain and live in peace, and prosperity, everyone and everything else yearns for the same too. In Sanskrit, the words *karuṇā* and *dayā* are synonyms for mercy or compassion. The word *dayā* implies the deep desire in one's heart to remove the sufferings or hardships of others, even at the cost of great effort and sacrifice on one's part. The well-known "hugging Mother," Mata Amritanandamayi from Kerala says:

> We have forgotten the love, compassion and mutual understanding taught by religion. The basic cause underlying all the problems that exist in the present-day world is the lack of love and compassion. Love and compassion, alone, will wipe out the darkness, bringing light and purity to the world... to show compassion towards suffering humanity is our obligation to God. Our spiritual quest should begin with selfless service to the world.[27]

Compassion for others is one of the central teachings of Mahayana Buddhism. "Contemplative reflection on the suffering of living beings is not enough; we must help diminish suffering through compassionate involvement..."[28] says the Buddhist scholar, Thich Nhat Hanh. The Tibetan spiritual leader, His Holiness the Dalai Lama says that our world needs ancient Indian values of non-violence and compassion. He was speaking to reporters ahead of the three-day Global Buddhist Congregation being held in Aurangabad in Maharashtra. Non-violence and compassion are helping people of many religions in India to live with peace and mutual respect, he said. "We can see conflicts everywhere. Whenever I hear about such conflicts, it pains me. At this moment, the world can live in peace if they follow values of compassion and non-violence."[29]

Jainism advocates compassion and care for every living being, including microscopic insects. Closely connected to the practice of *dayā* is *ahimsā* or non-violence. All being (*sat*) is divided into non-living (*ajiva*) and living (*jiva*) forms. Ancient Jain texts explain that it is the intention to harm, the absence of compassion or *dayā*, which makes an action violent. Jains also positively strive to cultivate an attitude of amity (*maitry*) towards all forms of life.

4. Remedy for the Wounded Human and the Broken World

In a world steeped in capitalistic patriarchal value system which denigrates what is feminine and gives less value to females and scant recognition to their contribution in every field, there is a need to emphasize the understanding of God, the sacred as a mother's womb, enfolding, with passion, tenderness and love. Mercy is the willingness to enter into the chaos of another as God enters into our chaos.[30] Jesus narrates the parable of the Good Samaritan in response to the question: "Who is my neighbour"? And, the answer turns out to be: "the neighbour is the one who shows mercy." This parable teaches us not to look for a neighbour who loves, but rather to be a neighbour who loves. This surprising shift to the agent of mercy has always made an enormous impact on hearers of the parable.

Chapter 25 of evangelist Matthew's gospel provides the roster of mercy: feed the hungry, give drink to the thirsty, shelter the homeless, clothe the naked, visit the sick, visit the imprisoned and bury the dead. The seventh one adds an early church practice, by which Christians buried not only their own members but others as well.[31]

> This Gospel call to practice mercy was made visible when Christianity revitalized life in Greco-Roman cities by providing new norms and new kinds of social relationships able to cope with many urgent urban problems. To cities filled with the homeless and impoverished, Christianity offered charity as well as hope. To cities filled with newcomers and strangers, Christianity offered an immediate basis for attachments. To cities filled with orphans and widows, Christianity provided a new and expanded sense of family.[32]

It is in this context that we need to understand the efforts which Pope Francis makes to restore mercy to the centre of his rule: not as doctrinal theme but rather in a 'multimedia' way. Mercy is a theme that returns in his speeches, in homilies and in documents, but it is also a personal attitude of his, a canonical choice, the operation of the imagination and of examples.[33] He writes: "I prefer a Church which is bruised, hurting and dirty because it has been out on the streets, rather than a Church which is unhealthy from being confined and from clinging to its own security."[34] At the dawn of the jubilee, in an interview, he stressed how the world is in need of "discovering that God is Father, that there is mercy, that cruelty isn't the way, that condemnation isn't the way." In the same interview the pope admitted that "the Church herself sometimes follows a hard line" and falls into the temptation of "stressing only the moral rules," thus excluding many people from the Good News of the Gospel.[35]

Further, the Church of Asia/India is to sit and learn from the Asian/Indian gurus of compassion. The Buddha advocated *karuna*, compassion to those who are suffering due to enforced poverty or enslaving religiosity. Confucius puts *ren* (translated as benevolence, love, humanity, mercy or compassion) as an ideal human virtue. This is achieved by following the golden rule: "The good man, what he wishes to achieve for himself, he helps others to achieve; what he wishes to obtain for himself, he enables others to obtain." Devout Hindus practice compassion (*karuna*), feeling one with the sufferer, leading to acts of kindness, mercy and charity in selfless service, especially to those in need and in pain. Finally, believing in Allah as "the Lord of Mercy, the Giver of Mercy," Muslims aspire to be merciful towards other Muslims and other groups that are seen as vulnerable, i.e., orphans, widows, poor beggars, and travellers.

More than anything else, the Church is to learn from the poor, listen to them, walk and be in solidarity with them in their journey towards the fullness of life. By the poor, I mean specially the women, the indigenous people, migrants, refugees and urban and rural workers, farmers and fisher people.[36] Learning from the Asian gurus (both the spiritual and the poor), the Church in Asia learns more intensely to follow Jesus who was compassion incarnate.[37]

Pope Francis says:

> We need constantly to contemplate the mystery of mercy. Mercy: the ultimate and supreme act by which God comes to meet us. Mercy: the fundamental law that dwells in the heart of every person who looks sincerely into the eyes of his brothers and sisters on the path of life. Mercy: the bridge that connects God and (hu)man, opening our hearts to the hope of being loved forever despite our sinfulness. (MV 2)

Moreover, we need to follow examples of people who took up works of mercy in our country. They include, Fr. Marianus Zelasek, a polish Divine Word Missionary in the early 1970s who worked among hundreds of leprosy patients in the temple town of Puri, Odisha. So also, Saint Mother Teresa of Kolkata and her Missionaries of Charity continue to give merciful service to many over the years. Fr. Joseph Idiayakunnel SJ from Gujarat communicated mercy through his legal aid work among the poor. Furthermore, we cannot forget the work of Blessed Rani Maria and Sr. Valsa John. We also have persons like Fr. William Wullner, another divine Word Missionary of German origin who went to Khandwa, M.P. and accepted the hospitality of the so-called outcastes of the town, staying in their houses, eating the *roti* and *daal* they offered and listening to their stories and woes.[38]

Conclusion

The world we inhabit is an ailing and broken one. We see many signs and symptoms of this brokenness. The only medicine that can cure the sick world with its inhabitants who are sick, broken, afflicted, greedy and selfish is to be like the Good Samaritan and be a merciful neighbour. Pope Francis is constantly inviting us to develop the feminine aspect of our psyche so that we may look at the ailing world with a maternal heart. Since we live among people who belong to many religious beliefs, and who upholds values like *daya, karuna, maitry* and *ahimsa*, there is a need to come together under the banner of these noble virtues and work for a world that practices these virtues and transform our common home into a beautiful and healthy one.

Endnotes

[1] Recently it was reported that it was the BJP, the ruling party, that received over 90 % of the electoral bonds.

[2] The recent happening in Maharashtra is a clear example of how every democratic institution is bent to suit the agenda of the ruling party according to their whims and fancies or vested interests.

[3] *The Hitavada*, Bhopal edition, Sunday, November 24, 2019, 1.

⁴ See Cedric Prakash, "In the Face of Conflict, Violence and War," in Jose Vallikatt, ed., *Communicating Mercy: Mercy, Communication, Encounter* (Delhi: ISPCK, 2016), 185-192 at 186.

⁵ See *The Hitavada* Bhopal edition, Sunday, November 24, 2019, 5.

⁶ Pope Francis, *Misericordiae Vultus* (Vatican City: Libreria Editrice Vaticana, 2015), n.4. Copy of the text is published in Jose Vallikatt, ed., *Communicating Mercy: Mercy, Communication, Encounter,* (Delhi: ISPCK, 2016), 17-42.

⁷ December 8, 2015 to November 20, 2016.

⁸ See Lisa Cahill, Diego Irarrazaval, Joao Vila-Cha, Editorial, *Concilium*, 2017, No.4, 7-8 at 8.

⁹ See Jacob Kavunkal SVD, "Showering Mercy to the World: Evangelization as Communication of Mercy," in Jose Vallikatt, ed., *Communicating Mercy*, 89-97 at 91-92.

¹⁰ See Leland Ryken, James C. Wilhoit and Tremper Longman III, eds., *Dictionary of Biblical Imagery* (Illinois and Leicester: Inter Varsity Press, 1998), 547-548.

¹¹ See Exodus 34:6, Psalms 86: 15; 103:8, etc.

¹² See Sofia Chipana Quispe, "The Connection with the Mercy and Compassion that Inhabits Us," (translated by Francis McDonagh) in *Concilium*, 2017, No.4, 11-20 at 13.

¹³ See J. Sheila Galligan, "Mercy's Mystery: Womb-Like Love," in *Spiritual Life* 56/1 (Spring 2010), 49-55. The author examines four specific ways in which merciful love can be appreciated as a form of 'womb-like' love.

¹⁴ See Ryken, et.al., eds., *Dictionary of Biblical Imagery*, 962.

¹⁵ Elizabeth A. Johnson, *She Who Is: The Mystery of God in Feminist Theological Discourse,* (New York: 1992), 39.

¹⁶ Johnson, *She Who Is*,139.

¹⁷ Quispe, "The Connection with the Mercy and Compassion that Inhabits Us," 14. We also need to be aware of situations in which pregnancies are the fruit of violence and pain as in the case of rape within or outside marriage.

¹⁸ As in the case of Rachel in the Book of Genesis 30: 22.

¹⁹ As in the case of Hannah in 1 Samuel 1: 5.

²⁰ See Francis Gonsalves, "Mercy and Compassion: The Womb of Interfaith Dialogue," in *Awakening to the Immensity of the Mystery: Theory and Practice in Inter Religious Relations,* edited by Packiam T. Samuel (Delhi: ISPCK/ Henry Martyn Institute (HMI, 2019), 323-335 at 327.

²¹ See Teresa Okure, "The New Testament Mercy, in *Concilium*, 2017, No.4, 21-29 at 23.

²² Pope Francis, *Misericordiae Vultus*, Bull of Indiction of the Extraordinary Jubilee of Mercy (Vatican City: Libereria Editrice Vaticana, 2016), no. 13.

²³ Okure, "The New Testament Mercy," 27.

[24] See Rotraud Wielandt, "Manifestations and Scope of God's Mercy in the Qur'an," in *Concilium*, 2017, No.4, 76-86 at 76.

[25] See Wielandt, "Manifestations and Scope of God's Mercy in the Qur'an," 78.

[26] See Gonsalves, "Mercy and Compassion: The Womb of Interfaith Dialogue," 328.

[27] Mata Amirtanandamayi, at the 2nd Parliament of World Religions held in Chicago in 1993. As quoted by Gonsalves, "Mercy and Compassion: The Womb of Interfaith Dialogue," 330.

[28] Thich Nhat Hanh, *Interbeing: Fourteen Gudielines for Engaged Buddhism*, rev. & ed. F. Eppsteiner (Berkeley, California, Parallax Press, 1993), 18. As quoted by Gonsalves, "Mercy and Compassion: The Womb of Interfaith Dialogue," 330.

[29] *The Hitavada*, Bhopal edition, Sunday, November 24, 2019, 3.

[30] See James Keenan, "The Evolution of the Works of Mercy," in *Concilium*, 2017, No.4, 33-43 at 33.

[31] See Keenan, "The Evolution of the Works of Mercy," 35.

[32] Rodney Stark, *The Rise of Christianity: A Sociologist Reconsiders History* (Princeton: Princeton University Press, 1996), 161. As quoted by Keenan, "The Evolution of the Works of Mercy," 38.

[33] See Stella Morraa, "Mercy (Re)forms the Church: a structural perspective," in *Concilium*, 2017, No.4, 44-53 at 50.

[34] Pope Francis, Apostolic Exhortation *Evangelii Gaudium* on the proclamation of the Gospel in today's world, (November 24, 2013), n. 49.

[35] The interview was published in the magazine *Credere*, 2 December 2015. For the English translation, cf. 'Text of Pope's Interview with Italian Jubilee Publication *"Credere"'* https://zenith.org).

[36] See Oscar Ante, OFM, "To be Missionary of Mercy, Servants of Compassion In Asia," in *Religious Life Asia*, Vol. 18/4 (October- December, 2016): 1-9 at 8.

[37] See Ante, OFM, "To be Missionary of Mercy," 9.

[38] Kavunkal SVD, "Showering Mercy to the World," 95.

11.

Pope Francis' Vision for a Youthful Church

An Ecclesiology for Young Millennials

Malleswararao Gh. (Jayaraj), SJ

Introduction

Pope Francis surprises everyone by his radical and relevant responses to the signs of the times. His announcement of a Synod of Bishops on young people in October 2018 was a memorable *Kairos* in the Catholic Church. The Synod engendered hope in young minds who strive for realistic guidelines for their present and the future. The purpose for the Synod is crystalized in the words of Cardinal Lorenzo Baldisseri, the Secretary General of the Secretariat of the Synod of Bishops, when he said that by discussing the theme for the Synod '*Youth, Faith and Vocational Discernment*' the Synod wishes to accompany young people along their existential journey by creating an opening for them to encounter God and humanity and actively take part in the building of the Church and society.

The whole process is a 'journey together' by the Church and the young people. It is a journey together towards fruitfulness in life and love. We perceive that during this journey, the Church not only looks to the young, rather "the Church in a special way sees herself in the young."[1] She is the real youth of the world for she "possesses what constitutes the strength and the charm of youth: the ability to rejoice with what is beginning, to give oneself unreservedly, to renew oneself and to set out again for new conquests."[2]

Therefore, in this paper I shall reflect on how the Church encounters young people and how Catholic young people envision a new Church that listens to their aspirations. The first part deals with the fraternal call by Pope Francis and shows how the Church encounters young Catholics in the postmodern world. In the second part, in order to build a foundation for a new model of the Church, certain aspects of the early Christian community and some of the renewed models of the Church envisioned in Vatican Council II (hereinafter VC II) will be highlighted. Finally, I explicate certain renewed attitudes of the Church in the light of the spirit of VC II and the Pope's summons, preparatory documents, Apostolic Exhortations such as *Evangelii Gaudium* (2013), *Christus Vivit* (2019) in order to draw out avenues for envisioning relevant models of church for young millennials. Pope Francis' vision for the young church is not a proposal for a new ecclesiology but a continuity with the spirit of VC II.

1. The State of Young People in a Postmodern World

The world is home to 1.8 billion young people. India has the world's largest youth population contributing to 41% of its population. It has more than 50% of its population below the age of 25 and more than 65% below the age of 35.[3] It is expected that, in 2020, the average age of an Indian will be 29 years. These numbers reveal to the Church in India that there is the abundance of youthful energy available at hand. Youth have the power to bring change and give hope to the hope-seeking nation and the Church in India.

Amidst the throwaway culture, globalization of indifference, technocracy, and fast-moving world, the young millennials are confused about how to choose what truly provides them lasting happiness. Even if they realize their capability to choose, it is confined only to the framework of industrial requirements. Beyond that, they seem lost in the world. Who is to blame? Certainly, not them! A tree has to be nurtured, a talent has to be developed, and a skill has to be mastered. Everything involves a process and a conducive atmosphere to grow and blossom.

For the country, youth are the trustees of prosperity. They are the power of prosperity. Nurture them, and they grow like a fruitful vine; if not, they erupt like a volcano. India saw the force of youth when they got involved in the Telangana movement, protested against the horrendous gang rape of Nirbhaya in 2012, raised an uproar against social discrimination of Rohit Vemula in 2016 and demanded a rollback of the fee-hike at Jawaharlal Nehru University (2019). These are only a few drops in the great ocean of youth power. Their involvement in politics improved civic engagement. 'Youth for Youth' was another realization that emerged out of these movements. The younger generation's fresh ideas and new leadership help the nation to overcome prevalent authoritarian practices. Protests led by youth leaders forced autocratic leaders to step down from power, allowing these youths to become part of formal decision-making processes.

In the postmodern world, the tendency is to brand youth as lost in the waywardness of modernity. This is tantamount to judging them unfairly. An old saying goes, 'Do not judge a book by its cover.' We do not judge them by their external living but delve into their attitudes and aspirations within. It is all about knowing what they seek. Their potential has to be awakened by continuous encouragement. We need to give them what they seek. Instead of repeating a litany of their weaknesses, applaud their new ideas, new capabilities and their search for a meaningful life. We need to allow them to build their future on their feet.

2. A Fraternal Call

'But forward, with courage,'[4] Pope Francis exhorted youth at the pre-synodal meet. His address unleashes the hidden power in youth to tell them the truth boldly. He invited them to speak courageously, and at the same time reminded them to listen with humility. Another call to young people was 'be brazen' with an assurance that their voice will be heard. He recognizes their potential saying that they are left alone many times but they are the builders of culture, with their style and with their originality.[5] He too gently pointed out the challenges lying before youth: lack of closeness (to one another and to the elders), neglecting the roots (not seizing the dreams of elders).[6] The upper most concern seems to be that 'they are in 'lack of a hand to hold on to'.

Having encouraged and challenged the youth, Pope Francis invites the shepherds of the flock to learn from them, to realize that they are protagonists, to discover the youthfulness of the Church and to tap the creativity of youth. His call truly is a parental concern of the Church to accompany her young children in their struggle to embrace the meaning of life amidst the complexities of choices placed before them during these 'times of uncertainty, volatility and insecurity.' Pre-synodal and post-synodal documents reflect broadly 'the specific realities, personalities, beliefs and experiences, the challenges and opportunities' of the young millennials of the world.

3. Encountering Young People

In his Apostolic Letter to the Youth of the World on the occasion of the International Youth Year, 1985, Pope John Paul II recognized the importance of youth in the Church with these words: "You young people are the ones who embody this youth: you are the youth of the nations and societies, the youth of every family and of all humanity; you are also the youth of the Church."[7] He said at an another occasion, "Young people are and ought to be encouraged to be active on behalf of the Church as leading characters in evangelization and participants in the renewal of society."[8] It is also befitting to add 'the renewal of the

Church." Young people are becoming more actively involved as leaders in the ecclesial community, above all through their membership in various groups.[9] According to Pudumaidoss, a theologian, analysis of Church law depicts youth as 'subjects on integral formation, youth as choice makers and youth as leaders'.[10] The Church too knows the basis of "the strength and beauty of young people, [namely] the ability to rejoice at the beginning of undertakings, to give oneself totally without going back, to pick oneself up and begin again in search of new conquests."[11]

Encounter involves listening to the voice of the youth and also understanding their identity, potential, involvement, relationships, challenges and opportunities in order to support them to live a meaningful, joyful and committed life for the common good. In this encounter, we learn who young people are and what the Church is.

3.1. Sense of Belonging

Young millennials have a sense of belonging. The preparatory document for the Synod for Youth held in October 2018 reiterates that the young people come from a multiplicity of worlds. This multiplicity could be geographical, historical and existential. Understanding youth from multiple terrains of backgrounds is always both an opportunity and a challenge for young people themselves as well as for the church. The document highlights 'belonging and participation' as one of the best characteristics of young people. However, there is always a swing between 'willingness and readiness to participate and commit themselves to concrete activities and their intolerance when they 'lack opportunities.' This leads to prominent struggles of the young people of 'resignation or fatigue in their will to desire, to dream and to plan, as seen in the diffusion of the phenomenon of NEET (not in education, employment or training).

At this juncture the basic means the Church could offer young people is the gift of discernment which involves the genuine actions of 'recognizing, interpreting and choosing' a life towards fullness of joy and setting a right example. The sense of belonging is one of the significant factors that lead to the shaping of one's identity. This sense of belonging and family sustains these young millennials on their journey. Pope Francis affirms that a common dream across continents and oceans is the desire to find a place where the young person can feel that he or she belongs. It is also expressed that without the anchor of community support and belonging, young people can feel isolated in the face of challenges.

3.2. Seeking a Living Example

Young millennials seek for role models who offer authentic examples of fruitful living. Young people look for persons of reference who are able to express empathy and offer them support, encouragement and help in recognizing their limits, but without making them feel they are being judged. The young cry out, 'many of us strongly want to know Jesus.' But in their struggle to build a true relationship they look out for 'authentic witnesses—men and women who vibrantly express their faith and relationship with Jesus while encouraging others to approach, meet, and fall in love with Jesus themselves.' They also seek for 'communities that empower them.' They seek 'to be listened to and not merely be spectators in society but active participants.'

When I asked a youth to come to the church, he replied, "What is there for me?" They are looking out for role models. They are striving to build a faith that brings meaning to their lives. 80% of Catholic youth leave the Church. The Church needs to continuously ask: 'why?' They are not a mere physical workforce of a parish. They are the potential spiritual force of the Church. The Church needs to accompany them to experience the love of Christ, in reality.

3.3. Striving for Higher Ideals

Young people work for better and higher ideals. They seek to engage with and address social justice issues of our time. They have a passion for political, civil and humanitarian activities. They opine that: 'We seek the opportunity to work towards building a better world.' It is evident that 'regardless of context, everyone shares the same innate desire for the higher ideals: peace, love, trust, equity, freedom and justice.' The radical involvement of Indian youth in social movements is a perfect example to such ethos of young people.

The focus in the Synod was on vocational discernment. The three verbs in *Evangelii Gaudium*, n.51 used to describe discernment are: "to recognize," "to interpret" and "to choose". They are invited to recognize the external and internal realities and interpret them in the light of faith and choose a path towards better life. When young people see this process of discernment as something to do with ideas, they are reminded that even in discernment, "realities are greater than ideas" (*Evangelii Gaudium*, n.231).

3.4. Digital Natives

Young millennials are digital natives. Young people say, "We are digital natives who could lead the way." Therefore, technology is another 'permanent part of the life of young people and must be understood as such.' Despite living in a hyper-connected world, there is a lack of spaces and opportunities to encounter difference. In addition, there exists a culture and dictatorship of appearances. The digital natives offer two concrete proposals regarding technology. They invite the Church to 'deepen her understanding of technology so as to assist us in discerning its usage' and to view technology as 'a fertile place for the New Evangelization'. It is necessary to offer formation to young people on how to live their digital lives.

3.5. Bound Together

Young men and women appreciate togetherness and collaboration with the opposite sex. A common perception that many young people have is an unclear role of women in the Church. They encourage the Church 'to deepen its understanding of the role of women. "What are the places where women can flourish within the Church and society?" ask young people. Some young women also feel that 'there is a lack of leading female role models within the Church.' They too wish to give their intellectual and professional gifts to the Church.

4. Criteria for Envisioning a New Model of the Church

Avery Dulles is convinced that a certain model always emerges from images within a paradigm, when he says, "When an image is employed reflectively and critically to deepen one's theoretical understanding of a reality it becomes what is today called a model."[12] According to him, "A model is accepted if it accounts for a large number of biblical and traditional data and accords with what history and experience tell us about the Christian life."[13] Thus, a good model must have:

> Basis in Scripture, basis in Christian tradition, capacity to give church members a sense of their corporate identity and mission, tendency to foster the virtues and values generally admired by Christians, correspondence with the religious experience of men (*sic*) today, theological fruitfulness, fruitfulness in enabling Church members to relate successfully to those outside their own group.[14]

Keeping the aforesaid guidelines for envisioning a model of the Church for young people, I proceed to explicate some of the liberative attitudes required for the Church. Those attitudes of the new Church envisioned by the young people are not exhaustive. The pilgrim Church continues to renew itself in order to respond to the signs of the times. Since every model of the Church has to resonate with the Biblical depiction of early Christian community I shall look into certain characteristics of the Church in early Christian Community.

Thomas G. Guirano says, "Models of the Church was far from anything like the notion that the Church needed to be remade in every generation."[15] I would definitely refute his understanding because Avery Dulles through his models of the Church clearly indicates that every model of church arose from the way it responded to the situations that challenged the Church.

4.1. *The Characteristics of the Early Church*

Acts 2:41-47 sums up the characteristics which marked the early Church. The early Church was 'a learning Church, a praying Church, a reverent Church, a happening Church, a sharing Church, a happy Church, a likable Church and a pilgrim Church.'[16] It is very clear how they kept listening to the teaching of the apostles (v. 42). Barclay states, "A real

Church is always a learning Church and a real Christian is always a learning Christian."[17] The Church learns about itself which we call self-retrospection and about the world. They not only persevere in listening to the apostles teach; they also persevered in prayer.

Whenever they faced with troubles, they knew that they could not face all this without the help which God could give them. We should always be reverent when we come to church because in the church in a very special sense we are in the presence of God. They too tell us that many wonders and signs were done by the apostles. It was a church where sick people were cured and where bad people were made good. In a real church things still happen. It was also a sharing Church. Those who were rich shared all they had with those who were poor.

Further, looking into the Gospels, we realize that "behind all the diversity and dynamism of the New Testament Church lies the common heritage of the Christian faith."[18] George Soares also presents certain attitudes of the early Church: eschatological detachment (1 Cor 7:29-31); social protest; taking up the stern warning uttered by Jesus in Mk 10:23-25; Mt 6:24; Lk 16:19-30) to reaffirmation of the privileged state of the poor (echoing the beatitudes of Jesus in Lk 6:20-21); and to a strong social protest against the oppressive actions of the rich (woes uttered by Jesus in Lk 6:24-25).[19] Another important attitude of ' love-communism' remains a unique experiment in the New Testament Church.[20] Ultimately, Soares emphasises that the Jesus community remains as the archetype of the Church. Jesus community is 'a community of radical freedom, radical universalism, radical sharing, radical service and radical equality.'[21]

Radical vision of Jesus community, the real Church of early Christian community should propel us to establish a prototype community here and now and a community that listens to the young people and responds to them by revisioning the attitudes of the Church for the youth.

5. Envisioning a Church for Young People

This involves knowing what kind of Church young people envision for themselves. Hearing their voices in the synodal documents, we could envisage a church that is dear to the young people.

5.1. A Welcoming Church

The Church oftentimes appears to be associated with excessive moralism. Sometimes, in the Church, it is hard to overcome the logic of 'it has always been done this way'. Young people feel that they need a Church that is always 'welcoming and merciful, which appreciates its roots and patrimony and which loves everyone, even those who are not following the perceived standards.'[22] *Lumen Gentium* clearly states that "At all times and every race God has given welcome to whosoever fears him and does what is right."[23] Church as the sacrament of the Kingdom of God which was compared to a seed growing into a big tree accommodating every bird of the air, requires to welcome young people providing them an abode of comfort and a sense of freedom.

5.2. A Healed and A Healing Church

The Church needs to better support the young and provide avenues to assist them in their healing. The Church can play a vital role in ensuring that the young are not marginalized but feel accepted. They also desire to see a Church that is 'empathetic and reaches out to those struggling on the margins, the persecuted and the poor.' We know that 'an attractive Church is a relational Church.'[24] In its relation to the people of God, she heals herself and heals young people. In the depiction of early Christian community, we acknowledged that it was a happening Church where healing and caring was part of the community living. An agapeic expression of Christian faith is always in getting healed by God and making that enduring grace of healing to people around you.

5.3. A Credible/Authentic Church

Today's young people are longing for an authentic Church. A credible Church is one which is not afraid to allow itself be vulnerable. Young people express a desire to see a Church that is a living testimony to what it teaches and witnesses to authenticity. They expect the leaders of the Church— ordained, religious, and lay—to be the finest example of this. They want the hierarchy of the Church, to be a 'transparent, welcoming, honest, inviting, communicative, accessible, joyful and interactive community.'[25] In short, the social and spiritual aspects of Church should complement each other.

5.4. *A Participatory Church*
Young people have difficulty finding a space in the Church where they can actively participate and lead. Young people interpret their experience of the Church as one where they are considered too young and inexperienced to lead or make decisions as they would only make mistakes. The Church needs to involve young people in its decision-making processes and offer them more leadership roles. These positions need to be on a parish, diocesan, national and international level, even on a commission to the Vatican. They wish that their 'prominent creative voice' is heard at all levels.

5.5. *A Street Church*
The demand on the Church is to 'walk with young people'. The Church is called to 'Go out, see and call.' This Gospel call of "going out", "seeing" and "calling" requires a willingness to spend time with them, to listen to the story of their lives and to be attentive to their joys, hopes, sadness and anxieties. They like the Church to meet them in the various places. Above all, the place in which they wish to be met by the Church is 'the streets, where all people are found'. The Church should try to find creative new ways to encounter people where they are comfortable and where they naturally socialize: bars, coffee shops, parks, gyms, stadiums and any other popular cultural center. In short, they should be met where they are: intellectually, emotionally, spiritually, socially and physically.

5.6. *An Accompanying Church*

The Church is self-examining herself on how to accompany young people to accept God's call to the joy of love and the fullness of life. Accompanying young people requires going beyond a preconceived framework, encountering young people where they are, adapting to their times and pace of life and taking them seriously. The demand on the Church is to 'walk with young people' wherein the Church is called to 'Go out, see and call.' In the task of accompanying the younger generation, the Church accepts her call to collaborate in the joy of young people rather than be tempted to take control of their faith (2 Cor 1:24). Walking with young people builds up the entire Christian community.

Conclusion

I have analysed how the Church encounters and understands young people. In her encounter with the young, the Church knows them. Catholic youth have the sense of belonging which permeates first in their own family and further spreads to the Church. They seek for an authentic example. They work for better and higher ideals. As they work for those higher ideals, they too express their need for discernment. The Church has begun to understand that youth see themselves as digital natives. Thus, the invitation is to make use of media as a vital instrument for new evangelisation. Youth like to be together and work together; as a consequence, they look for greater empowerment of women so as to enhance their participation in the decision-making processes of the Church.

Having encountered youth and having listened to their voices, after briefly looking back to the characteristics of the early Church in the Gospels, a new Church is envisioned by the young people. This new Church has to be one which is welcoming, accompanying, healing and healed, credible, authentic, participatory and ready to venture out into the streets where the poor are. These attributes and models resonate with the renewed spirit of VC II on the self-understanding of the Church as a communion of the people of God.

Pope Francis' fruitful journey of encountering young people and envisioning a youthful church for them clearly indicates that his vision of the Church for them is based on the spirit of the Gospel. It is clear that He is not writing a new text for a new ecclesiology, rather he is giving a practical application and concrete interpretation of what it means to be a youthful church. These attitudes may animate their faith and vocational discernment to make the Church in India come alive. These attitudes of the new Church envisioned by the young people are not exhaustive. The pilgrim church continues to renew itself in order to respond to the signs of the times. Indeed, it is an opportunity for the Church in India to realize Pope Francis' vision for young Indian millennials.

Endnotes

[1] John Paul II, *Dilecti Amici* (Apostolic Letter to the Youth of the World on the Occasion of the International Youth Year, March 3, 1985), n.15.

[2] John Paul II, *Dilecti Amici*, n.16.

[3] Ministry of Home Affairs of India, *Age Structure*, 2011 census data, http://censusindia.gov.in/Census_And_You/age_structure_and_marital_status.aspx (accessed on September 3, 2018).

[4] Pope Francis, 'Pre-synodal meeting with Young people at the International Pontifical College Maria Mater Ecclesiae', March 19, 2018, http://www.synod2018.va/content/synod2018/en.html (accessed on July 12, 2018).

[5] Ibid.

[6] Ibid.

[7] John Paul II, *Dilecti Amici*, n.1.

[8] John Paul II, *Christifideles Laici* (Post-synodal Apostolic Exhortation on the Vocation and the Mission of the Lay Faithful in the Church and in the World, December 30, 1988), n.46.

[9] John Paul II, *Pastores Dabo Vobis* (Post-synodal Apostolic Exhortation on the Formation of Priests in the Circumstances of the Present Day, March 25, 1992), n.9.

[10] Jesu Pudumaidoss, "The Portrait of Youth in Church Law," *Youth India: Situation, Challenges & Prospects*, ed. idem, F.V. Anthony, J. Vallabaraj, C. De Souza, J.S. Devadoss (Bangalore: Kristu Jyothi Publications, 2006), 302.

[11] Pope Paul VI, *Message of Vatican II to Young People* (Address to the Young Men and Women of the World, December 8, 1965).

¹² Avery Dulles, *Models of the Church* (New York: Doubleday & Company, 1974), 21.

¹³ Avery Dulles, *Models of the Church*, 22.

¹⁴ Avery Dulles, *Models of the Church*, 180-181.

¹⁵ Thomas G. Guirano, 'Why Avery Dulles Matters', *First things*, Issue archive (May,2009) http://www.firstthings.com/article/2009/04/why-avery-dulles-matters-1243317340 [accessed 8 September 2018].

¹⁶ William Barclay, *God's Young Church* (Edinburgh: The Saint Andrew Press, 1970), 17-24.

¹⁷ William Barclay, *God's Young Church*, 17.

¹⁸ George Soares Prabhu, "The New Testament Church and the Economic Liberation of Man," in *Collected Writings of George M. Soares Prabhu, S.J.*, ed. F. X. D'SA, vol. 4 (Jnana Deepa Vidyapeeth: Pune, 2001), 127.

¹⁹ Ibid., 129-132.

²⁰ Ibid., 133.

²¹ George Soares Prabhu, "Radical Beginnings: The Jesus Community as the Archetype of the Church," in *Collected Writings of George M. Soares Prabhu, S.J.*, ed. F. X. D'SA, vol.4 (Jnana Deepa Vidyapeeth: Pune, 2001),136-149.

²² *Instrumentum Laboris for Synod 2018,* 'Young People, The Faith and The Vocation Discernment', Pre-Synodal Meeting, Final Document, XV Ordinary General Assembly (Rome, 2018), http:// www. synod2018. va/content/synod 2018/en/ fede-discernimento-vocazione/instrumentum-laboris-for-the-synod-2018—young-people—the-faith.html (accessed on September 4, 2018).

²³ Second Vatican Council, *Lumen Gentium* [Dogmatic Constitution on the Church], November 21,1964, in *Vatican Council II: The Conciliar and Post Conciliar Documents*, ed. Austin Flannery, O.P. (Mumbai: St Pauls, 2001), n. 9.

²⁴ *Instrumentum Laboris* for Synod 2018, 5.

²⁵ Ibid., 7.

12.

Called to Be Friends of Christ

Pope Francis' Call to Youth to Humanize the World

Thomas Karimundackal, SJ

Introduction

Throughout his pontificate, Pope Francis has emphasised the role of youth in the Church and in society at large. Moreover, on many occasions he has shared how essential it is for young people to be open to the needs of society, listening to the elderly and learning from their own roots. In tone and approach, *Christus Vivit* (hereinafter *CV*)—the post-synodal apostolic exhortation published on April 2, 2019,[1] in response to the Ordinary Synod on Young People, the Faith, and Vocational Discernment held in October 2018—expresses the pope's concerns about today's 'youth reality' and his own suggestions for channelising their creative energy for humanising society. Thus, *Christus Vivit*, which is the fruit of a listening and discerning process, is born from the pope's desire to give a synodal orientation to the young people in the Church. The 182-page document reads like a compilation of wisdom sayings from a sage who is sharing his wisdom with youth, with great affection and encouragement.² Throughout the document the pope presents Jesus as the model par excellence for young people, and exhorts them to learn from Jesus, the ever young, to have a personal encounter and friendship with him, and finally to act and live like him to transform the society where they live. This paper is an attempt to read *Christus Vivit* to elicit the pope's dreams and concerns for Christ-centered youth in the Church and the world, at large.

1. **Christ-Centered Youth: The Core Message of *Christus Vivit***

The Christocentric nature of *Christus Vivit* can be vividly seen in the articulation of its title, and in its introduction and conclusion. While the title of the document, *Christus Vivit*, i.e., 'Christ is alive' highlights Pope Francis' desire to have a Christocentric focus to the document, the introduction and conclusion of the document serve as an *inclusio* to the theme already introduced in the title itself. While in the previous apostolic exhortations Pope Francis has used the theme of 'joy' as his starting point,³ in this exhortation he gives the reason for our joy: "Christ is alive!" (*CV* 1). That is to say, with the title *Christus Vivit*, he exemplifies his call for the kerygmatic evangelisation contained in his previous documents.⁴

The document begins with these introductory words: "Christ is alive! He is our hope, and in a wonderful way he brings youth to our world. The very first words, then, that I would like to say to every young Christian are these: Christ is alive and he wants you to be alive!" (*CV* 1). The phrase "Christ is alive" is used twice in these introductory verses to amplify the pope's focus in the document, i.e., "Christ is alive and he wants *you* (young people) to be alive!" Thus, the pope makes a clarion call to the young to be alive by relating reciprocally the 'living presence of the Risen Lord' in the world with their lively presence in the world. "Christ is alive!" As we understand it in the Scriptures, this was not only the experience of Jesus' disciples, apostles and the early Christian community, but it is also the faith experience of every Christian believer (cf. Jn 20:1-29; Heb 7:24-25; 1 Pet 3:18; Lk 24:1-53;

Mt 28:1-20; Mk 16:1-20; 1 Cor 15:3-8,14-21; Rom1:3-4; 6:3-11; 2 Tim 2:8). Therefore, the pope's invitation to youth to be alive is based on the Church's foundational experience of Christ's living presence in the world.

Our faith in the Risen Lord, i.e., Christ who is alive among us, leads us into a hope, because he himself becomes our hope (cf. 1 Cor 15:19; Col 1:27; 1 Pet 1:3-5). So, immediately after the dogmatic assertion, "Christ is alive," the pope relates the life of youth in the world to the hope that the Risen Lord radiates in the world: "He (Christ) is our hope, and in a wonderful way he brings youth to our world" (*CV* 1). We know that our hope in Christ will not disappoint us during our journey towards eternal life, because on that day when hope realizes its final fulfillment, we shall be like Him and see Him as He is (cf. Jn 3:16; 1 Jn 3:2-3; 5:13-14). Our hope in Christ causes us not to get discouraged, not to give up, because we have something to look forward to (cf. Phil 1:6; 3:13-14; 1 Pet 5:10; Tit 3:4-7), and we are saved in the hope of Christ alone (cf. Rom 8:24-25; Heb 3:6; 7:25). Therefore, the pope relates the hope of the young with Christ who is the hope itself.

Soon after these introductory words, Pope Francis continues in the document:

> He is in you, he is with you and he never abandons you. However far you may wander, he is always there, the Risen One. He calls you and he waits for you to return to him and start over again. When you feel you are growing old out of sorrow, resentment or fear, doubt or failure, he will always be there to restore your strength and your hope (*CV* 2).

Indeed, these words further reveal the Christo-centric nature of youth that the pope envisions in *Christus Vivit*. The pope affirms that the Risen Lord present in creation is very specifically and personally present in youth wherever and however they are: the clauses "he is in you, he is with you" will definitely remind us of the Johannine imagery of Christ's indwelling presence in the believers (Jn 14:20.23; 15:4-7; 17:23.26). Likewise, the pope's assertion: "he never abandons you ... he calls you and he waits for you to return to him and start over again" may invite us to recall the parable of the Good Samaritan (Lk 10:25-37), and the lost and found parables in Luke: lost sheep (a man celebrating with his friends; 15:4-7), lost coin (a woman celebrating with her friends; 15:8-10), climaxing with the lost son (a father celebrating with his household; 15:11-32). So the pope wants to tell young people that, like the Good Samaritan (Lk 10:25-37), Christ will never abandon them; like the Good Shepherd (Lk 15:4-7; Mt 18:12-14; Jn 10:1-21), Christ will always seek, care and protect them; like the Father who is prodigal in love (Lk 15:11-32), Christ will always wait for their return, and on their return will celebrate with them.

The all-enveloping presence of Christ is further explained by the next verse: "When you feel you are growing old out of sorrow, resentment or fear, doubt or failure, He will always be there to restore your strength and your hope" (*CV* 2). Certainly, the first imagery comes to our mind when we read this from Mt 11:28-30 where Jesus says, "Come to me, all you who are weary and burdened, and I will give you rest. Take my yoke upon you and learn from me; for I am gentle and humble in heart, and you will find rest for your souls. For my yoke is easy and my burden is light." It is very clear from Scripture that we find our strength in God alone (cf. Pss 6:1-3; 9:9-10; 32:7-8; 34:10b.17; Prov 18:10; Neh 8:10; Isa 26: 3-4; 30:15; 41:10; Ex 15:2; 33:14; Deut 31:8; 33:27; 1 Chr 16:11). It can be so easy to give in to worry, fear and despair, but with him we can find strength, and look forward to wonderful things. He gives us hope! (cf. Lk 12:25-26; Phil 4:6; Jn 14:27; 1 Pet 5:7; Josh 1:9; Isa 43:1-3; 12:2; Pss 34:4; 27:1-3; 145:18-19). Through faith in Christ we are given a spirit of power, love and discipline, and for that reason we have nothing to fear. We can hold on to his promises and be confident that he will see us through even in the darkest of days (cf. 2 Tim 1:7; Pss 138:3; 16:8; 62:1-2; 112:1, 7-8; 91:1-2; 112:1,7-8). Though we are not promised an easy life, we are told that Christ will be there with us when we believe in him, that he will not give us more than we can handle with his help, and even our hard times can be used to glorify God (2 Cor 12:9; Phil 4: 12-13; 2 Thess 3:3; 1 Pet 5: 10; Heb 4:16; 2 Thess 3:16).

In short, through the introductory verses of *Christus vivit* (*CV* 1-2) Pope Francis makes young people aware that they are to call on Christ, and that he will hear them and give them strength, hope and grace sufficient to carry them throughout their life. He will be their ever-present help when they are in need, and he can give them a peace that passes all understanding. For me that is extremely encouraging!

As a conclusion to *Christus vivit*, Pope Francis invites young people to keep running, attracted by the face of Christ who loves them so much:

> Dear young people, my joyful hope is to see you keep running the race before you, outstripping all those who are slow or fearful. Keep running, attracted by the face of Christ, whom we love so much, whom we adore in the Holy Eucharist and acknowledge in the flesh of our suffering brothers and sisters (*CV* 299).

Thus, keeping the Pauline imagery of running race for Christ in mind (cf. 2 Tim 4:7), the pope reminds young people to draw inspiration from the Risen Lord, who manifests himself in the Eucharist, and intervenes in the concrete flux of human history, especially giving hope and deliverance to every form of human suffering. In short, at the end of the document the pope wants young people to know that they are called to be alive as Christ is alive amongst them, with a heart capable of dreaming, of looking for great things and of committing themselves to build a better world. Throughout the exhortation, Pope Francis maintains this Christocentric focus by constantly inviting young people to have a personal encounter and friendship with Christ. Following is an attempt to read *Christus Vivit* in this perspective.

2. Jesus: The Inspiring Model

In the first chapter, Pope Francis presents the witness of youths whom God called throughout salvation history—with Jesus at the centre-stage—to show how often Scripture speaks of young people. Here the focus is to invite young people to live differently by committing themselves to Christ by drawing inspirations from the people who lived differently in the Old and New Testaments: the pope says, "we should never repent of spending our youth being good, opening our heart to the Lord, and living differently" (*CV* 17). In spite of the varied perceptions of the world, the pope says that God sees young people differently (cf. 1 Sam 16:7). He recalls that "in an age when young people were not highly regarded, some texts show that God sees them differently" (*CV* 6). He, then, briefly presents figures of young people from the Old Testament who lived differently from their contemporaries, namely Joseph and Gideon (*CV* 7), Samuel (*CV* 8), King David (*CV* 9), Solomon and Jeremiah (*CV* 10), the very young Jewish servant of Naaman, and the young Ruth (*CV* 11).

While citing the young who lived differently from the New Testament (*CV*12-21), the pope recalls that "Jesus, who is eternally young, wants to give us hearts that are ever young" (*CV* 13). As a parting shot in this chapter, the pope presents Jesus as 'the model par excellence' before the young people: "If you have lost your inner vitality, your dreams, your enthusiasm, your optimism and your generosity, Jesus stands before you as once he stood before the dead son of the widow, and with all the power of his resurrection he urges you: "Young man, I say to you, arise!" (Lk 7:14; *CV* 20).

3. Learn from Jesus, the Ever Young

As a continuation from the previous chapter, chapter two presents Jesus, ever young as the model par excellence for the youth of today. Quoting St Irenaeus, Pope writes: "Jesus is 'young among the young in order to be an example for the young and to consecrate them to the Lord'" (*CV* 22). The Pope begins with the Lukan narrative of the boy Jesus at the Temple where he is conversing with the teachers and elders of the community (Lk 2:41-52; *CV* 26). We should not think, the pope writes, that "Jesus was a withdrawn adolescent or a self-absorbed youth. His relationships were those of a young person who shared fully in the life of his family and his people", and "no one regarded him as unusual or set apart from others" (*CV* 28).

Quoting from his previous exhortation *Amoris Laetitia* (*AL* 384), the pope says that "Jesus did not grow up in a narrow and stifling relationship with Mary and Joseph, but readily interacted with the wider family, the relatives of his parents and their friends" (*CV* 29). The pope further points out the cordial relationship that Jesus enjoyed with his parents and others: "thanks to the trust of his parents", the adolescent Jesus, "can move freely and learn to journey with others" (*CV* 29) he says that these aspects of Jesus' life should not be ignored in youth ministry, "lest we create projects that isolate young people from their family and the larger community, or turn them into a select few, protected from all contamination" (*CV* 30). Rather, we need "projects that can strengthen them, accompany them and impel them to encounter others, to engage in generous service, in mission" (*CV* 30), because "the Lord is calling us to enkindle stars in the night of other young people" (*CV* 33).

Pope Francis further emphasises Jesus' presence with the young people saying that Jesus is not an outside reality but an indwelling reality, a youth he shares with the young people of the world today: [Jesus] "does not teach you, young people, from afar or from without, but from within your very youth, a youth he shares with you and in him many aspects typical of young hearts can be recognized" (*CV* 31). The pope further portrays Jesus as a source of inspiration for all their dreams, projects, ideals etc.: [With] "him at our side, we can drink from the true wellspring that keeps alive all our dreams, our projects, our great ideals, while impelling us to proclaim what makes life truly worthwhile" *(CV 32)*.

Pope Francis speaks of the youth of the Church as people who experience the daily presence of Christ and the power of his Spirit in their lives: "The Church is young when she is herself, when she receives ever anew the strength born of God's word, the Eucharist, and the daily presence of Christ and the power of his Spirit in our lives" (*CV* 35). Further, the pope exhorts the youth of the Church to reflect Christ in their day-to-day life: "as members of the Church, we should not stand apart from others", yet at the same time, "we must dare to be different, to point to ideal excessively caught up in herself but instead, and above all, reflect Jesus Christ" (*CV* 39). Therefore, he prays: "let us ask the

Lord to free the Church from those who would make her grow old, encase her in the past, hold her back or keep her at a standstill" (*CV* 35).

4. Youth are the 'Now' of Christ

Chapter three (*CV* 64-110) presents youth as the 'now' of God,' by presenting various factors that affect the youth of today, namely various ways of being young (*CV* 68-70) and experiences of young people (*CV* 71-85), the effects of digital environment (*CV* 86-90), migration (*CV* 91-94), every form of abuse (*CV* 95-102), and finally proposing a way out (*CV* 103-110). The title of the chapter, namely, "You are the 'now' of God" itself demonstrates God's (Christ's) active presence in the youth of today. Thus, once again Pope Francis affirms that young people are Christ's visible manifestation today. Therefore, at the outset of the chapter he says that we cannot just say that "young people are the future of our world", but "they are its present; even now, they are helping to enrich it" (*CV* 64). For this reason, the pope says that it is necessary to listen to them even if "there is a tendency to provide prepackaged answers and ready-made solutions, without allowing their real questions to emerge and facing the challenges they pose" (*CV* 65). Therefore, the pope exhorts to all who are involved in the care of young people to see them as God the Father sees them: "Whoever is called to be a father, pastor and youth guide should have the ability to discern pathways where others only see walls, to recognize potential where others see only peril. That is how God the Father sees things; He knows how to cherish and nurture the seeds of goodness sown in the hearts of the young" (*CV* 67).

Pope Francis reminds young people that "there is a way out" in all dark and painful situations (*CV* 103-110). Again, according to him this "way out" is Christ centered, because he reminds the young people that the Good News is received on the morning of the resurrection: "I remind you of the good news we received as a gift on the morning of the resurrection: that in all the dark or painful situations that we mentioned, there is a way out" (*CV* 104). Ultimately, the pope exhorts young people to trust in the Lord to renew them in all their dark and painful situations: "If you are young in years, but feel weak, weary or disillusioned, ask Jesus to renew you ... Jesus, brimming with life, wants to help you make your youth worthwhile" (*CV* 109). Finally, the pope asks them to grow in friendship, friendship with Christ and others, a theme that he has already developed in chapter two, otherwise he warns them that if we grow too isolated "it is very difficult to fight against... the snares and temptations of the devil, and the selfishness of the world" (*CV* 110) because "isolation ... saps our strength and exposes us to the worst evils of our time" (*CV* 110).

5. Christ is Alive Today

With the self-explanatory title, 'a great message for all young people', chapter four switches to a personal address aimed directly at the young. Pope Francis wants all young people to know that God loves them, Christ saves them and the Spirit of Jesus is alive today! In a very personal manner the pope says: "I now wish to speak to young people about what is essential, the one thing we should never keep quiet about. It is a message containing three great truths. [...]. The very first truth I would tell each of you is this: "God loves you". It makes no difference whether you have already heard it or not. [...] The second great truth is that Christ, out of love, sacrificed himself completely in order to save you. [...] Finally, there is a third truth, inseparable from the second: Christ is alive!" (*CV* 111, 112, 118, 124).

Pope Francis intently calls the attention of the young people to the tender love and compassion of God saying, "God loves you, never doubt this" (*CV* 112). You can "find security in the embrace of your heavenly Father" (*CV* 113). The Pope affirms that the memory of the Father "is not a 'hard disk' that 'saves' and 'archives' all our data. His memory is a heart filled with tender compassion, one that finds joy in 'deleting' from us every trace of evil. Because he loves you" (*CV* 115). His love, the pope says, is one that "has to do more with raising up than knocking down, with reconciling than forbidding, with offering new changes than condemning, with the future than the past" (*CV* 116).

While speaking about the second truth, "Christ saves you," Pope Francis once again emphasizes the need for a friendship with Christ. He exhorts the young people of today not to forget that "He forgives us seventy times seven. Time and time again, He bears us on his shoulders" (*CV* 119). The pope assures young people that Jesus loves them and saves them because "only what is loved can be saved. Only what is embraced can be transformed. The Lord's love is greater than all our problems, frailties and flaws" (*CV* 120). The pope further substantiates this idea with Christ's priceless love: "His forgiveness and salvation are not something we can buy, or that we have to acquire by our own works or efforts. He forgives us and sets us free without cost" (*CV* 121). In describing the salvation Jesus offers, the pope points to the beauty of the Christian message, "how valuable must you be, if you were redeemed by the precious blood of Christ! Dear young people, 'You are priceless! You are not up for sale!'" (*CV* 122*).* The Pope then provides a touching imagery to captivate the minds of young people, "keep your eyes fixed on the outstretched arms of Christ crucified" (*CV* 123).

While explaining the third truth "He is alive," Pope Francis once again calls their attention to the very title of his exhortation, which is the foundation of Christian faith itself: "He is alive!" He reminds them that "We need to keep reminding ourselves of this...because we can risk seeing Jesus Christ simply as a fine model from the distant past, as a memory, as someone who saved us two thousand years ago. But that would be of no use to us: it would leave us unchanged; it would not set us free" (*CV* 124). Therefore, the pope again appeals to the young to "see Jesus as happy, overflowing with joy. Rejoice with him as with a friend who has triumphed" (*CV* 126). Since he lives with us "there can be no doubt that goodness will have the upper hand in your life... then we can stop complaining and look to the future, for with him this is always possible" (*CV* 127). Thus, the pope presents with joy the central truth of the Christian faith: Jesus Christ is risen from the dead and offers us eternal life.

Affirming the centrality of our faith in the Risen Christ, Pope Francis states that "every other solution will prove inadequate and temporary [. . .]. with Jesus, on the other hand, our hearts experience a security that is firmly rooted and enduring" (*CV*128). The encounter and friendship with the risen Lord become the sustaining force of the entire Christian life. Here, the pope again relies upon a favourite quotation from his predecessor Pope Benedict XVI, "Being a Christian is not the result of an ethical choice or a lofty idea, but the encounter with an event, a person, which gives life a new horizon and a decisive direction" (*CV* 129; cf. *Deus Caritas Est* 1). The pope further emphatically states that an encounter and friendship with the living Christ is the only way of sustaining their entire Christian life: "If in your heart you can learn to appreciate the beauty of this message, if you are willing to encounter the Lord, if you are willing to let him love you and save you, if you can make friends with him and start to talk to him, the living Christ, about the realities of your life, then you will have a profound experience capable of sustaining your entire Christian life" (*CV* 129). This theme of encounter with the risen Lord repeats itself throughout the remainder of this Exhortation.

In these truths, where the role of the Father and Jesus is emphasized, the presence and role of the Holy Spirit is also articulated. Pope Francis says:

> Wherever the Father and the Son are, there too is the Holy Spirit. He is the one who quietly opens hearts to receive that message. He keeps alive our hope of salvation, and he will help you grow in joy if you are open to his working. The Holy Spirit fills the heart of the risen Christ and then flows over into your lives. When you receive the Spirit, he draws you ever more deeply into the heart of Christ, so that you can grow in his love, his life and his power" (*CV* 131).

Therefore, the pope asks to "invoke the Holy Spirit each day" (*CV* 131) so that "he can change your life, fill it with light and lead it along a better path. He takes nothing away from you, but instead helps you to find all that you need, and in the best possible way" (*CV* 131), for

"God's love has been poured into our hearts through the Holy Spirit who has been given to us" (*CV* 132).

6. Friendship with Christ is the Best Dream

The key to making the truths mentioned in chapter four in reality is friendship with the Lord. Therefore, the next chapter entitled "Paths of Youth" elaborates on the ways and means of making friendship with the Lord. At the outset of the chapter Pope Francis asks: "What does it mean to live the years of our youth in the transforming light of the Gospel?" (*CV* 134). Answering this query, he articulates the gracious status of youth: "youth, more than a source of pride, is a gift of God: To be young is a grace, a blessing. It is a gift that we can squander meaninglessly, or receive with gratitude and live to the full" (*CV* 134). He adds, "God is the giver of youth and he is at work in the life of each young person. Youth is a blessed time for the young and a grace for the Church and for the world. It is a joy, a song of hope and a blessing" (*CV* 135).

Having emphasized the gracious status of youth Pope Francis says that it is "a time of dreams and decisions" (*CV* 136-143), fuelled with "thirst for life and experience" (*CV* 144-149). The Pope states that "the love of God and our relationship with the living Christ does not hold us back from dreaming; they do not require us to narrow our horizons. On the contrary, that love elevates us, encourages us and inspires us to a better and more beautiful life" (*CV* 138). According to the pope, the best way to live fully the years of youth is to cultivate friendship with Christ (*CV* 150-157). The Pope reminds young people that they will not know the "deepest and fullest" meaning of their early years unless they encounter each day their best friend, the friend who is Jesus (*CV* 150). Having explained the beauty of true friendship (*CV* 151-152), the pope relates these qualities of friendship to Jesus' friendship with the young. He writes, "with the same love that Christ pours out on us, we can love him in turn and share his love with others, in the hope that they too will take their place in the community of friendship he established" (*CV* 153). "Friendship with Jesus cannot be broken. He never leaves us, even though at times it appears that he keeps silent"

(*CV* 154). "With a friend, we can speak and share our deepest secrets. With Jesus too, we can always have a conversation" (*CV* 155). Therefore, the pope asks youth: "Do not deprive your youth of this friendship. You will be able to feel him at your side" (*CV* 156). To begin and maintain this friendship, the pope encourages regular prayer, which he calls "both a challenge and an adventure." He writes: "prayer enables us to share with him every aspect of our lives and to rest confidently in his embrace. At the same time, it gives us a share in his own life and love. When we pray, "we open everything we do" to him, and we give him room "so that he can act, enter and claim victory"" (*CV* 155). Quoting Saint Oscar Romero, the pope further reveals Christ's personal love for every Christian: "Christianity is a person who loved me immensely, who demands and asks for my love. Christianity is Christ" (*CV* 156).

This chapter began with emphasizing the gracious status of youth as "a time of dreams and decisions" (*CV* 136-143) and in *CV* 157 the pope identifies Jesus as fullest form of dream that anyone can dream. He says:

> Jesus can bring all the young people of the Church together in a single dream, "a great dream, a dream with a place for everyone. The dream for which Jesus gave his life on the cross [....] A dream whose name is Jesus, planted by the Father in the confidence that it would grow and live in every heart. A concrete dream who is a person, running through our veins, thrilling our hearts and making them dance (*CV* 157).

Speaking of growth and maturity, Pope Francis explains the importance of seeking spiritual development, of seeking Christ and keeping his Word, of maintaining the connection with him:

> That is why you need to stay connected to Jesus, to "remain online" with him, since you will not grow happy and holy by your own efforts and intelligence alone. Just as you try not to lose your connection to the internet, make sure that you stay connected to the Lord. That means not cutting off dialogue, listening to him, sharing your life with him and, whenever you aren't sure what you should do, asking him: "Jesus, what would you do in my place? (*CV* 158).

While speaking about the richness of growing older, Pope Francis asks young people to keep "preserving and cherishing the most precious things about our youth" by letting "themselves be loved by God," and by sharing "more of his friendship, more fervour in prayer, more hunger for his word, more longing to receive Christ in the Eucharist, more desire to live by his Gospel, more inner strength, more peace and spiritual joy" (*CV* 161). Again, here the pope is concerned about forming young people who are deeply in friendship with Christ.

Friendship with Christ should lead young people to choose the paths of fraternity (*CV* 163-167), because the pope says that "spiritual growth is expressed above all by your growth in fraternal, generous and merciful love" (*CV* 163). Pope Francis further reiterates this saying, "the Holy Spirit wants to make us come out of ourselves, to embrace others with love and to seek their good" (*CV* 164). "[God] wants them especially to share in the joy of fraternal communion, the sublime joy felt by those who share with others, for "it is more blessed to give than to receive" (Acts 20:35) [...] Fraternal love multiplies our ability to experience joy, since it makes us rejoice in the good of others" (*CV* 167). The pope then wishes young people praying, "may your youthful spontaneity increasingly find expression in fraternal love and a constant readiness to forgive, to be generous, and to build community" (*CV* 167). According to the pope, "it involves living in the midst of society and the world in order to bring the Gospel everywhere, to work for the growth of peace, harmony, justice, human rights and mercy, and thus for the extension of God's kingdom in this world" (*CV* 168).

While asking the young people to commit themselves for the humanization of the world, Pope Francis asks them "to go beyond their small groups and to build "social friendship, where everyone works for the common good" (*CV* 169). When "the world is destroyed by enmity" he asks them dare to pursue with passion to "build bridges and make peace for the benefit of all" (*CV* 169), and to engage in various social programmes that build bridges between the peoples and uplift their socio-economic situations (*CV* 171-172). Here again the pope says that, they can confront these realities with creativity and hope with faith in the risen Lord (*CV* 173). Once again, the pope asks them to draw inspiration from Jesus who got involved in human history to be the protagonists of the transformation of society, and therefore, he encourages them saying:

> I want to encourage all of you in this effort, because I know that "your young hearts want to build a better world. [....] Please, do not leave it to others to be protagonists of change. You are the ones who hold the future! Through you, the future enters into the world. I ask you also to be protagonists of this transformation. [...] I ask you to build the future, to work for a better world. Dear young people, please, do not be bystanders in life. Get involved! Jesus was not a bystander. He got involved. Don't stand aloof, but immerse yourselves in the reality of life, as Jesus did (*CV* 174).

As agents of transformation, Pope Francis asks youth to be courageous missionaries (*CV* 175-178). He says, "filled with the love of Christ, young people are called to be witnesses of the Gospel wherever they find themselves, by the way they live" (*CV* 175). Quoting St Alberto Hurtado the pope says that "being an apostle does not mean wearing a lapel pin; it is not about speaking about the truth but living it, embodying it, being transformed in Christ. Being an apostle does not mean carrying a torch in hand, possessing the light, but being that light" (*CV* 175). In short, young people are called to be "courageous missionaries", witnessing everywhere to Christ with their own lives. The word, however, must not be silenced: "Learn to swim against the tide, learn how to share Jesus and the faith he has given you" (*CV* 176). The Christocentric and universal nature of mission is emphasized when the pope asks the young people:

> Where does Jesus send us? "There are no borders, no limits: he sends us everywhere. The Gospel is for everyone, not just for some. It is not only for those who seem closer to us, more receptive, more welcoming. It is for everyone. Do not be afraid to go and bring Christ into every area of life, to the fringes of society, even to those who seem farthest away and most indifferent. The Lord seeks all; he wants everyone to feel the warmth of his mercy and his love (*CV* 177).

7. 'Rooting' with Christ and Humanity

Having explained the intrinsic nature of being friends of Christ and friends of humans, Pope Francis now exhorts young people not to allow themselves to be uprooted from their culture and origins (*CV* 179-201). Such an uprooting unfortunately, according to him, will lend them to the danger of ideologies which encourage them to ignore history, rejecting the experience of their elders and look down on the past (*CV* 181). The pope calls these ideologies as masters of manipulation who despise all that is not young (*CV* 182). It finds expression in the so-called 'cult of youth' which sees growing old as a problem, blurring out what is distinctive about their origins. The Pope makes a clarion call that young people should reject this cult of youth as it promises a shallow life, and goes against the humanisation of the world to which they are called and send out (*CV* 184).

While rejecting the 'cult of youth', Pope Francis encourages youth to "care for their roots, because from the roots comes the strength that is going to make them grow, flourish and bear fruit" (*CV* 184). The pope then proceeds to emphasise the importance of a relationship with the elderly, who are the source of inspiration and wisdom (*CV* 187-192). As a conclusion to this chapter, the pope exhorts young people to, "Steer clear of young people who think that adults represent a meaningless past and those adults who always think that they know how young people should act. Together let us seek a better world, assisted by the Holy Spirit" (*CV* 201).

8. Christ Centered Care for the Youth

While speaking about youth ministry (*CV* 202-247), Pope Francis again clarifies the need for Christ-centered ministries for the care and formation of youth. At the outset of the chapter the pope says: "We should take into greater consideration those practices that have shown their value – the methods, language and aims that have proved truly effective in bringing young people to Christ and the Church. [...] What is important is that we make use of everything that has borne good fruit and effectively communicates the joy of the Gospel" (*CV*205). In our efforts to reach out to the young people, the pope says that "we have to give greater thought to ways of incarnating the *kerygma* in the language of today's youth" (*CV* 211).

According to Pope Francis "any educational project or path of growth for young people "must certainly include formation in Christian doctrine and morality", that must be centered on the *kerygma*, "the foundational experience of encounter with God through Jesus' death and resurrection", and on "growth in fraternal love, community life and service" (*CV* 213). Therefore, the pope says, "youth ministry should always include occasions for renewing and deepening our personal experience of the love of God and the living Christ" (*CV* 214). And as a model for the youth ministry the pope suggests to draw inspiration from the example of Jesus' interaction with the disciples of Emmaus (cf. Lk 24:13-35; *CV* 236-237).

9. Vocation: A Call to Friendship with Christ

Chapter eight of *Christus Vivit* deals with the important theme of vocation (*CV* 248 -277) "understood in a broad sense as a calling from God, including the call to life, the call to friendship with him, the call to holiness, and so forth (*CV* 248). In the light of Scripture and of the teachings of Vatican Council II, vocation is presented as a call for everyone – every existence is vocation – God's call to friendship with Christ (cf. *CV* 249-252): "The first thing we need to discern and discover is this: Jesus wants to be a friend to every young person" (*CV* 250). However, the pope emphasizes here "vocation in the strict sense, as a call to missionary service to others" (*CV* 253) in accord with his whole programmatic vision described in *Evangelii* Gaudium: communion-in-mission.

The Pope understands the very nature of vocation here on earth as mission: "I am a mission on this earth; that is the reason why I am here in this world" (*CV* 254). The challenge is then to ensure "that every form of pastoral activity, formation and spirituality should be seen in the light of our Christian vocation" (*CV* 254). Discerning one's vocation means exploring how young people can respond to the plan that God has for them. The pope further explains that discerning one's vocation "is a recognition of why I was made, why I am here on earth, and what the Lord's plan is for my life" (*CV* 256). It is, therefore, a way "to foster and develop all that we are" and "to bring out the best in yourself for the glory of God and the good of others" (*CV* 257). As a parting shot in this chapter, the pope focuses again on Jesus who is inviting young people to follow him more radically: "Jesus is walking in our midst, as he did in Galilee. He walks through our streets, and he quietly stops and looks into our eyes. His call is attractive and intriguing …. look more clearly at the world around you, and then, with Jesus, come to recognize the vocation that is yours in this world (*CV* 277).

10. Discernment: Having the Conscience of Christ

While speaking about discernment, Pope Francis asks young people to form a conscience in tune with the sentiments of Christ: "Forming our conscience is the work of a lifetime, in which we learn to cultivate the very sentiments of Jesus Christ, adopting the criteria behind his choices and the intentions behind his actions" (*CV* 281). In the process of discernment, the pope says, "we let ourselves be transformed by Christ" (*CV* 281). He emphasises the role of listening to the Lord in the process of discernment: "We must remember that prayerful discernment has to be born of an openness to listening—to the Lord and to others, and to reality itself, which always challenges us in new ways" (*CV* 284). The pope once again calls to our mind the role of friendship with the Lord in the process of discernment: "To discern our personal vocation, we have to realize that it is a calling from a friend, who is Jesus" (*CV* 287); "I want you to know that, when the Lord thinks of each of you and what he wants to give you, he sees you as his close friend" (*CV* 287); "More than rules and obligations, the choice that Jesus sets before us is to follow him as friends follow one another, seeking each other's company and spending time together out of pure friendship. Everything else will come in time, and even failures in life can be an invaluable way of experiencing that friendship, which will never be lost" (*CV* 290).

Conclusion

A careful reading of *Christus Vivit*, thus, shows the Christ centeredness of the apostolic exhortation and the pope's Christ centered programmatic vision for the young people of today. It is an invitation to youth to its vocation to be alive in and through and with Christ for the service of the humanisation of the world. "Learn from Jesus, the ever young", have an intimate personal "friendship with him", and "be at the service of humanity"—this is the call of Pope Francis in *Christus Vivit* to the youth of today.

The challenges facing the youth are real. But they find their antidote in three great truths, namely, that God loves them, Christ saves them, and Christ is alive among them. "Christ is alive", and is ready to accompany them in everything they do. He wants to be their best friend and, in that way, they will be fully alive as well! (cf. *CV* 124). Jesus' youthful days become an appropriate model for young people that teaches them the importance of a right relationship with God and humanity. Their missionary vocation calls for a concrete and faith-based commitment to the building of a new society. It involves living in the midst of society and the world in order to bring the Gospel everywhere, to work for the growth of peace, harmony, justice, human rights and mercy, and thus for the extension of God's kingdom in this world (cf. *CV* 168). Discerning one's vocation is how young people can respond to the plan the Lord has for them (cf. *CV* 287). In short, *Christus Vivit* is addressed to all, particularly to all Christian young people (*CV* 3), as a roadmap for a Church that strongly needs to be renewed and reformed.

Endnotes

[1] Given in Loreto, Shrine of the Holy House, on March 25, 2019, on the Solemnity of the Annunciation of the Lord.

[2] The document is composed of nine chapters divided into 299 paragraphs, where the pope explains that he allowed himself to be "inspired by the wealth of reflections and conversations of the Synod" on Young People (cf. *CV* 4).

[3] For example, *gaudium* (joy) in *Evangelii Gaudium*; *laetitia* (gladness, happiness) in *Amoris Laetitia*; and *gaudete* from *gaudere* (to rejoice) in *Gaudete et Exsultate* and *exsultate* from *exsultare* (to rejoice, to be glad) in *Gaudete et Exsultate*.

⁴ *Lumen Fidei* (Encyclical on the Light of Faith, 2013); *Evangelii Gaudium* (Apostolic Exhortation on the Joy of the Gospel, 2013); *Laudato Si'* (Encyclical on the Care for our Common Home, 2015); *Amoris Laetitia* (Post-synodal Apostolic Exhortation on Love in the Family, 2016); *Gaudete et Exsultate* (Apostolic Exhortation on the Call to Holiness in Today's World, 2018).

IV

Pope Francis' Poor Church for Migrants & Politically Marginalized

"To encounter the living God, it is necessary to tenderly kiss Jesus' wounds in our hungry, poor, sick and incarcerated brothers and sisters."

(Pope Francis)

13.

Can the Church Speak Out?

Pope Francis' Aggiornamento for Greater Global Involvement

Joseph Lobo, SJ

Introduction

Today, there is, without doubt, a strong and a well interwoven wave of political populism, dictatorship of the market economy and fascistic trends in significant parts of the globe. This paper explores the current specificities of these phenomena and their interlinks. The subtitle echoes the title of the celebrated essay of Gayatri C. Spivak: *Can the Subaltern Speak?* (Basingstoke: Macmillan, 1988). In this essay the author defines 'speaking' as an ability to create a meaningful discourse in a society. Whether it is acceptable for practice or not, such a discourse has to be accepted as a coherent set of utterances articulating a valid self-identity and interest for it to be 'speaking'. Since the subalterns are denied subjecthood in a society, the subaltern's speech is in principle and a priori rejected, stifled or 'unheard'. Therefore, according to her, subalterns cannot speak.[1]

Along a similar line of thought we ask: *Can the Church speak out* in a context as explicated above? Not that the Church as such is subaltern. But the question is, whether the Church can hold a coherent discourse, articulating a unique self-identity as a 'contrast community', and if her discourse can have an impact on wider society. It is tantamount to enquiring into the kind of speech and the speaker that are needed to be 'listened to' or to make an effective impact. Here, Pope Francis' political, economic and pastoral stances—which he acknowledges as the 'contextualization of some major thrusts of Vatican Council II' (hereinafter VC II) as authentic expressions of today's subalterns' identity and interests—and his personal charisma are significant. This paper brings out the peculiar situation in which the positions of Pope Francis and those of VC II find themselves in; despite concerted efforts by specific groups of people to ignore, ridicule, rebut and even attack them fiercely, they have nevertheless succeeded in having a significant impact on many. The point however, is to amplify and deepen the impact so as to bear fruit in the decades and centuries to come.

1. Three Anti-Reign Phenomena

Three global phenomena mentioned above—namely, political populism, dictatorship of the market economy and fascistic trends—seem to go against Jesus' vision of God's Reign. Let us discuss them briefly with regard to their dynamics and impact that they have on society.

1.1. Populism and the Post-truth Scenario

Traditionally 'populism' referred to any protest movement by the adversely affected people against the elite. But today in the post-truth scenario,[2] it has acquired a pejorative meaning, in the sense of reflecting a certain blind following of a leader on the basis of an acute emotional appeal that the leader has on the followers. Although at times the populist leader is suspected of lacking moral integrity, the followers may still accept, vote for, or 'venerate' him/her justifying that there are no other better alternatives.

The problem with populism is that it may identify a problematic situation correctly but draws out wrong inferences.³ For instance, a populist leader/government might rightly identify, say, an economic crisis, but in order to maintain himself/herself/itself in power, might blame a particular group of people for the crisis, thereby triggering off a kind of xenophobia. This goes a long way in facilitating the legitimization of the populist leader. Obviously, populism survives by distorting reality. The populist leader becomes a demagogue, and unaccountable to the general populace. If such populism begins to grow on a religious template, then it could demand and even receive an absolute submission from the followers. The religion built around the populist leader thus ends up being idolatry. Although populism plays high on nationalistic emotions and projects a pro-populace stance, ironically, it tramples on real democracy. And so, it is noted how Indian democracy has been systematically and "successfully hollowed out in the past five years. This will continue and accelerate, giving further impetus to the hollowing out of Indian democracy."⁴

Deliberately created mistrust among the people is part of the populist strategy; where "attitudes of rejection or forms of nationalism that call into question the fraternity of which our globalized world has such great need,"⁵ thrive unabatedly.

1.2. *The Dictatorship of Market Economy*
The unbridled capitalism and unregulated competitive market economy define the nature and dynamics of the current neo-liberalism. The age-old trickle-down theory, which is the offshoot of Adam Smith's 'invisible hand' through the uninterrupted self-interest-driven economic activity of individuals ushering in welfare for all, has miserably failed to ensure a just and equitable distribution of the unimaginable quantity of wealth produced by the industrial innovations within capitalism. Studies show that—although the quantity of absolute poverty is on the decline on the global scenario—the gap between a miniscule minority of 'super-haves' and a gigantic mass of 'have-nots' is on the rise, almost exponentially.⁶ Besides this, the adverse impact of a greed-based production on the

ecosystems is becoming uncontrollable, unmeasurable and irreversible. Loss of community, human dignity and ability for self-determination caused by displacement, commodification of the human person, increasing unemployment and periodic economic recessions have given rise to more and more inhuman and violent individual and social behaviours.

In this context, it is alarming to note the two recent global rankings that India has received: a. The 'Doing Business' report—earlier called 'Ease of Doing Business' (EoDB) published by the World Bank—ranks India 63rd which was 142 just five years ago and 77 in 2018.[7] This tells us how business friendly the regulations in India are. b. At the same time the 'Global Hunger Index' (GHI), published by International Food Policy Research Institute, ranks India 102nd out of 117 countries. We lag behind our 'poor neighbours': Pakistan (94th), Bangladesh (88th) and Sri Lanka (66th). The index is based on 4 components of which 3 are related to child hunger: undernourishment, child wasting (low weight for height), child stunting and child mortality.[8] The report claims that only 9.6% of the children in India below 23 months of age get adequate nutrition.[9]

Controversies apart, the hunger index report is corroborated by India's own Comprehensive National Nutrition Survey (CNNS), which is based on a sample of more than 1 lakh children across 30 states.[10] Although a direct correlation between the two rankings may not be possible, they certainly indicate our lopsided priorities.

1.3. *Fascistic Trends*

Although 'fascism' can be attributed to the specific political-economic-cultural complex that emerged in 1930's in Europe, ending up in the second world war, its close semblances are found even today in many parts of the world.

In general, factors that give rise to fascistic movements are related to economic distress, rise of populist leadership, and failure of any other types of constructive leadership. When a fascistic movement is allowed to manipulate religion(s), it becomes all the more unshakable by demanding and receiving a 'religious-type' of adherence from its followers. A fascistic movement that does not make religion intrinsic to itself becomes less tenable and lasting. In the current global scenario, there is a strong nexus among fascistic movements, populist leadership and big business corporates. Some of these nexuses have managed to harness religious and cultural support for their development and effective functioning.

2. Can the Church Speak Out? Pope Francis Shows a Way

By her very constitution the Church—as a historical development of the 1st century 'Jesus movement'—has to be a prophetic voice at all times. The fact that in various circumstances the Church has not lived up to this dimension of her vocation does not cancel it out. Hence in a situation where the populist-neo-liberal-fascistic nexus succeeds in forming the dominant and at times the only social discourse, the question naturally arises whether the prophetic voice of the Church can make any sense, let alone get a significant reception. Apparently, this doubt becomes stronger when we look at the responses got by Pope Francis' challenging appeals in recent times. It is reported that such appeals did not have much real impact beyond a certain admiration and respect for the person and ideas of the Pope. In fact, they were even vociferously countered and denounced by some.[11] We shall reflect later on the implications of such animosity.

As mentioned in the introduction, Gayatri Spivak is of the opinion that a subaltern cannot speak! But history, considered in sufficiently longer intervals, proves the contrary. Whether it is the case of Israelite subalterns in Egypt or Babylon, early Christian subalterns in the Roman Empire, subalterns of Latin America, subjugated women of the world, or Dalit and Tribal subalterns of India – all of these, with higher or lower degree of success, have made and are making themselves heard. In other words, history shows that subalterns can and do 'speak' in Spivak's sense of the word! Hence Spivak's position needs to be taken, as she herself has at times acknowledged, as a possibility, a warning, and an awakening call against any passivity, and not as a proven thesis.

With these considerations we set out interpreting the significance of Pope Francis' interventions beyond the current resistances, denunciations and lip service that they receive from some of the prominent world leaders and others.

2.1. Populism and Pope Francis

Against the current populist governments that try to silence every dissenting and critical voice through various punitive means, Pope Francis asserts the necessity of just denunciation:

> It's a matter of concerning oneself not with partisan politics, but with the great politics born of the Commandments and the Gospel. Denouncing human rights abuses, situations of exploitation or exclusion, or shortages in education or food, is not being partisan. Catholic social teaching is full of denunciations, yet it is not partisan.[12]

Among other strategies, populist leaders and governments create and maintain an 'other' in opposition to which the 'loyalists' are organized. The 'other' are then branded as 'anti-nationals', 'foreigners', 'burdens/hindrances to development', 'parasites' and so on. Such labelling can effectively sedate or blindfold the 'loyalists' against the failures of the populist government. Against such phenomena Francis asserts:

> Political addresses that tend to blame every evil on migrants and to deprive the poor of hope are unacceptable. Rather, there is a need to reaffirm that peace is based on respect for each person, whatever his or her background, on respect for the law and the common good, on respect for the environment entrusted to our care and for the richness of the moral tradition inherited from past generations.[13]

Further, while addressing a gathering of over twenty heads of states and governments in Rome on March 24, 2017, marking the 60th anniversary of the signing of the Treaty of Rome, Francis identified *solidarity* as the most effective antidote to modern forms of populism that try to drive a wedge between the created 'other' and the 'loyal we'. "Politics needs this kind of leadership, which avoids appealing to emotions to gain consent, but instead, in a spirit of solidarity and subsidiarity, devises policies that can make the Union as a whole develop harmoniously."[14] He named spiritual values as the "best antidote against the vacuum of values of our time, which provides a fertile terrain for every form of extremism."[15]

Populism thrives on media propaganda. Francis rightly points out:

> We are living in an information-driven society which bombards us indiscriminately with data – all treated as being of equal importance – and which leads to remarkable superficiality in the area of moral discernment. In response, we need to provide an education which teaches critical thinking and encourages the development of mature moral values.[16]

At a time when a large section of the media has become merely a propaganda machinery, his observations are spot on.

2.2. Dictatorship of Economy and Pope Francis

Although right from the days of Pope Leo XIII's *Rerum Novarum* (1891), the Catholic Church has upheld the right to private property, she has simultaneously subjected such a right to the common good; thereby envisaging it within a moral framework and denying it absolute validity. In today's world the hegemony of a neo-liberal capitalist economy is an undeniable fact. Human life itself, whether personal or social, seems to be permeated with economic ways of thinking. As a result, social inequalities are on the rise (*Gaudium et Spes* 63).

Evangelii Gaudium (hereinafter EG) begins with a strong appeal to the rich and the affluent to open their hearts to the harsh realities that the poor of the world face due to economic structures and systems of the day (EG 2-3). Such systems and structures are clearly responsible for the current socio-economic misery: "Today everything comes under the laws of competition and the survival of the fittest, where the powerful feed upon the powerless. As a consequence, masses of people find themselves excluded and marginalized: without work, without possibilities, without any means of escape" (EG 53). Addressing a reality by its name goes a long way in acting to transform it. Any distortion in this regard is detrimental to its transformation. And hence, Francis is honest in saying: "The worship of the golden calf of old (cf. Ex 32:15-34) has found a new and heartless image in the cult of money and the dictatorship of an economy which is faceless and lacking any truly humane goal."[17]

Growth and development cannot be measured only in economic terms. Hence, doctrines that resist necessary reforms under the guise of a false liberty are not acceptable (GS 65). Causes of conflict and discord that exist even in the absence of full-fledged wars are identified as excessive economic inequalities, desire to dominate others, human greed, distrust, pride, and other egotistical passions (GS 83).

The unbridled freedom and support for increasing one's profit in an uncontrolled competitive business gives rise to a situation where "[T]he thirst for power and possessions knows no limits. In this system, which tends to devour everything which stands in the way of increased profits, whatever is fragile, like the environment, is defenceless before the interests of a deified market, which become the only rule" (EG 56). Hence, the Smithian 'invisible hand' of the market needs to be replaced by conscious decisions made within the framework of inclusive and integral morality. Francis' analysis is astute in EG 204:

> We can no longer trust in the unseen forces and the invisible hand of the market. Growth in justice requires more than economic growth. It requires 'a better distribution of income' and creating jobs, not turning to remedies that are a new poison, such as attempting to increase profits by reducing the work force and thereby adding to the ranks of the excluded.

The active promotion of consumerism is essential to keep up the current form of global economy. Without a high consuming society, the markets would certainly experience a glut and profits would run down. Such a vicious circle is fuelled by human greed, which in the process reaches ever new depths. "The great danger in today's world, pervaded as it is by consumerism, is the desolation and anguish born of a complacent yet covetous heart, the feverish pursuit of frivolous pleasures, and a blunted conscience" (EG 2).

Such a situation creates more emptiness and a whole chain of related evils emerges. For "[W]henever our interior life becomes caught up in its own interests and concerns, there is no longer room for others, no place for the poor. God's voice is no longer heard, the quiet joy of his love is no longer felt, and the desire to do good fades" (EG 2). It is clear then, that the forces that are needed to keep up a competitive market are the same that dehumanize the 'haves' by their slavery to consumption and the 'have-nots' due to their inability to get even basic facilities for leading a dignified human life. In this context, Francis is acutely sensitive to one of the most devastating results of the present form of globalization: the "globalization of indifference", by which one's senses are deadened to perceive the cry of the poor and suffering (EG 54).

Against the oppressive nexus between economy and political power, Francis insists, "[I]f politics must truly be at the service of the human person, it follows that it cannot be a slave to the economy and finance."[18] Further, "[T]oday, it is the case that some economic sectors exercise more power than states themselves. But economics without politics cannot be justified, since this would make it impossible to favour other ways of handling the various aspects of the present crisis" (EG 196). Reiterating his stand on responsible economic development he minces no words in stressing the moral imperative to care for the environment and denouncing the profits "drenched in blood" from the arms industry.[19]

Some authors have pointed out that views of Francis should not be taken as merely reflecting an ideology (anti-capitalist or whatever) as such.[20] Rather, as truthful observations of the stark realities of the day ('exclusion' of many by the 'dictatorship of an impersonal economy' as Francis names them and the resulting misery for the masses) and an appeal for a more just and humane world.[21]

Other responses to Francis range from outright denunciation to a mere lip service in terms of some trivial course of action. Before boycotting the Pope's visit in 2015, the Republican Paul Gossar, a member of the US House of Representatives from Arizona, rejected Pope's views as 'misguided politics' as manifest in a "fool's errand of climate change."²² On the other hand, John Boehner, the Republican speaker was moved to tears by the Pope's words, and resigned on the very next day.²³ However, it is to be noted that despite all the rousing applause by many who attended Pope's address in the US, concrete action programmes hardly emerged.²⁴ In this context, it is interesting to note the Cuban president Raul Castro's response to Francis' political-economic stance—of which, playing a significant role in getting to close the Guantanamo Bay detention camp can be a glaring example. Castro, in anticipation of Francis' September 2015 visit to Cuba is reported to have said: "When the Pope comes to Cuba in September, I promise to go to all his Masses and I will be happy to do so …. if the Pope continues to talk as he does, sooner or later I will start praying again and return to the Catholic Church, and I am not kidding."²⁵

Numerous texts of *Laudato Si'* and parts of other addresses bring out Francis' insight into the structural character of today's social evils and the interrelated nature of politics, economy, ecology, technology, ethics, culture, theology and spirituality, which demand an integral approach in any meaningful response.²⁶ For instance, eschewing the path of hatred and violence, in his Address to the Joint Session of the United States Congress, he said:

> Our response must instead be one of hope and healing, of peace and justice. We are asked to summon the courage and the intelligence to resolve today's many geopolitical and economic crises… Our efforts must aim at restoring hope, righting wrongs, maintaining commitments, and thus promoting the well-being of individuals and of peoples. We must move forward together, as one, in a renewed spirit of fraternity and solidarity, cooperating generously for the common good.²⁷

Pope Francis is aware that for a sustainable response, solidarity and mutual understanding among nations/governments is of paramount importance. He writes in EG 164:

> A global consensus is essential for confronting the deeper problems, which cannot be resolved by unilateral actions on the part of individual countries. Such a consensus could lead, for example, to planning a sustainable and diversified agriculture, developing renewable and less polluting forms of energy, encouraging a more efficient use of energy, promoting a better

management of marine and forest resources, and ensuring universal access to drinking water.

Francis squarely critiques the anthropological presuppositions that lurk behind the current dictatorship of the market: "The worldwide crisis affecting finance and the economy lays bare their imbalances and, above all, their lack of real concern for human beings; man (*sic*) is reduced to one of his needs alone: consumption" (EG 55). This imbalance is the result of ideologies which defend the absolute autonomy of the marketplace and financial speculation.

The radicality of Francis' critique of the current economic system can be seen in its strong denunciation: "As long as the problems of the poor are not radically resolved by rejecting the absolute autonomy of markets and financial speculation and by attacking the structural causes of inequality…no solution will be found for the world's problems or, for that matter, to any problems. Inequality is the root of social ills" (EG 202). And therefore, a radical critique of the very founding presupposition of today's socio-economic-political-cultural system is the need of the hour.

2.3. Fascism and Pope Francis

Pope Francis' emphasis on the common good and concern for the poor—especially the migrants and refugees—makes him critique all forms of xenophobia that are epitomised in Fascism and narrow nationalism. "I am concerned because we hear speeches that resemble those of Hitler in 1934. 'Us first, we…we….' These are frightening thoughts."[28]

In these words, Francis reminded his audience, on the occasion of the centenary of the League of Nations about how there was a "resurgence of nationalist tendencies" today. It was such attitudes and movements that had ultimately sabotaged the League of Nations and had eventually led to World War II. Today's resurgence of Fascistic trends according to him partly "is a consequence of the reaction in some parts of the world to a globalization that has in some respects developed in too rapid and disorderly a manner."[29]

In the light of the above considerations, we now respond to the question – *Can the Church speak out?* Speaking out needs to be in terms of life-witness, deeds and words that can create an impact, a resonance, and a response. More than a reluctant acceptance, it is the acute animosity against the papal appeals that indicates that they are powerfully moving some unmoved convictions of the contemporary world! And so, the subaltern indeed has begun to 'speak', but is severely resisted. That is a good sign!

3. Pope Francis Provides Prerequisites for 'Speaking Out' Effectively

Pope Francis is, undoubtedly, a world leader who has relentlessly been raising his voice on the world stage on behalf of the world's voiceless majority. In his writings—especially in EG—one can decipher certain prerequisites for speaking out effectively, as follows:

1. Speaking out needs to be done from the position of interior strength and conviction and not out of fear and desperation. Such interior strength emerges from the realization that speaking out in words and deeds is part of the Lord's mission. Pope Francis writes in EG 12:

> [I]t is first and foremost the Lord's work, surpassing anything which we can see and understand.... This conviction enables us to maintain a spirit of joy in the midst of a task so demanding and challenging that it engages our entire life. God asks everything of us, yet at the same time he offers everything to us.

2. For the Church to speak out effectively, it is necessary that she gives up her interests, if any, of self-preservation. "I dream of a 'missionary option', that is, ...the Church's customs, ways of doing things, times and schedules, language and structures can be suitably channelled for the evangelization of today's world rather than for her self-preservation... [a bruised church] rather than a Church which is unhealthy from being confined and from clinging to its own security...while at our door people are starving and Jesus does not tire of saying to us: 'Give them something to eat' (Mk 6:37)" (EG 49).

3. Abandoning all forms of Dogmatism and Traditionalism that go against the discernment of reading the signs of the times and responding accordingly is necessary for a creative and critical response. Francis opens up a very important space for such possibilities when he says:

> Differing currents of thought in philosophy, theology and pastoral practice, if open to being reconciled by the Spirit in respect and love, can enable the Church to grow, since all of them help to express more clearly the immense riches of God's word. For those who long for a monolithic body of doctrine guarded by all and leaving no room for nuance, this might appear as undesirable and leading to confusion. But in fact, such variety serves to bring out and develop different facets of the inexhaustible riches of the Gospel (EG 40).

4. Patience more than expecting immediate results, processes more than pre-mature results, being realistic more than idealistic are some of the key requirements for a meaningful and enduring engagement, especially in a situation where a silver lining is not really visible at the horizon. Francis understands it better than many a Christian today, when he opines (EG 82):

> Some ... throw themselves into unrealistic projects and are not satisfied simply to do what they reasonably can. [Some] lack the patience to allow processes to mature; they want everything to fall from heaven... ... [Some] have lost real contact with people and so depersonalize their work that they are more concerned with the road map than with the journey itself. Today's obsession with immediate results makes it hard ... to tolerate anything that smacks of disagreement, possible failure, criticism, the cross.

What follows from such consideration is that a disciple of Jesus is called to lead a unique way of life, which is not fathomable to the prevalent thinking of the times. But there are reasons for Christian hope, which could appear even foolish to many. But that precisely constitutes being a 'contrast community'. Hence, Francis advises us in EG 271:

> It is true that in our dealings with the world, we are told to give reasons for our hope, but not as an enemy who critiques and condemns. We are told quite clearly: "do so with gentleness and reverence" (1 Pet 3:15) and "if possible, so far as it depends upon you, live peaceably with all" (Rom 12:18). We are also told to overcome "evil with good" (Rom 12:21) and to "work for the good of all" (Gal 6:10).

The hope that emerges from such a living is a deep conviction that:

> We can know quite well that our lives will be fruitful, without claiming to know how, or where, or when. We may be sure that none of our acts of love will be lost, nor any of our acts of sincere concern for others. No single act of love for God will be lost, no generous effort is meaningless, no painful endurance is wasted. All of these encircle our world like a vital force (EG 279).

5. The Church's mission among the poor needs to be seen as essential to her vitality:

> Any Church community, if it thinks it can comfortably go its own way without creative concern and effective cooperation in helping the poor to live with dignity and reaching out to everyone, will also risk breaking down, however much it may talk about social issues or criticize governments. It will easily drift into a spiritual worldliness camouflaged by religious practices, unproductive meetings and empty talk (EG 207).

Mission among the poor, indeed is a touchstone to verify our fidelity to the *missio dei* on the one hand and a protective gear from falling into a 'spiritual worldliness' on the other.

4. Characteristics of an Effective Speaking Out

The subaltern nature of the Church's speech consists in not being within the framework of intelligibility defined by the current global hegemonic forces. Such a situation can be resolved at least by two strategies: (a) by preventing the hegemonic frame of intelligibility from being the one and the only. This can be achieved by consciously making the subaltern discourse appear in many public forums and with greater frequency, and (b) through what Spivak calls an 'affirmative sabotage', namely, by using the very structures of the hegemonic world of intelligibility for its deconstruction. One can see the presence of both these strategies in varied forms and degrees in the responses of Pope Francis.

4.1. A Cultural Approach

An 'evangelized' culture seems to be a fitting antidote to all forms of culture of fatalism, apathy, hatred, greed and death. Pope Francis has clearly recognized that the roots of social tragedies lie in the cultural realm, where convictions are shaped. "The immense importance of a culture marked by faith cannot be overlooked...An evangelized popular culture contains values of faith and solidarity capable of encouraging the development of a more just and believing society and possesses a particular wisdom which ought to be gratefully acknowledged" (EG 68). This insight originates from *Gaudium et Spes*, when it recognizes that the human being "can achieve true and full humanity only by means of culture" (GS 53) and that culture needs to be at the service of integral human development and perfection. It is not to be made use of for some economic and political power (GS 59). And so, any 'deification' of culture, as in the case of fascist nationalism is excluded. Moreover, *Gaudium et Spes* also insists on the preservation of the uniqueness, wisdom and humanistic values enshrined in different cultures and on working against any process that obliterates such uniqueness (GS 56).

4.2. An Incarnated Political Spirituality

A 'political spirituality' that not only finds God in the authentic encounters with the 'polity' but also leads one to commit oneself for its welfare can be a highly motivating and energizing factor. Referring to the need of such a spirituality Francis laments, that at times, "... spiritual life comes to be identified with a few religious exercises which can offer a certain comfort but which do not encourage encounter with others, engagement with the world... As a result...even though they pray, a heightened individualism, a crisis of identity and a cooling of fervour [set in]. These are three evils which fuel one another" (EG 78). Contrary to an 'incarnated spirituality', "Many try to escape from others and take refuge in the comfort of their privacy or in a small circle of close friends, renouncing the realism of the social aspect of the Gospel" (EG 88). Faith in incarnation challenges us to shed all enslavements to virtual reality and such other escapism that is characteristic of today's world and open our senses to the realness of life.

For an effective response to our times we need a spirituality that has socio-political consequences. On the other hand, such a spirituality should be the very marrow of pastoral practice. And so, "[M]ystical notions without a solid social and missionary outreach are of no help to evangelization, nor are dissertations or social or pastoral practices which lack a spirituality, which can change hearts. These unilateral and incomplete proposals only reach a few groups and prove incapable of radiating beyond them because they curtail the Gospel" (EG 262). It is only an incarnated 'political spirituality' that can speak out effectively in our times. Such a spirituality makes us aware that political life needs to be participated by all including minorities. It empowers us to denounce the tendencies, ideologies, policies and movements that deny civic and religious freedom, thereby misusing power for the benefit of some sections at the cost of others (GS 73, 74).

Citizens are bound in conscience to obey the civil authorities when the exercise of their authority is done for the common good with a sense of responsibility and respect for the human individual. However, where citizens are oppressed by a public authority overstepping its competence, it is legitimate for them to defend their own rights against the abuse of this authority, keeping within those limits drawn by the natural law and the Gospels (GS 74). And so, citizens must take care not to vest excessive power in the hands of public authority and not to make exaggerated demands upon it in their own interests (GS 75). This consideration vehemently speaks against all types of populist and narrow nationalist governments.

An authentic 'political spirituality' encourages true patriotism, which in turn is opposed to any kind of narrow-mindedness. It consists in being concerned about "the welfare of the whole human family which is formed into one by various kinds of links between races, peoples and nations" (GS 75). Due to her specific role and competence the Church does not bind herself to any political system. Her role is to safeguard the transcendent character of the human person. The state or the political community addresses the other dimensions of the human person and community. Hence both need to collaborate for the integral welfare of all (GS 76).

4.3. With Solidarity and Collaboration

The herculean nature of the task before us today necessarily calls for collaboration. Francis is aptly practical here. "Greater possibilities for communication thus turn into greater possibilities for encounter and solidarity for everyone... To go out of ourselves and to join others is healthy for us. To be self-enclosed is to taste the bitter poison of immanence, and humanity will be worse for every selfish choice we make" (EG 87). Collaboration creates synergy, which is always more than the sum of individual efforts. Solidarity and collaboration act against the very cornerstone of the divisive tactics of vested interests. And so, the mere coming together and acting together does an effective speaking out.

A second type of solidarity is with the mission people. *Gaudium et Spes* in its preface considers 'solidarity of the Church with the whole human family' as the basis of her self-understanding (presence and mission) in the modern world (GS 1). Francis has been emphasizing this point in myriad ways, myriad times; for instance, in EG 270:

> Sometimes we are tempted to be that kind of Christian who keeps the Lord's wounds at arm's length. Yet Jesus wants us to touch human misery, to touch the suffering flesh of others. He hopes that we will stop looking for those personal or communal niches which shelter us from the maelstrom of human misfortune and instead enter into the reality of other people's lives and know the power of tenderness.

This type of solidarity, among other things, makes the mission of the Church more incarnate and the speaking out more effective.

4.4. A Mission Rediscovered

Despite an intensified sense of individual's autonomy, birth of a new humanism marks our times. It understands human person increasingly in terms of his/her responsibility towards fellow humans (GS 55).

The integral mission of Christ gains significance in the context of fragmented approaches to human 'development' that end up in human degradation. Francis points out "[T]oday, our challenge is not so much atheism as the need to respond adequately to many people's thirst for God, lest they try to satisfy it with alienating solutions or with a disembodied Jesus who demands nothing of us with regard to others" (EG 89). If the speaking out of the Church has to be effective, then she needs to address the deeper groaning of humanity and of creation. In order to do it effectively, she needs to get in touch with those groanings for real meaning and her response needs to shift from being abstract-universal to concrete-particular. For "[T]he ultimate aim should be that the Gospel, as preached in categories proper to each culture, will create a new synthesis with that particular culture" (EG 129).

4.5. Dialogue with all Knowledge Domains

Today, an effective speaking out demands that the Gospel be set on dialogue with diverse knowledge domains. For, these are the very ones that are misused to create anti-Reign realities. Pope Francis is deeply conscious of it. Hence, he points out: "Proclaiming the Gospel message to different cultures also involves proclaiming it to professional, scientific and academic circles. This means an encounter between faith, reason and the sciences with a view to developing new approaches and arguments on the issue of credibility, a creative apologetics (XIII Ordinary General Assembly of the Synod of Bishops gathered from 7-28 October 2012 to discuss the theme: The New Evangelization for the Transmission of the Christian Faith, proposition 17) which would encourage greater openness to the Gospel on the part of all" (EG 132).

Indeed, Francis exhibits great hope in the potential that religion and spirituality have to show us a way: "Why not turn to God and ask him to inspire their [of secular leaders] plans? I am firmly convinced that openness to the transcendent can bring about a new political and economic mindset which would help to break down the wall of separation between the economy and the common good of society" (EG 205). Religious classics across religions have great wisdom to provide for life here on earth. That needs to be tapped and set in dialogue with various 'development' models, political ideologies, religio-cultural movements of our times. That indeed would do another effective speaking out.

Conclusion

Can the Church speak out? We are reminded of Gandhiji's golden words: "First they ignore you, then they laugh at you, then they fight you, then you win."[30] Perhaps they may even 'accommodate' you in order to neutralize you. This is what happens when a subaltern begins to speak. Gandhiji's *ahimsa* was a subaltern discourse in the context of colonial might. It was ignored, then ridiculed, and then attacked by the British and finally Gandhiji won! Hence, they reflect a hope for any subaltern resistance.

The kind of resistance that the papal appeals for a more just and humane society face, and the sources from which it emerges, is truly unprecedented in the recent centuries. This implies that the papal appeals have reached the stage of 'attack' in the Gandhian scheme. That is a good sign. It also implies that the root causes of the unjust and inhuman realities have begun to feel the impact. It is analogous to the demoniac (the demon of 'all is well despite all wrongs') who was sitting quietly in the synagogue but began to get restless as Jesus entered there (Mk 1:22-23). The 'speaking out' therefore needs to be carried forward with a sense of humility, reliance on God, with a sense of unflinching commitment, and with collaboration with all those who want to make this world a better place to live in.

The Church is a mystery (LG 1); but the 'speaking Church' is also history! – the salt and light of the earth. The salt 'speaks out' by getting completely dissolved in the food and the light 'speaks out' by being on the lamp stand. But for that to happen the Church also needs to allow the 'subalterns' of her own fold to speak, by listening to their voices.

Endnotes

[1] Spivak clarifies: "It means that even when the subaltern makes an effort to the death to speak, she is not able to be heard, and speaking and hearing complete the

speech act." – Gayatri Chakravorty Spivak, *The Spivak Reader: Selected Works of Gayatri Chakravorty Spivak*, ed. Donna Landry and Gerald Mac Lean (New York: Routledge, 1996,) 292.

[2] Post-truth refers to a situation where appeal to emotions prevails over discursive reason in defining, perceiving and accepting what is true. This development stands in stark contrast to the modernity's perception of truth as that which can be established by the use of discursive reason.

[3] Jipson John, Jitheesh P. M, "Capitalism, Populism & Crisis of Liberalism: Interview with Akeel Bilgrami," *Frontline* (June 2019): 87.

[4] Teesta Setalvad, "Democracy was hollowed out in the past five years," *Frontline* (June 21, 2019): 32.

[5] Pope Francis, "Rejection and nationalism threaten peace: Pope Francis dedicates World Day Message to good politics," *L'Osservatore Romano* (online), 2577 (Dec. 21- 28, 2018): 5.

[6] For instance, Alan Kohler points out that over the past 40 years the income of the top 1% in the US has risen from 10 to 29 times that of the average income and is still on the rise. The average income of the 99 % has hardly seen any growth. See his "Two Great Vested Interests: Bankers and Communists", *Business Spectator*, December 2, 2013, www.businessspectator.com.au/print/698591. Referred to in Bruce Duncan, "Pope Francis's call for social justice in the global economy," *The Australasian Catholic Record* 91, no. 2 (April 2014): 12. Pope Francis' *Evangelii Gaudium* (n.54) debunks the 'trickle down' theory by pointing out that "this theory has never been proved by facts…it expresses a crude and naïve trust in the goodness of those wielding economic power and in the sacralised workings of the prevailing economic system." And so, "[T]he promise was that when the glass was full, it would overflow, benefitting the poor. But what happens instead, is that when the glass is full, it magically gets bigger (so that) nothing ever comes out for the poor" (n.55).

[7] https://iasscore.in/current-affairs/prelims/ease-of-doing-business-report-2019. Accessed on Oct. 29, 2019. India's 63rd rank for 2019 is mentioned in Ajit Ranade, "Question of Priorities: A Tale of Two Global Rankings", *Deccan Herald*, Oct. 29, 2019, 10.

[8] https://www.globalhungerindex.org/results.html, (accessed on 29th Oct. 2019).

[9] https://www.jagranjosh.com/current-affairs/global-hunger-index-2019-india-slips-to-102nd-place-pakistan-ranked-94-1571209500-1 (accessed on Oct. 29, 2019).

[10] Ajit Ranade, "Question of Priorities," ibid., 10.

[11] "'Marxist,' cried a few, and the charge echoed. The pope is 'confused,' declared others. And still others tried to deflect the pope's message by claiming that it was really directed to his own homeland, Argentina, rather than the United States. At least one wealthy individual threatened to withhold a donation for the renovation of St. Patrick's Cathedral in New York." See Jeffrey Sachs, "Market reformer: an economist considers Pope Francis's critique of capitalism", *America* 210/10 (Mar. 24, 2014): 18- 20. The conservative US radio commentator, Rush Limbaugh, accused the Pope of

sprouting 'pure Marxism', and of not knowing what he was talking about. See Vatican Insider, "Rush Limbaugh Lashes Out at Francis", *La Stampa*, Turin, Dec. 2, 2013. Cited in Bruce Duncan, 1. Rick Santorum has likened Francis' teaching on climate change to the Medieval Church's negative reaction to Galileo. See Rick Santorum, "Interview with Dom Giordano," Talk Radio 1210 WPHTPhiladelphia, June 1 2015; https://embed.radio.com/clip/59060539/7ref_url=http%3A%2F%2Fphiladelphia.cbslocal.com%2F2015%2F06%2F01%2Frick-santorum-on-pope-francis-letter-on-climate-change-leave-the-science-to-the-scientist%2F& station. id=121&rollup_ga_id=UA-2438645-53&ads_ga_page_track er=UA-1 74342 5 7-35# accessed March 18, 2016. Cited in Christopher Hrynkow, "The Planet, and Politics: A Mapping of How Francis Is Calling for More Than the Paris Agreement," *Journal of Church and State*, 59/3 (Summer 2017): 379. US Congress representative Paul Gossar, responding to Francis' speeches during his visit to the US between Sept. 21-27, 2015, "was upset with the pope's high-profile effort to combat global warming." See David Gibson, "Pope lays out political, ecclesial vision," *The Christian Century* 132/22 (Oct. 28, 2015): 14.

[12] Sergio Rubin and Francesca Ambrogetti, *Pope Francis: His Life in His Own Words: Conversations with Jorge Bergoglio* (New York: G. P. Putnam's Sons, 2013), 94; cited in Bruce Duncan, 7.

[13] Pope Francis, "Rejection and nationalism threaten peace: Pope Francis dedicates World Day Message to good politics," *L'Osservatore Romano* (online), 2577 (Dec 21- 28, 2018): 6.

[14] Charles Collings, "Pope Francis urges EU leaders to fight populism with solidarity," CRUX Taking Catholic Pulse, Mar. 24, 2017; https://cruxnow.com/vatican/2017/03/24/pope-francis-urges-eu-leaders-fight-populism-solidarity/ (accessed on Nov. 3, 2019).

[15] Ibid.

[16] Pope Francis, Apostolic Exhortation, *Evangelii Gaudium*, n. 64, November 2013.

[17] Pope Francis, "Address of Pope Francis to the New Non-Resident Ambassadors to the Holy See: Kyrgyzstan, Antigua and Barbuda, Luxembourg and Botswana," May 16, 2013; https://w2.vatican.va/content/francesco/en/speeches/ 2013/ may/documents/papa-francesco_20130516_nuovi-ambasciatori.html (accessed April 25, 2016); cited in Christopher Hrynkow, 391. Cf. *Evangelii Gaudium* 55.

[18] David Gibson, 14.

[19] David Gibson, 14.

[20] In his speech in Cuba, Francis placed service above ideology by saying, "Service is never ideological, for we do not serve ideas, we serve people." See Pope Francis, "Holy Mass Homily of His Holiness Pope Francis: Plaza de la Revolucion, Havana," Sept. 20, 2015; http://w2.vatican.va/content/francesco/en/ homilies/2015/documents/papa-francesco_20150920_cuba-omelia-la-habana. html (accessed March 18, 2016); cited in Christopher Hrynkow, 378.

[21] Russell R. Reno, "The Public Square," *First Things* 240 (Feb 2014): 3-4.

[22] Paul Gossar, "Why I Am Boycotting Pope Francis's Address to Congress," Sept. 18, 2015; http://time.com/4040743/paul-gosar-pope-francis-congress/ (accessed April 25, 2016); cited in Christopher Hrynkow, 391.

[23] Christopher Hrynkow, 391.

[24] US president Barak Obama himself lauded *Laudato Si'* and acknowledged the responsibility placed on world leaders like him towards preserving the global environment. See Barack Obama, "Statement by the President on Pope Francis's Encyclical", White House: Office of the Press Secretary, June 18, 2015; https://www.whitehouse.gov/the-press-office/2015/06/18/statement-president-pope-francis%E2%80%99s-encyclical (accessed April 25, 2016); cited in Christopher Hrynkow, 392.

[25] Raul Castro, quoted in Philip Pullella, "Raul Castro Meets Pope, Says Might Return to the Church," Reuters, May 10, 2015; http://uk.reuters.com/artide/2015/05/10/uk-pope-cuba-castro-idUKKBN0NV0AP20150510 (accessed March 18, 2016); cited in Christopher Hrynkow, 378.

[26] *Laudato Si*, nn. 10, 22, 26, 49, 53, 54, 57, 70, 139, 158, 166, 175, 177, 178, 181, 197, etc. Pope Francis, "Visit to the Joint Session of the United States Congress: Address of the Holy Father," September 24, 2016; https://w2.vatican.va/content/francesco/en/speeches/2015/september/documents/papa-francesco_20150924_usa-us-congress.html (accessed March 18, 2016); cited in Christopher Hrynkow, 389. Francis, "Meeting with the Members of the General Assembly of the United Nations Organization: Address of the Holy Father," September 25, 2015; http://w2.vatican.va/content/francesco/en/speeches/2015/september/documents/papa-francesco_20150925_onu-visita.html (accessed March 18, 2016); cited in Christopher Hrynkow, 389.

[27] Pope Francis, "Visit to the Joint Session of the United States Congress: Address of the Holy Father," Sept. 24, 2016; https://w2.vatican.va/content/francesco/en/speeches/2015/september/documents/papa-francesco_20150924_usa-us-congress.html (accessed March 18, 2016); cited in Christopher Hrynkow, 389, 390.

[28] "Pope Francis warns against 'us first' ideologies, previews Amazon synod," Cf. Interview given to La Stampa on on August 6, 2019; https://www.americamagazine.org/faith/2019/08/09/pope-francis-warns-against-us-first-ideologies-previews-amazon-synod (accessed on Sept. 26, 2019).

[29] Andrew Korybko, "Pope Francis is on a Crusade against Nationalism," The yearly talk of Pope Francis to Vatican diplomats, on Jan. 16, 2019; https://orientalreview.org/2019/01/16/pope-francis-is-on-a-crusade-against-nationalism/ (accessed on 26th September, 2019).

[30] https://www.reddit.com/r/GetMotivated/comments/3fqudm/image_first_they_ignore_you/ (accessed on Nov. 10, 2019). Typically, 'ignoring' may not be intentional. It is indicative of the unintelligibility of the subaltern speech from the point of view of the rest.

14.

The Authentic Option for the Poor

A Political Dimension of Pope Francis' Faith

George A. Sebastin Babu, HGN

Introduction: The Dire Need for a 'Political Pulpit

The Indian situation is worrying. On the one hand, poor farmers commit suicide, development-induced-displaced groups are homeless; infants die of hunger, violence against women and Dalits goes unchecked, natural resources are privatized; pro-corporate schemes are executed, unemployment rises, communalism and fundamentalism gets governmental sanction, caste-based atrocities are legitimized, democracy is being destroyed and the Constitution being rewritten to suit the powerful few. On the other hand, our country is being sold to corporates, court judgments are bought, elections are rigged and politicians turn into moneymakers.

The Indian Catholic Church which has an obligation "to enter into dialogue with all these different problems" (GS 3)[1] sadly continues building churches, erecting grottos, conducting novenas and publishing new translations of rites and rituals. Oftentimes, the Church's radical "Preferential Option for the Poor" (GS 69) and "working for the common good" (GS 74) are compromised with charitable works. Consequently, the Church evades the responsibility of "the accomplishment of the task of justice" (GS 72). Undoubtedly, the cultural, social, and economic dimensions of an individual encompass "a deep influence of political life" (GS 73) and none can repudiate polity. As all injustices have political dimension (GS 74), the 'world of poor' demands that the Church work towards political justice. The Catholic Church in India, a Political[2] church, ought to respond to the Indian political scenario to accomplish her stand for the poor.

Today, there is a need for a 'Political pulpit,' that courageously encounters and challenges oppressive political structures that cause poverty. With 'his clean hands', Pope Francis leads us by reiterating the spirit of Vatican Council II (hereinafter VC II) through his solidarity with political victims such as the poor, migrants, abused children, prisoners, vulnerable adults and mother earth. He meticulously sharpens his critiques against defrauders. His verbal and nonverbal gestures express the Political dimension of Christian faith, because an 'Authentic Option for the Poor' is necessarily an 'Authentic Political Stand'. Resonating with Pope Francis' thoughts, this paper explores the need for the Church's engagement in the Political dimension of faith, which would empower her to raise a voice for the voiceless in order to revamp the unjust political structures of society.

1. The Cry of the Poor for a Political Prophetic Voice

1.1. *Poverty Stricken World*

The Church is incarnate in a world where poverty, exploitation, and suffering abound. Her living conditions reveal oppression and the consequent need for radical changes in the political, social and economic structures.[3] While the wealthy become wealthier, the poor become poorer and the poorest suffer the most.[4] Quite often, poverty is associated with an inability to attain minimal standard of living which involves money, market, capacity to buy and sell.⁵ It would be unfair to limit multifaceted poverty to the economic aspect alone. In *The Interpreter's Dictionary of the Bible*, C. U. Wolf uses the Hebrew word *dal* not only to connote economic poverty but also to indicate psychological poverty, which implies those who are helpless.⁶ G. M. Soares-Prabhu explains that the poor in Bible are not to be understood exclusively in economic terms, but as referring to the state of being wretched of the earth; thus, potentially oppressed and exploited.⁷ In a wider understanding, the term 'poor' indicates all those who are helpless or those who are in need of help.

Ingeborg Gabriel enumerates different faces of poverty such as material poverty: lacking the satisfaction of basic needs; social poverty: lacking rights and social recognition; and cultural and religious poverty: lack of identity and orientation.⁸ Naturally, these faces of a multifaceted poverty become intertwined with human rights' violations, justified political repression, perpetuated social injustices, aggressive oppression, intellectual colonization, economic segregation, caste and racial discrimination, gender inequality, estranged migrants, abuse of children, minors, Dalits and tribals, devastation of nature, and so on. These barbarities make an individual or a group of people helpless or poor. Therefore, not only the economy but also individuals and society at large can produce poverty.

1.2. *Political Rootedness of Poverty*

Poverty doesn't exist independent of a structure. Daron Acemoglu and James A. Robinson argue that nothing around us happens automatically. Everything occurs with certain influencing factors.⁹ Thomas Sowell says, "There is nothing automatic about prosperity or poverty." For instance, the standard of living, which we take for granted today, has been achieved only within a minute fraction of human history. The low standard of living, what we consider to be poverty, has been a norm for untold thousands of years. Here the argument is not about poverty but the origin of inequality which has been ubiquitous as far back as history goes.¹⁰ Thus, poverty in any form, from the primitive age, never existed independently. Appadorai says that it rests on a structure which is designed by an elected administrative body for an orderly purpose. This elected administrative body holds the power to make laws and enforce them.[11] However, in most of the cases, as Dwight R. Lee says, the programmes of the government are resilient politically that do minimum to decrease the poverty rate, but a lot to increase the same. In doing so, government discourages independence and encourages dependence. Political pressure curtails any scheme. Naturally the failure of such schemes will not be perceived as intrinsically political. This is executed by political myopia.[12] Those possessing political power systematically preserve and sustain poverty to suit their vested interests. Thus, poverty is rooted in political structures.

1.3. *The Poor: Perpetual Political Victims*

'Big fish need small fish'[13] is the ideology functioning behind modern political systems. According to David Millwood, poverty has a network of power. The elite and the wealthy of society get their interests fulfilled by hook or crook whereas the poor become victims of political injustice. The bureaucrats of the state are relatively few, but their growth rate reaches the sky. Their importance, in terms of their privilege, power and influence, grows beyond proportion. This power and influence allow the elites to distort the allocation of resources and thereby impoverish the have-nots.[14] Consequently, Saleha S. Mahmood states that poverty increases the gap between the haves and the have-nots, nurtures propensities for violence and conflicts, and creates human rights crises, while human dignity and justice are at stake. The poor, the underprivileged, and those at the peripheries are increasingly marginalized and easily exploited. They suffer physical and psychological damage.[15] Thus 'the poor' are victimized politically.

1.4. *The Church's Option for the Poor: A Political Stand*

We know that politics breeds poverty. Consequently, anything done to eradicate poverty leads to a direct battle with politics. Charity alone doesn't help to win the battle. Paul Valley highlights the need to move from charity to justice.[16] The victims of political injustice long for a perpetual redemption by way of attaining social justice. Fighting for social justice forms an integral part of Catholic Social Teachings as it is affirmed in the encyclical *Sollicitudo Rei Socialis* (The Social Concern of the Church). J. G. Davies says that no one in this world can say that one is totally unconnected or unaffected by such circumstances.[17] The Church ought to confront the politically built structures that crush the poor mercilessly. It's 'option for the poor' is strongly founded on a political stand. Thus, to ensure long-term structural justice for the 'poor,' it is essential to work towards political justice (GS 74). Fighting poverty signifies Political action; and an option for the poor is a Political stand.

2. The Political Dimension of the Second Vatican Council

2.1. *The Essential Teaching of VC II*

In his inaugural address at VC II (*Gaudet Mater Ecclesia* – hereinafter GME), Pope John XXIII insisted on meeting the needs of the modern times (GME 16), wherein human beings labour under many difficulties (GME 17). He asserted that the teachings of the Church, which are predominantly pastoral in character, must be presented in an exceptional form to all people throughout the world, by keeping herself up-to-date where required. He simultaneously calls for a disagreement with the 'prophets of gloom' who are within the Church and are always forecasting disaster as though the end of the world was at hand. His intention, which demonstrates a way to fulfill our duties as citizens of earth and of heaven (GME 11), is clearly not one-sided. Rather, his political intervention exceptionally designates a new look at the present, and reflects on new conditions and new forms of life which ought to be introduced into the modern world (GME 12). John XXIII calls for a political engagement in order to resist the unjust surroundings and oppressive structures, thereby reconstructing them. *Gaudium et Spes* promotes a Political life inspired by inalienable moral values.[18] Certainly, a cry for a Political stand is a key component of VC II and the need of our contemporary world.

Similarly, VC II is very clear about whom it addresses as 'poor', viewing them from a concrete analysis of the happenings around the world: "...a huge proportion of the people of the world are plagued by hunger...totally illiterate...faced by new forms of slavery in living and thinking" (GS 4). The political rootedness of poverty is witnessed by GS 73. It states, "These (cultural, economic, social) transformations exercise a deep influence on political life..." A call to address poverty is found in GS 69. It states: "Men/women are bound to come to the aid of the poor..." and the Council asks the individuals and governments to remember the saying of the Fathers: "Feed the men/women dying of the hunger, because if you do not feed him/her you are killing him/her." Coming to the aid of the poor is nothing but bringing them justice. It is not an option but an obligation to all, especially the Church (Cf. *Evangelica Testifica*, 4). Finally, the mode of aid is stated in GS 73. "There is no better way to establish political life on a truly human basis than by encouraging an inward sense of justice, of goodwill, and of service to the common good." Thus, the Council, having analyzed the plagues of our times, responsibly calls for political engagement to ensure justice for the poor.

2.2. *Evangelization in Politics: Immediate Effect of VC II*

The Puebla Document of the Latin American Bishops' Conference (CELAM), which was published after VC II, states,

> The Church feels it has a duty and a right to be present in this area of reality. For Christianity is supposed to evangelize the whole human life, including the political dimension. So the Church criticizes those who would restrict the scope of faith to personal or family life; who would exclude the professional, economic, social, and political orders as if sin, love, prayer, and pardon had no relevance in them.

The same document also affirms that the need for the Church's presence in the political arena flows from the very core of the Christian faith. Referring to GS 36, the Puebla Document says that the purpose the Lord assigned to the Church's presence in the political arena is a religious one; it doesn't intervene in the socio-political arena with political, economic or social nature, but with a religious mission that structures and consolidates the human community according to the divine law (GS 42). Therefore, the political presence of the Church is for evangelization and for establishing the Kingdom of God.

2.3. New Signs of Our Times in a Broken Society

The world gives birth to new signs of concern from time to time. These are seen in human tears caused by socially and politically structured evils. In an interview Pope Francis said, "How can it be that it is not news item when an elderly person dies of exposure, but when the stock market loses two points, it is flashed as a great fall?"[19] How do we respond to these new signs of our time? Jacques Pulh opines that the living conditions we endure today hide from us these faces of God. In listening to them we will see how best to implement *Gaudium et Spes* today and open up new paths for evangelization. The Church, as mother, bears responsibility to respond. Indeed, the Church is called to be a "discoverer" of God in the face of the reality.[20] The cries of the little ones of our broken society are the new faces of our times that set paths for new evangelization so as to bring to the fore the political dimension of our faith.

2.4. The Political Dimension of Our Faith

The world of the poor opens up enormous opportunities for an evangelization that makes Christian faith real. It offers a reality check. St Oscar Romero says that the incarnation of the Gospel in the socio-political world is a must in which the social and political situation is judged from the standpoint of faith.[21] Through his incarnation, Jesus really took human flesh and made himself one with his brothers and sisters in suffering, in tears and in laments. It is an incarnation that is preferential and partial, an incarnation in the world of the poor. The world of the poor teaches us what the nature of Christian love is; a love that not only seeks peace but also unmasks false pacifism. The necessity of justice for the suffering ought to be meditated over. As per the lesson taught by GS 76, the Church should not run away from healthy conflicts. It also teaches that liberation is possible only when the poor themselves become masters of their own liberation by unmasking false authoritarianism, which includes ecclesiastical authoritarianism. The radical truth of faith is truly radical only when the Church enters into the life and death of her people.[22] Thus by being Political, the Church not only liberates the poor but also exposes injustice and oppression. It is a prophetic face of evangelization that testifies to faith in God.

Being political unveils the social responsibility of the Church. Kenneth R. Himes says that VC II initiated the church-state relationship.[23] This was clearly seen in the praxis of St Oscar Romero who said, "In fighting against multifaceted-poverty, the political dimension of faith is nothing but the Church's response to the demands of the socio-political world in which she exists. This demand is a fundamental one for the faith and the Church cannot ignore it."[24] The same understanding is emphasized in GS 74. Though the document states the autonomy and independence of the Church and political community (GS 76),[25] the Church that works for common good in collaboration with a political community to ensure justice for the poor, exposes its political nature in the world.[26] Thus, the teachings of VC II become incarnate in the political world, proclaiming good news to the poor, giving them hope, encouraging them to engage in liberating praxis and defending their cause. Romero also states that the Church that lives in a political world fulfills itself as a Church through politics, otherwise it cannot be the Church of Christ who fought for the poor, oppressed and repressed.[27] Thus, the Church's option for the poor authenticates the political dimension of our faith in its very core.

3. The Political Dimension of Pope Francis' Faith

3.1. *Pope Francis: A Son of Argentinian Soil*

Pope Francis—the first pope from Latin America—bases his priorities around the tenets of the Argentinian *'theology of the people'*[28] and gradually changes the view of the Church, including the role of religion in politics.[29] His land was at the forefront of liberation theology after VC II. Inspired by Saint Francis of Assisi, the Italian immigrant Cardinal

Jorge Mario Bergoglio chose the name 'Francis' for his pontificate. His motto, *Miserando atque eligendo* means "lowly but chosen," signaled a leadership style that is refreshingly humble, forgiving, and yet, optimistic and resolutely engaged with the world. For this reason, Pope Francis boldly embraces the poor, defends the marginalized, attacks the greedy, and champions the environment. In this regard, he is unapologetically political as he often rebukes world leaders and frequently comments on unjust global economic systems. He is truly a twenty-first-century pontiff.[30] Thus, his formation in Argentina in liberation theology is like the walls of the Red Sea in the Book of Exodus, rising up to protect and defend the 'poor'.

3.2. *The Effect of VC II on Pope Francis' Option for the Poor*

Thomas R. Rourke argues that Francis has concretely set a new course that retrieves the lost progressive heritage of VC II.[31] This Council, which had its impact on Argentinian soil, obviously affected Bergoglio too. Consequently, as Pope, he shows deep convictions in his option for the poor by walking the talk and getting the "smell of the sheep" (EG 198). St John XXIII's resolve: "to make use of the medicine of mercy rather than that of severity" (GME 16) leavens Francis' pontificate, and correspondingly, he never fails to disagree with the "prophets of gloom" (GME 8). Francis holds on to the conviction that mercy is the Lord's most powerful message and that we will not hear words of contempt from God, but only words of love and mercy that lead us to conversion.[32] For Francis, God's mercy, radically stands to challenge the oppressor's enslaving force, and gives birth to a thirst for liberation.[33] From the conclave to the latest post-Pan-Amazon Synodal working document *Instrumentum Laboris*, Pope Francis recapitulates this thirst that echoes the cry of the people and the earth for life (IL 18). Hence his pontificate carries forward St John XXIII's dream and VC II's vision.

Francis' mission realistically echoes the "preferential option for the poor". He embraces a commitment to the poor, upholds the creeds of VC II and the theology of the people, and rejects neo-Marxism.[34] The vibration is felt in and through his papacy. The urgent execution of option for the poor is found in *Evangelii Gaudium* where Pope Francis writes, "Among other important points, the need to resolve the structural causes of poverty cannot be delayed...because society needs to be cured of a sickness which is weakening it."[35] In *Laudato Si'*, he makes an integrated concern of the planet and the poor. For him, "ecological crisis is not so much to talk about the extinction of polar bears and exotic pandas but about the plight of millions of our less fortunate brothers and sisters."[36]

In dialogue with Dominique Wolton, Francis says that economic and social exclusion is a complete denial of human fraternity and a grave offence against human rights and the environment. The poorest are those who suffer most unjustly and they are the victims of the 'culture of waste'. Further, he demands the denunciation of the money god that causes poor to suffer.[37] He adds that the attack against life affects all humanity, especially the poor, the excluded, the marginalized and the persecuted (IL 44); and the ecological approach is always a social approach that raises the questions of justice, so as to hear both the cry of the poor and of the earth (IL 46). In both *Evangelii Gaudium* and *Laudato Si*,[38] Francis condemns the 'ideological colonization of globalization' that produces poverty. Indeed, "Pope Francis is fulfilling the primordial insight of Liberation Theology and promoting its registered trademark: the preferential option for the poor in favor of life and justice... For him, this option is not just rhetoric but a life choice and a spirituality."[39]

The spirituality of the option for the poor generated in Francis a desire for 'the poor church'. This was triggered when Archbishop Emeritus of Sao Paulo who sat next to Bergoglio during the conclave, hugged him and said 'Don't forget the poor.'[40] It reverberated in his heart to propose 'a poor church' for the poor. The meeting point of theology and politics transformed his understanding and urged him to call for a Church that is poor. His plain white cassock, pewter-coloured cross, dilapidated old black shoes, equal-footed platform, plain armchair and his residing among cardinals shattered the royal understanding of unreachable Pope. He expressed his displeasure over 'clericalism' saying, "It hurts my heart when I see a priest with latest model car and he warned the bishops to avoid 'the psychology of princes.'"[41] Paul Vallely recalls Francis saying, "The purpose of the Church is to surge forth to the existential peripheries where people grapple with sin, pain, injustice, ignorance, and indifference to religion and misery."[42]

To achieve this goal of poor church, Francis has shaken the complacencies and self-certainties of Vatican officials—deconstructing the monarchical model of papacy and declaring his desire for a poor Church for the poor people. Similarly, he denounced the injustices of those who oppress the poor.[43] However, his whip is used less or placed in the cold storage of the Indian Catholic Church often unaffected by the harsh realities of life. Thereby 'a poor Indian Catholic Church' remains a distant dream in India. Pope Francis condemns any 'lukewarm attitude'[44] and plainly says that the Church is not for those with a tepid faith. Basically, this attitude hinders anyone from engaging in Politics.

3.3. *Politics According to Pope Francis*

Pope Francis blends faith and politics very harmoniously. He says, "We are all Political animals, with a capital p. We are called to constructive political activity among the people. The preaching of human and religious values has political consequences. What is said from the pulpit refers to politics with capital P, to the politics of values. But the press frequently takes it out of context and takes advantage of it for the lowercase politics."[45] It is the spiritual dimension of the political action of the Church which Francis exercises.[46] Francis says that every individual or an institution throughout the world already has a politics. The politics of the Church is its own witness of going out of oneself. That's why the Church must serve politics by building bridges like Jesus. It's a diplomatic role that seeks something together through dialogue and it is at the heart of our faith.[47] However, it is not a party politics but big *P* politics, a *Politics of Values* that is oriented towards the common good of all. Pope Francis said in June 2013, "Getting involved in politics is a Christian duty, we Christians cannot be like Pilate and wash our hands clean of things..."[48] He further adds in another place, "Politics is dirty but the reason it has become dirty is that Christians didn't get deeply enough involved in the evangelical spirit. It's easy to find an excuse for this. Working for common good is a Christian duty."[49] Hence, Francis finds engagement in politics as the religious duty in order to realize VC II's vision of preferential option for the poor.

3.4. Pope Francis: A Political Prophet

Pope Francis' Political voice cries aloud and fights for the poor like the prophets of old. He has proven himself to be both a prophet and a politician. Vallely analyzes that the qualities needed for both have been manifested in different combinations.[50] The prophets functioned as the voice of conscience for the poor. They were constantly referring to the unjust structures in Israelite society and their need to be rectified.[51] This prophetic dimension emerges in his moral teachings and social concern, as Pope Francis clearly embraces a politically active papacy. He increases his potential to impact politics by his prophetic voice. This is a sign of the times in which he lives. Without wavering from traditional Catholic Church doctrine, he engages in transformative global political dialogues.[52] His papacy of forgiveness, mercy, and compassion uncompromisingly condemns the evil in the world prophetically.[53] Thus his Political voice resounds like a bugle calling for battle in order to accomplish God's saving mission for the poor.

In an interview with Skorka, Francis said that we are called to constructive Political activity among the people emphasizing on the *Politics of values*.[54] As a political leader of a state, Francis comes out sharply on the political policies of the nations. He commented on a Roman dinner saying 'food wasted is food stolen from the poor'.[55] He issued a fierce denunciation over unregulated capitalism and slave labour in connection with the Bangladeshi sweatshop factory collapse that killed thousands. He is not afraid to confront depravity in its den.[56] His diplomatic work with Obama, the then President of USA, played a crucial role in assuring peace in Cuba.[57] He has voiced opinion on issues such as climate change, poverty, inequality, and gay rights.[58]

Among his documents, *Amoris Laetitia* caused an uproar among conservative theologians because it followed more merciful application of church teachings, especially on divorce, sexual morality and access to communion. The encyclical *Laudato Si* has made observations on political conflicts related to global climate change.[59] He encounters not only other nations and organizations but also his own institution: church institutions and administrative bodies. In the Vatican, Francis broke the monarchy of papacy which was the turn at the core of VC II.[60] He permitted the agencies to investigate the Vatican Bank's deception and to summon any document and data they deemed necessary and they were told to report directly to Pope Francis bypassing the Vatican bureaucracy.[61] He is regular in his analysis and critiques of political occurrences. Thus, he proves to be a Political prophet very much in line with the Biblical prophetic tradition.

4. Church's Option for the Poor: Call to Indian Church for Political Involvement

The Indian Catholic Church (ICC) is well aware of the oppression and repression widespread in India today. She surely knows about the denial of justice, human rights, constitutional rights, democratic values, and so on to the citizens, especially to the poor in India. She also witnesses the same in the international arena. But it is painful and disheartening to note that the higher administrative bodies of the ICC keep silent in the face of oppression and injustice. We have a few examples of pastoral letters from Archbishop Thomas Macwan of Gandhinagar on November 21, 2017 and Archbishop Anil J. Couto of Delhi on May 22, 2018, who came out to support the common good, cautioning the faithful about dangers in society. They were targeted immediately by a biased media supported by political parties and communal forces. These initiatives have not got much support from the authorities of the ICC.

Would Pope Francis approve of the stance of the ICC? Not likely, since Francis affirms that political activism is essential. For him, being a Christian is not the result of an ethical choice or a lofty idea, but the encounter with an event which gives life a new horizon and decisive direction. As evidenced by his apostolic exhortations, for Francis, structural sin can be found in the concrete reality of economic structures that favour the rich at the expense of the poor and the marginalized. He focuses his attention on the need to address such systemic injustices in policy formation, especially in terms of the preferential option for the poor.[62] As the Pope and the head of a state, by his word and deeds, Francis calls the ICC for an active political engagement to authentically implement the preferential option for the poor through her Political pulpit. In this multi-religious Indian scenario, besides the Church being Political, she ought to necessarily encourage lay people to enter into politics with Christian values.

Conclusion

Traditionally, the Church is known to foster its spiritual dimension. But today, in a context with so much of injustice, the Church in general and the ICC in particular, is obliged to discover her political dimension to fulfill her prophetic mission of attaining justice. It is an incarnation that the world of poor expects today for its liberation. It is unbecoming of Christ's Church to 'washes her hands like Pilate. Having the mind of John XXIII and the spirit of VC II, Pope Francis incarnates the Church's teachings radically and shows us the way for praxis. By calling for an active political involvement, he theologizes on politics and harmonizes it with his faith. He calls for a *Politics of Values*. This is an expression of the political dimension of Pope Francis' faith that functions round the clock to authenticate his preferential option for the poor. This 'Political dimension of faith' principally demands 'clean hands' from every member of the Church. If we follow Pope Francis' example, we will truly become 'Political Prophets of the Poor'.

Endnotes

[1] Second Vatican Council, *Gaudium et Spes, Pastoral Constitution on the Church in the Modern World* (7 Dec 1965). Hereinafter this document will be referred to as *GS*.

[2] What Francis refers to here is Politics with capital P, to the Politics of values. See Alejandro Bermudez and Howard Goodman, trans., *On Heaven and Earth* (London: Bloomsbury, 2013), 136-137.

³ J. G. Davies, *Christians, Politics and Violent Revolution* (New York: Orbis Books, 1976), 2.

⁴ Saleha S. Mahmood, "Poverty and Injustice – Alarming Signs of the Present Crisis in Human Society Worldwide," in *Poverty and Injustice: Alarming Signs of the Present Crisis in Human Society Worldwide*, ed. Andreas Bsteh and Tahir Mehmood (Modling: Vienna International Christian-Islamic Round Table – 3, 2004), 121.

⁵ Francis P. Xavier, "Keynote Address from 'Poverty to Power'," in *Profiles of Poverty and Networks of Power*, ed. Anand Amaladoss (Madurai: DACA Publications, 2001), 13.

⁶ James Massey, *Downtrodden: The Struggles of India's Dalits for Identity, Solidarity and Liberation* (Geneva: Risk Book Series, 1997), 3.

⁷ George M. Soares-Prabhu, *Theology of Liberation: An Indian Biblical Perspective*, ed. Francis X. D'Sa, vol. 4 of *Collected Writings of George M. Soares-Prabhu* (Pune: Jnana-Deepa Vidyapeeth Theology Series, 2001), 87-92.

⁸ Ingeborg Gabriel, "The Different Faces of Poverty," in *Poverty and Injustice: Alarming Signs of the Present Crisis in Human Society Worldwide*, 27-31.

⁹ Daron Acemoglu and James A. Robinson, *Why Nations Fail: The Origins of Power, Prosperity and Poverty* (New York: Crown Business, 2012), 12.

¹⁰ Thomas Sowell, *Wealth, Poverty and Politics: An International Perspective* (New York: Basic Books, 2015), 33.

¹¹ A. Appadorai, *The Substance of Politics* (London: Oxford University Press, 1957), 4-5.

¹² Dwight R. Lee, "The Politics of Poverty and the Poverty of Politics," *The Cato Journal*, 33. https://pdfs.semanticscholar.org/698a/cd135853e9cc948d922543ee6266a73068ef.pdf (accessed October 13, 2019).

¹³ By this, the big fish control the system and the small fish compete with each other. See David Millwood, *The Poverty Makers* (Geneva: WCC, 1977), 5.

¹⁴ David Millwood, *The Poverty Makers*, 31.

¹⁵ Saleha S. Mahmood, "Poverty and Injustice – Alarming Signs of the present Crisis in Human Society Worldwide," in *Poverty and Injustice: Alarming Signs of the Present Crisis in Human Society Worldwide*, 121-30.

¹⁶ Paul Vallely, *Pope Francis: Untying the Knots, The Struggle for the Soul of Catholicism* (London: Bloomsbury, 2015), 138.

¹⁷ J. G. Davies, *Christians, Politics and Violent Revolution*, 4.

¹⁸ John Paul II, "*Gaudium et Spes*: The Ultimate Message: Christ, Redeemer of Man," in *Gaudium et Spes: Thirty Years Later, Loreto '95* (Vatican City: Laity Today, 1996), 13.

¹⁹ Vallely, *Pope Francis: Untying the Knots*, 324.

²⁰ Oscar Romero, *Voice of the Voiceless: The Four Pastoral Letters and Other Statements*, trans. Michael J. Walsh (New York: Orbis Books, 1985), 183-184.

²¹ Ibid.

[22] Ibid.

[23] Kenneth R. Himes, "Vatican II and Contemporary Politics," in *The Catholic Church and the Nation State*, 17.

[24] Romero, *Voice of the Voiceless: The Four Pastoral Letters and Other Statements*, 182.

[25] Mazowiecki, "Universal Values and he Concept of the Common Good," in *Gaudium et Spes: Thirty Years Later, Loreto '95*, 218.

[26] Third General Conference of Latin American Bishops, *Puebla: Evangelization at Present and in the Future of Latin America* (London: St. Paul Publication, 1980), 109.

[27] Oscar Romero, *Voice of the Voiceless: The Four Pastoral Letters and Other Statements*, 182-183.

[28] Historically this theological approach emerged from VC II, especially *Gaudium et Spes* which discusses the role of the Church in the world. It is founded on bottom-up theology where the sincere love of God is practiced by people at the local level. It emphasizes the need to place Christ, who lived among the poor and the socially marginalized, at the center of all activities. The theology of the people is subsequently detailed in *Evangelii Gaudium* (2013). See Paul Christopher Manuel, "How the Theological Priorities of Pope Francis Inform His Policy Goals," https://www.academia.edu/37277325/How_the_Theological_Priorities_of_Pope_Francis_Inform_His_Policy_Goals (accessed October 13, 2019).

[29] Ibid.

[30] Alynna J. Lyon, Christine A. Gustafson and Paul Christopher Manuel, "Eluding Established Categories: Toward an Understanding of Pope Francis," https://www.researchgate.net/publication/323013772_Pope_Francis_as_a_Global_Actor_Where_Politics_and_Theology_Meet (accessed October 13, 2019).

[31] Thomas R. Rourke, *The Roots of Pope Francis' Social and Political Thought: From Argentina to the Vatican* (Lanham: Rowman and Little field, 2016), 231.

[32] Vallely, *Pope Francis: Untying the Knots*, 124.

[33] Ibid., 124.

[34] Alynna J. Lyon, Christine A. Gustafson and Paul Christopher Manuel, "Eluding Established Categories: Toward an Understanding of Pope Francis," https://www.researchgate.net/publication/323013772_Pope_Francis_as_a_Global_Actor_Where_Politics_and_Theology_Meet (accessed October 13, 2019).

[35] Paul Christopher Manuel, "How the Theological Priorities of Pope Francis Inform His Policy Goals," https://www.academia.edu/37277325/How_the_Theological_Priorities_of_Pope_Francis_Inform_His_Policy_Goals (accessed October 13, 2019).

[36] Joshtrom Isaac Kureethandam, "Listening to the Cry of the Earth and of the Poor: Eco-Justice in *Laudato Si*," *Mission Today* 38/4 (Oct-Dec 2016): 292.

[37] Shaun Whiteside, trans., *Pope Francis with Dominique Wolton: The Path to Change, thoughts on Politics and Society* (London: Bluebird Books for Life, 2018), 27.

[38] Ibid., 19.

³⁹ Vallely, *Pope Francis: Untying the Knots*, 143.

⁴⁰ Marco Politi, *Pope Francis Among the Wolves: An Inside Story of Revolution* (New York: Columbia University Press, 2015), 17.

⁴¹ Vallely, *Pope Francis: Untying the Knots*, 183.

⁴² Vallely, *Pope Francis: Untying the Knots*, 151.

⁴³ Ibid., 413.

⁴⁴ Pope Francis, "The Church is not for the lukewarm," Morning Meditation in the Chapel of the Domus Sanctae Marthae, Tuesday, 23 May 2017. http://www.vatican.va/content/francesco/en/cotidie/2017/documents/papa-francesco-cotidie_20170523_the-church-is-not-for-the-lukewarm.html (accessed November 28, 2019).

⁴⁵ Alejandro Bermudez and Howard Goodman, trans., *On Heaven and Earth* (London: Bloomsbury, 2013), 136-137.

⁴⁶ Shaun Whiteside, trans., *Pope Francis with Dominique Wolton: The Path to Change, Thoughts on Politics and Society*, xii.

⁴⁷ Whiteside, trans., *Pope Francis with Dominique Wolton*, 7-13.

⁴⁸ Vallely, *Pope Francis: Untying the Knots*, 143.

⁴⁹ Ibid., 143-144.

⁵⁰ Ibid., 395-405.

⁵¹ Joy Philip Kakkanattu, "Biblical Prophets as Transformative Leaders," *Jeevadhara* 42/248 (March 2012): 123.

⁵² Lyon, Gustafson and Manuel, "Eluding Established Categories,"

⁵³ See Joy Philip Kakkanattu, "Biblical Prophets as Transformative Leaders," 130.

⁵⁴ Alejandro Bermudez and Howard Goodman, trans., *On Heaven and Earth*, 136.

⁵⁵ Vallely, *Pope Francis: Untying the Knots*, 174.

⁵⁶ Ibid., 184.

⁵⁷ Vallely, *Pope Francis: Untying the Knots*, 391.

⁵⁸ Walter Moss, "Is Pope Francis Too Political?" https://historynewsnetwork.org/article/158476 (accessed October 13, 2019).

⁵⁹ Lyon, Gustafson and Manuel, "Eluding Established Categories,"

⁶⁰ Marco Politi, *Pope Francis Among the Wolves: An Inside Story of Revolution*, 57.

⁶¹ Vallely, *Pope Francis: Untying the Knots*, 177.

⁶² Paul Christopher Manuel, "How the Theological Priorities of Pope Francis Inform His Policy Goals," https://www.academia.edu/37277325/How_the_Theological_Priorities_of_Pope_Francis_Inform_His_Policy_Goals (accessed October 13, 2019).

15.

Strangers No More

Pope Francis Carries the Torch of Vatican Council II

Mohan Doss, SVD

Introduction

Pope Francis has emerged as a champion of migrants and refugees in the contemporary world. Focusing on Asia's migration crisis, the Holy Father said in Bangkok on November 21, 2019, migration is "one of the defining signs of our time" and "one of the principal moral issues facing our generation."[1] However, it must be noted that migration has always existed. For instance, in the Judeo-Christian tradition, the history of salvation is but a history of migration. Nor can one forget that freedom of movement, the ability to leave one's own country and to return there, is a fundamental human right.[2]

The objective of this paper is to illustrate how Pope Francis has carried the flame of the Second Vatican Council (hereinafter VC II) and his predecessors' concern for the welfare of migrants and refugees through his passionate teachings and powerful symbolic actions. The paper consists of two parts. The first part deals with the magisterial teaching till the years of Pope Benedict XVI.³ The second part highlights Pope Francis' prophetic role in awakening the conscience of the world to accept migrants as brothers and sisters and embrace them as gifts to be nourished for the enrichment of human community.

1. Migrants and Migration: The Catholic Magisterium till 2013

The Church's genuine commitment to the welfare of migrants can be perceived from her social teaching from two perspectives. First, the Social Teaching of the Church makes human dignity its very centerpiece, because human dignity and human rights are integral to the proclamation of the reign of God. Human dignity is directly concerned with the issue of migration. Second, the recent magisterial social teachings are related to the issue of migration, and the Annual Migration Day Messages.

1.1. *Human Dignity: The Centerpiece of the Social Teaching of the Church*

The Social Teaching of the Church (hereinafter STC) is the outcome of the Church leaders' efforts to interpret God's Word in contemporary society. VC II's Pastoral Constitution on the Church in the Modern World, *Gaudium et Spes* (hereinafter GS) perceived it as the duty of the Church: "the Church carries the responsibility of reading the signs of the times and of interpreting them in the light of the Gospel, if it is to carry out its task" (GS 4). In his *Pacem in Terris* (Peace on Earth, 1963) Pope John XXIII asserted that the basic design of STC emerges from the sacredness of every human being to the full range of the human community.⁴ The STC affirms the rights and responsibilities of every person; emphasizes the necessity of the structures that protect these rights and fulfill these responsibilities, based on the values of the Gospel. Thus, the dignity of the human person is the centerpiece of the Social Teaching of the Church.

1.2. Church's Teachings on Migration

Let us have a quick look at some of the STC's of the past.

1.2.1. Exsul Familia: The Magna Charta for Migrants

The first great magisterial document on the subject of migration is *Constitutio Exsul Familia Nazarethana* (Families in Exile, 1952), of Pope Pius XII. It is referred as the *Magna Charta for Migrants*. It depicted the Holy Family of Nazareth in exile as the archetype of every refugee family,[5] and focused on Catholic immigrants and as well a wider horizon that validated a universalist vision of humans as individuals endowed with sacred rights. It acknowledged that "migration is an opportunity to transform suffering into something good. Immigrants look for a better life and are willing to contribute to the prosperity of their new homeland," and affirmed that "migrants have religious rights to keep their religion and identity and the Church has the duty to receive them in their new environment." It called on the international organizations to collaborate together for the welfare of migrants through international law and dialogues with the states.[6]

1.2.2. The Second Vatican Council[7]

VC II's *Gaudium et Spes* called on Christians in particular to be aware of the phenomenon of migration. The Council reaffirmed the dignity of migrant workers, the need to overcome inequalities in economic and social development (*GS* 63,65,66) and to respond to the genuine needs of the human person (*GS* 84). VC II attempted to present a balanced view by recognizing the right of the public authorities to regulate the flow of migration in a given context (*GS* 87).

The Decree on the Apostolate of Laity, *Apostolicam actuositatem*, gave a clarion call to the laity to extend their whole hearted cooperation and collaboration to all sectors of society (*AA* 10), and spoke of their inescapable duty to be the neighbour of every one in need, particularly of migrant workers and refugees (*GS* 27). Thus, the teaching of the Council is based on the biblical instruction: "The alien who resides with you shall be to you as the citizen among you, you shall love the alien as yourself" (Lev 19:34).

1.2.3. Post-Vatican Era: Pope Paul VI to Pope Benedict XVI

1.2.3.1. Pope Paul VI

Since VC II, the Catholic Church began to understand herself as a pilgrim church, a people on the move. This self-understanding of the Church had also enabled the faithful to see their life as a metaphorical journey, "whilst physically they could bring their faith to faraway places, or they could bring it at home by welcoming the world and being open towards foreigners. Local churches were called on to set up missions on their own territories."[8]

Pope Paul VI demonstrated the Church's commitment to the implementation of the Council's concern for migrants in his 'Motu proprio' *Pastoralis Migratorum Cura* and the Instruction *De Pastorali Migratorum Cura* (1969). The Pontifical Commission for the Pastoral Care of Migrants and Itinerant People continued to emphasize the necessity of pastoral ministry for migrants through its circular letter to the Episcopal Conferences entitled, *Church and Human Mobility* (1978).[9]

The documents *Populorum Progressio* (1967) and the *motu proprio* (1971) of Pope Paul VI underscored the role of migration towards building a "one universal human civilization".[10] These two documents affirmed peoples' right to move and asserted that it is a natural freedom; reminded of the duties of migrants; perceived migration as a global issue and called on the International Organizations to protect this right. These documents admitted that "states have the right to limit and regulate immigration, but their limitations should not be a way to stop states from discharging their duties towards migrants, they have to avoid ghettos, deportations, etc."[11] These documents exhorted Christians to welcome and accept migrants of other religious traditions also, because it offered an opportunity to 'love one's neighbor in need' as they are created in God's own image and likeness.[12]

1.2.3.2. Pope John Paul II

Starting from his first encyclical, *Redemptor Hominis* of 1979, Pope John Paul II gave the Church's defense of human rights an international dimension.¹³ His defense of human rights included several concerns of migrants. In his speech to the United Nations on October 2, 1979, he spoke of the right to freedom of movement and to internal and international migration, the right to nationality and residence, and the right to political participation. He emphasized the importance of cultural rights by asserting that they make up a person not only as an individual but also as person in a cultural society, i.e., at the collective level.¹⁴

In his *Laborem Exercens* of 1981 John Paul II emphasized one's right to emigrate together with one's family and the right to wellbeing that necessarily includes the right to respect one's identity. It affirmed also that the cultural heritage of migrants contributed to the cultural, spiritual, and human common good of the host societies.¹⁵ *Laborem Exercens* perceived human work as the key to the social question and addressed the human person as the subject: "Work must not be seen as an object, as a result or product. But rather work must be seen through the subject who performs the work. Work has human person as its subject" (LE 20). It categorically asserted the right of migrants to be treated as subjects with respect: "Migrants are workers, but they must not become the object of our concern, but rather they are the subject" (LE 23). It defended stating that the right to migrate supports the basic human freedom and the dignity of the person.

Being conscious of the lack of legal and social protection of illegal migrants particularly in the 1980s, the Catholic Magisterium denounced their insecure status, their struggle in obtaining visas and inability to have all their papers in order, the development of human trafficking and an eventual return to slavery.¹⁶ The Magisterium through its documents increasingly focused on the misery and the dignity of those without legal papers, and repeatedly emphasized that "the human persons caught in the migratory phenomenon should be the axis around which immigrant rights were constructed and not a last consideration when deciding the immigrants' fate and status."¹⁷ The 1984 Annual Migration Day Message tried to replace the term xenophobia (fear of strangers) with the newly coined word '*philoxemia*'. Philoxemia implies a sense of open and cordial hospitality which St Paul reminds the Christian community, "Extend hospitality to strangers" (Rom 12:13).

In his Message for the World Day of Migrants and Refugees in 1991 Pope John Paul II said: "Migration always has two aspects, diversity and universality. The former comes from the meeting between diverse individuals and groups of people and involves inevitable tension, latent rejection and open polemics. The latter is constituted by the harmonious meeting of diverse social subjects who discover themselves in the patrimony that is common to every human being formed as it is by the values of humanity and fraternity. There is a mutual enrichment when diverse cultures come into contact."[18] In his Annual Migration Day Message of 1993 he quoted his Apostolic Letter *Familaris Consortio* (1981): "The family of migrants... should be able to find a homeland everywhere in the Church" (FC 77).

In his Message for the World Day of Migration in 2002, Pope John Paul II emphasized the need for cultural preservation as well as cultural pluralism in the context of migration. The message rightly observed that most migrants often experience an identity crisis in the process of migration. They encounter a challenge to take on a new culture and it is a challenge to their own identity. Pope John Paul II suggested that they must defend and cherish their culture lest they miss something of their rich cultural identity.[19]

As against the popular perception of poor migrants as intruders, in his encyclical *Centesimus Annus* (1991) John Paul II asserted that "the poor as individuals and peoples...are not irksome intruders" (CA 28). He further affirmed that human dignity and human rights must necessarily be supported by subsidiarity and participation, and defended their right to be protected. He categorically stated that the dignity of migrants should not be sacrificed on the altar of legal correctness or discrimination, and emphatically asserted that migrants' humanity be taken into account before the illegal nature of their presence.[20]

In 2000, the Catholic Jubilee Year, John Paul II called for the regularization of those without legal papers in all countries as a gesture of reconciliation. In 2001, he wrote to the Director General of the International Organization for Migrations not to be afraid of confronting and denouncing those laws that infringed international norms, and concluded: "beyond all differences, all men and women are brothers and sisters in the one human family."[21] Moreover, in his annual message for World Migration Day 2005, he desired that as the Catholic immigrants are welcomed into the Catholic dioceses together with their linguistic and cultural differences, so also the immigrants in general are to be accepted together with their culture. They are called to contribute in some way to enrich the host societies. John Paul II was called "Pope of the Migrants" because of his uncompromising emphasis on the rights of the migrants.[22]

Erga migrantes Caritas Christi (The Love of Christ towards Migrants), the Instruction from Pontifical Council for the Pastoral Care of Migrant and Itinerant People in 2004, presented a series of pastoral guidelines to parishes and exhorted each parish to become a universal church by welcoming Catholic migrants, and be a home of everyone, a place for authentic human and Christian promotion. The active presence of migrants in a parish would make it an inter-ethnic, inter-cultural, and inter-ritual witness that Catholicity is not a mere concept but a tangible, cross-border, transnational, trans-ethnic reality.[23]

1.2.3.3. Pope Benedict XVI

In his *Caritas in Veritate*, Benedict XVI affirmed that the migration phenomenon has to be handled primarily through international cooperation and between departure and arrival countries. He pleaded that every migrant, legal or illegal, has to be respected by everyone and in all circumstances as a human person possessing fundamental and inalienable rights.[24]

Benedict XVI, in his message for the World Day of Migrants and Refugees in 2007, rightly affirmed that the World Day of Migrants and Refugees is "a useful occasion to build awareness, in the ecclesial community and public opinion, regarding the needs and problems, as well as the positive potentialities of migrant families." He further said that the choice of theme 'The Migrant Family' underlines, "the commitment of the Church not only in favour of the individual migrants, but also of his family, which is a place and resource of the culture of life and a factor for the integration of values. The family meets many difficulties. The distance of its members from one another.... New relationships are formed and new affections arise. Some migrants forget the past and their duties, as they are subjected to the hard trial of distance and solitude. If the migrant family is not ensured of real possibility of inclusion and participation, it is difficult to expect its harmonious development."[25] Indeed, the Messages for the World Day of Migrants and Refugees manifest the passionate commitment of the Church to the care of migrants and refugees in fidelity to the values of the Gospels.[26]

The Catholic Pastoral Magisterium established the following by the first decade in the new millennium:[27]

1. Legal migrants have to be protected against discrimination. Illegal migrants need special and respectful attention because they are not protected, are often victims of trafficking, etc. They are, before all other considerations, human beings.[28]

2. Migrants need to be welcomed in parish life. Each parish has to transform itself into a universal Church. It will be a proof that Catholicity is not a concept but a concrete transnational, trans-ethnic reality. Local parishes need also to become intercultural, with centers for migration studies.

3. Migrants of other religious traditions, especially Muslims are to be welcomed. The 2004 Instruction (*Erga migrantes caritas Christi*) made it obligatory to set up centers for interreligious welcome and dialogue in each diocese, non-discriminatory help by Catholic associations, and welcoming children of other religious traditions in Catholic schools.

2. Pope Francis: A Prophet of Our Times

Right from the start of his papacy in March 2013, Pope Francis emphasized his desire for "a poor Church for the poor" and respect for the sanctity of all life. These preferences have naturally led him speak on the experiences of migrants and refugees to decry the precarious, inhuman and intolerable conditions which they must often endure. Pope Francis is "effectively the first one to have taken such high-profile and lofty positions in favor of illegal migrants trying to enter Europe and the US."[29]

2.1. Pope Francis' Way of Promoting the Spirit of VC II

Pope Francis' contributions to carry the torch of VC II can be perceived notably in two ways: First, his pastoral approach characterizes a movement from doctrine through compassion to action—as referred by some "from orthodoxy through orthopathy to orthopraxis"—a movement from mere doctrinal theory to loving, affective personal engagement with the "other," the least, the lost and the excluded. Second, his reform of the Church can be characterized by a "revolution of mercy" that understands people's concerns "affectively through the lens of mercy and with love", and seeks "at every level to integrate faith with life through prayer and spiritual growth."[30]

Pope Francis' approach follows the spirit of *Lumen Gentium*, which in a way responded to the call, 'Church, define yourself in the contemporary context of the world'. This approach wants the Church move into the streets and realize her identity at the service of others, and follows faithfully the inspiration of the opening lines of *Gaudium et Spes* (1): "The joy and hope, the grief and anguish" of the people of our time, "especially of those who are poor or afflicted in any way, are the joy and hope, the grief and anguish of the followers of Christ as well."

2.2. Pope Francis' Passionate Concern for Migrants

Pope Francis' first pastoral visit outside Rome was to Lampedusa Island in Sicily, where he celebrated the Holy Mass to commemorate the thousands of migrants who had died crossing the Mediterranean. The purpose of his visit to Lampedusa was "to pray, to make a gesture of closeness, but also to reawaken our consciences so that what happened would not be repeated."[31] He denounced the European Union Security Policy as inhuman that lacked compassion and empathy for lost lives, for the terrible fate and excruciating pain endured by millions of people fleeing wars, persecution, and criminal environments. Pope Francis continually invites his listeners to treat migrants with acceptance and solidarity, to empathize with them and to recognize their value and human potential. He speaks unceasingly against the "globalization of indifference" and promotes a spirituality of solidarity.[32]

The term "the globalization of indifference" describes the callousness with which individuals and communities treat poor, desperate and marginal persons.[33] He has revisited this theme several times. For instance, in *Laudato Si* (25), he described widespread indifference to suffering and admitted that: "Our lack of response to these tragedies involving our brothers and sisters points to the loss of that sense of responsibility for our fellow men and women upon which all civil society is founded." [34]

Pope Francis' visit to Ciudad Juarez in Mexico in February 2016 during the US presidential campaign was highly symbolic. During the Holy Mass, close to the US metal border, he called for bridges not walls to be built. His clarion call for human solidarity was in opposition to Donald Trump's attitude towards illegal immigrants. For the Holy Thursday ritual, Pope Francis washed the feet of 11 migrants from a Roman Shelter in March 2016. Three of them were Muslims. In April, he went to Lesbos Island to visit temporary asylum seeker camps that were de facto prisons. His intention was obviously to denounce their very inhuman living conditions and the European countries' detention policies. On his return, he brought Muslim refugee families in his own plane back to Rome.[35]

Pope Francis denounces the mistreatment of migrants and speaks repeatedly on migration in his writings on other topics, including his encyclical *Laudato Si*, and the apostolic exhortation *Evangelii Gaudium*.[36]

In his writings, he often highlights the connections between issues like migration, poverty and development and global power structures. In *Laudato Si*, Pope Francis linked the issues of climate change, poverty and migration: "There has been a tragic rise in the number of migrants seeking to flee from the growing poverty caused by environmental degradation. They are not recognized by international conventions as refugees; they bear the loss of the lives they have left behind, without enjoying any legal protection whatsoever. Sadly, there is widespread indifference to such suffering" (LS 25). He dealt directly on the migration issues, for instance, in article 210 of *Evangelii Gaudium*:

> Migrants present a particular challenge for me, since I am the pastor of ... a Church which considers herself mother to all. For this reason, I exhort all countries to a generous openness which, rather than fearing the loss of local identity, will prove capable of creating new forms of cultural synthesis. How beautiful are those cities which overcome paralyzing mistrust, integrate those who are different and make this very integration a new factor of development!

On the occasion of the Mexico Holy See Colloquium on Human Migration and Development in July 2014,[37] Pope Francis highlighted poverty, climate change (LS 25) and violence as causes for migration, and emphasized the necessity and significance of solidarity and encounter for our times (EG 87). He spoke also on solidarity in the context of multiculturalism in his message for the 2015 World Day of Migrants and Refugees: "The multicultural character of society today…encourages the Church to take on new commitments of solidarity…. Migration movements…call us to deepen and strengthen the values needed to guarantee peaceful coexistence between persons and cultures." To the Holy Father, solidarity is not merely a matter of individual obligation but also central to a just world order: "[S]olidarity with migrants and refugees must be accompanied by the courage and creativity necessary to develop, on a worldwide level, a more just and equitable financial and economic order, as well as an increasing commitment to peace, the indispensable condition for all authentic progress."[38]

2.3. Pope Francis' Uncompromising Response to Human Trafficking

In 2014, together with leaders of other major religions, Pope Francis created the Global Freedom Network dedicated to eradicate slavery and human trafficking.[39] He has been particularly active and uncompromising in response to the scourge of human trafficking (LS 91; EG 75). In his address to the Participants of the International Conference on Combating Human Trafficking held in 2014, he described trafficking as, "an open wound on the body of contemporary society, a scourge upon the body of Christ. It is a crime against humanity." He emphasized the necessity of approaching the problem of trafficking both legally, through the activity of law enforcement authorities, and from a social and humanitarian standpoint, by providing victims with "human warmth and the possibility of building a new life."[40]

Pope Francis strongly condemned the traffickers in his homily at Lampedusa in 2013 and called them the exploiters of the poverty of others, for whom "the poverty of others is a source of income".[41] He argued in his statement on "Modern Slavery and Climate Change: The Commitment of the Cities" in July 2015: "Unemployment…has led to illegal work and human trafficking… everything has a rebound effect against the person himself. It can include human trafficking for purposes of slave labour or prostitution."[42]

In his *Amoris Laetitia* (2015), Pope Francis argued that human mobility can contribute to genuine enrichment of migrant families and as well of the countries that welcome them. He spoke also of the negative effects of migration on family life, particularly of "forced migration of families, resulting from situations of war, persecution, poverty and injustice, and marked by the vicissitudes of a journey that often puts lives at risk, traumatizes people and destabilizes families."[43] He insisted that the Church should have special pastoral programme for families that migrate and also to those members who remain behind. Such programmes "must be implemented with due respect for their cultures, for the human and religious formation from which they come and for the spiritual richness of their rites and traditions, even by means of a specific pastoral care". He contended rightly that "every effort should be encouraged, even in a practical way, to assist families and Christian communities to remain in their native lands" (AL 46).

2.4. Messages for the World Day Migrants and Refugees

Pope Francis' Messages for the World Day of Migrants and Refugees are not mere words but personal expressions of his passionate love and care for them that flow from deep down his heart and migrant roots. They are also his prophetic protest against the injustices meted out to them.

Criticizing the phenomenon of indifference, Pope Francis calls for a culture of encounter in his Message for the World Day of Migrants and Refugees in 2014: "A change of attitude towards migrants and refugees is needed on the part of everyone, moving away from attitudes of defensiveness and fear, indifference and marginalization – all typical of throwaway culture – towards attitudes based on a culture of encounter, the only culture capable of building a better, more just and fraternal world."[44] His message highlights the scandal of poverty in its various forms and linked poverty with migration among its other causes like persecution and violence. He calls for elimination of prejudices and presupposition against migrants and wants them to be seen not as problem but as brothers and sisters and above all as children of God. Thus, he seeks to move the world from an attitude of indifference to its opposite, which he calls a "culture of encounter."

In his message for the 2015 World Day of Migrants and Refugees, Pope Francis spoke of the Church without frontiers and as Mother to all. The Church lives her motherhood by spreading a culture of acceptance and solidarity. He condemns the hostile, suspicious and prejudiced reception of many migrants, which "conflict[s] with the biblical commandment of welcoming with respect and solidarity the stranger in need."[45] In addition, this treatment is inimical to the mission of the Catholic Church, which seeks to spread "throughout the world a culture of acceptance and solidarity, in which no one is seen as useless, out of place or disposable."[46] Since migration affects everyone[47] (*Caritas in Veritate* 62), Pope Francis promotes a globalization of charity and cooperation in the place of globalization of indifference.

Admitting that the phenomenon of migrants and refugees does challenge us today, Pope Francis advocates a response of mercy in his message for the Word Day of Migrants and Refugees in 2016. He promotes 'a culture of encounter' spelling out the following as its essential ingredients: (i). Fostering good relationship with others, (ii). Overcoming prejudice and fear, (iii). Magnanimous generosity to give and receive, (iv). Hospitality that thrives in a spirit of give and take in a society. He underscored further the need to promote the dignity of every person, particularly of migrants and refugees, and a grateful respect for host nations also. Stating that their departure from their homeland is often caused by poverty, persecution and violence, he pleaded that the flight of refugees should be averted in earliest stages and their right to live in their homeland must be defended at all cost. He called for vigilance against new forms of slavery that emerge crudely and shamelessly.[48] He reiterated the same ideas in *Amoris Laetitia* (46).

Along the lines of *Caritas in Veritate* (47), in his Message of 2018, Pope Francis emphasized the centrality of human person and called for a shared response that would include "Welcoming, Protecting, Promoting and Integrating" the migrants, which he called as 'FOUR VERBS'. Basing his reflections on Lev 19:34, he proposed that strangers in the host nations be treated as "the native among you."[49]

On the occasion of the unveiling of the monument "*Angels Unaware*" in St. Peter's Square on September 29, 2019, Pope Francis reminded the Christians on the need to "welcome, protect, promote and integrate" the migrants and added that the Church's mission should also extend to "all those living in the existential peripheries." He added: "If we put those four verbs into practice, we will promote the integral human development of all people."[50]

In his Message of 2019 Pope Francis wrote that one's fears of migrants influence one's way of thinking and in turn it affects one's attitude and actions. Further reflecting on various biblical texts, he spelt out deeper dimensions of faith.[51] Charity towards migrants is the highest form of charity to the vulnerable and poor. Charity cares for the whole person and excludes no one, and places the last and least in the first place. Faith includes one's attitude and actions in favour of migrants because it speaks of one's compassion to heal, save and help the neediest persons. Faith recognizes the equality of all, and aims at integral development that fosters "the development of each person and the whole of person."[52] Further, faith is about building the city of God and humans. He admits that the contemporary time is "an era of migration". But one must be aware that migrants are not problems to be solved. They are brothers and sisters to be welcomed, respected and loved. For him, migration is a God-given opportunity to humanity to build a better future together with all people.

2.5. Pope Francis Gives Greater Visibility to VC II

Taking into account Pope Francis' symbolic actions and words in favour of migrants and refugees against the backdrop of the documents of VC II and of his papal predecessors, one can state without any hesitation that he gives greater visibility to the Council.

Let me illustrate my standpoint with the following examples:

2.5.1. *Visibility to Exsul Familia*

On September 29, 2019, during a special Mass on the 105th World Day of Migrants and Refugees, Pope Francis unveiled a monument to migration in St Peter's Square as homage to the displaced. The monument titled, *Angels Unaware* depicts 140 migrants and refugees from various historical periods travelling on a boat and includes indigenous people, the Virgin Mary and Joseph, Jews fleeing Nazi Germany and those from war-torn countries. The monument *Angels Unaware* in St. Peter's Square gives visibility to *Exsul Familia* of 1952 in which Pope Pius XII spoke of the Holy Family of Nazareth in exile as the archetype of every refugee family.

During the unveiling ceremony of the statue, Pope Francis mentioned that it had been inspired by a passage from the Letter to the Hebrews: "Do not forget to show hospitality to strangers, for by so doing some people have shown hospitality to angels without knowing it" (Heb 13:2). He wanted the statue in St Peter's Square "so that all will be reminded of the evangelical challenge of hospitality."[53]

2.5.2. Visibility to *Gaudium et Spes*

The opening words of *Gaudium et Spes*, "The joy and hope, the grief and anguish of the people of our time are the joy and hope…of the followers of Christ", spring from Gal 2:10 which speaks of the "primordial concern for the poor". Pope John Paul II's call for the "Option for the Poor" was a retrieval of a constitutive dimension of the Church.[54] This paved the way for Pope Francis' persistent call to go to the existential peripheries, and for his passion to care for the disposable people, notably among them are migrants and refugees.[55]

Further, the opening lines of *Gaudium et Spes* imply also that the message of the gospel ought to be communicated in the dialect of the victims of sorrows. That is exactly what Pope Francis does,[56] and how he sets an example for all to follow. In a landmark visit in 2013 to the Mediterranean migrant hub of Lampedusa, he spoke like a relentless prophet: "The culture of well-being, that makes us think of ourselves, that makes us insensitive to the cries of others, that makes us live in soap bubbles, that are beautiful but are nothing, are illusions of futility, of the transient, that brings indifference to others, that brings even the globalization of indifference. In this world of globalization, we have fallen into a globalization of indifference. We are accustomed to the suffering of others, it doesn't concern us, and it's none of our business."[57]

Gaudium et Spes (22) speaks of one destiny and future for all people as all are God's children. In April 2016, Pope Francis flew to Lesbos Island and visited the temporary asylum seekers camps. He brought Muslim refugee families back to Rome on his own plane. Questions were raised: how he could come back with Muslim families when the

Christians of the Middle-East were persecuted and should be his priority. He clarified saying that he had not chosen between Christian or Muslim refugees, but had simply transported families who had regular papers. He added: "they are all Children of God".

The article 22 of GS indicates also the following as basis for interrelatedness of humanity: incarnational unity, unity that emerges from the paschal sacrifice of Christ, indwelling presence, and unity in destiny. Pope Francis emphasizes this unity of humanity in his writings, for instance, in *Laudato Si*, he speaks of relationality and interrelatedness of all beings (LS 120, 137-138). In his homily at Lampedusa in July 2013, he emphasized the interrelatedness of humanity in the context of migration: "So many of us, even including myself, are disoriented, we are no longer attentive to the world in which we live, we don't care, we don't protect that which God has created for all, and we are unable to care for one another.... (N)o one in the world feels responsible for this; we have lost the sense of fraternal responsibility."[58]

2.5.3. *Visibility to Lumen Gentium*

VC II spoke of the Church in chapter seven of *Lumen Gentium* as pilgrim Church, a journeying community of faith, and in article 6, among other images, as mother. In *Evangelii Gaudium* (210) and as well in his message for the World Day of Migrants in 2015, he spoke of the Church as a mother to all and without frontiers. In other words, the community of believers is never a settled community but people on the move. This comes as a sequel of his message of 2014, wherein he stated, "Migration can offer possibilities for a new evangelization, open vistas for the growth of a new humanity foreshadowed in the paschal mystery: a humanity for which every foreign country is a homeland and every homeland is a foreign country."[59]

2.5.4. *Visibility to Christus Dominus*

Christus Dominus (18) and *Ad Gentes* (20, 38) of VC II speak of the role of the Conferences of Bishops in the pastoral ministry to migrants, exiles, refugees and others on the existential peripheries.

Through his writings and symbolic actions, Pope Francis has set in motion effectively the bishops all over the world to care for migrants and open their institutions wherever feasible to migrants and refugees.

2.5.5. Visibility to the World Day of Migrants and Refugees

The celebration of the World Day of Migrants and Refugees was instituted in 1914 by Pope Pius X. The Messages were signed by the Secretary of State from 1974 to 1983. But since 1985 each message bears the signature of the Holy Father. Indeed, this shift in authorship emphasizes the genuine concern and passionate involvement of the Church in the welfare and pastoral care of migrants all over the world,[60] because they are vulnerable, exploited and voiceless. Pope Francis' Messages carry not only his signature but his very personal immersion into the situation of migrants and refugees, because he knows their situation personally and deeply as he lived his early life as one among them.

2.5.6. Visibility to the Social Teaching of the Church

The central piece and foundation of the STC is 'human dignity'. Pope Francis took the basis of the STC to its new heights symbolically in the Holy Thursday ritual of 'washing the feet' in 2016. He washed the feet of 11 migrants of whom three were Muslims. He underscored the same point in his 2014 Message for the World Day of Migrants and Refugees: "Every human being is a child of God! He or she bears the image of Christ! We ourselves need to see, and then to enable others to see, that migrants and refugees do not only represent a problem to be solved, but are brothers and sisters to be welcomed, respected and loved."[61]

2.6. Pope Francis' Powerful Reaffirmation of Pathways

Pope Francis' symbolic actions and teachings in favour of migrants and refugees, lets one trace the following powerful reaffirmation of pathways in accordance with the teachings of VC II and of his venerable predecessors. Through his words and deeds he powerfully does the following:

- emphasizes the need for "person-centered" and not politically-driven policies and responses to migrants and refugees;
- underscores the need for a "coordinated and effective response to forced migration". This effective response should be a shared response committed "to welcome, to protect, to promote and to integrate" migrants and refugees;
- advocates development programmes that "involve migrants as active protagonists". The programmes and policies that respond to migration crisis should take into account the autonomy, agency, cultural identity and the gifts of migrants and refugees;
- pleads for establishing effective structures to protect and integrate child migrants—who are vulnerable, voiceless and invisible—and work towards finding long term solutions for the problems faced by them. They are defenseless in three-fold ways, i.e., they are children, foreigners and unable to protect themselves;
- argues that human mobility can contribute to genuine enrichment of migrant families and as well of the countries that welcome them, and calls for measures to overcome the negative effects migration on family life (AL 46);
- proposes—in his Message for the World Day of Migrants, 2014—integration of migrants that is "neither assimilation nor incorporation", but "a two-way process, rooted essentially in the joint recognition of the other's cultural richness; it is not the superimposing of one culture over another, nor mutual isolation, with the insidious and dangerous risk of creating ghettos." The path of integration requires "a change of attitude towards migrants and refugees…on the part of every one, moving away from attitudes of defensiveness and fear, indifference and marginalization – all typical of a throwaway culture - towards attitudes based on culture of encounter, the only culture capable of building a better, more just and fraternal world".[62]

- promotes "welcoming, protecting, promoting and integrating" as the path of integration of migrants. Integration, according to his Message for 2018 World Day of Peace, entails reciprocal rights and duties. "Those who welcome are called to promote integral human development, while those who are welcomed must necessarily conform to the rules of the country offering them hospitality, with respect for its identity and values. Processes of integration must always keep the protection and advancement of persons, especially those in situations of vulnerability, at the centre of the rules governing various aspects of political and social life."[63]

- insists that efforts must be made to provide means for decent living in their countries of origins in order to avert migration caused by poverty.[64] However, this should go along with the right to human mobility.

Conclusion

Pope Francis consciously makes use of every opportunity and every form of his ministry to demonstrate his passionate concern for and uncompromising commitment to the welfare of migrants and refugees. His powerful symbolic actions and poignant pleas for their rights and dignity have made their concerns as the highest priority ever for the Universal Church. He has categorically emphasized the importance of a culture of solidarity, a culture of encounter against a culture of indifference. He did not hesitate to challenge powerful states and dormant international organizations for their indifference to inhuman policies and mistreatment of migrants.

Pope Francis' personal engagement together with the migrants and on behalf of them, and his impressive teachings have given greater visibility to the commitment of the Church to migrants and refugees ever since the publication of *Exsul Familia*. The Holy Father has effectively awakened the conscience of the people all over the globe for the cause of migrants and carries forward the flame of VC II by powerfully, personally and tangibly reaffirming the pathways in accordance with the teachings of the Council and of his predecessors.

Endnotes

[1] UCAN News Reporter, "Pope calls for an end to 'tragic exodus' of migrants," https://www.ucanews.org /news/pope-calls-for-an-end-to-tragic-exodus-of-migrants/86633 (accessed on November 21, 2019).

[2] Cf. Universal Declaration of Human Rights, art. 13.

[3] For a detailed expose on this, see, Mohan Doss, "Migrants in Theological Perspective: Strangers No More," in *Migration and Mission in India*, eds. L. Stanislaus and Jose Joseph (Delhi: Ishvani Kendra/ISPCK, 2007), 197-222.

[4] Pope John XXIII, *Pacem in Terris, Peace on Earth* (1963), http://www.vatican.va/content/john-xxiii/en/encyclicals/ documents/hf_j-xxiii_enc_11041963_pacem.html (accessed on 10 November 2019).

[5] Pope Pius XII, *Constitutio Exsul Familia Nazarethana* (1952), https://www.papalencyclicals.net/pius12/p12exsul.html (accessed on 23 October 2006).

[6] Blandine Chelini-Pont, "Catholic Migrant Initiatives Today" 2018 IRLA Meeting of Experts. Freedom of Religion or Belief in an Age of Unprecedented Human Mobility Forging New Approaches to the Conflict of Identities and Integration, November 2018, Cordoue, Spain. hal-02294791. https://hal-amu.archives-ouvertes.fr/hal-02294791 (accessed on 22 November 2019).

[7] Austin Flannery (ed.), *Vatican Council II: The Conciliar and Post Conciliar Documents*, (Mumbai: St. Pauls, 1995).

[8] Chelini-Pont, "Catholic Migrant Initiatives Today," hal-0229479.

[9] Pontifical Commission for the Pastoral Care of Migrants and Itinerant People, "Circular Letter to Episcopal Conferences - Church and Human Mobility (26 May 1978)," https://www.acmro.catholic.org.au/about/church-documents-on-migration/the-teaching-of-the-universal-church/other-vatican-documents/414-circular-letter-to-episcopal-conferences-church-and-human-mobility/file (accessed on 12 October 2019).

[10] Pope Paul VI, *Populorum Progressio, On the Development of Peoples* (1967), 73. http://www.vatican.va/content/paul-vi/en/encyclicals/documents/hf_p-vi_enc_26031967_populorum.html

[11] Chelini-Pont, "Catholic Migrant Initiatives Today," hal-0229479.

[12] Ibid.

[13] Pope John Paul II, *Redemptor Hominis* (1979); http://www.vatican.va/content/john-paul-ii/en/encyclicals/ documents/hf_jp-ii_enc_04031979_redemptor-hominis.html (accessed on 12 October 2019)

[14] Chelini-Pont, "Catholic Migrant Initiatives Today," hal-0229479.

[15] Ibid.

16 Chelini-Pont, "Catholic Migrant Initiatives Today," hal-0229479

17 Ibid.

18 Quoted in: DiMarzio, N. "John Paul II: Migrant Pope Teaches on Migration," www.uccb.org/mrs/ndjohnpaul.shtml (accessed on 10 October 2019).

19 Pope John Paul II, "Message of the Holy Father for the 88th World Day of Migrations: Migration and Inter-religious Dialogue, (2002)," https://www.vatican.va/content/john-paul-ii/en/messages/migration/documents/hf_ jp-ii_mes_ 20011018_world-migration-day-2002.html (accessed on 20 October 2019).

20 Pope John Paul II, *Encyclical Letter Centesimus Annus, On the Hundredth Anniversary of Rerum Novarum*, (1991), http://www.vatican.va/content/john-paul-ii/en/encyclicals/documents/hf_jp-ii_enc_01051991_centesimus-annus.html, accessed on 16 November 2019.

21 Pope John Paul II, "Letter to the Director of General of International Organization for Migrations" (22 November 2001), http://www.vatican.va/content/john-paul-ii/en/letters/2001/documents/hf_jp-ii_let_20011129_iom.html (accessed on 20 November 2019).

22 Chelini-Pont, "Catholic Migrant Initiatives Today," hal-0229479.

23 Pontifical Council for the Pastoral Care of Migrants and Itinerant People, *Instructions – Erga migrantes caritas Christi. The love of Christ towards migrants* (2001), 93-95; http://www.vatican.va/roman_ curia/pontifical _councils/migrants/documents/rc_pc_migrants_doc_20040514_erga-migrantes-caritas-christi-en. Html (accessed on 02 November 2019).

24 Pope Benedict XVI, Encyclical Letter *Caritas in Veritate* (2009), 62, also 67 and 21. http://www.vatican. va/content/benedict-xvi/en/encyclicals/documents/hf_ben xvi_enc_20090629_ caritas-in-veritate.html (accessed on 15 November 2019).

25 Pope Benedict XVI, "Message for the 93rd World Day of Migrants and Refugees – The migrant family" (2007);

https://w2.vatican.va/content/benedict-xvi/en/messages/migration/documents/hf_ ben-xvi_mes_20061018_ world-migrants-day.html (accessed on 20 November 2019).

26 For Asian Concern on Migrant Families, see, The FABC Papers No. 111: "The Asian Family towards a Culture of Integral Life." It emphasized the necessity of rendering greater pastoral service to the migrants and their families (2004: No. 15-17); http://www.fabc.org/fabc%20papers/fabc_paper_111.pdf (accessed on 12 November 2019).

27 Chelini-Pont, "Catholic Migrant Initiatives Today," hal-0229479.

28 Cf. John Paul II, "Letter to the Director General of International Organization for Migrations," (2001).

29 Donald Kerwin and Elizabeth Kilbride, "Pope Francis and Migrants: Honouring Human Dignity, Building Solidarity and Creating a Culture of Encounter," https://cmsny.org/pope-francis-and-migrants-honoring-human-dignity-building-solidarity-and-creating-a-culture-of-encounter/ (accessed on 20 November 2019).

³⁰ Allan Figueroa Deck, "Migrants and Refugees in Pope Francis's Transformative Vision of Church and Society," The Fr. Lydio F. Tomasi, C.S. Annual Lecture on International Migration, held on November 28, 2016, https://cmsny. org/publications/tomasilecture2016/ (accessed on 15 November 2019).

³¹ Kerwin and Kilbride, "Pope Francis and Migrants: Honouring Human Dignity, Building Solidarity and Creating a Culture of Encounter."

³² See, Pope Francis, *A Stranger and You Welcomed Me: A Call to Mercy and Solidarity with Migrants and Refugees*, ed. Robert Ellsberg (New York: Orbis Books, 2018).

³³ Pope Francis spoke on the theme of globalization of indifference during his visit to Lampedusa island in July 2013. "Pope Attacks the Globalization of Indifference," https://www.theguardian.com/world/2013/jul/08/pope-globalisation-of-indifference-lampedusa (accessed on 10 November 2019).

³⁴ Pope Francis, *Encyclical Letter Laudato Si' – On Care for Our Common Home* (2015), http://www.vatican.va/ content/francesco/en/encyclicals/documents/papa-francesco_20150524_enciclica-laudato-si.html (accessed on 12 November 2019).

³⁵ Chelini-Pont, "Catholic Migrant Initiatives Today," hal-0229479.

³⁶ Pope Francis, *Apostolic Exhortation Evangelii Gaudium - The Joy of the Gospel* (2013), http://www.vatican.va /content/francesco/en/apost_exhortations/documents/papa-francesco_esortazione-ap_20131124_evangelii-gaudium.html (accessed on 10 November 2019).

³⁷ See, http://www.vatican.va/content/francesco/en/messages/pont-messages/2014/documents/papa-francesco_ 20140711_messaggio-movilidad-humana.html (accessed on 8 November 2019).

³⁸ Pope Francis, "Message for the World Day of Migrants and Refugees – Church without frontiers, Mother to all," (2015), http://www.vatican.va/content/francesco/en/messages/migration/documents/papa-francesco 20140903_ world-migrants-day-2015.html (accessed on 15 November 2019).

³⁹ See, http://www.globalfreedomnetwork.org/

⁴⁰ Kerwin and Kilbride, "Pope Francis and Migrants: Honouring Human Dignity, Building Solidarity and Creating a Culture of Encounter," (accessed on November 20, 2019).

⁴¹ Pope Francis, "Homily of the Holy Father at Lampedusa," (2013), http://www.vatican.va/content/francesco/ en/homilies/2013/documents/papa-francesco_20130708_omelia-lampedusa.html (accessed on 18.11.2019).

⁴² http://www.vatican.va/content/francesco/en/speeches/2015/july/documents/papa-francesco_20150721_sind aci-grandi-citta.html (accessed on 10 November 2019).

⁴³ Pope Francis, *Post-Synodal Apostolic Exhortation Amoris Laetitia, On Love in the Family* (2015), https://w2.vatican.va/content/dam/francesco/pdf/apost_exhortations/documents/papa-francesco_esortazione-ap_20160319_amoris-laetitia_en.pdf (accessed on 20 November 2019), No. 46.

⁴⁴ Pope Francis, "Message for the World Day of Migrants and Refugees – Migrants and Refugees: Towards a better World (2014)," http://www.vatican.va/content/francesco/en/messages/migration/documents/papa-francesco_ 20130805_world-migrants-day.html (accessed on 15 November 2019).

⁴⁵ Francis, "Message for the World Day of Migrants and Refugees – Church without frontiers, Mother to all (2015).

⁴⁶ Francis, "Message for the World Day of Migrants and Refugees (2015).

⁴⁷ Benedict XVI, *Caritas in Veritate – On Integral Human Development in Charity and Truth* (2009), 62

⁴⁸ Pope Francis, "Message for the World Day of Migrants and Refugees - Migrants and Refugees Challenge Us. The Response of the Gospel of Mercy" (2016), http://www.vatican.va/content/francesco/en/messages/migration/ documents/papa-francesco_20150912_world-migrants-day-2016.html (accessed on 12 November 2019).

⁴⁹ Francis, "Message for the World Day of Migrants and Refugees - "Welcoming, protecting, promoting and

integrating migrants and refugees" (2018).

⁵⁰ See, "Pope Unveils Sculpture Commemorating Migrants and Refugees," https://www.vaticannews.va/en/pope /news/2019-09/pope-francis-world-day-migrants-refugees (accessed on 10 November 2019).

⁵¹ Pope Francis, "Message for the World Day of Migrants and Refugees – It is not just about migrants (2019)," http://www.vatican.va/content/francesco/en/messages/migration/documents/papa-francesco_20190527_world-migrants-day-2019.html (accessed on 14 November 2019).

⁵² Quoted from Pope Paul VI, Encyclical Letter *Populorum Progressio* (1967), 14.

⁵³ The monument was sculpted by the Canadian artist Timothy P. Schmalz. See, "Pope Unveils Sculpture Commemorating Migrants and Refugees," https://www.vaticannews.va/en/pope/news/2019-09/pope-francis-world-day-migrants-refugees (accessed on 10 November 2019).

⁵⁴ Cf. Pope John Paul II, *Centesimus Annus* (Rome: Libreria Editrice Vaticana, 1991), 11.

⁵⁵ Deck, "Migrants and Refugees in Pope Francis' Transformative Vision of Church and Society," https://cmsny.org/publications/tomasilecture2016/ (accessed on 18 November, 2019).

⁵⁶ Diego Fares, "How to Communicate in a Polarized Society?" https://www.laciviltacattolica.com/free-articles/ (accessed on 18 November 2019).

⁵⁷ Kerwin and Kilbride, "Pope Francis and Migrants: Honouring Human Dignity, Building Solidarity and Creating a Culture of Encounter."

⁵⁸ Francis, "Homily of the Holy Father at Lampedusa," (2013).

⁵⁹ Francis, "Message for World Day of Migrants and Refugees," (2014).

⁶⁰ N. DiMarzio, "John Paul II: Migrant Pope Teaches on Migration," www.uccb.org/mrs/ndjohnpaul.shtml (accessed on October 23, 2019).

⁶¹ Francis, "Message for the World Day of Migrants and Refugees," (2014).

⁶² Francis, "Message for the World Day of Migrants and Refugees," (2014).

⁶³ Pope Francis, "Message for the World Day of Peace - Migrants and refugees: men and women in search of peace (2018)," http://www.vatican.va/content/francesco/en/messages/peace/documents/papa-francesco_20171113 _messaggio-51giornatamondiale-pace2018.html

⁶⁴ Pope John Paul II, *Familiaris Consortio* (1981), 77. http://www.vatican.va/content/john-paul-ii/en/apost_ exhortations/documents/hf_jp-ii_exh_19811122_familiaris-consortio.html (accessed on 20.11.2019). The effective care of migrants and their families should begin in their places of origin. It is there human promotion should be guaranteed first, namely, the right to find in one's own homeland the conditions necessary for living a dignified life. Cf. Benedict XVI, "Message for the World Day of Migrants and Refugees," (accessed on 12 October 2019).

16.

Being a Poor Church of the Poor and the Periphery
The Contribution of Pope Francis

M. Surekha Lobo, BS

Introduction

There is a growing feeling in all of us that ours is a change of age and not an age of change. We are moving away from one way of living to a way of living that is totally different. We are living in a global and commercialized society. The rhythms of life seem to get faster with each passing year. Our advances in technology—in automation, communication and transportation—are making drastic changes in every sphere of life. Amidst these changes, Pope Francis highlights the worldwide crises of migrants, refugees, poor and the margins –being forced to leave their homelands to find safety from violence or to find food for their families. Pope Francis is well known as a 'common man's Pope.' He is the most discussed person on the Internet and the subject of street corner discussions because he comes down to the level of a common person and speaks in their own vocabulary. His messages are not a change in direction for the Church but a return to the core values of Christianity (Mt 5:17).

I am struck by Pope Francis' way of being compassionate like Jesus, promoting and safeguarding the principles of human dignity and solidarity. Ever since he assumed papal office, Pope Francis has been advocating a "poor church for the poor." What does this mean for us all? The renewed vision of the Church and the direction that he proposes is expressed in his desire: "How I long for a poor Church for the poor!" (EG 198). These words spell out his agenda for the Church and underscore a theme that is the core of his papacy. So, I ask: Is the Church seeing what is happening to the peripheries worldwide? What are the losses that we must offset in order to further the conciliar gains? Pope Francis' Twitter invitation[1] "to open the path towards a much greater joy: that of participating in God's own love,"[2] prompts me to delve deeper into this theme.

This paper articulates how Pope Francis is taking forward the agenda of Vatican Council II (hereinafter VC II) and its vision of Church and human family more concretely and radically in the footsteps of Jesus. This paper is divided into four parts: First, I begin with a reflection on the Exodus experience (Ex 2:23-24; 3:7-10) highlighting God's fundamental option towards human beings. Second, I shall draw up Jesus' vision of the poor as seen in the Gospels—concentrating on his walk with the poor and those on the periphery. Third, I shall examine the development of the idea of 'Church of the poor', especially focussing on how Pope Francis envisions a Church of the poor. Finally, I shall gauge how it is possible to embark upon building a poor Church for the poor, embodying the God of Jesus Christ walking with the poor and those at the periphery.

1. Remembering the God who Hears the Cry of the Poor

It is important to often reread the Bible to derive fresh insights and to make new inroads into the issues of today. A prime event of salvation is described in the Book of Exodus.[3] The very name 'Yahweh' is bound up with God's activity of liberating Israel from Egyptian slavery. That intervention is the basis of all the claims Yahweh makes to exclusive fidelity and to the practice of solidarity with all the oppressed. From the viewpoint of God and the people, this oppression was an evil that could not be tolerated. In their helplessness, the people cry out to God, who hears their cry. "As their cry for release went up to God, he heard their groaning and was mindful of his covenant" (Ex 2:23-24). The essence of the Exodus event seen through the eyes of faith and articulated in history is the basis of God's fundamental option towards humanity. In sum, God's covenant with Israel is a promise to walk with them and to protect them from their enemies. God therefore confronts the evil of injustice and sides with the poor.

In her article 'The Practical Trinity', Catherine LaCugna explains the doctrine of the Trinity and its centrality in understanding gospel demands for social transformation. Living the Trinitarian faith entails living as Jesus Christ did: with total confidence in God; as welcoming the outcast and the sinner. Therefore, living God's life demands contributing towards the unity of the Christian community and the harmony among all people of good will.[4] In sum, solidarity in the Bible is reflected in the drive against evil in which God sides with the poor and works through humanity to deliver them from their oppression. In so doing, God's goodness is made manifest. Solidarity is the very nature of God, which acquires a new meaning in the life and ministry of Jesus Christ.

2. Revisiting the Gospel Vision of Jesus

Jesus' identification with the poor and the marginalised was the hallmark of his life and mission. Realising his mission, Jesus identifies himself with the poor and the oppressed, in order to show them an active and effective concern.[5] From his birth right up to his dying on the Cross, Jesus is in search of and in solidarity with the marginalized of society. This can be summarized under five basic truths:

1. The annunciation as God's fundamental option for the poor (Lk 1:26-56);

2. Jesus' birth as sign of his identification with the poor (Lk 2:1-20);

3. Jesus' ministry unto the peripheries like Nazareth (Mt 2:23; Mk 1:9); Bethsaida (Mk 6:45; 8:22; Lk 9:10); Capernaum (Mt 9:1; Mk 1:21; 2:1; 9:33; Lk 10:15);

4. The temptations of Jesus and his Nazareth *Manifesto* as powers of resistance (Mt 4:1-11; Mk 1:12-13; Lk 4:1-13 and Lk 4:16-30); and

5. The paschal mystery as the essence of Jesus' solidarity (Mt 25:40; 2 Cor 12:9).

2.1. *The Annunciation and Incarnation: God's Fundamental Option for the Poor*

The mystery of God's choice to walk among humans is what stands out here. The very event of the Annunciation unfolds the mystery of God represented by the Angel, reaching out to all humanity, represented in the person of Mary, who is given the offer of being the mother of God.[6] "For in the Bible, the human person is never an isolated individual but always part of humankind. What happens to one, affects all. Humankind now becomes the locus of our encounter with God. 'What you do to the least of my brothers and sisters,' Jesus can truly say, 'you do to me.'"[7] The incarnation is always a call to follow Jesus in his solidarity with humankind, expressed concretely through his consistent and progressive identification with the poor. Jesus' incarnation is inclusive of all human beings irrespective of race, historical conditions or genders.[8]

2.2. *The Birth of Jesus: His Identification with the Poor*

Jesus the God become flesh entered into human history as a helpless, homeless, poor babe. He opted to be born as one among us—in a manger, which was a sign of his fundamental option for the poor and the marginalized. This ushered in a new and lasting expression of divine solidarity. The experience of solidarity makes Elizabeth proclaim, "This is what the Lord has done for me when he looked favorably on me and took away the disgrace I have endured among people" (Lk 1:25). The shepherds were the first beneficiaries of the Good News of Jesus' birth.

They worshiped the Babe born in a manger (Lk 2:8-20). Shepherds were the outcasts of society despised by others; and shepherding was a despised occupation in Jesus' time. Through these lowly shepherds God was reaching out to the peripheries.

2.3. Jesus' Ministry unto the Peripheries

Jesus may not have been as aware as we are today of the structural forces of evils of the society in which he lived. A very significant observation in Jesus' public ministry is the places he chose for his public ministry: remote villages such as Nazareth, not mentioned anywhere else outside the New Testament (Mt 2:23; Mk 1:9), Bethsaida (Mk 6:45; 8:22; Lk 9:10), which was a small remote fishing village and the rural township of Capernaum, which was sort of his headquarters during his Galilean ministry (Mt 9:1; Mk 1:21; 2:1; 9:33; Lk 10:15). The character of Jesus' solidarity is made more obvious when we understand a little more about the apparent nature of first century Palestinian society and the nature of Jesus' disputes with the Pharisees. But in his teaching and proclamation, Jesus is on the side of the voiceless and the victims of injustice and evil social structures. He was committed to justice and to structural change which is implied in the vision of the Reign of God.[9]

2.4. The Temptation of Jesus and the Nazareth Manifesto as Powers of Resistance

Jesus employed powers of resistance methods to communicate God's all-embracing love and he revealed God's justice through his very life and mission. Jesus' use of powers of resistance on the exploitative patriarchal power structures of his time is discussed in two narratives, the temptation of Jesus, and the Nazareth Manifesto.

Jesus' temptation stories (Mt 4:1-11; Mk 1:12-13 and Lk 4:1-13) show his struggle with the powers of evil in the wilderness, immediately after his baptism. Campbell discusses how in the wilderness Jesus encounters the domination system in all its power and is tempted to take the path of survival, domination, violence and idolatry. He further delineates the conflict between God's way and my way – the way of misuse of power. First, Jesus refuses to use his power to secure his own survival. Jesus says 'no' to making his own survival the fundamental priority and to using his power to meet his own needs. Second, Jesus says 'no' to use his power to establish a political empire grounded on the path of violence and domination. Third, Jesus refuses to test God and will not use God for his own ends; he says 'no' to idolatry. [10]

The Nazareth *Manifesto* as recorded in Lk 4:16-30 is considered by most scholars to be the programmatic statement of Jesus' vision statement.[11] In the inaugural sermon of Jesus is a 'mission manifesto' predicted in Isa 61:1-2. And the message is: "The Spirit of the Lord is upon me… to proclaim the year of the Lord's favour…"[12] This 'mission manifesto' of Jesus reveals the significance of his mission as proclamation of the good news, freeing those who are oppressed, offering sight to the blind and restoring health to the sick. "He subverts all notions of religious or ethnic superiority that hold people captive and cause them to denigrate and oppress" people and he offers an alternative way of promoting life.[13] His entire ministry challenges the powers and offers an alternative to their order of survival, domination and violence. Thus, Jesus redraws the map of his social world expanding it to embrace all, irrespective of class, colour, status and gender by identifying with the last and the least ones of the society. He unfailingly remains a close associate and a teacher to them.

2.5. *The Paschal Mystery: Essence of Solidarity*

The identification with the poor is complete, so complete that "in so far as you did this to one of the least of these brothers and sisters of mine, you did it to me" (Mt 25:40). What was begun at the incarnation now reaches its fulfillment — a total and radical identification with poor and the periphery — "where [God's] power is made perfect in weakness" (2 Cor 12:9). The words of Isaiah 53 find new meaning on Golgotha: "Yet ours were the sufferings He was carrying, while we thought of Him as someone being punished by God … having exposed Himself to death and … being counted as one of the rebellious, whereas He was bearing the sin of many and interceding for the rebellious" (Isa 53:5,12). George

M. Soares Prabhu draws a lesson from the story: "on the Cross Jesus is wholly poor and totally outcast. Identification and confrontation here have reached their furthest possible limits... The journey from the centre to the periphery, a journey which was the basic movement of his life and the basic thrust of his spirituality, comes here to its ultimate goal."[14]

Jesus' vision as presented in the gospels is clearly an option for the poor and the marginalized: an embodied reality. "To bring good news to the poor" was the commitment for the poor which Jesus spelled out right from his inaugural sermon as he began his public ministry (Lk 4:16-30). Who were the poor of Jesus' times? The Gospels tell that most of the poor of Jesus' times were the victims of social injustice, the women, the tax collectors, the sinners, the sick and the outcasts. They were subjected to "dehumanizing treatment by the hierarchical system of class, race, gender, age and status,"[15] affirms Walter Wink.

3. Church of the Poor Then and Now

The fact that Pope took the name 'Francis'—reminiscent of Francis of Assisi—confirms his understanding of evangelization primarily as assistance for the poor and the deprived, as protection of their dignity.[16] The concept of 'periphery' was put forward by Pope Francis in his address to the College of Cardinals before the papal election.[17] To understand the implications of the renewed vision of "being a Church of the poor and the periphery" it would be fitting to situate it in the context of Church of the poor then and now. This should enable the reader to pinpoint and appreciate the historical overview of how the Church of the poor and the periphery has evolved down the ages.

3.1. *A Church of the Poor since Vatican Council II*

The phrase "Church of the Poor" was first used by Pope John XXIII in his radio message to the world on September 11, 1962.[18] Fifty-seven years ago, on the eve of VC II, Pope John XXIII called on the faithful to be the "Church of the poor." He proclaimed that the Church is a "Church of all and in particular the Church of the poor."[19] It was later picked up by Asian Bishops at their historic first meeting in Manila in 1970.

Finally, it became the core message of the Second Plenary Council of the Philippines (PCP II) in 1991.[20] Since VC II's *Gaudium et Spes*, the Church has addressed issues of concern to everyone without limiting its reach to Christian believers alone:

> The joy and the hope, the grief and the anguish of the men of this age, especially of those who are poor or in any way afflicted, these are the joy and hope, the grief and anguish of the followers of Christ. Nothing that is genuinely human fails to raise an echo in their hearts. For theirs is a community composed of men [women]. United in Christ ...they have welcomed the news of salvation which is meant for every man [woman]. [21]

Likewise, John Paul II affirms that "the Church is firmly committed to their cause, for she considers it her mission, her service, a proof of her fidelity to Christ, so that she can be the 'Church of the poor.'"[22] Thus, 'the Church of the poor' was an identity of the whole mystical Body of Christ, with a rich history and development. *Lumen Gentium* teaches that the Church sees herself as called to follow the path of Jesus in bringing hope to all by re-presenting Christ anew. In the words of the council fathers: 'The Church encompasses with love all those afflicted by human infirmity and recognizes in those who are poor and who suffer the image of its poor and suffering founder. It does all it can to relieve their need and in them it strives to serve Christ.'[23]

Nevertheless, 'the Church of the poor' is a concept which has been central to the Church's self-understanding, mission, and pastoral priorities from her earliest history.

3.2. *A Church of the Poor since Pope Francis*

Pope Francis seems to be following the direction that God gave when Jesus was born. That lesson is reinforced not only because the Word was sent out to those shepherds—those on the periphery—but also because Jesus became part of them. Pope Francis' call for the faithful to embrace the periphery is explicitly Christocentric. According to him the poor are transfigured into Christ's own flesh which identifies Christian witness as a key constituent in evangelization as indicated by Pope Paul VI.[24]

Pope Francis seems to be incarnating the essence of Pope Paul VI's clarion call. His conception of poverty and the poor go far beyond conventional secular understandings of these subjects. Even though we all have a general idea of what poverty is, it is very difficult to define poverty in precise terms. However, Pope Francis has the following to say:

> For the Church, the option for the poor is primarily a theological category rather than a cultural, sociological, political or philosophical one. God shows the poor 'his first mercy'. This divine preference has consequences for the faith life of all Christians, since we are called to have 'this mind... which was in Jesus Christ' (Phil 2:5). Inspired by this, the Church has made an option for the poor which is understood as a 'special form of primacy in the exercise of Christian charity, to which the whole tradition of the Church bears witness.' This option – as Benedict XVI has taught – 'is implicit in our Christian faith in a God who became poor for us, so as to enrich us with his poverty'. This is why I want a Church which is poor and for the poor (EG 198).[25]

Quoting Pope Benedict XVI Pope Francis asserts that this option is implicit in our Christian faith after the example of God in Jesus, whose ultimate solidarity is shown by his self-emptying to the level of humankind to become human. Pope Francis has pursued his commitment to poverty at the periphery at various levels: at the level of written documents like *Evangelii Gaudium* and other verbal articulations; at the level of symbolic gestures (like washing and kissing the feet of prisoners); and at the level of institutional reforms (like financial management of the Vatican). His embrace of poverty at the periphery was particularly obvious in two symbolic gestures:

(i) On November 6, 2013, Vinicio Riva, a severely disfigured 52-year-old Italian man suffering from neurofibromatosis,[26] travelled with his aunt and dozens of others from northern Italy to Vatican City, where they attended a morning public audience held by Pope Francis. Pope Francis kissed Riva and blessed him. The severely disabled man, who has induced horror even in his doctors, described the encounter with the pope in glowing terms, saying that being caressed by Francis meant so much to him.[27] Pope Francis' embrace of Riva made an impact far beyond the Catholic Church.

(ii) On July 8, 2013, Pope Francis presided over Holy Mass for migrants in St Peter's Basilica on the tiny Sicilian island of Lampedusa, to commemorate thousands of migrants who have died crossing the sea from North Africa, underlining his drive to put the poor at the heart of his papacy. In his homily at Lampedusa, he lamented on what he called the anaesthesia of the heart: "We are a society which has forgotten how to weep, how to experience compassion – "suffering with" others; the globalization of indifference has taken from us the ability to weep!"[28] The poor and the marginalised are the chief source of theology, the chief record of God's self-revelation and intervention in world-history.

Moments like the above send edifying messages of a sense of openness and human solidarity to millions of women and men who are excluded on account of disease, poverty or affliction. Therefore, what we can perhaps envision is a Church of the poor and the periphery in India. It is a vision that will overlook the manmade differences on account of caste, creed, and gender and recognize the distinct identity of each person as persons created in the image and likeness of God. This is the key to being a Church of the poor in India and the world, at large.[29]

4. Guiding Lights for Birthing a Church of the Poor and the Periphery

Having looked at the First and Second Testaments for gaining insights on the 'option for the poor' and having gleaned Pope Francis' contributions to the same, how can we, today, strive to build this kind of a Church? The following guiding lights could assist us.

4.1. *Committed Pursuit of God in Contemplation*

One of the main challenges that the Church is facing today is to be God-conscious. God is more to be experienced in one's interior being than to be intellectually known in one's head. The traditional idea of a judging and punishing God needs to recede to the background and a 'youthful' idea of a loving, forgiving and affectionate God needs to be presented to the youth. For this, one has to encounter God in Jesus, a God who transcends petty divisions of caste, creed, clan, colour and gender.

Through contemplation one truly becomes like the one we contemplate. Contemplation is to become part of the world in order to reveal the hidden face of Christ to suffering humanity. A better understanding of the communion of the Triune God, will give a clearer understanding of God's redemptive plan for human communion, where people are in relationship with one another, co-workers in Christ, in communion with the Triune God: a single universal communion.

4.2. *Initiating a Counter-Cultural Solidarity*

There is still much to be said for the overall conditions of the poor and the periphery in the present era. Today the gap between rich and poor is even wider than what existed in 1962, the time of VC II. Sadly, one portion of the human race is included in progress and prosperity, while another is left behind in a crucible of growing violence where human dignity is threatened every day. The poor, along with the middle and working classes, have been the victims of a massive wealth and power grab. Therefore, in an alienating consumerist society the great divide poses a great challenge to the Church which seeks to affirm the equal dignity of all persons. Hence, the 'losses' that we must offset in order to further the conciliar gains is an imperative. Counter-culture solidarity for being a Church of the poor must be a counter-cultural community of solidarity and periphery sensitivity. The approach has to be premised not on self-centredness but on persons-for-others on a participative mode. What is required is a thorough breakthrough of the securities and comfort zones in order to become instruments of transformation and change.

4.3. *Church as the Passion for Periphery*

Mission was a passion for Jesus and at the same time a passion for his people. Jesus' command to "go forth", is addressed to every baptized person. It is to bear witness to the Lord Jesus by proclaiming the faith received as a gift, to proclaim the Gospel by their witness of life. The Church officially has advanced in successive ages of her history in dialoguing with fast-changing contexts. Obviously, no one can negate that the Church down the centuries were also dominated by patriarchy and struggles to uphold the place Jesus gave to the peripheries. The ministry of Jesus excludes no one, but the authenticating sign of this is that the Good news is preached to the poor.

Pope Francis radiates the joy of the annunciation. In his homily on March 19, 2013, he set the standard by saying that Jesus still wants to take on flesh. He urged the faithful not to be afraid of goodness and tenderness. At the heart of the Pope's social teaching, and at the heart of his repeated calls for to become a poor Church for the poor, there is the faith of incarnation, the faith that God took on human flesh and, in his body the Church, he still wishes to take on flesh… "Each of us is a link in this chain of love. And if we do not understand this, we have understood nothing of what the Church is."[30] Hence, what sets the tone for Pope Francis' preferential option for the poor is the Christian charism of inclusive love in action.[31]

4.4. *Greater Inclusion of Women for Effective Partnership in the Church*

The Christian faith understands each person irrespective of caste, creed and gender as made for communion, for a sharing in the life of the Trinity. So, actions of solidarity are part of the realisation of the divine plan and become sacraments of salvation along the way. The 28th Plenary Assembly of the Catholic Bishops' Conference of India (CBCI) held in Jamshedpur in February 2008, reflected on the theme 'Empowerment of Women in the Church and Society'. Moreover, on December 8, 2009, the CBCI issued a document titled 'Gender Policy of the Catholic Church of India'.[32] Women still feel controlled under a patriarchal and androcentric church, with men in the dominant roles and women in positions of subordination.[33] However, by contrast, Pope Francis calls for: "More widespread and inclusive female presence—many women involved in pastoral responsibilities, in the accompaniment of persons, families and groups as a well as in the theological reflection."[34]

Today, women themselves are collectively awakened globally and locally; yet, their voices are not heard, their experiences and abilities are not fully documented in the life of the Church. There is need for a greater inclusion of women in the process of decision making, planning and organizing. To change the attitude towards women may take years. Changes have to be affected in the minds of women and men, introduced in families and in schools. Finally, change has to come in women themselves by affirming their personhood with dignity. The Church needs to initiate creative dialogue with women, create space for women to share their views and visions, dreams and concerns. Moreover, more and more women ought to be seen in theological and pastoral formation and responsibilities. For this, the necessity of a structural change in the existing patriarchal system is very crucial. The Church in India will grow and flourish only when she recognizes the full potential of women's contribution to Church and Society.

4.5. *Decolonization of Minds and Hearts*

India today is undoubtedly ridden with violence and strife. Lack of equitable development and progress across the country has led to some youth taking up arms to demand justice and rights in many parts. At the same time, the innumerable insurgent groups have turned the less developed and segregated geographical parts of the Indian continent into a battle field. As a result, development is hampered. To reach out to the other in need and to people on the margins, one needs to decolonize one's mind from all that is "me and mine." One has to renounce, to let go of the selfish and limited self so as to enter into an to opening new realm in which "all life takes on a completely new meaning; the real sense of our own existence, which is normally veiled and distorted by the routine distractions of an alienated life…sees everything transfigured in God coming from God and working for God's creative redemptive love."[35] The transformation that is called for is similar to Newman's words, "In a higher world it is otherwise but here below to live is to change, and to be perfect is to have changed often."[36]

Conclusion

In our digitalized and highly consumeristic society, the Church is called to be an agent as well as witness to communicate the Gospel vision of Jesus Christ towards the human person and society, at large. An option for the poor has been an identity of the whole mystical Body of Christ, the Church, since her existence. Therefore, the Church is reminded by Pope Francis, to "go to the peripheries," to the margins, where no one dares to go. It cannot be denied that, the vision of a Church of the poor has been the defining factor in Pope Francis' pontificate. In our option for the periphery, we encounter the human face of God. Only when the Church lives in solidarity with the poor, can she become a poor church of the poor in the concrete reality of everyday life. By so doing, she will meaningfully participate in the ongoing evolution of God's salvific action.

Endnotes

[1] Pope Francis is one of the most-followed global leaders on the social networking platform, with close to 34 million followers spread across nine language accounts, according to analysis from Twiplomacy, a group that tracks the social media use of world leaders, reports *America Jesuit Review*. Michael J. O'Loughlin, "Pope Francis is the most-followed world leader on Twitter—but Trump is closing in" *America Jesuit Review* June 02, 2017, https://www.americamagazine.org/politics-society/2017/06/02/pope-francis-most-followed-world-leader-twitter -trump-closing, (accessed October 3, 2019).

[2] Pope Francis @Pontiff, *Tweeter*, September 1, 2019, https://twitter.com/Pontifex; (accessed September 6, 2019).

[3] The Exodus covers a period of just forty years, but these years were for Israel the era of revelation par excellence. In the events of these years Israel came to know the Lord. James Plastaras, *The God of Exodus: The Theology of the Exodus Narratives* (Milwaukee: The Bruce Publishing Company, 1966), 1.

[4] Catherine Mowry LaCugna, "The Practical Trinity," The *Christian Century* 109/22 (July 1992): 681-682.

[5] George M Soares Prabhu, "Jesus and the Poor," in *Collected Writings of George M. Soares Prabhu*, vol. 4, ed. Francis X. D'Sa (Pune: JDV Theological Series, 2001), 176.

[6] Thus, Mary of Nazareth, "found favor with God" so as to be elected as Jesus' mother. Hence Mary's simple but obedient and daring response was: "Behold, I am the handmaid of the Lord. May it be done to me according to your word" (Lk 1:38).

[7] George M. Soares-Prabhu, "The Spirituality of Jesus" in Scaria Kuthiralkkattel,

SVD, ed. *Biblical Spirituality of Liberative Action* (Pune: Jnana-Deepa Vidyapeeth, Theology Series, 2003), 100.

[8] Shane Claiborne writes, "Jesus came to show us what God is like in a way we can touch and follow. Jesus is the lens through which we look at the Bible and the world; everything is fulfilled in Christ." Shane Claiborne and Tony Campolo, *Red Letter Revolution: What If Jesus Really Meant What He Said?* (Nashville, Tennessee: Thomas Nelson, 2012), 7.

[9] Jacob Kavunkal, *Anthropophany: Mission as Making a New Humanity* (Delhi: ISPCK, 2008), 148-149.

[10] Charles L. Campbell, *The Word Before the Powers: An Ethic of Preaching* (Louisville, London; Westminster John Knox Press, 2002), 45-48.

[11] Chronologically, the Nazareth visit can be placed generally in the Galilean ministry and can be identified with that of Mt 13:54 and Mk 6:1. But Luke places it first because it is first, not chronologically but programmatically. Luke is not so much interested in chronological or geographical precision as in an orderly presentation of things Jesus said and did (Lk 1:3). Razouselie Lasetso, *The Nazareth Manifesto: The Theology of Jubilee and Its Trajectories in Luke-Acts* (Delhi: ISPCK, 2005), 82.

[12] Ladd, G. E. *A Theology of the New Testament* (Grand Rapids: W. B. Eerdmann Publishing Co., 1997), 240.

[13] Campbell, *The Word Before the Powers*, 50.

[14] Soares-Prabhu, "The Spirituality of Jesus", 100-101.

[15] Walter Wink, *Engaging the Powers: Discernment and Resistance in a world of Domination* (Minneapolis: Fortress Press, 1992), 176.

[16] Igor Rozin, "Pope Francis welcomed by Russian Orthodox Church," https://www.rbth.com/world/2013/03/ 15/pope_francis_wel comed_by_russian_orthodox_church_22967 (accessed September 19, 2019).

[17] To appraise how Pope Francis uses the term is to understand who he is, what kind of Church he envisions.

[18] Confronted by the under-developed countries, the Church presented herself the Church of all, and in particular the 'Church of the poor'. Adrian Hastings, *A Concise Guide to the Documents of the Second Vatican Council - Volume Two* (London: Darton, Longman & Todd, 1969), 212.

[19] This statement, from a radio address one month before the opening of Vatican II, was further developed in a number of council documents that articulated the nature and mission of the Church as responsible for, and accountable to, the poor and afflicted (*Ad Gentes* nos. 5 and 12). Cf. Marcus Mescher, "Fifty Years Later, Are We Still the Church of the Poor?" *Millennial Journal.com*, September 11, 2012, https:// millennialjournal.com/2012/09/11/fifty-years-later-are-we-still-the-church-of-the-poor/ (accessed October 2, 2019).

[20] Bishop Julio Xavier Labayen, *Revolution and the Church of the Poor* (Manila: Socio-Pastoral Institute and Claretian Publication, 1995), 2, quoted in Ferdinand M. Mangibin, "Church Of The Poor: Revisiting The Catholic Social Teachings Of The Church," *LUMINA*, Vol 20/2 , https://www.researchgate.net/publication/ 49600924_Church_Of_The_Poor_Revisiting_The_Catholic_Social_Teachings_Of_The_Church (accessed September 29, 2019).

[21] *Gaudium et Spes*, 1.

[22] John Paul II, Encyclical *Laborem Exercens: Human Work* [LE 8] (Bandra, Mumbai: St Pauls, 1981), 26.

[23] *Lumen Gentium*, 8.

[24] It is therefore primarily by her conduct and by her life that the Church evangelizes, in other words, by her living witness of fidelity to the Lord Jesus – the witness of poverty and detachment, of freedom in the face of the powers of this world, in short, the witness of sanctity (Paul VI, *Evangelii Nuntiandi*, 1975, 41).

[25] This is described by Pope Francis himself during the "question-and-answer session" held on the vigil of Pentecost, with ecclesial movements and communities on May 21, 2013. Pope Francis, "Pentecost Watch with Ecclesial Movements," http://w2.vatican.va/content/francesco/pt/speeches/2013/may/documents/papa-frances co_20130518veglia-pentecoste.html, (accessed September 7, 2019).

[26] Neurofibromatosis is a rare disease that covers the body with swelling growths and seeping sores. It's a genetic condition that causes painful growths and tumours throughout the body. Christopher J. Oldenburg, *The Rhetoric of Pope Francis: Critical Mercy and Conversion for the Twenty-First Century* (Lanham. Boulder. New York: Lexington Books, 2018), 50.

[27] The picture of their embrace saw the Pope being compared to St Francis of Assisi, who he took his name from, who was famously said to have embraced a leper. Hannah Strange, Pope Francis embraces disfigured man, *The Telegraph*, November 7, 2013; https://www.telegraph.co.uk/news/ worldnews/the-pope/10433948/Pope-Francis-embraces-disfigured-man.html (accessed September 3, 2019).

[28] Alessandro Bianchi, "Pope Francis Commemorates Migrant dead at Lampedusa," *Reuters* Homily July 8, 2013, https://www.reuters.com/article/us-pope-lampedusa/pope-francis-commemorates-migrant-dead-at-lampe dusa-idUSBRE9660KH20130708, (accessed September 8, 2019).

[29] However, it is essential that we understand the concepts as well as contextualize our understanding of the following as the key questions: What does it mean to be poor for our Church in the twenty first century? How can we draw up an effective and forward move in the direction to which Pope Francis is leading the Church to?

[30] Thomas C. Fox, "Pope Francis: 'the Church is a love story'" April 24, 2013 http://www.ncronline.org/blos/ ncr-today/pope-francis-church-love-story (accessed October 7, 2015).

³¹ Mohan Doss complements in saying that in taking the side of the periphery we are privileged to honour the dignity of the periphery, the poor, the marginalised and the exploited, and to recognise the presence and the operation of the life-giving Spirit of God. Mohan Doss, *Led by the Spirit: Mission, Spirituality and Formation* (DWS/ISPCK, 2008), 149.

³² CBCI Commission for Women, *Gender Policy of the Catholic Church of India* (Delhi: CBCI Centre, 2010).

³³ Inigo Joachim, "Empowering Women," Presented at Catholic Bishops Conference of India (CBCI) Meeting at Jamshedpur, Scriptural Spiritual and Theological Foundations, http://inigojoachim.com/empowering-women, (accessed October 23, 2007).

³⁴ Pope Francis, "Pope Francis: women must truly participate in Church and Society," https://www .youtube. com/watch?v+c7mt_WnQnqM, (accessed February 25, 2015).

³⁵ Kurien Kunnumpuram, ed. *In Spirit and Truth: Indian Christian Reflections on Spirituality and Worship: Selected Writings of Samuel Rayan, SJ.*, vol II (Bandra, Mumbai: St Pauls, 2012), 42-43.

³⁶ John Henry Newman, *An Essay in Aid of a Grammar of Assent* (New York: Catholic Publication Society, 1945), 39.

17.

The Political Involvement of the Church

Nishant A. Irudayadason

Politics: Boon or Bane for the Church?

Should the Church get involved in politics? Three approaches are possible to respond to this question. The first approach is that it is desirable for the Church to give opinions on the problems of the hour and the decisions to be taken. The second is that the Church must abstain from all political involvement because her vocation is purely spiritual. According to the third approach, the Church needs to remain politically neutral except in totally unacceptable situations, such as the extermination of Jews by the Nazis.

Disagreements are lively and profound among the advocates of these various positions, which makes the position of ecclesiastical leaders delicate. Whenever their statements reflect one of the three positions, they meet with criticism both from within and from outside. If they are silent, they are accused of cowardice and complicity. They are reproached for not making the Gospel message heard, and sometimes for betraying it by their silence. They are criticized for not using their moral authority to speak in favour of justice, human dignity and other cherished values. But when they do intervene, their intervention may be interpreted as a partisan act contrary to their mission. They can be accused of interfering with what does not concern them.

In this paper, I would like to address the question of relationship between the Church and politics, by making a four-step journey. The first will focus on the relationship between the gospel and the culture. The second will deal with the essence of Christianity. The third will briefly discuss the contemporary theological approaches and the last will outline some guidelines on the political role of the Church in our society.

1. Gospel and Culture

By culture, we mean institutions, customs, values, knowledge and behaviours that regulate social existence at a given point of time and place. Durkheim defines culture as "all the ways of thinking, feeling and acting through which a group gains symbolic unity." Politics is part of the culture thus defined. This is why any reflection on the attitude of the Church towards politics is to be situated in a broader context of the relationship between the gospel and culture. We witness in the history of Christianity three paradigms of this relationship.[1]

1.1. *Opposition*

The first paradigm can be described as apocalyptic or sectarian, which disapproves of culture and even condemns it. A well-known verse from the first epistle of John (2:15) is quoted: "Do not love the world or the things in the world. The love of the Father is not in those who love the world." People who follow this paradigm interpret this verse to conclude that Christians must distance themselves from culture.

Already in the third century, this position was found in the writings of an extremely talented North African Church Father and theologian named Tertullian, who advised Christians to avoid social encounters and social occupations as much as possible. He asked them to refuse all activity and responsibility in the city including commerce, philosophy, art (theatre, music), military service, industry, and of course any exercise of authority. In the sixteenth century, some advocates of the Radical Reformation wanted to cut all ties with the society of their time. "We who have been and shall be separated from the world in everything," says the Preamble of the Schleitheim Anabaptist Confession in 1527.[2]

This paradigm seems illusory and deceptive. Culture permeates us, much more than we think and it is theoretically impossible for us to isolate ourselves from culture. In democracies, it is impossible to step out of politics: even the one who abstains takes sides and weighs on the political game. Moreover, this attitude can be criticized for not taking seriously the doctrine of creation which calls for a positive appreciation of the world.

1.2. *Convergence*

The second attitude advocates an alliance between the gospel and culture. Church and society, though distinct, are inseparable. They converge and reinforce each other. Thus, in the second century, Justin Martyr, in his apologetic writings that address both the powerful and the scientists of his time, says that Christians are not rebels, protesters or outsiders. They submit and obey the authorities. They behave as good and loyal citizens, with irreproachable honesty. Their faith leads them to live in accordance with the moral and civic ideal of the Roman Empire. Their doctrines are not subversive but similar to what Greco-Latin philosophers and moralists teach. They do not question the values and ideals of the Roman culture, on the contrary, they reinforce them.

This ideal of a convergence between the gospel and the culture characterizes the Constantine era. A Christian is a good citizen who participates in the political life of his/her country and a good citizen is a good Christian. In the nineteenth century, in both Catholic and Protestant countries, it was often thought that the state and the Church should help and assist each other in an alliance between the throne and the Catholic altar or between the throne and the Protestant pulpit.

We can clearly see the danger posed by this attitude. It presents a gospel so well adapted, and integrated that it loses all power of prophetic challenge. It does not challenge unjust policies and practices of the government, but confirms them and complies with them. Christianity is used for political ends. We have an example of this in the *kulturprotestantismus*, which led the German churches to approve the war of 1870 and 1914 in the name of religious convictions.

1.3. *Separation*

The third position, called the "theory of the two kingdoms", is based on the famous saying of Jesus: "Give to Caesar what belongs to Caesar and give to God what belongs to God" (Mt 22:21). This has led to a clear separation between the temporal kingdom of culture governed by reason and law and the spiritual kingdom of the gospel governed by grace. Christians can belong simultaneously to both kingdoms. In the spiritual kingdom, they can love others as demanded by the Gospel. But their public and professional life must be led by the laws of the society. The gospel must not intervene in cultural, social and political issues.

This third position has the advantage of converging with the ideals of secularism, but it also has other disadvantages. The boundary between what is gospel and what depends on culture cannot easily be traced. Politics is not governed solely by reason, but also by ideologies, and therefore can contradict the gospel. Moreover, this attitude gives rise to serious abuses, as in the case of the Lutheran theologian Emmanuel Hirsch who took sides with Nazism. He believed that the state, in the name of cultural criteria, was right to exclude Jews from national life and he considered any intervention on the part of the Church as illegitimate. He also asserted that the state had no right to forbid him from having communion with a Christian Jew. It is strange argumentation that allowed him to approve the civil persecution of someone who in faith is considered a brother.

2. The Essence of the Christian Faith

2.1. *The Question of Essence*

To better evaluate these three paradigms, we need to dwell on the question of the essence of Christianity. By essence we mean the core that gives Christianity its identity. Christianity has undergone many changes over the past several centuries. Therefore, it is a difficult question, yet we need to give at least a partial and approximate character of the essence of Christian Faith.

2.2. *A Transcendence Presence*

It seems to me that at the heart of Christian faith lies the affirmative experience of a transcendent presence. The biblical God is not outside the world. He does not encounter people elsewhere and he is not indifferent to what happens in the world. He has an intimate connection to the world, especially to human history. He is interested and involved in history. Therefore, God's presence in the world is dynamic. The biblical story shows that God acts in the whole of reality without confining himself to a particular domain that we may term sacred as distinct from profane or mundane.

However, God is transcendent because he differs from the world and from its structures. He is not to be identified with nature, as some romanticists would like to think, nor with history as some Hegelians tend to think. Though he cannot be encountered elsewhere other than the world, he remains fundamentally distinct from it. He cannot become familiar or predictable. In an always unexpected way, he unsettles our categories, disturbs our taken-for-granted assumptions, challenges our habits. As Bultmann says, "God always remains beyond what has once been grasped, which means that the decision of faith is genuine only as actualized ever anew… as the one who demands my decision ever anew, God ever stands before me as the one who is coming, and this constant futurity of God is God's transcendence."[3] He comes to us but does not get enclosed in our religious, theological, philosophical, or political dwellings.

The difficulty for us is to think both the presence and transcendence of God without sacrificing one or the other. Two contrary temptations can threaten us. The first temptation eliminates or blurs the divine presence in the world, making religion a separate domain unrelated to the affairs of the world. The second temptation removes or masks the difference, making the gospel values getting fused with those of the culture. Fidelity to God gets identified with loyalty to one's nation and social class. As the French Protestant theologian Gabriel Vahanian says, "the religious or holy and the secular belong together." [4]

2.3. *The Bipolarity to Maintain*

Rather than the erasure of one of the two aspects, it would be necessary to establish between them a bipolar tension with a spirit of Vatican Council II. The council invites Christians "to strive to discharge their earthly duties conscientiously and in response to the Gospel spirit. They are mistaken who, knowing that we have here no abiding city but seek one which is to come, think that they may therefore shirk their earthly responsibilities" (GS 43).[5] Thus, the German theologian Ernst Troeltsch considers that, in order to remain alive, Christianity needs to maintain a balance between closure and openness.[6] Without its closure by remaining distinct, the gospel would be absorbed by culture and would become salt without flavour. Without its openness to get incarnated in a given culture, the Gospel would remain a utopia without possible concretization; it would be a salt that would not salt anything. The encounter between the gospel and the culture enables the gospel to remain alive, without getting dissolved in or getting isolated from the culture.

3. Contemporary Perspectives on Theology and Politics

Formerly, when we raised the question of relationship between the Church and the State, it was limited to the relationship of two powers—spiritual and temporal—claiming their rights over the same people who are both Christians and citizens. After Vatican Council II, since the Church is first and foremost the People of God, the question of relationship has become larger and more complex. It is the relationship between the Christian and the political society in which he/she lives. The political society in which the Christian lives is where the Christian is called to bear witness to the Gospel and accomplish his mission. Thus, the Church as the People of God is called to work for the whole of humanity.

3.1. *Politics of Agape*

It was in open opposition to the political theology of Metz and to all theologies which tried to gain a foothold in modernity that John Milbank, a British theologian of Anglican faith, launched in 1990 a very provocative thesis namely the scientific social theories are in themselves theologies or disguised anti-theologies.[7] They break from the authentically Christian understanding of relationship with God as a relationship of participation and substitute it with a legal relationship with an impersonal God, a legislator absent in the world, and an autonomous reality that we must consider *etsi Deus non daretur*. Whilst modern theologians interpret modernity (what Milbank calls *the secular*) and secularization as the result of an internal evolution in Christianity fulfilling its vocation in the context of modernity,[8] Milbank describes it as the consequence of a heresy which departs from the Christian orthodoxy in the decision of Duns Scotus to think God and world together, within the framework of a general ontology, instead of thinking ontology of the world from the ontology of its creator.[9] This break then deepens with nominalism and Reformation. The political philosophies of Hobbes and Machiavelli revive the pagan ontology based on the principle of an insurmountable original violence that virtue can only mitigate without having the ability for reconciliation.

While, in the account of Genesis, true freedom finds its condition in the participation of the ontology of human person in the ontology of God, which is also the foundation of the communion of people, Hobbes describes a world where everyone is at war with one another. This original conflict can be tempered by the political, but without ever extinguishing it, because, considered individually in the "state of nature", people who are supposed to be equals, are by the same fact eternally rival. According to Milbank, this places us in direct opposition to the Christian *agape*.[10] This opposition reaches its peak in the deconstruction of the idea of truth in the context of globalization of the market which generates a simulacrum society in which nothing is really desirable than desire itself. Even, because the market has no other end in itself than to excite the desire of the consumer.

Milbank uncompromisingly opposes these two ontologies as two global propositions of incompatible existence, between which the choice to be made. Therefore, he returns to the Christian ideals to develop a "counter-ethics", a "counter-ontology" and a "counter-kingdom",[11] by applying them to narrative, ritual and social practices. A simple adherence to the idea of non-violence is not enough, rather we need to put it into practice as a skill by learning to speak the language developed in the Bible and accomplished in Jesus and in the apparition of the Church that constitutes the concrete form of a non-antagonistic social practice *agape*.[12]

The perspective of Milbank finds an impressive illustration in the reflections of William T. Cavanaugh,[13] which draws the theological consequences from the Catholic Church's struggle against the dictatorship of General Pinochet in Chile. He rejects the distinction made by Jacques Maritain between the spiritual and the temporal leading the Church to think of itself as the soul of the world, and condemning it to impotence because it does not act as body neither in space nor in time. The same criticism can be addressed to Metz's attempt to think of the Church as an organ of social criticism acting as a member among others of civil society. In both cases, in fact, theological discourse has no hold on the political domain.[14]

The Church will find its hold on the political domain only after giving up considering herself as the soul of the world in order to unfold in the world in a corporeal fashion, making the body of Christ visible through concrete practices: "The Eucharist is not just a balm for the soul; it is a public act of the Church that disciplines the bodies of its members. Through the action of the Holy Spirit, the one body of Christ is formed, in which the sufferings of others become my sufferings and simultaneously the sufferings of Christ himself (1 Cor 12). The Eucharist produces a radical identification of three terms: Christ, those who suffer, and me (cf. Mt 25:31-46)."[15] In a daring confrontation of the Thomist theology of the Eucharist and Derridean deconstruction, Catherine Pickstock shows how the sacrament "dramatizes" the paradox of human existence as prey to doubt which seizes her when she thinks there is no physical or natural reality to which it is possible to place total trust. Only this radical Eucharistic dramatization makes it possible to overcome this paradox characteristic of postmodernity, by confronting the subject with this ultimate contradiction of dereliction and the glory of the Crucified One.[16]

It remains to be seen to what extent we are dealing with a theology capable of conceiving the advent of a political order conforming to the Gospel. In fact, for Milbank and the Radical Orthodoxy, the political action of the Church remains a prophetic action of resistance. It is true that the Radical Orthodoxy is marked, on the one hand, by a much more sustained attention to the specificity of the Christian message and to its polemical, even antagonistic position, with regard to contemporary nihilism.[17] and, on the other, to the mediating function of narrative and ritual practices most appropriate to faith in order to put into effect an effective "agapeic" resistance to the nihilistic reign of the single world market.

3.2. *Towards a De-Privatization of Theology*

In the writings of both Metz and Milbank, a real difficulty persists in developing a consistent thought of the "political" as they dominate the theme of "resistance" rather than that of proposition.[18] We wonder whether this apparently insurmountable limitation should be considered as a sign of failure. To address this, we need to explore the ideas of

José Casanova, American researcher in the sociology of religions in his critical resumption of the concept of secularization.[19]

Casanova's question is whether there is a possibility for Christian churches (and, more broadly, for the great religions of the world) to exist as "public" religions, overcoming the "sociological" curse which doomed to privatization and, consequently, to a fatal decline. His response is positive. He argues in two ways. First of all, he undertakes a fundamental critical reflection around the concept of secularization which he thinks that, despite its ambiguities, forces the theorist to situate his reflection in the genealogy of religious sociology in the nineteenth and twentieth centuries. But this concept must however be deconstructed because it articulates three planes that must be differentiated, if we want to interpret the contrasting transformations of religion today. First of all, secularization designates the process of empowerment of social practices in the place of religion; secondly it designates the fact that, by virtue of this process of empowerment, religion is excluded from the public sphere and can therefore only play a role in the private sphere; and finally it refers to the fact that religion thus reduced to the private sphere is engaged on the path of an irremediable decline.

Now, for Casanova, the first aspect of secularization well characterizes the ongoing, yet irreversible developments in religions at the end of the twentieth century. The other two correspond to an evolution in the place of religions in modern society that one may wish and therefore favour, but they cannot be deduced automatically from the first. There is no inexorable theoretical constraint which would force one to think that the incontestable process of autonomy of social practices would inevitably lead to a merciless reclusion of religions in the private sphere then to their decline. He substantiates this by analysing contrasting historical experiences in Catholicism around the world and in certain radical Protestant movements in the States United States.[20] This leads him to augur a global process of "de-privatization" of religions,[21] at least those who will have given up fighting against the separation of the Churches and the State and their own "de-establishment".

One of his theses, supported by his case studies is that the established churches (that is to say formally incorporated in the state apparatus) have become incompatible with modern differentiated states. In other words, "the fusion of the religious and political community is incompatible with the modern principle of citizenship."[22] From this point of view, the constitution of modern States certainly means the disappearance of the Church according to the ideal Weberian type, and the conformation of all the Churches to the ideal type of "Free Church" or "sect". But for the Churches which will have accepted this mutation, which presupposes acceptance of the framework and the fundamental values of modernity such as freedom of conscience and differentiation of society, this does not necessarily imply a retreat of the religious into the private. On the contrary, there is a possibility for them, provided that their own tradition makes it imperative, to opt for the exercise of a public role that Casanova describes as a critical function with regard to specific forms of institutionalization of modernity.

We find the theme of "critical resistance" to the normalization of traditional lifestyles and to the amoral functioning of the state and the market; resistance exercised in the name of the common good which cannot be reduced to the sum of subjective preferences and which must therefore be the subject of a public approval and possibly controversial. Insofar as, according to this critical resumption of the concept of secularization, the transition to the status of "public religion" supposes on the part of religions the renunciation of *the fusion of the religious and the political community*, it seems that one must conclude that all "political theology" in the strict sense has failed. However, it can be considered that Casanova's thesis equally sanctions the fruitfulness of the work of accompaniment accomplished by "political theologians", with a view to allowing the communities to which they belong, a thoughtful implementation of power of faith they confess, in order to contribute to the reconstruction of a new art of living together. From this point of view, their mission goes beyond the limited framework of the exercise of "critical resistance" and opens onto the broader perspective of a contribution to the "invention" of society. This is a task which we may well call "political", in a broader sense.

4. Guiding Principles

Based on discussion we had so far, we need to formulate some principles that can guide the Church in her relation to politics. I would like to suggest four principles based on the teachings of Vatican Council II which are further highlighted by the Papal documents with a special reference to the writings of Pope Francis.

4.1. *Maintaining Distance*

In Chapter IV of the Pastoral Constitution *Gaudium et Spes* expressly devoted to "the life of the political community", the first paragraph is devoted to "public life today" (GS 73) in which the foundations of truly human political life such as the dignity of human person, guarantee of human rights, concern for preserving the rights of minorities, respect for different opinions and religions are praised. The human person is distinct from the citizen and the guarantee of human rights conditions the participation of citizens in public affairs. In this way, the Church is not to be confused with a political community in any way, rather "she is at once a sign and a safeguard of the transcendent character of the human person" (GS 76, § 2).

The Church must always maintain a distance from the positions or practices of political parties and avoid the use of faith to endorse or legitimize them. No political position can claim to be the only option in accordance with the gospel. Fidelity to Christ is seen in many ways and Christians must refrain from absolutizing, idealizing, or sanctifying any of them.

4.2. *Knowing the Right Manner to Get Involved*

However, it is not enough to say that it is up to the faithful to take sides in politics individually, according to their religious convictions and analysis of the situation. We live in a society where communities can exert greater influence than individuals. Besides, if the ecclesial institutions remain silent and disregard politics, they will no longer be instruments of God. Hence it becomes necessary for the ecclesial authorities to challenge the government, that is to tell the government what is wrong (and in any society, there are always many things that go wrong) and to ask the government to provide remedies, even if they do not have to dictate a precise solution to the problems they perceive. They are better placed for this task than the political parties in opposition as they are not in the race for getting mandate to exercise power. In the same way, it seems necessary for the Church to challenge the citizens, warn them against dangers and abuses, and call them to choices that respect the human being.

The Church has been quite consistent on one point: for the sake of justice, we need to get involved in politics. The saintly Pope John XXIII says that "individual citizens and intermediate groups [...] must contribute their goods and their services as civil authorities have prescribed, in accord with the norms of justice and within the limits of their competence" *(Pacem in Terris* 53). This idea gets echoed in the Vatican Council II: "Prudently and honourably let them [citizens] fight against injustice and oppression, the arbitrary rule of one person or one party, and lack of tolerance. Let them devote themselves to the welfare of all sincerely and fairly, indeed with charity and political courage" (GS 75). As Pope Benedict XVI succinctly puts it, "justice is both the aim and the intrinsic criterion of all politics" *(Deus Caritas Est* 28). Pope Francis reiterates this: "Politics, though often denigrated, remains a lofty vocation and one of the highest forms of charity, inasmuch as it seeks the common good" *(Evangelii Gaudium* 205). This common good or justice is not limited only to human persons but extended also to the whole of creation as is exemplified by Pope Francis: "Unless citizens control political power – national, regional and municipal – it will not be possible to control damage to the environment" *(Laudato Si'* 179).

4.3. *Adopting a Critical Approach*

The dogmatic constitution *Lumen Gentium* exhorts Christians "to vigorously contribute their effort, so that created goods may be perfected by human labour, technical skill and civic culture for the benefit of all," but at the same time cautions us not to confound one's Christian duty with involvement in politics as there is a distinction between the affairs of the Church and of politics. The Church needs to challenge the political structure which can cause peril to our freedom including religious freedom (LG 36). "Christians should show in practice how authority can be reconciled with freedom, personal initiative with solidarity and the needs of the social framework as a whole, and the advantages of unity with the benefits of diversity" (GS 75).

The Church need not be revolutionary to campaign for the establishment of another system, but the Church must make protests against the excesses that threaten any system. While the revolutionary aims to replace the existing order by another order, the protester intends to mark the limit and the imperfection of any order. We may recall Camus' famous distinction between the "revolutionary" and the "rebellious". The Church is meant to rebel or protest against the unjust policies and programs played out in politics. It is in this sense that the Church can maintain a healthy critical relation to politics rather than swinging to either side of the spectrum, namely complicity and opposition.

4.4. *Inviting Reflection*

The ecclesial institution does not have to give instructions to the faithful, but it can and must help their reflection. It does so by organizing debates in parishes, councils, synods, publishing documents that are informative, and studies that deepen the issues on the agenda. "Civic and political education is today supremely necessary for the people, especially young people. Such education should be painstakingly provided, so that all citizens can make their contribution to the political community" (GS 75). In doing so, the Church does not leave her mission, rather she fulfils it. She contributes seriously to the commitment of the faithful. Sadly, today the political debate is more emotive than thoughtful, more spectacular than profound. Instinctive impulses take precedence over lucid and in-depth analysis, which means that we quickly slip into fanaticism, extremism and fundamentalism of all kinds. This applies to all areas including politics, and perhaps today especially for politics if we do not want politics to degenerate. "We should recognize how in a culture where each person wants to be bearer of his or her own subjective truth, it becomes difficult for citizens to devise a common plan which transcends individual gain and personal ambitions" (*Evangelii Gaudium* 61).

Conclusion

In the seventeenth century, a Puritan author wrote: "God loves adverbs, he cares more about how than about what." He explains that it does not matter to God whether one is married or single, clergy or laity, rich or poor. What matters to God is not what we do in life, but how we do it. The Church need not tell if Democrats are better than Republicans in the United States, if the Labour party is preferable to the Conservatives in Britain, if the left is superior to the right in France, if the UPA is a clear choice over NDA in India. On the contrary, the Church needs to be concerned about how any of these parties govern, whether their policies are humane and honest.

The Church need not intervene in the "substantives" that designate parties and political systems, but she must intervene in the "adverbs" that designate their ways of being and behaving. The transcendence of God means that he does not identify himself with any of our substantives, even if there are some whom he rejects. His presence manifests itself in our ways of being, therefore in the adverbs that qualify our choices and our behaviours.

Endnotes

[1] On this subject, it is useful to refer to the very enlightening and relevant work of R. Niebuhr titled *Christ and Culture* published in 1951.

[2] "The Schleitheim Confession of Faith, 1527", trans. J. C. Wenger, *The Mennonite Quarterly Review* 19/4 (October 1945): 247.

[3] Rudolf Bultmann, "Science and Existence," in *New Testament and Mythology and Other Basic Writings*, ed. Schubert M. Ogden (Philadelphia: Fortress, 1984), 144.

[4] Gabriel Vahanian, *Praise of the Secular* (Charlottesville: University of Virginia Press, 2008), 17.

[5] Reference to all council documents and Papal encyclicals will be given in parenthesis throughout this paper in the text itself.

[6] See Ernst Troeltsch, *The Absoluteness of Christianity and the History of Religions* (London: SCM, 1972); and Ernst Troeltsch, *Christian Thought: Its History and Application* (London: University of London Press, 1923).

[7] John Milbank, *Theology and Social Theories, Beyond Secular Reason* (Oxford: Basil Blackwell, 1990).

[8] See Max Weber, *The Protestant Ethics and the Spirit of Capitalism* (London: Routledge, 1997).

[9] John Milbank, "Knowledge, the Theological Critique of Philosophy in Hamman and Jacobi," in John Milbank, Catherine Pickstock, Graham Ward (eds.) *Radical Orthodoxy* (London: Routledge, 1999), 23-24. The title of this work, published as a manifesto by associating twelve Anglican and Catholic theologians close to Milbank, is sometimes used to designate a theological movement formed around his theses.

[10] Milbank, *Theology and Social Theories*, 9-26.

[11] Ibid., 398, 422, 432.

[12] Ibid., 398.

[13] William T. Cavanaugh, *Torture and Eucharist. Theology, Politics and the Body of Christ: Challenges in Contemporary Theology* (Maiden: Blackwell Publishers, 1998).

[14] William T. Cavanaugh, "The Body of Christ: The Eucharist and Politics," *Word & World* 22/2 (Spring 2002): 171-172.

[15] Ibid., 176

[16] Catherine Pickstock, "Thomas Aquinas and the Quest for the Eucharist," *Modern Theology* 15/2 (1999): 159-180.

[17] In the field of Christian theology of religions, the consequences of this position were drawn in an original way by Gavin D'Costa, *Theology and Religious Pluralism* (Oxford: Blackwell, 1986); *The Meeting of Religions and the Trinity* (Maryknoll: Orbis Books, 2000); Gavin D'Costa (ed.), *Christian Uniqueness Reconsidered* (Maryknoll: Orbis Books, 1990).

[18] Notice in the writings of Milbank the abundance of neologisms built on the prefix counter such as counter-kingdom, counter-narrative, counter-ethics, etc.

[19] José Casanova, *Public Religions in the Modern World* (Chicago: The University of Chicago Press, 1994).

[20] Casanova enumerates the passage of the Spanish Church from the status of State Church to that of "de-established" Church; changes in the status and self-awareness of the Church in Poland after the fall of communism; the transformation of the Brazilian Church which, from oligarchy, becomes the Church of the people; the transformation of Christian and radical sects in the United States giving birth to "the new Christian right"; finally, still in the United States, the passage of the Catholic Church from the status of "private denomination" to that of "public denomination".

[21] Casanova, *Public Religions in the Modern World*, 111.

[22] Ibid., 213.

V

Pope Francis' Renewal of Religious Life and Priesthood

"Men and women religious, like all other consecrated persons, have been called 'experts in communion'. So, I hope that the 'spirituality of communion' will become a reality and that you will be in the forefront of responding to the great challenge facing us in this new millennium: to make the Church the home and the school of communion."

(Pope Francis)

18.

Pope Francis' Call to Renew Consecrated Life in India By Reviewing Vatican Council II

Fabian Jose, UMI

Introduction: Pope Francis' Challenge to Religious Life in India

Consecrated life in the Catholic Church is a vital and healing presence in India. Consecrated men and women make a vital contribution to Indian society through their institutions in the fields of spirituality, theology, education, medical care, social services, and other charitable activities. In the present Indian context, however, consecrated men and women can experience challenges of identity and relevance in their vocations. Pope Francis has challenged the consecrated that "consecrated life is a call to counter mediocrity: to counter a devaluation of our spiritual life, to counter the temptation to reduce God's importance, to counter an accommodation to a comfortable and worldly life, to counter complaints – complaints! – dissatisfaction and self-pity, to counter a mentality of resignation and we have always done it this way: this is not God's way." Pope Francis has stressed the need for transformation in consecrated life, which is one of the signs of the Indian church.

Today, we have the immense task of the renewal of consecrated life by listening to the Church calling us to "a continuous return to the source of all Christian life," not only to the Charism of our founders and foundresses but specially to the Gospel, which is the 'fundamental norm in our following of Christ and for us the supreme law."[1] Further, the Decree on *Perfectae Caritatis* made a significant contribution to the renewal of consecrated life and it reflects: "One of its main contributions was defining renewal in terms of return to the sources: Scripture, the Church's tradition as well as the founding inspiration and sound traditions of the institute. Secondly, return to the sources should be in accordance with the signs of the time, that is, in dialogue with the contemporary world."[2] Today, Pope Francis is urging all the consecrated men and women to listen to the invitations of the council to renew our identity and relevance to place Jesus Christ as the center of our lives and to have an undying love for God's people. As authentic God-seekers and compassionate emissaries of God we are called to respond to the signs of the contemporary world. In this paper I will be highlighting the beauty, challenges, signs and relevance of consecrated life by revisiting Vatican II through the eyes of Pope Francis.

1. The Current Calls to Rediscover the Beauty of Consecrated Life

Consecrated life proclaims what God, the Father, through the Son and in the Spirit, brings about by his love, his goodness and his beauty. *Vita Consecrata* insists that "the consecrated life becomes one of the tangible seals which the Trinity impresses upon history, so that people can sense with longing the attraction of divine beauty."[3] We are called to live the consecrated life in its fullness by rediscovering the beauty and uniqueness of this chosen vocation which is centered on the person of Jesus Christ. Pope Francis asserts: "Together let us thank the Father, who called us to follow Jesus by fully embracing the Gospel and serving the Church, and poured into our hearts the Holy Spirit, the source of our joy and our witness to God's love and mercy before the world."[4]

We are called to discover the beauty of consecration by embracing and giving witness to the *Evangelii Gaudium*, the 'Joy of the Gospel' amidst the challenges and contradictions of Indian society. Indian spiritual writer Joe Mannath points out that it is "the desire to live as Jesus lived and taught, and finding the meaning of one's life in the life and teachings of Jesus that makes consecrated life enthusiastic and purposeful."[5] This is the beauty of consecrated life which we are called to live. Let us examine some of the calls which this entails today.

1.1. *A Call to Accept Jesus Christ as the Foundation of Consecrated Life*

The foundation of consecrated life is the person of Jesus Christ for whom consecrated men and women have dedicated their lives. Pope Francis urges consecrated people: "To ask ourselves: Is Jesus really our first and only love, as we promised he would be when we professed our vows?" He affirms: "Only if he is, will we be empowered to love, in truth and mercy, every person who crosses our path. For we will have learned from Jesus the meaning and practice of love. We will be able to love because we have his own heart." Only in and through the heart of Jesus the consecrated find their lasting joy and compassion to love and serve the Lord. The founders and foundresses of the religious orders were men and women who shared the compassion of Jesus "when Jesus saw the crowds who were like sheep without a shepherd."[6] Like Jesus, "who compassionately spoke his gracious word, healed the sick, gave bread to the hungry and offered his own life in sacrifice, so our founders and foundresses sought in different ways to be at the service of all those to whom the Spirit sent them." Through their prayers of intercession, their preaching of the Gospel, their works of catechesis, education, healing ministry, pastoral service and their service to the poor and the infirm found countless new ways of bringing joy of the Gospel to every culture and corner of the society.

1.2. A Call to be Rooted in Baptism

Every human being, created in the world out of the life-giving love of the Holy Trinity, has an irreplaceable role to play in the Heavenly Father's plan for the human salvation and destiny. As we continue our journey with God through life, we are led to discover our specific vocation, the exacting way in which the Lord calls us to be united with him and to participate in his work of redemption.[7] Pope Francis recalls the importance of baptism in the general audience that "the baptized are called to bring the light of Christ into the world through concrete signs. It is in this way that God's light and hope will reach all people, and fill a world that does not have hope and faith."[8] The baptized are called to be a sign even in the darkened corners of the world and manifest God's unconditional love to the humanity. Through the sacrament of baptism, a person receives a fundamental consecration. Rising from the baptismal font, every Christian is invited to hear again the voice that was once heard on the banks of the river Jordan: "You are my beloved Son; with you I am well pleased" (Lk 3:22).

The desire to make a gift of one's life to the Lord by the way of the evangelical counsels is a human response to the divine initiative one has received through baptism. Pope Francis exclaims with joy to the formators gathered in Rome: "Consecrated life is beautiful. It is one of the most precious treasures of the Church, rooted in the vocation of baptism." Thus, we have a mission to reflect the beauty of the compassionate face of God to all the people. As consecrated to God he reminds us through the sacrament of baptism that, we have been reborn as children of light, and faithful to our baptismal calling, let us share the new hope that Jesus brings. Our rootedness in baptism leads us to live the consecrated life, to recognize Jesus in the weakest and poorest and shed His light to all those who walk in the darkness in particular people of the periphery.

1.3. A Call to Live the Joy of the Gospel

Joy is the foundation of every human being. Every day people long to possess this joy which builds their personal life, homes, neighborhood, society, church and world. In his message *'To All Consecrated People'* he writes that "In their daily struggles, every man and woman tries to attain joy and abide in it from the teachings of Pope Francis, with the totality of their being. In the world there is often a lack of joy. We are not called to accomplish epic feats or to proclaim high-sounding words, but to give witness to the joy that arises from the certainty of knowing we are loved, from the confidence that we are saved."[9]

The limitations of our memories and fragile experiences often prevent us from searching for lasting joy where we can cherish and relish God's reflection. We have thousand reasons for remaining in joy. Its roots are nourished by listening with faith and perseverance to the Word of God. In the school of the Master we hear: "May my joy be in you and may your joy be complete" (Jn 15:11), and we are taught how to practice perfect joy. Pope Francis adds: "Joy is not born, does not come from the things one has!" *Evangelii Gaudium* reflects that, "The joy of the Gospel fills the heart and lives of all who encounter Jesus. With Jesus Christ joy is constantly born anew."[10] Consecrated people receive this lasting perfect joy to follow the Lord in a special way, in a prophetic way.

Pope Francis reminds the consecrated that wherever there are consecrated persons, seminarians, women and men religious, young people, there is joy, there is always joy. It's the joy of freshness; it's the joy of following Jesus; the joy that the Holy Spirit gives us, not the world's joy. Our meeting with Jesus lights up in us its original beauty, the beauty of the face on which the Father's glory shines (2 Cor 4:6), radiating happiness. In their finite humanity, on the margins, in their everyday struggles, consecrated men and women live out their fidelity, giving a reason for the joy that lives in them. So that they become splendid witnesses, effective proclaimers, companions and neighbors for the women and men with whom they share a common history and who want to find their Father's house in the Church.

1.4. *A Call to Proclaim God's Tender Love*

Throughout the history of Christianity, God has called men and women to follow Jesus Christ radically, to bear witness to His love and compassion in this world. Consecrated people have dedicated themselves to furthering the vision and mission of Jesus on earth by living as monks, hermits, priests, or women religious. Today, they are a mighty force in the Indian Church, spreading the good news of God's kingdom in a multi-religious, multi-linguistic, and multi-cultural nation. The consecrated in India bear witness to Jesus amidst the challenges of religious fundamentalism, persecution, and violence. They proclaim the Gospel of God's tenderness "among peoples who do not know Jesus Christ and the Gospel."[11] As followers of Christ, they "set aside their abilities, time, talents, work, the sweetness and goodness of their hearts, all for the service of others."[12] They share the pain and hope of the sick, suffering, poor, marginalized and oppressed brothers and sisters of society. In this way, "their words, their messages, the way they comfort the sorrowing and wipe the tears of those in pain are God's gifts and ways of expressing divine love."[13]

Gaudium et Spes emphasizes: "The joys and hopes, the grief and anguish of the people of our time, especially of those who are poor or afflicted, are the joys and hopes, the grief and anguish of the followers of Christ as well. Nothing that is genuinely human fails to find an echo in their hearts. For theirs is a community united in Christ and guided by the Holy Spirit in their pilgrimage towards the Father's Kingdom, bearers of the message of salvation for all humanity."[14] The whole world is involved in the reception and hermeneutics of this new way of being church, in dialogue with the world and its joys and sorrow.

Rooted in the joy of the Gospel and teachings of the church, Pope Francis emphasizes that: "People today certainly need words, but most of all they need us to bear witness to the mercy and tenderness of the Lord which warms the heart, rekindles hope, and attracts people towards the good. What a joy it is to bring God's consolation to others!"[15] He entrusts this mission to consecrated men and women: to discover the

Lord who comforts us like a mother, and to comfort the people of God by revealing the tender love of God. The men and women of our time are longing for words of consolation, the availability of forgiveness and true joy from the consecrated people.

2. Challenges to Consecrated Life in India

Like others of our day, consecrated men and women are exposed to and enticed by various pulls and pressures of a secular, consumerist and materialistic society, which challenges their call and commitment in various ways. Let us discuss some of the challenges.

2.1. *The Challenge to Renew a Contemplative Spirituality*

One of the major challenges the consecrated men and women encounter in India today is the need to renew the contemplative spirituality that lies at the heart of the rich spiritual heritage of India. Theologian Kurien Kunnumpuram remarks that there are many devotions and pious practices in Indian consecrated life, "but not enough spirituality."[16] Vandana Mataji, a Catholic nun who initiated the Christian Ashram movement in India, expressed that the consecrated people in India do not possess the "spirit of contemplation" that would enable them to "enter into relationship with others and to grasp what reality is." In her words, "Religious give themselves entirely to works or services at the cost of their contemplative dimension."[17] In the face of the demands of institutional life, apostolic ministries, and administrative tasks, consecrated people often fail to pursue the deeper dimensions of a contemplative spirituality.

Without blaming the predecessors of the Indian mission who were products of their times, consecrated people today have a solemn responsibility to rediscover the vital spiritual resources of India, which will equip them to grow as contemplative prophets so as to reflect a spirituality relevant to the context of India. *Perfectae Caritatis* aptly asserts: "The members of each institute, therefore, ought to seek God before all else, and solely; they should join in contemplation, by which they cleave to God by mind and heart, to apostolic love, by which they endeavor to be associated with the work of redemption and to spread the kingdom of God."[18] If we have such an experience of God's immense love for us, we will feel a great need to speak about this love. As St John says, "We speak of what we have seen and heard" (1 Jn 1:3). "But if this is to come about, we need to recover a contemplative spirit which can help us to realize ever anew that we have been entrusted with a treasure which makes us more human and helps us to lead a new life. There is nothing more precious which we can give to others."[19] Cultivating a contemplative spirituality is an urgent need for us to grow as more integrated persons to serve the people of God.

2.2. *The Challenge Posed by Over-Institutionalization of Consecrated Life*

The Catholic Church in general, and in India in particular, is an institutionalized, hierarchical structure, and seen by many as 'foreign' or 'Western'— an intrinsic part of colonial history. This is so because, as Indian ecclesiologist Kuncheria Pathil argues, the Church has failed to inculturate itself into the rich multi-cultural and local religious contexts of the Indian reality.[20] Rather, the historical churches in India are "mere 'extensions' or 'transplantations' from outside," and consequently, church structures and patterns of worship are likewise extrinsic, with "only minor adaptations . . . made to fit into [the Indian] context." Pathil explains that "many of the Church's huge impressive institutions were mostly funded by the West and it is alleged that many of the church's educational and health institutions cater exclusively to the needs of the rich and the super rich."[21] The Indian Church, therefore, "seems to be alienated from the Indian cultural, religious, and spiritual ethos."[22]

In *Evangelii Gaudium* Pope Francis emphasizes that "Through inculturation, the Church "introduces peoples, together with their cultures, into her own community," for "every culture offers positive values and forms which can enrich the way the Gospel is preached, understood and lived." In this way, the Church takes up the values of different cultures and becomes *sponsa ornata monilibus suis*, "the bride bedecked with her jewels" (Isa 61:10). He adds, "The Holy Spirit, sent by the Father and the Son, transforms our hearts and enables us to enter into the perfect communion of the blessed Trinity, where all things find their unity." The Holy Spirit is the one who builds communion and harmony among the people of God. Thus cultural diversity is not a hazard to the unity of the Church.[23] The various religious orders were founded in the church to bear witness to Christ's presence in the world and to serve the needs of the periphery through the various ministries of education, health care, the socio-pastoral apostolate, and evangelization. Yet, in the Indian Church, the institutional structures provide security and comfort to those in consecrated life, shielding them from the human powerlessness and poverty to which the Indian populations are subjected. It is this pervasive institutionalization that dulls the Church's prophetic edge.

2.3. *The Challenge of Decline of Religious Vocations to Consecrated Life*

Today, most religious communities in India are facing the challenge of declining vocations to consecrated life. Pope Francis encouraged consecrated men and women to "Respond to the crisis of vocations with intensified prayer, rather than despair or a lax admissions process." The failure of consecrated people to assume a contemplative-prophetic role has affected the church in India. However, as theologian John Sankarathil argues, the "vocation crisis" may be perceived as a "challenge rather than a tragedy," an "eye-opener and a call to every consecrated person and every Institute to re-examine their mission and vision and the particular charism of the founder in the modern world."[24] Sankarathil elucidates the contours of a vibrant, prophetic spirituality for consecrated life in India today, one which integrates the elements of prayer and prophetic witness: "Consecrated persons should possess a spirituality of profound commitment to God and concern for the poor and the less-privileged." Pope Francis challenges each consecrated person "not to distance myself from the people and live in comfort," but to be close to Christians and non-Christians in order to understand their problems and needs. They should shine forth as a beacon of hope in the lives of Christians and non-Christians by helping them to gain a better understanding of their faith commitment.

There is thus a fundamental relationship between vocation and mission. As *Vita Consecrata*, urges, "The mission of the consecrated life, as well as the vitality of institutes, undoubtedly depends on the faithful commitment with which consecrated persons respond to their vocation. But they have a future to the extent that still other men and women generously welcome the Lord's call."[25] God is speaking to consecrated men and women today through the signs of the times. The present issue is not whether the numbers are large or small, but whether consecrated people are "listening to what God is telling us today." Through the centuries, consecrated life has assumed many forms. Today, we are called to move beyond the outmoded—to "remain open to hear what God is telling us in the new, and to be challenged by what our contemporaries, especially the young, are telling us today. Keeping in touch with today's men and women, and listening to their needs with love, we will find the new forms that will revitalize religious life."[26] Joe Mannath sees hope in the present situation, saying, "Each change, each apparent death, is a new beginning."[27]

2.4. The Challenge of Hindutva and Religious Fundamentalism

India is a country characterized by its multi-religious, multi-cultural, and multi-linguistic elements, as well as its philosophy of non-violence (*ahimsa*).[28] Among the Hindu population, a resurgence of vicious religious nationalism and fundamentalism known as *Hindutva* has resulted in severe forms of discrimination against other religious traditions, notably Christians and Muslims. Theologian and sociologist Jacob Peenikaparambil, explains that, "Hindutva ideology is diametrically opposed to the values upheld by the Indian Constitution, particularly secular democracy." Its proponents aim to convert "India into a Hindu Rashtra, a theocratic state based on the tenets of Hindu religion, where the minorities will be treated as second class citizens, where there will be no freedom of the citizens to profess, practice and propagate the religion of their choice."[29] Therefore, fundamentalism is enforcing narrow sectarian practices for strengthening religious orthodoxy as well as achieving power, particularly political power. In order to consolidate political power, extreme coercion involving violence is used.[30]

To respond to the problem of religious fundamentalism, consecrated people have a responsibility to educate the young generation of India to discover the beauty and richness of their own religious traditions as well as to affirm the goodness and truth of other religious traditions.[31] Pluralism must be seen as a gift of God, and its promotion "the only way for building peace and human solidarity." The dream of India becoming an authentically developed country will be actualized only when the nation "preserves its pluralistic democracy."[32] Soares-Prabhu observes that in recent decades, the theology of India has shifted its focus from the "conquering mission" of the past to issues of "inculturation, interreligious dialogue, religious pluralism, ecumenical dialogue, communal harmony and liberation of the oppressed groups."[33] Whether these approaches will serve as antidotes to the hate campaigns of the fundamentalists remains to be seen. Nevertheless, the present circumstances have led many people belonging to all religions to serious introspection.[34]

2.5. *Challenges Arising on Account of Socio-Economic Disparities*
India has rich religious traditions, natural resources, and a unique cultural diversity; however, the nation faces serious challenges with regard to socio-economic disparities. In India, 28.5% of the people live below the poverty line. The poverty of India ostracizes the poor socially, economically, morally and religiously through the caste system, which presupposes an essential inequality among human beings. Poverty, caste, and religiosity in India are interrelated and their mutual influence affects the people socially, economically, and ethically.

The poor people of India desire to see consecrated men and women poor like them so that they may understand the struggles of the poor. In his apostolic exhortation *Evangelica Testificatio*, Pope Paul VI appealed to consecrated people to turn toward the poor: "You hear rising up, more pressing than ever, from their personal distress and collective misery, "the cry of the poor". . . In a world experiencing the full flood of development, this persistence of poverty-stricken masses and individuals constitutes a pressing call for "a conversion of minds and attitudes," especially for you who follow Christ more closely in this earthly condition of self-emptying."[35] In *Evangelii Gaudium* Pope Francis asserts that: "Our faith in Christ, who became poor, and was always close to the poor and the outcast, is the basis of our concern for the integral development of society's most neglected members."[36]

The millions of poor people in India pose a challenge to consecrated people to simplify their lives to witness Christ among the poor, to "dedicate to God all our spiritual labors to grow in holiness, all our intellectual efforts to acquire knowledge, all our work for evangelization, all our care to use things in the best possible way, all our efforts to earn enough for ourselves and for our apostolate and all our efforts to avoid waste, to preserve things and to handle them appropriately."[37] Therefore, according to Pope Francis, "Each individual Christian and every community is called to be an instrument of God for the liberation and promotion of the poor, and for enabling them to be fully a part of society." This demands that consecrated men and women be attentive to the cry of the poor and be responsive to come to their aid.[38]

2.6. *The Challenge of Discrimination against Women in Church and Society*

Today, women in Indian society are awakening to a new consciousness of their true identity. This collective awakening is occurring globally and locally, transcending the boundaries of nation, race, colour and creed. Women are discovering their strength and power, and thus mounting a courageous challenge to the male domination which exists in Indian society.[39] This transformation, however, belongs largely to the privileged and educated women of India. The status and power of women in India varies depending on their education level, economic status, and religious tradition.

The 28th Plenary Assembly of the Catholic Bishops' Conference of India (CBCI), held in Jamshedpur from February 13–20, 2008, explored the theme of 'Empowerment of Women in the Church and Society'. The religious leaders examined the social, economic, moral and religious status of women in India, especially those on the periphery of society. Women who belong to the minority groups and the backward castes and classes of Dalits and tribals, are victimized due to poverty, ill-health, lack of access to education, and appropriate knowledge. In various parts of India, "female feticide, infanticide, rape, molestation, kidnapping, abduction, battering, dowry deaths, murder, trafficking for sex and slavery" are evident even today. Women are often forced to migrate from their own lands and livelihoods to an insecure place where they are unable to find resources for survival. Women "suffer systemic and structural violence that enslaves them and dehumanizes them economically, socio-politically and religio-culturally."[40]

In a paper presented at the Plenary Assembly, Inigo Joachim, the former superior general of the congregation of St Anne, Madhavram, pointed out that the consecrated women of India are a powerful force in the Indian Church. They contribute immensely to the social transformation of society through their various ministries such as "educational and health services, legal advice, community development projects, communication media, inter-religious movements and other innovative ways of social and pastoral ministries to the needy and the marginalized in every nook and corner of the remote areas and cities of our country."[41] Though they contribute to the betterment of the social order as well as to the development of the church, they nevertheless continue to face the challenges of discrimination in Indian society.[42]

Today, Pope Francis calls for "a more widespread and incisive female presence" in the Church. Here the pope indicates the desirability of seeing "many women involved in the pastoral responsibilities, in the accompaniment of persons, families and groups, as well as in theological reflection."[43] The Church in India will flourish only when it recognizes the full potential of women's contribution to the Church and Society, and addresses the necessity of structural changes in the existing patriarchal systems.

2.7. The Challenges Arising from the Ecological Crises

India is a land of mountains, rivers, seas, valleys, forests, gardens, blessed with a unique bio-diversity. From the earliest times, the people of India lived in harmony with nature and with one another amidst great cultural and religious diversity, affirming the presence of the divine in the natural world. Ironically, as Indian moral theologian Clement Campos observes, "India is a strange mixture of the old and the new, a land of contradictions, where the majority of its people are expected each morning to beg pardon of the earth for stepping on it, while almost blissfully, its rivers are fouled up and its environment polluted."[44] Today, the people of India are losing this sense of the sacredness of nature in the drive toward destructive development and economic profit. Jesuit theologian Samuel Rayan warns that, "The earth system is being polluted and destroyed through wasteful, profligate and predatory practices by modern profit-oriented scientific-technological culture, be it industrial, agricultural, or communicational. The earth's standing, meaning, and history as the Home of Life are under threat of death."[45] The precise causes of ecological crisis are difficult to identify, as Kunnumpuram asserts, as it is a "complex phenomenon." However, he posits that "greed and selfishness, both individual and collective, as well as a utilitarian attitude to the cosmos are at the root of this crisis."[46]

In India today, Pope Francis's words ring especially true. India's environmental crisis is dire. In his encyclical *Laudato Si*, Pope Francis laments the abuse that we have inflicted upon the earth, our common home, though she is the mother who sustains us, and our sister with whom we share our life: "This sister now cries out to us because of the harm we have inflicted on her by our irresponsible use and abuse of the goods with which God has endowed her. We have come to see ourselves as her lords and masters, entitled to plunder her at will. The violence present in our hearts, wounded by sin, is also reflected in the symptoms of sickness evident in the soil, in the water, in the air and in all forms of life. This is why the earth herself, burdened and laid waste, is among the most abandoned and maltreated of our poor; she "groans in travail" (Rom 8:22). We have forgotten that we ourselves are dust of the earth (Gen 2:7); our very bodies are made up of her elements, we breathe her air and we receive life and refreshment from her waters."[47]

As Christian spiritual leaders, consecrated men and women have a mission to guide the people of India by drawing lessons from scripture and the sacred texts of other religious traditions, as well as the magisterial documents of the Church. Campos calls for a multi-religious approach to the environmental crisis in India, noting that in *Laudato Si*, Pope Francis cites a broad variety of sources, not only from his own tradition, but from several episcopal conferences, the Orthodox Patriarch Bartholomew, Sufi mysticism, the Rio Declaration on Environment and Development, and the Earth Charter. The pope expresses his "wish to address every person living on this planet," and to "to enter into dialogue with all people about our common home." [48] This dialogue can serve as a crucially important locus of collaboration among people of all faiths in India and a shared ethical response to protect and care for our Mother Earth.[49]

3. Guiding Lights to Illumine the Pathways of Consecrated Life

Having had a glimpse of the beauty of consecrated life as well as having discussed the many challenges that call for response and renewal, let us propose some guiding lights that will assist our consecrated life to remain relevant in the present times and in the future.

3.1. *The Need to Cultivate a Committed Prayer Life*

Holiness of every Christian comprises "in a habitual openness to the transcendent, expressed in prayer and adoration." In *Gaudete et Exsultate* Pope Francis says: "I do not believe in holiness without prayer, even though that prayer need not be lengthy or involve intense emotions." We need to be constant in prayer, and even amidst the bodily exercises do not abandon it. "Whether you eat, drink, talk with others, or do anything, always go to God and attach your heart to him."[50] Trust-filled prayer opens the heart of a person "to encounter God face to face." Prayer is the foundation to build relationship with God, cosmos, others and self.

For Pope Francis, consecrated people are called to cultivate a committed prayer life to grow in constant communion with the source of their consecration. This radical commitment, invites the consecrated to leave behind families, careers and everything that they hold very dear for the sake of the gospel. He holds that every prayer has to turn back to this to work for the Lord, not for one's own interests or for the institution in which one works; no, but for the Lord! He adds "prayer, in the consecrated life, is the air which makes us breathe that call, renew that call. Without this air we could not be good consecrated persons. We would be perhaps good persons, Christians, Catholics who do many works in the Church, but consecration you must continually renew, in prayer, in an encounter with the Lord."

Pope Francis holds that as Disciples of Christ it is essential to spend fruitful time with the Master, Jesus, to listen to his words, to learn from him always and to cultivate his lifestyle in our day-to-day life. "Contemplating the face of Jesus, died and risen, restores our humanity, even when it has been broken by the troubles of this life or marred by sin."[51] Unless the Lord warms our heart with his love and tenderness amidst the realities of life we will not be able to contemplate his face. The Pope identifies prayer as the source of the fruitfulness of the mission. Let us try to cultivate the contemplative aspect, even amidst the whirlwind of more urgent and heavy responsibilities. And the more the mission calls us to go out to the people of the periphery, let our heart be more closely united to Christ's heart, full of mercy love, and tenderness.[52] He repeats: "The Church needs men and women who pray, in this moment of great pain for humanity."

3.2. The Need to Foster Patience in Life

Patience is very often the focus of Pope Francis' homily at the daily Mass he celebrates at Casa Santa Marta. He emphasizes the importance of patience in consecrated life, which, is not just about bearing patiently with those with whom we live and work—it is also about bearing patiently with the sufferings of the world, "carrying it on our shoulders." Without patience, we grow tired and close our hearts to God's grace in a kind of spiritual euthanasia. The Pope recalls how God urged Abraham and his wife Sarah to be patient, even in their old age. In the same way, through patience, and prayer, God will bring fruitfulness in our personal and community lives.[53] "Enter into patience," because without patience "you cannot be magnanimous, you cannot follow the Lord."

Pope Francis insists that there must even be patience in the face of a lack of vocations. Choosing to stop accepting members and to sell off the community's property is a sign that the congregation "is close to death" and has become attached to money, rather than having the patience to pray for new vocations. This "art of dying well"—a congregation choosing not to pursue prospective vocations—is a "spiritual euthanasia" which "doesn't have the courage to follow the Lord. We follow Jesus to a certain point and by the first or second trial, goodbye." The pope accentuated that the consecrated men and women will certainly be fruitful if they are prayerful, poor, and patient.

3.3. The Need to Invigorate Religious Formation

Religious formation in consecrated life requires constant renewal in order for members to grow as integrated persons through contemplation and prophetic witness. Young men and women entering consecrated life in India carry with them the complex social, economic, spiritual, cultural, and emotional problems of Indian society. The formators are already making efforts to introduce integral formation programmes to their new members to help them face the challenges of consecrated life and to read the signs of the times.

Though much is being done, there is urgent need to focus more on the integral growth of the persons in consecrated life as Pope Francis enthused the formators assembled at the Vatican, on April 14, 2015: "The young must be formed in humble and intelligent freedom to let themselves be educated by God the Father every day of their life, at every age, both in the mission and in fraternity, both in action and in contemplation. There is not a vocations crisis where there are consecrated people able to transmit the beauty of consecration with their own witness." He added, "Well-formed vocations are more important than numerous vocations" emphasizing the need for quality rather than quantity. He also stressed on the formation of the mission to "form the passion of proclamation, the passion for going wherever, in every periphery, to tell everyone about the love of Jesus Christ, especially to those far from the Church, to the little ones, and to the poor, and let ourselves be evangelized by them."[54]

Living a God-centered life is the focus of the integral formation of the consecrated people of India today. Genuine religious formation "empowers the members to live their charism in radically new ways in the contemporary context."[55] Consecrated people need to cultivate openness, dialogue and collaboration with other religious orders and people of other faith traditions, so that our religious formation programmes may be fully equipped to read the signs of the time in India today. In the manner of Pope Francis, those in consecrated life are called to grow in prayer, deeper silence, solitude, discernment of the spirit, formation of the heart, love for the poor and contemplative-prophetic spirituality. They are called to find the presence of God in all things, to discover the true self, to read critically the signs of the times and to become a voice for the voiceless of the periphery in the current Indian society.

3.4. *The Need to Reach out to the Periphery through Social Justice*

Consecrated people are called to commit themselves to take the side of the poor and the marginalized. As a prophet of social justice Pope Francis encourages consecrated men and women to become daring prophets to serve God and His people. For him "option for the poor is a theological category rather than a cultural, sociological, political or philosophical one."[56] He reminds us in *Gaudete et Exsultate* that "many people have been and still are, persecuted simply because they struggle for justice, because they take seriously their commitment to God and to others."[57] At this point the words of St. John Paul II are apt to reflect, "If we truly start out anew from the contemplation of Christ, we must learn to see him especially in the faces of those with whom he himself wished to be identified."[58]

In the call to recognize Jesus in the poor and suffering humanity, we reflect the heart of Christ. Each individual consecrated person and all religious communities are called to be instruments of God for the liberation and promotion of the poor, enabling them to be fully part of society. In *Evangelii Gaudium* Pope Francis reiterates that: "We are called to find Christ in them, to lend our voice to their causes, but also to be their friends, to listen to them, to speak for them and to embrace the mysterious wisdom which God wishes to share with us through them."[59] This demands that we be attentive to the cry of the poor and that we come to their aid.

Today, in India, this means "working for systemic change, an approach to development based on the people's rights, and for sustainable development. We need to make the shift from developmental-and-charity model approach to that of transformative model."[60] According to George Kaitholil, the consecrated people of India are often afraid to risk their lives and security for the sake of the people on the periphery; instead, "most of us withdraw from the scene when we are faced with opposition from the powerful . . . Even if there are individuals who are ready, as a rule they do not get the needed support and encouragement from their institutes."[61] As the ultimate consequence of challenging and disturbing the economic and political status quo, one might even lose his or her life like Blessed Rani Maria and Sr Valsa John.

3.5. *The Need to Empower Women's Leadership in the Church*

Today, in India, consecrated women and men are called to work for gender equality in the church and in society. To address gender issues, men and women are called to relate to one another in creative reflection, dialogue, reconciliation, and respect.[62] *Gaudium et Spes* of VC II states, "With respect to the fundamental rights of the person, every type of discrimination, whether social or cultural, whether based on sex, race, color, social condition, language or religion, is to be overcome and eradicated as contrary to God's intent."[63] Since VC II, a number of outstanding women have emerged as theologians and biblical scholars. Through biblical and anthropological research, several remarkable women scholars are uncovering new data regarding women in history, Scripture and the early church community. In appointing seven women to the Vatican congregations, Pope Francis achieved a double win, namely, stressing the role of women in the church and the reform of the Vatican Curia.

Rekha Chennattu an Indian Biblical scholar encourages consecrated women to work for "new models of Christian leadership which are more participatory, creative, enabling and empowering."[64] The Church in India needs to recognize the crucial importance of women's leadership roles, at all levels. Sr Inigo concretely suggests that religious women should be "included in the diocesan and local level Councils and in the decision making process."[65] Furthermore, "we have to popularize inclusive language in liturgy, in the prayer of the Church, catechesis, homilies and should judiciously use more feminist and liberative passages: Deborah, Judith, Naomi and other women from the Old and New Testament. It should be announced from the pulpit that discrimination and violence against women is sinful. Parishes should involve women in the ministry of the proclamation of the Good News. Women should be included as co-workers and co-leaders by recognizing their leadership competence and intellectual and creative potentialities."[66] To improve the present status of women's leadership in the Church the 2019 Amazon Synod proposed the ordination of women deacons a type of ministry in the church that allows "for preaching, celebrating weddings and baptisms, but not consecrating the Eucharist."

3.7. The Need to Confront Social Evils through Interreligious Dialogue

Pope Francis is an eminent proponent of dialogue, seeing it as a contribution to peace. He highlights three areas of dialogue: (a) dialogue with states, (b) dialogue with society and (c) dialogue with believers who are not part of the Catholic Church. In each case, "the Church speaks from the light which faith offers." The Pope believes that "this light transcends human reason, yet it can prove meaningful and enriching to those who are not believers and it stimulates reason to broaden its perspectives."[67] The Indian churches' call for a deeper dialogue with other religions is one of the most significant signs of the times. Influenced by the religious fundamentalism of political leaders, communalism, caste system, gender inequalities and various other social evils our mother land and its people of different faiths are wounded in many ways.

Today, the consecrated people of India are called to be agents of reconciliation and conversation in this pluralistic country through the various ministries of education, social, health care and pastoral work. Reflecting on interreligious dialogue, lay writer Suresh reflects: "The serenity and compassion taught in Buddhism, the total renunciation and detachment preached by Jainism, the desire for right social order and the courageous life of Sikhism and the life of holiness and purity stressed in Zoroastrianism simply reflect the essential teachings of Christianity."[68] Today, 'New India' could be built again based on religious harmony, acceptance, respect, and dialogue with the people of different faiths. Our dialogue with the followers of other faiths must be characterized by an attitude of openness in truth and love.

Developing a hateful attitude towards the people of other faiths through fundamentalism and communalism by fanatics needs to be confronted by consecrated people in this pluralistic country. We are called to guide Christians to confront every form of violence and discrimination among people based on status, race or creed.⁶⁹ May the spirit of Christ and interreligious values of Pope Francis enable the church in India, together with the people of other faiths to work for religious harmony amidst religious diversities, to build unity and respect among all people irrespective of caste, colour, language, culture, etc. and above all to cultivate a magnanimous heart towards everyone and to read the signs of the times in addressing social problems. Today, in this 21st century, the mission of the Church in India is to build a 'New India' in alliance and dialogue with people of all faiths, to be a sign which reveals the reign of God established by Jesus Christ.

Conclusion: Look back with gratitude; live with passion; embrace the future with hope

In this article I have attempted to explore the beauty and challenges of consecrated life, attempting to give some guiding lights against the light provided by VC II and seen through the eyes of Pope Francis. I have mirrored the vital presence of consecrated life in the Indian Church and Society. Today, consecrated men and women often experience challenges of relevance and identity in their vocations. These concerns have their basis in the fundamental need for a renewal of consecrated life itself, one which embraces a Christ-centered spirituality and nurtures the prophetic charism that marks apostolic religious life. The Spirit is calling us in the context of India through Pope Francis to develop a new way of being Church.

Today, at this decisive time in the 21st century, Pope Francis challenges all consecrated men and women to ask themselves, "Is Jesus really our first and only love, as we promised he would be when we professed our vows? Only if he is, will we be empowered to love, in truth and mercy, every person who crosses our path. We will be able to love because we have his own heart."⁷⁰ Filled with the fire for Christ every consecrated man and woman is called to live a meaningful life by making Christ present in today's world. Pope Francis encourages the consecrated by recalling the words from *Vita Consecrata*: "You have not only a glorious history to remember and to recount, but also a great history still to be accomplished! Look to the future, where the Spirit is sending you in order to do even greater things."[71] The heartening words of Pope Francis enrapture our hearts and minds with a renewed vision and mission, "to look at the past with gratitude, to live the present with passion and to embrace the future with hope."

Endnotes

[1] *Perfectae Caritatis: Adaptation and Renewal of Religious Life*, Vatican City: Libreria Editrice Vaticana, October 28, 1965, 2; hereinafter cited as *PC*.

[2] Ibid.

[3] *Vita Consecrata*. Post Synodal Apostolic Exhortation on the Consecrated Life and its Mission in the Church and in the World (March 25, 1996), 20; hereinafter cited as *VC*.

[4] Pope Francis, Apostolic Letter of his holiness Pope Francis to all Consecrated People on the occasion of the Year of Consecrated Life, Vatican, November 21, 2014,1.

[5] Joe Mannath, *A Radical Love A Path of Light: The Beauty and Burden of Religious Life*, New Delhi, CRI House, 2013, 25.

[6] Apostolic Letter of Pope Francis to all Consecrated People, 2.

[7] Council of Major Superiors of Women Religious, *The Foundation of Religious Life: Revisiting the Vision*, Mumbai, Pauline Publications, 2009, 33.

[8] "Pope Francis address to formators of consecrated men and women gathered in Rome," https://zenit.org/articles/pope-francis-address-to-formators-of-consecrated-men-and-women/ 2015 April.

[9] Congregation for institutes of consecrated life and societies of apostolic life, *Rejoice*, A letter to consecrated men and women, *A message from the teachings of Pope Francis, Year of Consecrated Life* (Rome: 2 February 2014), 3.

[10] Pope Francis, Apostolic Exhortation *Evangelii Gaudium*, 2013,1; hereinafter cited as *EG*.

[11] Kurien Kunnumpuram, *Prophets of the Lord Friends of the Poor: Indian Christian Reflections on the Religious Life*, Mumbai, St. Pauls, 2014, 48.

[12] George Kaitholil, *Consecrated life: Challenges and Opportunities*, Bandra, Mumbai, St. Pauls, 2014, 23.

[13] Ibid.

[14] *Gaudium et Spes: Pastoral Constitution on the Church in the Modern World*, Documents of VC II, Vatican City, Libreria Editrice Vaticana, December 7, 1965,1; hereinafter cited as *GS*.

[15] *Rejoice*, A Letter to Consecrated Men and Women, 8.

[16] Kurien Kunnumpuram, *Prophets of the Lord Friends of the Poor*, 17.

[17] Shalini Mulackal, "Consecrated Life Today: Trends and Challenges in Society and Church" Paper presented at the *CRI National Consultation*, Organized by Streevani, Pune, January 24-25, 2009).

[18] *PC*, 5.

[19] *EG*, 264.

[20] Kuncheria Pathil, "Theological Reflections on the Church from India," in *Asian Horizons* 6/4 (December 2012): 689.

[21] Ibid, 690.

[22] Ibid.

[23] *EG*, 117.

[24] John Sankarathil, "Consecrated Life in India: The Asset of a Model, or A Challenge to Remodel," in *Vidyajyoti Journal of Theological Reflections* (March 2007): 189.

[25] *VC*, 64.

[26] Joe Mannath, *A Radical Love A Path of Light*, 175.

[27] Ibid.

[28] Sankarathil, "Consecrated Life in India," 185.

[29] Jacob Peenikaparambil, *The Saffron Surge: Humanistic Response to Hindutva*, Indore, Universal Solidarity Movement of Value Education for Peace, 2016, 8.

[30] Ibid., 134.

[31] Paul Parathazham, *Christianity in India: Sociological Investigations* , Bangalore, Dharmaram Publications, 2013, 61.

[32] Jacob Peenikaparambil, *The Saffron Surge,*136.

[33] Joseph Lobo, *Encountering Jesus Christ in India: An Alternative Way of Doing Christology in a Cry-for-Life Situation Based on the Writings of George M. Soares-Prabhu*, Bangalore, Asian Trading Corporation, 2005, 58.

[34] Ibid.

[35] Pope Paul VI, *Evangelica Testificatio*, Apostolic Exhortations on the Renewal of the religious life according to the teaching of the Second Vatican Council, Rome 1997, 17; hereinafter cited as *ET*.

[36] *EG*, 186.

[37] George Kaitholil, 81.

[38] *EG*,187.

[39] Kochurani Abraham, "The Place and Role of Women in the Catholic Church," in *Towards The Full Flowering of the Human*, ed. Kurien Kuumpuram, Mumbai, St. Pauls, 2011.

[40] The Universal Church celebrated the 20th anniversary of the Apostolic Letter of Pope John Paul II, *Mulieris Dignitatem*, on the Dignity of Women.

[41] Inigo Joachim, "Empowering Women," Presented at CBCI Meeting at Jamshedpur, Scriptural and Theological Foundations, February 13-20, 2008.

[42] Ibid.

[43] "Pope Francis: women must truly participate in Church and society," February 7, 2015.

[44] Clement Campos, "*Laudato Si*: An Indian Perspective," in *Theological Studies* 78/1 (March: 2017): 215.

[45] Samuel Rayan, "The Earth is the Lord's," in *Collected Writings of Samuel Ryan*, ed. Kurien Kunnumpuram, vol.1, Delhi, ISPCK, 2013, 19; cited Kunnumpuram, 263.

[46] Kurien Kunnumpuram, *Prophets of the Lord*, 263-264.

[47] Pope Francis, *Laudato Si: The Encyclical of Pope Francis on the Environment with Commentary*; by Sean McDonagh, NewYork, Orbis Books, 2016, 2; hereinafter cited as *LS*.

[48] Ibid., 216; *LS*, 3

[49] Ibid,, 217.

[50] *GE*, 148.

[51] Ibid., 151.

[52] *Rejoice*, 39.

[53] "Pope Francis urges religious to pursue prayer, poverty, patience," https://www.vaticannews.va/en/pope/news/2018-05/pope-francis-consecrated-life-prayer-poverty-patience.html.

[54] Pope Francis, "Vocations are about quality, not quantity," https://www.catholicnewsagency.com/news/pope-francis-vocations-are-about-quality-not-quantity-20907, (accessed 29/10/2019).

[55] Rekha M. Chennattu, "To be Rooted and Relevant a Call for a Paradigm Shift in the Life of Women Religious," in *AMOR* 15, Bangkok, Thailand, October 13-21, 2009, 56.

[56] *EG*, 198.

[57] *GE*, 63.

[58] Apostolic Letter, *Novo Millennio Ineunte*, January 6, 2001, 43; hereinafter cited as *NMI*.

[59] *EG*, 198

[60] Kaitholil, 159.

[61] Ibid.

[62] Ibid., 134-135.

[63] *GS*, 29.

[64] Rekha Chennattu, "To be Rooted and Relevant a Call for a Paradigm Shift in the Life of Women Religious, 58.

⁶⁵ Inigo Joachim, "Empowering Women as Evangelizers," *Asian Journal of Vocation and Formation*, 39/1 (Pune: January-June 2014), 35-36.

⁶⁶ Ibid.

⁶⁷ *NMI*, 50.

⁶⁸ A. Suresh, "Interfaith Dialogue in India," in *Journal of Dharma: Dharmaram Journal of Religions and Philosophies*, 25/1 (January-March 2000): 7-17.

⁶⁹ Pope Paul VI, *Nostra Aetate: Declaration on the Relation of the Church to Non-Christian Religions* (October 28, 1965), 5.

⁷⁰ Pope Francis, Witness of Joy: To Men and Women Religious for the Year of Consecrated Life, 3.

⁷¹ *VC*, 110.

19.

Actualization of the Conciliar Spring
Pope Francis' Vision of Ministry
Arjen Tete, SJ

Introduction: Springtime, Awaiting the Harvest

Vatican Council II (hereinafter VC II) was considered as "the work of the Holy Spirit" that brought "a new springtime in the Church." Spring is the time when new life begins to grow. It is not when everything is in full bloom and ready to be harvested. The solemn closing of VC II on December 8, 1965, was, therefore, a beginning, not an end. Much of the burden of the reception and implementation of the Council was shouldered by the local parish clergy, who were themselves ambivalent and confused. Assessing the situation of the time, Howland Sanks notes that the clergy "dutifully turned the altar round, removed the altar rail, and told the faithful to shake hands at the kiss of peace," and remarks that they did so "in the same authoritarian manner that had characterized much clerical behavior before the Council."[1]

Concerning disillusionment, Yves Congar, citing Cardinal John Henry Newman, remarks that "'it is rare for a Council not to be followed by great confusion'" and notes that the First Council of Nicaea (325) "was followed by fifty-six years of contentions punctuated by synods, excommunications, exiles (notably that of Hilary of Poitiers), interventions and imperial acts of violence."[2] But, unlike the conciliar documents of the Councils of Nicaea, Ephesus, Chalcedon, Trent—all of which defined solemn statements—VC II documents did not define any doctrine in a solemn way. They certainly unsettled the previously established certainties in many areas of church life. The changes initiated by VC II were felt most acutely by the clergy.

Positively, these documents provided Catholics a framework for theological work and for the Church to practice. Following these guidelines, the Church has been wading through the muddied waters of the (post)modern world. During his visit to Lithuania in September 2018, when a young Jesuit priest asked Pope Francis how they could help him, he replied:

> What needs to be done is to accompany the Church in a deep spiritual renewal. Historians tell us that it takes 100 years for a Council to be applied. We are halfway there. So, if you want to help me, act in such a way as to move the [Second Vatican] Council forward in the Church. And help me with your prayer.[3]

In order to actualize the dreams of the VC II, ever since his 2013 Apostolic Exhortation *Evangelii Gaudium* (hereinafter *EG*), Pope Francis has been calling for renewal and rethinking the way every person and every institution—from the Pope and the Roman Curia down the parish and its parishioners—live their faith and focus their energies.

This paper studies the document that addresses priesthood—*Presbyterorum Ordinis* (hereinafter *PO*)—through the lens of the primary doctrinal document of VC II, *Lumen Gentium* (hereinafter *LG*) and Pope Francis' *EG*. In order to appreciate the changes initiated for the clergy, we will first revisit the understanding of priesthood prior to VC II. Subsequently, we will map out the major focal points of *PO* and correlate them with pivotal points of Francis' "priestly thoughts." The paper will conclude demonstrating a definitive movement from cultic and sacerdotal dimension of priesthood to a broader vision of priestly ministry of preaching and pastoral activities so necessary for the full blooming of the Church.

1.   **Priesthood Prior to VC II**

From the sixth to the eleventh century, the Church in the Latin West functioned on the basis of feudalism. The spiritual and temporal functions were intricately intertwined. Commenting on the situation, John W. O'Malley writes: "Bishops and great abbots, who were often members of the local nobility, performed functions that we would today unhesitatingly describe as civic or political," and remarks that "lay magnates and kings sometimes convoked and almost invariably implemented synods, and they considered it their right in most cases to have a determining voice in the nomination of the prelates."[4] Nepotism was rampant and bribes were paid to be made bishops. Consequently, "unworthy men became bishops and abbots."[5]

As a reaction to such secular dominance and corruption of the Church, a reform movement, known as the Gregorian Reform, started in the eleventh century. Unfortunately, it also had an adverse effect on priesthood. O'Malley affirms that the reform party's initial goals were "the elimination of simony, clerical concubinage, and lay intervention in the designation of the bishop, including the bishop of Rome."[6] The reformers argued that "the laypersons must obey the clergy not only inside the church but outside, in the temporal orders as well... Since the Church and State actually form one body, Christendom—whose animating principle is faith—it can be directed to its final goal, eternal salvation, only by the priesthood."[7] Within the Church, they insisted on a clear distinction between the functions of the clergy and the laity. Until then the laity were quite active participants in the life and governance of the Church. It was only at this period that they became passive spectators. The active life of the Church was carried out by the clergy.

The period from Trent to VC II was a period of great institutional stability. The movements that contributed to the reform were the liturgical movement, the renewal movements of scriptural studies and the ecumenical movement. Greater emphasis was given to the training of priests. The spirituality of the priesthood at this period was greatly influenced by Pere de Berulle, Jean-Jacques Olier, and Saint-Sulpice. They advocated: "The priest was a man apart and a cleric separated from the lay people. Seminarians should be trained to keep themselves distinct from laypersons and separate from the nonspiritual life of the ordinary Christians."[8] It was this model that dominated the formation of priests till VC II.

2. Priesthood according to VC II

Priesthood was not a theme of discussion in the earliest agenda of VC II. The Mystery of the Church was the major theme of the Council. Hence, bishops and their role in the Church were in the agenda. Maryanne Confoy affirms that *PO* exists because "the bishops found the discussion of the priesthood contained in the documents of the Church, *Lumen Gentium* (LG) to be inadequate" and asserts that it is "a fruit of the bishops' deliberations, particularly during the latter period of the council."[9] Prior to study of this decree we look at the sketch of priesthood outlined in *Lumen Gentium*.

2.1. *Lumen Gentium* as Cornerstone

The priesthood is treated in two separate contexts in *Lumen Gentium*. First, it is dealt with in the chapter on the hierarchical structure of the Church, and secondly in the chapter on the universal vocation to holiness.

Lumen Gentium (nn.18-29) speaks of a "hierarchical communion" (bishops, priests, deacons) and fraternal relationship among the three. In a key passage from *LG* (21) we read: "Episcopal consecration confers, together with the office of sanctifying, the offices also of teaching and ruling, which, however, of their very nature can be exercised only in hierarchical communion with the head and members of the college... Bishops, eminently and visibly, take the place of Christ himself, teacher, shepherd and priest, and act in his person."[10] Bishops are seen in a collegial way and not in an individualistic way. *LG* (28) thus affirms that priests are equal to bishops in priestly dignity although they "do not have the supreme degree of pontifical office" and they "depend on the bishops for the exercise of their power." There is still a focus on the Eucharist as being the centre and focus of the priestly life (*LG* 26, 28). Priests are to consider preaching, teaching and counselling as essential to their ministry, not peripheral to their priesthood. *LG* 10 affirms the priesthood of all believers.

LG (nn.39-42) outlines the framework of God's universal call to holiness. *LG* (40) invites all Christians to follow Christ by devoting "themselves to the glory of God and to the service of their neighbour." Priests, like bishops whose priesthood they share, are invited to respond to God's call to holiness in the exercise of their ministry. *LG* (41) says that they can do so by bonding among themselves in priestly communion, giving witness about their priestly lives, and imitating those priests who have grown in holiness down the centuries. Priests' ministry has been raised to very core of the mystery of Jesus. Cunnane affirms that *LG* "remains in many ways the highest achievement of the Council," and notes that "subsequent decrees are largely developments of themes arising from the various sections of the Church Constitution."[11] Hence, let us revisit *PO* in the light of *LG* and discuss its actualization efforts by Pope Francis.

2.2. Juxtaposing *Presbyterorum Ordinis* and *Evangelii Gaudium*

Although VC II has spoken about priests on several occasions, *PO* discusses about them "at greater length and depth." The vision of priestly ministry is more expansively described in terms of the affirmation of Christ's "teaching, sanctifying and shepherding" role. Although the decree gives central place to the Eucharist in priests' life, it presents the sacred power of the priesthood as something wider than the purely cultic ministry.

Evangelii Gaudium is a call to renewal and an apostolic framework of the Church today. Its strength is in returning to the Vatican documents, refreshing them and offering them in a new presentation. Its emphasis is on the pastoral mission of the Church and the evangelizing discipleship reflected in personal witness. Picking up some of the energizing strengths of priesthood in *PO*, we underscore their actualization in the renewal efforts of Pope Francis.

2.2.1. *Communal Identity of Priesthood*

It is interesting to note that *PO* speaks of priests rather than of "the priest." The priest is not an isolated individual. VC II spoke of collegiality of bishops with the pope as its leader. It also speaks about a collegiality of priests called *presbyterium*. Priests trained to think of obedience as the primary virtue were expected to adopt a collegial and participatory style. Osborne writes:

> Priests are indeed coworkers of the bishop, and this is stressed again and again throughout the documents of the Vatican II. This is clearly what is meant by the presbyterium: a college of priests led by their local bishop. The priests alone as a group do not make up the presbyterium. Priests and bishops together make us the presbyterium.[12]

The call and the commission of priests are not delegated through the bishop; they come from the Lord himself. *PO* (1) stresses the importance of the priesthood and the triple-function of Christ's priesthood—prophet, priest, king—in which all partake. The stress on priests sharing in the same anointing of Christ and continuing the same mission is made in *PO* (2). The same is also true of all Christians. *PO* (2) affirms that priests are "ministers of Jesus Christ among the nations" who "act in the name of Christ the head." The Council calls on bishops to regard their priests as brothers and friends, and on priests to be as brothers among brothers and sisters vis-à-vis the laity (*PO* 3).

In *EG*, Pope Francis expresses the hope of VC II that episcopal conferences could "contribute in many and fruitful ways to the concrete realization of the collegial spirit" (*EG* 32).[13] In their "mission of fostering a dynamic, open and missionary communion," the pope exhorts the bishops "to encourage and develop the means of participation as proposed in the Code of Canon Law, and other forms of dialogue," in order "to listen to everyone" and not simply to those who would tell them what they like to hear" (*EG* 31). In his meetings with the bishops, he has been emphasizing collegiality, collaboration and communion between the bishops and priests for renewal and good governance of the Church.[14] He says that "the important thing is to not walk alone, but rely on each other as brothers and sisters, and especially under the leadership of the bishops, in a wise and realistic pastoral discernment" (*EG* 33). Pope Francis has been calling for a listening Church so that it does not become a museum.[15]

2.2.2. *The Spirituality of Priests*

PO says that "priests are made in the image of Christ the priest" (*PO* 12). The spirituality of priests is focused directly on Jesus. But, all Christians, whether ordained or non-ordained, are called to this holiness of growing unto the stature of Christ. The ordained ministers, however, commit themselves to be public holy persons in the holy Church. This implies being configured with Christ in his very mission and ministry.

The decree affirms that "it is through the sacred actions they perform everyday as through their whole ministry which they exercise in union with the bishop and their fellow-priests that they are set on the right course to perfection of life," while on the other hand, "the very holiness of priests is of the greatest benefit for the fruitful fulfillment of their ministry" (*PO* 12). The priestly ministry cannot be seen as disconnected from priestly spirituality. The document says that priests will be "more intimately united with Christ the Teacher and will be guided by the Spirit in the very act of teaching the word" (*PO* 13).

This spirituality calls priests to be balanced and integrated. Sometimes they can fall into the trap of juggling too many things which can cause them to be unfocused, superficial or burned out. Integrated priestly spirituality "cannot be achieved merely by an outward arrangement of ministerial tasks nor by the practices of spiritual exercises alone" (*PO* 14). Ratzinger sums up this tension: "Responsible activity in the service of [humankind] and intimacy with God are not in competition with each other. The service of others is the articulation of one's being-consumed for God, of one's being grasped by Him, of one's being-with-Him."[16] The document shows a definite modification in the dominant priestly spirituality since the Middle Ages which greatly emphasized on "the cultic aspects of priesthood, the correct, valid, and licit administration of sacraments, especially the offering of the sacrifice of the Mass, and the hearing of confessions."[17] The modification is towards the pastoral aspect of priestly spirituality.

Through his words in documents like *EG* and through his personal witness, Pope Francis has been demonstrating the essential characteristics of the spirituality of priests as: having a personal and intimate relationship with Jesus; devotion to sacramental ministry; proximity to their flock; offering a ministry of mercy; and living lives of service and humility. He directly invites everyone and priests in particular to encounter daily and experience love of God in the person of Jesus (*EG* 3). This encounter with God's love blossoms into an enriching friendship which liberates Christians from their "narrowness and self-absorption."

The spirituality of *EG* also denounces setbacks to ecclesial renewal and growth. It attacks hindrances like "complacency," "excessive clericalism," "spiritual worldliness" and those who act like "sourpusses" within the Church. This joy and confidence needed to tackle these challenges—both inside and outside the Church—is rooted and grounded in a deep relationship with Jesus Christ. Without that "personal encounter" with Jesus trying to spread the Gospel is useless. Priests must have, what *EG* calls, a "constantly renewed experience of savouring Christ's friendship and his message" (*EG* 266). Christians in general and priests in particular are challenged to be joyous people (*EG* 1) and not to appear as if they have just returned from a funeral (*EG* 10) or whose lives are like "Lent without Easter" (*EG* 6). Pope Francis uses such creative expressions to remind us of the centrality of joy in ministry.

2.2.3. *Celibacy of Priests*

Concerning celibacy there is nothing new in *PO*. It says that celibacy for clergy was quite optional for the early Church. Later, it was imposed by law. *PO* recognizes that celibacy is not "demanded of the priesthood by nature," but it does not alter the discipline of celibacy, which had been the major expression of separation from the world. Rather, the decree reiterates significance of celibacy affirming that it is "at once a sign of pastoral charity and an incentive to it as well as being in a special way a source of spiritual fruitfulness in the world" (*PO* 16). Pope Francis has reaffirmed the Catholic Church's centuries-old commitment to priestly celibacy.

2.2.4. Ministry of Priests

PO nn.4,5,6 together present the definition of priestly ministry, following the three offices of Christ as teacher, priest, and shepherd. Like Jesus, priests are teachers. They share in the teaching mission of the Jesus through ordination. In the threefold structure of Jesus' mission, the document gives first place to preaching the Word. The first task of the priests was "to preach the Gospel of God to all" (*PO* 4). The priestly or sanctifying function is given second place (*PO* 5). Finally, the shepherding function of the priest is discussed (*PO* 6).

O'Malley opines that unlike Trent, the decree "makes it clear correlation between priesthood and ministry" and "also attempts, not altogether successfully, to break the identification of priesthood with confection of the Eucharist and states that 'it is the first task of the priests' to preach the gospel."[18] The document is a shift away from the Tridentine emphasis essentially on the consecration of the Eucharist and the office of the power over the Mystical Body of Christ, the Church. Confoy rightly says:

> It is a movement towards broader vision of priestly ministry as whole: preaching and pastoral activities are now the primary tasks. These are directly connected with the people of God and not with the Eucharist. Only in this pastoral context is the sanctifying task of the priest determined. The three functions are to be understood in the light of the ecclesiology for which the service of the community is not just *a* function; it is *the* function of those who receive the priestly ministry through the sacrament of the holy orders.[19]

One notices that the spiritual dimension is intimately connected with the pastoral ministry. Priests in all that they are and do are missionary. The Council's renewed emphasis on the participation of the laity in the mission of the Church and the idea that the call to holiness is for all, not just for the religious or clerics, further calls into question the notion of the special or higher "vocation" of the priesthood.

In *EG*, Pope Francis proposes a profound missionary renewal of the entire Church; certainly, the clergy are central to this renewal. He affirms that pastoral workers "need to move 'from a pastoral ministry of mere conservation to a decidedly missionary pastoral ministry'" (*EG* 15). "Mere administration can no longer be enough. Throughout the world, let us be "permanently in a state of mission" (*EG* 25). The Pope exhorts that "all renewal in the Church must have mission as its goal if it is not to fall prey to a kind of ecclesial introversion" (*EG* 27).

Following the trajectory of VC II documents concerning the functions of priests, in *EG* Pope Francis has devoted twenty-five sections to the homily and preaching (*EG* 135-159). He says that a "preacher who does not prepare is not "spiritual"; he is dishonest and irresponsible with the gifts he has received" (*EG* 145). The Pope is also realistic. Being aware of the challenges faced in proclamation of the Gospel (*EG* 50-109), he asserts: "Challenges exist to be overcome! Let us be realists, but without losing our joy, our boldness and our hope-filled commitment. Let us not allow ourselves to be robbed of missionary vigor" (*EG* 109). Or again, "I repeat: Let us not allow ourselves to be robbed of the joy of evangelization" (*EG* 83).

Concerning priestly function, Pope Francis says that "the Church is called to be the house of the Father, with doors wide open... Everyone can share in some way in the life of the Church; everyone can be part of the community; nor should the doors of the sacrament [e.g. Baptism, Eucharist] be closed for simply any reason" (*EG* 47). In this context, *EG* says that the Church "has to go forth to everyone without exception." At the same time the document reminds us that "there is an inseparable bond between our faith and the poor" (*EG* 48). "God's heart has a special place for the poor" (*EG* 192). Hence, Pope Francis calls on the world's priests to stay close to the vulnerable, the marginalized and to be "shepherds living with the smell of the sheep." "Evangelisers thus take on the 'smell of the sheep' and the sheep are willing to hear their voice" (*EG* 24). "All of us are asked to obey His [Jesus'] call to go forth from our own comfort zone in order to reach all the "peripheries" in need of the light of the Gospel" (*EG* 20).

2.2.5. *Relationship of Priests with the Laity and the World*
PO (9) exhorts priests to "unite their efforts with those of the lay faithful and conduct themselves among them after the example of the Master." Those who had been separated and isolated from "the world" of everyday affairs are now expected to live among their fellow humans and to be in touch with the modern world. The virtues to be cultivated are "goodness of heart, sincerity, strength and constancy of character, zealous pursuit of justice, civility" (*PO* 3). Priests are encouraged to listen to the laity and recognize their experience and competence in different areas of life to read together the signs of the time. Consequently, the gap between priests and the laity, that had developed ever since the Middle Ages, is overcome, at least in theory, at VC II.

The term "missionary disciple," used throughout *EG*, holds in tension the need for a relationship with Jesus and the need to go to the margins to preach the Gospel. Every baptized member of the Catholic faith is called to evangelize and is called to be a missionary disciple. "In virtue of their baptism, all the members of the People of God have become missionary disciples (cf. Mt 28:19). All the baptized, whatever their position in the Church or their level of instruction in the faith, are agents of evangelization" (*EG* 120).

Scrutinizing "the signs of times," the Catholic Church has been regularly responding to missionary challenges through Vatican documents. But, a document is just a map not a territory; a menu is not a meal. Documents need to be translated into actions by every baptized

Christian but particularly by priests. The Indian Catholic Church is praised for its incredible transformative work for the poor, especially in the fields of education and health care. Education is seen as the most important tool for social transformation as it helps to impart values of compassion, morality and ethics. Yet, indifference of the privileged to the misery of others is quite striking in India.[20]

The Church is getting messier from within. The alleged involvement of bishops and priests in sexual abuse, fund swindling, land grabbing, etc., is discrediting disciple missionaries.[21] Money, power, and position seem to become matters of great importance. Priests accuse their bishops of functioning in an arbitrary manner with "little regard for internal democracy" and refuse transfer orders.[22] Falling prey to clericalism, corruption, careerism and comfort, priests lose their apostolic efficacy, vitality and solidarity with the laity. The laity fumes in anger. What could be the way forward for the leaders of the Indian Church today?

3. Charting a Way Forward

In the context of India today priests have to be revolutionaries, visionaries, animators, catalysts and community-builders. They are expected to be mature human persons. We see that personal issues that are not dealt with in a healthy way can and often do come back later in life and ministry to cause problems for priests themselves and for others. Hence, I propose some steppingstones to go forward.

3.1. *Attending to one's Humanity*

It is so important for priests to attend to their humanity which entails committing to ongoing growth in affective maturity, sexuality, and boundaries. It means being honest and transparent about their challenges and struggles, and grateful for who they are, exactly as God intended them to be. It implies priests cannot ignore their needs and their desires for meaningful and intimate friendship with fellow priests and other men and women, in the context of chastity and celibacy. They ought to strive to become fully human, growing unto the stature of Christ by freeing themselves from all external and internal attachments and freeing themselves for loving and building communities of love, sharing and justice.

3.2. Integrated Spirituality

A wise, old member of the staff in my Novitiate used to say to us: "If you don't pray, you won't stay." That may not necessarily be the case, but I do believe that if priests do not stay grounded in their primary relationship with Jesus, nurtured and nourished and deepened through a life of prayer, they run the risk of drying up or losing focus or falling in to the trap of thinking that this is all about them, rather than about God and serving God's people. Hence, to be balanced and integrated, they ought to be faithful to their daily personal prayer, daily Eucharist, spiritual direction, some regular silence and solitude, and whatever other devotional practices helps them be good men of prayer and discernment. This will not only assure success and productivity in compassionate mission and ministry but will also protect them from being burnt out. The laity, too, desires them to be men of prayer.

3.3. Well-informed and Well-formed

The role of ordained ministers in the Church is to be men of spiritual and intellectual depth, learned men who are well prepared and articulate, who can move beyond the surface of things into deeper meaning. Since they have ample opportunities for study and research, they ought to learn well and to prepare themselves to answer the questions that people actually have, not the questions that they or others think the laity should have. They should not dismissively say, "What does the laity know?" Today, they need to listen to the lay faithful more than ever before.

3.4. Men-with-Others

Priests ought to be men of communion in their relations with all peoples. They are called to be persons of mission and dialogue. They ought to have necessary skills for working collegially with their bishops, fellow pastors, other religious ministering in their region, lay leaders both men and women, and other members of the parish councils. They need to spend time with their collaborators for collective reflection and concerted action. They need to remember that they are neither master builders nor messiahs, but workers and ministers. They are "men-with-others."

3.5. Servants of the Word

Another thing the laity desire from the ordained ministers is good preaching. Priests ought to preach the word of God in ways that nurture faith, hope and love of the laity. To do so, they need to immerse themselves in the word of God. Priests in India ought to blend the word of God with important issues staring citizens in the face like poverty, unemployment, livelihood, health, and education. They ought to make use of the pulpit to awaken and alert their flocks about their rights and responsibilities as citizens. Sitting in the pews, I have heard priests give excellent homilies, founded on Scripture, dealing with the contemporary issues of great importance. But, once the homily is over, they rattle through the rest of the liturgy like an express train speeding up to reach its destination. Priests ought to realize that the faithful in the pews are also called to be a community at prayer.

3.6. Servants of the Marginalized

In India today, given the demand of being in solidarity with Dalits, Adivasis, migrant workers, women, and street youth, the priests are called to be compassionate servants of those who eke out existences at the margins. Compassion is more than mere affective sentimentality. It demands being in solidarity with suffering people and doing whatever one can to alleviate their suffering. This means that priests ought to practise not only charity, almsgiving and Good Samaritan work, but also ought to work for social change—so as to bring about a new social order where there is freedom, love, equality and justice. But, any attempt to empower tribals with rights and entitlements enshrined in the Constitution of India and various socially-relevant legislations is branded as seditious or criminal activity. Christian institutions are coming under increasing scrutiny as a means of harassment. Yet, priests in India, who have worked for nation building for years, serving all strata of society, must continue to stand with the people keeping in mind their mission of justice, reconciliation and peace.

4. Conclusion

Since VC II, the cultic and sacerdotal understanding of priesthood has moved towards priestly ministry of preaching and other pastoral activities. Although the Church and its priests are wading through muddied waters of (post)modern times, nonetheless, God desires to make all things "new" (Rev 21:5). Pope Francis says that the God who is "eternal newness," empowers the Church, through the Spirit, to construct a path of the future.[23] Priests' history is interwoven with God and fellow brothers and sisters. Hence, to go forth towards the future for full blooming of the Church, priests need to embrace Pope Francis' oft-repeated promotion of "boldness":

> Complacency is seductive; it tells us that there is no point in trying to change things, that there is nothing we can do, because this is the way things have always been and yet we manage to survive. ... Yet we allow the Lord to rouse us from our torpor, to free us from our inertia. Let us rethink our usual way of doing things; let us open our eyes and ears, and above all our hearts, so as not to be complacent about things as they are but unsettled by the living and effective word of the risen Lord.[24]

Endnotes

[1] T. Howland Sanks, *Salt, Leaven and Light: Community Called Church* (New York: Crossroad, 1992), 188.

[2] Yves Congar, "A Last Look at the Council," in *Vatican II by Those Who Were There*, ed. Alberic Stacpoole (London: Geoffrey Chapman, 1986), 349.

[3] The transcript of the conversation was published in the edition of *La Civiltà Cattolica* (17 October, 2018), http://www.laciviltacattolica.com/i-believe-the-lord-wants-a-change-in-the-church-a-private-dialogue-with-the-jesuits-in-the-baltics/ (accessed October 30, 2019).

[4] John W. O'Malley, *Tradition and Transition: Historical Perspective on Vatican II* (Wilmington, DE: Michael Glazier, Inc.), 95-96.

[5] Ibid., 96.

[6] Ibid., 90.

[7] Sanks, *Salt, Leaven, and Light*, 70.

⁸ Kenan B. Osborne, "Priestly Formation," in *From Trent to Vatican II: Historical and Theological Investigations*, ed. Raymond F. Bulman and Frederick J. Parrella (Oxford: Oxford University Press, 2006), 125.

⁹ Maryanne Confoy, *Religious Life and Priesthood: Perfectae Caritatis, Optatum Totius, Presbyterorum Ordinis* (New York: Paulist Press, 2008), 7.

¹⁰ For the Vatican II quotations cited in this paper, see Austin Flannery, *Vatican II: The Basic Sixteen Documents* (New York: Costello Publishing Company), 1996.

¹¹ Joseph Cunnane, "The Priest after Vatican II," *Vatican II on Priests and Seminaries*, Denis E. Hurley and Joseph Cunnane (Dublin: Scepter Books, 1967), 14-15.

¹² Kenan B. Orborne, *Priesthood: A History of Ordained Ministry and the Roman Catholic Church* (New York: Paulist Press, 1988), 331.

¹³ This collegial spirit is demonstrated and practised in *Evangelii Gaudium* itself, in which the bishops' conferences around the world serve as a major point of reference. Pope Francis cites 10 conferences in all, and the list is impressive in its geographical diversity: Africa, Asia, the United States, France, Oceania, Latin America, Brazil, the Philippines, the Congo and India.

¹⁴ Zenit Staff, "Pope's address to Italian Bishops' Conference," Zenit, (May 19, 2015), https://zenit.org/articles/pope-s-address-to-italian-bishops-conference-2/ (accessed November 9, 2019).

¹⁵ In his latest exhortation, *Christus Vivit (CV)*, Pope Francis says, "A Church always on the defensive, which loses her humility and stops listening to others, which leaves no room for questions, loses her youth and turns into a museum," (*CV* 41).

¹⁶ As quoted in Confoy, *Religious Life and Priesthood*, 40.

¹⁷ Sanks, *Salt, Leaven, and Light*, 148.

¹⁸ O'Malley, *Tradition and Transition*, 161.

¹⁹ Confoy, *Religious Life and Priesthood*, 30.

²⁰ Harsh Mander, *Looking Away: Inequality, Prejudice and Indifference in New India* (New Delhi: Speaking Tiger, 2015, xi; Harsh Mander, *Partitions of Heart: Unmaking of the Idea of India* (Gurgaon, Haryana: Penguin Random House, 2019), xix.

²¹ Nolan Pinto, "Mysuru priests accuse Bishop of sexual misconduct, corruption, shoot letter to Pope Francis," *India Today*, (5 November, 2019), https://www.indiatoday.in/india/story/mysuru-priests-accuse-bishop-of-sexual-misconduct-corruption-shoot-letter-to-pope-francis-1615989-2019-11-05 (accessed November 15, 2019).

²² Manoj Dattatreye More, "Some priests accuse Bishop of functioning in an arbitrary manner," *The Indian Express*, Pune (July 4, 2018), https://indianexpress.com/article/cities/pune/pune-some-priests-accuse-bishop-of-functioning-in-an-arbitrary-manner-5245065/ (accessed November 15, 2019).

²³ Pope Francis, *Gaudete Et Exsultate*, n.135.

²⁴ Pope Francis, *Gaudete Et Exsultate*, n.137.

20.

Tracing the Roots of Clericalism
Jesuraj Rayappan, SVD

Introduction

On October 7, 1964, as the third session of Vatican Council II (hereinafter VC II) was in progress, the late Archbishop Eugene D'Souza of Bhopal made his intervention on the theme of 'Apostolate of Laity' stating a radical reorganization was required, if laymen and laywomen were to fulfill their proper roles. He was even forthright when he broached, "are we—the Catholic clergy—truly prepared to abdicate clericalism? Are we prepared to consider the laity as brothers (sisters) in the Lord, equal to ourselves in dignity in the Mystical Body, if not in office? Are we prepared no longer to usurp, as formerly we did, the responsibilities which properly belong to them? Or rather—are we prepared to leave to them what is more pertinent to them, such as the fields of education, social services, administration of temporal goods, and the like?"[1]

The Archbishop demanded as to why the Church should always have to be represented on international bodies by clerics. Why cannot the lay faithful take the place of many of the clerics in the Roman Curia? Why cannot laity be admitted to the diplomatic service of the Holy See, and even become Nuncios? This way one can find numerous possibilities at various levels, i.e., on the world level, on the national level, on the diocesan level, and on the parish level. Such a substitution would obviously help the clergy "to devote themselves to the exercise of the sacred and sacramental office for which they were ordained." He predicted that such principles in the schema would open up a new era for the Church.[2] There was a thundering applause for the Archbishop's statement in the council hall. This was indeed a prophetic stance that had its ramifications in the church's life and mission.

In this paper, I would like to make a retrospective journey into the history of the church to identify some moments where clericalism reigned supreme, which, though claimed to have aided the church, had affected the church adversely. This would lead us to reflect on the epoch making Second Vatican Council that tried to correct some of these practices and, on the initiatives, taken by Pope Francis to continue with the reform measures of VC II.

1. The Concept of Clericalism

Clericalism, as a word, is used with increasing frequency among the members of the Catholic Church today. It is defined as a state of affairs in which there is an unnecessary or overly exaggerated importance given to clergy, in such a way that the clergy relate to laity as objects to be ruled rather than a people to be loved and pastorally cared for. Clericalism tends to be deeply a harmful reality among clergy and laity. Any form of clericalism is an aberration of the true call to be deacons, priests, and bishops in following Christ as ordained ministers or servants to serve God's people. Clericalism stands opposed to the life and values of Christ and its impact appears to be obstacles to the fruits of the Holy Spirit. Clericalism breeds a culture of death, in which the clergy seek to keep the focus and attention on themselves, an inappropriate self-centeredness extending even to the celebration of the Holy Mass. According to Pope Francis, this diminishes and undervalues the baptismal grace of our people. In doing so, it also downplays the equal dignity of every human person made in the image and likeness of God.

2. Clericalism in the History of the Church

Clericalism goes back to the very beginnings of Christianity, namely, Jesus Christ himself. George Soares-Prabhu writes, "Jesus appears in the Gospels as non-clerical, even as somewhat anti-clerical figure. He is not a priest, for he does not belong to a priestly family; and he is shown in continuing conflict with the priestly establishment which ultimately arranges for his death."[3] Jesus was indeed a victim of the clericalist mentality of his time and place. For having challenged the authority of the religious and social elite of a theocratic society, he paid with his life. The various pronouncements of Jesus against the exploitation in the name of religion by religious leaders of his time have to be seen as Jesus' anti-clerical propensity. Clericalist mentality was even prevalent among the disciples when they began arguing among themselves as to which of them was the greatest. According to Luke, Jesus did not try to pacify them with a power-sharing agreement or throw up his hands and walk away. Instead, he showed them a child and said: "Whoever receives this child in my name receives me, and whoever receives me receives the one who sent me. For the one who is least among all of you is the one who is the greatest" (Lk 9:48).

This spirit was clearly visible in the life of the apostles and in the early Christianity as the believers were expected to live a life of holiness awaiting the imminent Parousia. As George Soares-Prabhu comments, "Early Christianity does not know of a Christian priesthood in the traditional sense of the word."[4] The epistle of Clement of Rome to Corinthians written about the year 96 AD brings out a clear distinction between hierarchy and laity and reiterates their specific role in the community. Perhaps this is the first time the word laity is used in Christian literature.

St. Ignatius of Antioch says that the priest is like Jesus Christ to us, and the bishop, like God the Father. He also says that, "where the bishop is, there is the Catholic Church."[5] It does not indicate the exalted position of priests and bishops but impresses their call to radiate God's love for the flock. The elders of the early Church were motivated by

Apostolic simplicity, voluntary poverty by surrendering the property at the disposal of the Church, because of which they were greatly admired as centres of religious life of the community. In fact, they were truly pastors of soul as seen in the writings of St. Ignatius of Antioch, St. Cyprian of Carthage, etc.

3. The Turning Point

This situation changes with Constantinian turning point as Constantine the Great granted religious freedom and bestowed privileges on the persecuted Christianity and its officials.[6] The bishops and priests were exempted from statal tax and compulsory military service, and the church even began to inherit huge properties. The bishops who were seen as centers of religious life began to assume role that took away their time and energy for temporal affairs. Though the exercise of civil jurisdiction by bishops improved the quality of justice in the Empire, it obviously took away their time and energy leading them away from the primary purpose for which they were ordained, namely, the proclamation of the Gospel.[7] Here we see the beginning of an ecclesiastical forum that began to exercise one's power and the clergy inclined to constitute a special/separate class with their proper privileges, which later turned to be their rights. And in the following epoch, Martina writes, "The theological and canonical speculation of the following epoch gradually elaborated these privileges and had always defended it. It affirmed that it was not a statal concession granted to the clergy but an inherent right of the clergy."[8]

Together with richness came the increase of power and authority. The emperor did not stop donating his palace to the church but made sure that the cult was celebrated and that the churches were built. The clergy began to be associated with the sanctuary or stood behind the altar to celebrate the cult, while the laity stood in places away from the altar and participated in it passively. This paved the way for the privileged place of the clergy. It received a theological legitimation from Pseudo-Dionysius, a 6th century Syrian monk, who believed that the structure of the church on earth was meant to be a reflection of the structure in heaven. He taught that by holy ordinance the church is "made up of two ranked hierarchies (a superior clerical hierarchy made up of bishops, priests and deacons; and an inferior lay hierarchy made up of religious, laity and catechumens).

With the dawn of feudalism, the power and prestige of the clergy were highly exalted as bishops, abbots, priests, etc., were seen as representatives or vassals of the kings, who were entrusted with vast territory or landed property, which led to corruption, immorality and nepotism, in a way the Lay Investiture downgraded the spiritual dignity of the clergy. It goes without saying that on account of Lay Investiture unworthy persons were promoted to be the spiritual heads whose concern were most of the time centered on power and pleasure. Scandals of various kinds rocked the church and the church leadership was tainted with human weakness and mundane spirit.

As the ecclesiastics were drenched in mundane spirit and totally divorced from the spirit of Christ, God sent messengers to reform the church, i.e. Pope Gregory VII. Though he came with a set of reforms known as Gregorian Reforms, whose focus was to get rid of the interference of the political power in ecclesiastical affairs, he did not fail to uphold the dignity and prestige of the papacy and the clergy. This in fact increased the exalted position of the Roman Papacy and laid the foundation for a clericalized church. There were also individual men and groups, like Waldensians, Albigensians, etc., to challenge the worldly church, particularly the clergy.[9] But these were often branded as heretics and were dealt with cruelty never to be expected from followers of a gentle and loving Lord.

From the 5th to the 11th centuries, most of the popes were chosen from among the monks who had the spirit to ferment reform in the church, but due to the tinge of clericalism very little was done by way of reform. Scholasticism was thought to be a way forward in dealing with the clericalized church, but that too began to favour the officials. The existing division was further intensified in the Middle Ages with the introduction of the so-called state of perfection, which began to be associated with the life of celibacy, poverty and obedience. The Middle Ages was a time when the spiritual sphere was not only considered superior to the temporal but also subject to it. By getting rid of the concerns of life the perfect men were considered to be free for a life of prayer. This increased their prestige in the society as it brought recognition leading to an elitist spirituality, which the laity could not avail of.

The Renaissance and Humanism shattered the existing paradigm, under the influence of which the former Augustinian monk, Martin Luther, began to postulate some academic and practical questions regarding the faith and practice of the church which ended up in the split of the one church into several churches with its creeds and hierarchical structures. An analysis of the causes of the Reformation would reveal that there was a general decadence in the church administration, which in fact was due to clericalism. Corruption, immorality, nepotism, pastoral absenteeism, etc., were some of the factors that lead to the Reformation. Church laws were used to consolidate the power and position of clergy rather than to assist them to guide and shepherd the flock.

During the period of the Enlightenment, a host of European thinkers quite alienated from the church were sketching a paradigm which meant that the hitherto place held by the church was given to secularism. The principles they adhered to were no longer drawn from the Bible and tradition of the church but from the values of enlightenment, i.e., reason, progress and the state. In other words, Enlightenment once again came as a reaction to clericalism.

During the reforms of the Conciliar period, many Catholic thinkers believed that the pre-Vatican Council II Church had been characterized by an excessive clericalization. There were many arguments offered in favour of this view: the priest was so well respected that they were often feared rather than loved. The sacraments they administered were so revered that their power was almost magical. Liturgical functions were said to be too clericalist as well; by restricting the active parts of the Mass to only the ordained or those in minor orders, the laity were 'excluded' from participating in the worship of God. For centuries, the clergy have expected the lay faithful to 'pray, pay and obey'.

The lessons of history are encouraging. If the Church was able to foster, rather ignore the existence of, clericalism affecting it, then the Church should also be able to root it out. But it's also worth thinking about the internal social and political dynamics that have grown up around clericalism, and which may not necessarily yield to theological rethinking. Whether in secret or in public, clerical culture corrupts those who indulge in it and damages the ecclesial body politic in treacherous ways that we don't always see.

4. Resistance to Clericalism

Historically, almost all the anti-clerical movements in Europe were effectively anti-Catholic, in part because the Catholic Church was the largest, most widespread, and most powerful religious institution in the world. As we have noted earlier, there were individuals and groups that had tried to challenge clericalism: like Joachim of Fiore, John Wycliffe, John Hus, the Albigensians, Waldensians, etc. Mysticism that emerged during the Middle Ages came as a reaction to a worldly church, ritualism, external piety and academic theology. It was against authoritarianism. Meister Eckhart and Johannes Tauler were two great mystics of the time. Following the Reformation and continuing through the following centuries, there were movements in country after country to prohibit Catholic influence on civic affairs. Anti-clericalism took a violent form during the French Revolution. At the height of the revolution in France, during the Reign of Terror, anti-clericalists were busy butchering Catholic clergy and religious, desecrating churches, and enthroning the goddess of reason in the place of God. More than 30,000 priests were exiled and hundreds of priests were massacred.

In Austria, the Holy Roman Emperor Joseph II dissolved more than 500 monasteries in the late 18th century, using their wealth to create new parishes and taking over the education of priests in seminaries.[10] The *Kulturkampf* in Germany under Chancellor Otto von Bismarck had taken some anti-clerical measures, like suppression of some religious orders and monasteries.[11] Anti-clericalism had progressed by the late 19th century to the point where Catholicism was being publicly mocked and legally extricated from civic life. During the Spanish Civil War in the 1930s, there were many anti-clerical assaults by the Republican forces, as the Catholic Church supported the Nationalist forces. Over 6,000 clerics were killed. Anti-clericalism was an official policy of most Marxist and Communist governments, including that of the former Soviet Union and Cuba.

5. The Second Vatican Council: A Pastoral and Reforming Council

Many of the VC II reforms were initiated in the hope of ending clericalist monopoly on liturgy and worship and opening liturgy up to the laity. Summarizing the teaching of VC II, De Letter writes,

> Themes now stand out such as the church as mystery, people of God, not meant to dominate but to serve, church of the poor, church of sinners, a minority community in an ever more secularized world. Two trends appear: one stressing the church as an institution, the other as communion of life; but she is both. Collegiality means a sacramental rather than a juridical conception of the church... The collegiality of the bishops also came out in the discussion of the schema of bishops and the government of the dioceses. Hence decentralization and authority delegated to episcopal conferences.[12]

Having identified the key elements for a spirit-filled church, Bishop Frane from Yugoslavia spoke of poverty as a necessary condition for holiness of bishops. "When the Church was poor, it was holy. When it became rich, sanctity diminished accordingly (clericalism dominated). Bishops had a much greater obligation to be holy than all other members of the Church. Because as bishops we must sanctify others. Since the Middle Ages, most saints had come from the ranks of the religious orders, not from the ranks of the bishops. This would seem to indicate a lack of heroic sanctity among bishops. The reason for it is a lack of evangelical poverty. Diocesan priests and religious orders also needed to reform themselves in the matter of poverty."[13] Papal history tells that almost all the popes from the 5th to the 11th century were chosen from monasteries.

The openness of council fathers was seen when the lacuna of the first two sessions, namely, the absence of women was filled by the presence of women from the third session onwards. By the end of the third session, there were forty official auditors at the Council, seventeen of them were women, among them nine were nuns.[14]

5.1. The Vocation of the Faithful in VC II

The council fathers implicitly rejected all the three theological manifestations of clericalism in the VC II, which according to them were wrong.[15] This idea is further accentuated in the 'Decree on the Ministry and Life of Priests,' where we read: "Jesus gave his whole mystical body a share in the anointing of the Spirit with which he was anointed. In that body all the faithful are made a holy and kingly priesthood, they offer spiritual sacrifices to God through Jesus Christ ... therefore there is no such thing as a member who does not have a share in the mission of the whole body" (*Presbyterorum Ordinis* 2). The document clearly notes that each of the faithful, whether at the centre or periphery, has the potential to initiate a more dynamic expression of the living church.

To the idea that the priest celebrates the Eucharist and that the faithful are nourished from afar, the council insisted on the contrary: "The eucharistic celebration is the center of the assembly of the faithful over which the priest presides. Hence priests [must] teach the faithful to offer the divine victim to God the Father in the sacrifice of the Mass and with the victim to make an offering of their own lives" (*Presbyterorum Ordinis* 5). By offering themselves and their apostolic action in the world, the faithful bring the fruit of their baptismal priesthood (which is essentially non-liturgical and lived out in the world) to the church's fundamental act of sacrifice and self-offering to God at Mass. When this role of the faithful is denied, then Sunday Mass becomes the place where people assemble not as a priestly people offering their lives to God, but as individuals praying private devotions as they watch the priest offer sacred rites on a distant altar.

To the idea that the faithful are sanctified uniquely through the ministries of the ordained, the 'Dogmatic Constitution on the Church' clearly says: "The baptized, by regeneration and the anointing of the Holy Spirit, are consecrated a spiritual house and a holy priesthood, that through all their Christian activities they may offer spiritual sacrifices and proclaim the marvels of him who has called them out of darkness into his wonderful light" (*Lumen Gentium* 10). In other words, the vocation that the church offers to the faithful is not a secondary role. They are not clients of clerical ministries, but Spirit-filled participants in the church's role as herald of God's kingdom. Clericalism forgets that the visibility and the sacramentality of the Church belong to all the faithful people of God (*Lumen Gentium*, 9–14), not only to the few chosen and enlightened. Ministerial priesthood tends to eclipse the real nature and importance of common priesthood. The laypersons are neither peons nor servants nor employees of the clergy. They don't have to simply do whatever the clergy say. They have their rightful place in the church.

5.2. *Dissenting Voices at VC II*

In the Council itself there were contradictory forces that sometimes stood as stumbling blocks to the progress of the Council. We can identify some instances that might reveal such forces. Pope John XXIII, in line with the expressed desires of many Council Fathers, had decided to insert the name of St Joseph in the Canon of the Mass, immediately after the name of the Most Holy Virgin and to that effect Cardinal Secretary of State made an announcement on November 13, 1962. In some quarters Pope John was severely criticized for taking what was termed independent action while the Ecumenical Council was in session. A cursory reading of history indicates that the request, in fact, dates back to 1815, when tens and thousands of signatures of the hierarchy and the laity had been gathered and sent to the Vatican. The campaigns had become particularly intensive at the announcements of Vatican I by Pope Pius IX, and of Vatican Council II by Pope John.[16]

On December 1, 1962, six of the Council Fathers called for complete revision of the schema on the Church, lest it might lead to an outright rejection of the text as it stood. Ralph M. Wiltgen writes, "The schema was also criticized for being too theoretical, for being too legalistic, for identifying the Mystical Body purely and simply with the Catholic Church, for referring only condescendingly to the laity, for insisting excessively on the rights and authority of the hierarchy, and for lacking a charitable, missionary, and ecumenical approach… One of the speakers, Bishop De Smedt, summed up his criticism in three epithets: "the schema," he said, was guilty of "triumphalism, clericalism, and legalism."[17]

In defining the notion of episcopal collegiality there was opposition, particularly from two archbishops, namely, Archbishop Sigaud and Archbishop Marcel Lefebvre, who had formed a *piccolo comitato* (small committee) aimed at opposing certain ideas which they considered extreme. They invited individual bishops to join their alliance. Bishop Carli of Segni joined the group. Cardinal Döpfner later admitted that there was no bishop at the Council whom he feared more.[18] As the Council progressed, at least half a dozen organized opposition groups came into being and performed yeoman service by forcing the majority to take a closer and more careful look at schemas before accepting them. Besides these six organized opposition groups, there was the International Group of Fathers (in Latin, *Coetus Internationalis Patrum*), which was conservative and holding back the progressive elements in the Council.

The *Coetus Internationalis Patrum* group even purchased a small offset press, installed it near the Vatican, and hired an office staff. Three days after the meeting with Cardinal Santos, Archbishop Sigaud issued a bulletin announcing that this International Group of Fathers would sponsor a conference every Tuesday evening open to all Council Fathers. The purpose of these meetings, the announcement said, was to study the schemas of the Council—with the aid of theologians—in the light of the traditional doctrine of the Church and according to the teaching of the Sovereign Pontiffs.

Soon the International Group of Fathers became so active and influential that it aroused the indignation of the European alliance.

Archbishop Sigaud was considered to be an archconservative and some Catholic News Agencies depicted him and his group as working covertly against the aims of the Council. In spite of this, an almost endless flow of circular letters, commentaries on schemas, interventions, and qualifications flowed from his pen and those of the bishops and theologians whom he united through his group. Long before a schema came up for discussion, a careful program had been worked out, indicating exactly what aspects of the schema should be supported or attacked in written or in oral interventions.[19]

In response to the schema of *Gaudium et spes*, Archbishop Heenan of Westminster stated that the schema was "unworthy of an Ecumenical Council of the Church. He proposed that it should be taken away from the commission which was now handling it and referred to another commission, to be set up forthwith. Then, after three or four years, let the fourth and final session of the Council be convened to discuss all the social problems. The Council, which had spent so much time on "theological niceties," would become "a laughingstock in the eyes of the world if it now rushed breathlessly through a debate on world hunger, nuclear war and family life."[20]

The bestowal of the title 'Mother of the Church' had met with opposition. Some episcopal conferences, such as those from German-speaking and Scandinavian countries, had objected to the title. However, the Polish hierarchy sent a special request to the Pope and an International group of Fathers collected signatures and submitted them to the Pope with the view to declaring Mary as the Mother of the Church in the third session itself.[21]

Although it was clear that the Council would not seriously consider allowing priests to marry, a new suggestion was proposed that married men might be permitted to become priests. The advocates of this proposal drew their arguments from the circumstance that the Council, at the end of the third session, had decreed that the diaconate might be conferred, with the consent of the Roman Pontiff, "upon men of more mature age, even upon those living in the married state. If married men of mature age might become deacons, they argued, why might they not also become priests?"[22]

6. Pope Francis on Clericalism

Right from beginning of his Pontificate, Pope Francis has lit a strong critical light on clericalism in the Church today. In his 'Letter to the People of God' in August 2018, he wrote, "Clericalism, whether fostered by priests themselves or by lay persons, leads to an excision in the ecclesial body that supports and helps to perpetuate many of the evils that we are condemning today. To say 'no' to abuse is to say an emphatic 'no' to all forms of clericalism."[23] Pope Francis denounces clericalism as it is largely believed to be responsible for the sexual abuse committed by members of the clergy. In one of interviews Pope Francis reiterated that "It goes without saying that as long as there are clerics, there will always be clericalism. Of course, it worries me. That's why I say to priests – you will have read this – "Flee from clericalism!" Because clericalism distances you from people. "Flee from clericalism," and let me add: it is a plague in the Church. But here work needs to be done on catechesis too, the formation of conscience, dialogue and human values as well."[24]

In spite of human frailty, we need clerics to do their work in the Church. Still, this crisis will not pass without soul-reform: in a word, conversion—and more particularly—the conversion of the Church's hierarchical leadership. Since clericalism is a problem that affects every member of the church in one way or another, we need to seek a solution involving every member of the community. Addressing the pilgrims through video-message, Pope Francis denounced the temptation of clericalism in the following words:

> The temptation to clericalism, which greatly harms the Church in Latin America, is an obstacle to the development of Christian maturity and responsibility in a large section of the laity. Clericalism involves a self-referential attitude, implying a group mentality that weakens the impetus directed at an encounter with the Lord, who makes us his disciples, and our outreach to

men [*sic*] who await the proclamation of the Gospel. Therefore, I think it is important, even urgent, to form ministers who are capable of closeness, of encounter, who know how to move peoples' hearts, to walk with them, to enter into dialogue with their hopes and fears.[25]

Far from giving an impetus to various contributions and proposals, clericalism gradually extinguishes the prophetic flame to which the entire Church is called to bear witness. Clericalism forgets that the visibility and the sacramentality of the Church, belongs to the people of God (LG 9-14), not only to the few chosen and enlightened elites.

If clericalism is the disease, synodality is thought to be the cure. Only when the church embraces its identity as what VC II described of the People of God, can the clericalist mentality be erased. This means clergy and the hierarchy serving Christ in the people rather than the people serving the clergy as if they were Christ. Here the focus must change. It means the clerics must leave behind self-involvement that has led to so much desolation and denial, and place the poor, the hungry, and the abused back at the center of the Church's attention, which is their rightful place and privilege.

Realization of this mission belongs to the entire Church, and not only to the individual priest or bishop. Tomorrow's priests must be trained with a view to the future and they have to be trained in context, particularly because their ministry will be carried out in a secularized world. This in turn demands that the pastors discern how best they can prepare the people for carrying out their mission in these concrete situations of life. Their mission is carried out in fraternal unity with the people of good will. Therefore, the Pope opines that it must become the duty of all (clergy) to support and encourage the laity to realise their roles in the spirit of discernment and synodality, two of the essential features of the priests.

Conclusion

In order to overcome the abuses of priestly ministry, like authoritarianism, we need to return to *ad fontes* to reverse tide of sacerdotalism and clericalism that transformed the ordained ministers from servants/ pastors to cultic priests. We need to move away from the pre-VC II understanding of the priesthood as a clerical status to the New Testament and early Church's understanding of priesthood as a ministerial function done in the spirit of love and service.[26] In spite of the reality of clericalism, we need to look positively at the good works done by clerics in building up the kingdom of God. A continuous pessimistic or negative evaluation of priestly ministry might lead to a feeling of remorse, which is counterproductive. We had and still have great many church personnel who knew no other way but to serve God and God's people till the last breath of their lives. It is also equally true that the holy mother Church was tainted with men and women who gave into vanities and brought ill-repute.

As the sacrament of salvation in the world, the Church has responsibilities and obligations at every stage of human life: human being's need for daily bread; the administration and equal and just distribution of the world's goods; support to underdeveloped nations; a more profound application of the principles of brotherhood and love among men and women and nations; promoting the religious and moral aspects of procreation; indifferentism in religion and avoidance of pollicization of religion; the use of science and technology to raise the economic and spiritual standards of nations, etc.[27] The list is in fact endless. In order to realize the above-mentioned duties, the Church looks for men and women who must transcend self to understand the mission of the Church in bringing God's love to people. God has chosen weak and sinful human servants to continue the task of establishing God's reign among people. It is our profound faith that God who has called and commissioned God's servants to radiate God's love in the world will assist them with grace and accompany them till the end.

Endnotes

[1] Ralph M. Wiltgen, *The Inside Story of Vatican II: A Firsthand Account of Council's Inner Workings* (Charlotte: TAN Books, 2014), 278-279.

[2] Ibid.

[3] George M. Soares-Prabhu, "Christian Priesthood in India Today: A Biblical Reflection," in *A Biblical Theology for India: Collected Writings of George M. Soares-Prabhu*, vol. 2, ed. Scaria Kuthirakkattel (Pune: Jnana-Deepa Vidyapeeth, 1999), 222.

[4] Ibid., 222.

[5] To the Smyrneans, VIII.

[6] Soares-Prabhu writes, "When civic privileges granted to clergy encouraged the development of a clerical caste system and obscured the servant role that is prominent in the Gospels." Soares-Prabhu, "Christian Priesthood in India Today," 236.

[7] Giacomo Martina, *Storia della Chiesa* (Roma: Istituto Superiore di Scienze Religiose, Pontificia Universita Lateranense, 1980), 57-58

[8] Ibid., 58.

[9] Peter Waldo preached apostolic poverty as the way to perfection. Waldensians held that temporal offices and dignities were not meant for preachers of the Gospel. In addition to these their teachings were also tainted with heresy. Albigensianism was a revival of Manichaeism. Dualism was at the root of the movement. They were looking for a rule of moral life. They promoted the laity with the sharper realization of their dignity in the church. They questioned the wealthy church and insisted on preaching. They rejected warfare and such practices.

[10] Bihlmeyer and Hermann Tüchle, *Church History: Modern and Recent Times*, III (Paderborn: Ferdinand Schöningh, 1966), 282.

[11] Ibid., 402-407

[12] P. De Letter, *The Second Vatican Council: A Brief Historical Account* (Ranchi: Dharmik Sahitya Samiti, 1978), 14-15.

[13] Wiltgen, *The Inside Story of Vatican II*, 151.

[14] Ibid., 276-277.

[15] Here are three important aspects that promote clericalism in popular theology: (a) the priest represents Christ, while the people represent those to whom Christ ministered. However, equally important is the teaching of St. Paul that each of the baptized is an *alter Christus* — another Christ — and has a vocation to share the church's mission through an apostolic life in the ordinary world; (b) the ordained presbyter (priest) is understood to be the one who is active in the Eucharist as the agent of reenacting Holy Thursday and Good Friday, while the people are sacramentally passive as recipients of the priest's sacred action. This reduction of the laity to passive bystanders instead of active participants in Catholic worship is the most characteristic manifestation of clericalism and (c) One additional aspect of this implicit popular theology has to do with the Holy Spirit. It imagines that if

the Spirit is bestowed on the faithful, it will come exclusively through the ministry of the ordained. It presupposes that the faithful are directly dependent upon bishops and priests for their sanctification.

[16] Wiltgen, *The Inside Story of Vatican II*, 54.

[17] Ibid., 72-73.

[18] Ibid., 122-123.

[19] Ibid., 215-218.

[20] Ibid., 315-316.

[21] But the bishops of Germany and France, as well as Cardinal Bea, were known to be opposed to such a consecration, and it did not take place. While many Council Fathers were reassured by the proceedings of the public meeting, for others the last week of the third session remained Black Week. Wiltgen, *The Inside Story of Vatican II*, 365-367.

[22] One Council Father publicly took action in the matter early in the fourth session. He was Dutch-born Bishop Pedro Koop of Lins, Brazil, who gave wide distribution to an intervention on the subject which he planned to read in the Council hall. This intervention began: "If the Church is to be saved in our regions of Latin America, then there must be introduced among us as soon as possible a married clergy, formed from our best married men, but without introducing any change in the existing law of celibacy." A group of eighty-one professional men and women from around the world lent indirect support to the proposal by circulating among the Council Fathers a letter strongly advocating that married men should be allowed to become priests, and that priests should be allowed to marry. Their reasons against celibacy were the shortage of priests, their own dissatisfaction with "the manner in which priests are coming to terms with their vow of celibacy," and their claim that "priests are finding it increasingly difficult to radiate the new glory of the Church in a state of celibacy." Wiltgen, *The Inside Story of Vatican II*, 402-404.

[23] Letter of His Holiness Pope Francis to The People of God, 2, http://www.vatican.va/content/francesco/en/letters/2018/documents/papa-francesco_20180820_lettera-popolo-didio.html (accessed November 18, 2019).

[24] In-Flight Press Conference of His Holiness Pope Francis from Fatima to Rome, May 13, 2017, http://w2.vatican.va/content/francesco/en/speeches/2017/may/documents/papa-francesco_20170513_voloritorno-fatima.html (accessed November 18, 2019).

[25] Video-Message of Pope Francis to Participants in the Pilgrimage -Meeting at the shrine of Our Lady of Guadalupe, (Mexico City, 16-19 November 2013), Saturday, 16 November 2013, http://w2.vatican.va/content/francesco/en/messages/pont-messages/2013/documents/papa-francesco_20131116_videomessaggio-guadalupe.html (accessed November 19, 2019).

[26] Soares-Prabhu, "Christian Priesthood in India Today," 237.

[27] Wiltgen, *The Inside Story of Vatican II*, 309-310.

VI

Pope Francis' Dialogue with Religions and Science

"Approaching, speaking, listening, looking at,
coming to know and understand one another,
and to find common ground: all these things are
summed up in the one word 'dialogue'. If we want to
encounter and help one another, we have to dialogue."

(Pope Francis)

21.

Pope Francis' Encyclical *Laudato Si'* in Dialogue with Asian Religions
Peter C. Phan

Introduction: Viewing *Laudato Si'* with Asian Eyes

Environmental or ecological degradation, as part of a cluster of economic and social problems, was listed among the six most serious threats to global security and peace in the twenty-first century by the United Nations High-Level Panel on Threats, Challenges and Change in 2005.[1] While ecological degradation through depletion of natural resources, the destruction of ecosystems, habitat, and wildlife, and pollution, has long been studied as a scientific issue, it has only recently been investigated from the viewpoints of global security and peace and cultural, anthropological, and religious perspectives. Furthermore, it has been recognized that ecological destruction, though a direct result of the globalization of what is called the 'technocratic paradigm', has deep roots in modern anthropocentrism. Consequently, the solutions to ecological degradation must not be limited to science, technology, and economics, essential though these are, but must also be based on social, cultural, and religious convictions and values, in order that an 'integral ecology' may emerge.

Given the religious nature of the ecological crisis, it comes as no surprise that religious leaders have drawn from their own resources to contribute to its solution. Among these, the pride of place is to be given to Pope Francis, whose *Laudato Si': On Care for Our Common Home* (hereinafter *LS*), is the first papal encyclical devoted exclusively to the issue of ecology.[2] Of course, earlier popes have not been unconcerned about this threat to the survival of humanity and the cosmos. In the opening paragraphs of his encyclical (nos. 3-6), Francis recalls the teaching of his predecessors John XXIII, Paul VI, and Benedict XVI on the moral obligation to safeguard the environment. However, all of their statements on ecology are *obiter dicta*, and none of the earlier documents of Catholic social teaching offers a sustained treatment of the subject.[3]

In a sense, *LS* encapsulates the twin foci of Francis' pontificate, which are implied in his choice of 'Francis' as his name. Three days after his election to the papacy on March 13, 2013, he explained the reason for his choice: "Francis was a man of poverty, who loved and protected creation." Protection of the environment and love for the poor are the two basic themes of the encyclical, and they are strictly intertwined since, as the pope insists, it is the poor who suffer the most from ecological destruction: "The deterioration of the environment and society affects the most vulnerable people on the planet" (no. 21). The encyclical is an urgent clarion call to the whole world to heed the cry of the poor and the cry of the devastated Sister Earth that, in Francis' arresting description, "is beginning to look more and more like an immense pile of filth" (no. 21).

The intent of this article is not to summarize and evaluate the encyclical as a whole, which is unnecessary, as there is already a good number of studies, both popular and scholarly, that offer a summary and a critical analysis of it.[4] Rather my task is to read *LS* with Asian eyes, from the Asian perspective, in dialogue with Asian religions. The issue I would like to raise is: Are there any aspects of the teaching of *LS* that would be enriched by incorporating the teachings of the philosophical and religious traditions of Asia? Before broaching this question, I describe how Asia and Asian Catholics can read *LS* with great benefits as they take initiatives to save their continent from ecological destruction.

1. Asians as Addressee of *Laudato Si'*

Pope Francis addresses not only Catholics and other Christians but also the whole of humanity since "the environmental challenge we are undergoing, and its human roots, concern and affect us all" and since "all of us can cooperate as instruments of God for the care of creation, each according to his or her own culture, experience, involvements and talents" (no. 15). But there is a special sense in which the people of Asia will find *LS* to be of particular relevance for them in light of both its teachings on environmental protection and the ecological situation of their continent.

It is interesting to note that there is in Asia no leading politician or prominent business leader who would deny the reality of climate change and ecological destruction. All it takes for them to dispel any thought of climate change as a scientific and political hoax is to step outside their offices into the street in any Asian metropolis; they would be choked by smoke-filled air, assaulted by acrid smell, overwhelmed by wilting heat, and contaminated by disease-bearing water. In calling for environmental protection in Asia, Francis is thus preaching to the choir. However, the scientific information he provides on global warming (chapter one) is no less useful, his discussion of the "human roots of the ecological crisis" (chapter three) no less enlightening, his message about "integral ecology" (chapter four) no less apposite, and his call for "ecological conversion" and "ecological education and spirituality" (chapter six) no less urgent, given the fact that in all the areas in which human life is adversely affected by ecological degradation Asia is no doubt the most vulnerable continent.

By presenting a scientifically accurate and yet highly accessible explanation of how climate change results from human activities (chapter one) *LS* makes a great contribution—normally not expected of a religious document—to the diffusion of the much-needed understanding of the *causal connection* between the release of greenhouse gases (carbon dioxide, methane, nitrogen oxides, and others) into the atmosphere, the depletion of the ozone layer, global warming, the melting of the polar ice, the rise of the sea level on the one hand and human activities such as the burning of fossil fuel (coal, petroleum, and gas), deforestation, the dumping of industrial and nuclear waste and chemical products, and the increasing use of fertilizers, insecticides, fungicides, herbicides and agrotoxins on the other. Unless this causal connection between global warming and human activities is clearly understood and acknowledged, communal efforts "to resolve the tragic effects of environmental degradation on the lives of the world's poorest" (no. 13) in "a new and universal solidarity" (no. 14) would be impossible. Catholics, especially those who do not possess the requisite scientific knowledge—in fact, a majority of Asian Catholics—are not able to verify for themselves the fact of global warming, especially over against the denial of it by powerful interest groups. For them, the affirmation by the pope, the highest teaching authority of the church, that "our common home is falling into serious disrepair" (no. 61) serves as a rich and helpful source of information and an incentive for concerted action to promote an "*integral ecology*" (no. 137).

Thanks to Pope Francis' clarion call "to hear *both the cry of the earth and the cry of the poor*" (no. 49), Asian Catholics are now encouraged to pay attention to the catastrophic impact of global warming and climate change on the Asian poor, especially in three areas. First, there is a loss of safe habitable land. It was recently reported that 35 million people who live in the delta area of Bangladesh would be displaced and lose their livelihood if the global sea levels rise by one meter (3.3 feet).

Secondly, the lack of access to freshwater and the pollution of water is widespread. While 97.5 percent of the earth's water is found in its oceans, only 3 percent is freshwater. During the twentieth century, due to the threefold increase of the human population, industrialization, and irrigation of agriculture, water consumption jumped sevenfold, and it is predicted that by 2025, two-thirds of the world's population will experience water shortages. Sixty percent of the world's population lives in Asia, yet only 36 percent of the world's freshwater is available to them, and water scarcity drives up its price for the poor. (It was reported in 2002 that in Pakistan water costs 1.1 percent of the people's daily wage, whereas in the USA, only as little as 0.006 percent.).

Furthermore, as Pope Francis points out, "the quality of water available to the poor" is toxic: "Every day, unsafe water results in many deaths and the spread of water-related diseases, including those caused by microorganisms and chemical substances. Dysentery and cholera, linked to inadequate hygiene and water supplies, are a significant cause of suffering and infant mortality. Underground water sources in many places are threatened by the pollution produced by certain mining, farming, and industrial activities, especially in countries lacking adequate regulation or controls. It is not only a question of industrial waste. Detergents and chemical products, commonly used in many places of the world, continue to pour into our rivers, lakes, and seas" (no. 29). To those living or visiting Asia, sadly the pope's description of water pollution is all too familiar.

Water scarcity has caused conflicts not only in the Middle East over the Tigris-Euphrates Rivers and in Africa over the Nile but it is also a source of potential conflicts in Asia: between Pakistan and India (the Indus River), between India and Bangladesh (the Ganges and the Brahmaputra Rivers), among Thailand, Myanmar and China (the Salween River), and among Thailand, Cambodia, Laos, and Vietnam (the Mekong River). The melting of the glaciers on the Himalayas, which is caused by global warming, will affect the waters of the Ganges, Brahmaputra, Irrawaddy, Mekong, Salween, Yangtze, and Yellow Rivers. It has been said that in the international economy and politics water promises to be in the twenty-first century what oil was in the twentieth century. Finally, the pope goes on to note that "the control of water by large multinational businesses may become a major source of conflict in this century" (no. 31). Transnational water has become a highly profitable commodity and private companies have attempted to capture the 'water market'. Needless to say, privatizing water for profit further deprives the Asian poor of their right to safe water.

Thirdly, there is a loss of biodiversity. According to many scientists, in our time the earth is experiencing the sixth greatest extinction of life since life began 3.8 billion years ago. In 2015, the extinction of species was taking place one thousand times faster than at the end of the Ice Age, and this unprecedented loss of biodiversity is compounded by global warming. *LS* points out that "each year sees the disappearance of thousands of plant and animal species which we will never know, which our children will never see because they have been lost forever. The great majority become extinct for reasons related to human activities" (no. 33). In Asia, much of the biodiversity found in tropical countries is disappearing at an alarming rate. For example, the number of orangutans, which live only in Indonesia and Malaysia, is facing extinction by illegal logging and the clearance of their habitat for palm oil plantation. Golden-headed langurs and black-crested gibbons are disappearing in northeastern Vietnam.

Loss of biodiversity occurs not only on land but also in the waters. *LS* notes: "Oceans not only contains the bulk of our planet's water supply but also most of the immense variety of living creatures, many of them still unknown to us and threatened for various reasons. What is more, marine life in rivers, lakes, seas, and oceans, which feeds a great part of the world's population, is affected by uncontrolled fishing, leading to a drastic depletion of certain species" (no. 40). *LS* points out that "carbon dioxide increases the acidification of the ocean and compromises the marine food chain" (no. 24). In Asia, in a single year, the Yellow River can dump into the South China Sea 751 tons of heavy metals along with 21,000 tons of oil. In addition to acidification, climate change also contributes to the deoxygenation of seawater. Recent ocean models project that there will be a decline between one and seven percent in the global ocean oxygen in this century, which harms fish and other marine organisms.

Loss of biodiversity in the oceans is also caused by fishing with giant deep-sea-bottom trawlers, which is heavily subsidized by governments and which strips the oceans bare. A study by the International Union for the Conservation of Nature in 2012 found that 12 percent of all the marine species in the tropical eastern Pacific Ocean were threatened with extinction. In addition, mining for copper, manganese, nickel, cobalt, and rare metals on the floor of the Pacific Ocean at 2.5 miles beneath the surface will also do irreparable damage to marine life. Two marine ecosystems are especially at risk: the coral reefs and the mangrove forests. *LS* notes: "Many of the world's coral reefs are already barren or in a state of constant decline" (no. 41). Coral reefs, which are comparable to the great forests on dry land, provide shelter and livelihood security for nearly half a billion people across the globe. Like coral reefs, mangrove forests provide food and shelter for fish. Tragically, in the last forty years, millions of acres of mangrove areas have been destroyed. In Asia, Thailand has lost 27 percent of its mangrove forests; Malaysia 20 percent; the Philippines 45 percent; and Indonesia 40 percent.

From these brief considerations on the disastrous impact of global warming on Asia, and especially the Asian poor, in three areas, namely, habitable land, access to healthy water, and biodiversity, it is clear that *LS*, though not specifically written for Asia, is highly relevant for Asia. As the encyclical argues, not only has the "environmental, economic, and social ecology" been degraded (nos. 139-142) but also the "cultural ecology" (nos. 143-146) and the "ecology of daily life" (nos. 147-155) have been seriously harmed. These three ecologies constitute what *LS* terms "integral ecology" that must be preserved by means of a worldwide and concerted effort (chapter four). As *LS* points out somberly, ecological destruction has led to a decline in the quality of human life and the breakdown of society:

> The social dimension of global change includes effects of technological innovations on employment, social exclusion, inequitable distribution and consumption of energy and other services, social breakdown, increased violence and a rise in new forms of social aggression, drug trafficking, growing drug use by young people, and the loss of identity (no. 46).

Furthermore, ecological degradation has also led to "global inequality" between the rich countries of the Global North and the developing and poor countries of the Global South (nos. 48-52). A quick survey of the Asian contemporary social and economic scene will confirm Pope Francis' succinct litany of the challenges Asia is facing as a result of ecological degradation.

2. "The Great Sages of the Past": Toward an Interreligious Ecological Theology

In calling for the restoration of integral ecology Pope Francis appeals not only to the Judeo-Christian biblical tradition with its emphasis on the universe as God's creation (nos. 76-83), universal communion (nos. 89-92), and the common destination of goods (nos. 93-95), but also to the wisdom of Saint Francis of Assisi as expressed in his celebrated *Canticle of the Creatures* (no. 87), whose opening line *Laudato Si'* serves as the title of the encyclical. Furthermore, introducing a theological novelty, he cites the teaching of the Ecumenical Patriarch Bartholomew (nos.7-9) and twenty-one episcopal conferences, including those of the Philippines (no. 41), Japan (no. 85), and the Federation of Asian Bishops' Conferences (no. 116).

2.1. *The Federation of Asian Bishops' Conferences*

It is noteworthy that the Federation of Asian Bishops' Conferences (FABC) is probably the first official church body in the Catholic Church to be deeply concerned with ecology.[5] Already in 1988, at the Eleventh Bishops' Institute for Interreligious Affairs in Sukabumi, Indonesia, it was stated that "the ecological question or the harmony and balance of the natural environment in relation to the relation to the life of man [*sic*] is a fundamental one. The destiny of humankind is inextricably bound up with the way they cultivate the earth and share its resources. Harmony and peace call for respect for the earth. She is the mother of whose dust we are made and to whose womb we shall return. The usurpation of the fruit of the earth by some and the deprivation of others of the same results in the rupture of harmony among peoples."[6]

Among the Institute's many pastoral recommendations, there is one regarding the environment:

> Respect for nature and compassion for all living things are ingrained in the Asian religions and cultural traditions. Today in Asia owing to many factors, the natural environment with which man [sic] should be in harmony is being wantonly destroyed through deforestation, industrial pollution, depositing of nuclear wastes, etc. Christian life and witness should manifest greater sensitivity to nature and all sentiments. Hence we recommend that Christians join forces and cooperate with all movements of followers of other religions and secular groups engaged in maintaining balance and harmony in our ecosystem and protecting nature and its riches from destruction.[7]

Concern for the environment recurred as a constant refrain in the FABC's Plenary Assemblies and the various documents of its offices in the ensuing years. At the Sixth FABC Plenary Assembly on "Christian Discipleship in Asia Today" in 1995, it is stated in the Final Statement: "Ecology is once again brought to our pastoral attention. And urgently so, since we see in the countries of Asia the continuing and unabated destruction of our environment…. Life, especially in a third world setting, is sacrificed at the altar of short-term economic gains. The Lord, the Giver of Life, calls our discipleship in Asia into a question on the time bomb issue of ecology. Choosing life requires our discipleship to discern and act with other faiths and groups against the forces of ecological destruction."[8]

Note that the FABC's approach to ecology is framed in terms of 'harmony' and 'wholeness', which are said to be characteristic ideals of Asian peoples: "When we look into our traditional cultures and heritages, we note that they are inspired by a vision of unity. The universe is perceived as an organic whole with the web of relations knitting together each and every part of it. The nature and the human are not viewed as antagonistic to each other, but as chords in a universal symphony."[9] It is out of this sense of universal harmony and wholeness that concern for ecology is born and nourished. Indeed, there is a fourfold harmony to be achieved: with God, with oneself, with others, and with nature. A disturbance in any one of these four relations brings about disharmony in the other three; conversely, harmony in any one of them strengthens harmony in the other three. Thus, harmonious ecology is rooted in harmonious relations with God, with oneself, and with others. By the same token, there cannot be harmony with God, with oneself, and with others without harmonious ecology. Indeed, the idea of harmony is so central to Asian thought and life that the Theological Advisory Commission (now Office of Theological Concerns) has produced a 70-page document entitled *Asian Christian Perspectives on Harmony*, in which ecological degradation figures among the most destructive forces causing disharmony in Asia.[10]

Ecology is also discussed at the FABC's Seventh Plenary Assembly in 2000 with the theme "A Renewed Church in Asia: A Mission of Love and Service."[11] The Tenth Plenary Assembly in 2012, with the theme "A New Evangelization," notes how the ecological issue was brought to worldwide attention by the monumental disaster in Japan caused by a tsunami on March 11, 2011:

> Our Assembly has likewise noted the unabated abuse of creation due to selfish and shortsighted economic gains. Human causes contribute significantly to global warming and climate change, the impact of which affects the poor and the deprived more disastrously. The ecological concern, the care for the integrity of creation, including intergenerational justice and compassion, is fundamental to a spirituality of communion.[12]

As important as these FABC's documents are, they are not cited by *LS*. Instead, the encyclical quotes three other lesser-known texts. The first is a brief statement of the Colloquium on Faith and Science held in Tagaytay, the Philippines by the FABC Office of Education and Student Chaplaincies in 1993 entitled *Love for Creation, An Asian Response to the Ecological Crisis*.[13] The statement provides a helpful analysis of the ecological problem in its scientific, cultural, political, theological, and pastoral dimensions. The second document is the pastoral letter of the Conference of Catholic Bishops of the Philippines on ecology, whose title *What Is Happening to Our Beautiful Land* is echoed in the title of *LS*'s first chapter. "What Is Happening to Our Common Home." The letter begins with a graphic list of the ecological damages that have been done to the forests, seas, and land of the Philippines and ends with a recommendation of activities that can and must be undertaken by individuals, churches, and the government "to respect and defend life." The third document is a rather lengthy letter of the Catholic Bishops of Japan titled *Reverence for Life: A Message for the Twenty-First Century from the Catholic Bishops of Japan* (January 1, 2001). Chapter 3, titled "Life and Death," discusses eight issues, one of which being the environment. It recalls Rachel Carson's prophetic voice warning the world in 1962 about the "silent spring" and ends with the following beautiful words, which *LS* quotes (no. 85): "God cares even for the flowers of the field, dressing each with beauty and loving it. To sense each creature singing the hymn of its existence is to live joyfully in God's love and hope."[14]

So far we have only examined the teachings of the Catholic Church in Asia on ecology. However, the "Great Sages of the Past," to whom *LS* refers (no. 47) and from whom we can acquire "true wisdom, as the fruit of self-examination and generous encounter between persons" (no. 47) include also the spiritual masters of Asian religions. *LS* explicitly calls for dialogue and collaboration among religions for the defense of the earth, a call repeatedly made by the FABC: "The majority of people living on our planet profess to be believers. This should spur religions to dialogue among themselves for the sake of protecting nature, defending the poor, and building networks of respect and fraternity" (no. 201).

Among the many causes of the ecological crisis, Pope Francis highlights what he calls "the globalization of the technocratic paradigm" which "exalts the concept of a subject who, using logical and rational procedures, progressively approaches and gains control over an external object" (no. 106). In this case, the "external object" is the material world, which technocracy tries to dominate by means of "a technique of possession, mastery, and transformation" (no. 106). At the basis of this technocratic paradigm is the conception of the material world and everything existing therein as valuable only to the extent that they can be made to serve human needs and wants and not as valuable in themselves, by their independent existence and autonomous value. This conception is called "excessive anthropocentrism" (no. 1).

To counter the technocratic paradigm and excessive anthropocentrism the pope develops philosophical and theological arguments derived from the Christian sources (chapter 20). Starting from the Christian belief in God's creation of nature or the universe, Francis affirms the existence of a "universal communion": "All of us are linked by unseen bonds and together form a kind of universal family, a sublime communion which fills us with a sacred, affectionate and humble respect" (no. 89). The pope goes on to emphasize that "universal communion" includes the material universe: "Everything is related, and we human beings are united as brothers and sisters on a wonderful pilgrimage, woven together by the love God has for each of his creatures and which also unites us in fond affection with brother sun, sister moon, brother river, and mother earth" (no. 92).

Here I would like to extend Francis' reflections on universal communion by invoking the Buddhist and Daoist perspectives. Admittedly, Pope Francis' belief in a personal God and in God's creative act is fundamentally different from the non-theistic and non-creationist stance of Buddhism and Daoism. Yet, despite this difference, these two Asian religious traditions offer insights into reality that strengthen and enlarge the pope's position. In brief, the technocratic paradigm can be countered by the Buddhist notion of "interdependent/dependent co-arising/origination" (Sanskrit: *pratītyasamutpāda*), and excessive anthropocentrism by the Daoist view of universal harmony.

2.2. *The Buddhist Wisdom*

There has recently been significant production of scholarship, both general handbooks and specialized monographs, on Buddhism and ecology as well as a proliferation of Buddhist socio-political and spiritual associations of environmental activism.[15] This interest in ecological thought and practice in Buddhism has been dubbed the "Greening of Buddhism." In her helpful overview of the history and development of this movement, Stephanie Kaza acknowledges that "Buddhist environmental thought is both ancient and brand new."[16]

Buddhist ecological thought is ancient because it is rooted in the fundamental teachings of the earliest traditions of Buddhism, though of course, these teachings need to be re-interpreted to meet the threat of environmental destruction. In Theravada Buddhism, for instance, there is the central notion that suffering (*dukkha*) is caused by the desire of and attachment to things (*tanha*) born out of the ignorance of the impermanence of all beings. A remedy against desire and attachment and hence suffering is the practice of compassion (*karuna*) and loving-kindness, (*metta*), which is extended not only to all humans but also to all animals, plants, and even natural elements. The Noble Eightfold Path itself, which is intended as a guide for the individual to achieve enlightenment and liberation from suffering (*nirvana*) is interpreted as ways to prevent and relieve the suffering and destruction of not just individual beings but also the entire physical environment.

In particular, the precepts included in four paths, namely, right view, right speech, right action, and right livelihood have been reformulated to promote the protection of the environment. Right view implies not only the correct understanding of the impermanence of things and the connection between ignorance of this essential nature of things and suffering but also a correct understanding of the causal correlation between certain human activities such as fossil fuel and climate change. Not telling lies, under right speech, proscribes not only falsehood-telling but also misleading advertising to promote ecologically destructive consumerism. Not taking life, under right action, includes not only not killing human life but also doing no-harm (*ahimsa*) to all living beings and things. Right livelihood commands avoidance not only of life-killing professions but also the acquisition of unnecessary things. The remaining four paths—right effort, right mindfulness, right concentration, and right resolve—can also be interpreted in a way that is conducive to ecologically responsible living insofar as they train the individual mind to gain true insight into the nature of reality as suffering, impermanent, and interdependent.

The impermanence and interdependence of all things on one another bring us to the ecological thought present in Mahayana Buddhism. Central to this Buddhist tradition is the concept of "interdependent/dependent arising/origination" (*pratītyasamutpāda*) by which is meant that all things (*dharma*) do not exist as independent and permanent realities or "selves," but are constantly changing or "co-arising" (*samutpāda*) dependently (*pratītya*) on other things, which are also co-arising dependently on the things that co-arise dependently on them. The doctrine of interdependent origination is expressed in the following terse formula: "When this is, that is; This arising, that arises; When this is not, that is not; This ceasing, that ceases."[17] As a result of interdependent origination, there is nothing permanent, nothing substantial.

This doctrine is also expressed by the concept of "emptiness" (*śūnyāta*), or "no-self" (*ānatman*), which maintains that no self is independent of other selves. The Indian Buddhist philosopher Nāgārjuna points out that to say that a thing is "empty" is to say that it is dependently originated, marked by three characteristics: transient, unsatisfactory, and without inherent existence. Another representation of this Mahayana concept of the interdependence of all beings is the Jewel Net of Indra, which stretches through all space and time and connects an infinite number of jewels in the universe, with each jewel being infinitely multifaceted and reflecting every other jewel in the net.

In terms of ecological thought, the Buddhist concept of interdependent origination implicitly rejects the technocratic paradigm which views the world in terms of subject-object for domination and exploitation. Interdependent origination—as the term implies—affirms universal and mutual conditioning among all things. No being can exist without other: one person without all other persons; humanity without ecology; and vice versa, ecology without humanity.

This interdependence of all things is dramatically expressed by the Vietnamese Buddhist monk Thich Nhat Hanh. In a short post titled *Clouds in Each Paper* on Awakin.org March 25, 2000, he writes:

> If you are a poet, you will see clearly that there is a cloud floating in this sheet of paper. Without a cloud, there will be no rain; without rain, the trees cannot grow: and without trees, we cannot make paper. The cloud is essential for the paper to exist. If the cloud is not here, the sheet of paper cannot be here either. So we can say that the cloud and the paper inter-are.

"Interbeing" is a word that is not in the dictionary yet, but if we combine the prefix 'inter' with the verb 'to be', we have a new verb, 'inter-be'. Without a cloud, we cannot have paper, so we can say that the cloud and the sheet of paper 'inter-are'.

> If we look into this sheet of paper even more deeply, we can see the sunshine in it. If the sunshine is not there, the forest cannot grow. In fact nothing can grow. Even we cannot grow without sunshine. And so, we know that the sunshine is also in this sheet of paper. The paper and the sunshine inter-are. And if we continue to look we can see the logger who cut the tree and brought it to the mill to be transformed into paper. And we see the wheat. We know that the logger cannot exist without his daily bread, and therefore the wheat that became his bread is also in this sheet of paper. And the logger's father and mother are in it too. When we look in this way we see that without all of these things, this sheet of paper cannot exist.[18]

Because of interdependent origination humanity and ecology 'inter-are'. "Interbeing" is the only mode of existence possible, not only among humans themselves but also between humanity and ecology. The animals and the material world are not just 'objects' for us humans as 'subjects' to manipulate, dominate, and exploit. Their value and worth are not measured by their usefulness to humans; rather they possess their autonomous value in themselves because they and we co-arise interdependently. Without them, we cannot exist, and vice versa, without us they cannot exist. They and we 'inter-are'.

The FABC Theological Advisory Commission in its document *Asian Christian Perspectives on Harmony* already cited above explains how in the Mahayana tradition the historical Buddha becomes identified with the goal he reached, namely, *nirvāna*, the Ultimate "No-Self," or Absolute

"Emptiness," by destroying the twelve causes producing suffering. It goes on to say: "The human task is to follow the example of the historical Buddha and to reach this ultimate state of emptiness, which is stillness, quietness and limitless rest, but the dynamic stillness which reaches out in compassion to all living beings still in the throes of suffering."[19]

Despite profound resonances between Buddhist basic teachings, both in Theravada and Mahayana traditions, and contemporary ecological thought, it would be wrong to think that Buddhism is a religion of "nature" and immediately and inevitably leads to environmental protection activities.[20] (It is equally wrong to imagine that Christianity, with its theology of creation and incarnation naturally leads to the kind of ecological concerns as evinced by Pope Francis. There is always a gap between theory and practice, or more concretely, between what believers say and what they do. But this is no argument against the teachings of Buddhism per se; rather it calls for a concerted effort by believers of different traditions to draw from their own religious sources on ecological responsibility, to enrich their own insights with those of other religions and to help each other live up to their beliefs.[21]

2.3. *The Daoist Wisdom*

As mentioned earlier, the FABC regards harmony and wholeness as characteristic ideals of the Asian way of life. Daoism is both a philosophical school (*daojia*) and a religious practice (*daogiao*) that is distinguished from Confucianism and Buddhism (*fojiao*). The classics upon which Daoism is founded are the *Dao de jing*, also known as the *Laozi*, and the *Zhuangxi*. The defining concept of the Daoist religion is the Dao itself. Literally meaning the 'way' or the 'path', the Dao refers to the proper course of human conduct, especially as taught by the ancient sages. It soon came to be understood as the metaphysical basis of the natural order itself, primordial yet eternally present. In its primordial state Dao is described as 'nothingness', null and void. But the Dao also manifests itself and becomes present in the sensible world through *qi* (literally, breath, steam, vapor, or energy). *Qi*, both energy and matter, is the basic building block of all things in the universe, responsible for movement and energy, and is the vital substance of life. Daoist rituals and religious practices aim at preserving this *qi* by combatting the forces of aging, illness, and death. The goal, at one temporal and spatial, is to bring the various parts of the body back into unified harmony and thus to achieve immortality.

As with Buddhism, there are certain fundamental insights into humans and the natural world and basic ethical concepts in Daoism that can provide a consistent theoretical framework for an ecological ethics. Notable among these are the twin set of ideas *de* (virtue) and *dao* (way), *wuwei* (nonaction), and *ziran* (nature). Taken together, these two sets of concepts create an aesthetic order in which no one thing is assessed as better than another, everything (*de*) possessing its distinctive significance within the context of the whole (*dao*). As Karen L. Lai puts it succinctly:

> The Realization of each individual is meaningful only in the context of its relatedness and responsivity to others within the whole (*dao*). The affirmation of the value of individual beings *within the environmental context* feeds into a complex holism that emphasizes both the integrity and interdependence of individuals.[22]

A corollary of this ontological aesthetics is a decided rejection of anthropocentrism. Daoist environmentalism opposes any dualism that holds humans as discontinuous with, independent of, superior to, and even opposed to the environment. Instead, Daoism promotes both integrity or individuality (*de*) and holism or harmony (*dao*) in defining the individual. It sees the self as self-in-relation and self-in-context. In this combined integrity and holism, the whole is not simply the sum of its parts, nor is the whole more than its parts. Rather, the individuals cannot be what they are unless in harmony with the whole, and the whole cannot be what it is unless it is made up of the parts.[23]

Again, it is not necessary to delve into all the intricate philosophical and cosmological speculations and alchemy of Daoism here. Suffice it to note for our present purposes that central to Daoism as a religious practice is the ethics of 'noncontrivance' (*wu wei*). According to Zhuangxi, the Dao acts spontaneously in individuals, society, and nature. Similarly, humans must respect and submit to natural changes. In this way, they and the world can become one. By contrast, contrivance should be avoided because it is counter-productive and contrary to the spontaneity (*tzu-jan*) of the Dao. The ethic of noncontrivance means that humans must not act against nature; rather human action, like the Dao's, must be nonpurposive, nondeliberative and yet continuously transforming, as natural as water flowing downward and fire rising upward.

Clearly, such ethic of noncontrivance and spontaneity runs counter to the kind of anthropocentrism that makes humans the center or the summit of creation and technological domination of nature the goal of knowledge. Even though Daoist thought and practice are not based on the belief in God the Creator, they provide a powerful stimulus to "hear the cry of nature itself; everything is connected" (no. 117).

In light of the demographic explosion in Asian countries such as India, China, the Philippines, Indonesia, and Vietnam, and especially in the poorest countries of Asia, such a treatment of the impact of demographic explosion on the environment is little short of being cavalier. Perhaps *LS* is still hampered by the teaching of *Humane Vitae*, but the ecological crisis in 2018 is quite different from that in 1968 and should have provided an occasion for a serious re-examination of Pope Paul VI's admittedly non-infallible teaching on birth control. At any rate, what Pope Francis said on January 19, 2014 on his way back to Rome from the Philippines to the effect that one need not reproduce like rabbits in order to be good Catholics is a good place to start an open and honest discussion of 'responsible parenthood'.

Conclusion: The Call of LS to Heed Voices of The Great Sages of Asia

With the publication of *Laudato Si'* no one can accuse the leadership of the Catholic Church of turning a blind eye to an issue on which the survival not only of the human family but of the planet Earth itself depends. Pope Francis has sounded a clarion call for an "ecological conversion," a call addressed to the whole humanity, but also one that Asia will need to heed and respond actively and promptly because being a continent of the poorest of the poor, it has to respond to the cry of the earth to make a decent human life possible for its own people.

The pope's message is not a lone voice. It has been anticipated in many ways by the Asian bishops, not to mention many Asian theologians. Furthermore, Pope Francis' message about an integral ecology can be enriched by incorporating the wisdom of the "Great Sages" of Asia, in particular as embodied in Buddhism and Daoism. Thus, an Asian interreligious ecological theology can be formulated to encourage and accompany concerted efforts to save and "care for our common home."[24]

Endnotes

[1] See *Toward a More Secure World? The Report of the High-Level Panel on Threats, Challenges and Change* (2005). The Report lists six threats: (1) Economic and social threats, including poverty, infectious diseases and environmental degradation; (2) Interstate conflict; (3) Internal conflict, including civil war, genocide and other large-scale atrocities; (4) Nuclear, radiological, chemical and biological weapons; (5) Terrorism; and (6) Transnational organized crime

[2] Pope Francis, *Laudato Si': On Care for Our Common Home*, with Commentary by Sean McDonagh (Maryknoll, NY: Orbis Books, 2016, hereinafter *LS*).

[3] Of special note is John Paul II's World Day of Peace Message: *Peace with God the Creator, Peace with All Creation* (January, 1, 1990). For an extensive discussion of the earlier papal magisterium on the ecological crisis, see Kevin W. Irwin, *A Commentary on Laudato Si': Examining the Background, Contributions, Implementation, and Future of Pope Francis' Encyclical* Mahwah, NJ: Paulist Press, 2016), 1-93.

[4] See, for example, Donal Dorr, *Option for the Poor & for the Earth: From Leo XIII to Pope Francis* (Maryknoll, NY: Orbis Books, 2016); John Fleming & John Ozolins, *Laudato Si': A Critique* (Redland Bay, QLD: Conner Court Publications, 2016); Elizabeth-Anne Stewart, *Preaching & Teaching Laudato Si': On Care for Our Common Home* (Amazon Digital Services, 2016); Kevin Irwin, *A Commentary on Laudato Si': Examining the Background, Contributions, Implementation, and Future of Pope Francis' Encyclical* (Mahwah, NJ: Paulist Press, 2016); Nellie McLaughlin, *Life's Delicate Balance: Our Common Home and Laudato Si'* (Dublin: Veritas Publications, 2016); Anthony Kelly, *Laudato Si'* (Adelaide, SA: ATF Press, 2016).

[5] For a collection of the FABC's and its various offices' documents, see *For All Peoples of Asia: Federation of Asian Bishops' Conferences. Documents from 1970 to 1991*, vol.1, ed. Gaudencio Rosales and C. G. Arévalo (Maryknoll, NY: Orbis, 1991); *For All the Peoples of Asia: Federation of Asian Bishops' Conferences. Documents from 1992 to*

1996, vol. 2, ed. Franz-Josef Eilers (Quezon City, Philippines: Claretian Publications, 1997); *For All the Peoples of Asia: Federation of Asian Bishops' Conferences. Documents from 1997 to 2001*, vol. 3, ed. Franz-Josef Eilers (Quezon City, Philippines: Claretian Publications, 2002); *For All the Peoples of Asia: Federation of Asian Bishops' Conferences. Documents from 2002 to 2006*, vol. 4, ed. Franz-Josef Eilers (Quezon City, Philippines: Claretian Publications, 2007); and *For All the Peoples of Asia: Federation of Asian Bishops' Conferences. Documents from 2007 to 2012*, vol. 5, ed. Vimal Tirimanna (Quezon City, Philippines: Claretian Publications, 2013). These volumes will be cited as *For All Peoples of Asia*, followed by their respective years of publication.

[6] *For All the Peoples of Asia* (1992), 320.

[7] *For All the Peoples of Asia* (1992), 323.

[8] *For All the Peoples of Asia* (1997), 11.

[9] *For All the Peoples of Asia* (1992), 319.

[10] See *For All the Peoples of Asia* (1997), 237-238. The entire document is found on pp. 229-298.

[11] See *For All the Peoples of Asia* (2002), 7.

[12] See *For All the Peoples of Asia* (2014), 45.

[13] The text is available at http://www.usanews.com/story-archive.

[14] A new and revised version of this text was issued January 1, 2017. Chapter Three, titled "Threats to Life," in which environmental issues are discussed, has been much enlarged. It describes the changes in environmental problems and cites *LS* extensively in developing an "integral ecology."

[15] The following works are most helpful. On religion and ecology in general, see Roger S. Gottlieb, ed. *The Oxford Handbook of Religion and Ecology* (Oxford: Oxford University Press, 2006); Dale Jamieson, ed., *A Companion to Environmental Philosophy* (Oxford: Blackwell, 2001); and J. Baird Callicott and James McRae, eds., *Environmental Philosophy in Asian Tradition of Thought* (Albany: SUNY Press, 2014). On Buddhism and ecology in particular, two works stand out: Mary Evelyn Tucker and Duncan Ryūken Williams, eds. *Buddhism and Ecology: The Interconnection of Dharma and Deeds* (Cambridge, Mass. 1997) and Stephanie Kaza and Kenneth Kraft, eds., *Dharma Rain: Sources of Buddhist Environmentalism* (Boston: Shambala, 2000). All these works contain abundant bibliographies.

[16] See her "The Greening of Buddhism: Promise and Perils," in Roger S. Gottlieb, ed., *The Oxford Handbook of Religion and Ecology*, 184-206; here, 202. See also her "Acting with Compassion: Buddhism, Feminism, and the Environmental Crisis," in J. Baird Callicott and James McRae, eds., *Environmental Philosophy*, 71-98 and "American Buddhist Response to the Land: Ecological Practice at Two West Coast Retreat Centers," in Mary Evelyn Tucker and Duncan Ryūken Williams, eds., *Buddhism and Ecology*, 219-248.

[17] For a helpful explanation of "interdependent origination" in Buddhist thought, see Richard Gombrich, *What the Buddha Thought* (London: Equinox, 2009), 129-143

and Paul Williams with Anthony Tribe, *Buddhist Thought: A Complete Introduction to the Indian Tradition* (London: Routledge, 2000), 62-72.

[18] http://www.awakin.org/read/view.php?tid=222. See also Thich Nhat Hanh, *The Wisdom of That Nhat Hanh* (New York: One Spirit, 2000), 233-252.

[19] *For All the Peoples of Asia* (1997), 260.

[20] For a critique of the view that the Buddhist idea of "emptiness" and oneness of all things with nature make Buddhism an environmentally friendly religion, see Simon P. James, "Against Holism: Rethinking Buddhist Environmental Ethics," in J. Baird Callicott and Hames McRae, eds., *Environmental Philosophy*, 99-115. Instead of speaking about Buddhism as an environmentally friendly on account of its metaphysical concepts of emptiness, James argues that Buddhism is so because it commends a way of life, a set of virtues, in particular *karunā*, that promotes ecological responsibility.

[21] Stephanie Kaza has also enlisted feminist thought to enrich Buddhist and environmental thought and practice. See her "Acting with Compassion: Buddhism, Feminism, and the Environmental Crisis," J. Baird Callicott and James McRae, eds., *Environmental Philosophy*, 71-98.

[22] Karen L. Lai, "Conceptual Foundation for Environmental Ethics: A Daoist Perspective," J. Baird Callicott and James McRae, eds., *Environmental Philosophy*, 173-195; here 183. In addition to Lai's essay, see also the essays on Daoist ecology in this volume by R. P. Perrenboom, "Beyond Naturalism: A Reconstruction of Daoist Environmental Ethics," 149-172; Alan Fox, "Process Ecology and the 'Ideal' Dao," 197-207; Sandra A. Wawritko, "The Viability (*Dao*) and Virtuosity (*De*) of Daoist Ecology: Reversion (*Fu*) as Renewal," 209-224; and James Miller, "Ecology, Aesthetics and Daoist Body Cultivation," 225-243.

[23] For a study of Daoism and ecology, see N. J. Girardot, James Miller, and Liu Xiaogan, eds., *Daoism and Ecology: Ways within a Cosmic Landscape* (Cambridge: Center for the Study of World Religions, 2001). For a brief overview, se James Miller, "Daoism and Nature," Roger S. Gottlieb, ed., *The Oxford Handbook of Religion and Ecology,* 220-235.

[24] A longer version of this essay has been published under the title "An Ecological Theology for Asia: The Challenges of Pope Francis' encyclical *Laudato Si'*" in *Ecological Solidarities: Mobilizing Faith and Justice for an Entangled World*, ed. Krista E. Hughes, Dhawn B. Martins, and Elaine Padilla (University Park, Pennsylvania: The Pennsylvania State University Press, 2019), 147-165.

22.

The Documents of VC II:
Pope Francis' Springboard for Recovering Catholic Foundations for a Profitable Dialogue between Science and Catholic Theology and Science's Appropriate Place in Seminary Formation

Richard Benson, CM

Introduction: Reflecting Upon the Relationship between Science and Theology

I am deeply grateful to the organizers for inviting me to participate in this wonderful theological symposium which seeks to revisit the Spirit's work at the VC II (hereinafter VC II) as evident in the theological vision of Pope Francis.

In 1925 Alfred North Whitehead stated what is still pertinent to our contemporary culture and Church:

> When we consider what religion is for mankind [sic], and what science is, it is no exaggeration to say that the future course of history depends upon the decision of this generation as to the relations between them. We have here the two strongest general forces...which influence men [sic], and they seem to be set one against the other – the force of our religious institutions,

and the force of our impulse to accurate observation and logical deduction.[1]

In this paper I would like to take up the relationship between science and theology, and specifically Catholic theology. First and mainly as we find it described, albeit tangentially but authentically in several of the documents of VC II and secondly as those teachings on that relationship are reflected in the thought of Pope Francis.

I think it would be important to point out as we begin the examination of this topic that the Catholic Church has largely had a very positive relationship with science over the centuries. However, we do need to remember that 'science' as we know it and understand it today, the study of measurable phenomena that can be described and accounted for by physical laws, theorems and hypotheses and which can be tested by experimental methods is largely a post-Enlightenment development. Nevertheless, there is truth to the statement that the contemporary scientific method (observe, hypothesize, and test) does have authentic roots in the natural philosophy of Aristotle and that this methodology was accepted and utilized in Catholic theology and philosophy especially through Thomas Aquinas, despite the fact that 'modern science' is a rather late singularity. A careful study of the history of Catholic intellectual history, including natural philosophy and theology would demonstrate that the Church has generally had a 'cordial relationship' with science. For example, St Augustine and St Francis among others have pointed to creation as at least one source of authentic revelation.

1. Highlights of the Progress in the Dialogue between Science and Theology

To begin, let's take as a benign example of the intersection of science and Catholic theology, the Church's teaching on Darwin's theory of evolution. Pope Pius XII, a deeply conservative theologian directly addressed the issue of evolution in his 1950 encyclical, *Humani Generis*. The document makes plain the pope's fervent hope that evolution will prove to be a passing scientific fad, and it attacks those persons who "imprudently and indiscreetly hold that evolution ...explains the origin of all things." Nonetheless, Pius XII states that nothing in Catholic doctrine is contradicted by a theory that suggests one species might evolve into another—even if that species is man. The Pope declared: "The Teaching Authority of the Church does not forbid that, in conformity with the present state of human sciences and sacred theology, research and discussions, on the part of men experienced in both fields, take place with regard to the doctrine of evolution, in as far as it inquires into the origin of the human body as coming from pre-existent and living matter—for the Catholic faith obliges us to hold that souls are immediately created by God."

Fifty years later, Pope John Paul II addresses the same issue and is much less tentative in his acceptance of the scientific theory of evolution. He said: "Today, almost half a century after publication of the encyclical [*Humani Generis*], new knowledge has led to the recognition of the theory of evolution as more than a hypothesis." Evolution, a doctrine that Pope Pius XII only suggested was a possibility, Pope John Paul II accepts forty-six years later "as an effectively proven fact."[2] On the other hand, the Church has exhibited at times a hermeneutic of suspicion toward science or at least has ignored science and its conclusions when those suppositions seemed at odds with traditional theological maxims or a particular political ideology to which church leaders were wedded in some way.

The Galileo Affair is the preeminent example in most people's minds of this kind of anti-science bias.[3] Unfortunately this suspicion of science is still evident in some Catholic circles especially in discussions of human evolution. There remain Catholics who find evolution a thoroughly unorthodox theory. For example, Clement Butel in his piece 'Why Faithful Catholics should Oppose Evolution'[4] states the following:

> "For anyone who has searched, even only casually, for the relevant affirmative evidence, there can be no doubt that evolutionism invaded the Catholic Church during this century and is now firmly established as 'scientific fact' in almost all Catholic places of learning. ... In recent years (that is prior to 1990, when this essay was first published) a group of Catholic scientists has come

together for the purpose of exposing false evolutionist dogmatism. They are associated in a Catholic organization known under the acronym of CESHE (*Cercle Scientifique et Historique*).[5] CESHE, assuming that nothing known to science can be in conflict with the teachings of the Church, is mobilizing Catholic scientific opinion against evolutionist dogmatism.

In his encyclical letter *Laudato Si*,[6] Pope Francis has rekindled—to the consternation of some like Butel and others—that cordial relationship with science that was encouraged in the documents of VC II.

> Why should this document, addressed to all people of good will, include a chapter dealing with the convictions of believers? I am well aware that in the areas of politics and philosophy there are those who firmly reject the idea of a Creator, or consider it irrelevant, and consequently dismiss as irrational the rich contribution which religions can make towards an integral ecology and the full development of humanity. Others view religions simply as a subculture to be tolerated. Nonetheless, *science and religion, with their distinctive approaches to understanding reality, can enter into an intense dialogue fruitful for both.*[7]

Obviously, Pope Francis makes clear that our Catholic teaching is most accurate when it pays attention to and integrates scientific knowledge into its understanding of missionary discipleship. A rich dialogue between environmental science and Catholic Social Teaching leads the Pope to teach: "Each community can take from the bounty of the earth whatever it needs for subsistence, but it also has the duty to protect the earth and to ensure its fruitfulness for coming generations."[8] After summarizing the teachings on care for the environment by all our Popes from John XXIII through Benedict the XVI, Pope Francis suggests the importance of the voice of science in these papal teachings. "These statements of the Popes echo the reflections of numerous scientists, philosophers, theologians and civic groups, all of which have enriched the Church's thinking on these questions."[9] I would suggest that the Holy Spirit, so evident in Her work at VC II was able to refocus the Church away from some of the ideological misunderstandings that resulted from a suspicion of 'modernism'.[10] 'Science' when understood as an example of 'modernism' caused confusion in the ranks of the Church especially at the beginning of the twentieth century, a century in which many Catholics found themselves studying and using science in their careers and for the betterment of society. To be sure, if science is confused with 'scientism', the belief that science is the beginning and end of all truth and meaning, then the Church is right to condemn it, but St. John Paul II also points out in 'Fides et Ratio' that the same can be said when 'fideism' replaces 'faith'. A faith that rejects the wonder of creation is hardly a Catholic faith because it implicitly rejects the God who is the source of that very creation.

Challenges Posed by Some Scientific Developments
Apart from the evolution controversy it will be helpful for us to briefly review some scientific case studies that have arisen in both the twentieth and twenty-first centuries that inherently or at least apparently offer challenges to certain aspects of Catholic teachings:

1. In 1866 a simple Augustinian monk in Austria, Gregor Mendel, while teaching at a secondary school and with an intense interest in inheritance began a scientific revolution which continues down to our present day. He was the founder of modern genetics.[11] His work has led to fascinating scientific and medical breakthroughs in the human genome. At the same time his work also was the foundation for the discredited pseudo-science of eugenics and its unethical application by governments in Nazi Germany and in various cities and states in the United States of America.[12] While the pseudo-science of eugenics began in the first decade of the 20th century, no published Catholic challenge to it can be found until almost thirty years later,[13] long after it had been horribly established in Germany and in the United States as a scientific fact and was used in a futile attempt to "build a better society by building a better race." A British theologian, Robbins in 1931, was among the first Catholics to confront the eugenics movement on its own terms, that is, with cogent scientific facts. It is clear that Robbins had to be conversant with the science of Mendelian genetics in order to respond in a way that swept the foundation from underneath the pseudo-science of genetics. "Scientifically, eugenics stands or falls by the proof

of the proposition that it is possible to forecast with certainty the incidence of hereditary qualities and traits."[14] In this point, Robbins focusses on the real issue. Human Genes does not code for behavior. Later in the same text he makes it clear that there is no trajectory between Mendel's theories of heredity and the pseudo-science of eugenics. "Two things are therefore clear, that any eugenic proposals for intervention on the ground of heredity are, and will for a long time remain, a colossal begging of the whole question, and that the investigation of human heredity has at present no place outside the study."[15] It is remarkable for us to remember that Robbins is a theologian but he is using sophisticated science as the foundation for his ethical analysis. In that, he foreshadows the methodology espoused in VC II and taken up by Pope Francis. Here I simply want to make the point that in many cases Catholic theology is dependent on science in order to undertake a thorough and credible analysis of ethical issues that present themselves in an evolving world. I would suggest that we will see that Pope Francis understands this as his encyclical *Laudato Si* makes evident.

2. Today, genetic issues surround the conversations of Catholics who deal with the ethical dilemmas arising from genomic studies and applications. When our Catholic schools of theology, or our pastors or our Church leaders are ignorant of science they are ill prepared to respond in a cogent way to these important questions, consequently our Catholic community, especially our lay members working in the world of science, are left unaided. One of the most significant developments in twenty first century genetics is that of CRISPR. "By the end of 2014 some 1000 research papers had been published that mentioned CRISPR. The technology had been used to functionally inactivate genes in human cell lines and cells, to study Candida albicans, to modify yeasts used to make biofuels and to genetically modify crop strains. CRISPR can also be used to change mosquitos so they

cannot transmit diseases such as malaria. In July 2019, doctors in Mississippi, United States, used CRISPR to experimentally treat a patient with a genetic disorder. The patient was a 34-year-old woman with sickle cell disease. In the future, CRISPR gene editing could be used to create new species or revive extinct species from closely related ones."[16] CRISPR is also ethically controversial as a potential method to modify the human genome in embryos, either for therapeutic or enhancement outcomes. In fact, one Chinese scientist has claimed to do so.[17]

3. Recently, the internationally recognized journal, *Nature*,[18] published the largest study of its kind on same-sex attraction and genetics. It found that genes in fact do contribute to same-sex sexual behavior, but it also echoes research that says there are no specific genes that make people gay. How does this information contribute to a dialog with the Church's understanding and teaching about homosexuality? I don't propose to give an answer but I do suggest that we as Church need to pay attention to science and not ignore it or suggest that it can be dismissed as 'fake news'.

4. Similarly, can science help us navigate the shifting ethical landscape surrounding gender identity? The international publication, *National Geographic* published an entire special edition in 2017 dealing with the gender revolution.[19] The special issue asks the important question: "Can science help us navigate the shifting landscape of gender identity?" This of course is at the heart of the dialogue between science and theology. One instance documented by the *National Geographic* is the Samoan culture which identifies three genders; male, female and *fa'afafine*, a boy who generally takes on a girls' roles in play and family. As adults they remain anatomically male with feminine appearance and mannerisms. They help with household chores and childcare. Of course, one way to deal with the issue would be for the Church simply to dismiss gender identity as modern

'fantasy' and not a reality. "God made us male and female and so our bodies simply define the reality into which we are born," is one way to deal with the issue, but is that where science is taking us? How does the scientific study of genetics and gender affect the teachings of our Catholic Church?

5. Climate change also is denied by some as a 'politically correct' issue that is simply not real.[20] However, Pope Francis clearly disagrees. "The effects of global inaction are startling. About two weeks ago, several scientific research centers recorded the concentration of carbon dioxide in the atmosphere—one of the key global causes of global warming linked to human activity—as having reached 415 parts per million, the highest level ever recorded. Around the world, we are seeing heat waves, droughts, forest fires, floods and other extreme meteorological events, rising sea levels, the emergence of diseases and further problems that are only a dire premonition of things much worse to come, unless we act and act urgently."[21] His acceptance of science should provide us a point of departure for our further reflections.

3. The Aggiornamento of the Documents of VC II to Science

I would like at this point to review some of the documents of VC II to see what they may teach as the legitimate utilization of science by the Catholic Church. Does in fact the Church through her documents espouse a cordial relationship with science?

A quick analysis of *Gaudium et Spes* will remind us that one of the aspects of *aggiornamento* that resulted from the Council was the challenge to renew the Church's formerly positive relationship with science. Reading the signs of the times means a deep awareness of the effects of technology and the empirical sciences on human anthropology and culture.

> ...[I]ntellectual formation is ever increasingly based on the mathematical and natural sciences and on those dealing with man [sic] himself. ... This

> scientific spirit exerts a new kind of impact on the cultural sphere and on modes of thought. Technology is now transforming the face of the earth, and is already trying to master outer space. ... Advances in biology, psychology and the social sciences not only bring men hope of improved self-knowledge. In conjunction with technical methods, they are also helping men to exert direct influence on the life of social groups.[22]

The same encyclical goes on to propose that scientific study has a legitimate autonomy to "observe, hypothesize and test" in its quest for authentic knowledge.

> If by the autonomy of earthly affairs we mean that created things and societies themselves enjoy their own laws and values which must be gradually deciphered, put to use and regulated by men [sic], then it is entirely right to demand that autonomy. ... [A]ll things are endowed with their own stability, truth, goodness, proper laws and order. Man [sic] must respect these as he isolates them by the appropriate methods of the individual sciences or arts. Therefore, if methodical investigation within every branch of learning is carried out in a genuinely scientific manner and in accord with moral norms, it never truly conflicts with faith. For earthly matters and the concerns of faith derive from the same God. Indeed, whoever labors to penetrate the secrets of reality with a humble and steady mind, is, even unawares, being led by the hand of God, who holds all things in existence, and gives them their identity. Consequently, we cannot but deplore certain habits of mind, sometimes found too among Christians, which do not sufficiently attend to the rightful independence of science. The arguments and controversies which they spark lead many minds to conclude that faith and science are mutually opposed."[23]

Without a doubt we can see in these brief quotes from one document of the VC II the desire for the modern Church to revitalize the use of science for the betterment of culture and increase of knowledge and thus give it once again its proper place in the life of the Church. We can perceive here the foundations of the teachings of Pope John Paul II in his encyclical *Fides et Ratio* where he suggests that faith and reason (science) are two wings on a single bird.

Further along in *Gaudium et Spes* we find more encouragement for scientific inquiry. "Earthly progress must be carefully distinguished from the growth of Christ's kingdom. Nevertheless, to the extent that the former can contribute to the better ordering of human society, it is of vital concern to the kingdom of God."²⁴ Clearly, the Council Fathers had significant trust in the value of science for the development of human flourishing. "Thanks to the experience of past ages, the progress of the sciences, and the treasures hidden in the various forms of human culture, the nature of man himself is more clearly revealed and new roads to truth are opened."²⁵

Gaudium et Spes understands that the Church must integrate science into its theological research project because science is a legitimate source of knowledge. Also since it is also an integral part of contemporary society, the Church needs to be scientifically literate herself in order to bring the Good News of Jesus Christ into the contemporary world.. It was time to jettison any uncritical animosity toward science that had taken root in the Church in recent centuries.

> …[T]he culture of today possesses particular characteristics. For example, the so-called exact sciences sharpen critical judgement to a very fine edge. Recent psychological research explains human activity more profoundly. Historical studies make a signal contribution to bringing men to see things in their changeable and evolutionary aspects.²⁶

These statements, embedded into the Council document clearly pushed the Church to recover her traditional reverence for the authentic knowledge that results from legitimate scientific study and research. Far from a model of Church that retreats from the pursuit of modern science, the Church is encouraged to learn and integrate any authentic knowledge that results from scientific progress.

Much of the work of Pope Francis is founded upon the progressive and open vision of the documents of VC II. Indeed, *Gaudium et Spes*, pushes the concept even further. "…they can stimulate the mind to a more accurate and penetrating grasp of the faith. For recent studies and findings of science, history and philosophy raise new questions which influence life and demand new theological investigations."²⁷ Isn't this exactly what Pope Francis has modeled in his teachings and reflections on the environment and the understanding of sexual orientation, and the status of Catholics living together without the benefit of a sacramental marriage? Pope Francis' understanding of pastoral theology can be found in a seminal way in *Gaudium et Spes*. "In pastoral care, appropriate use must be made not only of theological principles, but also of the findings of the secular sciences, especially of psychology and sociology."[28]

4. The Vital Role of Science in Priestly Formation

Since Catholic priests can play a crucial role in modeling a healthy use of science in preaching and teaching, VC II addresses the science-theology issue once again in *Optatam Totius*: The 'Decree on Priestly Formation'. The decree suggests that seminarians, during their philosophical studies, should be conversant with traditional philosophy, contemporary philosophy and "recent scientific progress."[29] The document then reflects on the absolute importance of science for moral theology and its updating. "Special attention needs to be given to the development of moral theology. Its scientific exposition should be more thoroughly nourished ..."[30] While the comments on integrating science into the seminary curriculum are brief in this document they rely on the fact that all that was said about the importance and value of the empirical sciences in *Gaudium et Spes* is the context for the seminary curriculum and its focus on the pastoral care of the people of God in a culture that is scientifically literate.

The same concern with the integration of science into the seminary curriculum in *Optatam Totius* is picked up in the 2016 *Ratio Fundamentalis Institutionis Sacerdotalis* (The Gift of the Priestly Vocation). The *Ratio* states a general vision for seminary intellectual formation that encompasses more than the traditional knowledge of philosophy and theology as stand-alone areas of study.

> Intellectual formation is aimed at achieving for seminarians a solid competence in philosophy and theology, along with a more *general educational preparation*, enough to allow them to proclaim the Gospel message to the people of our day in a way that is credible and understood. It seeks to enable them to enter into fruitful dialogue with the contemporary world, and to uphold the truth of the faith by the light of reason.[31]

This focus by the latest *Ratio*, clearly carries both the vision of VC II and that of Pope Francis. When the Gospel is preached and the Gospel message is taught effectively in the contemporary world it demands that the priests of the Church be able to bring in the questions, challenges and insights of science. The people of God are scientifically literate and so the Church must speak to them with a reasonable modicum of scientific literacy and not from a hermeneutic of suspicion about science.

> This means that the development of all the faculties and dimensions of the person, including the rational dimension, through the vast array of acquired knowledge, contributes to the growth of the priest as the servant and witness of the Word in the Church and in the world. ....intellectual formation helps priests top listen profoundly to the Word, and also to the ecclesial community, in order to learn how to read the signs of the times.[32]

In returning to the beginning of our paper I would suggest that only if we utilize the understandings of modern science can we hope to do any kind of credible moral analysis of contemporary issues. I mentioned earlier some examples of a vast array of new and complex moral issues that present themselves to the Church for analysis. What is 'sexual orientation' and how can it be ethically respected? What is 'gender' and does our moral Tradition yet have the tools to address this as a 'reality'? How can we address those who consider climate change as 'fake news'? This paper never attempted to address these issues specifically but to use them to point out the importance of scientific knowledge to the Catholic theological enterprise in general and the Catholic moral enterprise in particular.

Conclusion

I would like to suggest by way of conclusion that our brief review of the documents of VC II do encourage a strong and cordial relationship between science and Catholic theology. They also clearly encourage the rehabilitation of science as an authentic source of knowledge and human flourishing that should be fully integrated into the seminary curriculum. Pope Francis' attitude toward the inherent value of scientific research and knowledge and his integral use of science in his encyclical *Laudato*

Si and many other reflections are not new additions to Catholic theology and magisterial teaching but a recovery of a long and well-respected tradition in the Church. While much more could be said and probably should have been said, it was my aim to simply reflect the reality and stability of the Church's traditional reverence for the authentic knowledge derived from scientific study and research and the Church's respect for that discipline especially as taught in the documents of VC II and as evident in the writings and teachings of Pope Francis.

> *[S]science and religion, different though they may be, share a common origin in the remote and mysterious fountainhead of a simple human desire to know. Both science and religion ultimately flow out of the same 'radical' eros for truth that lies at the heart of our existence. And so, it is because of their shared origin in this fundamental concern for truth that we may never allow them simply to go their separate ways.*[33]

Endnotes

[1] Alfred North Whitehead, *Science and the Modern World* (New York: The Free Press, 1967), pp 181-182 as quoted in John F. Haught, *Science and Religion* (Paulist Press, 1995), p 2.

[2] A letter released to the Pontifical Academy of Science meeting in October 1996.

[3] On June 22, 1633, the Church handed down the following order: "We pronounce, judge, and declare, that you, the said Galileo... have rendered yourself vehemently suspected by this Holy Office of heresy, that is, of having believed and held the doctrine (which is false and contrary to the Holy and Divine Scriptures) that the sun is the center of the world, and that it does not move from east to west, and that the earth does move, and is not the center of the world."

[4] http://www.theotokos.org.uk/pages/creation/cbutel/faithful.htm

[5] CESHE (Place du Palais de Justice 3 - B-7500, Tournai, Belgium) was founded to continue the work of Belgian scholar Fernand Crombette. It now has branches in France and the United Kingdom. Executive member: Peter Wilders, 42 Bd. d'Italie, Monaco. Website: http://www1.newsource.net/efob/

[6] Pope Francis, *Laudato Si, On Care for our Common Home*, Vatican Press, May 24, 2015.

[7] *Laudato Si*, no. 62 (emphasis mine).

[8] *Laudato Si*, ch. 2.

[9] *Laudato Si*, no. 7.

[10] A movement toward modifying traditional beliefs in accordance with modern ideas, especially in the Roman Catholic Church in the late 19th and early 20th centuries. The oath against modernism was required of "all clergy, pastors, confessors, preachers,

religious superiors, and professors in philosophical-theological seminaries" of the Catholic Church from 1910 until 1967.

[11] "Experiments in Plant Hybridization" (1866), by Johann Gregor Mendel.

[12] The eugenics movement took root in the United States in the early 1900's, led by Charles Davenport (1866-1944), the eugenics movement in the US quickly focused on eliminating negative traits. Not surprisingly, "undesirable" traits were concentrated in poor, uneducated, and minority populations. In an attempt to prevent these groups from propagating, eugenicists helped drive legislation for their forced sterilization. The first state to enact a sterilization law was Indiana in 1907, quickly followed by California and 28 other states by 1931. These laws resulted in the forced sterilization of over 64,000 people in the United States. In particular, California's program was so robust that the Nazi's turned to California for advice in perfecting their own efforts. Hitler proudly admitted to following the laws of several American states that allowed for the prevention of reproduction of the 'unfit'. *America's Hidden History: The Eugenics Movement* by Teryn Bouche and Laura Rivard.

[13] Robbins, H. *An Examination of Eugenics* (London: Burns Oates and Washbourne Ltd) 1931.

[14] Ibid, p. 9.

[15] Ibid, pp. 12-13.

[16] Wikipedia, https://en.wikipedia.org/wiki/CRISPR.

[17] Dr. He made his announcement on the eve of the Second International Summit on Human Genome Editing in Hong Kong, saying that he had recruited several couples in which the man had H.I.V. and then used in vitro fertilization to create human embryos that were resistant to the virus that causes AIDS. He said he did it by directing Crispr-Cas9 to deliberately disable a gene, known as CCR... , that is used to make a protein H.I.V. needs to enter cells.

[18] Ganna, Andrea et alii; "Large-scale GWAS reveals insights into the genetic architecture of same-sex sexual behavior" *Science*, 30 Aug 2019, vol. 365, issue 6456.

[19] *National Geographic*, "Special Issue: The Shifting Landscape of Gender" January 2017, vol. 231, no. 1.

[20] There is a list of scientists who have made statements that conflict with the scientific consensus on global warming as summarized by the Intergovernmental Panel on Climate Change and endorsed by other scientific bodies. A minority are climatologists. Nearly all publishing climate scientists (97–98% support the consensus on anthropogenic climate change. https://en.wikipedia.org/wiki/List_of_scientists_who_disagree_with_the_scientific_consensus_on_global_warming

[21] "Climate Change and New Evidence from Science, Engineering, and Policy," His Holiness Pope Francis, Casina Pio IV Monday, 27 May 2019.

[22] '*Gaudium et Spes*' no. 5, *The Documents of Vatican II*, W.M. Abbott, SJ, ed., America Press, 1966.

[23] Ibid, no. 36.
[24] Ibid, no. 39.
[25] Ibid, no. 44.
[26] Ibid, no. 54.
[27] Ibid, no. 62.
[28] Ibid, no. 62.
[29] The Decree on Priestly Formation, *Optatam Totius*, no. 15.
[30] Ibid, no. 16.
[31] *Ratio Fundamentalis Insitutionis Sacerdotalis, 2016,* no. 116.
[32] Ibid, no. 117.
[33] John F. Haught, *Science and Religion: From Conflict to Conversation*, Paulist Press, 1995, p. 203.

23.

Building Bridges between Religions: Reading *Nostra Aetate* through the Lens of Pope Francis

Midhun J. Francis, SJ

Introduction

In one of his daily homilies Pope Francis said, "The Lord has created us in His image and likeness, and has given us this commandment in the depths of our heart: do good and do not do evil."[1] He added: "The Lord has redeemed all of us, all of us, with the Blood of Christ: all of us, not just Catholics. Everyone! 'Father, the atheists?' Even the atheists. Everyone!"[2] In a pluralistic society, the vocation of a Christian is to proclaim the good news of 'peace on earth', which one has to actualize in one's day-to-day life. The Christian does this by embracing the other as brother and sister because each Christian is a co-pilgrim with the other.

At an interreligious meeting, Pope Francis said: "God is at the origin of the one human family. He who is the Creator of all things and of all persons wants us to live as brothers and sisters, dwelling in the common home of creation which he has given us."[3] He has also emphasized that 'human fraternity'[4] is established in creation; 'human fraternity' has its roots in 'common humanity; 'common humanity'[5] is the original plan of God in creation, and is actually 'a vocation contained in God's plan of creation.'[6] Here it means that human beings are created in dignity and no one can be a master or slave of the other. This paper has two parts. In the first part I will read the document *Nostra Aetate* (hereinafter NA) in the context of today's evangelization, and in the second, I will make an effort to elaborate Pope Francis' attempt to implement this document in his encyclicals and evangelization as the Servant of Servants.

I. The Spirit of *Nostra Aetate*

The history and development of NA indicate that it was never the intention of Vatican Council II (hereinafter VC II) to create a theology of religions. Rather, it was gradually developed as a document *for* the theology of other religions. However, NA is a document that is deeply theological.[7] It affirms that human beings look to their different religions for an answer to the unsolved riddles of human existence.[8] It also affirms our "human fraternity" and "common humanity."

Humankind's Common Origin and Destiny

The spirit of the creation story of humankind in the Book Genesis makes us aware that God not only creates human beings in the "image and likeness of God" (Gen 1:27) but also entrusts them the whole of creation to keep it as trustees: "God blessed them, and God said to them, Be fruitful and multiply, and fill the earth and subdue it; and have dominion over the fish of the sea and over the birds of the air and over every living thing that moves upon the earth" (Gen 1:28). 'Building bridges between religions' is important, not because we are called to tolerate the other, but because we have to become aware that we have the 'same origin and destiny' and a duty to "safeguard the other." NA states, "All men [and women] form but one community. This is so because all stem from the one stock which God created to populate the entire earth (cf. Acts 17; 26), and also because all share in a common destiny, namely God."[9]

Though NA is one of VC II's shortest documents, it still made a great impact on the life of the Church, especially with regard to interreligious dialogue. It opened up many doors of the Church for the people to know each other as brothers and sisters. It builds bridges between religions. It makes us understand better that the "origin and destiny" of all people is the same. It is not simply the documents that expect us to do this mission, but Jesus himself, who brought us together and is expecting each one of us to enter into dialogue with the other. In a commentary to the documents of VC II, John M. Oesterreicher writes: "The Church in fact believes that Christ, who 'is our peace', embraces Jews and Gentiles with one and the same love and that he made the two one (Eph 2:14). She rejoices that the union of these two 'in one body' (Eph 2:16) proclaims the whole world's reconciliation in Christ."[10] "It is Christ who saves us. But nonetheless, we are partakers in His great mission of evangelisation, that reminds us that we cannot limit Christ to Christianity alone. The Church carefully reflected the "revelation" and proclaimed that there is a 'ray of that truth' in other religions."[11]

Our Search for Truth and Holiness

Oesterreicher says, "In it (NA), a Council for the first time in history acknowledges the search for the absolute by other men (*sic*) and by whole races and peoples, and honours the truth and holiness in other religions as the work of the one living God."[12] The Catholic Church solemnly proclaimed that she "rejects nothing of what is true and holy in these religions. She has a high regard for the manner of life and conduct, the precepts and doctrine which, although differing in many ways from her own teaching, nevertheless, often reflect a ray of that truth which enlightens all men (*sic*)."[13] This is the 'revelation' the Church grasped through her reflections on other religions in the Council hall.

The Church always holds that she received the fullness of revelation in Christ. "Long ago God spoke to our ancestors in many and various ways by the prophets, but in these last days he has spoken to us by a Son, whom he appointed heir of all things, through whom he also created the worlds" (Heb 1:1-2). The revelation of that truth (Christ) is a free gift of God: it can be given to anyone, because it is God's act. This revelation cannot be grasped fully by human intellect because God is mystery. As God is both mystery and free, God can reveal Godself freely to our fellow human beings. This means that the Church cannot limit her evangelization to Christians alone; she has to evangelize herself as well as the entire humanity. She knows that Christ has to be proclaimed—not because she holds the fullness of truth, but because she has experienced God's love through Jesus Christ: the incarnated 'Logos'.

Dialogue with Love: Fundamental Duty of a Christian
The vocation of a Christian is to be faithful to our call to witness to the truth. In order to be faithful to our call, we must have a proper understanding of our traditions and scripture. NA says, "Yet she proclaims and is duty bound to proclaim without fail, Christ who is the way, the truth and the life (Jn 1:6). In him, in whom God reconciled all things to himself (cf. 2 Cor 5:18-19), people find the fullness of their religious life."[14] She has to proclaim "the truth that she has grasped with full commitment and charity because she understood it from the revelation that He (Jesus Christ) is the reflection of God's glory and the exact imprint of God's very being, and he sustains all things by his powerful word. When he had made purification for sins, he sat down at the right hand of the Majesty on high, having become as much superior to angels as the name he has inherited is more excellent than theirs" (Heb 1:3-4).

Therefore, the Church invites each member to enter into dialogue with others with prudence and charity, witnessing to his own faith commitment while 'preserving and encouraging' both spiritual and moral truths in other religions.[15] This commitment enriches her, helping her to realize that there is that "ray of that truth" in other religions. To be a Christian, one must embrace everyone into one's heart and proclaim the "truth".

Being a Christian, one cannot deny the "rays of truth" in other religions. It is the duty of a Christian to engage in interreligious dialogue.

Every religion's origin reminds us that there is an innermost quest for a supernatural power beyond us. This power is understood as a protective power from every natural calamity as well as inner tensions that human beings face.

> Throughout history even to the present day, there is found among different peoples a certain awareness of a hidden power, which lies behind the course of nature and the events of human life. At times, there is present even a recognition of a supreme being, or still more of a Father. This results in a way of life that is imbued with deep religious sense.[16]

A Christian is a co-pilgrim with all others on this earth. Being co-pilgrims, at certain times when others do not recognize their fundamental call to love, it is the duty of Christians to remind each other about this responsibility. This duty to love the other is a fundamental law of Christianity. In the Gospel of John Jesus says: "I give you a new commandment, that you love one another. Just as I have loved you, you also should love one another. By this everyone will know that you are my disciples, if you have love for one another" (Jn 13:34-35).

There were times that the Church deviated from her vocation to witness to the fundamental law called love, because, though the Church is also instituted in God's plan and grace, it is made up of human beings. Being human includes a possibility of forgetting our fundamental goal, which is God himself. NA speaks with contrition while reflecting on dialogue with Muslims: "Over the centuries many quarrels and dissensions have arisen between Christians and Muslims. The sacred council now pleads with all to forget the past, and urges that a sincere effort be made to achieve mutual understanding; for the benefit of all, let them together preserve peace, liberty, social justice and moral values."[17] This is another example of how Christians are expected to promote reconciliation between people of different faiths.

The Church calls for the building of bridges not only among Christians, but also among all other believers, even among atheists and agnostics. This is seen in the document *Gaudium et Spes,* particularly when it mentions atheism: "Although the church altogether rejects atheism, it nevertheless sincerely proclaims that all men and women, those who believe as well as those who do not, should help to establish right order in this world where all live together. This certainly cannot be done without a dialogue that is sincere and prudent."[18] It is not enough for us to live in peace on earth; indeed, it is our responsibility to make peace on earth for others to be able to live in, too. Every human being on this earth has a right to live in a peaceful manner, and Christians have a role in making this possible.

The 'Catholicity' and Universality of Redemption

The Church is a universal body; thus, she must be 'catholic' in her mission. Jesus entrusts her with this mission. "We know that Christ, being raised from the dead, will never die again; death no longer has dominion over him. The death he died, he died to sin, once for all; but the life he lives, he lives to God." (Rom 6:9-10). It is the Church's duty to make available this redemptive love for all. "It is clear that our former approach to missionary activity would need to be rethought, now that activity must aim at more than the conversion of others to Roman Catholicism. Rather, the first task must be to serve as presence of Christ among all nations, to be sign of the universality of Christian redemptions."[19] Because the church holds the position that there is a "ray of truth" in other religions, this enables her to accept the other as a co-pilgrim towards this universal redemption.

Human beings are created in the image and likeness of God (Gen 1:26), making them dignified persons. "Human dignity rests above all on the fact that humanity is called to communion with God."[20] The dignity of the human beings must be affirmed and they have the right to be part of this universal redemption because Christ has died for *all*. "The church holds that to acknowledge God is in no way to diminish human dignity, since such dignity is grounded and brought to perfection in God. Women and men have in fact been placed in world by God, who created them as intelligent and free beings; but over and above this they are called as daughters and sons to intimacy with God and to share in his happiness."[21] We are called to partake in this communion as brothers and sisters of one another and as sons and daughters of God, so that the universal salvation is brought about on the earth.

Catholicism vis-à-vis Other Religions

Even though one can say that NA acknowledges that every religion holds a "ray of truth", it mentions only major four religions by name. It begins with the Hinduism: "in Hinduism people explore the divine mystery and express it both in the limitless riches of myth and the accurately defined insights of philosophy. They seek release from the trials of the present life by ascetical practices, profound meditation and recourse to God in confidence and love."[22] This is not a full description of Hinduism; it instead demonstrates the richness of its spiritual values and its destinies, all of which enable the Church to dialogue with this religion, especially in a country like ours in India, where the majority are now in this category.[23] "A dialogue, therefore, has become inevitable, which in its turn demands a deep understanding and sympathetic appraisal of this extremely complex religions."[24]

Though VC II was not able to make particular statements on each branch of Buddhism, it made a profound general statement on Buddhism, saying, "Buddhism in its various forms testifies to the essential inadequacy of this changing world. It proposes a way of life by which people can, with confidence and trust, attain a state of perfect liberation and reach supreme illumination either through their own efforts or by the aid of divine help."[25]

The same paragraph in NA continues with a reference to other religions that are found throughout the world, without naming any of them individually. However, the document still speaks of these religions with esteem. "So, too, other religions which are found throughout the world attempt in different ways to overcome the restlessness of people's hearts by outlining a programme of life covering doctrine, moral precepts and sacred rites."[26] These religions include all tribal religions, but the document focuses on Islam and Judaism, which are considered by the council as Abrahamic religions along with Christianity.

The Council began the statement in NA affirming the Abrahamic origin of Islam. The document affirms that the Church has high regard for Muslims. It affirms that Muslims and Christians worship the same God, who is one living and subsistent, merciful and almighty, the Creator of heaven and earth, who has spoken to humanity.[27] Muslims try to commit to God through their 'five pillars'. The document emphasises that "they endeavour to submit themselves without reserve to the hidden decrees of God, just as Abraham, submitted himself to God's plan, to whose faith Muslims eagerly link their own."[28]

The document then shows the link between Islam and Christianity. "Although not acknowledging him as God, they venerate Jesus as a prophet; his virgin Mother they also honour, and even at times devoutly invoke."[29] They also await the day of judgment and the reward of God following the resurrection of the dead as result of their earthly pilgrim commitment.[30] "For this reason," the council says of the Muslims that "they highly esteem an upright life and worship God, especially by way of prayer, alms-deeds and fasting."[31] When the council acknowledges its agreement on Islam in regarding unity of God, it is also aware of the past wounds that have to be healed in a proper way with proper dialogue.

Though in the end, the document spoke about other religions, the initial intent was to create a document on Judaism. There have been so many unhealed wounds between Christians and Jews that have even been expressed in the liturgy and in the Catechism. On the eve of the Council's opening, the chief Rabbi of Rome stated that "the Jews hope that the Council, in accordance with the shining examples given by Pope John XXIII, will understand the need to eliminate all expressions still in use in the liturgy and in religious instruction which continue even today to evoke mistrust and ill-will towards the Jews."[32] Indeed, it was a hope that was fulfilled. VC II affirmed the common heritage of both the Church and the Jews.

The Council also encouraged the faithful to have a mutual understanding and appreciation.[33] "This can be achieved, especially, by way of biblical and theological enquiry and through friendly discussions."³⁴ The influence of the document on the forthcoming relationship of these Abrahamic religions was later seen when Pope Francis and King Mohammed VI signed an appeal regarding Jerusalem / *Al-Quds* the holy city and a place of encounter. The statement says, "We consider it important to preserve the Holy City of Jerusalem / Al-Quds Acharif as the common patrimony of humanity and especially the followers of the three monotheistic religions, as a place of encounter and as a symbol of peaceful coexistence, where mutual respect and dialogue can be cultivated."³⁵

II. Pope Francis and Other Religions

Pope Francis is known for his bold, prophetic actions. He travelled to many countries as a pilgrim and met many religious heads. "Pope Francis has travelled and addressed international questions much more than most would have expected at the beginning of his Pontificate."³⁶ During each visit he attempts to meet the heads of other Christian churches and religious groups and that country's most vulnerable people.

Archbishop Bernardito Auza says, "I see one golden thread tying all the words and actions of Pope Francis together, a unifying inspiration that has overarching implications not only on the pastoral and spiritual activities of the Church, but also on primary socioeconomic and political concerns of our time."³⁷ And "that golden thread would be the theme and practice of encounter, of dialogue, of building bridges rather than walls, of the globalization of solidarity over a globalization of indifference."³⁸ He has promoted the habit of dialogue among peoples and cultures. The archbishop affirmed again, "People pause to listen to his words and many act on them because, as Catholics and non-Catholics often they admit, they see him as a credible leader, a moral authority, a persuasive teacher, an authentic 'Pontifex' or bridge-builder."³⁹

Evangelii Gaudium: New Approach to Dialogue

Pope Francis' Apostolic Exhortation *Evangelii Gaudium* is a document on new evangelization. In this document he set apart a section called 'Social dialogue as a contribution to peace' [nos. 238-258] dedicated to the themes of dialogue and peace. He says, "A dialogue which seeks social peace and justice is in itself, beyond all merely practical considerations, an ethical commitment which brings about a new social situation. Efforts made in dealing with a specific theme can become a process in which, by mutual listening, both parts can be purified and enriched. These efforts, therefore, can also express love for truth."[40] The pope expects mutual respect and listening to one another in the dialogue with other religions. He expects it from both sides. He also said, "In this dialogue, ever friendly and sincere, attention must always be paid to the essential bond between dialogue and proclamation, which leads the Church to maintain and intensify her relationship with non-Christians."[41]

Friendship and Respect

During the plenary assembly of the Pontifical Council for Interreligious Dialogue on November 28, 2013, Pope Francis said that "the Catholic Church is aware of the value of promoting friendship and respect among men and women of different religious traditions. We increasingly understand its importance, both because in a certain sense the world has become 'smaller' and because the phenomenon of migration increases contact between persons and communities from various traditions, cultures and religions."[42]

Pope Francis has widened the Church's circle of friendships. Furthermore, he has embraced not only theists but also atheists into his circle. He has commented on homosexual people with respect, saying "who am I to judge them?" The Pope has also said, "The dialogue that we need cannot but be open and respectful, and thus prove fruitful. Mutual respect is the condition and, at the same time, the aim of interreligious dialogue: respecting others' right to life, to physical integrity, to fundamental freedoms, namely freedom of conscience, of thought, of expression and of religion."[43]

Pope Francis' respect for the other must be seen in the context of his reflection on Genesis 1:27 and on NA. Scripture and the NA document both speak about the 'origin of human beings from God'. The pope always gave importance for the diversity of cultures and embraced all. His words make it clear that God created every human being uniquely. He affirms this by saying that fraternity certainly "also embraces variety and differences between brothers and sisters, even though they are linked by birth and are of the same nature and dignity." Religious plurality is an expression of this; in such a context the right attitude is neither a forced uniformity nor a conciliatory syncretism."[44]

Openness in Evangelization

As we have already seen, NA emphasizes the "ray of truth" in other religions. Pope Francis explained this in *Evangelii Gaudium* explaining that "an attitude of openness in truth and in love must characterize the dialogue with the followers of non-Christian religions, in spite of various obstacles and difficulties, especially forms of fundamentalism on both sides."[45] Interreligious dialogue is not an optional mission for Pope Francis: "it is a necessary condition for peace in the world, and so it is a duty for Christians as well as other religious communities."[46] He goes on to explain that "this dialogue is in first place a conversation about human existence or simply, as the bishops of India have put it, a matter of "being open to them, sharing their joys and sorrows."[47] Making peace in the world is our fundamental duty as missionaries. And this peace must be made in love and respect, not with any violence. The Pope affirms, "In this way we learn to accept others and their different ways of living, thinking and speaking. We can then join one another in taking up the duty of serving justice and peace, which should become a basic principle of all our exchanges."[48]

Pope Francis continues that "true openness involves remaining steadfast in one's deepest convictions, clear and joyful in one's own identity, while at the same time being "open to understanding those of the other party and knowing that dialogue can enrich each side."[49] He also warns that this dialogue is not just for the benefit of keeping things calm and peaceful, but it is more about enriching relationships with the other. "What is not helpful is a diplomatic openness which says 'yes' to everything in order to avoid problems, for this would be a way of deceiving others and denying them the good which we have been given to share generously with others. Evangelization and interreligious dialogue, far from being opposed, mutually support and nourish one another."[50]

Pope Francis invites every Christian to encounter the other as a brother or sister with respect. He says:

> The world, looking to us believers, exhorts us to cooperate amongst ourselves and with the men and women of good will who profess no religion, asking us for effective responses regarding numerous issues: peace, hunger, the poverty that afflicts millions of people, the environmental crisis, violence, especially that committed in the name of religion, corruption, moral decay, the crisis of the family, of the economy, of finance, and especially of hope.[51]

"Human Fraternity for World Peace and Living Together"

A document on "Human Fraternity for World Peace and Living Together" was signed by His Holiness Pope Francis and the Grand Imam of Al-Azhar Ahamad al-Tayyib in Abu Dhabi on February 4, 2019. This document opens up by stressing our common brotherhood:

> In the name of God who has created all human beings equal in rights, duties and dignity, and who has called them to live together as brothers and sisters, to fill the earth and make known the values of goodness, love and peace. ..... In the name of human fraternity that embraces all human beings, unites them and renders them equal; In the name of this fraternity torn apart by policies of extremism and division, by systems of unrestrained profit or by hateful ideological tendencies that manipulate the actions and the future of men and women ....[52]

Just as NA refers to humanity's 'origin and destiny,' this document also speaks on human beings' final destiny as the result of the responsibility we undertake on this earth as brothers and sisters: "We, who believe in God and in the final meeting with Him and His judgment, on the basis of our religious and moral responsibility."[53] Moreover, it invites both Christians and Muslims "to work strenuously to spread the culture of tolerance and of living together in peace; to intervene at the earliest opportunity to stop the shedding of innocent blood and bring an end to wars, conflicts, environmental decay and the moral and cultural decline that the world is presently experiencing."[54] Indeed, the document on

Human Fraternity is an invitation to work as sons and daughters of same creator.

The document also explains that: "Dialogue among believers means coming together in the vast space of spiritual, human and shared social values and, from here, transmitting the highest moral virtues that religions aim for. It also means avoiding unproductive discussions."[55] Pope Francis has great hope for this document, which he affirmed in the interview on his return flight. He said, "The document was prepared with much reflection and indeed prayer. Both the Grand Imam with his team, and I with mine, prayed a great deal to make this document come to fruition. Because for me there is only one great danger at this moment: destruction, war, hatred among us." He lamented, "And if we believers are not able to shake hands, embrace, kiss one another and pray, then our faith will be defeated."[56]

Conclusion

Pope Francis proclaims in words and affirms through his deeds that "human beings are created in the image and likeness of God" (Gen 1:26). God forms 'Common Humanity' and 'Human Fraternity' in which diversity is not denied but appreciated and fostered. Human beings are equal in rights, duties and dignity, and God has called them to live together as brothers and sisters, to fill the earth and make known the values of goodness, love and peace.[57] The Pope invites all human beings to "God who is Father of all and Father of peace and condemns all destruction, all terrorism, from the first instance of terrorism in history, which is that of Cain."[58] The ultimate aim of every human person is to restore communion with the Creator and to remember that each person is created "in His image and likeness".

The mission to return to the Creator is not an isolated and individualistic mission, because we all are created in the world of plurality. Faith in the Creator enables the faithful to understand the plurality of the world. This plurality has to be understood in the context of culture and religion. The real believer will be the person who builds bridges between religions and cultures. Pope Francis has said that "religions cannot renounce the urgent task of building bridges between peoples and cultures."[59] Religion, however, is not meant only to *unmask evil*; it has an intrinsic vocation to promote peace, today, more than ever. Francis adds, "Without giving in to forms of facile syncretism, our task is that of praying for one another, imploring God the gift of peace in encountering one another; and engaging in dialogue and promoting harmony in the spirit of cooperation and friendship."[60]

Endnotes

[1] Pope Francis, Daily meditation on May 22, 2013, accessible at the website: http://www.vatican.va/content/francesco/en/cotidie/2013/documents/papa-francesco-cotidie_20130522_to-do-good.html

[2] Ibid.

[3] Pope Francis, Interreligious Meeting in Abu Dhabi, on February 4, 2019.

[4] Ibid.

[5] Ibid.

[6] Ibid.

[7] John M Oesterreicher, "Declaration on the Relationship of the Church to Non-Christian Religions," in *Commentary on the Documents of Vatican II*, ed. Herbert Vorgrimler (New York: Crossroad, 1989), 1.

[8] *Nostra Aetate* (NA), no. 1.

[9] Ibid.

[10] Oesterreicher, "Declaration on the Relationship of the Church," 40.

[11] NA 2.

[12] Oesterreicher, "Declaration on the Relationship of the Church," 1.

[13] NA 2.

[14] NA 2.

[15] Ibid.

[16] Ibid.

[17] NA 3.

[18] *Gaudium et Spes* (hereinafter GS), n. 21.

[19] Maureen Sullivan, *101 Questions and Answers on Vatican II* (Mahwah, NJ: Paulist Press, 2002), 61.

[20] GS 19.

[21] GS 20.

[22] NA 2.

[23] Cyril B. Papali, "Excursus on Hinduism," in *Commentary on the Documents of Vatican II*, ed. Herbert Vorgrimler (New York: Crossroad, 1989), 137.

[24] Ibid. 137.

[25] NA 2.

[26] NA 2.

[27] NA 3.

[28] Ibid.

[29] Ibid.

[30] Ibid.

[31] Ibid.

[32] Oesterreicher, "Declaration on the Relationship of the Church," 42.

[33] NA 4.

[34] NA 4.

[35] Appeal by His Majesty King Mohammed VI And His Holiness Pope Francis Regarding Jerusalem / Al-Quds The Holy City and A Place of Encounter, http://w2.vatican.va/content/francesco/en/speeches/2019/march/documents/papa-francesco_20190330_appello-marocco.html (accessed on November 9, 2019).

[36] Archbishop Bernardito Auza, "An Overview from the Point of View Pope Francis," *The Journal of Corporate Citizenship* (December 2016): 17.

[37] Ibid.

[38] Ibid.

[39] Ibid.

[40] *Evangelii Gaudium* (EG), n. 250.

[41] EG 51.

[42] Pope Francis, *Address of Pope Francis To Participants in The Plenary Assembly of The Pontifical Council for Interreligious Dialogue*, 28 November 2013, https://w2.vatican.va/content/francesco/en/speeches/2013/november/documents/papa-francesco_20131128_pc-dialogo-interreligioso.html (accessed November 9, 2019).

[43] Pope Francis, *On the Occasion of the 50th Anniversary of the Promulgation of the Conciliar Declaration "Nostra Aetate"*, 28 October 2015, http://w2.vatican.va/content/francesco/en/audiences/2015/documents/papa-francesco_20151028_udienza-generale.html (accessed November 9, 2019).

[44] Pope Francis, Interreligious Meeting in Abu Dhabi, on February 4, 2019.

[45] EG 250.

[46] Ibid.

[47] Ibid.

[48] Ibid.

⁴⁹ EG 251.

⁵⁰ Ibid.

⁵¹ Pope Francis, *On the Occasion of the 50ᵗʰ Anniversary of the Promulgation of the Conciliar Declaration "Nostra Aetate"* http://w2.vatican.va/content/francesco/en/audiences/2015/documents/papa-francesco_20151028_udienza-generale.html (accessed November 23, 2019).

⁵² Pope Francis and the Grand Imam of Al-Azhar Ahamad al-Tayyib, *Human Fraternity for World Peace and Living Together*, February 4, 2019.

⁵³ Ibid.

⁵⁴ Ibid.

⁵⁵ Pope Francis, Press Conference on the Return Flight from Abu Dhabi to Rome, February 5, 2019, http://w2.vatican.va/content/francesco/en/speeches/2019/february/documents/papa-francesco_20190205_emiratiarabi-voloritorno.html (accessed November 9, 2019).

⁵⁶ Ibid.

⁵⁷ Pope Francis and the Grand Imam of Al-Azhar Ahamad al-Tayyib, Human Fraternity for World Peace and Living Together, February 4, 2019.

⁵⁸ Pope Francis, Press Conference on the Return Flight from Abu Dhabi to Rome.

⁵⁹ Pope Francis, Speech Abu Dhabi on Feb. 4.

⁶⁰ Pope Francis, Francis, Speech at the International Peace Conference, April 28, 2017.

24.

The Joys and the Hopes, the Griefs and the Anxieties Being in, with and for our Common Home

Kuruvilla Pandikattu, SJ

The joys and the hopes, the griefs and the anxieties of the men [sic] of this age, especially those who are poor or in any way afflicted, these are the joys and hopes, the griefs and anxieties of the followers of Christ. Indeed, nothing genuinely human fails to raise an echo in their hearts.
(Vatican Council II, *Gaudium et Spes* n.1)
We have the power to make this the best generation of mankind in the history of the world or make it the last.
(John F. Kennedy)[1]

1. Inspired by Vatican Council II

This article tries to situate the prophetic message of Pope Francis in the broader context of Vatican Council II (hereinafter VC II) and specifically its landmark document *Gaudium et Spes* (Latin, meaning, joy and hope), which seeks to explore the relationship between the Church and the world. After exploring the challenges posed by VC II for both an inner and outer dialogue, we look at some of the joys and griefs of the present world. Then we try to connect the pope's message with the challenges facing the world today. Finally, we study the Amazon Synod and its significance for the Church and the world.

1.1. Pope Paul VI: VC II's Concluding Message to Thinkers and Scientists

I begin with the concluding words of Pope Paul VI on December 8, 1965, the last day of VC II, addressed to the "men of thought and science." He began with these words: "A very special greeting to you, seekers after truth, to you, men [sic] of thought and science, the explorers of man [sic], of the universe and of history, to all of you who are pilgrims enroute to the light and to those also who have stopped along the road, tired and disappointed by their vain search."[2]

The Pope summed up the activities of VC II as an "attentive search for and deepening of the message of truth entrusted to the Church and an effort at more perfect docility to the spirit of truth." So the path of the Church and that of the thinkers and scientists would cross. "Your road is ours. Your paths are never foreign to ours. We are the friends of your vocation as searchers, companions in your fatigues, admirers of your successes and, if necessary, consolers in your discouragement and your failures."[3]

He urged them: "Continue your search without tiring and without ever despairing of the truth. Recall the words of one of your great friends, St Augustine: 'Let us seek with the desire to find, and find with the desire to seek still more.' Happy are those who, while possessing the truth, search more earnestly for it in order to renew it, deepen it and transmit it to others. Happy also are those who, not having found it, are working toward it with a sincere heart. May they seek the light of tomorrow with the light of today until they reach the fullness of light."[4]

The Holy Father asserted that thinking is a great duty and responsibility. "Woe to those who voluntarily close their eyes to the light. Thinking is also a responsibility, so woe to those who darken the spirit by the thousand tricks which degrade it, make it proud, deceive and deform it. What other basic principle is there for men [sic] of science except to think rightly?"[5] In this holy search and thinking, the Holy Father offers scientists and thinkers, the mysterious lamp which is faith, entrusted to the Church by Jesus, who said, "I am the light of the world, I am the way, the truth and the life."

Never perhaps has there been so clear a possibility as today of a deep understanding between real science and real faith, mutual servants of one another in the one truth. He urged them to "have confidence in faith, this great friend of intelligence. Enlighten yourselves with its light in order to take hold of truth, the whole truth. This is the wish, the encouragement and the hope, which, before disbanding, is expressed to you by the Fathers of the entire world assembled at Rome in council."[6]

1.1. *The Trailblazing Gaudium et Spes (GS)*

Widely heralded as a landmark of Catholic social teaching, the wide-ranging document *Gaudium et Spes* was proclaimed just one day before the end of the Council: December 7, 1965. Divided into two parts, "The Church and Man's Calling" and "Some Problems of Special Urgency," this is one of the four Constitutions. Addressing "the whole of humanity," VC II "yearns to explain to everyone how it conceives of the presence and activity of the Church in the world of today" (GS 2).[7] I quote verbatim some of the sections of GS below:

1.1.1. *A New Age of Human History (GS 54)*

The circumstances of the life of human beings today have been so profoundly changed in their social and cultural aspects, that we can speak of a new age of human history. New ways are open, therefore, for the perfection and further extension of culture. These ways have been prepared by the enormous growth of natural, human and social sciences, by technical progress, and advances in developing and organizing means whereby men can communicate with one another. Hence the culture of today possesses particular characteristics: sciences which are called exact greatly develop critical judgment; the more recent psychological studies more profoundly explain human activity; historical studies make it much easier to see things in their mutable and evolutionary aspects, customs and usages are becoming more and more uniform; industrialization, urbanization, and other causes which promote community living create a mass-culture from which are born new ways of thinking, acting and making use of leisure. The increase of commerce between the various nations and human groups opens more widely to all the treasures of different civilizations and thus little by little, there develops a more universal form of human culture, which better promotes and expresses the unity of the human race to the degree that it preserves the particular aspects of the different civilizations.

1.1.2. *From Autonomy to Closer Bond between Religion and Society (GS 36)*

Now many of our contemporaries seem to fear that a closer bond between human activity and religion will work against the independence of men, of societies, or of the sciences. If by the autonomy of earthly affairs we mean that created things and societies themselves enjoy their own laws and values which must be gradually deciphered, put to use, and regulated by men, then it is entirely right to demand that autonomy. Such is not merely required by modern man, but harmonizes also with the will of the Creator. For by the very circumstance of their having been created, all things are endowed with their own stability, truth, goodness, proper laws and order. Man must respect these as he isolates them by the appropriate methods of the individual sciences or arts. Therefore, if methodical investigation within every branch of learning is carried out in a genuinely scientific manner and in accord with moral norms, it never truly conflicts with faith, for earthly matters and the concerns of faith derive from the same God. Indeed whoever labors to penetrate the secrets of reality with a humble and steady mind, even though he is unaware of the fact, is nevertheless being led by the hand of God, who holds all things in existence, and gives them their identity. Consequently, we cannot but deplore certain habits of mind, which are sometimes found too among Christians, which do not sufficiently attend to the rightful independence of science and which, from the arguments and controversies they spark, lead many minds to conclude that faith and science are mutually opposed.

1.1.3. Earthly Progress and Kingdom of God (GS 39)

Therefore, while we are warned that it profits a man nothing if he gain the whole world and lose himself, the expectation of a new earth must not weaken but rather stimulate our concern for cultivating this one. For here grows the body of a new human family, a body which even now is able to give some kind of foreshadowing of the new age. Hence, while earthly progress must be carefully distinguished from the growth of Christ's kingdom, to the extent that the former can contribute to the better ordering of human society, it is of vital concern to the kingdom of God.

1.3. Challenge for Inner and Outer Dialogue

Writing fifty years after the constitution, an American Jesuit David Hollenbach reflects on the impact of this document "Pastoral Constitution on the Church in the Modern World." According to him, this document "laid out the most challenging vision of the church's social mission of the modern era. It proclaimed that the Catholic community should be deeply engaged in promoting the dignity of every person, and this proclamation bore significant fruit in the church's participation in the struggle for human rights."[8]

The constitution presents a "hope-filled vision of the human condition and an inspiring call to move forward on the path to realize this vision."[9] Its inspiring message describes how Christ's grace could energize one's whole life, drawing mind and heart into the service of God and of those who suffer because of social neglect or exclusion. So, according to Hollenbach, the constitution calls for a two-fold dialogue:

> First, *Gaudium et Spes* saw dialogue with the secular world as a key source of the church's development of a deeper vision of its social role. The Catholic community and its leaders must listen to the many voices speaking about the

challenges we face, whether these voices come from Rome, from Washington, from the poor in our cities, in barrios or in refugee camps. We need to hear from Catholics and other Christians, from Jews, Muslims and Buddhists, and from those of no explicit faith at all as we seek to develop a more energetic response to challenges of justice and peace today.[10]

Indeed *GS* called the church to "step up this exchange" (GS 44) in order to formulate a more adequate Christian response to the needs of our world with deep hope and joy.

> Second, the church needs to develop structures to enable clergy and laity to enter into a more serious dialogue about how the Catholic community should respond to the challenges of public life today. Laypeople have deep experience of engagement in all facets of our public life, and the Catholic community must learn from this experience. ... Both the outer dialogue, with the larger society, and the inner dialogue, among members of the church, are essential to effective public engagement.[11]

> Finally, both of these forms of dialogue must be sustained by a radical trust that the world we seek to serve is truly God's world. God is the creator of all and is already present laboring in this world. Christ the redeemer and Christ's creator Spirit are already active within this world, beckoning it forward in grace and love. Despite the struggles and wounds of our social life, discerning engagement does not threaten our fidelity to the Gospel. Quite the opposite. Renewing the council's vision that we can really make a difference would once again bring us joy and hope as we work for justice and peace.[12]

2. Joys and Griefs of Our Present World

In the context of VC II and the necessity of the Church to encounter the world, we take up some concerns and joys of the contemporary world.

2.1. *Fourth Industrial Revolution (2016-)*

The mutual convergence of various technologies of the Third Industrial Revolution made the Fourth Revolution (hereinafter FIR) possible.[13] At this phase, FIR has moved away from the technological revolution to societal transformation. Life went from being all about the farm to all about the factory, and people moved from the country into town with the introduction of mechanical production. How people lived, worked and thought changed fundamentally with the discovery of electricity, electronics and mass production. The digital revolution altered nearly every industry, once again transforming how people live, work, and communicate.

Many dreams of people are being realised in unexpected ways: From robots to genetic sequencing and editing, artificial intelligence, miniaturized sensors, and 3D printing, etc. This is the beginning of the FIR! Klaus Schwab, Executive Chairman of the World Economic Forum first introduced this idea, taking into account the advances of AI, robotics, Internet of Things, machine learning and other technologies, which contribute to the FIR.[14]

Prof Schwab thinks that the world is on the verge of the FIR "that will fundamentally alter the way we live, work, and relate to one another. In its scale, scope, and complexity, the transformation will be unlike anything humankind has experienced before."[15] Internet of Things (IoT), artificial intelligence and the (im)perfect blend of the physical with the digital is poised to drive the FIR.

This Revolution can literally be disrupting every business, as we know it, and yet integrating every business in an odd way. How? Artificial intelligence, robotics, autonomous cars, advancement in biotech and genomics will all be part of the industrial revolution 4.0. Many economists are apprehensive of the FIR and its effect on job creation. According to MIT Sloan School of Management economists, Erik Brynjolfsson and Andrew McAfee, the revolution is likely "to increase inequality in the world as the spread of machines increases markets and disrupts labour markets."[16]

FIR focuses on smart technologies and connected devices. According to some reliable reports, by 2022, more than 28 billion devices will be connected. That's up from 18 billion devices in 2017. While these numbers can sound overwhelming, it also offers huge global opportunities, allowing people to securely connect to any device, on any network, to any application. That's the beauty of the rollout of 5G and Wi-Fi 6, which promise faster speeds and better reliability.[17]

The rate of current breakthroughs is historically unprecedented.[18] When compared with previous industrial revolutions, the FIR is evolving at an exponential rather than a linear pace. It may be claimed that FIR is conceptualised as an upgrade on the third revolution and is marked by a fusion of technologies straddling the physical, digital and biological worlds.

The FIR will change not only what we do but also who we are. It will affect our identity and all the issues associated with it: our sense of privacy, our notions of ownership, our consumption patterns, the time we devote to work and leisure, and how we develop our careers, cultivate our skills, meet people, and nurture relationships.[19]

Also, the revolutions occurring in biotechnology, which are redefining what it means to be human by pushing back the current thresholds of life span, health, cognition, and capabilities, will compel us to redefine our moral and ethical boundaries too. As to the challenges and possibilities posed by FIR: In its most pessimistic, dehumanized form, the FIR may indeed have the potential to "robotize" humanity and thus to deprive us of our heart and soul. But as a complement to the best parts of human nature—creativity, empathy, stewardship—it can also lift humanity into a new collective and moral consciousness based on a shared sense of destiny.[20] All of us are challenged to make sure the latter prevails. We should thus grasp the opportunity and power we have to shape the FIR and direct it toward a future that reflects our common objectives and values.[21] Are we ready to choose the optimistic and interconnected vision of the world? Or do we choose for a robotic world devoid of human values and even human beings?

2.2. *The Holocene Extinction (starting from 2000 AD)*

Otherwise referred to as the Sixth Mass Extinction or Anthropocene Extinction, this is an ongoing activity during the present Holocene epoch and is caused by human activity.[22] Alarming declines in the number of insects, vertebrates and plant species around the world have raised fears that we are in the midst of a sixth major extinction that could cause a collapse of the natural ecosystems we rely upon to survive.[23]

Urgent international action is needed to halt this potentially catastrophic decline in biodiversity, according to Professor Georgina Mace, head of the Centre for Biodiversity and Environmental Research at University College London, UK. While Prof. Mace believes that we're only on the brink of this extinction, she says the threat is so severe that biodiversity loss needs to be addressed on a global scale in a similar way to climate change.[24]

The warning was delivered by a British scientist, Professor Sir Robert Watson, chair of the UN's Intergovernmental Science-Policy Platform on Biodiversity and Ecosystem Services (IPBES), speaking in Paris. He told an IPBES meeting held to approve the summary of its new global assessment report on the state of life on Earth that the implications for human life were grave. The overwhelming evidence gathered in the assessment presented "an ominous picture. The health of ecosystems on which we and all other species depend is deteriorating more rapidly than ever.[25]

"We are eroding the very foundations of our economies, livelihoods, food security, health and quality of life worldwide." But Professor Watson, a previous chairperson of the UN's Intergovernmental Panel on Climate Change (IPCC), does not preach despair. Despite the "truly unsustainable rate" of species loss that would affect human wellbeing for this generation and for its descendants, despite the accelerating pace of extinction, he believes there is still hope.[26]

"We are in trouble if we don't act, but there are a range of actions that can be taken to protect nature and meet individual goals for health and development. It is not too late to make a difference, but only if we start now at every level from local to global." Transformative change, system-wide and including goals and values, could allow humankind to restore nature and to use it sustainably, he said. This might have been aided by the Christian vision of the world and human beings.[27]

"The essential, interconnected web of life on Earth is getting smaller and increasingly frayed," said Professor Josef Settele, one of the co-chairs of the global assessment, of the Helmholtz Centre for Environmental Research in Germany. "This loss is a direct result of human activity and constitutes a direct threat to human well-being in all regions of the world."[28] It holds that there are five main causes of the crisis. In descending order they are: changes in land and sea use; direct exploitation of animals and plants; climate change; pollution; and invasive alien species.[29]

Scientists point out that unlike the five earlier great waves of extinction to have occurred on the planet, this one is human-driven. IPBES has clearly explained that humankind and its activities are responsible for what is happening, and that we shall have to pay the price. "Fundamental changes on a planetary system scale have already begun," said co-author Peter Haff, a geologist and engineer with Duke University. "The very considerable uncertainty is how long these will last – whether they will simply be a brief, unique excursion in Earth history, or whether they will persist and evolve into a new, geologically long-lasting, planetary state."[30]

2.3. *The Best or the Last Generation*

It is here that we recall the prophetic words of the former American President, John F Kennedy. "We have the power to make this the best generation of mankind in the history of the world or make it the last." *Das Beste oder das Lezte!* The comforts we enjoy, the possibilities we possess, the information we own, the health and social securities we dream and political and economic structures we have created are unimaginable even for generations fifty years ago. We have the resources to make this the best! In terms of freedom, egalitarianism, security and well-being! At the same time, we are all aware that we can make of this the last! Tragic indeed!

It is said that the next 100 years of technological growth is equal to 20000 years of earlier growth. If we come together, we can truly create the most marvellous life for ourselves in terms of physical wellness, economic equality, psychological integration, intellectual openness and spiritual depth. We do have the resources at our disposal, which previous generations lacked. Can we truly realise our own strength and make of this world the best place for humanity (and other living beings)? If we decide collectively and give up our greed and avarice, we can!

3. Pope Francis' Prophetic Actions

It is in this context of the Church's openness to the world and the willingness to share its joys and joys, that we look at the work and words of Pope Francis. We limit ourselves only to three encounters.

3.1. *Mingling with Migrants at Lampedusa*

On July 8, 2013 just three months after his Papacy, Pope Francis celebrated mass on the tiny Sicilian island of Lampedusa on Monday to commemorate thousands of migrants who have died crossing the sea from North Africa, underlining his drive to put the poor at the heart of his papacy.[31] The choice of Lampedusa for his first official trip outside Rome was highly symbolic for the pontiff, who said news reports of the deaths of desperate people trying to reach a better life that had been like "a thorn in the heart."

Thousands of islanders waving caps and banners in the Vatican's yellow colors welcomed Francis at the fishing port where he arrived aboard a coastguard vessel accompanied by a flotilla of fishing boats and cast a wreath into the water.

He spoke to young African migrants before celebrating mass in a sports field that served as a reception center for tens of thousands of mainly Muslim migrants who fled the Arab Spring unrest in North Africa in 2011, greatly increasing an exodus that has gone on for years. His trip came at the start of the summer months when the island, one of the main points of entry into the European Union and just 113 kms (70 miles) from Tunisia, sees a steady flow of rickety and unsafe boats arriving on its shores.

He saluted the migrants, many of whom are preparing to fast during Ramadan, and thanked the people of Lampedusa for taking them in and setting an example of solidarity to a selfish society sliding into "the globalization of indifference." "We have become used to other people's suffering, it doesn't concern us, it doesn't interest us, it's none of our business!" he said during his homily from an altar built from an old fishing boat painted in Italy's red, green and white colors. He had harsh words for people smugglers who he said profited from the misery of others as well and asked pardon for "those, whose decisions at a global level have created the conditions which have led us to this drama."[32] During the mass he used a wooden chalice carved from the wood of a migrant vessel by a local carpenter.

3.2. Embracing the Man with Neurofibromatosis

Pope Francis embraced several people with severe skin disorders in Vatican City on Nov 7, 2013, and photos of him kissing the head of a disfigured man with neurofibromatosis have gone viral. Many say the present pope is a pope of the people and truly manifests Christian ideology of treating people with equality, taking to the streets to help the poor, and reaching out to stigmatized members of society. *The Washington Post* called his embrace of the neurofibromatosis victim as "the image worth a thousand words."

Neurofibromatosis is a rare genetic disorder that causes tumours— usually benign— to grow from the ends of nerves, and can cause severe disfiguration. Sometimes, the tumours can become cancerous, according to the National Institutes of Health. It can be both a physically and emotionally devastating disease.[33] Some people said that Pope Francis is living up to the ideals of his namesake, Francis of Assisi, a preeminent figure who considered himself a servant to the poor and destitute.[34]

3.3. Meeting with World Leaders and Scientists

In this spirit of humility and dialogue, the Pope has been meeting many world leaders, including Obama, Trump, Trudeau, Merkel and Putin. Some of the scientists he met are Stephen Hawking and Mark

Zuckerberg. Here I shall be focussing on two meetings the Pope had with scientists.

On May 27, 2019, the Pontifical Academy of Sciences and United Nations Initiative, SDSN, hosted a meeting between Pope Francis, Climate Scientists, and more than twenty Finance Ministers to discuss the Sustainable Development Goals and climate change. In line with Pope Francis' encyclical *Laudato Si'* (Care for our Common Home), the objective of the meeting was for climate experts and finance ministers to discuss new data and enhance awareness on climate change and sustainable development. The meeting specifically focused on the role of innovative climate financing as a critical next step to realize the Paris Agreement.[35]

In the context of the April launch of the Coalition of Finance Ministers for Climate Action, co-chaired by Chile and Finland, discussions taken place during this meeting provided additional perspectives for Finance Ministers to consider in their efforts to strengthen collective action on the matter. More specifically, the Coalition recently endorsed the Helsinki Principles, a set of six common principles that foster climate action, especially through the use of fiscal policy. Leading up to COP25 that will take place in Chile this December, discussions supported work geared towards the Santiago Action Plan, a set of concrete actions that will be taken to make tangible progress to tackle climate change.

In an earlier address to the Pontifical Academy of Science, Pope Francis acknowledged that the scientific world is more aware of how complex the world and human beings are. He noted that this has led science to be less isolated and more open to spiritual and religious values. "Commonly shared opinions" and the "desire for happiness" often influence scientific research, the Pope added. Therefore, the relationship between values and people, society and science "demands a rethinking" that promotes the "integral advancement" of each person and the common good. As a part of society, the scientific community is called to serve humanity and its integral development, the Pope said.[36]

Some areas Pope Francis named as "possible fruits" of that service of sciences are: climate change, nuclear arms, fossil fuels, and deforestation. Science has identified the risks in these areas, the Pope said, so they can also propose convincing solutions to the world's leaders.

4. A Case Study: The Amazon Synod

Openness to the world and the ability to rejoice and emphathise with it have been the hallmark of both VC II and Pope Francis. Paradoxically, such noble intent normally leads to opposition and criticism as well as appreciation. We can take the recently concluded Amazon Synod as a concrete case for this kind of mixed reception.

4.1. The Synod

The Amazon synod opened on Sunday, October 6, 2019, with Mass in St. Peter's Square. Like everything else in this pontificate, the synod is surrounded in controversy, not because it needs to be so, but because the professional haters of Pope Francis now insist that everything he does or says is wrong or evil or heretical.

Cardinal-designate Jesuit Fr. Michael Czerny and Dominican Bishop David Martínez de Aguirre did a fine job explaining the rationale for the synod in *La Civiltà Cattolica*. "*Laudato Si'* came out in June 2015. Over the years, numerous initiatives contributing to integral ecology have begun, many of them Church-based," they wrote. "Meanwhile, according to all indicators, the crisis has worsened significantly. The Amazon Synod is a conscious ecclesial effort to implement *Laudato Si'* in this fundamental human and natural environment."

The *instrumentum laboris* (working document) for the Amazon synod, like Francis' encyclical *Laudato Si'*, calls for an "integral ecology" or "integrated ecology." This implies the spiritual aspects of a situation are not segregated from the social aspects, and the social is not segregated from the economic, and none of it is any longer segregated from the demands of nature, especially when discussing the Earth's very "lungs."[37]

In addition to the synod being a chance to really apply *Laudato Si'* and to promote integral ecology, the simple of fact of the synod highlights another of this pontificate's themes, synodality itself. The pope could have issued a document about the challenges facing this region, and the relationship of those challenges to the broader culture and to the church, all on his own authority.[38]

That is not this pope's way. His method is that pioneered by Cardinal Joseph Cardijn: See, judge, act. And, in order to see more clearly, judge more fairly, and act in a more decisively Christian manner, you must listen and dialogue, listen and dialogue. That is what synodality is all about.

4.2. The Critics

All these have set Francis' critics on edge. Leading the pack is Cardinal Raymond Burke and Kazakhstan Auxiliary Bishop Athanasius Schneider. They have called for a 40-day crusade of prayer and fasting to prevent what they term "serious theological errors and heresies" in the *instrumentum laboris* from being adopted at the synod. The conservative duo is alarmed by the "implicit pantheism" in the *instrumentum laboris* and its openness to "pagan superstitions." So, they write: "The *Instrumentum Laboris* draws from its implicit pantheistic conception an erroneous concept of Divine Revelation, stating basically that God continues to self-communicate in history through the conscience of the peoples and the cries of nature," they write. These critics forget that St Augustine was employing Neo-Platonic philosophy to articulate his understanding of divine revelation, or when St Thomas Aquinas used Aristotelian concepts to do likewise.

Regrettably, the opposition is not limited to the two buffoonish prelates mentioned above. Some weeks ago, EWTN's Raymond Arroyo convoked his "papal posse" to discuss Francis and the synod. Especially ironic were their complaints about the possibility that the synod might make celibacy optional in certain circumstances. "This is a subversion. ... It would be a total disaster to make celibacy optional. ... Basically, it's an abandonment of what Jesus himself lived," frothed Fr. Gerald Murray. It may be recalled that Pope Benedict XVI issued *Anglicanorum Coetibus*, which allowed married clergy from the Anglican Communion to join the ranks of the Catholic clergy. Was Benedict permitting an "abandonment of what Jesus himself lived"? National Catholic Reporter, Michael Sen Winters ask: Are our Eastern Orthodox and Byzantine Catholic brothers committing a similar abandonment when they permit married clergy?[39]

It is fine to entertain criticisms of the synod's *instrumentum laboris*. I found it terribly dry at points. And I would like a more explicit connection between some of the anthropological perspectives contained here and the anthropology articulated in VC II's *Gaudium et Spes*. Winters alleges that the "hysterical allegations of heresy and error tell us more about the accusers than the accused. And the haters are not few nor are they insignificant."

4.3. The Aftermath

It is very sad that these forces have been focussing almost exclusively on the minor controversies (Pachamama statue) and in the process eclipsing its major contribution to the universal Church. It has found very positive responses from diverse places. Further, it has important implications for the Church in Asia. San Diego Bishop Robert McElroy, urged the Church in America to embrace the type of synodal pathway that the church in the Amazon has been undergoing. McElroy was chosen by Pope Francis to attend the Amazon synod, a gathering that the U.S. bishop found marked by "deep and broad consultation, the willingness to accept arduous choices, the search for renewal and reform at every level, and unswerving faith in the constancy of God's presence in the community," reports the National Catholic Reporter.

Bishop Franz-Josef Bode of Osnabrück, Germany, told the National Catholic Reporter that the recent synod's push for married priests and women deacons 'complies with our reflections' for the German Church's upcoming 'Synodal Path.' Besides accepting the "synodal path," we in India have a lot to learn from it, leading to an ecological conversion respecting the earth and the indigenous mentality. Regarding the

Synod's proposal to adopt an "Amazonian rite" Cardinal Beniamino Stella, Prefect of the Congregation for the Clergy, said it was natural for people to want to communicate through their "local language and symbols, colours, and stories." He recalled how the bishops of the Amazon Region are dealing with "diversified realities" that are multi-ethnic and multi-linguistic. Any rite expresses the history and the spirituality of a people, he said.

Fr Eleazar Lòpez Hernández, an expert in indigenous theology, and a member of the Zapoteca people in Mexico, confirmed that the Churches of Latin America need to express their faith according to their traditions. This is what the proposal for an Amazonian rite is based on, he said. We need to generate something that is "in tune with local traditions", added Fr Hernández. "Our people have their own religious experiences that give meaning to their lives." We cannot focus on only one culture or follow a single pathway, he explained.

5. Concluding Thoughts

We have started with the Pope who concluded the VC II. May be it is good to end it with the Pope who began it. Pope John XIII's Decalogue is inspiring to deal with the Joys and the hopes, the griefs and the anxieties of our times. His "Only for Today" challenges us to be involved in the world with joy, hope and serenity.

1. *Only for today*, I will seek to live the livelong day positively without wishing to solve the problems of my life all at once.[40]

2. *Only for today*, I will take the greatest care of my appearance: I will dress modestly; I will not raise my voice; I will be courteous in my behavior; I will not criticize anyone; I will not claim to improve or to discipline anyone except myself.

3. *Only for today*, I will be happy in the certainty that I was created to be happy, not only in the other world but also in this one.

4. *Only for today*, I will adapt to circumstances, without requiring all circumstances to be adapted to my own wishes.

5. *Only for today*, I will devote ten minutes of my time to some good reading, remembering that just as food is necessary to the life of the body, so good reading is necessary to the life of the soul.

6. *Only for today*, I will do one good deed and not tell anyone about it.

7. *Only for today*, I will do at least one thing I do not like doing; and if my feelings are hurt, I will make sure that no one notices.

8. *Only for today*, I will make a plan for myself: I may not follow it to the letter, but I will make it. And I will be on guard against two evils: hastiness and indecision.

9. *Only for today*, I will firmly believe, despite appearances, that the good providence of God cares for me as no one else who exists in this world.

10. *Only for today*, I will have no fears. In particular, I will not be afraid to enjoy what is beautiful and to believe in goodness. Indeed, for twelve hours I can certainly do what might cause me consternation were I to believe I had to do it all my life.

May we be inspired from VC II. May we be involved in the world like Pope Francis. May we be transformed to be messengers of peace who will share in the "joys and the hopes, the griefs and the anxieties," of our world! Then we can be in, with and for our common home, the Mother Earth!

Endnotes

[1] Kennedy, John F. "John F. Kennedy Quotes." BrainyQuote. Accessed November 8, 2020.

https://www.brainyquote.com/quotes/john_f_kennedy_125481.

[2] Paul VI, Pope. "Closing Speech at Vatican II." EWTN Global Catholic Television Network, December 8, 1965. https://www.ewtn.com/catholicism/library/closing-speech-at-vatican-ii-8983.

[3] Paul VI, 1965.

[4] Paul VI, 1965.

[5] Paul VI, 1965.

[6] Paul VI, 1965.

[7] Paul VI. (1965). *Pastoral Constitution on the Church in the Modern World: Gaudium et spes*. Retrieved from http://www.vatican.va/archive/hist_councils/ii_vatican_council/documents/vat-ii_const_19651207_gaudium-et-spes_en.html

[8] David Hollenbach, "Joy and Hope, Grief and Anguish." *America Magazine*, December 5, 2005. https://www.americamagazine.org/issue/553/article/joy-and-hope-grief-and-anguish.

[9] Ibid.

[10] Ibid.

[11] Ibid.

[12] Ibid.

[13] Earlier about twenty years ago, we used to talk about NBIC Convergence (Nano-, Bio-, Information- and Cognitive Technology Convergnce). It has become dated now, since the convergence in technologies is much more all-inclusive and all-pervasive.

[14] Klaus Schwab and Nicholas G. Smith, *The Fourth Industrial Revolution*, New York, Random House, 2017.

[15] Klaus Schwab, "The Four Industrial Revolutions," *Trailhead*. Accessed September 16, 2019. https://trailhead.salesforce.com/en/content/learn/modules/learn-about-the-fourth-industrial-revolution.

[16] Erik Brynjolfsson and Andrew McAfee, "Will Humans Go the Way of Horses?," September 5, 2016. https://www.foreignaffairs.com/articles/2015-06-16/will-humans-go-way-horses.

[17] Max Neufeind, Jacqueline O'Reilly and Florian Ranft, *Work in the Digital Age: Challenges of the Fourth Industrial Revolution*, 2018.

[18] Gavin Weightman, *The Industrial Revolutionaries: The Making of the Modern World, 1776-1914*, New York, Grove Press, 2007.

[19] Jon-Arild Johannessen, *Automation, Innovation and Economic Crisis: Surviving the Fourth Industrial Revolution*, 2018.

[20] William Rosen, *The Most Powerful Idea in the World: A Story of Steam, Industry, and Invention*, New York, Random House, 2010.

[21] Insights. "Insights into Editorial: Fourth Industrial Revolution: What It Means, Why It's Being Discussed - INSIGHTS," January 23, 2016. https://www.insightsonindia.com/2016/01/23/insights-into-editorial-fourth-industrial-revolution-what-it-means-why-its-being-discussed/.

[22] James Rollins, *The Sixth Extinction*, London, Orion Books, 2015.

[23] Elizabeth Kolbert and Anne Twomey, *The Sixth Extinction*, New York, Simon & Schuster Audio, 2014.

[24] Richard Gray, "Sixth Mass Extinction Could Destroy Life as We Know It– Biodiversity Expert." Horizon: The EU Research & Innovation Magazine. March 4, 2019. https://horizon-magazine.eu/article/sixth-mass-extinction-could-destroy-life-we-know-it-biodiversity-expert.html. See also John Leslie, *The End of the World: The Science and Ethics of Human Extinction*, London, Routledge, 2008.

[25] Genese M. Sodikoff, *The Anthropology of Extinction: Essays on Culture and Species Death*, Bloomington, Indiana University Press, 2012.

[26] Franz J. Broswimmer, *Ecocide: A Short History of Mass Extinction of Species*, London, Pluto Press, 2002.

[27] Theo Van Gogh, *Biblical Bullshit: Christianity and the Accelerating Risk of a Sixth Mass Extinction*, Cork, BookBaby, 2017.

[28] "UN Report: Nature's Dangerous Decline 'Unprecedented'; Species Extinction Rates 'Accelerating.'" *United Nations Sustainable Development* (blog), May 6, 2019. https://www.un.org/sustainabledevelopment/blog/2019/05/nature-decline-unprecedented-report.

[29] https://physicsworld.com/a/humans-drive-sixth-mass-extinction-wave/

[30] Jeremy Hance, "How Humans Are Driving the Sixth Mass Extinction | Environment | The Guardian." The Guardian. Accessed September 16, 2019. https://www.theguardian.com/environment/radical-conservation/2015/oct/20/the-four-horsemen-of-the-sixth-mass-extinction.

[31] Alessandro Bianchi, "Pope Francis Commemorates Migrant Dead at Lampedusa." *Reuters*, July 8, 2013. https://www.reuters.com/article/us-pope-lampedusa-idUSBRE9660KH20130708.

[32] Ibid.

[33] Lecia Bushak, "Pope Francis Comforts Man With Neurofibromatosis, Kisses Head Full Of Tumors," *Medical Daily*. November 9, 2013. https://www.medicaldaily.com/pope-francis-comforts-man-neurofibromatosis-kisses-head-full-tumors-262464.

[34] Faith Karimi, "Pope Francis' Embrace of a Severely Disfigured Man Touches World." CNN. November 7, 2013. https://www.cnn.com/2013/11/07/world/europe/pope-francis-embrace/index.html.

[35] Elene Crete, "A Special Address with the Pope: Climate Change and New Evidence from Science, Engineering, and Policy." May 29, 2019. http://unsdsn.org/news/2019/05/29/a-special-address-with-the-pope-climate-change-and-new-evidence-from-science-engineering-and-policy/.

[36] Bernadette Mary Reis, "Pope to PAS: Science Provides the 'Charity of Knowledge' - Vatican News." November 12, 2018. https://www.vaticannews.va/en/pope/news/2018-11/pontifical-academy-science-pope-plenary.html.

[37] Michael Sean Winters, "Amazon Synod Has Set Pope Francis' Professional Haters on Edge." *National Catholic Reporter*. October 2, 2019. https://www.ncronline.org/news/opinion/distinctly-catholic/amazon-synod-has-set-pope-francis-professional-haters-edge.

[38] Winters, 2019.

[39] Winters, 2019.

[40] Pope John XIII, "The Daily Decalogue of Pope John XXIII." October 11, 2015. http://www.appleseeds.org/Decalogue_John-23.htm.

VII

Pope Francis & the Oikos: Ecumenism and Ecology

"An integral ecology includes taking time to recover a serene harmony with creation, reflecting on our lifestyle and our ideals, and contemplating the Creator who lives among us and surrounds us, whose presence must not be contrived but found, uncovered."

(Pope Francis)

25.

Pope Francis' Enriching of the Ecumenical Movement

Moving Ahead after Vatican Council II

Archbishop Felix Machado

Although the ecumenical movement has been functioning formally for over a hundred years, it has been deepened and enriched by different events or persons in the course of time. Pope Francis' contribution to this deepening and enriching of the ecumenical movement is significant. Deeply rooted in the teachings of the Second Vatican Council (hereinafter VC II), Pope Francis began his Petrine ministry by quoting the inaugural address of St Pope John XXIII, which he had delivered to the Fathers of the Council on October 11, 1962. Determined to promote unity in the Christian and human family, Pope John XXIII had said:

> This concern of the Church in promoting and defending the truth derives from the fact that, in the plan of God 'who wills all persons to be saved and to come to the knowledge of the truth' (1 Tim 2:4), unless they are assisted by the whole of revealed doctrine, people cannot come to that absolute and most firm unity of minds with which true peace and eternal salvation are linked. Unfortunately, the whole family of Christians has not yet fully and perfectly attained this visible unity in the truth.[1]

Pope Francis began his universal ministry by repeating those words of St John XXIII and reminding Christians of the gift of Baptism which they have received so that they render witness of their lives freely to the cause of unity among Christians.[2] He said, "I cannot forget all that the [Second Vatican] Council meant for the progress of ecumenism. Here I would recall the words of St John XXIII: 'The Catholic Church considers it her duty to work actively for the fulfilment of the great mystery of that unity for which Jesus Christ prayed so ardently to his heavenly Father on the eve of his great sacrifice; the knowledge that she is so intimately associated with that prayer is for her an occasion of ineffable peace and joy.'"[3]

I would identify two principal points to define the essence of the ecumenical movement: (1) the divine gift of common faith which the Holy Spirit has infused into the Christians through the sacrament of Baptism and to which Christians are asked to bear witness to in their daily life, and (2) the obstacle which the visible division of Christians represents to the proclamation of the Gospel today.

During the 'Week of Prayer for Christian Unity' (January 18–25), Pope Francis emphasised that the common divine gift of faith which all Christians have received is of the fundamental equality among us, Christians. He said: "It is easy to forget the fundamental equality existing among us: that once we were all slaves to sin, that the Lord saved us in baptism and called us his children. It is easy to think that the spiritual grace granted us is our property. It is a grave sin to belittle or despise the gifts that the Lord has given our brothers and sisters, and to think that God somehow holds them in less esteem. When we entertain such thoughts, we allow the very grace we have received to become a source of pride, injustice and division. And how can we then enter the promised Kingdom of God?"[4]

It is necessary that Christians acknowledge with humility that we are responsible for the divisions among us. At an ecumenical gathering for prayer, Pope Francis declared:

> As the Bishop of Rome and the Shepherd of the Catholic Church, I want to ask forgiveness and mercy for any behavior on the part of Catholics towards Christians of other Churches that did not reflect the values of the Gospel. At the same time, I invite Catholic brothers and sisters to forgive if, today or in the past, they have suffered offences from other Christians. We cannot erase what is past, nor do we wish to allow the weight of past transgressions to continue to pollute our relationships. The mercy of God will renew our relationships.[5]

Lest we become indifferent to the divided Church, it is also necessary to continuously remind ourselves that, "The Church established by Christ the Lord is, indeed, one and unique…Without doubt, this divided Church openly contradicts the will of Christ, provides a stumbling block to the world, and inflicts damage on the most holy cause of proclaiming the good news to every creature."[6] We must make every effort to heal the wounds of division. The division among us is disobedience to Christ and sin against the mystical Body of Christ.

Pope Francis finds theological reasons for our commitment to ecumenism. The essential nature of the Church is to be one (unity). He understands theology as promptings of God in a particular existential situation so that Christians can live a meaningful life, totally obedient to our Lord. The theological reason for ecumenism is the Blessed Trinity: The Father, the Son and the Holy Spirit. He invites Christians to reflect on the actual problem of divisions in the light of the Trinitarian God, saying:

> So many past controversies between Christians can be overcome when we put aside all polemical or apologetic approaches, and seek instead to grasp more fully what unites us, namely, our call to share in the mystery of the Father's love revealed to us by the Son through the Holy Spirit. Christian unity—we are convinced—will not be the fruit of subtle theoretical discussions in which each party tries to convince the other of the soundness of their opinions. When the Son of Man comes, he will find us still discussing! We need to realize that, to plumb the depths of the mystery of God, we need one another, we need to encounter one another and to challenge one another under the guidance of the Holy Spirit, who harmonizes diversities, overcomes conflicts, reconciles differences.[7]

Pope Francis proposes a concrete path to follow in order to achieve the unity which is desired by Christ. This path of unity is our constant conversion to Christ. Our efforts cannot remain limited to only a horizontal level. It is through Christ that we achieve our conversion. Christ is the centre of history and humanity (St Bonaventure). Christ is the fullness of human life and he gathers fragmented humanity into his Body, the Church (Rom 5:12). The Church is ever in need of reform. The most effective concrete path to unity is, to 'sing the mercies of God forever' as the Psalm teaches us; for, in his words:

> [God] never tires of casting open the doors of his heart and of repeating that he loves us and wants to share his love with us. The Church feels the urgent need to proclaim God's mercy. Her life is authentic and credible only when she becomes a convincing herald of mercy. She knows that her primary task, especially at a moment full of great hopes and signs of contradiction, is to introduce everyone to the great mystery of God's mercy by contemplating the face of Christ. The Church is called above all to be a credible witness to mercy, professing it and living it as the core of the revelation of Jesus Christ. From the heart of the Trinity, from the depths of the mystery of God, the great river of mercy wells up and overflows unceasingly. It is a spring that will never run dry, no matter how many people draw from it.[8]

Unity cannot be achieved by changing the structures of the Church or trusting in logical and clear reasoning. Alluding to the ancient heresies of Pelagianism and Gnosticism,[9] Pope Francis explains that:

> Pelagianism leads us to trust in structures, in organizations, in planning that is perfect because it is abstract. Often it also leads us to assume a controlling, harsh and normative manner. Norms give Pelagianism the security of feeling superior, of having a precise bearing. This is where it finds its strength, not in the lightness of the Spirit's breath. Before the evils or problems of the Church it is useless to seek solutions in conservatism and fundamentalism, in the restoration of obsolete practices and forms that even culturally lack the capacity to be meaningful. Christian doctrine is not a closed system, incapable of raising questions, doubts, inquiries, but is living, is able to unsettle, is able to enliven. It has a face that is supple, a body that moves and develops, flesh that is tender: Christian doctrine is called Jesus Christ. The reform of the Church then — and the Church is *semper reformanda* — is foreign to Pelagianism. She is not exhausted in the countless plans to change her structures. It instead means being implanted and rooted in Christ, allowing herself to be led by the Spirit. Thus, everything will be possible with genius and creativity.[10]

Gnosticism, too, leads to trusting in logical and clear reasoning, which nonetheless loses the tenderness of a brother's flesh. The attraction of Gnosticism is that of "a purely subjective faith whose only interest is a certain experience or a set of ideas and bits of information which are meant to console and enlighten, but which ultimately keep one imprisoned in his or her own thoughts and feelings" (*Evangelii Gaudium*, n. 94). Gnosticism cannot transcend. The difference between Christian transcendence and any form of gnostic spiritualism lies in the mystery of the incarnation. Not putting into practice, not leading the Word into reality, means building on sand, staying within pure idea and decaying into intimism that bears no fruit, that renders its dynamism barren.

Nothing can replace the 'personal encounter with Christ of the Gospels' on the part of Christians who are committed to ecumenism; in fact, that is the launching pad to remain involved in ecumenism. Pope Francis spells this out clearly:

> The best incentive for sharing the Gospel comes from contemplating it with love, lingering over its pages and reading it with the heart. If we approach it in this way, its beauty will amaze and constantly excite us. But if this is to come about, we need to recover a contemplative spirit which can help us to realize ever anew that we have been entrusted with a treasure which makes us more human and helps us to lead a new life. There is nothing more precious which we can give to others.[11]

There are Christians in different churches and ecclesial communities, who manifest great enthusiasm to share the Gospel with others and thus try to bring people to Christ. These Christians and/or groups can cause great harm to the unity and credibility of the Gospel of Jesus Christ. We cannot forget that the Holy Spirit is the protagonist of evangelization. Pope Francis gave a stern warning to such people who sometimes say to him: "'Father I am going to evangelize' — 'Yes, what do you do?' — 'Oh, I proclaim the Gospel and I say who Jesus is; I try to convince people that Jesus is God'. My dear, this is not evangelization. If there is no Holy Spirit, there is no evangelization. This may be proselytism, advertising.... But evangelization is allowing yourself to be guided by the Holy Spirit, letting him lead you to proclamation, to proclamation with witness, even with martyrdom, even with words."[12]

Further specifying what ecumenism requires, Pope Francis exhorts Christians to live a life of prayer and holiness. A life of holiness requires that we choose sacrifices. There is no unity without prayer and holiness of life. The union with Christ is the universal vocation of all the baptized. Pope Francis invites us to ask ourselves: "How do we proclaim the Gospel of reconciliation after centuries of division? Paul himself helps us to find the way. He makes clear that reconciliation in Christ *requires sacrifice*. Jesus gave his life by dying for all. Similarly, ambassadors of reconciliation are called, in his name, to lay down their lives, to live no more for themselves but for Christ who died and was raised for them (cf. 2 Cor 5:14-15). As Jesus teaches, it is only when we lose our lives for love of him that we truly save them (cf. Lk 9:24). This was the revolution experienced by Paul, but it is, and always has been, the Christian revolution. We live no longer for ourselves, for our own interests and "image", but in the image of Christ, *for* him and *following* him, *with* his love and *in* his love."[13]

We often think that we must make our own plans for achieving Christian unity. This is because we mistakenly think that we are the makers of the unity of the Church. Pope Francis corrects our mistaken thinking. In a homily at the close of the 'Christian Unity Week' he said:

> For the Church, for every Christian confession, this is an invitation not to be caught up with programmes, plans and advantages, not to look to the prospects and fashions of the moment, but rather to find the way by constantly looking to the Lord's cross. For there we discover our programme of life. It is an invitation to leave behind every form of isolation, to overcome all those temptations to self-absorption that prevent us from perceiving how the Holy Spirit is at work outside our familiar surroundings. Authentic reconciliation between Christians will only be achieved when we can acknowledge each other's gifts and learn from one another, with humility and docility, without waiting for the others to learn first.[14]

Following in the teaching of his predecessors, St Paul VI and St John Paul II, Pope Francis invites Christians to live the 'ecumenism of blood'.

This way of ecumenism will come as a result of our conversion to Christ who willingly chose the cross: "For the love of Christ controls us, because we are convinced that one had died for all; therefore, all have died. And he died for all, that those who live might live no longer for themselves but for him who for their sake died and was raised" (2 Cor 5:14-15). In this context, Pope Francis draws our attention to concrete difficulties and obstacles in the path of ecumenism. He wants us to remember the martyrs, the martyrs of today. "They are witnesses to Jesus Christ, and they are persecuted and killed because they are Christians. Those who persecute them make no distinction between the religious communities to which they belong. They are Christians and for that they are persecuted. This, brothers and sisters, is the ecumenism of blood."[15]

As a member of the 'Global Christian Forum' I was present at the Plenary Gathering Consultation held in Tirana, Albania, from November 2-4, 2015, along with Cardinal Kurt Koch. The theme chosen was *'Discrimination, Persecution, Martyrdom: Following Christ Together'*. Pope Francis sent the following message to the Forum through Cardinal Koch:

> I extend greetings to you all .... In a particular way, I wish to greet our brothers and sisters of different Christian traditions who represent communities suffering for their profession of faith in Jesus Christ, our Lord and Saviour. I think with great sadness of the escalating discrimination and persecution against Christians in the Middle East, Africa, Asia and elsewhere throughout the world. Your gathering shows that, as Christians, we are not indifferent to our suffering brothers and sisters. In various parts of the world, the witness to Christ, even to the shedding of blood, has become a shared experience of Catholics, Orthodox, Anglicans, Protestants, Evangelicals and Pentecostals, which is deeper and stronger than the differences which still separate our Churches and Ecclesial Communities. The *communio martyrum* is the greatest sign of our journeying together. At the same time, your gathering will give voice to the victims of such injustice and violence and, seek to show the path that will lead the human family out of this tragic situation. With these sentiments, I assure you of my spiritual closeness. May the martyrs of today, belonging to many Christian traditions, help us to understand that all the baptised are members of the same Body of Christ, his Church (cf. 1 Cor 12:12-30). Let us see this profound truth as a call to persevere on our ecumenical journey towards full and visible communion, growing more and more in love and mutual understanding.[16]

Echoing similar sentiments, in his 1995 encyclical letter, *Ut Unum Sint*, St John Paul II suggested that: "Albeit in an invisible way, the communion between our Communities, even if still incomplete, is truly and solidly grounded in the full communion of the Saints—those who, at the end of a life faithful to grace, are in communion with Christ in glory. These *Saints* come from all the Churches and Ecclesial Communities which gave them entrance into the communion of salvation."[17] He explains,

> In a theocentric vision, we Christians already have a common *Martyrology*. This also includes the martyrs of our own century, more numerous than one might think, and it shows how, at a profound level, God preserves communion among the baptized in the supreme demand of faith, manifested in the sacrifice of life itself. The fact that one can die for the faith shows that other demands of the faith can also be met. I have already remarked, and with deep joy, how an imperfect but real communion is preserved and is growing at many levels of ecclesial life. I now add that this communion is already perfect in what we all consider the highest point of the life of grace, *martyria* unto death, the truest communion possible with Christ who shed his Blood, and by that sacrifice brings near those who once were far off (cf. Eph 2:13).
>
> While for all Christian communities the martyrs are the proof of the power of grace, they are not the only ones to bear witness to that power. When we speak of a common heritage, we must acknowledge as part of it not only the institutions, rites, means of salvation and the traditions which all the communities have preserved and by which they have been shaped, but first and foremost this reality of holiness.
>
> In the radiance of the "heritage of the saints" belonging to all Communities, the "dialogue of conversion" towards full and visible unity thus appears as a source of hope. This universal presence of the Saints is in fact a proof of the transcendent power of the Spirit. It is the sign and proof of God's victory over the forces of evil which divide humanity.
>
> Where there is a sincere desire to follow Christ, the Spirit is often able to pour out his grace in extraordinary ways. The experience of ecumenism has enabled us to understand this better. If, in the interior spiritual space described above, Communities are able truly to "be converted" to the quest for full and visible communion, God will do for them what he did for their Saints. He will overcome the obstacles inherited from the past and will lead Communities along his paths to where he wills: to the visible *koinonia* which is both praise of his glory and service of his plan of salvation.[18]

The Anglican-Roman Catholic dialogue received a very strong boost when St Paul VI received Archbishop Michael Ramsey, the then Archbishop of Canterbury, in a private audience and founded the Anglican Centre in Rome some fifty years ago. In subsequent years Anglican-Roman Catholic dialogue received an impetus. The Anglican-Roman Catholic International Commission (ARCIC, formed in 1970) was already in existence and had drawn up statements on the Eucharist. In 2002 a group was added to the ARCIC. It is known as the International Anglican-Roman Catholic Commission for Unity of Mission (IARCCUM). I am a member of this group together with Bishop Royce M. Victor from India. The mandate of the IARCCUM is threefold: (1) to write the common statement to be agreed upon and signed at the highest levels of our Churches; (2) to promote the reception of ARCIC documents; and (3) to foster tangible initiatives arising from the level of communion we already share.

The Holy See and Canterbury convoked a joint meeting—the first part of the meeting was held in Canterbury and the second part in Rome. Pope Francis, together with Archbishop Justin Welby, Archbishop of Canterbury, received the joint group—i.e., pairs of Anglican and Roman Catholic bishops of the 19 countries—on October 5, 2016, for the Vespers in the Church of San Gregorio Al Celio in Rome. Pope Francis expressed his desire that while we continue to hope for the full and visible unity, we must not interrupt proclamation of the Gospel of Jesus Christ to all nations and work jointly, untiringly and urgently to bring the mercy of God to our wounded world. In his homily he said:

> To work always and everywhere as instruments of communion is a great calling. It involves working for the unity of both the Christian family and the human family. These two goals are not only not opposed to but are mutually enriching. When, as disciples of Jesus, we serve together side by side, when we promote openness and encounter, and reject the temptation to narrow mindedness and isolation, we are working both for the unity of Christians and for the unity of the human family. We acknowledge one another as brothers and sisters with different traditions but inspired by the same Gospel to undertake the same mission to the world. It would always be good, before

> beginning a particular activity, to ask ourselves the following questions: Can we not do this together with our Anglican brothers and sisters? The mission of shepherds is to help the sheep entrusted to them to go forth and actively proclaim the joy of the Gospel, not to remain huddled in closed circles, in ecclesial 'micro-climates' which would bring us back to the days of clouds and thick darkness... The Church is reinvigorated when she goes out of herself in order to practice and proclaim the Gospel on the byways of the world. The ecumenical movement is truly the fire of mission that made it possible to surmount barriers and tear down walls which kept us apart and made a common path unthinkable.[19]

Pope Francis has taken the ecumenical movement from spiritual to concrete dialogue of truth. His emphasis on the "mercy of God" is now known as the "ecumenism of mercy". The 500th anniversary of the Protestant Reform occurred in 2017. On that occasion Pope Francis invited all Christians to seize the opportunity in order to use it fruitfully for closer ecumenical ties with Lutherans and others. Pope Francis travelled to Lund, Sweden, to commemorate the 500 years of the Protestant Reformation. The aim of this journey was clearly to serve together those who suffer most, to show God's mercy to all, to strive to overcome violence and join efforts to safeguard creation for future generations in our common home, the earth. In his homily in Lund the Pope said, "Unity is established as we journey together...We must look with love and honesty at our past, recognizing error and seeking forgiveness, for God alone is our judge... Lutherans and Catholics must let themselves continuously be transformed by the encounter with the other and by the mutual witness of faith."[20] Pope Francis, together with the General Secretary of the World Lutheran Federation, signed the 'Joint Declaration' from Lund on October 31, 2016. It is expected that this declaration is put into practice locally. The Declaration "calls upon all Lutheran and Catholic parishes and communities to be bold and creative, joyful and hopeful in their commitment to continue the great adventure ahead of us."[21]

Some Concluding Remarks

When our vision is open to the mission of God, ecumenism becomes a necessity. Mission comprises 'all activities of the Church'. When our vision is restricted, narrowed down and lopsided, due to human factors, like, fear and anxiety we may hardly feel any importance for ecumenical encounters in our local churches. Besides VC II emphasising the importance of ecumenism in the life of every Christian, all the Pontiffs from Pope Leo XIII down to Pope Francis have also worked hard to communicate the importance of ecumenism to all the faithful. The Supreme Pontiffs taught that unity was imperative both by the very nature of the Church and also by the command of our Lord Jesus Christ. This command is more binding on us, especially the leaders in the Church, who have the responsibility within the Church to guide the faithful towards full and visible unity of all Christians.

Ecumenism is all about efforts which Christians make to continue living their life faithfully in their respective church traditions with newness. Both continuity and newness in our Christian life is what ecumenical movement is all about. Defining how we must understand tradition, Olivier Clement—noted theologian of the Russian Orthodox Church and Professor at Saint Serge in Paris, France—writes: "The tradition is the life of the Spirit in the Church. On the one hand, the Holy Spirit is the memory of the Church and the faculty of discernment within the Church; but on the other hand, the Spirit is equally holding in balance the eschatological tension ('already' and 'not yet') and the Church is therefore also her perpetual newness."

Christianity is not a system or an ideology. Christianity is Someone: Jesus Christ. Consequently, to be a Christian is to have a personal encounter with Christ who is himself the Truth. The whole idea of the Truth needs to be re-examined, because we nearly always think of the Truth as a system or an ideology. Now, ideologies or words can clash, and that is not a very good approach to Christian truth. Here, we have to reverse our perspectives: dialogue can only be founded on this reality of communion. And communion cannot be separated from the truth; in fact, it is itself the way into the heart of the Truth, in the mystery of the Blessed Trinity.

Christians really need to be told that if they enter 'communion', they would experience the profoundest part of the Christian faith. The best and the most central part of the Christian faith is not a doctrine; it is this encounter, this love, this communion. From this core perspective, what might have appeared central often becomes peripheral and what might have appeared peripheral often becomes central.

We need to address common challenges we all face today. Let us strive to become one with Christ, for we are called to common witness and service to the downtrodden. By belonging to Christ, we belong to one another, to each other. Let us not stop at 'polite ecumenism'; mutual bickering within us must cease as we 'let mutual (brotherly-sisterly) love continue' (Heb 13:1). Our vision of unity must be: (1) relational, not so much organizational; (2) missional and therefore, purposeful; and (3) spiritual, that is life-giving, empowering the weak and the marginalized. The unity we seek is not supernatural synergy, i.e., many can be more forceful than a few.

The following practical suggestions could serve to foster ecumenical initiatives:

1. meeting ecumenically for a concrete need;
2. mutual respect for one another, because every voice is important;
3. diversity should not divide – let us embrace the essentials;
4. promote intergenerational connectivity;
5. mission is critical, therefore, do not just meet; rather, *do something* together: limit activities and get involved in love-compelling actions;
6. contextualisation and decentralisation are important Do not just multiply big meetings; rather emphasise more of relational networking than organisational networking;
7. leadership is the most important factor to success. Good leadership is necessary for sound and solid ecumenism.

Pope Francis has been emphasising that dogma has nearly always been formulated by a negative or apophatic approach; it has never claimed to articulate the mystery, but to safeguard our encounter with Christ. Among Christians it is extremely important to discover and to learn to love the other person's way of approaching Christ and of loving Christ. There is no reason not to reach agreement in theology; a doctrinal question can never become completely stuck. People want to be doctrinaire because they are afraid. We are living at a time when people are uptight about identity, when each denomination is trying to assert itself in what is most specific to it; and denominations are seeking to define themselves by returning to the past, that is, thinking of themselves as being in opposition to someone/something. This tendency needs to be combatted by an attitude which is both faithful and open, and by an awareness that in the end there is only one Church, a Church which we are wounding, a Church whose one seamless garment we are tearing apart. The theological aspects are blown up out of proportion by the realm of passions, and then everything comes to take place in the realm of passions and emotions. It is essential then, for us to let the passions subside and to discover what really matters, that is communion. We need to understand once and for all that communion is not a matter of sentiment, but that it is the most fundamental of all.

That is why we cannot make speculations about ecumenism, but ecumenism itself is to be made real by the way we live our day-to-day Christian life. The undivided Church is here in our midst, showing through; it is already experienced in the community by the existence of the community itself, and that is something that should fill us with joy.

Endnotes

[1] St John XXIII, Opening Discourse of the Second Vatican Council, St Peter's Basilica, October 11, 1962.

[2] Pope Francis, Discourse to the Representatives of the Churches and Ecclesial Communities and Different Religions, Sala Clementina, Vatican, March 20, 2013.

³ Pope Francis, Discourse to the Representatives of the Churches and Ecclesial Communities and Different Religions, Sala Clementina, Vatican, March 20, 2013.

⁴ Pope Francis, Homily at the Vespers on January 18, 2019, Basilica of St Paul Outside the Walls, Rome.

⁵ Pope Francis, Homily at Vespers on January 25, 2016, Basilica of St Paul Outside the Walls, Rome.

⁶ *Unitatis Redintegratio* (UR), Decree of the Second Vatican Council, n.1.

⁷ Pope Francis, Homily during the Vespers on January 25, 2015, Basilica of St Paul's Outside the Walls, Rome.

⁸ Pope Francis, *Misericordiae Vultus*, (MV), Bull on the Occasion of the Convocation of the Extraordinary Jubilee of Mercy, April 11, 2015, n.25.

⁹ Congregation for the Doctrine of the Faith, Letter to Bishops of the Catholic Church about Some Aspects of Christian Salvation, *Placuit Deo*, March 1, 2018.

¹⁰ Pope Francis, Address at the Meeting with the Participants in the Fifth Convention of the Italian Church at the Cathedral of Santa Maria del Fiore, Florence, Tuesday, 10 November 2015. Full text available at: http://www.vatican.va/content/francesco/en/speeches/2015/november/documents/papa-francesco_20151110_firenze-convegno-chiesa-italiana.html

¹¹ Pope Francis, Apostolic Exhortation *Evangelii Gaudium* (EG), November 24, 2013, n.264.

¹² Pope Francis, General Audience, October 2, 2019, St Peter's Square, Rome.

¹³ Homily during the Vespers on January 25, 2017, Basilica of St Paul Outside the Walls, Rome. Full text at: http://www.vatican.va/content/francesco/en/homilies/2017/documents/papa-francesco_20170125_vespri-conversione-san-paolo.html

¹⁴ Pope Francis, ibid.

¹⁵ Homily during the Vespers on the Solemnity of the Conversion of St Paul, January 25, 2015, Basilica of St Paul Outside the Walls, Rome. Full text at: https://w2.vatican.va/content/francesco/en/homilies/2015/documents/papa-francesco_20150125_vespri-conversione-san-paolo.pdf

¹⁶ Pope Francis, Message to Cardinal Kurt Koch, President of Pontifical Council for Promoting Christian Unity, on the Occasion of the Plenary of Global Christian Forum, Tirana, Albania, November 2-4, 2015.

¹⁷ See John Paul II, *Ut Unum Sint*, (UUS), May 25, 1995, n.84.

¹⁸ Ibid.

¹⁹ Homily of Pope Francis in the Church of San Gregorio Al Celio during Vespers for IARCCUM Members, September 30 – October 7, 2016 in Canterbury and Rome.

²⁰ For more details see the website: http://www.vatican.va/roman_curia/pontifical_councils/chrstuni/lutheran-fed-docs/rc_pc_chrstuni_doc_2013_dal-conflitto-alla-comunione_en.html

[21] See Joint Declaration on the Doctrine of Justification by the Lutheran World Federation and Catholic Church: https://www.vatican.va/roman_curia/pontifical_councils/chrstuni/documents/rc_pc_chrstuni_doc_31101999_cath-luth-joint-declaration_en.html

26.

Pope Francis Charts a Different Ecological Way

Bishop Allwyn D'Silva

Introduction

There is little doubt that we are facing an ecological crisis of unimaginable proportions. In the midst of darkness and a sense of helplessness, some persons provide rays of hope by raising their voice on behalf of the poor of the earth, thereby giving us roadmaps to respond to this crisis. Pope Francis is one such person. In this paper, I will first highlight the ecological problems that we are facing worldwide. Second, I will show how Pope Francis' eco-theology—especially as seen in *Laudato Si'*—provides us with insight to respond to these crises. Drawing inspiration from this, third, I shall chart some roadmaps for those in priestly formation. Fourth, I shall describe some 'Green Initiatives' that the Archdiocese of Mumbai has started to effectively combat this crisis. Finally, I will offer a few practical suggestions for an eco-friendly lifestyle.

1. **The Ecological Crisis**

The past year saw an unprecedented surge in awareness of and engagement with the climate emergency, with Collins Dictionary naming 'climate strike' as their 2019 Word of the Year.[1] This is a reflection of the momentum of school climate strikes and Extinction Rebellion protests that are applying pressure to both governments as well as the private sector to act on the climate crisis.[2] *The Guardian* newspaper reported that two-thirds of people in the United Kingdom now consider the climate emergency to be the biggest issue facing humankind while Italian schools will include climate change as a topic in curricula from next year.[3] The world over, universities and academic institutions are divesting from fossil fuels and scrutinising their carbon footprints.[4]

Closer home, Maharashtra's grape growers are grappling with heavy crop losses caused by unseasonal heavy rain.[5] Last year, Jambutke village in Dindori taluka, Nashik district, faced heavy rains from the third week of October to just after the first week of November.[6] These rains created cracks in the tender grape berries sown on a 16-acre plot, which subsequently turned black and rotted away.[7] Though the landowner says that he will not be able to harvest even a single kilogram from 15 out of his 16 acres, he will have to continue applying crop protection chemicals to keep the vines free from fungal attacks.[8] Having spent over Rs. 1.5 lakh per acre on fungicides, pesticides, fertilisers and micronutrients; he compares the expenses incurred to maintaining a cow yielding no milk.[9] This is the third time in five years that he has lost grapes at a nascent growth stage.[10]

A new research report states that instead of the previously thought 80 million, "300 million people are now living on land that is likely to flood at least once a year on average by mid-century without adequate sea defences, even if governments manage to make sharp cuts in emissions".[11] Climate Central points out that 150 million people live on land that may go permanently below the high tide line due to sea level rise by 2050.[12] Mumbai, Kolkata and Shanghai are among the global cities that face the risk of being wiped out; and the countries of China,

Bangladesh, India, Vietnam, Indonesia, Thailand, the Philippines, and Japan account for the bulk of the at-risk population.[13]

Philip Alston, the United Nations Special Rapporteur on extreme poverty and human rights, made it clear in a report released in June 2018 that climate change will have devastating consequences for people in poverty, yet "authorities have a history of prioritising wealthier areas for protection, further endangering people in poverty."[14] It is frightening that:

> Even under the best-case scenario, hundreds of millions will face food insecurity, forced migration, disease, and death. Climate change threatens the future of human rights and risks undoing the last fifty years of progress in development, global health, and poverty reduction... It will have the most severe impacts in poor countries and regions, and the places poor people live and work. Developing countries will bear an estimated 75-80 percent of the costs of climate change.
>
> The poor lose relatively more when affected; have fewer resources to mitigate the effects; and get less support from social safety nets or the financial system to prevent or recover from the impact... Eight hundred million in South Asia alone live in climate hotspots and will see their living conditions decline sharply by 2050.
>
> 100-400 million more people will be put at risk of hunger and 1-2 billion more people may no longer have adequate water... Between 2030 and 2050, [climate change] is expected to cause approximately 250,000 additional deaths per year from malnutrition, malaria, diarrhoea, and heat stress... 2017 saw 18.8 million people displaced due to disasters in 135 countries—almost twice the number displaced by conflict.[15]

Despite these impacts, and warnings from scientists and advocates since the 1970s, action has been lacking and not commensurate with what needs to be done. In addition, we have an unfortunate track record of underestimating the rate of climate change impacts.[16] With thirty years of conventions seeming to have resulted in little, governments have failed us and instead crossed several climate change thresholds.[17] Big businesses, especially fossil fuel industries—which account for 91 percent of global industrial greenhouse emissions and 70 percent of all human-made emissions—have been complicit, by taking no action to change their business models.[18] The Alston report has constructive proposals on how to move forward:

Addressing climate change will require a fundamental shift in the global economy and how States have historically sought prosperity, decoupling improvements in economic well-being and poverty reduction from resource depletion, fossil fuel emissions, and waste production. This will entail radical and systemic changes including incentives, pricing, regulation, and resource allocation, in order to disrupt unsustainable approaches and reflect environmental costs in entire economic subsystems including energy, agriculture, manufacturing, construction, and transportation.[19]

The Intergovernmental Panel on Climate Change (IPCC) published a special report in 2018 which, in essence, finds that: "we only have until 2030 to transform the global economy to avoid the worst impacts of climate change by 2050."[20] Given the magnitude of climate change impacts, the time has come for the global community, our governments, our cities and all our provinces to declare a climate emergency—a total of 722 localities in 15 countries have already done so.[21] Diplomatic engagement on climate change must be prioritised and emphasised rather the minimised.[22] The climate threat is existential and capable of annihilating most people on earth.[23]

Not just people, but all life on earth is threatened by the climate emergency. The 2019 Global Assessment Report on Biodiversity and Ecosystem Services by the Intergovernmental Science-Policy Platform on Biodiversity and Ecosystem Services, makes clear that climate change accelerates the destruction of ecosystems and the extinction of species.[24] Its authors conclude that a million species face extinction; climate changes is the third biggest driver of this extinction – behind changes in land and sea use and direct exploitation of organisms but ahead of pollution and invasive alien species.[25]

Though time is running out to address the climate emergency, "vested interests are running the biggest disinformation campaign in history"[26] and "a corrupting influence on politicians and the media and are prepared to spend millions of dollars to block action".[27] Faced with the possible loss of their research funding, "climate scientists are pressured to understate the risks".[28] Even IPCC reports are couched in reticence and caution and downplay the more damaging and the more extreme outcomes.[29]

In this situation, climate scientist Kate Marvel opines that rather than hope, courage is needed to face climate change.[30] Given that humanity is at a crucial juncture, our hope to solve the climate crisis must be grounded in courage for things to change, since hope is false without courage.[31] There is insufficient time to debate "whether the current climate trajectory is an emergency or can be addressed with gradual change. The forecasts are compelling and the scenarios are devastating. It's time to move straight to the most important question of our times: how to restore a safe climate at emergency speed."[32]

Solutions are needed now. As questioned by Yeb Sano at the 2013 United Nations Climate Summit at Warsaw: "If not us, then who? If not now, then when?".[33] At the January 2019 World Economic Forum at Davos, teenage activist Greta Thunberg urged world leaders to act on climate, saying, "I don't want you to be hopeful. I want you to panic. I want you to feel the fear I feel every day. And then I want you to act. I want you to act as you would in a crisis. I want you to act as if our house is on fire. Because it is."[34]

Apart from the climate crisis, other environmental concerns such as biodiversity loss, water pollution and scarcity, land degradation, deterioration of air quality, toxins in food, all threaten life as we know it.

2. Theological Reflection

The protection of our environment is no longer optional or secondary to Christian life. This care for the common home comes from a genuine relationship with God who is the Creator of all things. Despite the many challenges and obstacles that one may face, the care for the common home is an integral part of the human vocation and living our vocation to be protectors of God's handiwork is essential to a life of virtue. In this, we draw on the Gospel teachings of love, and on the need for renewing and revival under the guidance of the Holy Spirit;

for the challenge is not easy. Pope Francis reminds us in the opening words of chapter six of *Laudato Si'*:

> Many things have to change course, but it is we human beings above all who need to change. We lack an awareness of our common origin, of our mutual belonging, and of a future to be shared with everyone. This basic awareness would enable the development of new convictions, attitudes and forms of life. A great cultural, spiritual and educational challenge stands before us, and it will demand that we set out on the long path of renewal.[35]

Despite the cultural, spiritual and educational challenges that are put before us, Pope Francis is asking us to look at the care of the common home as "an integral ecology [which] includes taking time to recover a serene harmony with creation, reflecting on our lifestyle and our ideals, and contemplating the Creator who lives among us and surrounds us, whose presence must not be contrived but found, uncovered."[36] *Laudato Si'* calls for a kind of harmony that must be reflected in our lifestyle and ideals that includes a contemplation on God which is inclusive of all other realities around us, and for a concrete and profound conversion that impacts life and everything that life was intended for and that which flows from it.[37]

3. Responding to the Signs of the Times: A Roadmap for Priestly Formation[38]

Pastorally, Pope Francis hopes that seminaries and houses of formation "will provide an education in responsible simplicity of life, in grateful contemplation of God's world, and in concern for the needs of the poor and the protection of the environment".[39] With reference to seminary formation, it would seem that *Laudato Si'* is geared towards four goals: (1) simplicity of life; (2) contemplation of God; (3) concern for the poor; (4) protection of the environment.

3.1. *Simplicity of Life*

In this post-modern era, our lives are impacted by consumerism. No one can claim that consumerism has not affected one's life. In fact, consumerism is one of the strongest forces affecting our lives in the modern world. Everyone knows that we live in a culture of consumerism but only a few people understand the full extent of the problems it causes or the effects that it has on each one of us. Whether we live in urban, suburban or even rural areas, consumerism not only affects us but more worryingly it defines what the good life is— fundamentally consumerism promotes material goods.

In one study, it was documented that on an average, every day, each of us is bombarded with around 1,600 commercial messages. This sounds like a massive number, but when you think of a typical day in your life, it is quite possible. A typical day might feature the following activities: waking up, reading the newspaper (featuring advertisements), listening to the radio (advertisements), traveling to work (roadside advertisements), arriving at work (advertisements of the internet, email, social media, etc.), and the whole process continues as you return home to relax and turn on the TV (advertisements). How impossible it is to isolate ourselves from this phenomenon!

Laudato Si' uses the phrase "less is more"[40] and therefore brings together the need for personal conversion and corporate responsibility. Institutions of Christian inspiration such as seminaries and houses of formation need to be wary of an unhealthy obsession with consumption and material prosperity for its own sake. *Laudato Si'* warns that "obsession with a consumerist lifestyle, above all when few people are capable of maintaining it, can only lead to violence and mutual destruction."[41] The encyclical calls for a new lifestyle. Primarily the shift has to be from a 'throwaway culture', in terms of both material things and relationships, to a 'life-giving culture'. Much of the relationships that we engage in can be considered pragmatic and even utilitarian. Human relationships are seen in terms of usefulness and not beyond. Seminary formation needs to promote relationships that are life-giving, within the seminary and outside it, too.

We must promote a counter-consumeristic worldview—not merely reduce, reuse, recycle—and in doing so, choose a life that promotes the gospel values of humility and simplicity. Thus, we should: "cultivate the spirit of poverty in practical ways…be formed to imitate the heart of Christ, who, *"became poor although he was rich,"* in order to enrich us."[42] Seminarians in particular "should seek to acquire the freedom and docility of sons of God, attaining to the spiritual self-mastery that is needed for a proper relationship with the world and worldly good... Already being used to sacrifice willingly and generously what is not needed, they ought to be witnesses to poverty through simplicity and austerity of life, so as to become sincere and credible promoters of true justice".[43]

3.2. *Contemplation of God*

In *Laudato Si'*, the idea of contemplation is focussed more to the ability to seeing the beauty of God in His Creation. In doing so, not only the sense of appreciation increases but also a deep respect for the creative power of God. This is because contemplation of Creation leads to a discovery of a teaching of God in each thing: "for the believer, to contemplate creation is to hear a message, to listen to a paradoxical and silent voice".[44] This ability to contemplate in the context of *Laudato Si'* is to be able to read, feel and respond the signs of the times. In the words of Saint Bonaventure, as quoted in *Laudato Si'*, "contemplation deepens the more we feel the working of God's grace within our hearts, and the better we learn to encounter God in creatures outside ourselves".[45] Contemplation offers the searching heart an "alternative understanding of the quality of life, and encourages a prophetic and contemplative lifestyle, one capable of deep enjoyment free of the obsession with consumption,"[46] – contemplation for the purpose of a renewed lifestyle.

3.3. *Concern for the Poor*

In the late sixties and right through the seventies, the theme of the poor dominated most theological discussions. The poor at that time was in reference to those who are economically poor. However today, the description of the 'poor' can be widened to include many other aspects of poverty. For instance, poverty in Asia shows its face in many different forms: hunger, discrimination and violence against women, abuse of children and the vulnerable, destruction of the unborn life, natural disasters and climate change, forced migration, the rise of rural and urban poor, human trafficking, corruption and abuse of power, illiteracy, oppression of the indigenous communities, and many others. Despite the progress in some Asian countries, poverty remains the greatest challenge across Asia.

Laudato Si' primarily speaks of the economically poor, the marginalised, and the unjust situations caused by capitalism. The word 'poor' appears 44 times in the document and perhaps it is the group that is most mentioned and cared for in the encyclical. In the case of seminarians, seminary formation should find ways to help them be "permeated by a pastoral spirit"[47] because this will "make them able to demonstrate the same compassion, generosity, love for all, especially the poor..."[48]

3.4. *Protection of the Environment*

The 2016 *Ratio Fundamentalis Institutionis Sacerdotalis* states that "protecting the environment and caring for our common home – the Earth – belongs fully to the Christian outlook on man and reality. They constitute in some way the basis for a sound ecology of human relations".[49] The greatest demand above all today is for a "profound interior conversion. It must be said that some committed and prayerful Christians, with the excuse of realism and pragmatism, tend to ridicule expressions of concern for the environment. Others are passive; they choose not to change their habits and thus become inconsistent. So what they all need is an 'ecological conversion', whereby the effects of their encounter with Jesus Christ become evident in their relationship with the world around them. Living our vocation to be protectors of God's handiwork is essential to a life of virtue; it is not optional or secondary aspect of our Christian experience".[50]

As we all know, the call to care for our common home comes from the concept of stewardship that is found in the creation accounts in the book of Genesis. This idea of stewardship is also integral to Catholic Social Teaching. The interplay between stewardship and Creation needs to be widened so as to provide a broader inclusiveness for the purpose of an integral ecology that begins with a personal conversion. Primarily, stewardship is to be understood as a mission of the Church, and therefore the care of the common home has to be an integral part of the Church's mission. The mission is then based on the building of relationships: with God, self, the other, and the cosmos.

The Christian understanding of stewardship is founded on a relationship with God which defines human beings and founds their relationships with other created beings. It is this relationship that defines us as the *imago Dei*. For priests, it is within this communion of love that the mystery of all being, as embraced by God, finds its fullest meaning, both theologically and pastorally-spiritually. Stewardship is the way of priestly life which characterises the ministerial journey as "servants of God and stewards of God's mysteries".[51]

3.5. *Dialogue*

Intercultural-interfaith dialogue can be a key feature in the Asian reality. Dialogue in this context offers an opportunity to encounter others the Catholic way: "The majority of people living on our planet profess to be believers. This should spur religions to dialogue among themselves for the sake of protecting nature, defending the poor, and building networks of respect and fraternity."[52] *Laudato Si'* opens the pathway for dialogue—the capacity to enter into meaningful conversations. Interreligious dialogue must be characterised by "an attitude of openness in truth and in love [...] in spite of various obstacles and difficulties, especially forms of fundamentalism on both sides. Interreligious dialogue is a necessary condition for peace in the world, and so it is a duty for Christians as well as other religious communities."[53]

Inter-disciplinary and cross-disciplinary conversations are equally important. The theology of Creation must be in constant conversation with other sciences in order to provide a grounded rationale for the care of the common home: "Dialogue among the various sciences is likewise needed, since each can tend to become enclosed in its own language, while specialisation leads to a certain isolation and the absolutisation of its own field of knowledge. This prevents us from confronting environmental problems effectively. An open and respectful dialogue is also needed between the various ecological movements, among which ideological conflicts are not infrequently encountered. The gravity of the ecological crisis demands that we all look to the common good, embarking on a path of dialogue which demands patience, self-discipline and generosity, always keeping in mind that realities are greater than ideas."[54]

4. Responding to Signs of the Times: Green Diocese Initiative of Bombay Archdiocese

Recognising the ecological crisis as a major threat facing the world today, Oswald Cardinal Gracias, the Archbishop of Bombay, initiated and launched a process to make the Archdiocese of Bombay a 'Green Diocese' on September 1, 2018 (on the occasion of the World Day of Prayer for the Care of Creation).[55] This is a long-term initiative that will be developed over a period of several years. It envisages the lowering of the carbon footprint of the Archdiocese of Bombay, and that the diocese contributes positively to the environment. A core group of twelve persons comprising the Bishop-In-charge, office bearers of the Archdiocesan Office for Environment, priests and laity animate the Green Diocese initiative.

One of the first tasks of the core group was to evolve a five-point thrust: Spirituality, Education, Engagement (Concrete Actions), Networking and Advocacy, and Personal Lifestyles (with a focus of reducing consumption of goods) for steering the initiative. In the first two years, the focus has been on Spirituality, Education and Personal Lifestyles—which will enable the Archdiocese to take up Concrete Actions and get involved in Networking and Advocacy.

Via workshops and seminars, awareness has been created amongst parishioners of various parishes and other target groups about the impact of climate change, and the urgent need to embrace eco-friendly personal lifestyles. Prayer services and meditations are being conducted in the Archdiocese, and liturgical resources are periodically developed. Creation Chapels have been set up in a couple of parishes in order to pray with and amidst creation. Educative excursions and youth camps have been undertaken in rural areas to understand how people live in harmony with creation.

Several individuals/organisations are contributors to the initiative in terms of hands-on experience. Experts in the field have been invited to share their knowledge at awareness programmes organised by the Archdiocesan Office for Environment so as to draw on the expertise of knowledgeable individuals in order to educate our people and sustain the initiative. Eco-friendly practices are already underway in several parishes. Reporting of such efforts is being encouraged to inspire all parishes to get on board. Reported initiatives feature on the quarterly e-newsletter made available on the website of the Archdiocesan Office for Environment. As part of capacity building, a certificate course has been launched in the Archdiocese and 38 persons are training to become Eco Ambassadors. Sharing of ideas is encouraged during meetings and training programmes to allow new ideas for implementation to develop from the stakeholders themselves.

The core group is in the process of developing parameters to evaluate the Green Diocese process. Evolving such a means of assessing impact is an acceptance of our responsibility and provides direction to our work towards enabling all generations to enjoy the fruit of God's creation. The evaluative parameters will also serve as a reflection of the commitment to enrich our surroundings and protect it from further harm. The core group will engage more extensively with a higher percentage of parishes in the Archdiocese and plans to actively network with secular groups in the future.

5. Responding to the Signs of the Times: Daily Commitments for Individuals

Tony La Vina suggests the following low-carbon lifestyle choices that people can take on weekdays to reduce climate change:

Meat Free Mondays – Choose Meat Free Meals: Halving your meaty days from 7 per week to 3 or 4 will annually reduce your carbon footprint by up to 1.5 tonnes.

Short Tuesdays – Shorter Showers, Ditch the Bath: Reducing your showering from 7 to 4 minutes will reduce your carbon footprint by 100 kg of CO_2.

Warm Wednesdays – Save Energy at Home: Turn your temperature down by 1°C and save 10% on your heating bills.

Seasonable Thursdays – Eat Seasonable Foods: Seasonal fruit and vegetables have a small carbon footprint. They are grown in natural conditions with fewer fertilisers and food miles.

Fuel Free Fridays – Choose a More Sustainable Way to Travel: Walk, cycle, take the bus or carpool.[56]

Conclusion

Hans Joachim Schellnhuber—a leading climate change researcher and founding director of the Potsdam Institute for Climate Impact Research—opines: "The Asian countries hold Earth's future in their hands. If they choose to protect themselves against dangerous climate change, they will help to save the entire planet".[57] The Church in Asia has its task set before her. The Church has to take up a pivotal role in the restoration of Mother Earth—to play a critical and prophetic role in restoring the planet's equilibrium.[58] In her efforts in restoring the face of the earth, the Church must respond to its cry: "[Mother Earth] now cries out to us because of the harm we have inflicted on her by our irresponsible use and abuse of the goods with which God has endowed her. We have come to see ourselves as her lords and masters, entitled to plunder her at will. The violence present in our hearts, wounded by sin, is also reflected in the symptoms of sickness evident in the soil, in the water, in the air and in all forms of life. This is why the earth herself, burdened and laid waste, is among the most abandoned and maltreated of our poor..."[59]

There is always a need for an ongoing personal conversion, which includes an 'ecological conversion' to inspire us to greater creativity and enthusiasm in resolving the world's problems and in offering ourselves to God "as a living sacrifice, holy and acceptable."[60] This then is our mission—to have courage and go in a different ecological way, undeterred by opposing forces.

Endnotes

[1] Editorial, "Health and climate change: making the link matter," *The Lancet* 394, No. 10211 p1780. DOI: https://doi.org/10.1016/S0140-6736(19)32756-4

[2] Ibid.

[3] Ibid.

[4] Ibid.

[5] Parthasarathi Biswas, "Climate change: A story gone sour," *The Indian Express*, November 14, 2019, https://indianexpress.com/article/india/maharashtra-farmers-grape-farming-climate-change-wineyard-6118371/

[6] Ibid.

[7] Ibid.

[8] Ibid.

[9] Ibid.

[10] Ibid.

[11] Nikhil Agarwal, "Mumbai, Kolkata could be wiped out by the sea by 2050, warns new report," Livemint. https://www.livemint.com/news/india/mumbai-could-be-wiped-out-by-the-sea-in-the-next-30-years-warns-new-report-11572413315187.html (accessed November 2, 2019).

[12] Ibid.

[13] Ibid.

[14] Tony La Vina, "Climate emergency and the poor," manilastandard.net. http://manilastandard.net/opinion/columns/eagle-eyes-by-tony-la-vina/299660/climate-emergency-and-the-poor.html (accessed October 16, 2019).

[15] Ibid.

[16] Michael Mann, "The 'Fat Tail' of Climate Change Risk," Huffpost. https://www.huffpost.com/entry/the-fat-tail-of-climate-change-risk_b_8116264 (accessed November 4, 2019).

[17] Tony La Vina, *Climate emergency and the poor.*

[18] Ibid.

[19] Ibid.

[20] Tony La Vina, "Time to declare a climate emergency," *The Standard*, July 9, 2019.

[21] Ibid.

[22] Ibid.

²³ Ibid.

²⁴ Ibid.

²⁵ Ibid.

²⁶ Jane Morton, *Don't Mention the Emergency?* (Australia: Darebin Climate Action Now, 2018). https://climateemergencydeclaration.org/wp-content/uploads/2018/09/DontMentionTheEmergency2018.pdf (accessed November 4, 2019)

²⁷ Ibid.

²⁸ Ibid.

²⁹ Ibid.

³⁰ Kate Marvel, "We need courage, not hope, to face climate change," *On Being*. https://onbeing.org/blog/kate-marvel-we-need-courage-not-hope-to-face-climate-change/ (accessed November 4, 2019).

³¹ Tony La Vina, *Time to declare a climate emergency.*

³² Morton, *Don't Mention the Emergency?*

³³ UNRIC, "Philippine negotiator to fast for the Climate," United Nations Regional Information Centre for Western Europe. https://www.unric.org/en/latest-un-buzz/28834-philippine-negotiator-to-fast-until-progress-is-made-at-climate-conference- (accessed November 14, 2019).

³⁴ Greta Thunberg edited speech, "Our house is on fire," *The Guardian*. https://www.theguardian.com/environment/2019/jan/25/our-house-is-on-fire-greta-thunberg16-urges-leaders-to-act-on-climate (accessed November 14, 2019).

³⁵ Pope Francis, *Laudato Si'* (hereinafter LS) 202.

³⁶ *LS* 225.

³⁷ Clarence Devadass, "*Laudato Si'* and Its Implication in Seminary Formation." Paper presented at the Seminar on Awakening Climate Change Concern in Seminaries for Bishops and Seminary Formators of Priests in Asia, Hua Hin, Thailand, November 2019.

³⁸ This section is drawn from: Devadass, *Laudato Si' and Its Implication in Seminary Formation*, 2019.

³⁹ *LS* 214.

⁴⁰ *LS* 222.

⁴¹ *LS* 204.

⁴² *Ratio Fundamentalis Institutionis Sacerdotalis* (RF) 111.

⁴³ Ibid.

⁴⁴ *LS* 85.

⁴⁵ *LS* 233.

⁴⁶ *LS* 222.

⁴⁷ *RF* 119.

⁴⁸ Ibid.

⁴⁹ *RF* 172.

⁵⁰ *LS* 217 as quoted in *RF* 172.

⁵¹ 1 Cor 4:1.

⁵² *LS* 201.

⁵³ Pope Francis, *Evangelii Gaudium* (EG) 250.

⁵⁴ *LS* 201.

⁵⁵ Oswald Cardinal Gracias, *Official-I* on the occasion of the Solemnity of the Assumption of the Blessed Virgin Mary. August 15, 2018.

⁵⁶ Antonio La Vina, "Climate Emergency". Presentation at the Seminar on Awakening Climate Change Concern in Seminaries for Bishops and Seminary Formators of Priests in Asia, Hua Hin, Thailand, November 2019.

⁵⁷ ADB, "Wake-up Call: Asia-Pacific Needs to Act Now on Climate Change." Asian Development Bank. https://www.adb.org/news/features/wake-call-asia-pacific-needs-act-now-climate-change (accessed November 14, 2019)

⁵⁸ Devadass, *Laudato Si' and Its Implication in Seminary Formation*. 2019.

⁵⁹ *LS* 2.

⁶⁰ Rom 12:1.

27.

Self-Concern versus Concern for Christ

Pope Francis' Impetus to the Ecumenical Movement

Shajan Kuttiyil, OIC

Introduction

Unitatis Redintegratio (hereinafter UR)—the decree on ecumenism of the Second Vatican Council (hereinafter VC II) promulgated on November 21, 1964—was a great milestone in the history of the Church towards unity. The first statement of the decree itself highlights the thrust of VC II, especially its main focus on communion ecclesiology: "The restoration of unity among all Christians is one of the principal concerns of the Second Vatican Council."[1] The Council invites the Catholic faithful to identify and appreciate the rich heritage of other churches and ecclesial communities. The documents of VC II, especially *Lumen Gentium* (hereinafter LG), *Orientalium Ecclesiarum* (hereinafter OE) and *Unitatis Redintegratio* make the Catholic Church's approach to other churches and ecclesial communities clear. The rigid and more legalistic approach of the Church in the past was replaced with a more pastoral one of 'communion.' The Catholic Church is fully aware of its mission of unity and demands that her faithful work tirelessly for the total communion of all the churches by prayer, their example, scrupulous fidelity to the ancient traditions of the East, better knowledge of each other, working together and by a brotherly attitude.[2]

This paper seeks to offer only a bird's eye view of Pope Francis' views on ecumenism, particularly focussing on his pastoral approach, which is Christocentric and deeply rooted in the teachings of VC II. His approach and his way of communicating with other churches is one of 'a heart speaking to the heart (*cor ad cor loquitor*) but which avoids sentimentalism and emotional ploys.' In his communication and dialogue with other churches, it is beyond doubt that his whole person is involved—mind, heart and body, showing his genuine and sincere efforts towards fostering unity and communion.[3] Indeed, Pope Francis gives more of a simple, practical and concrete answer to the question: "What can we do together for a common witness to the world by way of unity and communion among the churches and ecclesial communities?"

Love and Friendship: The Basics of Ecumenism
Love builds communion between individuals and communities. VC II's documents—especially OE and UR, which are really promoting the unity and communion of all the churches—aim at unity by way of newness of attitudes of mind, from self-denial and unstinted love.[4] The Council's decree on OE concludes with the exhortation taken from the epistle of St Paul to the Romans: "Let us all love each other with the love of sisters and brothers, outdoing each other in showing honour" (Rom 12:10). Pope John XXIII, the initiator of VC II, believed that a simple gesture of friendship would usher in a real ecumenical movement in the Church.

Echoing Pope John XXIII's thrust, Pope Francis speaks about the importance of love and friendship in our onward journey to unity. He says, "Wealth can encourage the erection of walls, create divisions and discriminations but it is not those who have so many riches who bear fruit, but those who create and keep so many bonds, so many relationships, so many friendships through the different 'riches' that is the different gifts with which God has endowed them."⁵ This means that no doctrinal coherence or theoretical exposition will endear others to our faith, but it is our lived experiences of love that will attract others to the Christian faith. The criticism of the conservatives in the Church against Pope Francis is that he is soft on doctrine and strong on compassion and that he is primarily considered as a pastor rather than a doctrinal, dogmatic, religious head.⁶ Pope Francis makes repeated exhortations that it is only through mutual love translated into the service of our needy brothers and sisters that we can give authentic witness to Jesus and His teachings.

Pope Francis invites all Catholics to be grateful and say, "'thank you, Lord' for the other person who is different from me because each and everyone is a gift for my Church."⁷ He talks about the gift of uniqueness of individuals and the plurality of the communities with which the Church of Christ is adorned and embellished. He reminds us that only those who can appreciate unity in diversity in the multi-religious context can respect and accommodate others and avoid the scandal of division and give common witness through Gospel preaching and diverse apostolic activities. He defines dialogue as: "the courage to accept differences, because those who are different either culturally or religiously, should not be seen or treated as enemies, rather welcomed as fellow-travelers, in the genuine conviction that the good of each resides in the good of all."⁸

Pope Francis believes that the true 'face of love' is mercy and compassion towards other human beings in need and the attitude of such persons proves that they are people gentle and meek. It is true that 'gentle persons are attractive to many people. They have to neither convince persons of different faiths of their orthodoxy nor do they have the need of proselytizing. Their gentleness itself is a sufficient testimony for Christ. Only when men and women have become gentle, merciful and deal compassionately with their fellow human beings do they bear witness to a spirituality that is in keeping with Christ.'⁹ 'To speak truth in love' (*caritatis et veritate*) is the first step and also the basis of all our attempts at dialogue for unity. It is only through personal friendship and the bond of love with others—talking, listening, learning, working and growing together in a spirit of mutual trust—that true communion is achieved.

Ecumenism: An Act of Operating at a Loss

Pope Francis reiterates that to walk together is not merely a ploy either to strengthen one's own positions or to entertain personal interests but it is rather an act of obedience to Jesus and His love for the world. Only by reflecting on the love of Christ, who emptied Himself and laid down His life for us, can one think of losing oneself and entering into dialogue and communion with others by kindling and instilling the love of Jesus in them. It is an act of losing in order to gain. He adds that the devil always succeeded in his role and had no difficulty in separating us, because the direction we had been taking was that of the flesh and not of the Holy Spirit. Once we are driven by our instincts, we become slaves to unbridled consumerism. God's voice is then gradually silenced and there is no chance for dialogue and communion.

Pope Francis caution us against the attitude of pretending to love each other and really only to be looking for our own interest. He believes "to walk together is to 'operate at a loss', since it does not adequately protect the interest of the individuals but only caters to the Will of our Lord for unity and perfect communion."[10] He warned about the dangers involved in it that self-interest and hypocrisy destroy the Church. To fail in the sincerity of sharing, in the sincerity of love, means to cultivate hypocrisy, move away from the truth, to become selfish, to extinguish the fire of communion and turn to frost of interior death.[11]

Ecumenism: An Act of Building Bridges

Pope Francis always talks about building bridges between nations, churches, ecclesial communities, families and individuals. The most basic need of any human and ecclesiastical communion is the personal association of the individual members of different churches and ecclesial communities. The closeness and intimacy of the personal association of the individual members will certainly lead to a communal association and further to an ecclesial communion. In contexts of diversity—where there are different churches and ecclesial communities which are not in communion with each other, but share the same common patrimony—importance must be given to the personal association of the members of the different churches. It is a fact that the majority of the members belonging to different churches are family members but unfortunately dispersed in different churches and communities. Nonetheless, it is a societal and social need to come together and share many of their communal events. The family get-together and celebrations clubbed with ecclesial celebrations—like Baptism, First Holy Communion, Marriage, House blessings and so on—are to be considered as privileged moments of ecumenism between individuals, families, different ecclesial communities and other denominations.

It is true that much has been achieved over the last decades in our ecumenical journey and separated Christians no longer consider one another as strangers, competitors or even enemies but as brothers and sisters. The former lack of understanding, prejudice and indifference have been largely removed and now the Churches at least come together to pray and work for a common cause in order to give witness together to their common faith. The underlying factor behind all these efforts is the realization that 'what unites us is much greater than what divides us.' In order to have such a fellowship, one needs to have only a confession of faith in the Lord Jesus Christ. Pope Francis invites all the faithful to rediscover the joy of being brothers and sisters in the Church. He said how good it is to know that we belong to each other, because we share the same faith, the same love, the same hope and the same Lord. He encourages us to appreciate the qualities of others, to recognize the gifts of others without malice and without envy. "Envy causes bitterness inside; it is vinegar on the heart."[12]

While addressing the gathering of the World Council of Churches (WCC), Pope Francis appreciated the contributions of those who have taken the initiatives and paved the way to bring all the separated churches together. He said that it is "out of love for Jesus they did not allow themselves to be mired in disagreements, but instead looked courageously to the future, believing in unity and breaking down barriers of suspicion and of fear."[13] To a certain extent, the new developments in the field of ecumenism, especially the pastoral approach initiated and promoted by Pope Francis, help the faithful break the barriers of division and bring them together to an ecclesial communion. He invites the Christian faithful to engage in a 'culture of encounter', seeing it as an act of building bridges that will surely enhance the efforts to Christian unity.

Change of Vocabulary – From Exclusion to Inclusion

There has been a radical change in the Catholic Church's attitude towards the non-Catholic Churches and communities since VC II. The broadening of the vocabulary in the usage of the Catholic Church to address the separated churches and other ecclesial denominations itself is indicative of a significant change. The exclusive identification of the Catholic Church with the One Church of Christ "*extra ecclesiam nulla salus*" (no salvation outside the Church) was replaced by an inclusive concept of the Church: "*ecclesia vera subsistit in ecclesia catholica*" (true Church of Christ subsists in the Catholic Church).

The shift in the approach from exclusion to inclusion and the ecumenical vision of communion expressed by VC II helps the churches to work towards the unity underlying the diversity and variety and at the same time upholding the identity and autonomous nature of each Church *sui iuris*.[14] Since VC II, the Catholic Church has held the view that there are ecclesial values outside the Church, and communion is understood not merely as the dominion of one Church over other Churches but as the communion of different Churches. There is already a paradigm shift in the understanding of the ministry of primacy in the Catholic Church: not an exercise of power—an *anathema sit* approach—but understood as service in love and exercised in the spirit of communion and collegiality.[15]

Unity Entails Repentance and Forgiveness

Pope John XXIII, who conceived of VC II, was the first to officially confess the Church's repentance in public for the responsibility of the divisions on her part and to forgive the faithful of other Churches for their mistakes. Pope Francis keeps on asking forgiveness for the sins committed in the past and urges the Churches to come together for the common witness in today's broken world. Pope Francis repeats the principles of VC II and believes that the separated Christians alone cannot be accused of the sin of separation in the past for the Catholic Church, too, has to share the burden of past divisions. On account of this realization, the Catholic Church now considers ecumenism not as a return to the past but as a search for future repentance and reconciliation. Therefore, the ecumenical movement is to be seen as a mutual rapprochement and as walking together with our friends, appreciating the riches and good qualities in them and inviting them to divine truths and to total communion.

At an ecumenical meeting held at Geneva, Pope Francis pointed to the Biblical significance of the number 70, noting how in the Gospel Jesus tells his disciple to forgive one another 'not only seven times, but seventy times.' That number, the pope said, is not a limit nor does it quantify justice, but rather, it opens up a vast horizon and serves as the measure of charity capable of infinite forgiveness.[16] He speaks of division as one of the most serious sins because it does not allow God to act and what God wants from us is that we forgive and love each other so as to become more and more like God, who is perfect communion and love (Trinitarian communion). Both forgiveness and repentance are necessary; for they complement each other on our way to total communion.

Supremacy and Absolutism – Obstacles to Unity

VC II urged a self-evaluation on the part of the Catholic Church, especially in her relationship with other churches and ecclesial communities. This must be seen against the backdrop of the attitude of the Catholic Church to put herself always at the centre while labelling all other churches and ecclesial communities as heretic/schismatic/separated brethren/uniate churches, etc., thereby treating them as inferior. All those terms with which other churches were addressed are clear indication of the Catholic Church's attitude of discrimination and a sign of an exclusive, holier-than-thou mentality. But the attitude has now changed and the shift is based on the understanding that the churches should never develop a fundamentalist attitude which supposes a world that is fully complete and immune to historical evolution. Fundamentalism can creep into the Church at the moment in which some norms are absolutised without regard for the community as a whole.

The new ecclesiological developments that took place at VC II gave a new vision of the Church as a communion of churches and as a result, the churches have come closer to each other, recognizing each other as sister churches and communities. The Church of Jesus Christ is One, Holy, Catholic and Apostolic. The communion of the churches demands uniformity of faith in Jesus Christ but at the same time, it promotes diversity and includes a multitude of churches and communities. In order to achieve this desired aim, the Church has always to be in the process of *reformanda* or *aggiornamento,* which does not mean that the Church sacrifices the truth, but rather is open to the truth of unity of churches. The document of the Amazon Synod held in Rome and approved on October 26, 2019, which was submitted to the Pope, clearly mentions that "legitimate diversity does not harm the communion and unity of the Church, but expresses and serves it."[17]

Pope Francis continues to talk about avoiding the temptation to absolutize certain cultural paradigms and getting caught up in partisan interests. It is quite possible that the churches enter into long term dialogue and waste time by discussing trivial matters presuming them to be absolute and eternal truths. As the old saying goes 'absolute power corrupts absolutely.' The question asked by Pope Francis 'who am I to judge others?' is a question that helps us to relate with others without prejudice and pre-conditioned programmes. He encouraged Catholics to think first about their own hardness of heart, and not about the sins of others.[18] He said it is more troubling to see the certainty shown by some who consider their own blessings as clear sign of God's predilection rather than a summons to responsible service of the human family and the protection of creation.[19]

The Catholic Church needs to act with discretion in her exclusive claim to be the wholesale seller of supreme and absolute truths. "While acknowledging that the fullness of truth has been revealed in Jesus Christ, individual Christians have no guarantee that they have grasped the truth fully, and so there must be openness to an ever deepening knowledge of that Truth."[20] The Church of Jesus Christ can be proud to be one Church of Christ only when the prayer of Jesus becomes realized: 'that they may be one.' As Christians, everyone is obliged not to create new obstacles with the claim of absolutism or with a fundamentalist attitude excluding others, but to search constantly for ways that will help pave ways for new horizons of unity.

Prayer: Oxygen and Roadmap of Ecumenism
VC II's documents affirm that the unity of the churches is the work of the Holy Spirit. Thus, we have to be at the disposal of the Holy Spirit and wait in prayer until the Holy Spirit works within us and brings about unity among the divided Christian faithful. The Catholic faithful are exhorted to imbibe the great example of the early Christians who, even in the midst of difficulties and persecutions, gained strength and courage through their home get-togethers and communion with each other by means of prayer, sharing of the property and breaking of the bread (Acts 4:23-31). Prayer is not merely considered as an expression of the Church's faith but also of her confidence that God will bring to perfection the work that God has begun. It is true that when Christians pray together, the goal of unity comes closer. Yves Congar is of the opinion that when the separated Christians pray together, by that very act their hearts are transformed for the better and opened wide to their brothers and sisters who are astray from them.[21]

Pope Francis talks of prayer as the oxygen of ecumenism: Whenever we say 'Our Father' we feel an echo within us not only of our being sons and daughters but also our being brothers and sisters. The Lord's Prayer is the prayer of the Church, confirming a person's identity as a beloved child of God and reminding Catholics of the responsibility owed toward their brothers and sisters in Christ. He speaks of 'Our Father' as a roadmap for the spiritual life to consider each other as God's beloved sons and daughters. He reminds the Christians that "where the Father is present, no one is excluded" and he reminds us to love others like the Father who loves us without counting the cost.[22] He pointed out that it is hard to attain the perfect communion without prayer because there, we prevent the wind of the Holy Spirit from driving us forward.

Ecumenism of Mission – A Prerequisite to Unity
Pope Francis says that Christian unity in many ways depends on a willingness to go out of oneself to meet the needs of others. He called for a 'new evangelical outreach' among Christian communities. He laments that ecumenism is divorced from missionary outreach today and he reiterates that the mission aspect of Christianity can neither be neglected nor emptied of its content. He talks about a 'new evangelical outreach' needed among Christians of different confessions who are called to be one people that experience and share the joy of the same Gospel. Moreover, he dreams of an ecumenical spring, which despite the 'constant vacillations' among different denominational communities, would allow them to gather together around Jesus Christ. He pointed out that 'walking, praying and working together' is an important theme and walking is a twofold movement which implies both going in and out, which means going in towards the centre, which is Christ, and out toward 'the existential peripheries' of the world.[23]

Pope Francis puts forward the 'ecumenism of mission' as an obligatory option for communion and unity. It is not much concerned with the theological debate done by the experts on certain controversial doctrinal matters; rather it affects the concrete life of the Christians of different confessions living side-by-side and facing the same realities around them. It is called an ecumenism of witness and mission. The 'ecumenism of mission' becomes a sign of unity and peace for the people of all denominations and the whole world.[24] He declared the month of October 2019 as an extraordinary Mission month in the Catholic Church with the view that "missionary outreach is paradigmatic for all the Church's activity" and also "to give fresh evangelical impulse to her work of preaching" with the collaboration of all the Christian faithful, and bringing to the world the salvation of Jesus Christ.

Ecumenism of Blood – Pride of Christians and Bond of Communion

VC II clearly speaks about the need of recognizing the riches of Christ and virtuous works in the lives of others who are bearing witness to Christ sometimes even to the shedding of their blood.[25] Pope Francis repeats the teachings of VC II and speaks of an 'ecumenism of blood' against the background of the killing of Christians at the hands of ISI in the Middle East and elsewhere. Pope Francis mentions that, despite their division, conflicts and doctrinal controversies, churches are already united by martyrdom and persecution in the 'ecumenism of blood': in which persecutors make no distinction when attacking believers in Christ and their places of prayer.[26] He was referring to the blood of martyrs who endured suffering for the name of Jesus.

Pope Francis invites the Christians "to see what we can do concretely, rather than grow discouraged about what we cannot and to look to our many brothers and sisters in various parts of the world, particularly in the Middle East, who suffer because they are Christians. He invites all the faithful to draw close to them and never to forget that our ecumenical journey is preceded and accompanied by an ecumenism already realized the ecumenism of blood, which urges to go forward."[27] He tries to instill confidence and courage in the minds of the Christian faithful irrespective of their theological or ecclesiological differences but united in the faith in Jesus Christ.

Ecumenism of Poor – A Common Witness

The VC II document UR speaks clearly on the dignity of the human person—that the Church should use every possible means to relieve the afflictions of our times, such as famine, natural disasters, illiteracy, poverty, lack of housing and unequal distribution of wealth. It is hoped that through such cooperation all believers in Christ are able to learn easily how they can understand each other better and esteem each other more, and how the road to the unity of Christians may be made smooth.[28] Through every single gesture of his, Pope Francis speaks for the poorest of the poor in the world. He speaks of an 'ecumenism of poor' as a call to journey and act together in order to bear witness to the Lord, particularly by serving the poorest and most neglected of our brothers and sisters in whom Jesus is present.[29]

Pope Francis is firm in his option for the poor. He calls for concrete action for the more vulnerable who are increasingly marginalized, lacking their daily food, employment and a future. Therefore he said: let us be challenged to compassion by the cry of those who suffer.[30] He criticized the Church for putting dogma before love and for prioritizing moral doctrines over serving the poor and marginalized.[31] He draws the attention of the Christian faithful to the fact that the cry of the poor is growing louder and embraces the entire earth. As a credible response on the part of the Church, he puts forward the 'ecumenism of the poor' as the preferential option for the poor in order to give them real hope in their life and to put a smile on their faces.

Conclusion

Pope Francis echoes the voice and the incarnation (*avatar*) of the teachings of VC II, giving flesh and life to ecumenism in the concrete situations of the Church today. From his very first words and gestures as bishop of Rome, he has lived out the teachings of the Council on unity even without referring to them explicitly. He gives confidence, courage and example to every Christian to follow the footsteps of Jesus rather than being preoccupied with doctrinal controversies that widen the division and discord among Christians. He exhorts Christians to look forward to a bright future with hope irrespective of what has happened in the past. He reminds us of the mission of the Church that Christian unity is not optional and the Church cannot stop its mission of unity until she attains perfect communion.

Pope Francis strongly believes that ultimately unity is a gift of God's Spirit and of God's guidance. It cannot be achieved by human effort alone. Unity is neither a mere academic nor a diplomatic matter to be used as a plot to strengthen the personal interests or positions; rather its soul is spiritual. Christ must be prioritized over any differences that might get in the way of unity. Pope Francis' approach of 'a heart speaking to the heart' (*cor ad cor loquitor*) has already won the hearts of many. It transcends all borders and boundaries and opens wide horizons of communion. He has a big heart that creates waves and reaches out to others and makes an impact on others' lives. Wherever the Will of Christ prevails and self-concern is transformed to the concern for Christ, there arises a new horizon of communion and unity.

Endnotes

[1] *Unitatis Redintegratio* (UR), n.1.

[2] *Orientalium Ecclesiarum* (OE), n.24.

[3] Rocco D' Ambrosio, "Will Francis pull it off?" *Charisms in Unity* 26/3 (July-September 2018): 42.

[4] UR no. 7.

[5] https://www.catholicnewsagency.com/news/pope-francis-true-wealth-is-found-in-friendship-not-things-31040.

[6] Chhotebhai, "Is Pope Francis a heretic?" *Indian Currents* 31 (September 2019): 38.

[7] https://www.catholicnewsagency.com/news/pope-francis-the-catholic-church-belongs-to-christ-32419.

[8] Michael Amaladoss, "Dialoguing with the Muslims: Saint Francis and Pope Francis," *Vidyajyoti Journal of Theological Reflection* 89/10 (October 2019): 749.

[9] Anselm Gruen, *Heaven begins within you* (New York, The Cross Road Publishing Company, 2011), 118.

[10] https://www.vaticannews.va/en/pope/news/2018-06/pope-francis-geneva-wcc.html.

[11] https://www.catholicnewsagency.com/news/pope-francis-seld-interest-and-hypocrisy-destroy-the-church-206879.

[12] https://www.catholicnewsagency.com/news/pope-francis-the-catholic-church-belongs-to-christ-32419.

[13] https://www.vaticannews.va/en/pope/news/2018-06/pope-francis-geneva-wcc.html.

[14] CIC uses the term 'Ritual Church *sui iuris*' but CCEO uses the term 'Church *sui iuris*' that refers to a Church's legal status in as much as it is recognized to have the capacity or right to govern itself according to its own law.

[15] John Berchmans, "Ecumenical Re-reading of Some New Testament Texts (45–70)," in *That they all may be one*, ed. Philip Vysanethu & George Thomas (Bethany Vedavijnana Peeth, Pune, 2013), 63.

[16] https://www.catholicnewsagency.com/news/-mission-is-a-prerequisite-to-unity-pope-says-in-geneva-62886.

[17] https:/www.catholicnewsagency.com/news/amazon-synod-document-calls-for-married-priests-and-increased-role-for-women-20862.

[18] https://www.catholicnewsagency.com/news/pope-francis-judge-your-own-heart-first-not-that-of-those-in-need-89254

[19] https://www.catholicnewsagency.com/news/-mission-is-a-prerequisite-to-unity-pope-says-in-geneva-62886.

[20] *Information Service*, 111/125 (2007): 146.

[21] Ian Randall, "Unity in the Gospel: Catholic – Evangelical Relationships," *One in Christ* 39/27–28 (2003): 76

[22] https://www.catholicnewsagency.com/news/pope-francis-the-our-father-is-spiritual-roadmap-15326.

[23] https://www.catholicnewsagency.com/news/-mission-is-a-prerequisite-to-unity-pope-says-in-geneva-62886.

[24] https://www.vaticannews.va/en/pope/news/2019-05/editorial-tornielli-pope-francis-bulgaria-orthodox-ecumensim.html.

[25] UR n.4.

[26] https://www.vaticannews.va/en/pope/news/2019-05/editorial-tornielli-pope-francis-bulgaria-orthodox-ecumensim.html.

[27] https://www.vaticannews.va/en/pope/news/2018-06/pope-francis-geneva-wcc.html.

[28] UR n.12.

[29] https://catholicherald.co.uk/news/2019/05/06/pope-francis-catholics-and-orthodox-are-unite-by-ecumenism-of-blood/

[30] https://www.vaticannews.va/en/pope/news/2018-06/pope-francis-geneva-wcc.html.

[31] Chhotebhai, "Pope Francis: Asthmatic, Charismatic or Schismatic?" *Indian Currents* 31 (Sept. 2019): 33.

28.

Towards an Environmental Spirituality in the Light of *Laudato Si'*
Isaac Parackal, OIC

Introduction: The Perilous State of Our Planet

The contemporary age is characterized by rapid growth at all levels of life. Ours is especially an age of scientific and economic progress and growth. However, there is a degeneration in relationships and value systems. Progress leads us to a kind of alienation. The sense of precariousness and insecurity makes humans greedy and selfish. The scientific mind feels threatened at the very thought of *mystery*. It wants to *master* everything and conquer the mysteries of nature.[1] *Experiment* has taken the place of *experience*. The contemporary human person wants to experiment rather than to experience at the heart level. *Human beings try to misuse nature for selfish motives.* They forget to recognize the intrinsic value of nature and try to exploit her in all possible ways. So, *agriculture* has become *agribusiness*. Previously it was a labour of love with the soil producing optimum yield but now it has become an enterprise of maximum exploitation with modern technologies.[2] The egoistic mentality makes humans forget their ultimate role in the universe. They fail to realize that *nature is not a slave to be raped but a partner to be cherished*. Nowadays, even the deserts are not deserted as they are locus of dangerous atomic experiments. The radical relativity in the universe urges us to think in terms of an environmental spirituality that integrates all beings in the thread of harmony and love. This article is an analysis of Pope Francis' eco vision depicted in his 2015 encyclical letter *Laudato Si'*.

1. The Ecological Legacy of Christianity: A Brief Overview

The theme of ecoclogcial consciousness is not a new idea in the Christian tradition. The early Church Fathers have begun this environmental study, which was furthered by Vatical Council II (hereinafter VC II) and Pope John Paul II, and perfected by Pope Francis. A general overview of the Church Fathers reveals a theme of respect and even adoration of God's creation.[3] For many of the Church Fathers revelation begins by observing God's creative activity in nature as part of the same revelation provided more directly in scripture.[4]

In his writings, St Clement of Rome emphasizes that creation reveals the bounty and goodness of the creator.[5] St Irenaeus draws a beautiful picture of the world where human beings grow into the image and likeness of their Creator using their freedom.[6] He envisages a process of regeneration of the human and cosmic body through the word and spirit: the two hands of God. He sees the entire cosmos becoming blessed and eventually immortalized by being ever more fully united with its divine source of being.[7] His famous statement "The glory of God is the human being fully alive" reveals sensitivity and enthusiasm that one must show towards one's fellow beings and nature.

Clement of Alexandria, known as the 'Educator of Souls' says, "The initial step of a soul to come to knowledge of God is contemplation of nature."[8] He puts great emphasis on the reflection of nature for understanding its Creator. In his teachings Tertullian affirms that nature teaches us to abide by the law of God, because nature is the revelation of God.[9] Origen asserts that a person reflecting on the scriptures and reflecting on nature must arrive at the same conclusion because both are coming from the same God.[10] According to him, the hand of God has not neglected even the bodies of the smallest creatures as each one of them is seen to possess some features that are unique to them. For St Athanasius, there is no inconsistency between *creation* and *salvation*, for the Heavenly Father has employed the same agent for both works, his "*Word*." Therefore, to destroy God's creation is to destroy a profound divine revelation. We are the stewards of this world.[11]

Citing Genesis chapters 2 and 3, St Ephrem expresses his awareness of the sacramental character of the created world, and of the potential of everything in the created world to act as a witness and pointer to the Creator. God's two witnesses, says Ephrem, are "Nature, through man's use of it, and Scripture, through his reading it."[12] Almost all the early Church Fathers have made great theological contributions in fostering ecological consciousness and emphasised the divine revelation in creation.

VC II reminds us that created things have their own laws and values which human beings have to learn.[13] An ecological worldview sees all forms of life as having their own worth and not just usefulness for humans. The whole existence possesses intrinsic quality and worth. There is a certain right for everything and everyone.[14] At the heart of the deepest feelings of those who care for the fate of the planet is a sense that the earth is seen as having its wondrous and absolute value independent of us. Our duty is to live in harmony with it. We, humans have to use our intelligence along with the gifts given by the Holy Spirit to complete and perfect God's work of creation through our activities with a view to the betterment of society, and that of the whole creation.[15] The present condition of opulence of the minority and the destitution of the majority is against the plan of God. So, VC II advocates the option for the poor and the just, and an equal distribution of natural resources. Harmony between humans and nature will be restored only when people determine to "be more" rather than "have more."[16]

In 1971, the document *Justice in the World* issued by the Synod of Bishops represents a major step in the development of Catholic teaching on environment. It emphasises the close link between ecology and justice considering "the option for the poor" with an "option for the earth".[17] In his writings Pope John Paul II affirmed the need for fostering ecological consciousness. In his pastoral jouneys, he urged all people especially in the developed countries to restrain from selfish tendencies and embrace a simpler way of life with great respect for nature. A recurring theme in his sermons was that ecological problems are first spiritual problems.[18] He calls all people to undergo "an ecological conversion", a change of heart and mind which would allow all people to join in the great ecological challenge of the 21st century.[19] If an appreciation of the value of life is lacking, we would lose our concern for others and for nature itself. If there is a lack of respect for nature by plundering of natural resources, the life in the planet is threatened. So, discipline, simplicity and the spirit of sacrifice must become a part of daily life to foster the qulaity of life.[20] It is through work that we respond to God's gift of the earth and cooperate with God in yielding the fruits of the earth.[21]

In his Encyclical *Caritas in Veritate* Pope Benedict XVI reminded us that our duty towards the environment and duty towards human persons are interlinked and we should take great care in maintaining them.[22] We see a great legacy in nurturing environmental consciousness in the church. In this context, *Laudato Si'* throws more light to our study of nature.

2. The Ecological Crisis

In his encyclical *Laudato Si'* Pope Francis elaborates the ecological theme, lamenting over the present terrible condition of the earth: "The sister (earth) now cries out to us because of the harm we have inflicted on her by our irresponsible use and abuse of goods with which God has endowed her."[23] The "mastery mentality" of human beings made her sick in all possible ways. Humans have disfigured the face of the earth by plundering her at will. "The earth, our home, is beginning to look more and more like an immense pile of filth."[24]

The soil, water, air and all forms of life have been sickened by constant exploitation. Human beings have, the Pope writes, forgotten the fact that they are made up of the earthly elements. Pollution caused by non-biodegradable waste from the industrial sources and business establishments is a matter of great concern because it covers the beautiful landscapes with toxic rubbish.[25] The laxity in recycling and reusing waste causes pollution of the soil. Climatic change and global warming aggravate the situation. The greenhouse gases that cause global warming are released mainly as a result of human activity. Intensive use of fossil fuels and deforestation add to the polluting levels.[26] A rise in the sea level due to the melting of the polar ice caps can create a serious situation as a quarter of the population lives in the coastal areas.[27]

Climate change, the Pope observes, is a global problem with crucial implications: "It represents one of the principal challenges facing humanity today."[28] Water pollution is another serious problem. The contamination of water resources by industrial toxic materials causes dramatic consequences.[29] The oceans that contain the bulk of our planet's water supply are contaminated and a variety of marine creatures is badly affected and drastically depleted. The uncontrolled fishing threatens marine organisms such as plankton, coral reefs, and thereby breaks the ocean food chain. The oceans, Pope Francis feels, have been turned into a cemetery of species by unbridled human exploitation. The same is true with rivers and lakes.[30]

Deforestation, for the Pope, is another area of serious concern. The vast forests, the bio-diverse lungs of the planet are burned down or levelled for purposes of cultivation and have frequently become wastelands. This entails the loss of countless species of beings.[31] Many cities and urban areas are congested with huge inefficient structures, excessively wasteful of energy and water and they really lack sufficient green space. He cautions, "We were not meant to be inundated by cement, asphalt, glass and metal, and deprived of physical contact with nature."[32] These structures are so chaotic that they create visual and sound pollution, too. The multinational companies, he observes, operate their business establishments in the developing countries and leave behind great human and environmental liabilities such as unemployment, abandoned towns, the depletion of natural reserves, deforestation, the impoverishment of agriculture and local stock breeding.[33] The selfishness of human beings makes the planet be squeezed dry beyond every limit.[34] "Never have we so hurt and mistreated our common home as we have in the last two hundred years."[35]

Pope Francis beautifully draws a picture of modern media and the digital world and how it many a times hinders us from hearing the wise advice of the great sages of the past. "The overloaded accumulation of unwanted information by media and digital world aggravates the situation by preventing people from thinking and reflecting wisely, respecting the other and loving generously. Personal relationships are replaced by internet relations that lead people to a sort of mental pollution."[36] True wisdom, he reminds us, is not a product of mere accumulation of overloaded data but it is the fruit of self-examination, dialogue and generous interactions between persons. In this scenario, the Pope analyses the role of human person in the world to overcome the present crisis. He affirms without doubt that the human person has the sacred vocation to fulfil the mission of God.

3. The Role of Human Beings in Caring for Creation

Human beings have a privileged role in creation as they are the only creatures capable of relating with the Creator. Since God is immanently present in the world, the world is to be recognized as the manifestation of God's action. Thus, the human attitude towards nature should be one of respect. Human being's role in nature should not be a 'dominion' but a 'caring' which promotes the betterment of the created world. The human being is not dominator but priest, trustee, and protector of creation.

3.1. *Priest of Creation*

Human being's role in creation can be seen as that of a priest of creation. Pope Francis observes that the complex of proper responses of humans to nature suggests that the human being's role in nature may be perceived as that of priest of creation, as a result of whose activity the sacrament of creation is reverenced and dignified.[37] Since anyone alone is conscious of God, oneself and nature, one can mediate between insentient nature and God – for a priest is characterised by activity directed towards God on behalf of others.

Human beings alone can reflect on the purposes of God and they alone can fulfil those purposes cooperating with God.[38] Humans alone can contemplate and offer the action of the created world to God. However, a priest is also active towards others on God's behalf and in this sense, too, the human being is the priest of creation. S/he alone, having reflected and contemplated on God's intentions and plans, can be active in and with the created world consciously seeking to enhance and fulfil God's purposes.[39] S/he is to live with reverence for all creation giving equal value to all.[40] The ultimate destiny of the universe is the fullness of God which is realized in the resurrection of Christ. The human being endowed with intelligence and love, and drawn by the fullness of Christ has the sacred duty to revere nature as s/he does to other persons and so lead the whole universe back to the creator.[41]

Pope Francis brings out the cosmic characteristic of the Eucharist which joins heaven and earth. It embraces and penetrates all creation.[42] To be a priest means to be a mediator. So human beings as priests of creation have been entrusted with the sacred vocation to gather together the offering of creation and present it back to God.[43] In this sense, the human being is an intermediary between God and Nature and this divine vocation matures and sanctifies the human person.[44] Human beings cooperate with God in the creative activity and fulfil God's purposes within it.[45] "Thus the Eucharist is also a source of light and motivation for our concerns for the environment, directing us to be stewards of all creation."[46]

3.2. *Steward of Creation*

For Pope Francis, nature is a divine gift given to the "care" of humanity.[47] He repeats this "caring notion" to assert the responsibility of humankind towards God, the giver of the gift.[48] In the creation story of Genesis, the human being is presented as having 'dominion' over the creation. This has encouraged unbridled exploitation of nature.[49] However, it is a "caring dominion" rather than an "authoritative domination." The term 'dominion' has a kingly reference. Caring and preserving are part of kingly qualities. A king is supposed to look after his kingdom and the subjects. He is not expected to exploit his people for his own selfish purposes.[50]

The Pope reminds us that the two biblical concepts "tilling" and "keeping" also should be understood in the proper context. "Tilling" refers to cultivating, ploughing or working, while "keeping" means caring, protecting, overseeing and preserving."[51] In this sense, creation is entrusted to the proper care and concern of human beings and they are answerable and accountable to God for the faithful preservation and maintenance of it.[52] Pope Francis gives a spirituality by drawing a "Father figure" of God who creates and owns the land and to whom human beings are accountable.[53] This spirituality, he thinks, is the best way to restore humans to their rightful and proper place in the universe.[54] The world we live in is a common home which is entrusted to the care of human beings.[55]

3.3. *Human Being as Symbiont with Reverence for Creation*

According to Pope Francis the world manifests God's continuing presence and so it commands admiration and awe.[56] Emphasizing the interdependent, symbiotic character of life he suggests that our attitude to nature should not be manipulative. It is a partnership between human beings and the world where one acts as a *symbiont—the one who makes harmony*. The Pope elaborates this marvellous harmonious relation: "An integral ecology includes taking time to recover a serene harmony with creation, reflecting on our life style and our ideals, and contemplating the Creator who lives among us and surrounds us…"[57] Further, he adds, "The human person grows more, matures more and is sanctified more to the extent that he or she enters into relationships, going out from themselves to live in communion with God, with others and with all creatures."[58]

Quoting from the book of Genesis, the Pope argues that human life is grounded in three fundamental and closely intertwined relationships with God, with our neighbour and with earth itself.[59] However, this vital relationship has been broken outwardly and within. This rupture he calls sin, and it has resulted in the loss of harmony.[60] The originally harmonious relations have become conflictual and confrontational. In this context, the call to be a *symbiont* to regain the lost relationship becomes significant. The Pope stresses the interconnectedness of the cosmic family as he states: "Because all creatures are connected, each must be cherished with love and respect, for all of us as living creatures are dependent on one another."[61] The Buddhist concept of *radical relatedness of all beings (pratītyasamudpāda)* is much echoed here in the words of Pope Francis.[62] Creatures exist only in dependence on each other, to complete each other and in the service of each other that "throughout the universe we can find any number of constant and secretly interwoven relationships."[63]

All life is interdependent, indeed many creatures can only live in concert with, and often literally on, particular other organisms (*symbiosis*).[64] Although we are often not aware of it, we depend on other beings for our own existence.[65] "Everything is related, and we human beings are united as brothers and sisters on a wonderful pilgrimage, woven together by the love God has for each of his creatures..."[66] This love of God, the Pope states, "unites us in the bond of affection with brother sun, sister moon, brother river and mother earth."[67] He affirms that the human being has the sacred duty to conserve and protect nature which is unique and irreplaceable.[68] The Earth is a precious home for all of us and it deserves our love.[69]

3.4. *Human Being as Interpreter and Prophet of Creation*
For Pope Francis, as Creator, God expresses the divine intentions and purposes and unveils the divine meaning in the various and distinctive

levels of the created natural world and in its processes. The human being is capable of seeing and hearing it. The natural world is seen as the symbol of God's meaning and it is conceived as the means whereby God's intentions and purposes are made known. In other words, the world is seen as a sacrament.[70] "Hence, there is a mystical meaning to be found in a leaf, in a mountain trail, in a dewdrop and in a poor person's face."[71] This concept of sacrament, according to Pope Francis "serves to emphasize another aspect of human function, namely, human being as *interpreter* of creation's meaning, value, beauty and destiny. He beautifully writes: "Standing awestruck before a mountain, he or she cannot separate this experience from God and perceives that the interior awe being lived has to be entrusted to the Lord."[72] As Jesus made his way throughout the land, he contemplated the beauty of creation and invited others to perceive a divine message in it.[73] The flowers of the field and the birds which his human eyes contemplated and admired are imbued with his radiant presence.[74] Every creature presents then the radiance of God.

As interpreter of God's meaning in creation attributes to human being the prophetic function which is a complementary aspect of the priestly role of the human person.[75] A prophet is one who reads the signs of the times and interprets them for the future. So, human beings are the interpreters of God, and as such, they act as *prophets*, a role which historically has always complemented the priestly in human's corporate relation to God. The human being as prophet reads the signs of nature and interprets them for the betterment of the world. Faith allows us to interpret the divine meaning and the beauty of what is unfolding. The whole universe is open to God's transcendence within which it develops.[76] "The universe unfolds in God, who fills it completely."[77]

The Pope observes that God has written a precious book whose letters are of created things present in the universe.[78] From electromagnetic to Divine and from vegetal to human, all are intertwined and every creature manifests the continuous divine revelation.[79] This contemplation of creation allows us to discover each thing as a teaching which God wishes to hand on to us. Humans have to listen to this subtle voice, understand the message and interpret the meaning for the whole world.[80] The Pope asserts that "the divine and the human meet in the slightest detail in the seamless garment of God's creation, in the last speck of dust of our planet."[81]

4.5. Human Being as Co-creator, Co-worker and Co-explorer with God

God, for Pope Francis, respects human freedom and is intimately present to every being without impinging on its autonomy. "God, who wishes to work with us and who counts on our cooperation, can also bring good out of the evil we have done."[82] The Holy Spirit has filled the earth with various possibilities and therefore from the very heart of being something new can always emerge. So there is creativity and novelty in nature as in the case of an art work.[83] Human excellence could be seen as the human being making his/her distinctive human contribution as *co-creator* to that ceaseless activity of creation which is God's action in and for the world.[84]

Creating a world in need of development God in some way sought to limit Godself so that the so called evils, sufferings and dangers are part of the childbirth which God uses to draw humans into the act of cooperation with Him.[85] In the scene of creation one stands with one's creative energies within oneself and in relation to nature. Creation is of an order- an order of love (*ṛta*).[86] This order extends a free choice before human beings. "We are free to apply our intelligence, towards things evolving positively, or towards adding new ills, new causes of suffering and real setbacks."[87] The human being can either create a world "in which freedom, growth, salvation and love can blossom, or lead towards decadence and mutual destruction."[88]

The Pope cautions us that in a technocratic paradigm, human freedom to take decisions and make space for creativity is substantially diminished. In this context he urges us to take a balanced position that would enhance human creativity to flourish in the advancement of science and technology on the one hand, while creating an attitude to control the negative effects of intervention in the eco-system on the other hand. In other words, our intention should not merely be profit-oriented but other-oriented. Quoting his predecessor, Pope Francis undoubtedly affirms that the scientific and technological progress is an evidence of "the nobility of the human vocation to participate responsibly in God's creative actions."[89]

Pope Francis acknowledges that technology has remedied countless evils that used to harm and limit human beings. He also appreciates the work of many scientists who contributed to the welfare of the human race.[90] In this sense, the human being is acting as a creative participant in creation, as it were the leader of the orchestra of creation, in the performance of which is God's continuing composition. Moreover, human beings offer themselves with dedication in the creative process. Techno science, the Pope admits, can produce important means to improve the quality of human life.[91] In short, humans have the opportunity of consciously becoming *co-creators* and *co-workers* with God in His work on earth.[92]

The Pope urges us to uncover (or dis-cover) God's presence in creation.[93] Technology helps the human being fulfil his/her personal and social development in cooperation with God. "Human creativity cannot be suppressed."[94] For him, science and technology are wonderful products of a God-given creativity.[95] Techno science "can produce art and enable men and women immersed in the material world to "leap" into the world of beauty."[96] He gives the example of an artist who cannot be stopped from using his or her creativity. In the same way, human beings who possess particular gifts for the progress of science and technology cannot be prevented from using their God-given talents for the welfare of the world. Through science and technology they explore with God the creative possibilities within the universe God has brought into being. This is to see human beings as *co-explorers* with God.[97] This cooperation of humans in the creative processes is not a passive involvement but an intelligent and active participation – an authentic collaboration with the

Creator. "It is an attitude of the heart, one which approaches life with serene attentiveness, which is capable of being fully present to someone without thinking of what comes next, which accepts each moment as a gift from God to be lived to the full."⁹⁸

Work, according to Pope Francis has an ennobling and sanctifying role that contributes to the overall well-being of the whole world. It matures and sanctifies the life of human beings.⁹⁹ Quoting from the Bible he shows how Jesus being a carpenter sanctified human work. Through his work Jesus lived in full harmony with nature and lent it an attention, full of fondness and wonder.¹⁰⁰ The correct understanding of work, Pope reminds us, is an essential aspect of integral ecological relationship between human beings and the world.

4. A Spirituality of Radical Conversion (*Metanoia*)

We have seen how Pope Francis raises his prophetic voice against the egoistic tendencies of human beings who try to exploit the natural resources for the selfish motives. "When people become self-centred and self-enclosed, their greed increases."¹⁰¹ He observes that the current global situation engenders a feeling of insecurity and uncertainty which can become 'a seedbed for collective selfishness. He perceptively notes: "The emptier a person's heart is, the more he or she needs things to buy, own and consume."¹⁰² He cautions that obsession with a consumerist life style can only lead to violence and mutual destruction especially when it is a monopoly of a few.

Pope Francis encourages us to rise above all these limitations of greed, consumerism and materialism by choosing what is good. He urges humanity to make a new start and turn away from our destructive tendencies of self-centredness.¹⁰³ He calls for a spirituality of radical *metanoia* (turning back). It is a commitment and conviction.¹⁰⁴ It is a radical conversion of heart, mind and spirit.¹⁰⁵ He calls it the ecological conversion or *metanoia*.¹⁰⁶ It is a *metanoia* from our old life styles and selfish attitudes to a new understanding of reality (from dualism to inclusivism- *dvaita* to *advaita*). It is a *metanoia* from self-elevation to self-expending. It is a *metanoia* from our mental and social conditioning to a new path of freedom and openness towards goodness, truth and beauty.[107] It is a *metanoia* from life negation to life affirmation.[108] It is a *metanoia* from individualism to togetherness.[109] It is a *metanoia* from self-affirming to other-affirming.[110] It is a *metanoia* from knowing the instrumental value of nature to knowing the intrinsic value of nature.[111] It is a new awareness that makes us awaken to new horizons of freedom and joyful celebration of life.[112]

Ecological conversion "can inspire us to greater creativity and enthusiasm in resolving the world's problems and in offering ourselves to God 'as a living sacrifice, holy and acceptable.'"[113] This conversion calls for a number of attitudes which together foster a spirit of generous care, love and full of tenderness.[114] Pope Francis emphasizes the significance of education that can bring this new awareness.[115] He observes, "There is nobility in the duty to care for creation through little daily actions, and it is wonderful how education can bring about real changes in life style."[116] Education in environmental responsibility can encourage ways of acting that can directly and significantly affect the world around us. He elaborates a number of practical ways such as avoiding the use of plastic, reducing water consumption, planting trees, care for other beings, etc.[117] This ecological awareness through education must be translated into new habits and be made into practical at different levels—at schools, in families, in the media, in the political institutions, in catechesis and elsewhere.[118]

Pope Francis urges everyone to take up an ancient lesson found in different religious traditions together with the Bible. It is a life style with the conviction that "less is more."[119] He cautions, "A constant flood of consumer goods can baffle the heart and prevent us from cherishing each thing and each moment."[120] So, a life of simplicity marked by moderation can help us appreciate the small things and be grateful for the same. It helps us live our life to the full and be serenely present to the beauty of reality with humility.[121] Quoting Saint Francis of Assisi, Saint Therese of Lisieux, Saint John of the Cross and Saint Bonaventure,

Pope Francis proposes to live a spirituality that cherishes a "culture of care" towards the "other" as each creature bears in itself a Trinitarian structure.[122] To be totally open to this "Trinitarian epiphany" of reality is the sum and substance of the ecological spirituality that leads us to life fulfilment: "Everything is interconnected, and this invites us to develop a spirituality of that global solidarity which flows from the mystery of the Trinity."[123]

Pope Francis' eco-vision is not only to pass "from the exterior to interior to discover the action of God in the soul but also to discover God in all things."[124] This eco-vision is in a way learning to encounter God in all creatures which bear in themselves a specifically Trinitarian structure and reveal the mystery of the Trinity in a unique manner.[125] It is a vision that "entails learning to give, and not simply to give up."[126] The Pope writes, "When we can see God reflected in all that exists, our hearts are moved to praise the Lord for all his creatures and worship him in union with them."[127]

I conclude this article with a prayer of our great ancient sages of the Indian tradition, *Lokāsamasthā sukhino bhavanthu* which means, "*Let there be peace and happiness in the whole world.*" Together with Pope Francis, let us also wish the same for the whole world with the prayer, *"Praise be to you, Lord."*

Endnotes

[1] Pope Francis, Encyclical Letter *Laudato Si'* 2015, no. 116; hereinafter LS with the number denoting paragraph.

[2] LS 190.

[3] Steven Bauma Prediger, *The Greening of Theology* (Georgia: Scholar Press, 1995), 39.

[4] Bishop Kallistos Bare, *The Orthodox Way* (Fairford: St. Vladimir's Seminary Press, 1995), 53-55.

[5] Clement of Rome, "Letter to Corinthians" 1:20, translation: *Early Church Fathers Series* (Brussels, 1987), 44-45.

[6] Wallace Hadrill, *The Greek Patristic View of Nature* (Manchester: Manchester University Press, 1968), 114.

[7] Paul Santmire, *The Travail of Nature* (Minneapolis: Fortress Press 1985), 41.

[8] *Early Church Fathers Series*, 45.

[9] Andrew Linzey, *Compassion for Animals* (London: SPCK Publications, 1988) 6-7.

[10] Paul Santmire, *The Travail of Nature*, 87. Wallace Hadrill, *The Greek Patristic View of Nature*, 137.

[11] *Ibid*, 86-87,

[12] Andrew Linsey, *Compassion for Animals*: *Reading and Prayers*, 89. See also Sebastian Brocke, *St. Ephrem the Syrian: Hymns On Paradise* (Fairford: St. Vladimir's Seminary Press, 1917).

[13] Vatican Council II, *Gaudium et Spes*, ed. Austin Flannery (NY: Costello 1996), 36.

[14] *Ibid*, 39.

[15] *Ibid*, 41.

[16] *Ibid*, 69.

[17] Synod of Bishops, *Justice in the World*: Antilles Episcopal Conference, Pastoral Letter, Caring for the Earth (April 2005), 2.

[18] Pope John Paul II, "Peace with God the Creator, Peace with all Creation", "*Message for the World Day of Peace* (1 January 1990), 6.

[19] Pope John Paul II, *Redemptor Hominis, The Redeemer of Man* (Bangalore: St. Paul Editions 1979) 12.

[20] *Ibid*, 12-13.

[21] Pope John Paul II, *Encyclical Letter on Hundredth Anniversary of Rerum Novarum* (May 1, 1991), 31.

[22] Pope Benedict XVI, *Caritas in Veritate* (2009), 48.

[23] LS 2.

[24] LS 21.

[25] LS 21.

[26] LS 23.

[27] LS 24.

[28] LS 25.

[29] LS 29.

[30] LS 40-41.

[31] LS 38.

[32] LS 44.

[33] LS 51.

[34] LS 106.

[35] LS 53.

[36] LS 47.
[37] LS 83.
[38] LS 66.
[39] LS 233-236.
[40] LS 69.
[41] LS 83.
[42] LS 236.
[43] LS 80-81.
[44] LS 231.
[45] LS 83.
[46] LS 236.
[47] LS 228.
[48] LS 55.
[49] LS 67.
[50] LS 5, 6,11,106.
[51] LS 67.
[52] LS 200.
[53] LS 92, 53.
[54] LS 75, 68.
[55] LS 232.
[56] LS 93-96; 233-234, 238.
[57] LS 225.
[58] LS 240.
[59] LS 66.
[60] LS 66.
[61] LS 42.
[62] LS 164, 240.
[63] LS 240.
[64] LS 86, 138.
[65] LS 140.
[66] LS 92.
[67] LS 92.
[68] LS 34.
[69] LS 164.
[70] LS 234.

[71] LS 233.
[72] LS 234.
[73] LS 97, 100.
[74] LS 100.
[75] LS 222.
[76] LS 79.
[77] LS 178.
[78] LS 85.
[79] LS 138.
[80] LS 85, 225. The Pope laments that the subtle words of love in nature are not heard in today's noisy, busy, imbalanced and distracted life style. It is a call to recover the serene harmony with creation and thereby with the Creator Himself.
[81] LS 9.
[82] LS 80.
[83] LS 80.
[84] LS 53.
[85] LS 80.
[86] LS 77. It is a cosmic order of love, see 236.
[87] LS 79.
[88] LS 79.
[89] LS 131.
[90] LS 102.
[91] LS 103.
[92] LS 117.
[93] LS225.
[94] LS 131.
[95] LS 102.
[96] LS 103.
[97] LS 131, 132.
[98] LS 226.
[99] LS 231.
[100] LS 98.
[101] LS 204.
[102] LS 204.
[103] LS 207.
[104] LS 52, 216-218.

[105] LS 217.
[106] LS 220.
[107] LS 205.
[108] LS 9.
[109] LS 9, "It is a way of loving, of moving gradually away from what I want to what God's world needs."
[110] LS 208.
[111] LS 140.
[112] LS 207.
[113] LS 220.
[114] LS 220.
[115] LS 211-215.
[116] LS 211.
[117] LS 210, 211.
[118] LS 209-215.
[119] LS 222.
[120] LS 222.
[121] LS 223.
[122] LS 218-240.
[123] LS 240.
[124] LS 233.
[125] LS 239, 234.
[126] LS 9.
[127] LS 87.

29.

From *Cenozoic* Period to *Ecozoic* Era: A New Consciousness on Eco-justice

George Kalapurackal

Introduction

"Who is truly concerned with environmental problems?" Paul Haffner poses this question in his treatise *Towards a Theology of the Environment*; and answers: "Certainly the Catholic Church."[1] In the midst of increasing ecological problems, the Church is called to respond to the ecological crisis. As the creation of God continues in Christ (*Pleroma*)[2] through the Church, the Church must respond to the environmental crisis. Optimistically, the Church got an impetus for ecological concerns from the pre-Vatican Council II (hereinafter VC II) era to the post-VC II period. Moreover, Pope Francis actualizes the teachings of VC II, forming a new consciousness of eco-justice. This new consciousness is from an understanding of the sacredness of nature which is closely related to the sacramental, Eucharistic, pneumatological and moral dimensions of creation. This article seeks to depict the sacredness of creation actualized in the teachings of Pope Francis.

1. Redefining the Traditional Concept

In Antiquity, trees, springs, streams, and hills have their own *genius loci*[3] as guardian spirit; and these spirits were like centaurs, fauns and mermaids. It was important to calm down the spirit in charge of the situation before cutting a tree, damming a brook or mining a mountain. Later, Christianity began to exploit nature by considering it as mere object. Christianity exposed nature as not divine and strongly held the anthropocentric view, seeing human beings as ordained ones to dominate all other species in nature. It relegated nature to a low status. Critics would say that animism was replaced by the cult of saints in the Church.[4] Further, science and technology developed very fast in the West and religion was also influenced by it. Therefore, the conquest of nature spread in western Christianity more easily than in eastern Christianity. However, in the early Church, nature was conceived as a symbolic means through which God speaks to humans. For instance, the ant was considered as a sermon to sluggards and the rising flame was the symbol of the soul's aspiration. This nature-centered view was artistic rather than scientific.[5]

The traditional understanding of the Scriptures may not be sufficient enough to awaken in us a new sense of sacred. Therefore, we need a new process of adaptation "not only through the awesome qualities of the universe as experienced immediately, but also through the immense story of the universe and its long series of transformations."[6] For realizing a new sense of the sacred, we need to establish rituals which would involve the primordial moment of emergence of the universe. The discovery of photosynthesis of respiration, the appearances of trees and flowering plants, the emergence of life especially of humans are moments that evoke the sacred sense. This new sense of sacred will inspire us to have a new approach to the modern world. This sense of sacred will enable us to discover all things around us as objects of our intelligence. We find them as the miracle of existence. Moreover, we will experience the existence of God in every being through its good qualities.[7] This new understanding will not tempt us to dominate nature. On the contrary, we would realize the fact that humans and other creatures are part of the same creation. Moreover, (wo)man will begin to treat natural world with mercy of God and with divine compassion.

2. The Sacred and Sacramental Nature of Creation

There has been tremendous change in the traditional understanding of sacraments during the twentieth century. The general understanding has changed from the metaphysical dimension to the profound ecological character. The universe reveals the signs of transcendence and immanence. People get a conscious experience of divine presence by walking in creation in a new way. "All places can become sacramental to people who see signs of the Spirit in them."[8] An ecocentric ethical order strives to bring equilibrium in the entire cosmic community. The Spirit ever urges humankind to have a mystical relation with the universe as a whole. According to Boff, "[t]o be spiritual means living in accordance with the thrust of life toward and in unison with society and nature."[9] Mystics like Maximus the Confessor experienced the Spirit in the cosmos and had a reverential attitude towards it.[10] This creates a sense of sacredness of creation.

2.1. *Sacredness of Creation*

The icon of sacredness of nature "constitutes the epiphany of God in the world and the existence of the world in the presence of God."[11] John of Damascus says: "I do not venerate the creation instead of the creator, but I venerate the Creator, created for my sake, who came down to his creation without being lowered or weakened."[12] It is through matter that "God has worked out our salvation."[13] We have missed this salvific power of the environment today which we need to have rediscovered. In the Greek Fathers' view the 'image of God' within a human person depicts the specific value of freedom. The human person must be associated with the created world and thus the created world must be transformed to God.[14] A reclaiming of the sacredness of creation is required to begin a new covenant with the earth. Unfortunately, the universe has shrunk to mechanical, mathematical and lifeless by 'dehallowing' nature.[15]

In classical cosmology, we find that God and world are set facing one another. By contrast, process thinkers like Alfred North Whitehead (1861-1947) have tried to understand the world in a new way: as an evolutionary cosmos. Here God is seen as within the process of the cosmos and the world is reflected within God's process. The world and God are perichoretically involved in one another. This leads to a mystery that the perichoretic circularity is not yet complete. We can see here a mutual relationship between God and the world, but each one preserving its identity and difference. The Creator is not identified with the world and the world is not identified with God. However, the universe is identified in God.[16] "We must keep in mind, however, that sacramentality must not aim simply at a vertical vision of God and the universe but must be directed at the horizontal—God as process of evolutionary cosmogenesis. No being is completed; all are open to new advances and hence to new revelations."[17] This denotes that sacredness in fact is in process and it is open to new kinds of manifestation of the mystery of the Creator. What we require today is a more holistic and mystical understanding of the universe as we see in wisdom theology. Wisdom theology tries to integrate all parts of cosmos into a single and meaningful whole by respecting the divine mystery. "[it] brings back to our theological work and our cosmology the elements of feeling, intuition, bodylines and connectedness to earth that have been marginalized."[18]

Nature can be understood in relation to God that is as the presence of God in nature and of the openness of nature to God. The Latin expression *'finitum capax infinitum'*—"the finite is open to the infinite"—specifies the sacredness of nature as the sacrality of nature.[19] When we speak of sacrality of nature in relation to sacramentality of nature, confusion may occur as we compare it with the particular theological meaning of 'sacrament.' The term sacrament refers to the forgiveness of sins, life and salvation by realizing the real presence of Christ in the liturgy where the believer enters into an I-Thou relationship with Christ. In the sacramentality of nature, we find a new relationship between humans and nature.

Paul Santmire's understanding of I–Thou relationship between humankind and creation is in tune with the thought of Martin Buber. Santmire proposes a new type of human relatedness called I-*Ens* relationship; '*ens*' meaning 'being.'[20] "An I-*Ens* relationship is akin to an I–Thou relationship in almost every respect—on some occasions even a kind of reciprocity can be identified—except that there is no speech, no verbal communication between the I and the Ens."[21] This I-*Ens* relationship can be accounted for in the relationship between a human being and a tree. If one contemplates the tree, then one sees not only the tree but also the presence of Christ. This is the very Christ whom I experience in the Eucharist and "who personally addresses me in the proclaimed Word and who personally cares for me through the works of mercy of my brothers and sisters in Christ."[22] Christ is not present in, with and under the tree. But when one cares for the tree, then it is in some way appropriate to its particularity and also appropriate to the '*tree-ness*' of the tree. Therefore, "nature is sacral to me because nature is where I encounter the same Christ whom I know personally."[23]

2.2. *Eucharist and Creation-Ecology*

In the midst of the ecological crisis today, what is the relation between the Eucharistic meal and Creator/Creation? The Bread and Wine used as the Eucharistic meal are gifts of creation and the fulfillment in God's new Creation.[24] The Bible affirms that God gave people manna when they were hungry, which ceased when people possessed the land. By occupying the land people had to work for food. Therefore, manna has been the expectation of the Promised Land. This implies a reality that bread has the dimension of the fertility of the land because people were collecting bread by cultivating the land. The grain and wine are mentioned in the Bible as signs of God's care. God's gracious action includes the growth of grain, the fertility of land, the wine and oil.[25] The wine too is related to the promise of the land. The people of Israel were led to the land where vines were growing. They were sent to examine the quality of land by testing whether the land is good or not and whether there is wood or not in which they had to find their living place. The book of Numbers configures this story.[26]

Further, Eucharistic prayers in the liturgy of the Eastern Church present God as Creator who loves His Creation, which is to be renewed through endeavours of the creatures and thereby a new Creation is to be inaugurated.[27] The Orthodox view of Christianity is deeply rooted in the Eucharist and this view opposes ecological destruction because the Orthodox believe that God created the world not only for humans but also for nature. "Divine and human meet in every human being and in every detail of this created world."[28] The prayers of the Anaphora in the Orthodox tradition "refer to the creation in two senses: creation/ *ktisis* of God which came into being *ex nihilo* and a new creation which is a gift of God's grace."[29] The use of sacramentality in a panentheist manner indicates that the things of the earth signify not only divine love but also a sense of active participation in the Divine. Panentheistically, the whole material world is as a vehicle through which God reveals himself.[30] According to Teilhard de Chardin, one of the two dimensions of priesthood is mediation between the world and God. Eucharist is a place of exchange between the world and God, where the Redeemer and the redeemed meet.[31] A priestly offering encompasses thanksgiving as the fulfillment of creation's promise and redemption. The earthly things are lifted up for God's blessing.

3. The Moral Dimension of the Earth

There are three moral schemas in the sacredness of the earth: creational, intrinsic, and unenchanted. The *creational schema* functions with the belief that a Divine or Supreme Being created nature. As a result, we believe that nature is sacred.[32] Those who hold this view set up moral boundaries to protect sacred creation. This schema taps both theological concepts and religious traditions. The intrinsic schema functions with a moral belief that nature is sacred in itself. Therefore, we have the responsibility to protect nature. In this schema, belief in God is not an essential condition for attributing sacredness to objects.[33] Sometimes, those who hold this view are nonreligious. Here the source of sacredness has changed but moral boundaries are there because sacredness is still present. The unenchanted schema operates with the belief that nature is not sacred.[34] Individuals with this view may have reasons to protect nature, but reason without considering sacred moral beliefs. However, sacredness of nature is addressed in the patterns of the activity of people.[35]

Thomas Berry argues that we are ending the Cenozoic period of the earth's development and entering the Ecozoic phase of the earth. Cenozoic period is that the period of the expansion of life in the full brilliance of its expression. The Ecozoic period is that the new human-earth relations are hopefully being shaped. This shift demands a change in our consciousness or a transformation from anthropocentric norms to biocentric norms. The Ecozoic era reminds us that the cosmos is not a collection of objects, but a communion of subjects. This entails that each component of the cosmos has the right to fulfill its role in the changing process of the earth.

4. Ecozoic Era: A Change in Consciousness

According to Berry an account of the past is necessary to provide an adequate response to the present and guidance for the future. As a critique of Western Christian culture, his solution is a cultural one. Berry replaced the 'ecological age' with the term 'Ecozoic era,' which represents a change in consciousness that takes place in human beings. It also represents a transition between scientifically designated ages of the earth which are Paleozoic (up to 220 million years ago), Mesozoic (220 to 65 million years ago) and Cenozoic (65 million years to the present).[36] The mammals became dominant on earth in the Cenozoic era. The Cenozoic era is divided into two periods: Tertiary and Quaternary. The Tertiary period borders the Mesozoic and humans developed during the Quaternary period.[37]

According to Nicholsen, "[T]he Cenozoic era which we have been living, an era marked by a magnificent flowering of species, is waning and will not return."[38] Ecozoic era will be a time to change the lifestyle and behaviour of humanity if it needs to face ecological crises. Berry opines that we need a new cosmological understanding. The traditional story of the universe provided us with life purposes, shaped our emotional attitudes and energized our actions.[39] However "it did not take away the pains and stupidities of life or did not make unfailing warmth in human association."[40] Berry considered this new story of the universe as revelatory and religious. His idea of revelation includes not only the Christian sense of revelation but also the North American people's land mystique, Teilhard's personal archetypal dimension of the earth, the Mother Earth Goddess. According to him, the ultimate form of human wisdom was encompassed in the *Logos* concept in the Greek world, the *rita* concept in Hinduism and *dharma* in Buddhism.[41]

The new Ecozoic era invites our attention to new cosmological reflections on the meaning, value and place of humans in the universe. It always encourages us to have an other-oriented approach to nature. Plants, animals and human beings have equal roles for the sustenance of the cosmos. Ultimately, we should have the aim of caring for all species on the earth, thereby preserving the health of the earth. The new cosmological dimension also asserts the need of revitalizing our religious experience and healing the human psyche. As we find a single sacred community, we have to develop an ecological spirituality. Therefore, religious traditions, women, science, classical humanistic traditions will have important roles for redefining value, meaning and norms for the Ecozoic era. The integration of all these realities will help to formulate a new approach to the environment.[42]

In this context, it is relevant to gauge the development of ecological concerns since VC II to see how the Church transformed from an anthropocentric attitude towards ecological concerns.

5. Environment and VC II

Humanity has the responsibility to maintain cosmic order as stewards of nature. *Gaudium et Spes* tries to emphasize this in its teaching.[43] It implicitly speaks of the protection of earth and insists that the human person must take care of the goods of the earth with love and responsibility (GS 37). It stresses that all created beings have their own rules and values and human beings must learn them because all persons "always recognized the voice and the revelation of God in the language of creatures" (n.36). *Gaudium et Spes* follows the thought of *Lumen Gentium*. By referring to biblical texts, *Lumen Gentium* states that redemption is for all creation; not exclusively for humankind. The whole of creation is part of redemption. There is also the need for better distribution while exploiting the goods of the earth (LG 36,41,48). Notably, both these VC II documents explicate the need of caring for the earth. Citing these references, Keenan opines that these significant documents give ample importance to the growing environmental crisis.[44]

Further, the document articulates an intimate relationship between nature and culture. People become aware of their humanity only through agriculture and understanding values of environment. Only through culture can humans achieve full humanity (n.55). Culture has relation to values and nature. Therefore, humanity is much influenced by culture and nature. Keeping the harmony is the responsibility of humankind.[45] As a principle for the proper development of culture, the document says that when one engages in building activity upon the earth in order to get fruit one "carries out the design of God manifested at the beginning of time, that one should subdue the earth, perfect creation and develop oneself."[46] Moreover, it holds that God intended the earth for all human beings. Created goods should be for all in abundance under justice and charity. Whatever be the forms of property, attention must be given to the universal destination of earthly goods. When one uses or possesses earthly goods, the benefit should go not only to oneself, but also to all people. Sadly, the anthropocentric concerns of the document count humans as rulers of the earth, not stewards of nature and its wealth. In other words, it permits human being to accumulate goods of the earth, even without considering the true value of the earth.[47]

Dignitatis Humanae stresses that human beings must act by making use of responsible freedom, motivated by a sense of duty and not be driven by coercion. As everyone is endowed with reason and free will, one has the moral obligation to seek the truth. It is the duty of all to seek the truth with true judgments of conscience by using all suitable means.[48] "Furthermore, society has the right to defend itself against possible abuses committed on the pretext of freedom of religion."[49] Thus, the faithful are supposed to have a responsible attitude towards creation too.

6. Development of Ecological Thinking in the post-Conciliar Period

In the post-conciliar period, the anthropological stress consists of three types of justice: distributive justice, commutative justice and the social justice. Social justice affirmed the individual's duty to the whole of society.[50] Social commitment of the individual includes the right environmental perspective. Concerned with the ecological social teachings in this period, Popes John Paul II, Benedict XVI and Francis have given remarkable contributions. Pope Paul VI opened channels to their ecological vision, even though his attention was on integral human development.

In his *Address to the International Labor Organization* on June 10, 1969, Paul VI pointed out the relationship between human beings and the environment. He highlighted new aspects in relation to creation. It is the duty of the creature who exploited nature, to humanize the earth as it was. Thus, humanity can enjoy the fruits of the earth as gift from God.[51] According to him, the totality of (wo)man is beyond science and technology. Most significantly, in an exceptional way he speaks about the environmental concern of the church. This is the first time that the Catholic social teaching recognizes the threat of human activity to the environment. This aspect is described under the title "The Environment."[52] Paul VI exposes the unanticipated outcome of human activity. Because of the unexpected changes in the environment, (wo)man is becoming aware that the exploitation of nature risks her/his existence on earth and humanity is turning into a victim of this degradation. He sees this as a "dramatic and unexpected consequence of human activity, which amounts to an ill-considered exploitation of nature."[53] He anticipates the dangerous situation in future that the environmental issues may create intolerable ecological crises.

Pope John Paul II laid a strong theological foundation for environmental concerns. In *Redemptor Hominis,* he relates the creation narrative of Genesis to the incarnation of Christ. Jesus Christ restored not only broken humanity but also the broken earth as well. When sin entered into the world, coupled with the dominion of (wo)man over the world, the world was subjected to futility. Jesus Christ, the redeemer of the world, recuperated its original relationship with the Almighty.[54] According to Deane-Drummond, *Redemptor Hominis* comments not only about what is going wrong in the fundamental relationship between humanity and nature, but also about how we need to understand right relationship, in the context of the dominion over nature.[55] John Paul II articulates in *Sollicitudo Rei Socialis* that "the task is 'to have dominion' over the other created beings, 'to cultivate the garden.'"[56] It is to be done within the framework of obedience to the divine law and thereby becoming the means of perfection of human beings. He elucidates that destruction of natural environment leads to the destruction of human environment. People are worried about the preservation of natural environment because they have realized that each species contributes to keeping the balance of nature. But very little effort is made to protect the moral settings for an authentic human ecology.[57] The ecological crisis is, in fact, a moral problem because it is to be understood as a problem of resources. As a moral problem it is concerned with equal allocation of resources to all and thus a question of justice. Therefore, the environmental crisis should be addressed in terms of a human-earth relationship.[58] In *Pastores Gregis* John Paul II points out that the call for solidarity involves the question of safeguarding creation and the resources of the earth. The interests of production and profit take priority over the good of individuals and of humanity. The result of these interests is the pollution and environmental destruction.[59]

In his World Day of Peace Message in 2007, citing *Centesimus Annus*, Pope Benedict XVI affirms the ecology of nature. He points out that as a response to *Centesimus Annus*, all of us have to unite to bring peace in the world. "Alongside the ecology of nature, there exists what can be called a 'human' ecology, which in turn demands a 'social' ecology. This means that humanity, if it truly desires peace, must increasingly be conscious of the links between natural ecology, or respect for nature, and human ecology."[60] The expression 'human ecology' conveys a necessary idea that human beings are not divorced from nature, but that they are part of creation.

7. Pope Francis: An *Ecozoic* Conscience of the Time

According to Pope Francis, the ecological slant is a sociological approach and hence it must integrate questions of justice in relation with the environment so that the cry of the earth has to be heard as the cry of the poor. In his encyclical, *Laudato Si* (LS), he admits that climate change is a global problem of environmental, social, economic and political implications.[61] He asserts that an ecological debt exists globally with roots in current and historical patterns of exploitation (n.51). He observes that modern anthropocentrism misplaced human beings in forms of technological progress which cannot be equated with the progress of humanity and history (n.113). However, he adds that this does not mean rejection of the possibilities of technology or return to the Stone Age (n.114). He observes that technology, economics, and political orders can be improperly oriented and become the end of human flourishing than the means of human flourishing.

Further, turning to the social dimensions of ecology, Francis criticizes the 'throwaway culture' of consumerism (n.43). According to him, one of the moral burdens of environmental degradation is the impact on the poor people as they are 'the excluded' (n.48). The 'rampant individualism,' consumerism, and today's culture of 'self-centered gratification,' are signs of ethical and cultural decline. LS also speaks of human rights in terms of environment. With regard to human rights, water is considered very fundamental to the achievement of any other right. It speaks of environmental degradation and injustice in the case of water as it faces social burdens (n. 29). He underlines that "each creature has its own purpose. None is superfluous," and the nature is "the locus of God's presence" (n. 84). Therefore, our vocation is to protect the handiwork of God which is essential for a virtuous life, not an optional or secondary aspect of Christian life.

Conclusion

We saw that the Cenozoic period of the earth's development is ending and we are entering the Ecozoic phase. This shift demands a change in our consciousness or a transformation from anthropocentric norms to biocentric norms. This transformation of consciousness can be called an ecological conversion. Ecozoic era will be a time to change the lifestyle and behaviour of humanity. In the traditional eschatological view, we were looking at a completely different world as a place of fulfillment where the cosmos itself had no future. But when we consider the creation as the promise of the Kingdom of God, then the world as creation belongs to the history of the Kingdom of God. Therefore, we need an inclusive eschatological cosmology as the basis of Christian environmental theology.

It is imperative for humanity to develop other-oriented thinking patterns in the direction of 'the new heaven and the new earth'. This new awareness of humanity will inspire us to safeguard nature for justice, human rights, eradication of poverty, equality, etc. The Catholic Church has the responsibility to frame a new contemporary environmental ethics. That is what we see in the teachings of VC II culminating in Pope Francis who gives a new radiance to the environmental concerns of the Church. He reminds each of us: "I am speaking of creation as a whole. We human beings are not only the beneficiaries but also the stewards of other creatures."[62]

Endnotes

[1] Paul Haffner, *Towards a Theology of the Environment* (Herefordshire: Gracewing, 2008), 71.

[2] Pierre Teilhard de Chardin, *The Divine Milieu: An Essay on the Interior Life* (New York: Harper and Row, 1960), 122.

[3] In classical Roman religion a *genius locus* was the protective spirit of a place, often depicted in religious iconography as a figure holding attributes such as a cornucopia, patera or snake.

[4] Lynn White, "The Historical Roots of Our Ecological Crisis," in *This Sacred Earth: Religion, Nature, Environment*, ed. R. S. Gottlieb (New York: Routledge, 1996), 189.

[5] Ibid., 190.

[6] Thomas Berry, "Into the Future," in *This Sacred Earth*, 412.

[7] Frithjof Schuon, "Seeing God Everywhere," in *Seeing God Everywhere: Essays on Nature and the Sacred*, ed. B. McDonald (Indiana, IN: World Wisdom, 2003), 1.

[8] John Hart, *Sacramental Commons* (Maryland: Rowman & Littlefield Publishers, 2006), xiii.

[9] Leonardo Boff, *Ecology and Liberation* (New York: Orbis Books, 1995), 137.

[10] Maximus the Confessor (c. 580 – 662) was a Christian monk, theologian and scholar. According to him, the divine economy is expressed and fulfilled by a threefold presence of logos: in the cosmos, in scripture and in the person of Jesus Christ. The cosmic embodiment is effected through the *logoi* of created beings and a creature (he says, for instance, an animal) is participating in the Life, Being and Goodness of God. (Torstein Theodor Tollefsen, *The Christocentric Cosmology of St. Maximus the Confessor* (Oxford: University Press, 2008).

[11] John Chryssavgis, "The World of the Icon and Creation: An Orthodox Perspective on Ecology and Pneumatology," in *Christianity and Ecology: Seeking the Well-Being of Earth and Humans*, ed. D. T. Hessel and R. R. Ruether (Cambridge: Harvard University Press, 2000), 84.

[12] John Damascus, *Three Treatises on the Divine Images* (New York: St. Vladimir's Seminary Press, 2003), 22.

[13] Ibid., 30.

[14] Chryssavgis, "The World of the Icon and Creation: An Orthodox Perspective on Ecology and Pneumatology," 85.

[15] Leonardo Boff, *Cry of the Earth, Cry of the Poor* (New York: Orbis Books, 1997), 115.

[16] Ibid., 147.

[17] Ibid., 152.

[18] Paulina Kainulainen, "Wisdom Theology and Symbols Powerful Enough," in *Ecothee: Ecological Theology and Environmental Ethics*, ed. K. Kenanidis and A.P.L. Andrianos (Kolymbari: Orthodox Academy of Crete, 2009), 297.

[19] H. Paul Santmire, *Ritualizing Nature: Renewing Christian Liturgy in a Time of Crisis* (Minneapolis: Fortress, 2008), 107.

[20] Ibid., 122.

[21] Ibid., 122.

[22] Ibid., 123

[23] Ibid., 123.

[24] See *Spirituality, Creation and the Ecology of the Eucharist*, Reflections of an International Consultation Convened by the European Christian Environmental Network (ECEN) from April 2 to 6 (Geneva: Centre International Reformed John Knox, 2007), 27.

[25] Lucas Vischer, "Bread and Wine—Signs of God's Creation and New Creation," in *Spirituality, Creation and the Ecology of the Eucharist* (Geneva: John Knox International Reformed Centre, 2007), 41-42.

[26] Vischer, "Bread and Wine—Signs of God's Creation," 46-47.

[27] Tamara Grdzelidze, "The Eucharist and the Creation – an Orthodox View" in *Spirituality, Creation and the Ecology of the Eucharist*, 53.

[28] Ecumenical Patriarch Bartholomew I, "Spirit and Human Rights"- address during the conference of an honorary doctorate at Southern Methodist University, November 5, 1997 in *Cosmic Grace, Humble Prayer, The Ecological Vision of the Green Patriarch Bartholomew I*, ed., J. Chryssavgis (Cambridge: Eerdmans, 2003), 214.

[29] Vischer, "Bread and Wine – Signs of God's Creation and New Creation," 56.

[30] Philip Knights, "'The Whole Earth My Altar': A Sacramental Trajectory for Ecological Mission," *Mission Studies* 25 (2008): 60.

[31] Pierre Teilhard de Chardin, *Writings in Time of War* (London: Collins, 1968), 219.

[32] Justin Farrel, "Environmental Activism and Moral Schemas: Cultural Components of Differential Participation," *Environment and Behavior* 45/3 (2011), 405.

[33] Ibid., 405.

[34] Ibid., 405.

[35] According to Milton, environmental activism is characterized by four kinds of ecological piety; monastic, sectarian, churchly and folk. Monastic piety leads a life with minimum harmful impact on nature. Sectarian piety was directed at social change rather than renunciation. Churchly piety supported environmental organizations, making donations and paying subscriptions. Folk piety was experiencing green consumerism: a kind of reutilization of everyday titbits. See Kay Milton, "Nature Is Already Sacred," *Environmental Values* 8/4 (1999), 441.

[36] Anne Marie Dalton, *A Theology for the Earth: The Contributions of Thomas Berry and Bernard Lonergan* (Ottawa: University of Ottawa Press, 1999), 118.

[37] Allan D. Sills, *Earth Science the Easy Way* (New York: Barron's Educational Series, 2003), 125.

[38] Shierry Weber Nicholsen, *The Love of Nature and the End of the World: The Unspoken Dimensions of Environmental Concern* (Massachusetts, MA: Massachusetts Institute of Technology, 2003), 177.

[39] Thomas Berry, *The Dream of the Earth* (San Francisco: Sierra Club Books, 1988), 123.

[40] Ibid., 123.

[41] Ibid., 20.

[42] Thomas Berry, (2009, January 1). Twelve Understandings Concerning the Ecozoic Era: Center for Ecozoic Studies; available from http://www.ecozoicstudies.org/index.php?option=com_content&view=article&id=22:twelve-understandings-concerning-the-ecozoic-era&catid=11:statements&Itemid=110 (accessed on 27 October 2019). According to Jensen, three principles are vital for the Ecozoic era: (a) recognizing that the universe is not a collection of objects but a communion of subjects; (b) the universe of humans and nonhumans is a single sacred community; (c) the universe is primary and the human is a derivative. Thus, medicine must first serve the planet, not humans, because if the planet is unhealthy, humans cannot be healthy. See Derrick Jensen, *Listening to the Land: Conversations About Nature, Culture, and Eros* (White River, VT: Chelsea Green Publishing Company, 2004), 39.

[43] *Gaudium et Spes* gives more theological grounds for the Church's social teachings than earlier social encyclicals because it promotes the dignity of the person, reflecting on the creation of (wo)man in the image of God and endorses the communal and social dimension of humanity to build solidarity with others. See David Hollenbach, "Commentary on Gaudium et Spes," in *Modern Catholic Social Teaching: Commentaries and Interpretations*, ed. K. R. Himes (Washington, DC: Georgetown University Press, 2005), 267.

[44] Marjorie Keenan, *From Stockholm to Johannesburg: An Historical Overview of the Concern of the Holy See for the Environment 1972-2002* (Vatican City: Pontifical Council for Justice and Peace, 2002), 14.

[45] *Gaudium et Spes* n.55.

[46] GS n.57.

[47] GS n.69.

[48] *Dignitatis Humanae*, nn. 1,2,3. Available from http://www.vatican.va/archive/hist_councils/ii_vatican_council/documents/vat-ii_decl_19651207_dignitatis-humanae_en.html. (Accessed on 10 October 2019).

[49] Ibid., n. 7.

[50] Charles E. Curran, *Catholic Moral Theology in the United States: A History* (Washington, DC: Georgetown University Press, 2008), 250.

[51] Paul VI, *Address to the International Labor organization*, 10 June 1969; available from http://www.vatican.va/holy_father/paul_vi/travels/sub-index/index_ginevra.htm (accessed on 12 October 2019).

⁵² It exhorts that "[w]hile the horizon of man is thus being modified according to the images that are chosen for him, another transformation is making itself felt, one which is the dramatic and unexpected consequence of human activity. Man is suddenly becoming aware that by an ill-considered exploitation of nature he risks destroying it and becoming in his turn the victim of this degradation. Not only is the material environment becoming a permanent menace - pollution and refuse, new illness and absolute destructive capacity - but the human framework is no longer under man's control, thus creating an environment for tomorrow which may well be intolerable. This is a wide-ranging social problem which concerns the entire human family. The Christian must turn to these new perceptions in order to take on responsibility, together with the rest of men, for a destiny which from now on is shared by all." (Paul VI, *Octogesima Adveniens*, n.21).

⁵³ Celia Deane-Drummond, "Joining in the Dance: Catholic Social Teaching and Ecology," *New Blackfriars* 93, no. 1044 (2012), 193 212; available from http://onlinelibrary.wiley.com/doi/10.1111/j.1741 2005.2011.01476.x/abstract, 195 (accessed 10 October 2019).

⁵⁴ John Paul II, *Redemptor Hominis*, n.8.

⁵⁵ Deane-Drummond, "Joining in the Dance: Catholic Social Teaching and Ecology," 197.

⁵⁶ John Paul II, *Sollicitudo Rei Socialis*, n.30.

⁵⁷ John Paul II, *Centesimus Annus*, n.38. The term 'human ecology' was used by Ellen Swallow Richards in the work *Sanitation in Daily Life*, published in 1907. In this work human ecology is defined as "the study of the surroundings of human beings and the effects they produce on the lives of men." (Ellen H. Richards, *Sanitation in Daily Life* (Boston: Whitcomb and Barrows, 1907), v.)

⁵⁸ Heather Eaton, "Forces of Nature: Aesthetics and Ethics," in *Aesth/Ethics in Environmental Change: Hiking through the Arts, Ecology, Religion and Ethics of the Environment*, ed. Irmgard Blindow, Sigurd Bergmann, Konrad Ott (Munster: LIT Verlag), 109.

⁵⁹John Paul II, *Pastores Gregis*, Post Synodal Apostolic Exhortation, n. 70; available from http://www.vatican.va/holy_father/john_paul_ii/apost_exhortations/documents/hf_jp-ii_exh_20031016_pastores-gregis_en.html (accessed 4 October 2019).

⁶⁰ Benedict XVI, *World Day of Peace Message*, 2007, n. 8; available from http://www.vatican.va/holy_father/benedict_xvi/messages/peace/documents/hf_ben-xvi_mes_20061208_xl-world-day-peace_en.html (accessed October 7, 2019).

⁶¹ Pope Francis, *Laudato Si'* n.25.

⁶² Pope Francis, *Evangelii Gaudium* n.215; available from http://www.vatican.va/evangelii-gaudium/en/#2 (accessed October 12, 2019).

Contributors

1. **Prof. Dr Felix Wilfred** is founder-director of the Asian Centre for Cross-Cultural Studies, Chennai. Earlier he was Chair of the School of Philosophy and Religious Thought, University of Madras, and President of the International Theological Review Concilium. He was a member of the Vatican International Theological Commission, then chaired by Cardinal Ratzinger. He was visiting Professor in several universities. He was on deputation by the Government of India, served as ICCR Professor of Indian Studies, Trinity College, Dublin. He edited a landmark volume: *The Oxford Handbook of Christianity in Asia* (Oxford University Press, New York). He is also the chief editor of the *International Journal of Asian Christianity* (IJAC), Brill, The Netherlands. His latest book *Religious Identities in the Global Age: A Southern Perspective* is in print. Email: felixwilfred@gmail.com

2. **Prof. Dr Aloysius Pieris, SJ**, is a theologian as well as an Indologist. Of his many books, *An Asian Theology of Liberation*, (Maryknoll, Orbis Books 1988) and *Studies in the Philosophy and Literature Pali Abhidhammika Buddhism* (Colombo 2004) represent his two fields of research. He has held visiting chairs of theology in Catholic as well as Protestant faculties in USA and has served as examiner in Buddhist studies in the University of Kelaniya and is a member of the Sri Lanka Association of Buddhist studies. He is founder-

director of the Tulana Research Centre for Encounter and Dialogue at Kelaniya. Email: aloypsj@gmail.com

3. **Prof. Dr Massimo Faggioli** is Professor in the Department of Theology and Religious Studies at Villanova University, Philadelphia, USA. His books and articles have been published in more than ten languages. He is a columnist for the globally acclaimed *Commonweal* and *La Croix International* magazines. His most recent publications include the following books: *A Council for the Global Church. Receiving Vatican II in History* (Fortress, 2015); *Catholicism and Citizenship: Political Cultures of the Church in the Twenty-First Century* (Liturgical, 2017); *The Liminal Papacy of Pope Francis. Moving Toward Global Catholicity* (Orbis, 2020). He is co-editing with Catherine Clifford *The Oxford Handbook of Vatican II* (Oxford University Press, 2021). Email: massimo.faggioli@gmail.com

4. **Prof. Dr Michael Amaladoss, SJ**, from India, has a Ph.D. in Sacramental Theology from Paris. He has been a Professor at Vidyajyoti College of Theology in Delhi and has taught in many theological and pastoral centres in Asia, Europe and North America. He has been the President of the International Association of Mission Studies and a Consultor to three secretariats at the Vatican and one in the World Council of Churches. He was the Founder-Director of the Institute of Dialogue with Cultures and Religions (IDCR), Chennai, India. He is the author of 34 books and about 500 articles in many languages. Email: michamal@gmail.com

5. **Prof. Dr Francis Gonsalves, SJ**, has a Licentiate from the Gregorian University, Rome, and Ph.D. from the University of Madras. He has been a Professor and Principal at the Vidyajyoti College of Theology, Delhi. He has taught theology at the Sogang University, Seoul, South Korea, and at the Jesuit School of Theology, Berkeley, affiliated to the Santa Clara University, USA. He has also served as the Executive Secretary of the Indian Theological Association (ITA). Currently, he is the President of JD, Pune, as well the Executive Secretary of the Conference of Catholic Bishops of India (CCBI).

He has authored seven books, edited eight others, and published over 200 scholarly articles in various publications in India and abroad. He has been contributing articles on religion, spirituality and social-justice issues in a column called 'Mystic Mantra' for *The Asian Age* and *The Deccan Chronicle* national dailies. Email: francis.gonsalves@jdv.edu.in

6. **Dr Anil Thomas, CM**, is currently serving as the provincial superior of the South Indian Province of the Congregation of Mission (CM). He was recruited by JD to teach in the faculty of theology. Having obtained a Licentiate and Doctorate in Missiology from the Pontifical Gregorian University, Rome, he has been teaching Missiology, Ecumenism and Dialogue in the faculty of theology at JD and has served as the head of the department of Systematic Theology. Email: anil.thomas@jdv.edu.in

7. **Prof. Dr Joseph Scaria Palakeel, MST**, is the Dean of Theology at Ruhalaya Seminary in Ujjain, M.P. He has his Doctorate in Theology with specialization in fundamental theology from the Pontifical Gregorian University, Rome (1995). His areas of expertise and research interest are: Media, Religion and Culture. He has been the Co-founder and Executive Editor of *Jnanatirtha, A Journal of the Scriptures* (2000-2005). Currently, he is its associate editor. He has authored four books and edited two. He has participated and presented papers in various national and international conferences and his scholarly articles have appeared in national and international journals. Email: josepalakeel@gmail.com

8. **Deacon Jaime & Ligia da Fonseca** are married since 1980 and have two children. They are members of the ecclesial movement '*Couples For Christ*' (CFC) since 1991 and have been ministering to and counselling married couples and youth since 1998. Jaime was ordained Permanent Deacon on In April 2009 by Oswald Cardinal Gracias. Since June 2013, he has been serving at Our Lady of Fatima Parish, Sewri. In Sept. 2009, they were appointed by Pope Benedict XVI, Members of the Pontifical Council for the Family (PCF) for a

period of five years. At the invitation of Vatican, they have attended consecutively three Plenary Assembly of the Pontifical Council for the Family in Rome (XIX in Feb 2010; XX in Nov/Dec 2011; XXI in Oct 2013). Jaime and Ligia have represented India at the FABC (Federation of Asian Bishops' Conferences) gatherings on Family since 2007. Email: jaime.ligia@gmail.com

9. **Dr Patricia Santos, RJM**, belongs to the Congregation of the Religious of Jesus and Mary, Pune Province. She has a MA in Psychology from Pune University, a Licentiate in Systematic Theology from Boston School of Theology and Ministry and a Doctorate in Pastoral and Empirical Theology from Catholic University of Leuven, Belgium. She is currently a theology lecturer at Jnana Deepa, Pune and Coordinator of the Diploma programme in Theology for Sisters. She is a member of the Ecclesia of Women in Asia (EWA), Indian Women Theologians' Forum (IWTF), Indian Theological Association (ITA) and Catholic Conference of Psychologists of India (CCPI). Email: patricia.santos@jdv.edu.in

10. **Prof. Dr Shalini Mulackal, PBVM**, is a Presentation Sister, teaching systematic theology at Vidyajyoti College of Theology, since 1999. She is also a visiting professor to a number of other Seminaries and theological institutes in India. She is an active member of the Indian Theological Association (ITA) and has served the Association as Vice-President and also as its first woman President. She has served as coordinator of the Indian Women Theologians Forum (IWTF) and Ecclesia of Women of Asia (EWA). She has published a number of articles with special emphasis on women empowerment in Church and Society. She has also contributed to the Dalit Bible commentary series published by Centre for Dalit Studies, Delhi. She has also co-edited three books of the ITA. Email: smulackal@gmail.com

11. **Fr Malleswararao Gh. (Jayaraj), SJ**, is a Jesuit from Andhra Province. Having completed his Masters' degree in Systematic Theology at JD, Pune, he taught Christology in JD as part of his

probationary teaching. His research areas of interest are Relational Christology, Contextual Christology, and Communion centered Ecclesiology. Email: jayaraj23sj@gmail.com

12. **Dr Thomas Karimundackal, SJ**, teaches Scripture and serves as the Head of the department of Scripture Studies and as the coordinator of the Masters Programme in Biblical Studies at JD, Pune. He has presented research papers in many national and international conferences, and published many articles in national and international Journals as well as in edited books. His book "A Call to Commitment: An Exegetical and Theological Study of Deut 10,12-11,32" has received wide reviews. He also has co-edited three books: Melodies from the Flute: Dialogue among Religions and Cultures – Memorial Volume for Indian Christian Philosopher Rev Noel Sheth SJ (2018); Logic and Love: Reflecting on Professor John Vattanky's Contribution to Indian Philosophy and Spirituality (2019); Fully Human, Fully Spiritual: Fostering Diverse Spiritual Experiences – Essays in Honour of Dr Stephen Chundamthadam SJ (2019). Email: thomas.karimundackal@jdv.edu.in

13. **Dr Joseph Lobo, SJ**, the ex-director of Karnataka Jesuit Regional Theological Center, Bengaluru, has a Master's degree in Sociology from Pune University and a Doctorate in Systematic Theology from the University of Innsbruck, Austria. He has published many articles mainly in theological journals and co-edited a few books. He has been a visiting faculty at JD, Pune, Vidayjyoti, Delhi, and a few other seminaries in India. He has taught courses at Jesuit School of Theology, Berkeley, and at the University of Innsbruck, Austria. Email: jlobosj@gmail.com

14. **Fr George A. Sebastin Babu, HGN**, has a Bachelor's degree in Civil Engineering from Anna University, Chennai, and Master's degree in Mathematics from Periyar University, Salem. He has authored a book on Oscar Romero in Tamil. Currently, he is pursuing his doctoral studies in Systematic Theology, in JD, Pune. Email: asbabuji19@gmail.com

15. **Prof. Dr Mohan Doss, SVD**, has Master's Degrees in Sociology, English Literature and Systematic Theology. He completed his doctorate in Systematic Theology in Albert-Ludwigs University in Freiburg, Germany in 2000. He is the author of the book, *Christ in the Spirit*. He has edited a few books, contributed scholarly articles in anthropology, sociology and theology to national and international journals, and presented papers in national and international conferences in India and abroad. He has represented Vatican twice at the International Colloquiums. Since 2000 he has been teaching Systematic Theology at JD, Pune. He was the dean of theology at JD from October 2014 to April 2018. Email: mohan.doss@jdv.edu.in

16. **Dr Surekha Lobo, BS**, having successfully defended her Doctoral Thesis on the topic "Presence-Solidarity: A Paradigm for a Kenotic Mission: The Significance of Jesus Christ for India today in the Writings of Samuel Rayan and Elisabeth Schüssler Fiorenza," taught theology at Jnana Deepa, Pune. She has participated in many conferences and published numerous articles in various journals. Email: surekhabs@gmail.com

17. **Prof. Dr Nishant Alphonse Irudayadason** is a Professor of Philosophy at JD, Pune. After having obtained two doctorates on Ethics and Postmodernity from *Université Paris-Est* and from *Institut Catholique de Paris*, France, he has been actively pursuing academic life. He has authored two books and over 30 scholarly articles both in national and international journals and has presented papers in many academic conferences both in India and abroad. He is also a visiting faculty in many colleges and universities in India. He is a regular contributor to contemporary political analysis in "Light of Truth," a bimonthly published from Kochi. Email: nishant.irudayadason@jdv.edu.in

18. **Dr Fabian Jose, UMI**, has completed her BTh in Vidya-Deep, Bangalore, MTh in JD, Pune, and Doctorate from the Jesuit School of Theology at Berkeley of Santa Clara University, California,

USA. Currently, she is a lecturer in spirituality, Coordinator of the MTh in Spirituality and the Animator of the women's forum in JD, Pune. She has published two books *Renewed Vision for Consecrated life: Mystics, Prophets and Jesus Christ, The Relevance of Thomas Merton's Spirituality for the Consecrated Life in India*. Email: fabian.jose@jdv.edu.in

19. **Dr Arjen Tete, SJ**, has been teaching Systematic Theology since 2015 at JD, Pune. He belongs to Calcutta Province and resides in De Nobili College, Pune. He has a Bachelor's degree in Sanskrit from the University of Calcutta and Master's degree in Cultural Anthropology from the University of Pune. He is a graduate with a doctorate in Sacred Theology from the Jesuit School of Theology of Santa Clara University, California. He was in the organizing committee of the symposium "Towards Renewing Church and the World: Revisiting Vatican II through the Eyes of Pope Francis" held at JD. Email: arjen.tete@jdv.edu.in

20. **Dr Jesuraj Rayappan, SVD**, is a Professor of Church History and Patrology at JD, Pune. He has been the resident professor of Khristo Jyoti Mohavidyaloyo, Sason, Odisha and the Dean and Vice Rector of Khrist Premalay Regional Theologate, Ashta, MP. He has also been a visiting faculty to many other Indian seminaries. He has authored a book, *The Original Fire and New Flames: History of the Catholic Church in Orissa: 1850-1922* and published several articles. Email: jesuraj.rayappan@jdv.edu.in

21. **Prof. Dr Peter C. Phan**, who has earned three doctorates, is the inaugural holder of the Ignacio Ellacuria Chair of Catholic Social Thought at Georgetown University, USA. His research deals with the theology of icon in Orthodox theology, patristic theology, eschatology, the history of Christian missions in Asia, and liberation, inculturation and interreligious dialogue. He has published over 30 books and over 300 essays. His writings have been translated into many languages, and have received many awards from learned societies. He is the first non-Anglo to be elected President of

Catholic Theological Society of America and President of American Theological Society. In 2010 he received the John Courtney Murray Award, the highest honour bestowed by the Catholic Theological Society of America for outstanding achievement in theology. Email: Peter.C.Phan@georgetown.edu

22. **Prof. Dr Richard Benson, CM**—member of the Congregation of the Mission (Vincentians, abbreviated as CM)—is Vice President and Academic Dean of the Catholic Theological Union (CTU), Chicago. He was Adjunct Professor in the Religious Studies Department, at DePaul University, Chicago, and served at St John's Seminary, Camarillo, California, as Academic Dean (1995-2010) and Chair of the Moral Theology Department (1994-2010). He was singled out by the Carnegie Foundation for an excellent model of pedagogy for seminarians. He has a B.A. in Philosophy, a Master of Divinity Degree, a Master of Arts (Theology), a Master of Arts (Biological Sciences), a Licentiate and a Doctorate in Sacred Theology from the Catholic University of Louvain, Belgium. Email: rbenson7@depaul.edu

23. **Fr Midhun J Francis, SJ**, is working among Muslims for the "Christian-Muslim relationship" as the mission of the South Asian Conference of the Society of Jesus. He has completed his MA in Philosophy from the University of Madras and MTh in Systematic theology from JD, Pune. Email: midhunkochu@jesuits.net

24. **Prof. Dr Kuruvilla Pandikattu, SJ**, is a professor of Physics, Philosophy and Religion at JD, Pune. Currently, he is the Dean of the Faculty of Philosophy and Director of JD Centre for Science-Religion Studies (JCSR) and Association of Science, Society and Religion (ASSR), Pune. He has been actively involved in dialogue between science and religion. He has been involved as co-founder and co-publisher with two journals, *Jnanadeepa: Pune Journal of Religious Studies* and *AUC: Asian Journal of Religious Studies*. He has authored over 40 books and 210 academic articles. Email: kuru@jdv.edu.in

25. **Archbishop Felix Machado** was appointed as Bishop of the Diocese of Nasik—with personal title of Archbishop—in 2008, and is Bishop of the Vasai Diocese since 2009. He has a Licentiate from the Catholic Faculty of Theology, Lyon, France; Master of Arts in Theology from Maryknoll School of Theology, New York; and a Doctorate from Fordham University, New York. He has taught in several faculties in India and abroad and has published numerous articles in Indian and foreign journals. He was also the editor of '*Pro Dialogue*': a Vatican publication. Archbishop Machado had delivered lectures at international seminars and conferences. He was Chairperson for the CBCI's 'Office of Interreligious Dialogue and Desk for Ecumenism' and CCBI's Chairperson for the 'Commission of Ecumenism'. He is currently the Chairperson for the Office of Ecumenical and Interreligious Affairs (OEIA) of Federation of Asian Bishops' Conferences (FABC). Email: archbp.48@gmail.com

26. **Bishop Allwyn D'Silva** was appointed Auxiliary Bishop by Pope Francis on December 20, 2016, and was ordained Bishop by Oswald Cardinal Gracias on January 28, 2017. Currently, he is in-charge of the Justice and Peace Commission for the Archdiocese of Bombay and coordinator of the Prison Ministry as well as the Secretary of the Climate Change Desk and Human Development Office for the Federation of Asian Bishops' Conferences (FABC). As part of his priestly ministry, Bishop Allwyn spent 21 years in the slums of Mumbai where he was deeply involved in Human Rights issues, social concerns and more recently, in environmental matters at the local, regional and national levels. He has co-edited, published and presented a number of articles and papers. Email: bpadsilva2017@gmail.com

27. **Dr Shajan Kuttiyil, OIC**, has a doctorate in Oriental Canon Law from Pontifical Oriental Institute, Rome (2005). His thesis was "*Communicatio in Sacris*: A Juridical-Theological Study in the Context of Catholic and Non-Catholic Eastern Churches in India." Currently, he is the Director of Bethany Vedavijnana Peeth, Pune

(2018 -). He has also been visiting staff member at JD, Pune and Malankara Major Seminary, Trivandrum. Email: kuttiyil1968@gmail.com

28. **Dr Isaac Parackal, OIC**, holds a doctorate in Philosophy (Metaphysics and Anthropology) from the University of St. Thomas Aquinas, Rome. Since 2002 he has been teaching Metaphysics, Ancient and Medieval Philosophy and Ecology in different cycles of philosophical studies such as Bachelor's, Master's and Doctorate levels at JD. He has served as Head of the Department of Systematic Philosophy and Coordinator of Masters' programme. Currently, he is a member of the Doctoral Committee and Academic Senate. He has published many books and articles. He is also a visiting Professor in different institutes. Email: isaac.parackal@jdv.edu.in

29. **Fr George Kalapurackal** belongs to the Archdiocese of Ernakulam-Angamaly (Kerala) and ordained for the same archdiocese on January 1, 2005. He studied philosophy and theology at St. Thomas Apostolic Seminary, Kottayam, Kerala. His Licentiate was done at Catholic University, Leuven, Belgium. Now he is doing doctoral studies in Moral Theology at Jnana Deepa, Pune. Email: kalapurasunny@gmail.com

www.ingramcontent.com/pod-product-compliance
Lightning Source LLC
Chambersburg PA
CBHW030328240426
43661CB00052B/1565